More Praise
Academic Dean or Provost

"*The Essential Academic Dean or Provost* is an expansive yet highly readable text for the novice as well as experienced administrators. The text provides concise advice on the breadth of issues that an academic administrator encounters on a daily basis, from interaction with department chairs to working with upper administration of the university and beyond. Buller has done an admirable job in this significant revision of his highly regarded earlier work, *The Essential Academic Dean*. I strongly recommend this text, particularly to department chairs seeking higher level administrative and management positions."

—*REZA LANGARI, professor and JR Thompson Department Head Chair, Engineering Technology and Industrial Distribution (ETID), Texas A&M University*

THE ESSENTIAL ACADEMIC DEAN
OR PROVOST

THE ESSENTIAL ACADEMIC DEAN OR PROVOST

A Comprehensive Desk Reference

Jeffrey L. Buller

JB JOSSEY-BASS™
A Wiley Brand

Published by Jossey-Bass
A Wiley Brand
One Montgomery Street, Suite 1000, San Francisco, CA 94104-4594-www.josseybass.com

Jossey-Bass books and products are available through most bookstores. To contact Jossey-Bass directly call our Customer Care Department within the U.S. at 800–956–7739, outside the U.S. at 317–572–3986, or fax 317–572–4002.

Wiley publishes in a variety of print and electronic formats and by print-on-demand. Some material included with standard print versions of this book may not be included in e-books or in print-on-demand. If this book refers to media such as a CD or DVD that is not included in the version you purchased, you may download this material at http://booksupport.wiley.com. For more information about Wiley products, visit www.wiley.com.

Library of Congress Cataloging-in-Publication Data

Buller, Jeffrey L.
 [Essential academic dean]
 The essential academic dean or provost : a comprehensive desk reference / Jeffrey L. Buller. –
Second edition.
     1 online resource. – (Jossey-Bass resources for department chairs)
 Revised edition of: The essential academic dean. 2007.
 Includes index.
 Description based on print version record and CIP data provided by publisher; resource not viewed.
  ISBN 978-1-118-76215-8 (pdf) – ISBN 978-1-118-76219-6 (epub) – ISBN
978-1-118-76216-5 (paperback) 1. Deans (Education) 2. Universities and colleges–
Administration. I. Title.
 LB2341
 378.1'11–dc23

                                                                            2015027575

Cover design by Wiley

Cover image: ©Marilyn Nieves/iStockphoto

Printed in the United States of America
SECOND EDITION
PB Printing   10 9 8 7 6 5 4 3 2 1

CONTENTS

PART FOUR
The Academic Leader as Supervisor

PART FIVE
The Budget of the College or University

PART SIX
The Opportunities and Challenges of Being an Academic Leader

PART SEVEN
The Next Step for the Provost or Dean

To my current and former colleagues at Florida Atlantic University who have taught me more about effective academic leadership than I could have learned in years of graduate seminars.

- *Daniel Gropper and the late Dennis Coates of the College of Business*
- *Gary W. Perry and Russell Ivy of the Charles E. Schmidt College of Science*
- *David Bjorkman and Michael Friedland of the Charles E. Schmidt College of Medicine*
- *Anne Boykin and Marlaine Smith of the Christine E. Lynn College of Nursing*
- *Rosalyn Carter of the College for Design and Social Inquiry*
- *Gregory F. Aloia and Val Bristor of the College of Education*
- *Karl K. Stevens and Mohammed Ilyas of the College of Engineering and Computer Science*
- *Heather Coltman of the Dorothy F. Schmidt College of Arts and Letters*

ABOUT THE AUTHOR

JEFFREY L. BULLER has served in administrative positions ranging from department chair to vice president for academic affairs at a diverse group of institutions: Loras College, Georgia Southern University, Mary Baldwin College, and Florida Atlantic University. He is the author of *The Essential Department Chair: A Comprehensive Desk Reference, Academic Leadership Day by Day: Small Steps That Lead to Great Success, The Essential College Professor: A Practical Guide to an Academic Career, Best Practices in Faculty Evaluation: A Practical Guide for Academic Leaders, Positive Academic Leadership: How to Stop Putting Out Fires and Start Making a Difference, Change Leadership in Higher Education: A Practical Guide to Academic Transformation* (with Walter H. Gmelch), *Building Academic Leadership Capacity: A Guide to Best Practices*, and (with Robert E. Cipriano) *A Toolkit for Department Chairs*. Dr. Buller has also written more than two hundred articles on Greek and Latin literature, nineteenth- and twentieth-century opera, and college administration. From 2003 to 2005, he served as the principal English-language lecturer at the International Wagner Festival in Bayreuth, Germany. More recently, he has been active as a consultant to the Ministry of Education in Saudi Arabia, where he is assisting with the creation of a kingdomwide Academic Leadership Center. Along with Robert E. Cipriano, Buller is a senior partner in ATLAS: Academic Training, Leadership, & Assessment Services, through which he has presented numerous training workshops on academic leadership for deans and provosts.

PREFACE

If academic leaders in higher education were like their depictions in the movies, few of us would willingly show our faces in public. Consider, for instance, the following unfortunate role models:

- Dean Peter Morgan Sr. (Charles Coburn) in *Vivacious Lady* (1938)
- Dean Vernon Wormer (John Vernon) in *Animal House* (1978)
- Dean Bradley (Eddie Albert) in *Stitches* (1985)
- Dean Martin (Ned Beatty) in *Back to School* (1986)
- Dean Walcott (Bob Gunton) in *Patch Adams* (1998)
- Dean Carl Cain (Obba Babatundé) in *How High* (2001)
- Dean Gordon "Cheese" Pritchard (Jeremy Piven) in *Old School* (2003)
- Dean Van Horne (Anthony Heald) in *Accepted* (2006)
- Dean Leakey (William Bogert) in *Tenure* (2008)

You can probably add several more of your favorite fictional deans to this list. Every single one of them is stuffy, stupid, mean, or all three. If a dean appears in most American movies, that dean will be the character who stands in the way of the young hero's desire to fulfill a dream. Fictional deans are often symbols of a hidebound tradition that undermines the true spirit of higher education; they end up as figures of ridicule because they're proven to be completely wrong about absolutely everything.

This is a book about how *not* to become that sort of dean.

Being a provost is even worse. Academic vice presidents are practically nonexistent in movies and on television. Outside of higher education, very few people even know that they exist. I once served with the title "dean of the college" and, in a year without raises, was asked if I wanted a title change since my work couldn't be compensated with added salary. "Sure!" I remember replying, "Make me the provost." When I was asked why I wanted that particular title, I replied, "Because every angry parent who calls the school always says, 'Get me the dean!' No one ever says, 'Get me the provost!'" Sadly, however, that anonymity is one of the few redeeming features of the position. At many institutions, being provost can feel like the worst job on campus. If a faculty member wins an award, the president gets to convey the honor; if a faculty member has to be fired, the provost has to convey the news. If someone receives a promotion, the letter comes from the president; if someone is denied a promotion, the letter comes from the provost. You get the picture: service as chief academic officer can often be a thankless business. But it's also a very important business, and the consequences of not being effective in the job are enormous.

While there are all kinds of differences in the work that deans and provosts do, there is one overriding similarity: they are the leading academic officer of a complex organization, either an independent college, a college within a university, or the university itself. It's also the case that although there are many career pathways to a presidency, the vast majority of provosts once were deans. Many of the personnel and budgetary issues that deans and provosts deal with are similar in nature even if they occur at different organizational levels. For this reason, it makes sense to address many of their responsibilities in the same book, and that's the approach I pursue here. I'll occasionally use the term *dean* as a shorthand way of saying "chief academic officer of an entity such as a college or university" because you can imagine how annoying the latter expression could become in a book of this length. While I'll try as much as possible to point out where strategies might diverge between what the provost or the dean does, in most cases I'll trust readers to make appropriate mental translations when my use of the word *dean* means something more like *provosts, deans, directors,* or *anyone else in charge of a complex academic program.*

Like its two companion volumes, *The Essential Department Chair: A Comprehensive Desk Reference* (2012) and *The Essential College Professor: A Practical Guide to an Academic Career* (2010), *The Essential Academic Dean or Provost* presents not academic theories about administrative leadership, but real-life situations that academic leaders face day in and day out. Its intended audience includes:

○ Graduate students who are studying higher education administration and want to learn about the actual practice of college leadership as a complement to the theories they encounter in other works

○ Faculty members and department chairs who are considering whether they might wish to pursue a higher administrative role and want to know how to prepare for these responsibilities and understand what they entail

o Current deans and provosts who want a reference manual in which they can find brief but highly informative discussions of the topics most relevant to their success as academic leaders

I recommend that those who are not yet deans or provosts consider working their way through this book sequentially; the first three chapters provide these readers with a good introduction to what they'll need to know in order to be prepared for a higher administrative role. The subsequent parts build on this earlier material and cover many duties that deans and provosts have. More experienced administrators will probably want to plunge right in and start with whatever topics are of immediate interest to them. This second edition contains an index (an important feature, missing from the first edition, which truly makes this version a comprehensive desk reference), as well as updated sources, material reflecting some recent changes in higher education, and improved cross-references designed to help those who read the book out of sequence locate where technical terms have been defined or related concepts have been discussed.

A number of resources have appeared since the release of this book's first edition, and I've benefited greatly from the insights of these authors and administrators. Since provosts and deans can benefit from their own library of important books on academic leadership, I acknowledge the following recent works that were particularly helpful to me and recommend that readers of this book also explore them:

o Dianne Dorland and Patricia Mosto's *A Toolkit for Deans* (Lanham, MD: Rowman & Littlefield, 2014)

o Larry Nielsen's *Provost: Experiences, Reflections, and Advice from a Former "Number Two" on Campus* (Sterling, VA: Stylus, 2013)

o The third edition of Laura Behling's *The Resource Handbook for Academic Deans* (San Francisco, CA: Jossey-Bass, 2014)

Each chapter of *The Essential Academic Dean or Provost* is as brief and self-contained as possible. My goal has been to provide readers with clear, concise recommendations that can be absorbed in ten minutes or less. You're busy, and I know that time is of the essence. One special feature of this book, pioneered in the first edition, is the scenario analysis that concludes each major part. In a scenario analysis, academic leaders are provided with a hypothetical case study designed to apply the principles explored in the previous chapters in that part, several considerations that may cause them to reevaluate how they might handle that situation, and a few recommendations about where to begin solving the problem presented by the study. It can be particularly beneficial to discuss a scenario analysis with a fellow administrator or a trusted mentor in order to determine how different administrative approaches might be brought to bear on the same challenging problem.

Scattered throughout the book are a number of essential principles that are formatted as follows.

> Essential principles are the key rules that can help you succeed in a variety of administrative situations. These are the principles to which you'll want to give extra attention when you face your own administrative challenges. If you remember nothing else from this book, be sure that you've mastered all of these suggestions.

Essential principles are designed to be short and easily remembered, but they're not mere platitudes. They've all been tested in actual administrative situations and have proven their value. Even if you end up disagreeing with a few of these guidelines, they deserve your serious and thoughtful attention. Don't ignore them. At the request of many readers (including the anonymous reviewers for this edition), this edition has significantly more essential principles than the first edition did. They can provide a useful way of identifying parts in the book that are most relevant to your position. As you flip through the pages, notice which essential principles catch your eye. They're often keys to the chapters you'll find most valuable. If several of these observations have a particular resonance for you, consider writing them on sticky notes and attaching them to your door or computer monitor. They'll provide a daily reminder of what you can do to make continual progress in improving your academic leadership.

There are many people I want to thank for their roles in making *The Essential Academic Dean or Provost* possible. Carolyn Allard and Sheryl Fullerton, who served as editors for the first edition, and David Brightman, who served as editor of the second edition, made many valuable suggestions (and sometimes just resigned themselves to the inevitable when I was too stubborn to change). Lawrence Glick, senior associate general counsel at Florida Atlantic University, was a useful resource on issues that had legal implications, which means pretty much every issue a dean or a provost ever deals with. D. Parker Young, professor emeritus of higher education at the University of Georgia, has provided workshops on higher education law for more than thirty years, greatly influencing my approach to legal issues at colleges and universities and reinforcing my respect for what he routinely calls "creating a climate where the incentives for legalism are reduced." I also thank Magna Publications for allowing me to adapt and reuse in chapter 8 some material that originally appeared in *Academic Leader*. (Reprint permission was granted by Magna Publications and *Academic Leader*.) Sandy Ogden deserves some kind of canonization for proofreading the entire manuscript (in addition to a slew of other manuscripts while also doing her day job) since I'm simultaneously the world's fastest writer and worst typist. (The two achievements are not unrelated.)

Whether you're hoping to serve as a university provost or academic dean someday, have recently accepted such a position, or are already well along in your administrative career, you're certain to discover that academic leadership offers you exciting, frequently changing opportunities to apply your creativity, initiative, and problem-solving skills. While this book has been designed to focus on the day-to-day nuts and bolts of being an academic administrator, remember that it does so primarily to make you more efficient at these tasks so that you can develop your own vision for your college. College administration shouldn't be a matter of rudimentary problem solving and paper shuffling. It should be about building toward a vision of the future. So if you have problems to solve and papers to shuffle, why not get those tasks out of the way as quickly and effectively as possible?

Each day in our administrative careers may be regarded as merely a step we take in an extended pilgrimage of self-discovery. As you turn the page to continue your journey, I hope that it's an amazing and fruitful trip wherever your own path takes you.

Jupiter, Florida   JEFFREY L. BULLER
January 1, 2015   *Florida Atlantic University*

The premium online content for this book includes additional scenario analyses, along with field-tested advice for working in unique academic environments. To access this bonus content, visit www.wiley.com/go/Buller.

PART ONE

THE ACADEMIC LEADER'S ROLE

BEING #1 IN THE #2 BUSINESS

Harry Carter, who long served as provost at Georgia Southern University and the Citadel, loved to mention the septic tank company that posted a large billboard greeting drivers as they entered Augusta, Georgia, along Highway 25: "We're #1 in the #2 Business."

There are all kinds of ways in which university provosts and academic deans can feel as though they're in the #2 business. Many of the issues they have to deal with may make them feel as though they're wading into the academic equivalent of a septic tank. But even more important, they're always #2 to someone else who's #1: the person who serves as the visible face and symbol of the institution. Larry Nielsen even devotes an entire chapter to the topic of "Being Number Two" in his book *Provost* (2013). And so although they're often lumped together with other members of "the upper administration" by students, faculty members, and even at times department chairs, the nature of the position held by the provost or dean is intended to be middle management. While provosts and deans may have a great deal of independence in certain areas, they ultimately report to someone—a specific person who serves as their supervisor—rather than to a governing board, as presidents and chancellors do. At the same time, they are themselves supervisors, evaluating the performance of others, recommending appropriate salary adjustments, and trying to unite them all into a single academic team.

Hundreds of books have been written about the principles of leadership or how to get things done from the top. There's also an expanding literature on how to serve most effectively as an employee, mastering the techniques of *followership*, a term coined by Robert E. Kelley (1992) and elaborated on in more comprehensive studies by Kellerman (2008), Riggio, Chaleff, and Lipman-Blumen (2008), and Bligh and Kohles (2012). But how can provosts and deans be expected to lead from the middle? How can they become #1 in the #2 business?

As a way of answering these questions, it might be useful to begin with recognizing that no one is ever #1—not really. They may think they are, or the organization chart may say they are, but shared governance in higher education means that no one person has authority over every aspect of what goes on at a college or university. As one way of viewing this idea, the first essential principle in this book is perhaps the most important one you'll encounter when it comes to academic administration:

> All leadership entails leadership from the middle. When you understand how organizations really work, you realize that everybody reports to somebody.

Standard organizational charts, adapted as they are from military and corporate environments where they often make more sense, tend to distort this issue. On paper, faculty members report to chairs. Department chairs in turn report to you, if you're a dean, or to your deans, if you're a provost. Either way, you eventually report to the president, directly or through the chief academic officer. The president reports to a board. The board is subject to bylaws and other applicable regulations. You can never climb to the top of this chart and be in charge of it all.

> Climbing to the pinnacle of each organizational pyramid simply takes you to the base of the next pyramid.

Moreover, authority is decentralized in higher education in a way that's not practical in other organizational cultures. The faculty is ultimately responsible for the curriculum. The president and governing board are ultimately responsible for the budget. When people overlook that long-standing division of power, problems start to arise. And yet the system usually works. Decisions are made. Policies are developed. New initiatives get under way. But those initiatives don't always come from the top. We've all known a provost, dean, department chair, or faculty member whose energy, insight, or personal charm completely transformed a school. Institutional leadership can arise from any level of the hierarchy. You don't have to be in charge to be influential.

That's a good thing, because provosts and deans have always had a view from the middle. The English word *provost* is ultimately derived from two Latin roots, *pro-* ("in front of") and *positus* (the perfect-passive participle of the verb *ponere*, "to put." Provosts were thus originally officers who were "put in front of" other people in ecclesiastical, academic, or political life. But they didn't occupy the highest rung on the organizational ladder. In a church, the provost might be the minister of the largest church in a town. At a university, the provost might be the head of a particular college or school. And in government, the provost might be something like a mayor. In each case, the provost's position, while important, did not possess ultimate authority and always reported to someone else whose powers and responsibilities were considerably greater.

In a similar way, our word *dean* comes to English from Norman French via the Latin word *decanus*, meaning an officer in charge of ten people (from the Latin *decem* or the Greek *deka*, "ten"). A dean thus had far less authority, in etymological terms at least, than a centurion, who was in charge of one hundred people. At the same time, the dean had far more responsibility than any of the ten subordinates. During the Middle Ages, deans ceased to have a military connection, and the term became adopted by the church to describe the priest who supervised ten monks in a monastery, the head of a chapter in a cathedral church, or a member of the religious hierarchy through whom clerics reported to an archbishop. Given the religious origins of universities like Oxford and Cambridge, the word required only a slight shift in emphasis as it moved from ecclesiastical to academic circles. The dean thus became the administrator in charge of the behavior and academic progress of students in a college. As the organizational structures of colleges and universities became more complex, deans became elected members of the faculty who provided administrative guidance, management, and vision to their institutions. By the twentieth century, deans in the United States were already being viewed more as administrators than teachers. They almost always had academic backgrounds, but they were appointed (and less frequently elected) because they demonstrated potential for making their colleges and schools run effectively.

From their origin, therefore, provosts and deans have always had responsibilities that draw them in two directions simultaneously: they are advocates for and supervisors of the people over whom they have authority; they report to and serve as the representatives of some higher administrative level that sets the limits within which they themselves can operate. Performing both responsibilities effectively is one of the perennial challenges facing provosts and deans. Few other aspects of their role are as important as the ability to see the needs of the institution from the middle and to address those needs adequately. So how do you do that? Here are nine basic principles to keep in mind as you begin developing your own approach to providing leadership from the middle.

Principle 1: Develop Collegial Candor

As an academic leader, you want your own supervisor to treat you with respect, give your views a fair hearing even if they're not ultimately accepted, and share information with you freely, particularly when having that information is essential for you to do your job. Is it unreasonable, therefore, to assume that those who report to you are looking for the same considerations from your office? Your method of interacting with department chairs, division directors, and the faculty members at your institution should be a reflection of the role you wish to play in the larger institutional structure. In fact, how you treat others may even help shape that role.

Developing an atmosphere of collegial candor means taking steps to create a working environment where individuals feel safe to provide their perspectives on various issues, understand that you'll agree or disagree with these views on the basis of their arguments' merits and not the individual advancing them, and recognize that the overall mission of the institution is the guiding principle behind all deliberations, not the personal convenience of a particular administrator. You therefore have an obligation to apply this philosophy to all your discussions with your president, governing body, and members of the community. You have no less of an obligation to adhere to these same principles when dealing with the members of your school or college.

The people who report to you rely on you as a sounding board for their ideas and insights, even if their behavior doesn't always suggest that they themselves are open to other perspectives. Disagreement with one's boss shouldn't be confrontational, and it's rarely the case that job security results from blindly accepting every suggestion your superior makes. Phrased in a collegial manner—"Now, that might be true, but another way of looking at it could be . . . " or, "Perhaps, though, we should also consider whether . . . "—disagreements can broaden a discussion and help decision makers avoid a serious mistake. Certainly administrators can be frustrated when those who report to them constantly and inconsiderately disagree with every idea they propose, every suggestion they make, or every improvement they consider. But it can also be frustrating when people see it as their responsibility to agree merely for the sake of agreement, avoiding any serious attempt to explore whether the merits of a proposal are offset by any disadvantages. Effective provosts and deans tend to be those who speak freely when it's important to do so but also understand how to provide alternatives in a constructive, consensus-building manner. It's not hypocritical to refrain from expressing a strong opinion on every subject; sometimes that's just the most diplomatic and beneficial strategy to pursue. It's a technique sometimes called *strategic nonengagement.*

Creating an open atmosphere in a college means making it clear that department chairs and faculty members are free to express points of view that are different from yours, even in open meetings, as long as the discussion remains civil and focused on substantive issues, not personalities, private disputes, or "ancient history." No one should tolerate grandstanding or outright insubordination; your supervisor wouldn't tolerate such behavior from you, and you can't be expected to tolerate it from a chair or faculty member. But it's important to promote an open exchange of ideas with those both above you and below you in the institutional hierarchy. Only in this way are you likely to learn what you need in order to perform your job effectively. Open channels of communication are also the only way for the institution to avoid embarking on disastrous courses of activity because no one felt free to say that the ideas being discussed were unsound.

Principle 2: Clarify Your Vision

The president and governing board of your institution are likely to have articulated a vision for the future direction of your college or university; perhaps these ideas are contained in a formal strategic plan or in a vision statement. Your faculty members also have a vision of how they would like their academic areas to develop, their students to learn, and their research to progress. None of those visions can be realized, however, without your view from the middle. The president will need assistance in determining how his or her overarching goals for the institution are best realized and measured in academic units. The faculty will need assistance in seeing how their individual goals stand in the larger priorities of your institution and how they can play a significant role in making the strategic plan a reality.

One aspect of your job as an academic leader is thus to serve as a catalyst in clarifying or crystallizing these visions. For example, if one of the president's strategic goals is to develop more undergraduate research at the same time that students improve their understanding of global issues, how can these two issues be combined in your programs' curricula? Can you lead your programs toward the adoption of a new capstone experience for students that will include a substantial component of original research? Can you spearhead a review of all course curricula to strengthen international perspectives wherever possible? Can you suggest alternative requirements for majors so that students who study abroad are less likely to be delayed in their progress toward graduation? As a provost or dean, you understand the individual needs, methods, and philosophies of your disciplines far better than do many members of your governing board or legislature. As a result, you are in a unique position to crystallize the institution's larger vision into a plan that fits the ways in which disciplines actually work in your area.

Similarly, faculty members at your school may be interested in greater flexibility in workload, revisions to evaluation procedures that will suit their jobs more adequately, better compensation, or improved facilities. You have an opportunity to serve as an advocate for these needs—when you, in your professional judgment, see them as valid—by clarifying how they might serve to advance the institution's strategic plan. So if improved student advisement, enhanced civic engagement, and collaborative endeavors between academic affairs and the office of student life are institutional goals, how are initiatives in these areas being rewarded in your current faculty evaluation system? As Bob Cipriano, the author of *Facilitating a Collegial Department in Higher Education: Strategies for Success* (2011), is fond of saying:

> What gets rewarded gets repeated.

You'll get more of anything you specifically measure, recognize, and compensate people for. As a result, you can help bridge the middle ground between upper administration and faculty by finding points of overlap where strategic goals (what the president wants) can be used to advance the aims of the faculty (what professors want). If you implement a reward structure in which promotions, tenure, and annual increases are based at least in part on advancing the institution's strategic goals, you're more likely to see those goals achieved in a timely manner. I have a lot more to say about clarifying or crystalizing an academic vision in chapter 4.

Principle 3: Be Neither a Lackey nor a Shop Steward

You may be asked, "Whose representative are you: the board's or the faculty's?" This question really poses a false dichotomy. It's usually asked by someone who's either trying to bait you (to see if your response will end up on the wrong side of his or her personal litmus test) or who's particularly knowledgeable about how colleges and universities actually work. Your most important duty as provost or dean is to *serve as the advocate for the academic programs you supervise*. At times, this advocacy will consist of making the case for certain programs or individuals who report to you as forcefully and eloquently as you can. At other times, the best advocacy you can provide your unit is to clarify for your department chairs and faculty members why certain perceived needs can't or shouldn't be addressed. Good academic leaders sometimes have to say no. They're neither the lackeys of the president, legislature, or governing board (i.e., serving merely as a conduit that conveys to the faculty the decisions made by those at the top of the organization chart) nor the shop stewards of their faculty (pressing for the adoption of every request, demand, and desire they receive). Your view from the middle requires you to be both your own person and responsive to the perspectives of those above and below you. It's a demonstration of good judgment to know when one of these must take precedence over the other.

Principle 4: Be Consistent without Becoming Inflexible

Both your supervisor and your faculty want to know what you stand for. They want to know your core beliefs, the things that are nonnegotiable for you, and your sense of vision for your programs. In most cases, people actually feel more comfortable when they believe that an area is headed in the wrong direction than when they believe it's not headed in any direction. For this reason, you'll be expected to speak regularly about your values and vision. Be reasonably consistent in responding to these requests; academic leaders who seem enamored of every new trend that arises seem as aimless as those who can't find any particular cause to get behind. In most cases, both your president and department chairs want to know that they can predict the general thrust of your thinking on a subject. They'll feel there's a greater sense of purpose in your school if you convey a clear sense of your priorities and proceed to act on them in a consistent manner.

> Being firm isn't the same as being rigid, and being authoritative isn't the same as being authoritarian. Provosts and deans need backbone, but the most valuable part of a backbone is that it's strong enough to stiffen when necessary and flexible enough to bend a little when compromise is required.

In striving to be reasonably consistent, remember that it's important to be reasonable as well as consistent. Administrators who never change their minds can be as destructive to institutions as deans who change their minds whenever they're presented with an alternative point of view. Reliability shouldn't be synonymous with stubbornness. People will excuse an occasional change of direction or the rescinding of a decision as long as they know the reasons for the change and you're candid about the process that led to the new decision. Avoid giving the impression that you simply caved in to pressure or that someone "got to you." Be clear about why the new course is necessary and how it still fits in with your overall plan for your unit. The only proviso is that if you find yourself having to explain these changes too often, it's time to reconsider how sound your original plan for your area may have been.

Principle 5: Try to See Issues from the Perspectives of Others

Everyone at your institution has a different perspective based on his or her individual role. Thus the president wants you to see how your programs fit into the big picture. Your faculty members want you to see things in terms of their workloads and career paths. Deans often see the university as a pie: if someone gets a bigger slice, someone else's slice has to be smaller. The key to being a successful academic leader is the ability to see all these points of view simultaneously and then to move forward with the best possible judgment. No issue can ever be solely about the university; there are times when your individual school or college is going to have to come first in the decision that's being made. But your perspective can't always be limited to your individual unit either; sometimes your students will be better served if another dean receives a new faculty line or a major new facility. Being a team player means knowing the right moment to claim the glory and the right moment to share it.

Principle 6: Become Known for Something

Peter Northouse, author of one of the most widely used textbooks in leadership studies, distinguishes two types of leadership: assigned leadership, which people hold because of their titles and job descriptions, and emergent leadership, which people are granted by others because their views are respected due to what they know and how they act. (See, for example, Northouse, 2013. For more on Northouse's views on leadership, see chapter 8 in this book.) One of the secrets to leading from the middle is developing your stock of emergent leadership by being known as *the* expert in some area. Exactly what you're known for will depend a great deal on your own background and interests. But you might consider developing a distinctive reputation at your institution by selecting at least one of the following three areas: expertise, values, or vision. While there's a great deal of overlap among these categories, they're useful for providing a starting point in our analysis of ways in which you can develop your own niche of proficiency.

Being known for your expertise

This involves reaching a level of knowledge or skill in an area that distinguishes you from your peers. Because you know more about some particular area, you become the go-to person whenever advice or insight in that area is needed. For instance, every institution needs gurus in various areas of technology, assessment, faculty development, course evaluation, fundraising, program review, the intricacies of budgeting, and so on. By developing expertise in one of these areas, you establish your reputation not just as an effective advocate for your disciplinary area, but also as someone who works on behalf of the institution as a whole. "Oh, well," people will say, "if your question involves distance learning, you really ought to talk to Dr. [Name]; she's the expert when it comes to anything involving online education." Moreover, by developing an area of expertise that transcends your own college, you'll have a platform that allows you to speak quite broadly on a host of institutional issues. As a result, you'll begin to function—and to be seen—as a leader beyond the boundaries of your college.

Being known for your values

This means establishing a clear identity because of the principles and practices you advocate. Some academic leaders are known as "the conscience of the institution," framing each discussion within its moral or ethical implications. Perhaps the values you believe in most are protecting the environment, looking out for the underrepresented, promoting professionalism, representing the interests of the faculty (or student body or staff), supporting collegiality throughout the institution, or exploring creative new solutions to perennial problems.

Perhaps your values take you in a different direction, establishing your identity as an early adopter of new technology or institutional initiatives, the person who always remembers other people's birthdays or sends congratulatory notes when good things happen in their lives, or the advocate for typographical and grammatical perfection in every public document. Whatever values most resonate with you can become the basis for a identity as the institutional specialist in that area.

Being known for your vision

This identity entails the ability to see beyond what is and imagine what could be. As the campus visionary, you would be the person who always thinks in terms of larger possibilities and future directions. Good vision is, of course, not wholly divorced from practicality, so you'll need to amass a certain amount of evidence in support of the vision you promote. For instance, based on the demographics of your region or enrollment trends at peer institutions, you could be the person who begins to position your institution in such a way as to be ahead of the curve when new developments arise. Student populations change over time in terms of their need for specific student services, their likelihood to gravitate toward particular majors, and their relationships with both the institution and their parents. As a visionary leader, you might be the person who's aware of how each new generation of students will differ from its predecessors and can help guide your institution in preparing for those changes. (See Watson, 2013, and Williams and Drew, 2012.)

Principle 7: Radiate Positive Energy

Some of the best administrative advice any academic leader can hear comes from what most people would regard as an unusual source—the actor Cary Grant: "I think that being relaxed at all times, and I mean relaxed, not collapsed, can add to the happiness and duration of one's life and looks. And relaxed people are fun to be around" (Nelson, 2003, 25).

Certainly no one can deny it's often very stressful to serve as a provost or dean. There are times in which the implications of the decisions we make, the intensity of the criticism we receive, and the pressure we're under to succeed on a wide variety of fronts can shake our confidence, resulting in a high level of anxiety. In addition, some academic leaders (like many others in positions of authority) believe that they *should* feel constantly harried, always rushing off from one important meeting to the next. After all, if their positions weren't stressful, anyone could succeed at the job, and then how could you justify the higher salary that comes with administrative assignments?

What deans and provosts need to realize is that by conveying a sense of anxiety, tension, or frenzy from excessive work, they can undermine their position as a campus leader. As Cary Grant suggested, people naturally gravitate toward others who are relaxed, confident, and self-assured. When their leaders have a relaxed demeanor, they give faculty, students, and staff a sense that even if matters are difficult now, everything will work out in the end. People thus acquire the confidence that they need in order to make matters actually work out in the end. Administrators who function in crisis mode all the time give the impression that they can't distinguish between truly serious matters—an imminent threat to the life or safety of a member of the campus community or a situation of financial exigency so dire that it threatens either the entire institution—and the more routine challenges that colleges and universities face every day.

Leadership from the middle therefore sometimes begins with nothing more than maintaining an attitude of calm and confidence when everyone else appears to be on the verge of panic. The pressures of the academic year create these periods of Sturm und Drang on a schedule we can almost predict. As each semester draws to a close and nerves are frayed from the pressure of final exams, grades that are due, reports that must be completed, and dozens of deadlines that must all be met at once, the mood on campus changes dramatically. Tempers flare. Despair sets in. What seemed insignificant before suddenly seems insurmountable. It's at times like these that leadership needs to be demonstrated through quiet confidence, an attitude that "we can do this, and the result will be fantastic," and a gentle optimism that today's momentary frustrations are worthwhile because they'll result in something wonderful.

Being #1 in the #2 business requires a high level of confidence. Rather than stoking the fires of anxiety, effective leaders approach difficulties as simply part of the job and convey an attitude that solving problems provides an opportunity to engage their creativity. If you follow this principle, you'll notice that people throughout the entire institution will begin to view you as a confident, reliable leader. This type of positive energy doesn't have to be limited to your president, chancellor, or chair of the governing board. In fact, if your CEO tends not to project a positive and confident demeanor, it's even more important for you do so. It's this type of leadership that you as a dean or provost can quite effectively demonstrate from your position in the middle of the hierarchy (See Buller, 2013).

Collins (2001) notes that the highest caliber of "leaders embody a paradoxical mix of personal humility and professional will" (39). In this way, another essential ingredient in leading from the middle is discovering a way to combine an invigorating attitude of confidence that obstacles will be overcome with an ability to be unassuming, humble, even self-deprecating about your own accomplishments. Strong academics are usually very serious about fulfilling their college's mission, but they rarely take themselves too seriously. Confidence that comes across as arrogance or pretentiousness alienates others; it doesn't make them more eager to follow the direction the dean or provost has charted. Academic leaders who insist too often that they must stand on their dignity can end up with very little dignity left as they become mere caricatures of the supercilious dean we're familiar with from television and movies. Everyone's personality is different, of course, but most deans discover that allowing themselves to be seen having a good time on occasion, even if the humor is sometimes at their own expense, enhances rather than diminishes their authority.

Principle 8: Unite Your Own Dreams and Vision with Those of Others

Leadership isn't synonymous with power. Power is the ability to get what you want. Leadership is the act of helping others achieve what they need. Weak and ineffective leaders insist on moving only in the direction they regard as important; they may seem successful in the short term because power can cause things to appear as though they're changing, but these leaders are unlikely to remain effective for very long. The best leaders help others develop and attain their own shared visions of a better future. Those leaders may be the catalyst for creating the image of an exciting future, and they may contribute to certain aspects of it, but they don't view themselves as the only source of good ideas. Effective leaders recognize that part of their job is to build a culture that is optimistic about the future, regardless of whether the leaders will receive credit for that vision themselves. As administrators who lead from the middle, those of us in the #2 business have to look for ways to achieve the goals of our programs with the overall strategic goals of the institution.

A good place to start is to look for ways of building partnerships between departments, colleges, and divisions of the institution. Since resources are limited, presidents and boards look favorably on proposals that benefit more than one area. Moreover, the traditional organization of universities into departments, schools, colleges, and divisions tends to fragment institutions. Your cooperative efforts can help reverse this silo mentality and foster a new culture of cooperation. Mandating that type of programming from the top down rarely works; chancellors and presidents are often far less effective in doing so than are visionary provosts and deans. For this reason, building bridges between areas is a perfect way to establish yourself as a university leader who's conscious of fiscal realities.

The type of collaborative effort that you propose is likely to be determined by the individual needs of your institution. Nevertheless, a large number of themes can be used to initiate such an effort. For instance, you might propose a new initiative in creativity, innovation, and entrepreneurship that draws together the arts, sciences, engineering, and business under a single umbrella to explore how people discover what is truly original and expose others to the importance of this discovery (Buller, 2011).

An initiative in the area of leadership could combine the theoretical and historical study of major leaders, managers, and visionaries with practical experience in leading on-campus organizations, small start-up businesses, and committees within the university's own hierarchy. Indeed, certain important developments in scholarship fall between the lines where traditional departments begin and end: bioengineering draws on expertise in both biology and engineering; digital publication incorporates studio art, computer information systems, design, printing, and marketing; and neuroscience spans psychology, biology, medicine, and philosophy. These interdisciplinary endeavors can lead to the exploration of entirely new forms of intercollegiate cooperation. Moreover, the very type of collaborative endeavor you propose with other colleges could assume a unique shape. It could range from something as simple as a lecture series or single team-taught course to something as ambitious as a new center, program, or endowed professorship. Whatever you propose, it's probably best to simply ask yourself what visions of the future you already share with other units at your institution and then think creatively about how you can work together to pursue these common interests.

Principle 9: Give More Than You Receive

An old saying goes:

If you give more than you receive, eventually you'll receive more than you give.

That maxim, which is frequently interpreted as, "If you work harder than you're paid, eventually you'll be paid more than you work," is actually true for more than just the salary a person earns. Provosts and deans can demonstrate effective leadership from the middle by focusing on the true nature of all leadership: working on behalf of their stakeholders, not simply reaping the benefits of their positions. Truly effective leaders are always motivated by a desire to do what's in the best interest of those for whom they're responsible. Once academic leaders start viewing their programs as personal fiefdoms, they begin to lose their effectiveness as leaders. To be #1 in the #2 business, you need to think broadly in terms of servant leadership and the way you can benefit your institution as a whole (Wheeler, 2012). For instance, if you discover that students are doing well in their courses but not developing the personal skills they need to succeed, you have a number of choices. You can view the situation as just a student affairs problem, or you can do something to help. An initiative that broadens the definition of what constitutes student success, a peer mentoring group that addresses issues both within and outside the classroom, a task force that explores ways in which academic affairs and student affairs can better partner together, or simply a constructive conversation with other campus leaders about what can be done to improve the student experience at your institution all demonstrate true leadership. Leaders reach out to others to address their needs, and that practice can start anywhere in an institutional hierarchy, not merely with the person who's #1.

Conclusion

Provost and deans need to be able to consider both the good of the whole and the good of each individual part simultaneously. Just as every issue can't be about the entire institution, not every decision you make can be only about what benefits a particular professor, department, or college. An excess of equality may end up not being equitable at all. There will be times when one of your programs—or even one individual in your program—is going to have to receive more space, equipment, or resources simply because there's a need for more. That's not favoritism; that's just good academic leadership. It's not regarded as inequitable in a hospital if patients in the intensive care unit receive more resources than do outpatients; at that particular moment, the greater needs of the seriously ill call for greater care. The same principle is true of academic programs: needs will at times be greater for one college, department, or person than they are for others. It'll be a test of your judgment as an academic leader to recognize when those occasions arise.

Serving as the #2 at most universities, provosts and deans have many opportunities that are unique to their roles. Within their own spheres of authority, they are perfectly positioned to communicate the mission and vision of their disciplines. With their fellow administrators, they can act as mentors and examples. With the president and board, they can demonstrate leadership by knowing when to advocate for the needs of their stakeholders and when to put the needs of the whole institution first. Being at the middle of a hierarchy does not, in other words, restrict opportunities for leadership. To the contrary, it multiplies the number of directions in which you can demonstrate your leadership.

REFERENCES

Bligh, M. C., & Kohles, J. C. (2012). *Followercentric approaches to leadership*. Toronto, Canada: Hogrefe.

Buller, J. L. (2011). The need for linking innovation, creativity, and entrepreneurship. *Academic Leader*, 27(5), 4–5.

Buller, J. L. (2013). *Positive academic leadership: How to stop putting out fires and begin making a difference*. San Francisco, CA: Jossey-Bass.

Cipriano, R. E. (2011). *Facilitating a collegial department in higher education: Strategies for success*. San Francisco, CA: Jossey-Bass.

Collins, J. (2001). *Good to great: Why some companies make the leap . . . and others don't*. New York, NY: HarperCollins.

Kellerman, B. (2008). *Followership: How followers are creating change and changing leaders*. Boston, MA: Harvard Business School Press.

Kelley R. E. (1992). *The power of followership*. New York, NY: Doubleday/Currency.

Nielsen, L. A. (2013). *Provost: Experiences, reflections, and advice from a former "number two" on campus*. Sterling, VA: Stylus.

Nelson, N. (2003). *Evenings with Cary Grant*. New York, NY: Citadel Press.

Northouse, P. G. (2013). *Leadership: Theory and practice*. Thousand Oaks, CA: Sage.

Riggio, R. E., Chaleff, I., & Lipman-Blumen, J. (2008). *The art of followership: How great followers create great leaders and organizations*. San Francisco, CA: Jossey-Bass.

Watson, E. (2013). *Generation X professors speak: Voices from academia*. Lanham, MD: Scarecrow Press.

Wheeler, D. W. (2012). *Servant leadership for higher education: Principles and practices*. San Francisco, CA: Jossey-Bass

Williams, R. H., & Drew, M. R. (2012). *Pendulum: How past generations shape our present and predict our future*. New York, NY: Vanguard Press.

RESOURCES

Bright, D. F., & Richards, M. P. (2001). *The academic deanship: Individual careers and institutional roles*. San Francisco: Jossey-Bass.

Kouzes, J. M., & Posner, B. Z. (2003). *The Jossey-Bass academic administrator's guide to exemplary leadership*. San Francisco: Jossey-Bass.

Krahenbuhl, G. S. (2004). *Building the academic deanship: Strategies for success*. Portsmouth, NH: Praeger.

Maxwell, J. C. (2005). *The 360° leader: Developing your influence from anywhere in the organization*. Nashville, TN: Nelson Business.

Wolverton, M., & Gmelch, W. H. (2002). *College deans: Leading from within*. Phoenix, AZ: American Council on Education/Oryx Press.

Wolverton, M., Gmelch, W. H., Montez, J., & Nies, C. T. (2001). *The changing nature of the academic deanship. ASHE-ERIC Higher Education Research Report*, vol. 28, no. 1. San Francisco: Jossey-Bass.

2

PREPARING FOR A LEADERSHIP ROLE

Although there's no one type of person who's perfect for all aspects of academic leadership, there are certain personal qualities that are frequently associated with effective provosts and deans. Academic leaders should be able to:

○ Cope with a large amount of detailed information while not becoming bogged down in insignificant matters. Effective leaders know an amazing amount about every single tree, but they never lose sight of the forest itself.

○ Delegate effectively, valuing the contributions of others and not mistaking the empowerment of others with loss of their own authority.

Delegation always implies a certain loss of control. The report or decision that's delegated to someone else is unlikely to be exactly the same as if it were your own. But that's a good thing. Too much uniformity of ideas or style leads to stagnation.

○ Serve as advocates not just of their own academic disciplines, but of all the fields they represent. At times deans and provosts may even act as advocates for areas outside academic affairs, regarding the needs of the entire institution as vitally important.

○ Follow recent trends in higher education without jumping on every bandwagon that appears. Effective academic leaders are selectively responsive to new ideas and emerging best practices, realizing that some "hot new developments" are merely fads and others may not be appropriate for their institutions.

- ○ Make hard decisions, defend them, and admit when their decisions are wrong.
- ○ Communicate excellently, understanding that communication goes both ways. In other words, it's just as important to listen well as it is to speak and write well.

Why Would Anyone Want to Become a Dean or Provost?

People are attracted to academic leadership positions for all kinds of reasons, not all of them particularly appropriate. For example, being a dean or provost almost always entitles you to a higher salary and certain benefits like a larger office, a designated parking space, membership in various clubs or professional organizations, opportunities to travel to interesting places, and free admission to many events. While these advantages are undeniably attractive, they should never be *the* reason for seeking a deanship. Individuals who are attracted to administrative positions by the benefits they bring rather than the nature of the position frequently become frustrated by the long hours, twelve-month contracts, complexity of the problems to be solved, varied constituencies to be satisfied, and the realization that the benefits aren't really as attractive as they'd hoped. Similarly, people who apply for leadership positions because there's one burning issue they wish to solve—such as the inadequacy of faculty salaries, the decline of academic standards, the lack of respect given their discipline, or the intransigence of the governing board—often discover that the problem is more complicated than they had initially believed and that their lack of interest in other pressing problems is making them ineffective in their full range of responsibilities.

If you're considering the possibility of becoming a provost or dean, it's time to take serious stock of your reasons for wanting to assume this responsibility, what you hope to gain by it, and what you believe you'll be offering others through this position. Ask yourself these questions and provide completely candid answers:

- ○ If I were offered a leadership position but only at my current salary, would I still be interested?
- ○ How would I feel if, for whatever reason, I found myself facing a great deal of anger and hostility at a meeting of faculty, students, or administrators, all of whom were directing their rancor at me personally?

○ Am I a caregiver? How do I feel when I'm on the receiving end of a seemingly endless series of complaints, requests, demands, and needs day after day?

○ Do I enjoy solving problems, even when the vast majority of those problems may be either very difficult to address or, at the other extreme, so minor that the time required to solve them seems inefficient?

○ How do I feel about attending meetings? Do I get bored easily when matters not directly related to my academic field are discussed at great length? Do I feel that numerous meetings and appointments take me away from my "real work"?

○ When I think of the most important things my institution does, what immediately comes to mind? Do I think only of faculty concerns and academic issues, or do I also think more broadly in terms of student development and student life issues, the overall strategic direction of the institution, the school's relationship with external constituencies (trustees, legislators, advisory groups, donors, accrediting bodies, and so on), staff needs and concerns, and other such matters?

○ Can I let things go easily once a decision is made even if it hasn't gone my way? Do I need to revisit issues continually and justify my perspectives repeatedly?

○ How do I handle isolation? How do I feel when I'm not really being part of a group and have to face challenges on my own?

Make no mistake: there are many wonderful opportunities that come to those in leadership positions, and for the right people, it's the best job in the world. But being a provost or dean also requires attendance at plenty of meetings, reading seemingly endless reports, being confronted by angry parents/students/faculty members, having to come up with coherent rationales for institutional policies on the spur of the moment, spending long days devoted to complex and frustrating issues, and having to deal with things that you'd really prefer not to know about.

Ten Essential Preparations

If, despite all the disadvantages associated with positions of academic leadership, you still believe that you are attracted to the possibility of serving as a dean or provost, how do you begin preparing for such a position? While there are degree programs in higher education administration, most deans rise to their positions through the faculty, with little or no advance preparation for the work they'll have to do. In light of that, what sort of steps can you take to prepare yourself better for being successful as a dean?

Volunteer for leadership roles

One of the most important steps you can take in preparing to be a dean is to gain a variety of experiences that teach you about leading groups of different kinds. Look for opportunities to serve on curriculum committees, both inside and outside your academic area. Volunteer for committee assignments that provide a great deal of challenge and give you an opportunity to develop your leadership skills. Don't limit your exposure to easy successes or areas that you already know reasonably well. Rather, seek out opportunities beyond what you've already done, particularly if you have relatively little experience in conducting promotion and tenure reviews, grievance hearings, reviews of complex programs outside your area (even nonacademic programs, if that's possible), large-scale curriculum reforms (such as revisions to the general education program, conversion to or from the semester system, implementation of new standards across the curriculum), and similar activities. Try to get elected to your faculty senate or whatever your institution calls the body that addresses matters of importance to the faculty as a whole. Volunteer to serve on committees in other colleges that require outside representation.

Once you've sought out these leadership roles, begin to assess your level of success and satisfaction in fulfilling these duties. Were you able to identify areas of common ground where others saw only discord? Did you find it easy to look beyond the immediate needs of your discipline and see the big picture? If your work consisted mostly of this type of leadership opportunity—with significantly less time allocated to teaching, scholarship, and advising students—would you be satisfied in such a role? Can you provide evidence that you would be good at it?

Seek to assume support roles

In addition to pursuing opportunities for developing your leadership potential, you may wish to prepare for your future role by learning as much as possible about the types of issues deans are asked to address. Support roles for an academic leader's office—positions such as director of faculty development, special assistant to the president for strategic planning, credentialing liaison, and the like—can provide you with a great deal of information about how academic leaders do their work and what these types of assignments involve.

At the same time that you learn the many technical details of the job, you may also have an opportunity to work with a mentor—someone in a senior administrative position who can provide you with on-the-job training. As issues or problems arise, you can compare what you would have done with how the mentor you're working with approached the situation. In cases where you would have chosen a radically different course of action, discuss the issue with your mentor and explore why your approach wouldn't have been the same. Use your support role to determine which aspects of administrative work you have particular talent for and which may require additional training or experience. In certain cases, you might find a particular niche—for example, you might become the budget guru, long-range planning expert, curriculum authority, assessment diva, or mediation czar—that you can parlay into a full-time position either at your own institution or elsewhere.

Volunteer for accreditation review committees

Both regional accrediting bodies (such as the Southern Association of Colleges and Schools, the Middle States Association of Colleges and Schools, the Western Association of Schools and Colleges, and so on) and specialized bodies that offer accreditation or certification in individual disciplines (e.g., the National Council for Accreditation of Teacher Education, Association to Advance Collegiate Schools of Business, and National Association of Schools of Music) are almost always in need of qualified individuals who can review institutions' applications for accreditation. Some of these opportunities involve off-site review of the documentation that institutions have submitted for a new or renewed accreditation status. Other opportunities may require travel to the schools being reviewed in order to determine the accuracy of their self-studies, compliance reports, or responses to concerns that have been raised. In either case, the experience will provide you with a great deal of information about current issues in higher education policy, the ways in which different colleges and universities address the challenges that arise in offering superior academic programs, and interaction with personnel at other institutions who can serve as good resources for you as you develop your administrative portfolio.

Learn in detail how your institution works

While you probably already have a good sense of how your institution works in general, as a provost or dean you'll need detailed insight into where various decisions are made and how. Aside from curricular matters and other issues vital to your school's academic programs, who is responsible for the various tasks assigned such areas as student life, institutional advancement, public relations, security, the registrar's office, and physical plant? You may be right to assume that the position you're interested in doesn't become involved in such issues as student disputes with roommates, concerns about safety in the residence halls, off-campus programming, and corporate fundraising, but you need to have a clear conception of who does address these matters on your campus. After all, you may be asked.

Administrative offices frequently become clearinghouses of information, so the more information you have, the better. Frequently students and their parents don't distinguish between the academic side of their experience and other aspects of college life, such as paying their bills, engaging in cocurricular activities, and balancing the demands of their job and their studies. They might not expect you to know all the answers, but they do want you to know where the answers can be found. Similarly, parents with concerns about charges for services or the behavior of a child's roommate aren't going to call the central switchboard and ask for the bursar, the provost, or the residence life office. They may not even know those terms. They're going to assume that you'll know where to direct them, even if they don't expect you to solve all their problems. Besides, the better you understand how your institution operates, the more positive examples of efficiencies and effective leadership styles you're likely to encounter.

Stay apprised of ongoing issues in academia

No institution functions in a vacuum. The challenges you're facing at your school have parallels at literally dozens of other colleges and universities across the country. The best practices of these peer institutions can help guide your own decisions. The problems they're addressing may well arrive at your own college in a year or two, so you need to know what trends are emerging in higher education. Are the students who are enrolling in colleges for the next few years more likely to be focused on a career or interested in serving the greater good? Are there implications of federal law that'll need to be addressed on your campus? What are some of the recent developments in the areas of academic freedom, intellectual property, students with disabilities, and similar issues? To extend your expertise in these areas, you should be consulting the following resources on a regular basis:

- *Chronicle of Higher Education*, published weekly from administrative offices in Washington, D.C. Each issue covers a broad range of academic and administrative issues and contains a large section of advertisements for positions, including positions for deans and provosts. The *Chronicle*'s website (www.chronicle.com) provides access to many of the articles and job listings of the print version, along with a variety of forums, discussion groups, and other information valuable to higher education professionals.

- *Journal of Higher Education*, published bimonthly by the Ohio State University Press. Each issue contains peer-reviewed scholarly articles on matters of concern in higher education, as well as reviews of recently published books on significant issues in the field.

- *Dean and Provost*, published monthly by John Wiley; this concise newsletter provides timely updates on legal rulings of interest to higher education administrators, profiles of current deans and provosts, news of concern to academic leaders, and suggestions about how to be more effective in your job. It is available in print, online, and as a PDF delivery.

- *Change: The Magazine of Higher Learning*, published bimonthly by the Taylor & Francis Group in Philadelphia. This journal is a key resource on issues of higher education policy, improving the quality of instruction, and recent trends in academia.

- *Academe*, the official journal of the American Association of University Professors. It appears bimonthly and features articles, editorials, and book reviews, often examining issues from a faculty perspective.

- *Academic Leader*, published monthly by Magna Publications in Madison, Wisconsin. This eight-page newsletter contains highly focused articles on the practicalities and theories of higher education. Its target audience is everyone from department chairs through system chancellors.

- *Leader to Leader*, published quarterly by John Wiley. This journal is not restricted to issues in higher education alone. Rather, by examining new thought about leadership in a broad range of organizational contexts, it provides administrators with insights into the similarities and differences among leaders in different types of institutional environments.

○ *Peer Review*, the quarterly publication of the American Association of Colleges and Universities. Although it focuses primarily on undergraduate liberal education, it is also useful to graduate deans and administrators of professional programs because of its analysis of recent trends in education practice. Each issue focuses on a central topic of critical concern to academics.

○ The websites of major publishers in the field of academic administration, such as Jossey-Bass (www.josseybass.com), Magna (www.magnapubs.com), Stylus (stylus.styluspub.com), and ABC-Clio (www.abc-clio.com/). Simply browsing the recent books being released by publishers such as these can provide an overview of current administrative topics of major importance. Selecting the books that interest you for your own administrative library is a useful way to begin expanding your knowledge of the issues that are involved in being a dean or provost.

Promote interdisciplinary work

One way of practicing problem solving, building ties among different academic areas, and developing a vision for the future is to become active in expanding interdisciplinary programs. Interdisciplinary studies frequently provide clear administrative challenges—belonging to no one department, they often are seen as belonging to no one at all—that can give you an opportunity to polish your administrative skills while filling a genuine institutional need. They will also give you the chance to work with other departments on a wide variety of administrative challenges (developing new courses, achieving equity in load, securing funding, drafting written proposals, and the like) that you will need in further leadership roles. In addition, success in promoting interdisciplinary programs provides you with a broad area of achievement outside your own academic discipline that can help you make the case that you are qualified to accept the challenges of a position as provost or dean.

Attend events widely

Another way of increasing your knowledge of different disciplines and how your school works is to attend events widely across campus. Everyone has his or her own interests, of course, and there are likely to be lectures, concerts, athletic events, seminars, discussions, and gatherings that you ordinarily would not attend, even though you've been invited, because these aren't closely related to your field or areas of interest. As a dean or provost, however, you'll be expected to understand the role that scholarship and cultural activities play in a wide variety of disciplines. You'll be expected to demonstrate support for all the programs under your supervision, not just for your own academic area. The sooner you begin to attend campus events widely, the sooner you will begin to appreciate the complex contributions of different fields. As an added advantage, you'll also come to be seen as an individual who has a broad view of what's important at your institution. Of greatest value to you will be the expanded network of contacts and perspectives that you will gain through your increased campus activity.

Develop budgetary experience

One area that academic leaders can never master too thoroughly is budgeting, particularly when it comes to planning, proposing, and supervising how funds are to be spent. If there are budgetary workshops offered by your institution or the professional organization of your discipline, enroll in them regularly. If you can't find any appropriate training opportunities, begin reviewing some reference works or surveys that deal with academic budgeting, such as Barr and McClellan (2011), Buller (2012), Goldstein (2012), and Kretovics (2011), and be certain that you are familiar with the basic terminology and principles of academic budgeting.

Attend workshops for academic leaders

Many organizations provide training sessions for deans, several of which are open to department chairs and other individuals who are interested in exploring the possibility of a deanship. These workshops will expose you to a large number of current best practices in higher education while also allowing you to ask the specific questions you may have about the dean's role. The American Council on Education (www.acenet.edu/leadership/) offers a number of programs for new, aspiring, and experienced chief academic officers. The Council of Academic Deans from Research Education Institutions conducts a New Deans Institute (www.cadrei.org), the American Association of Community Colleges sponsors the John E. Roueche Future Leaders Institute (www.aacc.nche.edu/newsevents/Events/leader shipsuite/Pages/FutureLeadersInstitute.aspx), and the Council of Graduate Schools holds a New Deans Institute each summer (www. cgsnet .org /events).

If a sufficient number of administrators at your school are interested in the same program, it can be more cost-effective to bring the training to you than to send a large group to a workshop. The Academy for Academic Leadership (www.academicleaders.org), ATLAS: Academic Training, Leadership, and Assessment Services (www.atlasleadership.com), and Keeling and Associates (www.keelingassociates.com) all tailor programs to meet the specific needs of the host institution. Webinars sponsored by the Wiley Learning Institute (wileylearninginstitute.com) and Magna Publications (www.magnapubs.com/online/seminars) provide programs in which you can participate without leaving your home or office.

Seeking out training opportunities like these will help put you in contact with much of the information that you will need in your future role as dean. In addition, your participation in such workshops will announce your interest in further administrative responsibility to others who may be able to help you in your career. You'll also begin forming a network of alliances with whom to interact as you assume new duties.

Reorganize your résumé

The curriculum vitae of an administrator should be organized somewhat differently from that of a faculty member. Whereas professors are likely to emphasize scholarly achievements, success in teaching, and service activity in their résumé, an administrator should give precedence to important accomplishments in leading programs to greater success, managing resources, and supervising employees. Review your vita, therefore, and ask yourself what picture emerges from its pages. Is it clear that the person whose work is reflected in that document has the experience needed to serve as an academic leader? If not, how could you reorganize your material in such a way as to call attention to your administrative achievements? Consider separating your administrative experience from your academic experience at the beginning of your vita. What accomplishments clearly belong in the first category rather than the second? After the introductory material of the résumé (your contact information, degrees, positions held, and so on), it may be useful to include a section titled "Administrative Highlights" in which you outline your achievements in such areas as these:

o Academic programs

o Faculty relations

o Finance and budget

o Technological innovation

o External relations

o Organizational efficiency

o Policies and procedures

Sections in which you have relatively few entries will indicate where you might need additional training or experience as you prepare for your first position as provost or dean. You may also wish to consider introducing this entire section of your vita with a brief "Philosophy of Administration" in which you outline your approach to academic leadership. Here's an example of this type of statement:

> Effective administrators combine their dedication to collegiality and professionalism with an ability to inspire those whom they serve. Through collegiality and their willingness to build consensus, administrators model for students the highest form of leadership and benefit from the creativity, talent, and insights of every member of their community. Through professionalism, administrators set an essential, institution-wide standard that tasks must be accomplished on time and at a high level of quality, that confidences must be kept, and that even the smallest details of a plan must be addressed. Through the ability to inspire others, administrators both build a community and help that community fulfill its shared vision.

By developing your statement of philosophy, you'll help clarify for yourself (and for the people who will eventually interview you) how you view your administrative position and your role in advancing your institution's mission.

Sample Interview Questions

Once you feel you've made adequate progress on the ten suggestions outlined, you can begin to think about applying for and pursuing higher administrative positions at your own institution or elsewhere. A crucial part of that process will be engaging in what's likely to be an extensive series of interviews that people will use to determine whether you might be a good fit for the challenges facing their next provost or dean. To help get you ready for that process, following are some of the most common questions asked during interviews of candidates for dean or provost positions:

1. Why are you interested in this job?
2. How do you view the role of the dean [provost]?
3. What successes have you had in fundraising?

4. What do you expect that you'll like least about being a dean [provost]? What do you expect that you'll do best?

5. How might you promote greater unity or focus in our programs?

6. What evidence can you provide of your support for all the academic areas that report to this position (such as fine arts, natural sciences, humanities, social sciences, business administration, education, engineering, health careers, law, and so on)?

7. What is the most interesting book you've read in the last six months?

8. How would you preserve the special nature and traditions of this institution?

9. What makes you unique as an individual?

10. How would you judge the success of a dean [provost]?

11. What should be included in the curriculum we offer?

12. Which of the current trends in higher education do you believe will last? Which trends do you regard as mere fads?

13. How would you improve the retention of our minority students? How would you improve our retention overall?

14. What do you do to relax?

15. How do you attract a diverse student body? A diverse faculty?

16. Where do you see yourself in five years? ten years?

17. What is the biggest challenge facing academic administration today?

18. What is the most significant accomplishment in your current job?

19. How do you go about internationalizing the curriculum? How do you go about internationalizing the student body?

20. What do people who don't like you say about you?

21. How do you handle salary compression or salary inversion?

22. What approach would you take toward faculty development?

23. Who should initiate curricular matters: administrators or the faculty?

24. Describe a mistake you made. What did you learn from it?

25. How do you handle community relations?

26. How do you handle programs with low enrollments?

27. What have you done in the area of community service [or, if appropriate, service-learning]?

28. Would you have an open-door policy?

29. What is the proper balance between research and teaching? How should service enter into this balance?

30. What achievement would you like to look back on after your first year as dean [provost]?

31. Describe a tough decision you've made. What made it so difficult?

32. Describe a problem you've solved.

33. How do you go about allocating resources when you're planning a budget?

34. What is your stand on academic freedom?

35. How would you describe yourself? How would the faculty you work with describe you? How would members of the staff describe you?

36. How will I know when you're angry? serious? joking?

37. What are some examples of your creativity and innovation?

38. Why do you want to leave teaching?

39. Describe an unpopular decision and its result.

40. What is your favorite word in the English language? Why?

Conclusion

Perhaps the best advice for prospective academic leaders came from the late John McDaniel, dean of liberal arts at Middle Tennessee State University, who, when I asked him about what he had learned in many years of successful administrative work, said, "It all comes down to humility, integrity, humor, perspective, and service. A good dean can figure out how to do the 'best' thing when it's just not possible to do the 'right' thing because resources, politics, and personalities are what they are. That's the perennial challenge for deans. It usually starts with the first day on the job and ends only with the assignment itself."

REFERENCES

Barr, M. J., & McClellan, G. S. (2011). *Budgets and financial management in higher education*. San Francisco, CA: Jossey-Bass.

Buller, J. L. (2012). *The essential department chair: A comprehensive desk reference*. San Francisco, CA: Jossey-Bass.

Goldstein, L. (2012). *A guide to college and university budgeting: Foundations for institutional effectiveness*. Washington, DC: NACUBO.

Kretovics, M. A. (2011). *Business practices in higher education: A guide for today's administrators*. New York, NY: Routledge.

RESOURCES

Bolman, L. G., & Gallos, J. V. (2011). *Reframing academic leadership*. San Francisco, CA: Jossey-Bass

Bolton, A. (2000). *Managing the academic unit*. Maidenhead, Berkshire, UK: Open University Press/McGraw-Hill.

Bryant, P. T. (2005). *Confessions of a habitual administrator: An academic survival manual*. Bolton, MA: Anker.

Buller, J. L. (2011). *Academic leadership day by day: Small steps that lead to great success*. San Francisco, CA: Jossey-Bass.

Buller, J. L. (2013). *Positive academic leadership: How to stop putting out fires and begin making a difference*. San Francisco, CA: Jossey-Bass.

Gunsalus, C. K. (2006). *The college administrator's survival guide*. Cambridge, MA: Harvard University Press.

Little, L., & McDaniel, T. (2003). *Lessons in leadership/dean's dialogue*. Madison, WI: Magna.

Martin, J., & Samels, J. E. (2015). *The provost's handbook: The role of the chief academic officer*. Baltimore, MD: Johns Hopkins University Press.

Roy, M. M. (2014). Preparing for a successful role in academic leadership: Understanding your role. In L. L. Behling (Ed.), *The resource handbook for academic deans* (pp. 3–8). San Francisco, CA: Jossey-Bass.

Zappe, C. J., & Gerdes, E. J. (2012). Temporary insanity: Deciding to be a dean. *Academic Leader*, 24(12), 1, 6.

3

IDENTIFYING YOUR LEADERSHIP STYLE

Every now and then someone may ask you, "What's your leadership style?" Depending on your relationship with the speaker, his or her tone of voice, and exactly what you've been up to lately, the thrust of this question can vary quite a bit. For instance, in an interview, the people asking you about your style may be trying to ascertain where you see yourself more as:

- A *catalyst* for innovation. (If you say, "I'm a change agent," others may hear, "I'm someone who's going to eliminate everything you like about this place.")
- A *champion* for your area. (If you say, "I'm an advocate for our programs," others may hear, "I'm someone who's going to pick fights with the president and governing board.")
- A *conduit* from the faculty to the rest of the university. (If you say, "I'm a bridge builder," others may hear, "I'm someone who's going to be the president's lapdog.")
- An action-oriented *coach* rather than a mere talker or dreamer. (If you say, "I'm a hands-on kind of leader who likes to work with people one-on-one," others may hear, "I'm someone who's going to micromanage all of you within an inch of your lives.")

Along this same line of thinking, Timothy J. Fogarty (2006) outlines four major types of "bad deans" that search committees may try to weed out during their screening:

- The *indecisive dean* who has difficulty making any kind of decision
- The *clueless dean* who can't understand either academic administration as a whole or the local political culture

○ The *hoarder* who can't delegate authority
○ The *shaker* who promotes change simply for its own sake, not because change is actually needed

At times questions about your leadership style are a kind of trap. If you don't say exactly what's in the questioner's mind, he or she may decide that you're not the type of leader the program needs right now.

In other contexts, the question may arise when someone is simply curious about how you make decisions. For example, do you see yourself more as an administrator who still may teach and do a bit of research or as an academic who happens to have some administrative duties at the moment? Still others may be wondering whether you're a carbon copy of the person formerly in that position (who may have been much beloved, universally hated, or something in between) or a new type of boss they'll have to spend endless hours figuring out. There will even be those who ask you this question because you just did or said something that surprised, shocked, or dismayed them. (The latter use tends to have a recognizable inflection of its own, something along the lines of "What kind of leader *are* you?" Ending this question with a somewhat exasperated *anyway* is optional but extremely common.)

For this reason, since you're all but certain to be asked about your leadership style on a regular basis, it pays to remember the following essential principle:

> Good provosts and deans develop a clear understanding of how they view their roles, what they're trying to accomplish as academic leaders, and who they think they are in terms of their own careers and their place within their institution's overall culture.

While we all believe we already know who we are, this issue becomes more complex the longer you reflect on it. Too often, our concept of what we want others to believe we stand for clouds our understanding of what we actually believe. The answers we give in interviews tend to be shaped by what we believe people want to hear. If you provide those answers often enough, you can start to believe your own press releases and lose track of your true strengths, preferences, and approaches to stressful situations. You have to be aware of your own weaknesses and areas of inexperience in order to build an effective leadership team. So let's return to the initial question: "What's your leadership style?"

Kim Cameron and Robert Quinn (2011) have developed a taxonomy of leadership styles based on the competing values framework. In its simplest form, leaders are classified on the basis of where they fall on two scales:

1. Whether they are more flexible and adaptable in their approaches or prefer their environments to remain more stable and controlled
2. Whether their focus tends to be on the internal processes of the organization they work for or on the external constituents who are served by that organization

Combining the leader's scores on these two scales suggests that the leader's style falls into one of four categories:

1. *Collaborative* (highly flexible and adaptable with an internal focus): Leaders who emphasize building community and promoting teamwork while seeing their roles as those of facilitators or mentors
2. *Creative* (highly flexible and adaptable with an external focus): Leaders who emphasize vision and innovation while seeing their roles as those of innovators or power brokers
3. *Competitive* (favoring a stable and controlled environment with an external focus): Leaders who emphasize speed and decisiveness while seeing their roles as those of producers or directors
4. *Control* (favoring a stable and controlled environment with an internal focus): Leaders who emphasize efficiency and practicality while seeing their roles as those of coordinators and monitors

A number of instruments exist for identifying your leadership style in accordance with this framework, including the Octogram (www. octogram.net) and the Management Skills Assessment Inventory (www. josseybass.com/go/cameron).

Although the four leadership styles addressed by the competing values framework provide a useful taxonomy, they represent only one of many systems that attempt to identify the different ways in which people lead others. Following are just a few representative leadership styles that are discussed by scholars who study organizational behavior:

Hierarchical leaders   Focus on the chain of command. They insist that reporting relationships be strictly followed and value decisiveness in supervisors and unquestioned obedience in employees.

Collaborative leaders	Work side-by-side with employees in setting and achieving goals. They see themselves either as a peer or as first among equals with others in the group, frequently giving their own opinion no more weight than that of anyone else.
Charismatic leaders	Obtain power through the force of their own personality. They have willing followers rather than mere subordinates and may not even hold an assigned position of leadership.
Laissez-faire leaders	Make a conscious decision to employees to develop their own solutions to a problem. They believe that groups are more creative when they are left to their own devices than when they are merely expected to follow instructions.
Parental leaders	Take a paternalistic or maternalistic attitude toward employees. They continually look out for the needs of those who report to them and intervene as necessary to make their jobs easier.
Situational leaders	Assume that no two opportunities or challenges are alike and that each situation calls for a different leadership approach. They regard each problem as unique and often adopt whatever approach they believe will be most effective in solving it.
Transactional leaders	Follow existing policies and procedures to the letter. They tend to be most effective when an organization has experienced a severe loss of confidence in its previous leadership or feels that prior administrations have played favorites and worked outside the established system.
Coaching leaders	Empower employees and delegate meaningful responsibilities to them. They see their role not as someone who tells people what to do but as a mentor who guides others in making more effective decisions.
Servant leaders	See themselves as existing primarily to help those they lead. They often eschew the traditional trappings of leadership and insist that the focus remain on the employees' achievements, not their own.

These leadership styles are not mutually exclusive—we can easily imagine a charismatic, collaborative, coaching leader or a hierarchical, parental, transactional leader—and it's possible to add dozens of other styles to this list. But even this short sample provides evidence that not everyone has to lead in the same way and no single way of leading is equally effective in every organization. (See Northouse, 2013; Kippenberger, 2002; and Hyun, Lee, and Miller, 2014.)

Another way of understanding your leadership style is to take advantage of one of the personality assessment tools available that can help provide insight into characteristics that affect your preferences and approaches to making decisions. (For general information on several of these inventories, including the Myers-Briggs Type Indicator, the Keirsey Temperament Sorter, and the DiSC Personal Profile, see Buller, 2012.) This kind of assessment tool can identify aspects of your personality that make you who you are, explain why you tend to solve problems in a particular way, and suggest certain skills your staff may need in order to compensate for your personal challenges and limitations. The truth is that almost any inventory that deals with personality, leadership style, or administrative strategy will be valuable in helping you reflect on how you can capitalize on your strengths and remediate your weaknesses. The goal is simply to become systematic in thinking about how your leadership strategies help or hinder what you are trying to accomplish in your position.

As useful as general inventories of personality traits may be, it can be beneficial to supplement them with tools that deal specifically with the role you'll be playing as provost or dean. The scenario analyses that conclude each part of this book provide one way for assessing your administrative style. Although a few suggestions for how to respond to each challenge are outlined for you, the situations in the analyses don't have a single correct solution and can be addressed effectively in different ways by different academic leaders. In addition, you might find it useful to perform an informal but candid self-assessment of your own strengths and weaknesses. To help you do that, we'll consider three very different types of administrative style inventories. You may prefer one more than the others, or you may find each one gives you different kinds of insights from the other two.

Leadership Spectrum Inventory

The Leadership Spectrum Inventory in exhibit 3.1 is a quick self-assessment tool. Since it takes only a few minutes to complete, it can be a useful exercise to complete at the start or end of each academic year

Exhibit 3.1 Leadership Spectrum Inventory

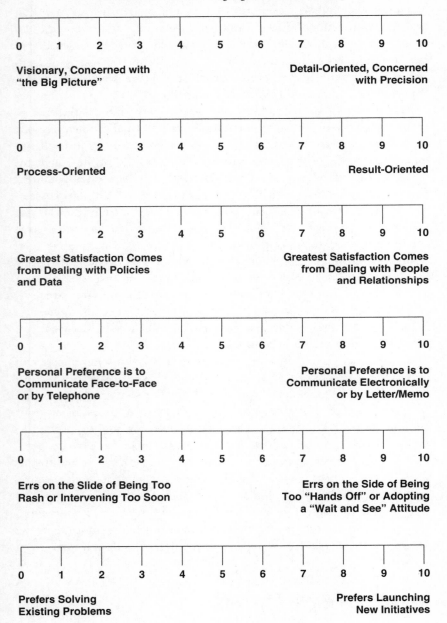

just to see whether your responses change over time. For each question, provide a candid response that indicates how you really feel, not how you believe deans are "supposed" to feel. Don't overthink each question. As in most other personality inventories, your first impulse is probably your most revealing. Each question consists of a spectrum between two administrative styles. Circle a number on each spectrum that indicates where your personal approach falls between the two styles. By circling a number rather than placing an X anywhere on the line, you'll have an answer that'll be easier to compare to one you'll create in a later exercise. If you're absolutely torn between the two choices, circle 5. But try not to do so too often. Very few people fall in exactly the middle of the spectrum.

Remember that all of us fall somewhere on each of these spectrums, so there's no one right place for "a good dean" to be. As is always the case with style inventories, the goal isn't to answer the question "right"; it's to explore how you really tend to approach administrative situations.

Stark Contrasts

The second inventory provides a useful complement to the Leadership Spectrum Inventory, or it may be taken independently. The basic concept will be familiar to you if you've ever played the party game "Would You Rather?" (For some examples of questions commonly posed in this game, such as "Would you rather go to jail for one year or have your best friend go to jail for ten years?" and "Would you rather have X-ray vision or be able to control the weather?" see www.wouldyourather.com. Gomberg and Heimberg (1997) provide additional popular examples of the dilemmas used in this game, as does their board game version distributed by Zobmondo. For each item, you must choose between two difficult alternatives. Once again, be sure to answer honestly, not simply according to how you believe you "ought" to answer. Also, responses like "I don't know" or "The two choices seem equally (un)pleasant" aren't allowed in this exercise, and you can't invent your own third choice (such as a compromise between the two alternatives). For each question, simply record which of the two statements you are more inclined to agree with and also the level of difficulty you found in making your choice. Score 1 for an extremely easy choice, 10 for an almost impossible choice, and rank the other possibilities in between.

1. Which of the following two statements is closer to your own opinion?
   a. Colleges and universities tend to be run too loosely. They are businesses created to produce a "product" (the education of

students and the development of new scholarship), not "families" or benevolent organizations run for the benefit of faculty members and other employees. Accountability and adherence to policy should be emphasized.

b. Colleges and universities are unique organizations that can prosper only if they make the needs of faculty members and other employees an important priority. Family-friendly and employee-friendly policies (and exceptions to policies when waiving a requirement benefits the employee) must take precedence over efficiency, productivity, and other concepts from the business world that are not really appropriate in academic life.

2. You are complaining to your spouse, best friend, or closest confidant that "they just don't get it. They simply don't have the right perspective to understand how this issue affects me and my college as a whole." The *they* in these sentences most likely refers to:

a. Members of the upper administration.

b. Members of the faculty.

3. Because of your increasing job responsibilities, you are forced to give up one of the following forever. You decide that you will never again:

a. Teach.

b. Conduct research, scholarship, or creative activity.

4. You must offer a new full-time faculty position to one of the following two departments.

a. The department with the larger number of majors

b. The department that generates the highest number of student credit hours because it offers a large number of service or general education courses

5. Would you rather ...

a. Retain every one of the department chairs in your area, with absolutely no option to replace them in the future?

b. Have a system where you must replace every one of the department chairs in your area each year and where chairs aren't ever permitted to succeed themselves or extend their terms?

6. Which of the following two statements is closer to your own opinion?

a. College students today increasingly have special psychological needs and learning disabilities that must radically alter the way we fulfill our mission. Furthermore, societal norms for the behavior and dress of students have become so flexible that attempting to enforce strict standards is counterproductive. Our duty must be to respond to students' needs and to "meet them where they are" rather than attempt to adhere to a set of standards that is impossible to realize in today's world.

b. Our duty as a college is to prepare students for life, and one important part of that preparation is to insist that educated people adhere to certain expectations in their behavior and scholarship. We do students a disservice by failing to enforce high enough standards. We should require more of our students, even if this policy increases our rate of attrition.

7. Enrollment at your institution is undergoing a massive but temporary increase. You must do one of the following:

a. Enforce existing maximum enrollment limits per section (maintaining a hard-won level of instructional quality but compelling students to take courses from other institutions or possibly even to transfer).

b. "Open the floodgates" in all courses (meeting student demand, but significantly increasing student-to-faculty ratios).

8. Would you rather … :

a. Remain a full-time administrator from now until your retirement?

b. Return to the faculty immediately with no possibility of ever having another administrative appointment?

9. You receive an unexpected telephone call "about a serious problem." You are told that the caller is extremely angry, and when you learn the caller's identity, you feel your anxiety level rise dramatically. Which of the following is more likely to have made you more nervous?

a. The president of your institution

b. An angry parent of one of your students

10. Would you rather … :

a. Keep the same curriculum for all of the disciplines in your area from now until you retire with no changes whatsoever (i.e., no new courses, no new programs, no alteration of any syllabus except for updated editions of current textbooks)?

b. Be required to replace every course, major, and requirement with a radically new approach, curriculum, and syllabus every five years?

11. Which of the following two statements is closer to your own opinion?

    a. In today's litigious climate, colleges must go out of their way to control substance abuse, rowdy behavior, and sexual misconduct. It's a different and more dangerous world than when we went to college, so it's important for institutions to enforce strict zero-tolerance policies on many types of behavior.

    b. One of the most important aspects of the college experience is the opportunity for all students to experiment and discover what is proper for themselves in the areas of alcohol consumption, drug use, and sexual activity. Rowdy behavior was and always will be a part of collegiate life. It's futile to try to control it, and setting limits too strictly can even interfere with the maturation process that students undergo at college.

12. You are lured away from your current position by one of the following career opportunities. Which is it?

    a. Serving as the founding dean of a college (or first provost at a university) where there will be serious and unpleasant birth pangs but an opportunity to be innovative and to leave a lasting legacy.

    b. Serving as the chief academic officer of a well-established, well-funded unit or institution that has most of its very difficult decisions behind it. It's an easy job, but most people won't remember you after you're gone.

13. Would you rather … :

    a. Fire someone, endure a long, frustrating grievance process and lawsuit, and ultimately have your decision vindicated?

    b. Have your own job placed in jeopardy even though you know it will all work out in the end?

14. Which of the following scenarios would make you more uncomfortable?

    a. Arriving at your office in the morning to find it taken over by an angry delegation of students

    b. Finding out that your office was taken over by the students while you are traveling outside the country

15. Would you rather … :

    a. Have your duties revised so that all you did all day, every day was to check and recheck each unit's actual expenditures against its annual budgetary allocation to be certain that it was remaining in budget?

b. Have your job constantly on the line based on your ability to successfully and creatively develop a never-ending series of innovative academic programs that aren't offered by any other institution in the country?

16. You have just learned that the provost at a peer institution and one of his or her deans have had a serious disagreement. One side is clearly in the right; the other side is clearly in the wrong. Based on no more information than that, your initial assumption is that the person most likely to be at fault is the

a. provost.

b. dean.

17. In which of the following would you seriously take the greatest pride?

a. A book of your own that received only modest reviews and limited sales

b. A major grant proposal that was successfully submitted by a group of other faculty members in your area

18. There's only one hour left before you leave campus for the summer in order to participate in an in-depth leadership training program for academic leaders. You can devote your time to only one of the following:

a. Solving a serious problem that arose only today

b. Launching a major new initiative that has the possibility of producing long-term benefits for your institution

19. A new facility will soon be ready for occupancy by one of your disciplines. The building has been one of your most important projects for several years, and you see it as an important part of your legacy. Unfortunately, you've learned that you must be away from campus on crucial business for more than a month after the building is completed. Which of the following alternatives would you choose?

a. Delegating the unveiling of the new facility to someone else at your institution

b. Delaying the opening until you can be present

20. You learn that a student and a faculty member are in a dispute. Based on no more information than that, which side do you immediately feel is more likely to be at fault?

a. The student

b. The faculty member

21. There's a severe budget crisis, and you're forced to do one of the following:

    a. Impose substantial salary cuts on all employees

    b. Terminate the faculty member with the least seniority in each program

22. Which of the following two statements is closer to your own opinion?

    a. It is preferable to keep admission standards flexible enough that we can meet our enrollment targets, even if this policy lowers the quality of the student body. It's only to be expected that certain students will end up flunking out. At least we gave them an opportunity.

    b. It's preferable to preserve high admission standards, even if this policy results in significantly lower enrollment, flat or declining budgets, and reductions of faculty lines. It's immoral to admit a student for whom there's not a high likelihood of success.

23. Would you rather … :

    a. Spend an entire week involved in one very unpleasant, angry confrontation after another?

    b. Have no other work to do for a month except the one activity that bores you most?

24. Following a national search, one of your departments presents you the names of two highly recommended candidates for a faculty position. Do you hire:

    a. The applicant who is demonstrably the better teacher?

    b. The applicant whose teaching ability is weaker but who will immediately bring your institution substantial research income?

25. A problem arises that has an 80 percent chance of fixing itself and a 75 percent chance that if you intervene, you'll make the problem worse. But there's a 20 percent chance it'll become worse anyway and a 25 percent chance that only you can fix it. What do you do?

    a. Intervene even though the odds are that you'll make matters worse, agreeing with Karl von Clausewitz that "it is … better to act quickly and err than to hesitate until the time of action is past" (Hamilton, 1921, 200).

    b. Wait and see, even though it's possible you'll end up with a real disaster on your hands, agreeing with Lewis Thomas (1974) that "the great secret, known to internists, … but still hidden from the public, is that most things get better by themselves. Most things, in fact, are better in the morning" (85).

26. You have an opportunity to leave your position for a new job with a significantly higher salary in a better location. The problem is that this new position is at an undistinguished institution and your new title is so unimpressive that most of your current colleagues will probably view the new opportunity as a demotion. Which do you choose?

   a. The higher salary, better location, and superficially less prestigious position

   b. Your current position, which has more prestige but a lower salary

27. A faculty member in your area must be reprimanded. How do you deliver this message?

   a. In writing so that you can leave a paper trail

   b. Orally so that you can use the occasion for mentoring

28. Someone who works in your area arrives at your office visibly distraught. You find out that the employee is desperate to talk to you about a very difficult personal problem. Nevertheless, you're scheduled to appear before your governing board to make a routine presentation; in fact, the members of the board are already waiting for you. What do you do?

   a. Keep your commitment to the governing board, even though it means temporarily abandoning the distressed employee

   b. Help your employee, even though it means keeping the board waiting and making its members angry

29. Two problems have arisen, both severe enough that you must address them immediately. You have a trusted subordinate who can help you with one of them. Which issue do you take on yourself, delegating the other to your subordinate?

   a. A messy but not particularly challenging personnel problem

   b. An important but not particularly complex report that your president has requested

30. It's your first meeting on a significant new initiative. To which of the following two activities do you devote most of your meeting time?

   a. Charging the committee, giving a great deal of attention to the nature of the result you hope they'll achieve

   b. Discussing the best procedures for the committee to use in doing its work, developing an action plan, and setting a meeting schedule

As is readily apparent, the vast majority of these choices are really false dichotomies. They don't represent the sort of dilemmas academic leaders usually face—at least not with such a high degree of inflexibility. Nevertheless, the limitations of time, budget, and our own talents do impose on us periodic choices that are somewhat similar to the thirty problems you just encountered. The alternatives you chose in this exercise, even if they seemed a bit strained at times, reveal something important about what kind of academic leader you are. That information will help you uncover where your unacknowledged biases and undiscovered strengths lie. It will also highlight your own default positions, suggesting where your views may need to be expanding by consulting with others who see matters differently.

This exercise in stark contrasts can help in a number of ways. First, it serves as either a reinforcement of or a correct to the view of your leadership style that emerged from the Leadership Spectrum Inventory. To review, here are the six areas covered by that inventory:

A. A visionary versus a detail orientation

B. A process versus a result orientation

C. A policies-and-date versus a people-and-relationships orientation

D. An in-person or oral communication style versus an electronic or indirect communication style

E. A charge-in orientation versus a hang-back orientation

F. A "fix-what's-here" versus a "start-something-new" orientation

Many of the stark contrasts deal with these same perspectives. To create a score in each category, start by assigning yourself a 5 for each perspective, A through F. Then increase or decrease that score according to table 3.1. Any score below 0 counts as 0, and any score above 10 counts as 10.

Now compare those six numbers to the ones you circled on the corresponding lines of the Leadership Spectrum Inventory. Were there any areas in which your two numbers were significantly different? Were there other elements in how the two stark contrasts were phrased that led you to reply in a manner that would seem contrary to your self-image? (If so, what were these factors? Knowing what they are is important because they suggest attractions or aversions that may tend to override your usual approaches to situations.) If there were no extraneous elements that you can identify in the alternatives, how might you account for the discrepancy? Are there ways in which your self-image is perhaps not quite accurate when you are confronted by actual situations?

Table 3.1. Scoring Guide for Stark Contrasts

A   Subtract 2 each time you chose *b* for items 15 and/or 18. Subtract 1 each time you chose *a* for items 12 and/or 28.

Add 2 each time you chose *a* for items 15 and/or 18. Add 1 each time you chose *b* for items 12 and/or 28.

B   Subtract 3 if you chose *b* for item 30. Subtract 2 if you chose *b* for item 1.

Add 3 if you chose *a* for item 30. Add 2 if you chose *a* for item 1.

C   Subtract 2 each time you chose *a* for item 28 and/or *b* for item 29. Subtract 1 if you chose *a* for item 1.

Add 2 each time you chose *b* for item 28 and/or *a* for item 29. Add 1 if you chose *b* for item 1.

D   Subtract 3 if you chose *b* for item 27. Subtract 1 each time you chose *a* for items 3 and/or 29.

Add 3 if you chose *a* for item 27. Add 1 each time you chose *b* for items 3 and/or 29.

E   Subtract 2 each time you chose *a* for items 14 and/or 25. Subtract 1 if you chose *b* for item 6. Subtract 1 if you chose *a* for item 11.

Add 2 each time you chose *b* for items 14 and/or 25. Add 1 if you chose *a* for item 6. Add 1 if you chose *b* for item 11.

F   Subtract 2 each time you chose *a* for items 10 and/or 18. Subtract 1 if you chose *b* for item 12. Subtract 1 if you chose *a* for item 15.

Add 2 each time you chose *b* for items 10 and/or 18. Add 1 if you chose *a* for item 12. Add 1 if you chose *b* for item 15.

Your administrative profile

A second way in which this exercise in stark contrasts can be useful derives from what these questions tell you about your personal administrative profile. Review your choices to each of the thirty items and identify the patterns that emerge in each of the following areas:

a. *Where your natural sympathies lie in the administrative hierarchy* (items 2, 3, 8, 9, 16, 20, 24, 28, and 29)? While the title listed on our business cards may be dean or provost, we all have other roles that we play simultaneously, even if we're not aware of them. We may be acting in a way that makes others think of us as a friend of the faculty, defender of the student, future president, advocate for excellence in teaching, or something similar. It's useful to know where your sympathies lie so that you can compensate for the limitations of these default tendencies when it's necessary and play a different role when it's appropriate. In addition, knowing what your natural bias is likely to be in specific situations can encourage you to go out of your way to hear the other side when you need to do so, an approach that will make you a better leader.

b. *What professional responsibility holds your greatest interest—and perhaps earns your highest respect* (items 3, 8, 9, 15, 16, 17, 20, 24, and 28)? Provosts and deans have to divide their time among duties involving various aspects of administration, teaching, scholarship, and service. Some administrators believe that it's inappropriate for them to have a personal share in the limited resources available to full-time faculty members for instruction and research. Others feel that remaining active as a teacher and scholar brings them greater credibility with faculty members, students, and potential donors. Both perspectives have merit in certain situations and for certain individuals. But it's important to know where you fall on this continuum in order to explain your perspective to those who may challenge it. Also, if you find that your answers suggest that you are, for example, "too administration focused" or "too faculty focused" not sufficiently sensitive to the needs and interests of students, this knowledge can guide you to seek other perspectives in order to develop a more balanced understanding of each issue as it comes your way.

c. *How comfortable you are with innovation or change* (items 5, 6, 10, 11, 12, and 15)? We all vary in our capacity to feel comfortable in a shifting and ambiguous environment. Some administrators thrive on change; they may even love it too much, unnecessarily altering policies and programs simply to "shake things up." Other administrators are overly averse to change; they'll stick to a decision even when it's apparent that the decision isn't working or has been counterproductive. It can help to be aware of your own leadership style when it comes to tolerating change. If you know how you're likely to react in times of upheaval, you can compensate for any tendencies to move too quickly or too slowly when more or less stability seems desirable.

d. *Is a significant part of your job satisfaction derived from personal recognition or from group achievements* (items 17, 19, and 26)? Academic leaders are motivated by many things: money, praise, the delight of solving a thorny problem, the excitement of creating something new, personal recognition, and the success of the institution as a whole. Since so much that provosts and deans accomplish is necessarily less tied to personal achievements than to work done by the faculty and students, it's important for you to know whether you'll find sufficient fulfillment in other people's glory. Many a dean has been dissatisfied because it was the faculty of the college, not the dean, that was honored as the recipients of the prestigious fellowships, teaching awards, and book contracts. And many provosts have felt that exchanging success as a researcher for days filled with meetings was too great a sacrifice. It can be helpful for you to know how you might feel should such a situation occur.

e. *What are your personal priorities?* Several of the questions on the inventory pose stark contrasts that force you to choose between competing priorities, much in the way that your work as an academic leader sometimes forces you to make choices among lesser evils or greater goods. For example, deans and provosts are regularly asked whether they approach the institution as though they were running a business (item 1), assign greater importance to the total number of majors in a program or its contribution to the generation of student credit hours (item 4), are sympathetic to the needs of students (item 6), care more about providing students with access to academic programs or maintaining high academic standards (item 7), and so on.

While the dichotomies created by this exercise are often strained, they're helpful in clarifying your position on issues. Which items were most challenging? Which choices were the hardest? The items that you found particularly difficult—as well as the items that you found so clear-cut that it seemed almost ridiculous to ask the question—tell you a great deal about your leadership approach to various issues. If a choice seems too easy, this may be an area in which you'll want to seek out other perspectives. If a choice was too hard, see it as an opportunity to analyze the implications of each alternative and decide how you or the college would fare as a result of the choice you make.

Your Administrative Quadrant

The final leadership inventory, the Administrative Quadrant (AQ) is designed to determine how academic leaders tend to deal with making decisions. For each question, choose the one response (a, b, c, or d) that seems closest to how you would actually react to the situation. As with the other exercises, force yourself to select only one option and answer according to what you actually believe, not how you think "a good academic leader" would respond:

1. In response to budget reductions, your supervisor has insisted that all full-time faculty members must now teach one extra course per term. You're told that there'll be absolutely no exceptions, and it'll be taken very seriously if any administrator fails to apply this policy across the board. Despite this warning, you are aware of a faculty member who's a single parent of three young children and the sole caregiver to her aged parents, both of whom suffer from Alzheimer's disease. Increasing this faculty member's load would cause her severe hardship. You try to raise

the issue with your supervisor, who replies, "I said no exceptions, and I mean no exceptions. The policy is what it is." What do you do?

a. Raise the faculty member's teaching load. You did all you could, but as your boss says, "The policy is what it is."

b. Discreetly keep the faculty member's teaching load low, hope that your decision goes unnoticed, but resolve that you'll simply face the consequences if your supervisor finds out.

c. Tell the faculty member you're sorry, but you'll need to follow the new policy. You'll help the best you can with an additional teaching assistant and a slightly reduced service load.

d. Raise the faculty member's teaching load and try to help her behind the scenes. For instance, on her load report, you count one large section as equivalent to teaching two regular sections, discreetly send her information about the employee assistance program and the county's social services agency, and help in other ways that won't seem obvious either to the provost or the faculty member.

2. One of your faculty members wants to try her hand at administration. She accepts a deanship at another university but pleads with you to grant her a year's leave of absence so that she has a backup plan in case things don't work out. You're not fond of this idea because if she doesn't resign, she'll tie up a precious tenure-track line for an entire year. Nevertheless, you eventually give in and grant the leave of absence. The academic year gets under way, and the date arrives when the faculty member promised to give you an answer about whether she'd resign or return. On the phone she says, "I just need more time. The president and provost here are awful. The atmosphere is positively toxic. But there's a good likelihood the board's going to force them out by the end of the year, and things would improve tremendously then. The rumor is that they may even make me the new provost. I hate to ask, but I really need one more year of leave." Which of the following are you *most* likely to say?

a. "I just can't wait another whole year without doing a tenure-track search. It's hurting the program, and if I don't start a search now, I could end up losing that line next year should you decide not to return. But the deadline for me to start a search is still four months away. I'll give you a four-month extension, but that's the best I can do."

b. "Oh, I don't know. That really is going to create a problem for us. But I do understand what you're saying, and it does sound like too good an opportunity to miss. Okay, I'll grant you another year's leave."

c. "Well, I think we might be able to reach a compromise. I'm going to initiate a tenure-track search on your line, but I'll set the interview dates for a year and one week from today. I'll call you back in a year, and if you say you're coming back, I'll cancel the search before we do interviews. We'll have lost a little money placing those ads, but at least we won't have paid any travel expenses for the candidates."

d. "Look, it was hard enough giving you one year; two years is completely out of the question. I need to know right now whether you're resigning or staying."

3. At the registrar's request, the president of your institution implemented a policy several years ago that professors won't be allowed to change their classrooms once the semester has begun. In part, this rule has been adopted for security reasons: the school wants to be able to account for any individual student or faculty member in the event of an emergency. But in part, the policy is simply practical: after the semester begins, the registrar's office is far too busy to make all the room changes that faculty members typically request; each change has to be entered into the system manually, and the registrar's staff isn't large enough to handle this work. One semester, a faculty member comes to you: he is teaching two courses back-to-back, and the registrar's office has scheduled these classes on opposite sides of the campus. The professor has a lot of equipment that he needs to move from one class to the next, and with the schedule as it is, he'll probably need to end the first class early each day, then start the second class late. Even worse, you're worried that some of the very expensive equipment used in these courses will be damaged from being moved back and forth so frequently. Which of the following is *closest* to the action you'd be likely to take?

a. You'd call the registrar and insist that an exception be made since it was the registrar's own room-scheduling decision that caused this problem.

b. You'd locate a vacant room close to the professor's first classroom, and since the registrar refuses to move the class officially, ask the faculty member simply to switch to the new room unofficially and keep quiet about this change.

c. You'd tell the faculty member that there are valid safety and logistical reasons for the president's policy, so even though it's a huge inconvenience, he'll have to teach in the rooms he's been assigned.

d. You'd reduce your travel budget to purchase a duplicate set of equipment, even though it's very expensive, thus making the faculty member's trip across campus much faster since he doesn't have to pack up and move the equipment.

4. One of your most important initiatives has been to boost the research productivity of the faculty. At the same time, you're also hoping to improve the visibility of your institution by encouraging the faculty to present their research at major national and international conferences. For this reason, even though the budget has been very tight, you've made some difficult and unpopular cuts so that you can set aside two special funds. The first contains a certain amount of research funding for each faculty member in the college; the second contains a pool of travel funding for each faculty member. Because the money was so hard to obtain, you've imposed special requirements. In order to qualify for the research money, the faculty member must demonstrate that the project to be funded will lead to a peer-reviewed publication or significant grant application. In order to qualify for the travel money, the faculty member must be presenting a paper at a major conference. Most departments have accepted these restrictions, but one of your chairs comes to you with a proposal: "Look, you know I inherited a program that really hasn't emphasized research for many years. I want to change that, but I'm still a long way from the point where we're ready to use the special funding you've created. But I think it could provide the way to get us there. There's a research opportunity overseas this summer that I can get my entire department involved it. It'll kick-start our research and put us on track for grants and publications in a year or two, but not immediately. The problem is that I'd need to divert the new research and travel funding to do so. I know it isn't what you had in mind, but it *is* research and travel. And it does ultimately achieve your goal." Which of the following are you most likely to say in response?

a. "My problem is that what you propose isn't really what I said we'd do with the money. But I tell you what: make this proposal at our next chairs' meeting. We'll see if the other chairs have any reasonable objections. Maybe one or more of them might want this flexibility too. I think that as long as we're open about it and submit it to a formal vote, we might be able to achieve what you want to do."

b. "Well, the whole point of my initiative was to improve our research productivity. One size doesn't fit all, I guess. So, sure. Let's go ahead and pursue your plan. Just give me your assurance that this is the best possible way to boost research in your area."

c. "I really want to help you, but I've already made it clear to everyone how the new funding is to be used. I can't go making special deals now. But let's set up a meeting where we can go through your budget, and I'll look carefully through mine, and let's see if there isn't some other way we can fund your project for at least part of your faculty."

d. "I know you think you've got a great idea. And maybe you do. But it just isn't what I designed these funds for. I fought hard and angered a lot of people to get the money for one purpose and one purpose only. I just can't pull a bait-and-switch like that."

5. A faculty member has applied for tenure. Although he's an excellent teacher with a solid record in research, he's just slightly under what's generally considered the minimum requirement in research when tenure is granted. The votes at the department, college, and university level have been so split and contentious that the president, who trusts your judgment, has decided to leave the matter up to you. What's your initial impulse?

a. "This person's a wonderful teacher but also doesn't meet the criteria for success in research. I feel I have to vote against tenure, but I'm going to make a special effort to help this person find a position where tenure is based largely on excellence in teaching."

b. "I hate to lose such a great teacher. And this faculty member was so close to meeting the standard for research. If I can get a waiver that allows this person an extra year or two on the tenure clock, I bet a good mentor can help this faculty member more than fulfill our research requirement."

c. "Tenure is a serious matter, a very long-term investment. We need to do better than award it to people who just squeak by. I'm inclined to vote against tenure."

d. "The choice is about someone's career and livelihood. My thought is that when a decision is this close, you always give the benefit of the doubt to the faculty member. I'm inclined to vote in favor of tenure."

Scoring and interpreting the AQ

Your AQ is the function of two numbers, which we'll call your E and F scores. Here's how you calculate them.

Both E and F start at 0: $E = 0$ $F = 0$

- Question 1. If you answered:

  a. Add 1 to E and subtract 1 from F.
  b. Subtract 1 from E and add 1 to F.
  c. Add 1 to both E and F.
  d. Subtract 1 from both E and F.

  $E = $ _____ $F = $ _____

- Question 2. If you answered:

  a. Add 1 to both E and F.
  b. Subtract 1 from E and add 1 to F.
  c. Subtract 1 from both E and F.
  d. Add 1 to E and subtract 1 from F.

  $E = $ _____ $F = $ _____

- Question 3. If you answered:

  a. Subtract 1 from both E and F.
  b. Subtract 1 from E and add 1 to F.
  c. Add 1 to E and subtract 1 from F.
  d. Add 1 to both E and F.

  $E = $ _____ $F = $ _____

- Question 4. If you answered:

  a. Subtract 1 from both E and F.
  b. Subtract 1 from E and add 1 to F.
  c. Add 1 to both E and F.
  d. Add 1 to E and subtract 1 from F.

  $E = $ _____ $F = $ _____

- Question 5. If you answered:

  a. Add 1 to both E and F.
  b. Subtract 1 from both E and F.

   c. Add 1 to E and subtract 1 from F.

   d. Subtract 1 from E and add 1 to F.

E = _____   F = _____

Your final E and F scores: E = _____   F = _____

Each of the two scores should be between −5 and +5. It is not possible to score a 0. If your scores don't adhere to both principles, check your addition. Then use the grid in figure 3.1 to circle each number on its appropriate line. Draw the shortest possible line between these two numbers. The section of the grid that your line crosses reveals your AQ. The title of each quadrant appears in figure 3.2.

Here's what your AQ reveals. Your E score relates to your tendency either to *enforce* policies or to *enable* people to find exceptions to policies. The higher your E number, the more likely you are to insist that a policy be followed. The lower your E number, the more willing you are to bend (or even ignore) the rules.

F relates to your administrative *focus*. A high F score means that your focus tends to be on *people-oriented* solutions. A low F number means that your focus tends to be on *procedural* or *systemic* solutions. Putting

Figure 3.1 Administrative Quadrant Grid

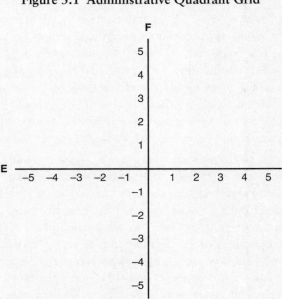

Figure 3.2 Administrative Quadrant with Labels

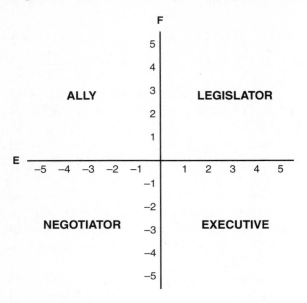

these two aspects of your administrative style together places you in one of the following four categories.

Ally: Allies have low E scores and high F scores. They tend to seek win-win solutions by working directly with people rather than by focusing too exclusively on what the policies say. They're most effective when situations allow for a great deal of personal interaction and enough time for them to work out solutions. They may run into problems, however, when they try to be everyone's friends, put too positive a spin on bad news when they deliver it, or fail to take aggressive action because they don't want to upset someone.

Legislator: Legislators have high scores for both E and F. They want people to be able to obtain the resources they need in order to do their jobs effectively, but they often do so behind the scenes, working on the level of policy whenever possible. Negotiators do best when they're able to develop new procedures in response to changing circumstances. They can thus be very effective in situations when an institution is undergoing a great deal of change. However, they may be limited by their natural inclination to work things out behind closed doors. It may not occur to them that they need to keep a larger circle of stakeholders in the loop or share their thought processes with others.

Negotiator: Negotiators have low scores in both E and F. They often view their role as "chief exception maker," recognizing the importance of good rules and policies but also seeing the advantage of being able to bend those rules when necessary. Negotiators can be very effective in situations requiring diplomacy *if* they have all the authority they need to grant the exemptions. Negotiators may get into trouble occasionally by breaking the rules a few too many times, creating an environment in which no one takes written policies very seriously.

Executive: Executives have a high E score and a low F score. They place a great deal of confidence in policies and procedures and feel that colleges and universities tend to develop rules for a very good reason. With executives, students and faculty members always know where they stand on an issue, and the executive can be counted on to honor his or her word. Executives need to be careful, however, that their consistency doesn't harden into sheer inflexibility; they're well advised to rely on confidants or mentors who can warn them whenever they're running the risk of being hidebound and mistaking the letter of the law for its spirit.

Conclusion

Knowing your leadership style doesn't tell you whether you'll be successful as a dean or provost. No one style of leadership is most effective for every person at every institution in every type of situation. Some leadership styles are more effective when we're creating programs, and others are preferable when we're trying to maintain programs that are already well established. Some academic leaders see their job as working closely with students and faculty members, while others focus more on external donors and implementing the goals of the upper administration. Either approach can work, depending on the circumstances. Leadership styles are not something that we're forced to adopt because of who we are or how we're wired. They're more like tools in a toolbox that you can pick up or put down as you need them. As long as you're aware of what you're doing, sometimes it can be very effective to act in a way that contradicts our customary approach to a situation. But doing so requires us to be aware of what our customary approach actually is. The different leadership style inventories presented in this chapter are effective techniques of assessing how we tend to lead most of the time and where we may need help in broadening our typical point of view.

REFERENCES

Buller, J. L. (2012). *The essential department chair: A comprehensive desk reference*. San Francisco, CA: Jossey-Bass.

Cameron, K. S., & Quinn, R. E. (2011). *Diagnosing and changing organizational culture: Based on the competing values framework* (3rd ed.). San Francisco, CA: Jossey-Bass.

Fogarty, T. J. (2006). The good, the bad, and the ugly: Knowing your dean. *Department Chair, 17*(1), 10–11.

Gomberg, D., & Heimberg, J. (1997). *Would you rather? Over 200 absolutely absurd dilemmas to ponder*. New York, NY: Plume/Penguin.

Hamilton, I. (1921). *The soul and body of an army*. London: E. Arnold.

Hyun, J., Lee, A. S., & Miller, L. (2014). *Flex: The new playbook for managing across differences*. New York, NY: HarperBusiness.

Kippenberger, T. (2002). *Leadership styles*. Oxford: Capstone.

Northouse, P. G. (2013). *Leadership: Theory and practice* (6th ed.). Thousand Oaks, CA: Sage.

Thomas, L. (1974). *The lives of a cell: Notes of a biology watcher*. New York, NY: Viking Press.

Would you rather ... ? CA: Zobmondo. Board game. www.wouldyourather.com.

RESOURCES

Alessandra, A. J., & O'Connor, M. J. (1996). *The platinum rule: Discover the four basic business personalities—and how they can lead you to success*. New York, NY: Warner Books.

Beck, J.D.W., & Yeager, N. M. (1994). *The leader's window: Mastering the four styles of leadership to build high-performing teams*. New York, NY: Wiley.

Diamond, R. M. (Ed.). (2002). *Field guide to academic leadership*. San Francisco, CA: Jossey-Bass.

Glanz, J. (2002). *Finding your leadership style: A guide for educators*. Alexandria, VA: Association for Supervision and Curriculum Development.

Kippenberger, T. (2002). *Leadership styles*. Minneapolis, MN: Capstone.

Leaming, D. (2003). *Managing people: A guide for department chairs and deans*. Bolton, MA: Anker.

Leaming, D. (2007). *Academic leadership: A practical guide to chairing the department* (2nd ed.). Bolton, MA: Anker.

4

CREATING A SHARED VISION

Since there's no one "best" leadership style for a dean or provost, it's perfectly acceptable that all of us bring a variety of strengths and weaknesses to these positions. Some of us are better at managing day-to-day details, others excel at large-scale strategic planning, and still others make their greatest contributions in specific areas like fundraising, curricular revision, or policy development. One way of compensating for the skills we lack as academic leaders—or lack in sufficient measure—is through team building. The administrators, assistants, and faculty members we hire can bring a better balance to those areas of responsibility for which we need additional support. Another way of addressing our weaknesses is to seek out additional training or information that helps us acquire the skills we lack.

Some administrative skills, like effective budgeting and the best ways to conduct an interview, can be learned by reading a book like this one or attending a workshop. Others, such as developing and promoting a compelling vision for the college, may seem all but impossible if you don't regard yourself as a "visionary person." In fact, many people believe that a sense of vision is innate and that those who are born without this gift can never develop it. President George H. W. Bush once spoke dismissively of "the vision thing" when reporters repeatedly asked him what he hoped to achieve in his presidency besides serving as a caretaker for the Reagan revolution. In a similar way, even the most managerial sort of academic leader, the type of person who's more comfortable completing an expense report than creating a long-term plan, will occasionally be asked, "What's your vision for the future? Where do you see your programs going? What would you like your legacy to be?" Any provost or dean who can't answer these questions compellingly enough may be regarded, at least by certain stakeholders, as ineffective. In extreme cases, the lack of a vision can cripple an administrative career.

A Visioning Exercise

If you've never thought of yourself as a particularly visionary person, how do you cope with "the vision thing"? How can you acquire this seemingly elusive skill? *Can* you even acquire it? As in most areas of life, certain people will have a greater facility for creativity than others; nevertheless, developing a shared vision is possible for anyone who's willing to put a little time into the activity. You can think of the following steps as a kind of "visioning exercise."

The vision steps

STEP 1: OUTLINE THE WAYS IN WHICH YOUR PROGRAMS ARE DISTINCTIVE NOW.   Take a blank sheet of paper and write down as many adjectives or phrases you can think of that describe how the programs you supervise are different from others. What sets them apart from other programs you've worked with or known about? What are your area's core values, the principles that if they were to change or be removed, would cause your area to stop being what it has always been? Keep working at this exercise until you've filled the entire sheet of paper. Then rank all your adjectives and phrases from the most important to the least important. After you've finished ranking these qualities, the top three to five descriptors should tell you something fundamental about your program's unique identity. But before we get to that point, check to see if statements similar to the following appear anywhere on your list:

- "Excellent faculty"
- "We care about our students"
- "Small class size"
- "Student oriented"
- "Superb curriculum"
- "Inadequate funding"

If you find statements like these on your list, cross them off and move the next item up in your rankings. The reason that those six phrases aren't very informative is that every college or university in the world believes those things about itself. Even schools where courses aren't allowed to run unless they enroll at least five hundred believe that they're dedicated to small class sizes ("At least we don't have those online courses that each contain three thousand students"), and even schools with massive endowments and high tuition feel they're underfunded. We all think our faculty is amazing and believe we care about our students. We helped design our curriculum, so we all naturally believe it's first rate. Though you may not believe these things about your peers and competitors, the faculty members and administrators at those schools certainly believe them. So if those were the only six items on your list, keep probing for more distinctive features. Don't move past this step until you have a list of no fewer than ten qualities that truly set your programs apart from others.

STEP 2: EXTRAPOLATE FROM THE CORE STRENGTHS YOU FOUND. After you've developed your list of truly unique attributes—and remember that every set of programs is unique in certain ways—you're ready to see what you can build based on your current strengths. For instance, if the opportunity to engage in undergraduate research is a distinctive feature of your college, what are the logical next steps that can be developed from that strength? Is every senior given an opportunity for substantive research before graduation? If you've already attained that goal, can these opportunities be extended downward through your program? Or can you guarantee a dedicated research space (an office, lab, or studio) to every student majoring in one of your programs? Do they all work extensively with full-time faculty members as their mentors? Do they present their findings at professional conferences or research symposia? Are those trips fully funded? Are students encouraged or required to submit written versions of their research to undergraduate or peer-reviewed journals? Do they all receive training in how to submit articles and book proposals to academic publishers? What, in other words, can you do to build on an existing strength so as to make the programs in your college truly exciting for students who wish to enroll, for potential donors who wish to contribute, and for senior administrators who want the colleges in their institution to be successful?

STEP 3: EXPLORE THE POSSIBILITY OF A VISION STATEMENT FOR YOUR OWN AREA BASED ON YOUR INSTITUTION'S STRATEGIC PLAN OR MISSION STATEMENT. Presidents and governing boards are expected to have visions for their institutions. For this reason, it may be possible to base a new vision for your area on something that's already been established for the entire university. The advantages of such an approach are that it will strengthen the institution as a whole (since there's greater alignment among the goals of its various units) and that it makes it far more likely your vision statement will receive support, perhaps even additional funding, from your supervisor. It illustrates that you're thinking in terms of the big picture rather than your own specific area. So if improving international opportunities for our students is a central theme in the president's strategic plan, how can you work with the faculty to develop a vision that promotes this objective? Can you provide an opportunity for every student who majors in one of your programs to travel abroad at a reduced cost before graduation? Can you include an international component in every course taught in your curriculum? Is it possible to establish an international center dedicated to the specific needs of your programs? Can you aggressively seek visiting scholars from other countries to teach in your programs? Can you work with the staff to ensure that all your programs' websites and publications are available in multiple languages?

Similarly, if increasing experiential learning is one of your president's most cherished goals, how can you build a shared vision around this desire? Are internships available in all of your majors? Could you incorporate community service learning into more of your introductory courses? Are there ways of substituting traditional lecture courses with practica, labs, or simulations? Is there a way of developing a senior capstone requirement that uses an experiential activity to help students draw together what they have learned in your programs? In short, take whatever the vision is for your institution and reflect on how you can ratchet it up in a way that's relevant to the area you supervise.

STEP 4: INVESTIGATE WAYS OF BASING YOUR VISION ON INNOVATIVE FORMS OF TEACHING, SCHOLARSHIP, OR SERVICE. Ernest Boyer's landmark book, *Scholarship Reconsidered* (1990), suggested that the way in which higher education traditionally looked at scholarship (i.e., as research) was only one of several different kinds of scholarship found in academia. In addition to this Scholarship of Discovery, as Boyer calls conventional research, he also identified activities that he called the Scholarship of Integration (which includes such activities as combining the techniques of different fields through interdisciplinary approaches), the Scholarship of Application (which uses the discoveries made within a discipline to solve a practical problem or to produce a tangible benefit), and the Scholarship of Teaching (which makes pedagogy more effective).

As you seek to develop a vision for the programs you supervise, you might consider basing your ideas on one of these alternative forms of scholarship or on similar efforts to transcend the boundaries of traditional research. For example, your vision might involve the Scholarship of Innovation (which deals not with discovering something that already exists but creating something that did not yet exist), the Scholarship of Service (which produces new insights through experiential activities such as community-based projects), or the Scholarship of Leadership (which involves influencing scholars in a discipline to move in a common direction toward a visionary goal).

Begin by asking questions like, "How can we incorporate innovations in instruction such as simulations, content provided via massive open online courses/MOOCs or iTunes U, immersion courses, case studies, internships, and the like across our entire curriculum?" or, "What type of capstone project would most benefit our students if their course work regularly included service-learning, community engaged scholarship, social entrepreneurship, or other means of helping the community?" In other words, while the content of your curriculum may not be all that much different from that of similar programs at other institutions, your area's unique vision might be derived from the manner in which that content is applied to practical situations or shared with those who need it.

STEP 5: USE A FOCUSED BRAINSTORMING EXERCISE TO EXPLORE IDEAS THAT CAN FORM THE BASIS OF A VISION FOR THE FUTURE. One well-known and effective technique that you can use in developing possible directions for your programs' future growth and advancement is to brainstorm possible ideas. Focused brainstorming refines this approach even further so as to make it more immediately practical. You focus a brainstorming exercise when you impose certain limits on the ideas that people generate. For example, you might choose an arbitrary date in the future (ten, twenty-five, or fifty years out) and begin jotting down ideas about what your institution's best-case scenario would be at that date. What internal steps could you then begin taking that would start your unit moving in that direction? Another focused brainstorming activity could be to take the acronym commonly used for your college or program (CLAS, COBA, CHSS, HRP, and the like) or the standard abbreviation used for your institution (UCLA, USC, UW, BYU, and so on) as the basis for a list of positive adjectives or nouns that can serve to crystallize the essence of a strategic vision.

As unusual as this activity may sound, it works. It was used in 2003 to provide Mary Baldwin College (MBC) with its theme of Mind—Body—Character when that school was searching for a way to express its transformative, holistic approach to undergraduate education. It was used again in 2012 at Florida Atlantic University when, as part of its regional accreditation, the school was developing its Quality Enhancement plan (QEP) in the area of undergraduate research; the acronym QEP was rebranded as "Question. Explore. Pursue." thus providing an easily remembered focus for the QEP's marketing campaign. In a similar way, pairing adjectives and nouns or adverbs and adjectives so as to provide a striking oxymoron (such as "Innovative Tradition, Where People Do the Impossible Daily, Whimsical Practicality") can help reveal the ways in which your program's characteristic identity can provide guidance for its future. Even the combination of commonplace, noncontradictory nouns and adjectives can help clarify your college's vision. For a time in the 1990s, Georgia Southern University's College of Liberal Arts and Social Sciences used this approach to adopt the phrase "The College of the Creative Mind" as it planned for the future.

STEP 6: EXAMINE THE POSSIBILITY OF A VISION IN WHICH YOUR INSTI-TUTION ACHIEVES NATIONAL OR EVEN INTERNATIONAL RECOGNITION BECAUSE IT'S ASSOCIATED WITH A SIGNIFICANT AWARD, EVENT, OR DISTINCTION.   One of the quickest ways to establish a clear identity, while at the same time drawing media attention, is to offer a highly publicized award in some area. (See chapter 42.) For instance, if your institution has a particular strength in the area of advising, you might consider an award that honors the person or program that has made the greatest contribution to student advising anywhere in the world. Bringing the recipient to campus, providing an honorarium and lodging, and creating a suitable award are all expenses that can more than pay for themselves in the publicity they bring. Suddenly you'll have tied your school's name to high-quality advising. That identity will then give you a basis for expanding this vision in the future.

Any area in which your institution already excels—or wishes to excel—can provide the basis for such an award. Possibilities include high medical school placement rates, a record of promoting leadership among women, a history of developing creativity, a tradition of serving first-generation college students, and achievements in publishing student research.

In a similar way, an event that either occurs annually or is critical to your institution's history can provide a vision for the future. A good example of this practice is Westminster College in Fulton, Missouri, the site of Winston Churchill's famous iron curtain speech in 1946. The col-lege has long parlayed this historic event into its vision of serving as an American center for Churchill studies and memorabilia. Whittier College has established the Nixon Fellows Program, named after Richard Nixon, the college's most famous graduate. If your institution doesn't have any alumni whose names are instantly recognizable and few, if any, histori-cal events associated with it, you can still begin developing a vision by planning a recurring event: a lecture series, annual day of commemora-tion, or conference could bring individuals from all over the world to your college, who would take home the notion that your programs are particularly noted for the theme of the recurring event you have created.

Sharing the vision

Once you've developed a clear sense of what you'd like your vision to be, it'll become critically important for you to allow others to buy into it, enrich it with their own perspectives and ideas, and truly share throughout the programs you supervise. After all, a vision that doesn't inspire your faculty members, students, and donors is unlikely to be successful, even if it has received substantial support from the president and governing board. As you begin to share your vision and work with others toward fulfilling it, it's advisable to keep in mind a few additional principles.

BE CONSISTENT.   Speak about your vision for the future as often as possible, and be certain to relate new developments and opportunities to the long-term goals you've adopted. At times, you may begin to feel like a broken record, repeating the same thing over and over. At other times, people may grumble that you seem to have only one idea and they feel they can begin to recite your mantra with you. These criticisms, while they may be annoying, are preferable to a situation in which no one can ever guess what the dean's values are or where the college is going. Academic leaders who appear to have a new vision every week come across as not really committed to anything and only frustrate the people who are still trying to fulfill the last great plan.

BE FLEXIBLE.   Being consistent isn't the same as being rigid. Members of the faculty, and perhaps even your president and other stakeholders, will undoubtedly have suggestions about the precise direction your vision should take and how it might be implemented. Give a respectful ear to every voice. Although not every suggestion may be worth adopting, they're all worth hearing. Allowing people to help shape the vision as it develops extends your base of support and makes it more likely that your initiatives can be achieved in a timely manner. Be aware that there'll probably be plenty of naysayers who will announce, at times quite loudly, that instead of doing what you've proposed, the institution will be better off doing something completely different (which usually involves increasing that person's salary and/or lowering his or her workload). But you shouldn't let these voices distract you if you don't find them persuasive. In most cases, the naysayers are simply fixated on one of their own pet projects that don't benefit the entire institution. Be respectful of these voices, incorporate anything useful they have to say into your planning, and give credit where credit is due, but don't let them cause you to give up on your vision.

BE PRACTICAL.   A properly conceived vision should be both inspiring and attainable. It should inspire people to reach just a little further than they thought possible without draining resources from critical areas or imposing a goal that's completely beyond the realm of possibility. A true vision should excite people to move in a direction that will take some time to achieve. The goal may not be reached even within your tenure as dean or provost. But the vision should not simply be pie in the sky. Always seek a balance between the challenging and the realistic, and strive to preserve an attitude that "we can do this if we put our hearts into it."

Creating Buy-In

When people play an active role in the creation and fulfillment of a shared vision, they become more invested in its success. In addition, moving together in a common direction tends to increase morale and collegiality, with the result that the vision benefits the college in a way that extends far beyond the initiative itself.

PAY AS MUCH ATTENTION TO THE ENVIRONMENT YOU CREATE AS YOU DO TO THE VISION ITSELF.   Although people will often turn to you as an academic leader for a sense of where your programs are heading, it's not necessary for you to develop every initiative yourself. In fact, you'll be more effective if you work to create an atmosphere in which people feel free to create and share their own ideas about the future. It won't be possible, of course, to change the culture overnight if people have grown accustomed to strong centralized authority and to following rather than leading. But as a long-term strategy it's much more productive for you to create an environment where everyone feels empowered to engage in the creation of a vision than for you to have to do all the visionary work yourself.

BEGIN WITH A FOCUS ON SHARED VALUES.   Even in the most politicized academic environment, there will be certain fundamental principles that a vast majority of the faculty members in your programs can agree on. Just as earlier in this chapter I asked you to think about the core values of your programs, the nonnegotiables that make you who you are, so can it be beneficial to engage the entire faculty and staff in this exercise. In a retreat or at the opening meeting of the year, set aside some time for people to explore what your college is as a means of discovering where it needs to go. In a small enough unit, this activity can be done as a brainstorming exercise, with ideas recorded on a whiteboard, flip chart, or PowerPoint presentation. In larger units, breakout sessions of twelve to twenty faculty members each might discuss this issue and then report their ideas to the entire group. Challenge people to think of everything they can that they regard as essential to the identity of your programs and institution. Their results may include basic principles, elements of pedagogy or research methods, commitments to certain student-to-faculty ratios, cherished programs such as a longstanding lecture series, senior requirements, outreach efforts, cherished traditions, distinguished alumni, and the like—anything that comes to mind when a majority of people think of the question, "Who are we?"

HELP PEOPLE TO DISCOVER AREAS OF DISTINCTION WITHIN YOUR PROGRAMS. A subsequent step would be to ask not simply, "Who are we?" but, "What makes us better than our peers?" In *Good to Great* (2001), Jim Collins encourages organizations to ask themselves, "What can we be best in the world at?" and, "What are we deeply passionate about?" (95). In a similar way, ask members of your faculty and staff to compare your programs to those at peer and aspirational institutions. How are you different from those? If it seems too extreme to ask, "How are we unique?" (since this question would imply that you are truly one of a kind), then at least ask what makes your programs special in some way.

When students are thinking about majoring in one discipline instead of another, what would members of your faculty and staff say to confirm the students' good impression of what they do? What would graduates of your institution say? If a student was thinking of transferring to another university, how might you make the case that what you offer is really the better choice? It may be that your curriculum is structured more sensibly than that of your peers, that you have more (or fewer) required courses in your programs, that you have a better placement rate of students into graduate programs or careers of their choice, that you provide students with better access to senior faculty members even in introductory courses, that you offer opportunities for students to travel more widely (either to conferences in their field or to study abroad), or that you are distinctive in a way that others outside your program cannot even imagine.

However any of your stakeholders might legitimately answer the question, "How are we better than others who are like us?," their responses give you insight into the ways in which your programs are distinctive.

ASK WHETHER YOUR CORE VALUES AND AREAS OF DISTINCTION POINT THE WAY TO AN IMPROVED FUTURE.   Perhaps at the same retreat or faculty meeting, perhaps at a separate event (such as a series of lunches with mixed groups of faculty and staff, several focus group sessions, an online threaded discussion or listserv, or whichever means best suits your local culture), explore with members of the faculty, staff, and student body possible answers to the question, "Based on who we are and where we are now, where should we go from here?" Get as many ideas from as many different constituencies as possible. Consider with them what steps you need to take to preserve your current strengths and identity. Ask about new opportunities that may arise for the disciplines in your area over the next few years. Are there curricular areas or productive lines of research that are not currently being addressed but seem to be emerging as important? Are there ways you can bring greater visibility to existing programs of distinction so as to make your entire unit stronger as you compete for students, resources, and recognition?

At this stage in the process, don't spend a lot of time weighing and evaluating suggestions. The important thing is for all your stakeholders to have a voice, to get as many ideas on the table as possible, and to see what elements of a potential new vision might emerge through the combined efforts of everyone in your area.

AFTER LISTING ALL THE POSSIBLE ELEMENTS OF A SHARED VISION, PROMOTE WIDESPREAD DISCUSSION OF THESE IDEAS.   Once a large number of ideas are on the table, it's time to begin sorting through them in order to see which suggestions have the greatest potential. This activity of discussing a potential new vision for people to share can itself be an important team-building exercise. The process of building consensus for any type of plan encourages people to discover issues of shared concern and understand ways in which their own pet projects may not have the widespread support they imagined. This part of your long-range planning is probably best done not in a single meeting or retreat, but in a series of sessions that extend over several weeks or months. The idea that seems hot one day may not, after all, stand the test of time. Consider beginning the process with four or five mixed sessions of faculty members, students, staff employees, alumni, and other external constituents (such as parents of students, consistent donors to your college, or representatives from an advisory or governing board). Pay close attention to areas where there is widespread agreement across the different groups and where suggestions tend to splinter people into clear factions.

ALIGN EXISTING REWARD STRUCTURES WITH THE NEW VISION.   A favorite saying of my friend Bob Cipriano, author of *Facilitating a Collegial*

Department in Higher Education: Strategies for Success (2011), is:

> What gets rewarded gets repeated.

We see this idea at work in faculty evaluations. In systems where publications are counted for the purposes of promotion and salary increases, faculty members tend to produce larger numbers of individual works, even when those publications are brief or of relatively minor significance. In structures where pages of published scholarship are tallied, faculty members tend to produce longer works, although not necessarily a greater number of total works. That same strategy works when you're developing support for the vision that people in your programs have developed.

It'll be extremely difficult for any genuine progress to be made toward fulfilling this vision if that progress doesn't "count" in your institution's evaluation procedures. One way of pursuing this strategy might be to organize a faculty committee that can recommend ways in which existing evaluation criteria can be revised in order to reflect the significance of the new vision. For instance, if the goal is to become nationally recognized for internationalizing the curriculum, you might change the format of people's annual report so that faculty members know they'll be given credit for contributing to the global dimensions of existing courses, applying for Fulbright Fellowships and other international travel grants, mentoring students in seeking international study opportunities, and making arrangements for foreign faculty members to take visiting positions in various programs. By tracking and rewarding progress toward fulfilling this new shared vision, you'll help maintain the amount of buy-in that was created when you gave people an opportunity to help develop the vision in the first place.

ENLIST ADDITIONAL SUPPORT FOR THE NEW VISION. One effective way of building momentum toward the attainment of your goal is to seek support from an outside college or institution for the vision that you, your faculty, and staff have developed. Taking advantage of external support is a doubly effective strategy since it both brings you additional enthusiasm, resources, and excitement for the collective new vision and holds your feet to the fire because tangible results will now be expected. Once you go public with your vision, in other words, you and others will regularly be asked, "How's that new plan coming?" and you will be extremely uncomfortable if you have little progress to report.

Moreover, by tying the vision to the institution's strategic plan, one of your president's initiatives, or a goal important to your governing board, you'll obtain strong allies that can help you make these dreams a reality.

You may become eligible for sources of funding that are targeted toward fulfillment of the strategic plan or special initiatives. You may prompt the staff in your office of advancement to begin thinking about potential donors who can help you achieve your goals. Similarly, those who are involved with sponsored programs may know of other sources to help fund the new vision. At the very least, you'll gain the reputation of being a team player because rather than moving in a radically different direction from the rest of your institution, you've taken the appropriate steps to align your goals with those of the institution as a whole.

BE GENEROUS IN ACKNOWLEDGING THE CONTRIBUTIONS OF OTHERS. An important way to secure the continued support of your faculty and staff for making this shared vision a reality is to reiterate how important everyone is to the plan's fulfillment. Public acknowledgment of someone's contributions both rewards that person for all the effort he or she has given your initiative and motivates others to work even harder on the plan. People begin to understand that their efforts in fulfilling the vision aren't taken for granted but appreciated in a public and satisfying way. Those who haven't yet given their full support to the new initiative will be encouraged to do so when they see their peers being commended for their accomplishments. These public recognitions make it clear that the vision for the future isn't just your personal vision for the institution, but something that's widely supported and embraced.

Moreover, these public recognitions are good ways of getting people to know that progress is being made. A sense that "things really are changing for the better" can help create a positive atmosphere that will improve morale, promote retention of your most valued faculty members and your most capable students, and strengthen your institution's reputation for excellence. Remember that as a dean or provost, your success is measured by the success of those who work for you and enroll in your programs even more than by what you achieve on your own (June, 2013).

TAKE ADVANTAGE OF EVERY OPPORTUNITY TO PRESERVE MOMENTUM IN ATTAINING THE VISION. In higher education, we frequently make a great deal of initial progress in developing a new plan for the future, only to see these developments quickly stall as new demands are made on our time. You're more likely to preserve momentum toward turning your vision into a reality if you take steps to reinforce its importance whenever possible. Regular reference to the plan and its progress at meetings of your faculty and staff will help confirm the notion that achieving the new vision is an ongoing priority. Here are some other ways in which you can preserve the momentum toward fulfilling the goals of the plan:

- Develop a web page that's devoted exclusively to the vision. Update this site frequently (at least once a week), and be sure that it contains important and exciting developments.

- Take advantage of social media to post frequent updates on progress, success stories, and other good news about the plan to help preserve the sense of excitement and accomplishment. Encourage others to do so as well. An inexpensive way of achieving this goal is to hire a student worker to post at least ten updates on the plan every week though various social media sites.

- Establish some form of internal recognition tied directly to the vision, perhaps along the lines of "achievement of the month" or "annual award for innovation." This public recognition will give you a recurring occasion on which to draw attention to progress being made on the plan and will provide repeated opportunities to reward those whose contributions are making the vision a reality.

Conclusion

Properly conducted, the systematic development of ambitious but attainable visions can build esprit de corps, improve morale, provide a sense of direction to your unit, and help attract positive attention to your institution's most important activities. A positive vision diverts attention from the sort of grousing about minor issues that's all too frequent in higher education and focuses energy on your programs' clear potential for the future. It provides you with an opportunity for constructive delegation, development of leadership skills in members of your faculty and staff, and occasions for external constituencies to become more active in the life (and financial support) of your institution. It brings you in touch with prospects for securing additional external funding through grants, sponsored research, and awards from foundations. And it reinforces your reputation as a visionary dean or provost.

REFERENCES

Boyer, E. L. (1990). *Scholarship reconsidered: Priorities of the professoriate.* Princeton, NJ: Carnegie Foundation for the Advancement of Teaching.

Cipriano, R. E. (2011). *Facilitating a collegial department in higher education: Strategies for success.* San Francisco, CA: Jossey-Bass.

Collins, J. C. (2001). *Good to great: Why some companies make the leap—and others don't.* New York, NY: HarperBusiness.

June, A. W. (2013, July 26). Administrators measure their success quietly. *Chronicle of Higher Education*, A40–41.

RESOURCES

Bensimon, E. M., & Neumann, A. (1994). *Redesigning collegiate leadership: Teams and teamwork in higher education.* Baltimore, MD: Johns Hopkins University Press.

Buller, J. L. (2009). High impact administration. *Academic Leader, 25*(1), 2–3.

Hill, C. (2004). *Leading lights.* Madison, WI: Magna.

Katzenbach, J. E., & Smith D. K. (2003). *The wisdom of teams: Creating the high-performance organization.* New York, NY: Collins Reprints.

Keller, G. (1983). *Academic strategy: The management revolution in American higher education.* Baltimore, MD: Johns Hopkins University Press.

Keller, G. (2004). *Transforming a college: The story of a little-known college's strategic climb to national distinction.* Baltimore, MD: Johns Hopkins University Press.

Koutzes, J. M., & Posner, B. Z. (2003). *The Jossey-Bass academic administrator's guide to exemplary leadership.* San Francisco, CA: Jossey-Bass.

Lewis, C. P. (1996). *Building a shared vision: A leader's guide to aligning the organization.* University Park, IL: Productivity Press.

London, M. (1995). *Achieving performance excellence in university administration: A team approach to organizational change and employee development.* Westport, CT: Praeger.

Percy S. L., Zimpher, N. L., & Brukardt, M. J. (Eds.). (2006). *Creating a new kind of university: Institutionalizing community-university engagement.* Bolton, MA: Anker.

Rowley, D. J., Lujan, H. D., & Dolence, M. J. (1997a). *Strategic change in colleges and universities: Planning to survive and prosper.* San Francisco, CA: Jossey-Bass.

Rowley, D. J., Lujan, H. D., & Dolence, M. J. (1997b). *Working toward strategic change: A step-by-step guide to the planning process.* San Francisco, CA: Jossey-Bass.

Tucker, D. (2014). Building a shared vision of your institution. In L. L. Behling (Ed.), *The resource handbook for academic deans* (pp. 89–92). San Francisco, CA: Jossey-Bass.

Watson, D. (2000). *Managing strategy.* Maidenhead, Berkshire, UK: Open University Press/McGraw-Hill.

Zimpher N. L., Percy, S. L., & Brukardt, M. J. (2002). *A time for boldness: A story of institutional change.* Bolton, MA: Anker.

5

LEADING CHANGE

As part of your effort to advance a new vision at your college or university, you'll inevitably want to bring about some changes. The initiatives you have in mind might include the development of new academic programs, large-scale reform of existing programs, the creation of a new honor code or college creed (Buller, 2012), the establishment of some much-needed faculty development efforts, plans for additional facilities, the drafting of new policies, or any of a number of other improvements that will benefit the school. Implementing these changes can, if done well, strengthen your institution and bring an important boost to your own career. But launching an initiative that fails or causes the program to appear adrift may, in the worst-case scenario, open you and your institution to ridicule, embarrassment, and even financial disaster.

Many academic leaders are attracted by the possibility of promoting an initiative as a way of leaving their stamp on the institution. It can bring a sense of excitement and momentum to the people you work with, open opportunities for new funding, and help to solve problems that have been hampering the success of your programs. But as you consider proposing any significant change, here are fifteen guidelines you may want to keep in mind.

Never Seek Change for Its Own Sake

Initiatives are most widely accepted where there's a genuine problem to be solved. Administrators, particularly those who are new to their positions, may feel pressure to do something, just to avoid the impression that they're not doing anything. They may wish to make some changes not because they're necessary under the circumstances, but merely because they want to develop a name for themselves, build their résumé, or make

73

a difference. Wanting to leave your programs better off than when you found them is commendable. But although imposing changes just "to shake things up" does not always guarantee disaster, it does make disaster more likely. Even under the best conditions, unnecessary change rarely results in smooth, consistent progress. Unless you can give a compelling answer to the question, "What are we trying to solve by doing this?" you probably don't have a situation that calls for radical change.

As a short experiment, try writing a summary, in twenty-five words or fewer, of what critical challenge you're facing that can't be solved without a major new initiative. If you find that you can't identify the problem clearly and concisely within that word limit, you probably haven't thought through the issue enough to be able to explain it to others. In fact, the problem may not really be a problem at all.

Ask yourself some follow-up questions.

o Do you have a low rate of student retention that your school's current recruitment plan is incapable of addressing?

o Do your assessment efforts repeatedly suggest that the curriculum isn't meeting the student learning outcomes you've set?

o Are faculty members too frequently denied tenure and promotion, even though their peers at other institution have not faced this challenge?

o Has your school been liable to lawsuits or successful grievances because you don't have policies and procedures to deal adequately with the situations that occurred?

If you can answer yes to questions like these, you may find it relatively easy to say, "In order to solve the problem we have with X, we must consider doing Y." But if this thought experiment has left you struggling to identify exactly what problem you're trying to solve, you may need to reconsider whether you're ready to launch a major initiative. Successful revolutions in higher education rarely occur just because someone believes that "all change is good."

By imposing an unnecessary change, deans and provosts often learn just how undesirable and destructive ill-conceived initiatives can be. The law of unintended consequences, which states that you can't predict all the effects a change will have, is particularly true in an institution as complex as a college or university. Institutional change can be difficult enough when it's necessary. It's far more likely to be a waste of time and resources when we try to fix a problem that really doesn't exist.

Expect Mixed Messages

Few people, if any, are ready for as much change as they say they want.

New provosts and deans are frequently surprised by a common occurrence. Throughout their interviews or their first few meetings with faculty members, they hear repeatedly, "We need someone with some bold new ideas. People here are hungry for change, and we're all counting on you for some clear leadership about where we need to go. Believe me, change can't happen fast enough for any of us!" As a result, they regard these conversations as a mandate to launch important initiatives from the very beginning of their positions and immediately start laying the groundwork for the changes they believe everyone will welcome. But soon after beginning to implement a few changes, they discover resistance to their ideas even from (or perhaps *especially* from) the very people who claimed they were so enthusiastic about a bold new direction. The fact is that people who work at colleges and universities, like people who work nearly everywhere else, are sometimes fascinated by the idea of change but less comfortable with the reality of change. Organizations favor inertia. That, after all, is their purpose: to provide consistency to procedures. That's why we have policy manuals and faculty handbooks. So when people say that they want radical change, what they often mean is that they want *other* people to change and become more like themselves. Unless your initiative involves offering people more money, a lighter workload, or additional opportunities for personal recognition, they often fear and resist change.

In studying the readiness of most groups to adopt new ideas, Everett M. Rogers (2005) of the University of New Mexico found that most populations fall into five identifiable groups:

1. *Innovators*: Those who are venturesome and bring about change—approximately 2.5 percent of the population
2. *Early adopters*: Those who respect innovation and quickly include proposed changes in their own activities—approximately 13.5 percent of the population
3. *Early majority*: Those who deliberate for a time about the value of a change but do come to accept it—approximately 34 percent of the population
4. *Late majority*: Those who are long skeptical of the need for change but eventually accept it, albeit grudgingly—approximately 34 percent of the population

5. *Laggards*: Those who resist change at all cost, are highly traditional in their views, and often are regarded as old-fashioned or behind the times—approximately 16 percent of the population

Because roughly half of any population is likely to be skeptical of or resist any change that's proposed, academic leaders need to gauge carefully the amount of institutional change they believe their stakeholders can reasonably sustain.

In higher education, we often say that teaching and research are our highest priorities. Since change processes often divert resources from teaching and research, they need to be worth the cost. This argument may make it appear as though change is never possible in higher education. But there's a corollary to the caution we must bring to launching new initiatives: even in cases where people seem openly hostile to doing things differently, provosts and deans don't have to abandon all hope of improving their programs. They just have to enter these processes with their eyes fully open. A great deal of work may be required behind the scenes to bring people along and help them to understand that their current way of doing things isn't working. You may need to present your ideas with some diplomacy; rather than talking about change, your stakeholders may find it more palatable if you talk about "building on the established strengths of our school." (On the importance of relating new ideas to a program's history and points of pride, see chapter 47.) You may need to invest time in conversations with people one-on-one in order to learn precisely what their anxieties are so that you can allay them. At the very least, you should be prepared for there to be more resistance to your initiatives than you initially expect. A good rule of thumb is:

Change processes are almost always harder and take longer than anyone believes they will at the beginning.

Do Your Homework

It's important to do a lot of groundwork behind the scenes, but you also want to avoid giving the impression that you're privileging certain people with information. Change processes that are perceived as being foisted on people from the top down will understandably meet with resistance. People will view the proposal as simply another scheme to make administrators look important while creating additional work for everyone else.

You can avoid this problem by doing some initial work behind the scenes. Try to gauge a sense of what the major concerns and objections will be. A good way to gain this information is to work with the opinion leaders among the faculty and staff. Whose views matter to their peers? Meet with these individuals one-on-one or in small groups to talk about the need for the change and explore with them how the change helps them or makes it possible to solve a problem they're facing. In these preliminary sessions, it's not a good idea to outline in detail what you see as the end result of the change process. For one thing, the very people you're meeting with are those who are most likely to have useful suggestions about possible alternatives. For another, you don't want to give the impression that you're playing favorites by giving insider information to a select few individuals. Instead, talk about the problem you're trying to solve and why a solution is important. Listen to their ideas. What concerns do they have? What suggestions can they make for getting others involved in this initiative? What practical advice do they have for working with standing committees and groups like the faculty senate? Remember that your goal isn't to sell the opinion leaders on a process that moves in lockstep with your preconceived ideas about what should be done. These opinion leaders will bring you a perspective you'll need in order to make the change process a success.

Pay Attention to Trends, But Don't be Trendy

Certain developments in higher education redefine the entire environment in which we work; others turn out to have been mere fads. Assessment has proven to be a game changer; Total Quality Management was a fad. Online distance education has continued to provide educational access to new populations of students; the Gopher protocol, a system for distributing documents over the Internet that caused some excitement at universities in the early 1990s, was a fad. The degree to which service learning, social entrepreneurship, massive open online courses (MOOCs), and performance-based budgeting will be widely accepted or seem quaint within a decade or two is still uncertain. So pay attention to trends as you pursue your change initiative. After all, not every innovation at your own school has to be something that hasn't already been tested elsewhere—but you should avoid pursuing an initiative simply because it seems hot at the moment. The key test is whether it makes sense for your institution and solves a genuine problem you have.

Get an Objective View

Now that you know what some of the issues affecting the change process are likely to be, it's time to speak to those who have absolutely no vested interest in the success of your initiative. They can give you a candid appraisal of whether the potential benefits of the process will be worth the cost, effort, and risk of failure. If you've never led a change process before, you can seek advice on how best to handle the challenges that will arise. Possible sources of objective advice include professional organizations, accrediting bodies, and peer or aspirational institutions. You might consider hiring a consultant, but consultants are frequently suspected of "saying whatever they're being paid to say." Particularly if they're from a rival institution, people may think that they don't have your own school's best interests at heart.

The only absolute criterion for the person you choose to advise you is that he or she must be willing to speak his or her mind freely and not simply tell you what you want to hear. If the change process is a bad idea, it's better for you to know that now than when it's well under way. Finally, make sure that your own supervisor is behind your idea. If he or she is not going to support it, now is the best time to know it.

Go Public

After receiving insights from opinion leaders inside your institution and at least one objective party outside your institution, you're ready to go public with your ideas. What you want to describe at this point is the problem you're trying to solve and a process for solving it, not any one specific solution. Ideas still need to be generated, and you may not yet be in possession of the best possible plan. For this reason, present a general overview of the issue at an appropriate venue. The group should be large enough that no one feels blindsided by learning of your intentions only through rumor. A full faculty meeting is one good place; an open forum of faculty, staff, and students is another.

Based on the ideas you've received from the opinion leaders and your objective external advisor, feel free to propose a few more specific ideas about how the change process will come about and which groups will be charged with implementing it. Continue to be receptive to ideas about how the process can be modified so as to make it more successful. Allow people to buy into the process by contributing to it in ways that don't detract from its overall focus or direction. Frequently a change in nomenclature or timing may be all that's required to help people begin seeing the change process as something they can readily support.

Celebrate Wins along the Way

Leading a successful change initiative involves setting a realistic timetable that includes plenty of intermediate goals to mark your progress. One of the mistakes academic leaders too frequently make during change processes is to present fulfillment of a large-scale plan as the only goal. The problem with this approach is that it's difficult to see tangible results in a highly complex project that may come to fruition only five to ten years from now. Initial enthusiasm for the idea is likely to dissipate as other concerns arise without any apparent progress being made toward the ultimate goal of the process.

The way to avoid this problem is to break a complex plan into a number of smaller plans, each with its own identified goals. For example, rather than presenting the creation and implementation of a new graduate degree program as your initiative, it may be wiser to see that as a long-term goal but with more immediate objectives at various points along the way—such as conducting a needs assessment, completing a review of best practices for this type of degree, holding focus group sessions on the structure of the curriculum, formulating staffing plans, seeking external funds to defray start-up costs, and so on. Since each goal is achievable within a short time, people will see progress occurring very quickly.

Even more important, if for any reason it proves undesirable to continue the plan for the proposed new degree program, that doesn't mean that the change process itself has failed. You'll be able to say things like, "Remember that all we set out to do was to complete a needs assessment. Well, we did that and discovered that for an institution our size, with the sort of funding we're likely to have for the foreseeable future, and the pool of students we'd be drawing from, a new graduate program wouldn't be sustainable. I'm not about to weaken our current strengths by committing us to any program for which we can't provide adequate funding in accordance with our standards for quality. I'm certainly not going to mortgage our future on a program that we don't think we can maintain. Now, one good thing that came out of this change process is that the needs assessment told us a few things about how we can strengthen our existing programs and better serve our students. So with this information in hand, let's start working together to make a few modifications based on what we learned."

In this way, you don't tie the success of the change process to the achievement of any specific long-term goal. What you had believed would be simply a step along the way has cautioned you about the desirability of undertaking such an ambitious endeavor and enables you to transform a potentially disastrous move into a far more positive experience.

Communicate Broadly, Frankly, and Often

Although change is always difficult, most people accept it if they understand why it's needed and how it benefits them. Academic leaders may embark on a change process because they have information that other stakeholders lack. They see how the budget is organized, hear complaints from students and their parents, see course evaluations from every program that reports to them, and meet with donors and other supporters. As the change process continues, they may also be getting reports from committees and work groups. But they can't assume that everyone at the institution knows all these things.

Without adequate communication, people will assume that nothing is being done, too much is being done, or the wrong things are being done. They may misunderstand that the provost or dean is implementing a policy that their colleagues recommended, not simply because he or she was acting unilaterally. Frequent open communication of both successes and failures of the change process helps avoid the impression that secret deals are being cut "by a cabal" or "in a star chamber." Speak freely at meetings of the faculty, staff, and students about how things are going, who's doing what, and unexpected glitches that have arisen. Discuss with different groups possible alternatives that are being considered. Make sure that everyone knows how far along the change process is at the moment, whom they can contact if they have questions or suggestions, and at what point final decisions are going to be made. You may feel that you're reporting many of the same updates over and over, but doing so is essential.

Remember That Costs Include Many Things

When we're in the midst of a change process (particularly one that we initiated), we can have a tendency to become fixated on the benefits that will result from the change. But changes also come with costs, and not all costs are financial. There are opportunity costs—chances missed for doing one thing because we've chosen to do something else. There are costs associated with the time, human effort, and information capital that have to be invested in any change process. Moreover, the costs that are financial in nature can be substantial. Inefficient workload assignments result in the need to hire additional full- or part-time faculty. Publishing glossy reports about the initiative may consume resources that could have been used for other purposes if most communications were handled electronically.

For these reasons, think broadly in terms of the costs associated with the process and the change that will eventually emerge from it. Are there current activities that are lower in priority than the proposed change? If so, you may be able to redirect some financial, space, and human resources from a lower to a higher priority. Ask yourself frequently, "Do the benefits that are likely to result from this change justify these costs? If they don't, what reason do we have for continuing?"

Use Focus Groups

Unless the change that's being considered is extremely time sensitive, it's almost always useful to meet periodically throughout the change process and try out the ideas being generated on mixed focus groups of faculty members, staff representatives, and selected students. This approach avoids several problems. First, committees and work groups develop tunnel vision; they latch onto one idea and fail to see flaws that outsiders can spot quickly. Second, unless you field-test ideas, you may end up solving one problem only to create three or four new ones. Particularly in processes where it's not possible for committees to include representatives from every constituency, focus groups give you insight into how ideas play among different stakeholders. Does a curricular reform that the faculty loves delay students in their plans to graduate in a timely manner or leave them no time for internships they feel they need? Does a schedule revision create conflicts with other events? Does a reassignment of responsibilities that produces a more equitable workload in one area result in unforeseen inequities elsewhere? Will certain constituencies resist the change because they didn't feel sufficiently in the loop as it was being planned? Holding periodic focus group discussions is a way of identifying and dealing with potential problems before they become serious. Moreover, by giving stakeholders a chance to respond to and shape ideas while the process is still ongoing, they may well have greater buy-in when the change is eventually launched.

Consider Alternatives

Your process will be smoother if you give fair consideration to all possible approaches before embarking on a plan. Provosts and deans tend to be problem solvers: when confronted with a challenge, they want to develop a plan to overcome it as soon as possible. When dealing with change processes, however, it can be disastrous to move precipitously, particularly without considering all of your options. Academic leaders who are new to their positions may be especially susceptible to forming opinions about the best way to solve problems, perhaps because they're familiar with a certain approach that worked when they were in a previous position or at another institution. There can also be a temptation to act quickly in the belief that it will appear as though they are acting decisively. But even experienced administrators can benefit from being cautious during change initiatives and remembering to ask, "Is there more than one way of achieving this goal?" If you have an advisory council (particularly a group consisting of experienced academic professionals rather than those involved in very different lines of work), it can be helpful to explore with the council different ways that similar issues have been addressed elsewhere. Are there clear patterns of best practices that emerge? Even if the conclusion is to go ahead with the original plan, this discussion will have been a useful investment. As you explain the idea to faculty members and other constituents, you'll now know various reasons that other alternatives were less desirable or simply not feasible.

Follow Through

Successful change leaders put as much energy into following through on initiatives as you do on launching them. It's easy for faculty members to become jaded by repeatedly hearing about bold new plans from administrators, only to see those plans languish soon after the initial enthusiasm for them has cooled. People grow weary of reports that simply lie on the shelf and impressive-sounding proposals that can never become reality. It can be particularly damaging to morale when new administrators arrive from outside an institution, launch a new initiative, and then leave for another position before there's any hope of their plans coming to fruition. For this reason, it's important for deans and provosts to ask themselves several questions when they prepare to launch change processes:

o *What are the realistic possibilities that this institution can put in place the changes I am proposing?* This question should not imply that it's never appropriate for a college or university to stretch beyond what it's always done or to seek to overcome difficult challenges. Nevertheless, there's an important distinction between striving for what's difficult to obtain and wasting resources on what's all but impossible to achieve. Even the most exciting dream for the future will inspire others only if you have some reasonable chance of seeing it come true. If your goal proves to be unrealistic, embarking on this change process will end up doing your institution—and perhaps your career—a disservice.

o *Is it possible to bring about this change within my likely tenure at this institution or in my position?* Once again, this question shouldn't imply that it's never advisable to begin a project that will come to fruition only under your successor. You should, however, avoid initiatives where you're the one who will reap the excitement of the project's initial launch and publicity while those who come after you must deal with the thorny issues of funding, implementation, and sustainability. Never embark on an initiative that you wouldn't want to see through if you were to remain at the institution, and remember that most initiatives should be attainable within the span of your current position. (On the matter of how long that tenure might be, see chapter 46.)

○ *What will be our exit strategy for concluding this initiative?* It's wise to decide in advance what indicators you'll use to tell you when you've arrived at your goal of bringing about this change. What will success look like? Be sure, too, to have plans in mind about how you'll modify or abandon the project if serious, unforeseen problems arise. If the funding you project doesn't materialize or student enrollment declines significantly, will the plan still be feasible? If not, how will you change it or conclude the change process early? Is there a way of abandoning certain goals if they no longer seem desirable while still achieving the overall intent of the project?

In addition to asking yourself these questions, be certain that your initiative is important and exciting enough that both you and your principal stakeholders will want to see it through. It's counterproductive for the programs you supervise to be dismissed as never finishing what they start. And you certainly don't want your legacy to be that of a leader who "came up with new initiatives every week, none of which ever went anywhere." It's important for the goals of a major change process to balance stretching beyond what's already in place with being reasonable about what's ultimately possible. Your possession of a high degree of common sense will help you to find balance between your desire for vision and your need for practicality.

Provide Incentives

As we've seen, people are frequently reluctant to change because they're comfortable with their current situation, unwilling to learn the new skills, afraid they'll lose something they value, or concerned about a possible increase in workload. One of the ways in which to respond to this reluctance is to help people see that change is beneficial, not simply to the institution, but also to them personally. While you want to avoid even the impression that you're cutting private deals with individuals, there may be situations in which incentives can be provided either to everyone or to select offices at the institution in order to bring them onboard the initiative.

For instance, in a program where limited faculty development funding has been an issue, you might want to explore whether any cost savings resulting from a new plan could be invested in additional support for faculty research and travel. Similarly, if faculty members in an area are struggling with research productivity because all of them have a large number of course preparations every term, you might consider coupling the proposed change with permitting larger section sizes in appropriate courses and reducing classroom time to promote greater research. Regardless of the problem you're trying to solve with the proposed change, identify the stakeholders you need to support it and ask yourself, "How can this reform be presented in such a way that it helps alleviate a serious concern of this constituency? How can it serve to benefit these stakeholder groups for their valuable contributions and remove a difficulty that they're facing?"

Understand Individual Differences

People are likely to respond to change differently depending on their gender, age, background, and other factors. Although each person is unique, there's been a great deal of research into the ways in which different groups of people tend to handle change. For example, studies have suggested that women are more likely to approach change from a process perspective: Who needs to be consulted, what procedures are to be followed as the change is being considered, and how much consensus is possible as the plan is put into effect? Men are much more likely to look at change from a result perspective: What needs to be done, when does it need to be done, and what can we do with the benefits once the change has been made (Brooks and MacKinnon, 2001; Eggins, 1997)? Generations too respond differently to change. Younger members of the faculty and staff, who are accustomed to viewing rapid changes in technology as an ever-expanding series of improved features and new opportunities, tend to see change as synonymous with progress, whereas older employees may be frustrated by having to learn how to use new software just when they're getting comfortable with its previous version (Buller, 2015).

In addition, a person's role at the university may affect the way he or she looks at change. Those in management or leadership positions often view change as an exciting opportunity, while employees who don't have explicit leadership responsibilities frequently see change as an unwelcome disruption of their routines (Strebel, 2006). Deans and provosts need to be aware of how various groups of stakeholders may respond differently to change. The men you work with may become frustrated with a process that seems to be taking too long or seeks to bring everyone on board: "Why do we keep talking this to death? Let's just put it to a vote." The women you work with may feel less engaged if they feel the change process is so focused on reaching a goal quickly that it rides roughshod over people: "Why are we so engrossed with just this one possibility? Can't we talk about the issue some more and get some other perspectives on the table?" Understanding how people view change differently can help you conduct the process in a way that better reflects their interests and needs.

Be Generous

If you wait to recognize the success of an initiative until its final goal has been realized, people's enthusiasm for the process is likely to flag. It's important to celebrate each of the steps along the way to fulfilling the overall goal of change. It's also important to give as many people as possible a chance to share credit for the achievement. No matter how much the initiative may have been your own doing, it won't be as successful as it can be until it's widely embraced as the institution's initiative. For this reason, as the process begins to bear fruit, it's useful to herald its success openly (so as to bring attention to the positive aspects of change) and widely (so as to include as many people in the success of the plan).

In fact, it's probably wise to play down your role in leading this effort. The change won't really take hold until people begin to identify with it, and that is unlikely to happen if they're constantly reminded that this idea was "yours." Acknowledge each person's efforts publicly by name and at sufficient length so as to demonstrate that you really did notice and appreciate what he or she has done. You might consider combining a few formal awards that celebrate the contribution made by an individual or program with impromptu acknowledgments at meetings. You might say, "And while we're on the subject of the gen ed revision, I'd just like to say that none of what we just talked about could've been done without the work of...." Particularly in situations where you can't sufficiently reward people's contributions through stipends and other tangible means, these public acknowledgments go a long way toward improving morale. It's also a nice surprise to be able to say to someone occasionally, "You know, I realize how hard you've been working to get this proposal ready for the faculty meeting. Why don't you head home now and get a head start on the weekend?" Sometimes, too, you can reward people for important contributions with a new computer, flexibility in work schedules, funding for a conference, or other creative ways that have an impact far in excess of their cost.

Conclusion

Approached in this way, change processes can bring about some much-needed improvements, build morale, and leave your stakeholders with a sense that your programs are moving in the right direction. Not every provost or dean needs to be engaged in a major change process all the time. Some years it's preferable for programs to lie fallow so that people can recover their energy and reap the benefits from the resources that are in place. When a bold new direction is needed, however, following the guidelines presented in this chapter will help make your task easier and more successful.

Change requires the various constituencies of a college or university to think about their roles in new ways, exert their creativity, and tolerate a certain amount of ambiguity until the likely outcome is clear. Leading a change produces anxiety. No matter how unsuccessful or unpopular the previous approach may have been, there will always be those who find it difficult to give it up. It thus requires not merely good problem-solving skills in order to decide what needs to be done, but also good people skills in order to conduct the process in the most constructive way possible.

REFERENCES

Brooks, A., & MacKinnon, A. (Eds.), (2001). *Gender and the restructured university: Changing management and culture in higher education.* Philadelphia, PA: Open University Press.

Buller, J. L. (2012). *The essential department chair: A comprehensive desk reference.* San Francisco, CA: Jossey-Bass.

Buller, J. L. (2015). *Change leadership in higher education: A practical guide to academic transformation.* San Francisco, CA: Jossey-Bass.

Eggins, H. (Ed.). (1997). *Women as leaders and managers in higher education.* Ballmoor, Buckingham, England: Open University Press.

Rogers, E. M. (2005). *Diffusion of innovations* (5th ed.). New York, NY: Free Press.

Strebel, P. (2006). Why do employees resist change? In Harvard Business School. *Harvard Business Review*, leading through change (pp. 45–63). Boston, MA: Harvard Business School Publishing Corporation.

RESOURCES

Cameron, K. S., & Quinn, R. E. (2011). *Diagnosing and changing organizational culture: Based on the competing values framework* (3rd ed.). San Francisco, CA: Jossey-Bass.

Clark, B. R. (2007). *Sustaining change in universities*. Maidenhead: McGraw-Hill International.

Dew, J. R., & Nearing, M. M. (2004). *Continuous quality improvement in higher education*. Westport, CT: Praeger.

Freed, J. E., & Klugman, M. R. (1997). *Quality principles and practices in higher education: Different questions for different times*. Phoenix, AZ: American Council on Education/Oryx Press.

Judson, A. S. (1996) *Making strategy happen: Transforming plans into reality* (2nd ed.). Malden, MA: Blackwell Publishers.

Rowley, D. J., & Sherman, H. (2001) *From strategy to change: Implementing the plan in higher education*. San Francisco, CA: Jossey-Bass.

Shapiro, N. S., & Levine, J. H. (1999). *Creating learning communities: A practical guide to winning support, organizing for change, and implementing programs*. San Francisco, CA: Jossey-Bass.

6

PROMOTING DIVERSITY

One of higher education's greatest strengths is its diversity. Students can choose from among public or private universities, those with secular or religious perspectives, those dedicated to career preparation or to liberal education, online colleges, traditional colleges, a combination of online and traditional course work, and so on. Despite ongoing accusations in books like *ProfScam* (Sykes, 1988), *Tenured Radicals* (Kimball, 1990), and *One-Party Classroom* (Horowitz and Laksin, 2013), the political leanings of college professors are anything but homogeneous. Those of us who work in higher education know that on any given day, students are likely to be taught by faculty members representing the full spectrum of political views: conservative, libertarian, liberal, radical, middle of the road, and any other perspective that can be imagined.

The students themselves are highly diverse. At the vast majority of universities, scholarships and financial aid mean that students will be in courses with people from a wide range of socioeconomic backgrounds. Efforts to diversify the faculty and student body in terms of race and ethnicity have paid off, with most campuses being far more inclusive than they were several decades ago. In 2011, 44 percent of the college faculty in the United States consisted of white men, 35 percent white women, 6 percent black, 4 percent Hispanic, and 9 percent Asian/Pacific Islander. Precisely comparable data for earlier periods are difficult to obtain, but as recently as 1987, only 33.2 percent of the faculty in the United States consisted of women of any ethnicity whatsoever. (See nces.ed.gov/fastfacts/display.asp?id=61 and nces.ed.gov/programs/digest/d12/tables/dt12_290.asp.) In 2009–2010, 72.9 percent of the students graduating with a baccalaureate degree were white, 10.3 percent were black, 8.8 percent were Hispanic, 7.3 percent were Asian/Pacific Islander, and 0.7 percent were American Indian/Alaska

Native. (See nces.ed.gov/fastfacts/display.asp?id=61.) Those results are roughly comparable to the US population generally in 2010, when 74.8 percent of the people who identified themselves as belonging to a single race described themselves as white on the national census, 12.6 percent as black, 19.5 percent as Hispanic, 5.0 percent as Asian or Pacific Islander, and 0.9 percent as American Indian/Alaska Native. (See http://www.census.gov/prod/cen2010/briefs/c2010br-02.pdf.) Note that these figures total more than 100 percent since the US Census treats being Hispanic as a matter of national origin, not as a separate race or ethnicity.

> From 1999–2000 to 2009–10, the number of degrees earned among U.S. residents increased for students of all racial/ethnic groups for each level of degree, but at varying rates. For associate's, bachelor's, and master's degrees, the change in percentage distribution of degree recipients was characterized by an increase in the numbers of degrees conferred to Black and Hispanic students. For doctor's degrees, the change in percentage distribution of degree recipients was characterized by an increase in the numbers of degrees conferred to Hispanic and Asian/Pacific Islander students. (http://nces.ed.gov/fast facts/display.asp?id=72)

Gender equity continues to be a challenge, with slightly more women than men completing baccalaureate degrees (in 2009–2010, 42.6 percent of the students graduating were men, and 57.4 percent were women) but with greater disparities among particular ethnic groups. In the same year, only 34.1 percent of the students who identified themselves as black and graduated with a bachelor's degree were men. That disproportion increases at the master's level, where only 28.9 percent of the graduates are men. (See nces.ed.gov/fastfacts/display.asp?id=72.) Gender inequality also persists in certain disciplines, with the National Science Foundation reporting that only 15.5 percent of engineering doctorate holders in 2008 were women (www.nsf.gov/statistics/seind 12/append/c5/at05–17.pdf), while other studies report that only 10.4 percent of nursing students nationally are men (www.thedp.com/article/2011 /11/nursing_and_engineering_tackle_gender_inequality).

In addition, economic inequality has been an increasingly visible problem in higher education. The Georgetown Center has found that "since 1995, 82 percent of new white enrollments have gone to the 468 most selective colleges, while 72 percent of new Hispanic enrollment and 68 percent of new African-American enrollment have gone to the two-year open-access schools" (cew.georgetown.edu/separateandunequal). That discrepancy is, however, not a matter of ethnic discrimination but a function of sheer economics. For example, the Harvard *Crimson's* study of the class of 2017 found that more than half of the students came from families in which parental income was $125,000 or more, with a full 14 percent of the students coming from families earning at least $500,000 (www.thecrimson.com/article/2013/9/4/freshman-survey-admissions-aid/). By contrast, an analysis conducted by the National Center for Public Policy and Higher Education found that 44 percent of the students attending community colleges came from families with a combined income of $25,000 or less, while only 15 percent of students came from families earning $100,00 or more a year (ccrc.tc.columbia.edu/Community-College-FAQs.html and nces.ed.gov/pubs2013/2013165.pdf).

While it's common to describe this situation as a crisis in higher education, these results need to be interpreted within their proper context. The fact is that American higher education has always been a highly imperfect work in progress. There have been constant attempts to include groups as societal values have evolved. The Morrill Land Grant Acts of 1862 and 1890, the GI bill of 1944, the desegregation of universities in the 1950s and 1960s, the conversion of many single-sex institutions to coeducational institutions in the 1970s, and Title IX in 1972 were all designed to bring educational opportunities to excluded or underrepresented groups. Moreover, efforts to provide more educational opportunities to working-class Americans, African Americans, and women still continue. As states reduce their level of funding to public universities and the cost of tuition rises, it's only natural for income inequality to become a more central theme in the nation's continuing quest for a fair and inclusive system of higher education. Many of the policies that affect this effort are made by legislatures, governing boards, and university presidents, but there's also a great deal that deans and provosts can do.

Reasons for Promoting Diversity

If you examine the diversity plans in place at a representative sample of colleges and universities across the country, you'll discover at least three philosophical principles that institutions use to justify their quest for diversity and the ways in which they pursue it.

At some institutions, the need to increase diversity is tied primarily to the school's *instructional* mission. Because students need to succeed in a highly diverse world, we are told, part of the institution's pedagogical duty is to help students prepare for that environment before they graduate.

At other institutions, diversity tends to be tied more closely to the *scholarly or research mission* of the college or university. One of the most important aspects of higher education, it's argued, is that students are exposed to a multitude of competing ideas, compelling them to work their way through different perspectives on the world and its problems. Without encountering the points of view that may be brought to bear by individuals of different cultures, races, socioeconomic classes, genders, nationalities, and sexual orientations, the scholarly context that we provide to students—and the perspectives that are developed by members of the faculty and other scholars—cannot be sufficiently rich.

Still other institutions see their commitment to diversity as arising out of their *service mission.* American colleges and universities have long played a role in improving their communities. One of the hallmarks of higher education, after all, is that it doesn't merely study society but also transforms it by increasing the knowledge, skill levels, or breadth of worldview of all its students. By reaching out to groups that were formerly underrepresented in American higher education, colleges and universities are continuing their traditional roles as change agents in society.

These three bases for diversity plans in higher education often overlap. Nevertheless, even when they do, different assumptions about why diversity is important can lead to variations in how institutions attempt to fulfill their goals in this area. For instance, schools that base their commitment to diversity largely on their service missions tend to develop plans that emphasize admissions strategies or faculty and staff recruitment. Schools that tie diversity more to their pedagogical or scholarly missions may give more attention to curricular development or services that can be provided to faculty and students. In the discussion that follows, we'll explore several ways that deans can help move from the general goals established by their institutions to diversity plans that are more specifically tied to the missions of their individual colleges.

Communicating This Philosophy

As a provost or dean, you have an important responsibility to share with your stakeholders the reasons that your institution values diversity. People are much more likely to be energetic in their pursuit of a goal if they understand why that goal is important to them. For instance, as we saw in chapter 5, few faculty members are likely to devote their time to supporting a change if they don't understand the importance of the problem that change is trying to solve. Equally few faculty members are going to contribute to the college's annual fund if they don't understand why participation rates are important to donors. (See chapter 25.) In the same way, you're likely to get little more than lip-service in terms of broad support for your diversity goals until you become proficient at explaining why diversity should be important to every student, faculty member, parent, staff member, and donor you serve. We saw that the philosophical basis for promoting diversity may differ from institution to institution and that these rationales tend to fall largely into three categories. Once you fully understand the reasons behind your institution's plan for diversity, you'll be in a much better position to help that plan succeed. You'll be able to convince people to make the extra effort that is often required because you'll know the reasons that those efforts are important and be in a good position to explain that importance to others.

Mentoring your faculty and staff in the reasons for actively pursuing diversity isn't a task that you can attempt once and then assume the work is complete. Stressing the way in which your institution's mission benefits from increased diversity is something that you need to consider every time you meet to plan a strategy for student recruitment, develop a job description, write a search announcement, or review your curriculum. In each of these cases, there's likely to be someone present who understands that achieving diversity seems to be important to the institution for some reason or another but really hasn't internalized the benefits derived from this activity. At times, such a person will say something like, "Why can't we just try to attract the best possible people we can into the pool and let diversity take care of itself?" More frequently, however, someone will simply think these thoughts silently, but their attitude will affect the process anyway. By taking the initiative and making certain that people are always aware of both the institution's overall diversity plan and the philosophical basis for it, you'll be much more likely to see energetic and genuine follow-through on your college's diversity efforts.

Promoting Diversity in Searches

Affirmative action and equal opportunity provisions have long been components of most searches at American colleges and universities, and they've been responsible for a great deal of progress. Higher education is now far more diverse than it was in the mid-twentieth century. But in many cases, these efforts are limited to making sure that the search committee is diverse, placing a statement welcoming applicants from underrepresented groups in all advertisements, determining whether the finalist pool is sufficiently diverse, and so on. Those efforts can do a great deal, but they're also limited in their impact. Certain disciplines may not be able to staff a diverse search committee precisely because they're in need of greater diversity. Moreover, in areas where only a few women or African Americans are employed, they often are asked to participate in a large number of searches as a way of providing a diverse perspective. (We'll examine the problem this practice causes for minority provosts and deans later in this chapter.) The language intended to promote diverse applicant pools in search announcements is often a fairly bland: "Women and minorities are encouraged to apply," or "Ideal State University is an Affirmative Action/Equal Opportunity Employer." Determining that a group of finalists isn't sufficiently diverse often comes too late in the process to do much good; a significant part of the search season may already be over, and the search committee may be forced into a difficult choice between continuing the search into the next academic year or hiring a highly qualified candidate that doesn't help the program's diversity.

One useful way of avoiding some of these problems is to look at each faculty search from the very beginning through the lens of diversity. For example, is the specialty in which the search will be conducted likely to be one in which the prospect pool is diverse? If not, is that precise specialty so crucial to the program that it can't be modified in such a way as to broaden the group of applicants who qualify? In many cases, professional organizations track the dissertation topics of graduate students along with demographic information such as race and gender. By looking at information of this sort, you may discover that even a slight modification of the position description will be likely to attract a far more diverse applicant pool. In addition, requirements like "PhD in hand at the time of application" may cause you to miss out on candidates who are in the process of earning an EdD, DA, PsyD, MFA, or other terminal degree. By rephrasing this requirement as, "Terminal degree in a relevant discipline required by the starting date of this position, August 1, [year]," you'll be able to attract a much broader (and possibly more diverse) set of candidates. Finally, although you'll need official transcripts of the person you eventually hire for the position, is it necessary for you to require all applicants to send you official transcripts? The fees that some universities charge for printing and mailing official transcripts is relatively high. Even a modest fee can begin to add up for people who may be applying for fifty or more positions in a tough job market. By requiring official transcripts rather than photocopies of transcripts issued to the student, you may unintentionally be discouraging candidates with limited resources from applying for your position and thus narrowing your pool to a more homogeneous group in terms of socioeconomic background.

The way in which a search announcement indicates that the institution supports diversity can make a great deal of difference. Unadorned statements—for example, "Applicants from underrepresented groups are encouraged to apply"—or reference to the school's affirmative action policy are now so common as to have relatively little impact. It's far better to include a statement about why diversity is important in the search: "Because of Select Private College's dedication to diversity and inclusiveness across the curriculum, applications from all qualified candidates are welcome, regardless of their age, gender, religion, race, ethnicity, national origin, physical challenge, sexual orientation, and marital or family status." The precise list of protected classes you mention is likely to be a function of your institution's specific mission and diversity statement (see the section on religious institutions below), but providing a bit more detail will probably yield better results than a terse "Select Private College is an AA/EEO institution." (Certain readers of the ad might not even recognize the reference to affirmative action/equal employment opportunity.)

In addition, some institutions feel that they've done their part in promoting diversity by listing positions in publications targeted at specific minority groups. While use of these publications may help broaden a candidate pool, they are rarely sufficient to attract a large number of female and minority applicants. They may even backfire with candidates who find it offensive that an institution acts as though women and minorities read only specialized publications and not trade journals intended for everyone in the profession.

Providing Adequate Infrastructure

There's an old joke about a college professor who dies and is standing before the Pearly Gates. St. Peter says, "Well, this has never happened before. In your lifetime, you did exactly as much good as evil. So we'll give you a choice: Spend all day tomorrow in heaven, the next day in hell, and then tell me the day after that which one you prefer." The professor goes to heaven on the following day and finds that it's nice but rather boring. Everyone is dressed in white. There's constant harp music. And there are no vices to provide a break in the routine. On the next day, the professor is greeted in hell with a huge reception. One of the devils says, "Oh, I read your book, and it was *fantastic, brilliant!*" Everyone treats the professor like a celebrity. Lunch is expertly catered, and the drinks are unlimited. When the two visits are over, St. Peter asks which place the professor prefers. "On the whole," he replies, "I actually think I had a better time in hell." St. Peter thinks that an odd choice, but the decision has been made, and the professor is immediately sent to hell. All around there's nothing but fire and brimstone. People either ignore the professor entirely or utter rude remarks in passing. Finally, the professor finds the devil who had been so enthusiastic about the book and asks, "What's wrong? Everyone was so nice yesterday." The devil looks confused for a moment and then realizes what had happened. "Oh, that?" he replies. "You see, yesterday we were interviewing you. Today you're faculty."

While that joke contains a truth that relates to almost anyone who's ever interviewed for a job—that highly congenial department that conducted the interview often seems to vanish as soon as you actually arrive for work—it can be especially difficult for minority faculty members. Too often all the institution's efforts seem to be concentrated on the front end: seeking a diverse group of applicants, making a good impression on the finalists, and putting together a competitive offer. But once the faculty member is hired, people sometimes act as though their job is done. The candidate who was wooed during the interviews can feel abandoned once he or she arrives at the start of the semester.

Particularly in environments that are trying to overcome a severe lack of diversity, being among the first people hired from underrepresented groups can be a lonely experience. It's not that members of minority groups can relate only to other members of the same group or that women in a male-dominated field (or vice versa) only want to socialize with others of their gender. And it's certainly not the case that people will automatically form close bonds or even have a lot in common simply because they're of the same gender or ethnicity. Rather it's a matter of being attentive to the needs and desires of the faculty members as individuals. Some of these pioneering faculty members may want additional mentoring as they make the transition to a new institution with values and expectations that may be different from those elsewhere. Some, if they're in their first faculty position, may wish to have access to a confidant with whom they can share concerns, frustrations, and triumphs. Some may prefer to be left alone.

The goal is to provide enough infrastructure to support the added challenges that faculty members from underrepresented groups may experience, but only to the extent that the person finds helpful. If you do too little, the faculty member may well feel isolated. If you do too much, it may appear as though you don't trust the faculty member to succeed on his or her own. The key is simply to keep in touch regularly, find out what the person needs, and convey your willingness to be supportive in any way you can. (Of course, that's probably a good message to send to *all* your faculty members.)

Don't assume that you can figure out on your own everything that people need and simply provide it. Every institution is different, and the specific needs of your faculty, staff, and students are going to vary somewhat from what you may regard as most important. One of the best ways to start addressing this situation is to hold a series of conversations, either one-on-one or in small groups, to discover what needs are not being met or what problems are arising. With members of the faculty and staff, you can probably do this best through informal conversations every few weeks, coupled with several small discussion groups built into your regular faculty and staff training program. With students, it's probably better to gather this information through peer-conducted support groups or regular discussions that occur as part of an introduction to college class, orientation, or other type of first-year experience activity. Allow the issues to emerge naturally in the course of these conversations or discussions. The person who's leading them should ask general questions, such as, "How have things been going? Is there anything that seems to be getting in the way of your satisfaction or success here? Are there any resources you wish you had access to?" The answers to these questions are not likely to arise immediately. Don't be surprised if the initial answer is, "Everything's fine. I don't need anything." No one, after all, wants to be perceived as weak or a failure. If you keep probing, however, you may eventually reach some problem areas: "Do you feel as though you're fitting in? Have you found a group of friends you meet with regularly? Do you have someone to talk to if you have a problem?" The degree to which the answers to these questions are specific or vague will also tell you a great deal. If you do discover that the individual has a need that is not being met, you can either help the person get in touch with appropriate resources that are already available or start seeking the type of services that could help address these unmet needs.

It's also important to review existing policies and activities with an eye toward how they promote or discourage diversity. Conduct an internal audit by asking questions like these:

o Are our policies on class attendance and personal leave flexible enough for members of the student body or employees who may be members of religious faiths not dominant at our institution?

o Does the food served in the dining hall, faculty club, and locations for major events take into account the dietary preferences of members of other faiths, as well as those with food allergies or dietary restrictions based on philosophical beliefs?

○ How often does our benefits office review what they offer to make sure that the opportunities available to those who work here accommodate lifestyles and family structures outside the mainstream?

○ Do our employment plans include such family-friendly measures as a tenure stop-clock policy, spousal placement policy, and residence assistance plan? (See chapter 17.)

○ Do we have a committee that regularly reviews all faculty, staff, and student policies with a view toward, "What problems would this policy cause me if I were less than full time?"

○ Do we allow flexible work hours for every position in which there is no reason to require set hours?

○ Do we review the course schedule to ensure that those who wish or need to pursue degrees at nontraditional times are able to graduate in a timely manner?

○ Do we provide as much course work as possible through multiple means of delivery (such as online courses and asynchronous distance learning, in addition to traditional classroom courses) so that people may attend your institution even if they have complex work schedules or alternative learning styles?

○ Do we have a forgiveness policy for students whose work is negatively affected by a circumstance beyond their control?

Certain stakeholders may be reluctant to consider revising these policies, assuming that they imply a decline in standards or allowing "everyone to do whatever they want." Nevertheless, if you explain that diversity comes in all forms and reflects the individual needs of each person, you can better explain how removing needless obstacles can create a richer blend of individuals at your institution. If you assume that everyone has the same needs, you'll be more likely to recruit only students, faculty, and staff members who have the same needs and outlook you do. But if you develop policies that compensate for individual differences, you develop a community that deeply respects the different contributions that each of us brings to our community.

Supporting Events That Promote Diversity

As you'll see a number of times in this book, provosts and deans don't just have organizational roles; they also have symbolic roles. The organizational roles of academic leaders consist of the responsibilities outlined in their job descriptions along with all the other duties that tend to accrue to deans and provosts at universities everywhere. Their symbolic roles derive from their status as the face and voice of their areas. The provost serves as the representative of academic standards at the institution. The dean serves as the representative of the programs that fall within his or her college. As a result, the presence or absence of these academic leaders sends a message, intended or not, about what is regarded as important at the institution. If the provost attends a basketball game but not a football game, there will be those who will conclude that basketball is somehow being favored over football. In the same way, if the dean attends the men's basketball game but not the women's basketball game, there will be those who conclude that the dean suffers from a gender bias.

The same phenomenon is true when it comes to events celebrating diversity on campus. The presence or absence of academic leaders is interpreted by many people as an indication of how important the administration regards those causes. Naturally you can't be everywhere. The sheer number of events at the typical college or university means that many schedules overlap, and the responsibilities assigned to a dean or provost often occupy far more than the average working day. Nevertheless, the symbolic nature of these positions means that your support of public events is viewed as a declaration of your priorities. At times, too, an e-mail or memo to the faculty encouraging their attendance at important events can underscore how important you regard those activities and the causes they represent. For example, the National Day of Silence is an annual event designed "to call attention to the silencing effect of anti-LGBT bullying and harassment in schools" (www.dayofsilence.org/resources/). During that event, participants pledge not to speak as a sign of support of people of all sexual orientations and preferences despite continued public discrimination and periodic violence. To explain their position, students print cards that they can hand to anyone who questions them or seems confused:

> Please understand my reasons for not speaking today. I am participating in the Day of Silence (DOS), a national youth movement bringing attention to the silence faced by lesbian, gay, bisexual and transgender people and their allies. My deliberate silence echoes that silence, which is caused by anti-LGBT bullying, name-calling and harassment. I believe that ending the silence is the first step toward building awareness and making a commitment to address these injustices. Think about the voices you ARE NOT hearing today. (www.dayofsilence.org/PDFs/dos_palmcard.pdf)

One challenge is that in many college courses, oral participation is an integral component of the pedagogy. In many foreign language, communication, law, drama, music, and other courses, students who don't speak aren't actively participating in the class. For this reason, students are permitted to break their silence in class whenever a professor needs them to do so, and it's recommended that they work with the instructor in advance to see if arrangements can be made that permit them not to speak on that one day. If a dean or provost sends an e-mail to the faculty encouraging them to respect the students' rights to participate in the Day of Silence to whatever extent it's pedagogically possible, that statement provides a clear signal that the academic leader values the importance of a diverse student and faculty community. The following is sample text that you could adopt to suit your own style:

> On [date], a number of students at our institution will be participating in the National Day of Silence. In case you have not yet heard of it, the Day of Silence is an activity that occurs on a large number of high school and college campuses. Its purpose is to heighten awareness of issues that affect members of the LGBTQA community by illustrating, for just one day, what the world would be like if the voices of this community were silenced. Students (most of whom should be wearing buttons or pins indicating their participation in this activity) may hand you a card outlining their reasons for keeping silent that day. While I encourage you to accommodate these students to whatever extent possible, the Day of Silence is not intended to interfere with or restrict the educational activities of your classes. If, as the professor of the course, you decide that the students need to speak in your class, simply say so, knowing they have been encouraged to comply with your request. In addition, the participants will all be instructed as they sign their pledge cards that this event is not to be disruptive in any way. The Day of Silence should, in other words, enhance and not detract from the educational mission of our community.

You may see such terms as *LGBT*, *LGBTQ*, *LGBTQA*, and *LGBTQI* seemingly used interchangeably. While *LGBT* is universally accepted as standing for lesbian, gay, bisexual, and transgender, the significance of the other letters depends on the user. *Q* is sometimes said to stand for questioning (those who are not yet sure of their sexual identity) and sometimes for Queer (an attempt to take back and neutralize a term once used in hate speech). *A* may be regarded as standing for asexual, allied, all, aromantic, or advocates. *I* stands for intersexual and is not as commonly used as the other letters, at least in the United States.

Being Holistic in Your Approach to Diversity

Diversity includes a wide range of ways in which stakeholders can be different from one another. When most people think of diversity, they tend to see this issue only in terms of race, ethnicity, and gender. But the concept of diversity is far broader than that. As a result, it's often helpful to think in the broadest possible terms of groups that you'd like to attract and retain among students, faculty, and staff. What type of diversity are you most lacking that would provide a richer experience for everyone who lives and works at your institution? Gender? Racial? Socioeconomic? Ethnic? Sexual orientation? Physical capability? Religion? Age? Political views? Family situation? Once you have identified the groups that appear to be underrepresented in your college, ask yourself:

○ How would the curriculum that my college offers look to members of these target groups? Do we offer courses and programs that appeal to a broad range of students, or are we unintentionally alienating some of the very groups we say we're trying to attract?

○ Do we offer cocurricular and extracurricular activities that would appeal to our target audience? Do our public lectures, organizations, and celebrations speak broadly to the full range of students we are trying to attract?

○ Is there curriculum already in place that would attract a diverse faculty to my institution? Have I taken steps to ensure that my reward structures and recognitions provide encouragement to newer faculty members (who may be significantly more diverse than the senior faculty)?

Long-Term Strategies

Institutions sometimes lament the way in which competition for highly qualified graduate students and faculty members from minority groups becomes so intense that they have difficulty making the progress that they want. While many institutions exist in service areas where the local population is at least 25 percent nonwhite, they discover that fewer than 5 percent of the graduates each year in many disciplines are nonwhite. Rather than simply giving up when faced with odds like this, the solution that many institutions have found most effective is to "grow their own."

Since the student body is likely to be more diverse at the undergraduate than the graduate level, explore the possibility of granting scholarships that will attract a diverse and talented group of faculty members or graduate students. One of the ways this approach can work is to seek a donor who will fund all or part of a student's graduate program if that student returns to the institution as a faculty member for a specified time after graduation. Some of the postdoctoral instructors supported in this way will turn out to be so talented that they'll be highly competitive candidates when tenure-track positions become available. (In fact, since this approach provides them with several years of guaranteed full-time experience after completing their graduate programs, they may well be highly competitive against less-experienced candidates.) Even instructors whom you can't retain indefinitely will increase the diversity of your staff for a time, probably also increasing their dedication to your institution because of the opportunity you gave them. None of these strategies will pay off immediately, of course. Nevertheless, if you are dedicated to promoting diversity for the long term, they can be important parts of your overall diversity plan.

Diversity at Religious Institutions

Private colleges and universities with ties to particular religious traditions approach promoting diversity differently from public institutions. For example, some religious schools require all members of the faculty and staff (and sometimes students too) to draft and file a faith statement outlining their beliefs and promise to uphold the principles of that religion. For example, Shorter University in Rome, Georgia, requires all employees to be committed Christians and notes that all applicants for positions "are expected to sign and adhere to" a personal lifestyle statement before they are hired. That statement indicates that the person will not use illegal drugs, "use alcoholic beverages in the presence of students" or in public settings such as restaurants and stadiums, and "reject as acceptable all sexual activity not in agreement with the Bible, including, but not limited to, premarital sex, adultery, and homosexuality" (su.shorter.edu/wp-content/uploads/personal_lifestyle_statement.pdf). The university's employment opportunity website also provides links to two other types of personal statement that members of the Shorter community can sign and submit:

- A *Statement of Faith*, which outlines the university's commitment to the belief that the Bible is inerrant and infallible, Jesus Christ is the eternal Son of God and source of salvation, and Christians must live lives "consistent with Scripture in their character and in their conduct." (su.shorter.edu/wp-content/uploads/statement_of_faith.pdf)

- A *Statement on the Integration of Faith and Learning*, which presents the university's expectation that "employees will encourage the spiritual development of our students by sharing with them the biblical message of Jesus Christ and by encouraging them to implement biblical truths in their daily lives and decisions." (su.shorter.edu/wp-content/uploads/faith_integration.pdf)

In such a context, it would not be possible to advocate on behalf of diversity in religion, sexual orientation, or family status. That's perfectly acceptable because Shorter University is a private institution where students and faculty members know in advance exactly what the expectations and experience will be like. In fact, it's even better than acceptable because it adds to the diversity of choices available in American higher education. There will be faculty members, students, and parents who believe that the best form of higher education occurs in an environment where every member subscribes to a given set of values. There will also be faculty members, students, and parents who don't share that belief. Religious institutions add to the overall diversity of a complex system of higher education by providing opportunities that aren't available elsewhere. They also often support other types of diversity, such as offering a supportive environment for people of all ages, races, ethnicities, national origins, and physical conditions.

Something similar may be said for single-sex institutions. They may not support gender diversity, but they add to the overall diversity of American higher education by offering students and faculty members as choice. Gallaudet University doesn't violate the spirit of diversity by focusing its programs on the needs of deaf and hearing-impaired students, and the Hadley School doesn't violate the spirit of diversity by concentrating on the needs of the blind. Like Spelman College, Howard University, and other historically black colleges and universities, they contribute an important component of diversity to the higher education system as a whole. So if you are a provost or dean at an institution that due to its special mission, privileges certain categories of students or employees over others, it doesn't necessarily mean that you're not promoting diversity. It simply means that you need to encourage people to see the larger picture of how your programs and institution contribute to the tapestry of choices that is American higher education.

Special Challenges for Minority Provosts and Deans

We saw that minority administrators are often asked to serve on a large number of search committees. Out of a well-intentioned desire to bring minority perspectives to every hiring decision, members of underrepresented groups find themselves receiving far more than their share of opportunities to serve. This practice isn't limited to faculty search committees. Because of the need of many institutions to diversify the curriculum, student body, administration, cultural programming, and promotion guidelines, minority provosts and deans often find that their entire day is taken up with meetings. Many of those meetings are relatively low level and not the best use of the administrator's time. But if a policy explicitly states that diversity on a committee is required or if a relatively homogeneous institution is trying its best to diversity its staff, the limited number of minority administrators at the institution are going to be very busy. At its best, this practice provides an opportunity for the academic leader to make a difference on a wide variety of issues. At its worst, it smacks of tokenism, wastes time, and leaves the administrators feeling that they've been taken advantage of.

Minority provosts and deans also face the challenge of filling multiple symbolic roles simultaneously. We already saw that being a member of the administration carries symbolic weight. Everything you say, from official announcements to the most offhand remark, is now something "the dean [or provost] said." If you add minority status to that role, the symbolism grows astronomically. You may well be the first black, Hispanic, or woman dean the college has ever had. If you don't succeed, there will be those who will conclude, as completely unfair as it is to do so, that your failure is more than just personal. The next time the institution sets out to hire a black, Hispanic, or woman dean, some people may say, "Well, we tried that, and it didn't work." Those deplorable attitudes are changing, but they do exist, and they'll probably exist at least temporarily for each new minority group that gradually finds acceptance within our larger culture. There's an important symbolic role that accompanies these positions too, in that students may be viewing the provost or dean as a role model and wondering if they can see themselves in your position someday. For this reason, the stakes and the pressure can be great at times, but so can the impact. While it's advantageous for every academic leader to have a mentor and confidant, it can be especially beneficial for minority provosts and deans to have someone with whom they can speak candidly about their challenges, vent their frustrations, and get constructive advice whenever they need it.

New Issues in Gender Balance

For many years, American higher education has focused on opening educational opportunities to women. In fact, Title IX and the change in the 1970s of most colleges and universities that accepted only men to full coeducational status were attempts to achieve precisely this goal. But enrollment patterns have changed over the past several decades. According to the National Center for Education Statistics, the ratio of women to men enrolled at all four-year postsecondary institutions that qualified for federal student financial aid in fall 2010 was 56.7 percent to 43.3 percent, while at two-year institutions it was 57.4 percent to 42.6 percent. In 2010–2011, women outpaced men in both the rates at which they were earning bachelor's degrees (57.2 percent to 42.8 percent) and doctorates (51.4 percent to 48.6 percent) (nces.ed.gov/programs/digest/d12/tables/dt12_219.asp.).

The problem now isn't primarily one of giving women access to education but of addressing gender imbalance in certain programs and determining why men are choosing not to go to college at the same rates as women. One study found that in 2011, baccalaureate disciplines such as engineering (17.2 percent women to 82.8 percent men), computer and information sciences (17.6 percent women to 82.4 percent men), and philosophy and religious studies (36.5 percent women to 63.5 percent men) were heavily dominated by men, while those such as the health professions (85 percent women to 15 percent men), psychology (77 percent women to 23 percent men), and foreign languages (69 percent women to 31 percent men) were overwhelmingly preferred by women. "For the College Class of 2011, women significantly outnumbered men in 15 academic disciplines, men outnumbered women in nine academic fields, and there was approximate gender parity in five disciplines" (www.aei-ideas.org/2013/01/college-class-of-2011-by-academic-discipline-and-gender-the-selective-concern-about-gender-imbalances-is-imbalanced/).

The conclusion to draw isn't necessarily that academic leaders should support a new national initiative to attract men to college or campaigns to force gender equality in every discipline, but that new diversity challenges will arise all the time.

Promoting diversity in higher education will always be a work in progress.

As provosts and deans, we have an obligation to track the demographics of our students, faculty, and staff; note patterns where diversity is either increasing or diminishing over time; and take steps to address those issues that hamper our ability to fulfill our mission. Since each institution's mission varies, the way in which the emergence of a new majority group that has the potential to increase homogeneity will affect each school differently. A pool of faculty candidates that overwhelming describes itself as completely secular by conviction may not be of any concern at a large public research university, but it may pose a severe problem for a small, conservative Christian college. Since promoting diversity entails being aware of this issue in terms of both how it affects our own institution and how it relates to demographic patterns in higher education generally, it is important for provosts and deans at every type of college and university to remain well informed about evolving trends globally.

Conclusion

Promoting diversity in higher education is an ongoing challenge. Since one of the most important aspects of the college experience is exposing students to a broad spectrum of views and the people who support those views, provosts and deans have an important role to play in maintaining the type of environment in which this experience will occur. Different institutional missions mean that diversity won't manifest itself in exactly the same way at every school. Moreover, there are times when we have to take a systems approach to promoting diversity, keeping in mind how patterns develop in higher education generally rather than just at our own institutions or in our own programs. Nevertheless, as provosts and deans, we can never afford to think of diversity as a problem that will at some point be solved. Rather, like maintaining high academic standards and keeping the curriculum up to date, it is a part of our jobs that will continue as long as we are in our positions.

REFERENCES

Horowitz, D., & Laksin, J. (2013). *One-party classroom: How radical professors at America's top colleges indoctrinate students and undermine our democracy*. New York, NY: Crown Forum.
Kimball, R. (1990). *Tenured radicals: How politics has corrupted our higher education*. New York, NY: Harper.
Sykes, C. J. (1988). *ProfScam: Professors and the demise of higher education*. Washington, DC: Regnery Gateway.

RESOURCES

Adams, M. (Ed.). (1992). *Promoting diversity in college classrooms: Innovative responses for the curriculum, faculty, and institutions*. San Francisco, CA: Jossey-Bass.

Adams, M. (1997). *Teaching for diversity and social justice*. New York, NY: Routledge.

Behling, L. L. (2014). Diversifying the campus: Some steps for deans to take. In L. L. Behling (Ed.), *The resource handbook for academic deans* (pp. 269–276). San Francisco, CA: Jossey-Bass.

Cooper, T. L. (2006). *The sista' network: African-American women faculty successfully negotiating the road to tenure*. Bolton, MA: Anker.

Chun, E. B., & Evans, A. (2012). *Diverse administrators in peril: The new indentured class in higher education*. Boulder, CO: Paradigm.

Flowers, L. A. (Ed.). (2004). *Diversity issues in American colleges and universities: Case studies for higher education and student affairs professionals*. Springfield, IL: Charles C. Thomas.

Goodman, D. J. (2000). *Promoting diversity and social justice: Educating people from privileged groups*. Thousand Oaks, CA: Sage.

Johns, A. M., & Sipp, M. K. (Eds.). (2004). *Diversity in college classrooms: Practices for today's campuses*. Ann Arbor, MI: University of Michigan Press/ESL.

Kirwan, W. E., & Hale, Jr.,, F. W. (Eds.). (2003). *What makes racial diversity work in higher education: Academic leaders present successful policies and strategies*. Sterling, VA: Stylus.

Rai, K. B., & Critzer, J. W. (2000). *Affirmative action and the university: Race, ethnicity, and gender in higher education employment*. Lincoln: University of Nebraska Press.

Smith, D. G. (2009). *Diversity's promise for higher education: Making it work*. Baltimore, MD: Johns Hopkins University Press

Smith, D. G. (2014). *Diversity and inclusion in higher education: Emerging perspectives on institutional transformation*. New York, NY: Routledge.

Smith, D. G., Wolf, L. E., & Busenberg, B. E. (1996). *Achieving faculty diversity: Debunking the myths*. Washington, DC: Association of American Colleges and Universities.

Turner, C.S.V. (2002). *Diversifying the faculty: A guidebook for search committees*. Washington, DC: Association of American Colleges and Universities.

Valverde, L. A. (2003). *Leaders of color in higher education: Unrecognized triumphs in harsh institutions*. Walnut Creek, CA: AltaMira Press.

Watson, L., Terrell, M. C., Wright, D. J., Bonner II, F., Cuyjet, M., Gold, J., . . . Person, D. R. (2002). *How minority students experience college: Implications for planning and policy*. Sterling, VA: Stylus.

Williams, D. A. (2013). *Strategic diversity leadership: Activating change and transformation in higher education*. Sterling, VA: Stylus.

Wood, P. (2004) *Diversity: The invention of a concept*. San Francisco, CA: Encounter.

7

A SCENARIO ANALYSIS ON THE ACADEMIC LEADER'S ROLE

This chapter is the first of seven scenario analyses in this book and the online content that accompanies it. Exercises of this kind are useful tools to help deans and provosts develop their skills as academic leaders, consider other alternatives to difficult problems, and prepare for challenging situations even before they arise. Each scenario analysis has three complementary parts:

○ *Case study*: A fictional though plausible situation depicting one or more challenges similar to those that academic leaders actually face.

○ *Considerations*: Questions that may cause you to see the case study in a different light or to alter how you would respond to it.

○ *Suggestions*: A critique of the case study itself and ideas about possible actions to take in order to remedy a similar situation or to lessen its severity. While the case studies by their very nature do not lend themselves to right or wrong answers or to only one solution for all administrators and all institutions, this section is based on practical and field-tested responses to similar challenges. The suggestions provided should not be regarded as the only answers but rather should prompt further consideration as to what you would do to find the best possible solution to a difficult problem.

One way to improve your administrative skills through scenario analyses is to compare your analysis with those of your peers. Critique together the suggestions given, propose your own solutions, see how the questions posed in the "Considerations" section might alter your responses, and identify what your own approaches teach you about your style of management.

For each part of the book, there is one scenario analysis for deans and another for provosts. If the case study for deans appears here in the book, you'll find the one for provosts online and vice versa. This first exercise is a scenario analysis for deans. A scenario analysis for provosts appears in the online content accompanying this book.

Case Study for Deans

A tenure-track faculty member in your college who has an extremely poor record in research received a negative annual evaluation from the chair, concluding that insufficient progress was being made toward tenure. The faculty member meets with you to appeal the chair's decision. "I'm being discriminated against by my chair," the faculty member claims. "I'm continually placed in a position where it's impossible for me to succeed. You see, every qualified graduate student the chair accepts into our program is either homosexual or transgendered, and the traditions of my religion, as well as those of my country of origin, forbid me from condoning or having any contact with individuals who engage in 'deviant' sexual practices. So I never have an opportunity to put together a research team. I have to do everything myself. The result is that I have inadequate research assistance and cannot possibly achieve the results the chair demands. I want you to overturn the chair's evaluation, rate me as at least satisfactory in research, and demand that the chair diversify the department by recruiting some normal, heterosexual men with whom I will be able to work."

You're taken aback by the directness of the faculty member's claim and proceed to explain the institution's policy on unlawful discrimination, but the faculty member counters, "That's hypocrisy. You can't enforce the equal opportunity rights of the students without violating mine. The very policy you just cited says that you won't allow discrimination against religion or country of origin, and here you are discriminating against *my* religion and *my* country of origin. If I'm ultimately denied tenure based on this issue, it'll certainly result in a major lawsuit and unfavorable publicity for this institution, my department, and you personally."

How do you handle this situation?

Considerations

1. Do you attempt to resolve this issue on your own, or would you involve other offices at the institution?
   a. If you decide to resolve the issue on your own, what do you say to the faculty member?

    b. If you decide to involve other offices, which ones do you contact, and why?

2. Does your answer change if one or more of the following are true?
   a. You work at a conservative religious college that has an institutional policy stating that homosexuality is immoral.
   b. The faculty member's religion has dietary restrictions and forbids the consumption of alcohol, but you have witnessed the faculty member violate both of those constraints on multiple occasions.
   c. The chair of the faculty member's department disputes the allegation that all graduate students in the program are homosexual or transgendered.
   d. You suspect that the chair has a bias against the faculty member's religion and know that the chair opposed hiring this faculty member from the beginning.
   e. The faculty member has a reputation for appealing every negative decision even when clearly in the wrong.
   f. There has been a history of conflict between the chair and the faculty member for several years.

Suggestions

Issues of diversity frequently bring one person's rights into conflict with another's. Although both sets of rights in these issues often have equal merit, that does not appear to be the case in this situation. If the school's diversity policy prohibits discrimination on the basis of sexual orientation, then the faculty member has no right to insist that the department seek out heterosexual men as graduate students to work on the professor's research team. The faculty member does have a right to his or her own religious beliefs but chose to take a job at an institution that was not limited to members of that faith. He or she should have known from the start of the position that due to the school's commitment to diversity, there was a high probability of interaction with students of various sexual orientations. Moreover, that interaction is inherent in the nature of the job the faculty member accepted. So while student rights and faculty rights appear to be in conflict here, they aren't truly parallel: the students' rights trump those of the faculty member, and the faculty member has created a false dichotomy by equating them.

All of this changes if the university is private and adheres to the values of a particular religious tradition. Moreover, the situation is dramatically different if the school requires a faith statement or personal lifestyle statement such as those we saw in chapter 6. If those statements preclude supporting, engaging in, or condoning homosexual activity, then you will certainly want to investigate the faculty member's claim that "every qualified graduate student the chair accepts into [the] program is either homosexual or transgendered." Blanket statements of this kind are rarely true or, at least, rarely the entire story. Moreover, it would be strange indeed for a chair to admit only students who had to lie on their personal lifestyle statements. There's probably a great deal more to this situation than the faculty member is telling you, and you won't want to accept this claim on face value.

Regardless of the type of institution where the situation occurs, however, the issue of competing rights shouldn't obscure the specific focus of the negative evaluation: the faculty member's poor research performance. If research is an important criterion for evaluation at the university, you have an obligation to address that problem in addition to any issues of competing rights that may be involved. It is natural for people to be defensive when they are told that their performance was unsatisfactory, and the faculty may be raising the issue of religious beliefs as a smokescreen. As a result, you should be sensitive and respectful to the faculty member's beliefs but not allow the issue that he or she has raised to distract you from the performance problem at the heart of the matter.

PART TWO

THE NATURE
OF ACADEMIC
LEADERSHIP

8

LEADERSHIP AND MANAGEMENT

In chapter 1, we saw how the organizational structure of a university means that deans and provosts necessarily lead from the middle. But what does it mean to be a leader? Many colleges of businesses prepare executives for key roles in the corporate world through their departments of management. Is management any different from leadership? If so, do provosts and deans lead or manage their areas? Or is it different for the two positions, with provosts in a leadership role while deans primarily manage their areas or vice versa? Certainly a case can be made for any of these positions, depending on the definitions of leadership and management we adopt. But the position I'll adopt in this book is that *leadership and management are distinct but complementary skills, both of which are essential to the success of provosts and deans.* Probably the most famous statement distinguishing these two skills is Warren Bennis and Burt Nanus's (1985) observation: "Managers are people who do things right and leaders are people who do the right things" (221). But what does this actually mean? And don't we really want our academic leaders to do the right things right? In other words, don't we want them to make good decisions and then implement those decisions in the best possible way?

In *Leadership: Theory and Practice* (2013), that exhaustive study of research on leadership mentioned in chapter 1, Peter G. Northouse defines *leadership* as "a process whereby an individual influences a group of individuals to achieve a common good" (p. 5).

This definition has four important components:

1. *Leadership is a process.* It's not a trait you have to be born with or a mysterious quality that resists all attempts to understand it. As a process, leadership can be studied. We can conduct research to determine

how to perform this process better. And we can improve our own leadership skills by applying what we learn.

2. *Leadership involves influence.* When we influence others, we produce change. For this reason, all leadership is change leadership, at least to a certain degree. Leaders cause their organizations (or at least their units within those organizations) to do things differently, improve their processes, and seek higher goals. While power causes change through the threat of force, leadership causes change through authority and influence.

3. *Leadership affects groups of people.* You can't lead alone in your office (even though we've all met deans and provosts who try to do exactly that). Leadership is an interactive and social process that affects other people. Although you'll see in the next chapter that academic leadership is sometimes exhibited one-on-one, the actions made by a provost or dean almost always involve groups of faculty members, students, or other stakeholders.

4. *Leadership entails pursuit of a common good.* Notice that the definition does not state that the good being pursued must be initiated by the leader. Effective leaders recognize that others also have useful ideas and are willing to pursue those ideas when they have the potential to benefit the organization. The important aspect to observe is that leaders want people to move toward a common good, not merely something that benefits them personally.

These four components begin to clarify what makes leadership different from management. In their widely used textbook for college business courses, Angelo Kinicki and Brian Williams (2013, p. 5) define *management* as "the pursuit of organizational goals efficiently and effectively by integrating the work of people through planning, organizing, leading, and controlling organizational resources."

That definition is almost identical to the one proposed by Richard L. Daft in *Management* (2014, 6), who describes his topic as "the attainment of organizational goals in an effective and efficient manner through planning, organizing, leading, and controlling organizational resources."

Distinguishing Management from Leadership

Setting aside for a moment the reference to leading within these definitions, we can analyze four essential components that begin to help us distinguish management from leadership.

1. *Management concerns the attainment of some objective.* Both leadership and management involve the pursuit of some goal. But whereas leadership emphasizes the pursuit, leadership emphasizes the goal. For example, heroic failures are often seen as inspiring examples even though they never achieved their objective. "At least they tried to attain something lofty," people may say. "You have to admire that." Yet no one admires a manager who tries to complete a project within a budget but fails or attempts to launch a successful product but has disastrous results. Leaders may inspire people to move toward unattainable dreams; managers have to be sure the bills get paid.

2. *Management focuses on effectiveness and efficiency.* Effectiveness is about producing results; efficiency is about doing so with a minimum expenditure of resources. Good managers combine these skills. They not only attain their objectives but do so in a way that doesn't waste time, money, or effort. Leadership is less about effectiveness and efficiency than it is about inspiration and team building. The poet and activist Sarojini Naidu (2013) once said of the great Indian leader Mahatma Gandhi, "We have to spend lakhs of rupees [the equivalent of saying "millions of dollars"] to keep Gandhi poor." (p. 21; see also Mehta, 1997. The comment is also sometimes attributed to Winston Churchill, Jawaharlal Nehru, and others.) Many things that Gandhi did weren't efficient. Some of them weren't even very effective—at least not immediately. But he was still an inspirational leader.

3. *Management emphasizes the use of skills.* Daft (2014) notes that managers achieve their goals effectively and efficiently through planning, organizing, and controlling the assets they have available. Becoming more effective as a manager involves developing greater skills in these areas. One can learn to plan more strategically, organize resources more proficiently, and control activities more capably. In fact, much of the curriculum in management programs is about the practice and improvement of these very skills.

4. *Management is resource oriented.* The whole idea of efficient management is using resources efficiently. While leaders can afford to dismiss those who continually focus on the bottom line as "mere bean counters," managers never have that luxury. They are responsible for keeping every activity under their supervision on time and within budget. For this reason, management deals extensively with resources—not just funding but also equipment, facilities, information, and human resources—in order to make sure that the job gets done properly.

As you read this list of management components, you may well have thought, "That's a lot of what I do, but I think of myself as an academic leader, not an academic manager." But recall what I said at the beginning of this chapter: leadership and management are distinct but complementary skills, and in order to be successful at your job, you have to be good at both. In fact, Daft regarded leadership as an essential skill for managers, and we could easily say that even the best leaders are expected to manage a good part of the time.

While we have probably all known managers whose work never really rose to the level of leadership, very few people have the luxury of leading twenty-four hours a day. Regardless of how visionary someone's ideas may be, sooner or later that person has to work on the practical details of implementation. Leadership and management balance one another. Put another way, think of them as the yin and the yang of what makes an effective academic administrator, but also as skills that support and lead into one another. (See figure 8.1.) In other words, you need to manage your resources well in order to lead your programs toward new visions. That new level of success then gives you an expanded or improved set of programs to manage, and the process continues. Another

Figure 8.1 The Relationship between Leadership and Management

way of looking at this relationship is to see the twin skills of leadership and management as supporting and completing one another in four major ways:

1. Their approach to stability or continuity
2. Their origin and development
3. Their orientation
4. Their attitude toward risk

These four differences are so important that they're best addressed individually.

Stability or continuity

Management strives for continuity; leadership strives for change. Leadership always involves influencing people, and that influence causes them to make different choices or to act in different ways. Since management is resource oriented, it involves finding ways of saving money, time, and other limited assets. Leadership, however, often involves taking calculated risks. Those risks, no matter how carefully they are calculated, sometimes do not work out. As a result, leadership occasionally results in the loss of resources, the very goal that management seeks to avoid. When the risks do prove beneficial, however, change is all but inevitable. So whereas management tends to be all about stability or continuity, leadership is frequently about growth, progress, and change.

Origin and development

Management authority arises from the organizational chart. Someone is assigned a managerial role and thus has supervisory duties toward subordinates: those who occupy a lower position on that branch of the organizational chart. Although we sometimes speak of leadership roles being allotted in this way, much of academic leadership is independent of our title and job description. (Recall Northouse's distinction between *assigned leadership* and *emergent leadership* from chapter 1. See Northouse, 2013.) As with all emergent leadership, a great deal of the authority we have as academic leaders arises because people have decided that our ideas are worth pursuing. In other words, if managers have subordinates, leaders have followers. Policies can require a subordinate to do what the manager says, but being a follower is much more voluntary. It means that the person is willingly being influenced by the vision of the leader. As a result, the relationship that managers have with their subordinates is different from that which leaders have with their followers. It's the manager's task to monitor and direct subordinates so that they may achieve specific goals effectively and efficiently. The role of the leader, however, is to inspire and motivate followers so that they'll move closer toward a vision that leaves them in a better place than they were originally even if it's never attained.

Orientation

Managers are resource oriented: their focus tends to be on tasks and projects. They develop tactics that help them reach short-term goals. They devote a great deal of their time to measuring their area's expenditure of resources, return on investment, speed at which progress is being made, and success in completing the tasks it's been assigned. Leaders, by contrast, are more people oriented. They work with others to develop strategies that help them reach long-term goals. They devote a great deal of their time to cultivating their teams, arousing positive emotions in others, directing people's vision toward the future, and working for change and improvement.

Attitude toward risk

Management is risk averse. In fact, the cautious approach that businesses take toward risk is even called *risk management*. Managers try to avoid problems and, by maintaining consistency, keep situations predictable and (in a word) *manageable*. Leaders take calculated risks. They're more interested in solving problems than avoiding them, shaking things up than lapsing into inertia. Although leaders certainly hope that the vast majority of risks will pay off, they're aware that not all of them will. They understand that in order to achieve great results, you sometimes have to experience great failure.

Importance of Leadership and Management for Academic Leaders

How does knowing all of this help provosts and deans? First, it provides them with a more holistic view of what their work will actually be. Although we often speak of academic leadership, no one can really lead 100 percent of the time. Too much change, risk, and uncertainty creates anxiety in an organization. People need time to catch their breath, savor their victories, and simply continue doing the things they're good at.

But if this stability continues too long, people start to feel as though progress isn't being made. They worry that the institution or their units in it aren't achieving everything they're capable of.

For this reason, provosts and deans need to balance their leadership and management roles. Although it can seem disappointing to a newly promoted academic leader who's eager to lead the area to greater and greater successes, the real job of the dean or provost is only about 5 percent leadership and 95 percent management. Colleges and universities are just too complicated as organizations for anyone in middle management to be successful implementing one radical change after another. The vast majority of the job is making sure that the operation of the area is running efficiently and effectively, as dull as that may sound. And yet that 5 percent sliver of leadership that also comes with the job can be incredibly important. It's here that you'll leave your legacy, improve student learning and faculty research, and come away from your position with satisfaction that your time was well spent.

Second, it helps clarify the true nature of academic leadership. Although most of what deans and provosts do falls under the heading of management, the actions they take that make programs truly distinctive tend to occur when they are acting as leaders. And remember what's involved in that leadership: bringing about change, focusing on our stakeholders, working in ways that may go beyond the job description, and taking risks. In *Developing Academic Leadership: Best Practices and Emerging Paradigms* (2015), Walt Gmelch and I proposed the following definition of *academic leadership*: "Academic leadership is the act of empowering members of the faculty and staff by working with them collegially to achieve common goals, build a community of scholars, and sustain a high level of morale" (43).

Unlike other types of leadership that are directed downward in a strict hierarchy, academic leadership flows in many different directions at once. It empowers others, providing them not merely direction but also responsibility and the authority they need to fulfill that responsibility. It involves collegiality and working to sustain morale, treating people not as subordinates, but as partners in a common enterprise. It seeks to engage others in a community with shared purpose, common goals, and mutual respect. If we ever forget that, we run the risk of losing our effectiveness as academic leaders.

Third, and most important, it illustrates that you have to focus your leadership initiatives on what really matters. Since only about 5 percent of your time is devoted to leadership instead of management, you need to choose your battles so that your effort really counts. I once worked in a college where an interim dean was appointed from outside the unit during the year when a national search for a new dean was conducted. At the opening meeting of the faculty that fall, he announced that since he had only a year in the position, he knew he couldn't accomplish everything he wanted. But he didn't want the college to languish for a year either. During his tour of our facilities that summer, he had noticed that certain buildings were looking shabby due to deferred maintenance and others just seemed a bit dated. He would devote his year to doing everything possible to improve those facilities so that faculty and students would have a better environment in which to work. And that's exactly what happened.

Like any other dean, most of his time had to be devoted to management issues like interviewing and hiring new faculty members, making sure that syllabi and personnel evaluations were completed on schedule, allocating funds for the college, and representing our interests to the provost and president. But when it came to leadership, his energy was entirely focused on improving the college's facilities. By the end of the year, the college was high on the priority list for several major renovations and developing plans for at least one new building. I've known a number of deans who served many years and still had much less of a legacy than he left after just twelve months. He did it by focusing his leadership on what mattered.

Academic Leadership as Empowering Others

Provosts and deans lead by empowering others, not by directing, ordering, or commanding them. While a provost or dean may technically be someone's boss on an organizational chart, little of what we do in these positions is telling other people what to do. While it is true that we are at times called on to establish policies or decide which among several options to pursue, we rarely give someone a direct order. In fact, on occasions when we do have to resort to leading by command, it is almost always an indication that something has gone wrong. Either we've been ineffective in resolving the matter in other ways, the employee is being obstinate and thus in danger of greater sanctions, or we're letting our emotions interfere with our judgment; whatever the reason, something isn't functioning as it should. In most situations, we demonstrate our leadership as provosts and deans by persuading others to act in a certain way or delegating them sufficient authority and responsibility to make the decision themselves. It's this act of entrusting others with the ability to chart their own course that I have in mind when I speak of academic leadership as the act of empowering members of the faculty and staff.

You can better understand how empowerment relates to academic leadership by thinking of your work as something like working in a garden. The gardener doesn't bear the fruit or produce the blooms, but he or she does tend the conditions that make the fruit and foliage possible. You can tell a tomato plant to produce more tomatoes all you want, but if you haven't prepared the soil, provided just the right amount of water, and protected the plant from predators, you're not going to achieve the goal you had in mind. Even worse, you can tell a tomato plant to produce cucumbers all you want, but you'll just be wasting your effort. Being a good gardener involves more than just the gardener alone. He or she has to produce the right conditions, care for the plants, and give them what they need in order to thrive in the environment. No one may see all the effort that went into producing the prize tomato or breathtaking orchid. But the gardener knows, and in any case he or she is far more interested in the tomato or the orchid itself than in the credit that comes from growing it.

True academic leaders take much the same approach. They don't teach all the classes, publish all the books, or serve on all the committees, but they do create the conditions that make all that productivity possible. They know that you don't get more creativity simply by telling people to be more creative. They know too that different people may have different strengths and that their star teacher may not be their star researcher. It's pointless (and poor leadership) to assume that everyone has to be excellent in precisely the same way. So they spend their time producing the conditions that make excellence possible, not telling people what to do.

If you see your job as a provost or dean as telling the faculty and staff what to do, at best they'll do only exactly what you tell them and not a bit more. If instead you empower them by giving them some freedom, they're likely to come up with something far more creative and wonderful than you could ever have dreamed of yourself. No one may see all the effort that went into producing the winning grant proposal or the game-changing book. But the academic leader knows, and in any case he or she is far more interested in the success of the faculty and students than in the credit that comes from leading them.

Limitations of the Metaphor

The idea of the academic leader as gardener does have its limitations. If we get carried away with the metaphor and start talking about how we sometimes have to "prune" programs to make them stronger and "sow the seeds" of our ideas, we're likely to find ourselves accused of taking on yet another function of the busy gardener: just spreading a lot manure. More seriously, however, there's one way in which too keen an insistence on the metaphor of leading as gardening can yield exactly the opposite result from what we intended: when we assume that gardeners are judged by the "productivity" of their gardens. The more vegetables and the more bouquets that come out of a garden, we may think, the better the garden is, and thus the better the gardener's skill. In a similar way, we can fall into the trap of thinking that the more student credit hours, refereed articles, funded grants, and timely graduates a program produces, the better the program is and thus the better the skill of the academic leader.

Approaching work in this way simply drives us back to the fallacy of thinking that we can lead our areas by telling people what to do. We start thinking of our role as setting goals for our programs while leaving it to others to determine how they can possibly meet those goals. We forget that our academic programs exist to produce understanding, insight, and new ideas, not simply degrees and student credit hours for their own sake. We start evaluating our programs—and ourselves—by the "bushels" of articles our faculty produces or the "acres" of students who graduate within a set period. And so we revert to telling our faculty members that they're not excellent unless their productivity is abundant and continuous. We expect our students to complete their programs on a timetable that made perfect sense for students in the 1950s and 1960s, not those today who often have to work full-time jobs to pay even a portion of their tuition.

Understanding the relationship between academic leadership and empowerment of others means recognizing that the administrator's job is to create an environment that is most conducive to the development of understanding, insight, and new ideas. It means seeing our jobs as weeding out not "inefficient" programs, but obstacles that simply make the work of students and faculty more difficult. It means that our default approach to most situations is to help our stakeholders discover how they *can* do something, not why they can't. And it means devoting many more hours each day to asking, mentoring, and assisting than to telling people what to do.

Conclusion

Being a provost or dean involves both leadership and management. We manage our areas well so that we'll have the resources we need when we have an opportunity to lead our programs to greater success. But that success doesn't come about simply by imposing our ideas on a reluctant faculty, staff, or student body, ordering them and driving them in a direction they have no interest in going. It comes about by creating a culture in which people understand they're empowered to make decisions about their own destiny and trusting them to make the right decisions.

REFERENCES

Bennis, W. G., & Nanus, B. (1985). *Leaders: The strategies for taking charge.* New York, NY: Harper.

Daft, R. L. (2014). *Management* (11th ed.). Mason, OH: South-Western Cengage Learning.

Gmelch, W. H., & Buller, J. L. (2015). *Building academic leadership capacity: A guide to best practices.* San Francisco, CA: Jossey-Bass.

Kinicki, A., & Williams, B. K. (2013). *Management: A practical introduction* (6th ed.). New York, NY: McGraw-Hill/Irwin.

Mehta, G. (1997). *Snakes and ladders: Glimpses of modern India.* New York, NY: Doubleday.

Northouse, P. G. (2013). *Leadership: Theory and practice* (6th ed.) Thousand Oaks, CA: Sage.

Singh, S. (2013). *Bewildered leader—M. K. Gandhi: Arabinda poddar.* Bloomington, IN: Xlibris.

RESOURCES

Buller, J. L. (2014). Tellin' ain't leadin.' *Academic Leader, 30*(2), 1, 6.

Bush, T. (2011). *Theories of educational leadership and management* (4th ed.) Thousand Oaks, CA: Sage.

Kotter, J. P. (1990). *A force for change: How leadership differs from management.* New York, NY: Free Press.

9

LEADERSHIP WITH INDIVIDUALS

In some ways, the very concept of exercising leadership with individuals seems a contradiction in terms. In chapter 8, I adopted Peter Northouse's definition of leadership as "a process whereby an individual influences a *group* of individuals to achieve a common good" (2013, 5, emphasis added). So if leadership always involves a group, how can we be said to be leading when we're interacting with only one other person? The answer lies in the difference between the purpose and the process of leadership.

In terms of its purpose, deans and provosts lead their academic programs by having an effect, direct or indirect, on all the stakeholders of those programs. Moreover, as Don Chu notes in *The Department Chair Primer* (2012), that group of stakeholders is a lot broader than we sometimes believe. We get in the habit of thinking of our programs as closed systems: all of the stakeholders, like the faculty and students, are internal members of that system. But higher education actually functions as an open system: its stakeholders include a lot of people who are outside the system: parents, legislators, accrediting bodies, professional organizations, and the like. When provosts and deans lead, they have an effect on all these groups. They don't merely lead downward, as occurs in a hierarchical organization like a corporation or military unit. They also lead upward, laterally, and outward, engaging in a process that I've called *centrifugal leadership* (Buller, 2013). But none of this means that academic leaders always interact with all these stakeholders all the time. The process of leadership sometimes means large assemblies, working with midsized committees, chairing small work groups, and meeting with people one-on-one.

Some of the most challenging meetings on the academic leader's schedule consist of individual appointments. One-on-one meetings might include regular appointments with supervisors, unexpected encounters with a faculty member or student who comes in to lodge a complaint, formal meetings with the parent who wishes to talk to the dean or provost about a serious issue, interviews with a candidate who is being considered for a position, tense sessions with an employee who is being reprimanded or dismissed, and a wide variety of other such interactions. Most of these conversations are relatively routine, a part of a normal day's work. But some of them are extremely stressful, emotion filled, or simply uncomfortable. In certain instances, the other person in these meetings may be angry, and you may even feel threatened by the intensity of the antagonism being displayed. At other times, emotions are simply vented because the two of you are alone, and pretense can fall when there is no audience.

In light of all these forms that the one-on-one meeting can take, what's the best way to prepare for these encounters? Moreover, how can you demonstrate leadership in such situations, guiding the focus to the issues that are important to you and your programs even as you address the other person's problem or concern? Leadership with individuals becomes much more effective if you can keep in mind the following ideas.

Plan Carefully

Whenever it's possible, plan as carefully for one-on-one meetings as you do for formal presentations before large groups. There's a tendency, when we see individual appointments on our calendars, to treat these conversations as somehow less critical than the formal meetings with committees, boards, and similar groups. After all, individual meetings occur all the time, so how much preparation do we require simply to talk to someone? In fact, some of the most important—and anxiety-producing—meetings take place in one-on-one conversations. Without others present, people say things that they may never admit in a public setting. They also feel free to bring up the "truly important" matters that they are reluctant to broach before groups of people. For this reason, dismissing an individual appointment as "just a casual conversation" is rarely a good idea. At best, you may miss an opportunity to discuss ideas that can advance your area. At worst, you will be unprepared for a situation that could turn disastrous (or at least unpleasant) because you hadn't taken the time to prepare.

At the level of the dean or provost, it's probably a bad idea to walk into any meeting when you're unaware of the topic to be discussed. Issues that reach your level tend to be so important and so varied that you need time to refocus your attention from the last topic of concern to the issue at hand. Even more important, there may be documents or types of information that could clarify matters quickly that you'll want available, and you'll be at a disadvantage if you don't know the topic of the meeting in advance. For this reason, ask your staff always to request the purpose of a meeting when placing it on your calendar. Even a brief notation, such as "10:00 am: Prof. Jones [re: salary concerns]," can help you prepare for the conversation and make the meeting time more productive.

Whenever possible, consider in advance what you'd like your basic message to be in the one-on-one meeting. Reflecting on this central topic in advance doesn't mean that you're going to be inflexible, ignoring any valid points and observations your interlocutor might raise. It's merely a way of reinforcing your initial starting point so that the other person's passion or rhetoric doesn't catch you completely off guard. All too often, if we fail to reflect on what we hope our central theme will be in a conversation, we fail to have any theme at all and end up allowing others to set the agenda for us. A conversation is, of course, always a matter of give and take, and some well-considered reflection on the thoughts you will contribute on your end can make the entire conversation more productive.

Prepare to Be Unprepared

Not every conversation, of course, gives you time for preparation. Some occur on the spur of the moment. Others surprise you because their focus is not what you had anticipated. For instance, your calendar reads, "10:00 am: Prof. Jones [re: salary concerns]," but the concerns that are raised are not about Prof. Smith's own salary, but about clerical salaries that Prof. Smith feels have been rising too rapidly. At times, too, someone will make an appointment to talk about one issue, only to raise a second, and far more important, issue in the course of the meeting. (Every dean and provost is familiar with the phrase, "While I've got you here, I also wanted to ask you about....") In situations like these, unless you are already well prepared to discuss the issue that is suddenly introduced, your best approach is probably to listen to the issues being presented, ask questions to make sure that you understand the matter, and respond that you'll get back to the person very soon. As you've probably already discovered, nearly every situation has more than one side to it, and since you were unaware that this topic would come up, you had no opportunity to explore those other perspectives. Before making a firm commitment, therefore, you'll want at least to gather some facts, think through the matter carefully, and examine the issue from a broader perspective.

When pressed for an immediate reaction in these situations, it's best to respond in a general, philosophical, or procedural manner. You can say something like, "I haven't looked into your case in particular relative to other assistant professors in our college. But let me explain what approach I generally take when I consider matters of salary inequity...." Then take down the particulars of the individual's situation, examine the larger picture, develop a clear plan of action, and get back to the person who brought the situation to your attention. Although being caught off guard in a conversation like this can be stressful, you can still exert leadership if you simply remember the following essential principle:

> In conversation, you may find that the other person has already seized the initiative by setting the agenda. Nevertheless, if you consistently operate on the basis of clear convictions and your core beliefs as an administrator, you can still guide the direction of that agenda.

In other words, don't be forced against your will into making a commitment to any particular course of action without considering the larger picture. By focusing on how you'll make a decision in all such cases, you'll clarify your basic principles and make it clear that while you consider suggestions or requests when they are made, you don't make private deals.

Concern Is Not Commitment

Frequently when you're caught off guard in a one-on-one meeting, you and the person you're meeting with will want entirely different outcomes for the conversation. The other person will want a commitment that the problem will be solved or the favor granted. You'll want to avoid making any commitment until you learn more about the issue, consider carefully the implications of any decision, and explore all the options. Yielding to one request for a salary adjustment may, for instance, create an even greater problem of inequity than the other person realizes. Moreover, there may be policy restrictions that prevent you from solving the other person's problem in precisely the manner that he or she wishes. There may be, in other words, a large number of compelling reasons that you don't want to make an immediate commitment or promise a remedy that you'll really not be able to provide. Nevertheless, your promises to "look into it" or to "see what we can do" will frequently come across as cold and indifferent to the person who has raised the issue. He or she may feel that you're simply stalling or putting him or her off when all you really want to do is gather information and reflect on the broader implications of this decision.

The appropriate middle ground in a situation like this is to demonstrate your full concern for the person who's raising the issue, while explaining why you're unable to make a commitment now. You'll start to lose credibility very quickly if you adopt this approach only as a stalling technique. Be sincere about your desire to get back to the person quickly. Make a note on your calendar, reminding yourself to do so in the next day or two. Gather the information you need thoroughly, but understand that the other person is waiting for your reply. What may seem like "only a few days" to you will be seen as "several whole days without any reply" to the other person. You'll begin developing a reputation as a dean who "doesn't get back to people" and who "only pretends to be concerned about their issues" unless you follow through quickly after the initial conversation.

Stick to Your Principles

Second only to failing to get back to someone after promising to do so, nothing so damages the credibility of an administrator as giving the appearance of cutting private deals with a small group of "favorites." Indeed, one of your most important reasons for not making an immediate decision when blindsided by someone is to avoid creating greater inequity by granting an individual request without due attention paid to the larger context of those affected by this decision. You don't want people to have even the perception that you're cutting special deals with this person because you favor the individual more than others or that "only the squeaky wheels get the grease" around here. For this reason, be very clear that any decision you make as the result of an individual request both adheres to your overall policies and values and is understood as adhering to those policies and values. For this reason, be sure to explain your decision—whether positive or negative—in light of your core principles. Don't assume that the other person will automatically make this connection. You may need to make explicit how the current situation relates to your overall administrative philosophy—for example:

○ *Equity*: "As you know, I try to treat all my department chairs as fairly as possible, understanding that each of their situations is quite different. So after carefully examining not only their salaries but also their years of experience, number of people they supervise, ways in which they contribute to the college and the larger institutional mission, and number of students whom they serve, what I've decided is … "

○ *Collegiality*: "I've never believed that members of a college all have to agree with one another or even like one another in the same way that we like our personal friends. But I do believe that we have to work together efficiently and productively, meeting each other's professional needs to the best of our abilities. That's why, in the interests of this type of collegiality, I've decided to … "

○ *Professionalism*: "More and more throughout my administrative career, I've come to place a priority on true academic professionalism, by which I mean respecting the importance of confidential information, getting the training that each of us needs to keep current in our jobs and to perform our functions effectively, and not letting our personal differences get in the way of doing what needs to be done to achieve our core mission. So when I considered this matter in that light, I realized that what I needed to do is … "

○ *Integrity*: "If there's anything I've seen that proves destructive to a faculty, it's when academic leaders don't keep their promises and act with transparency. I'm a strong believer in what's sometimes called authentic academic leadership. That means that I try to base every decision I make on principles that I could defend to anyone. Because of that, it seems that my only choice is to … "

○ *Transparency*: "I've always believed that when you disagree with someone, you have an obligation to tell that person candidly and completely why you've made a decision he or she may not like. You may not always accept my reasons, but I think you have the right to know them. That's why, in this case, the issues that I think are most important are … "

Be Willing to Repeat Yourself

At times when you follow up with someone and render your decision, the person to whom you're speaking won't accept the result as final and wants to keep arguing a point or reviewing matters that you have already considered. This problem is particularly acute for provosts and at institutions where the avenues of appeal beyond the dean are limited. (See chapter 44.) Even in other academic environments, however, unwillingness to accept a negative decision often occurs in one-on-one meetings because there aren't other people present who can reiterate and amplify the arguments that you've made, demonstrate to the person you're talking to that he or she doesn't have universal support on the matter in question, and clarify that it's not simply you as an individual who's unwilling to grant this request; it's the institution itself. In private conversations, people sometimes feel that if they keep arguing long enough and passionately enough, you'll eventually give in—if only perhaps to get the person out of your office. When faced with obstinate people of this kind, you might consider resorting to the following strategy:

o Make it clear that your decision is final if your mind is indeed already made up on the issue. Say something like, "I'm sorry but as I've told you, that's my final decision, and I won't be reconsidering the matter."

o Adopt the "stuck record" strategy if nothing else is effective. You may need to repeat yourself over and over until it finally sinks in to the other person that the discussion is at an end. "I understand your arguments," you might say, "but as I've said before … "

o If no other approach is effective, bring the conversation to a close and mention any recourse that the individual may have. You don't want to give the impression that you're "throwing someone out of your office," but in the most extreme of situations, you may need to end the conversation when it's clearly no longer productive. You can do so in a polite and effective manner by saying something like, "I'm sorry, but I can see that my reasons don't satisfy you, even though I've tried to explain them as clearly as I can. I think it's best, therefore, that we simply conclude this meeting. If you feel that you must pursue this matter further, your next step would be to … "

Conclusion

We sometimes imagine leadership as taking place only in crises or when we are debating major issues before large groups of people. It's possible, however, to demonstrate leadership even in the individual conversations that deans have with constituencies throughout their days. Basing each decision on a compelling set of core principles and making it clear that your decisions are always firmly grounded in those principles is one of the most important aspects of leadership that deans can possess.

REFERENCES

Buller, J. L. (2013). *Positive academic leadership: How to stop putting out fires and start making a difference.* San Francisco, CA: Jossey-Bass.

Chu, D. (2012). *The department chair primer: Leading and managing academic departments* (2nd ed.). San Francisco, CA: Jossey-Bass.

Northouse, P. G. (2013). *Leadership: Theory and practice.* (6th ed.) Thousand Oaks, CA: Sage.

10

LEADERSHIP WITH GROUPS

In chapter 9 we saw that one of the best ways for provosts and deans to demonstrate leadership is by relating whatever topic happens to be under discussion to their own set of core administrative principles. A key goal of academic leadership, in other words, is making sure that people understand the connection between decisions that need to be made and the basic operating principles of the person who makes those decisions. This rule also applies to situations where you are dealing with groups such as committees, councils, boards, task forces, and informal gatherings. True group leadership begins in authentic leadership, just as when you're talking with a person one-on-one. When the other members of a group are aware of guiding principles, their work becomes easier because they understand what to expect from you, and you provide a type of professional development for them by modeling an example of effective organizational leadership. Nevertheless, while basing your interactions with the group on a clear set of guiding principles is an important place to begin, there are also several other factors to keep in mind when working with committees and other groups.

Master the Group's Operating Procedures

Working with a group becomes far easier if you understand its established procedures for making decisions and implementing policies. While many people assume that meetings at a college or university must follow Robert's Rules of Order (Robert, Evans, Honemann, and Balch, 2011), that's actually not true. Unless required to do otherwise by their institution's bylaws or operating manual, committees and other working groups are free to follow any set of procedures that works best for them (Buller, 2014). If a committee decides to define a quorum as "however many people attend the meeting," it is usually free to do so—unless the institution or division to which that committee reports has a different policy.

Nevertheless, most groups choose to follow Robert's Rules of Order since these procedures are time-tested and widely known. For this reason, it pays for an academic leader to become well acquainted with this approach to parliamentary procedure, as well as any others that may be in effect at your institution. Even if the group already has an officially appointed parliamentarian, as an academic leader you'll be expected to know at least the rudiments of how groups work. This knowledge will help you understand the complexities of when discussion of various matters is or is not appropriate, how to amend or table motions when necessary, and how to take votes. It's frequently the case that in the heat of a particularly intense debate, claims are made that the established procedure requires this or that; since most people have only a general sense of whether the claim may be true, decisions can be made that could have been more effectively challenged or debated. For this reason, such materials as Robert et al. (2011), Jones (1990), and Sturgis (2000) will give you all the background you need to know about the basics of conducting meetings and the priority of various types of motions.

In addition, numerous websites can help you to review most aspects of committee procedure and organization. Among the best of these websites are the Official Roberts Rules of Order website (www.robertsrules .com), Roberts Rules of Order Online (www.rulesonline.com), and an excellent, concise online resource developed by the Student Activities Office of California State University, Chico (www.csuchico.edu/sac/ parliament.html). Finally, the American Institute of Parliamentarians (www.parliamentaryprocedure.org) and the National Association of Parliamentarians (www.parliamentarians.org) offer a wide range of information and training materials, including opportunities for workshops and distance learning, that can provide you with even more detailed knowledge of how parliamentary procedure is best applied to committee meetings.

Make Meetings Task Oriented

Every dean or provost needs to participate in meetings every now and then that are conducted primarily to exchange information rather than to produce results. Getting together for face-to-face updates of what's going on in our areas is one of the most common ways in which administrators and faculty members stay in touch. Nevertheless, with the wide range of methods for disseminating information electronically and through internal newsletters, it's helpful to avoid abusing the time set aside for meetings with a long list of updates and the exchange of routine information. One of the most common complaints people have about meetings is, "I'd have time to do all the work that at these meetings we keep saying needs to be done—if only I didn't have all of these meetings." For this reason, it's a matter of respect for how busy the members of your committee are to reduce as far as possible the number of updates and announcements. Focus on critical information only, while keeping most committee time free for discussion of issues, decision making, and planning.

Before every meeting of a committee you chair, consider asking yourself, "What is it that I hope our group will accomplish during this meeting? What should be our 'product'?" If you can't answer that question clearly and succinctly before you call the meeting to order, you're highly unlikely to accomplish anything that's worth your members' time. In addition, you're increasing the likelihood that a particularly strong-willed committee member with an agenda of his or her own will hijack your meeting by diverting attention to issues that the other members won't regard as important.

In general, committee meetings are much more productive when we create and stick to a written agenda. Whenever possible, this agenda should be distributed to the other members of the committee at least forty-eight hours before the meeting begins. Advance notice of the issues that'll be discussed allows attendees to begin thinking through each one, perhaps even gathering data or supporting materials to bring to the meeting. If you've done sufficient advance preparation before the meeting that you've identified a clear purpose for it, stating that purpose right on the printed agenda so that everyone will come to the meeting aware of what they are expected to accomplish is highly useful. A well-constructed meeting agenda should thus look something like exhibit 10.1:

Exhibit 10.1 Sample Committee Agenda

AGENDA

College Curriculum Committee

November 8, 20xx

3:00 pm

Hunter Classroom Building, Room 302

Purpose: to review proposals for possible new courses and course changes and to consider a draft proposal for a new policy on minimum standards for independent study courses.

I. Call to Order	3:00 pm
II. Approval of minutes, meeting of October 15, 20xx.	3:00–3:05 pm
III. New Course Proposals	3:05–3:20 pm

    a. *PARL 101: Introduction to Parliamentary Procedure (carried over from meeting of 10/15/xx due to lack of departmental signatures).*

    b. *PARL 201: Intermediate Parliamentary Procedure.*

    c. *PEDN 460: Capstone Project in Pedantry.*

IV. Course Change Proposals	3:20–3:25 pm

    a. *Possible renumbering of PEDN 218: Advanced Pedantry to PEDN 318 (carried over from meeting of 10/15/xx due to lack of quorum).*

    b. *Possible elimination of prerequisites for PEDN 212: Survey of American Pedantry.*

V. Policy on Minimum Standards for Independent Study Courses	3:30–3:50 pm

    a. *Review of policies in place at peer and aspirational institutions (see materials distributed at meeting of 10/15xx).*   3:30–3:40 pm

    b. *Review of draft policy proposed by subcommittee (B. Rogers, chair; H. David, J. Tompkins; see material attached to this agenda).*   3:40–3:50 pm

VI. Development of Action Plan for Meeting of 12/1/xx (3:00 pm; 205 Hunter Classroom Building: NOTE CHANGE OF LOCATION)	3:50–3:55 pm
VII. Announcements	3:55–4:00 pm
VIII. Adjournment	4:00 pm

As you review the sample agenda, you'll notice several differences from those that are more common at meetings in higher education. One difference is that major items have both start and end times indicated. Listing times for each activity on the agenda is good practice for a number of reasons. First, it is an indication to as to whether you've tried to schedule too much for a single meeting. The phenomenon known as the planning fallacy means that we tend to be overly optimistic about how long things will take. If you discover that despite a tendency to succumb to the planning fallacy, you still can't fit everything you'd like into the time allowed for the meeting, it's clear that you're trying to schedule too much. Either focus only on the highest priorities, break one meeting down into several, or consider lengthening the meeting time.

Second, the agenda provides a guide to the members about how long each item is expected to take. No one will expect the agenda to flow precisely as scheduled, of course, but the time indications do provide guidelines. On the sample agenda, for instance, the chair expects that the course change discussions will be very brief; only five minutes is allotted to two of them. That suggests to the participants that if they have serious reservations about these changes, they may wish to move to table those items to reconsider when more time is available. Notice, too, that not every item is given a set time. It would be ridiculous, for instance, to suggest that the discussion of changing the course number for PEDN 218 will take place precisely between 3:20 and 3:22. Breaking items into increments smaller than five or ten minutes is unnecessary. Remember that the point is merely to indicate your expectations as meeting chair, not to establish an inflexible limit.

Another difference is that the agenda does not divide items into old business and new business, but places them in a general order of priority. Because even with the suggested times for each item listed, meetings do sometimes run long, it's far better to place items in priority order than to use any other system. In that way, if time does run out, you'll have spent the meeting discussing the items of the greatest importance. In addition, all business discussed in a formal meeting is technically new business. Some of it may have been discussed at a previous meeting (what is usually meant by the term *old business*), but if no decision has been made, the item remains subject to discussion and resolution. By creating an artificial division between so-called old and new business, committee chairs give precedence to the continuation of earlier discussions, which may be far less important than other items on the agenda.

Finally, the date for the next meeting is clearly indicated on the agenda. By knowing in advance when the next meeting is scheduled, those attending can check their calendars and let the chair know whether they have a conflict. In fact, the agenda provides a substantial amount of information about nearly everything members need to know about the meeting: its date, time, location, and duration. Documents needed for the meeting are clearly specified and identified with boldface type. Enough detail is provided so that people won't waste time at the meeting asking questions like, "Which course is PEDN 460 again?" Distributed in electronic form before the meeting, the agenda makes it easy for attendees to cut and paste information directly onto their calendars. Distributed in hard copy at the meeting itself, the agenda is easy to follow so that everyone in attendance knows exactly what will be discussed and why.

When preparing an agenda, it's helpful to remember that the word *agenda* is a Latin term meaning "things that must be done." The agenda format outlined in the sample specifies the purpose of the meeting and the "products" that are expected to result from the group's time together. Without set agendas, meetings often get sidetracked by overly long discussions about whichever items happen to be addressed first. In other words, if committee members don't have a clear understanding of what's expected of them, it's no surprise that they don't use their time together productively. As the committee's chair, you should remember the following essential principle for demonstrating leadership in this type of setting:

Just as good fences make good neighbors, so do good agendas make good meetings.

Delegate Responsibly

Being a leader in groups doesn't mean doing everything yourself. Delegating certain tasks to others helps both you and the members of your committee. That's a lesson too many academic leaders forget. In their haste to get done quickly, accurately, and creatively, many deans and provosts take on too many of the group's tasks themselves. They'll approach the group with a draft of a report or proposal that's largely complete and ask, "What do you think?" This strategy may be useful at times (particularly when a deadline is looming) but is often counterproductive. Because of the academic leader's title, certain members of the group may not feel free to express their opinions even if they have serious concerns or objections. At the other extreme, certain faculty members may object quite vigorously to aspects of your proposal simply because you *are* the dean or provost; they may be posturing before their peers or simply feel disenfranchised by the way in which you've so aggressively taken charge of the process.

In addition, failure to delegate also deprives your committee members of an important opportunity to develop their own skills as leaders and members of an administrative team.

Just as good agendas make good meetings, so does good delegation make good leadership.

In order to delegate tasks effectively, you don't simply reassign the duties that you yourself don't want to fulfill. You delegate tasks to give others valuable experience in leadership, take advantage of as many people's creativity as you can, and help your group function as efficiently as possible. Inevitably, of course, certain members of any group will perform their delegated tasks more effectively than others. But never lose sight of the essential principle that we saw in chapter 2: *delegation always implies a certain loss of control.* The report or decision that's delegated to someone else is unlikely to be exactly the same as if it were your own. And that's a good thing. Too much uniformity of ideas or style leads to stagnation. The group's review of a proposal, report, or document that's different from what you would have created—which may even be, from your perspective, not nearly as good as what you could have created yourself—is actually a constructive aspect of committee work. You may see that there are alternative ways of approaching an issue or that there's far less consensus about approaches than you had originally believed. Working through an imperfect draft can be a useful process for a group as it develops new suggestions in response to flawed proposals and works together as a team to sort through complex issues. Just as you don't expect a student group to get it right the first time they try a complex task, so you shouldn't expect a committee to accomplish its task without a learning curve. Delegation of responsibilities helps the members of the committee improve their own skills of collaboration, teamwork, and creative problem solving, even as it frees you from the burden of having to complete the entire assignment on your own.

Allow All Perspectives to Be Heard

One of the most important duties of committee leadership is making certain that all voices are heard and all perspectives are given due consideration. In fact, of the commonly cited ten "General Principles of Parliamentary Procedure" (cited, for example, at people.ehe.osu .edu/dgranello/files/2008/11/parliamentary-procedure-full-notes.pdf and www.asu.edu/clubs/naacp/form/Standing%20Committee%20Handbook .pdf), four of the guidelines deal explicitly with this goal.

1. All members have equal rights, privileges, and obligations; rules must be administered impartially.

2. The minority has rights which must be protected.

3. Full and free discussion of all motions, reports, and other items of business is a right of all members. ...

9. Members must not attack or question the motives of other members. Customarily, all remarks are addressed to the presiding officer.

While in larger or more formal groups, you may wish to enforce the rule that "all remarks are addressed to the presiding officer," that solution is not practical for most committees and task forces in higher education. The exchange of comments and reactions is often too free-flowing even to make it possible in most groups for the presiding officer to recognize each speaker in turn. How then do you go about creating a committee environment in which all opinions are heard and given due consideration? Partly you set a good example, sincerely asking for alternative points of view, treating opposing views with respect when they're offered, and discussing each idea on its merits, not as a reflection of the intellect or character of the person who introduced it. Partly, too, you make sure all voices are heard by insisting on a high standard of collegiality in group discussions, intervening quickly if one of your committee members deviates from these standards, and maintaining an atmosphere that rewards people for the free exchange of ideas.

If you're chairing a committee, you'll need at times to serve as the advocate or defender of a member of the committee who may be coerced into silence by the more vocal members of the committee. Part of being a good leader in groups involves being proactive in protecting those who don't always have the power, status, or personality to protect themselves, and that goal can't be achieved if certain members of the committee are intimidating others into silence. In situations where certain members of the group are shut down repeatedly, you may even need to have a quiet conversation with the more aggressive members of the group, explaining how their behavior is counterproductive to the group's work and reiterating your own commitment to the free exchange of ideas.

Leading Informal Groups

Most of this discussion so far has been based on the assumption that the groups you're leading are organized formally, like committees and task forces. But how do you lead a group of people when you're not formally in charge of it? For instance, is it appropriate to demonstrate leadership if you are one provost among many peers at a statewide meeting of a dean casually meeting with your fellow deans for coffee? Or suppose you're having a conversation with a mixed group of people, with some of those present members of the community, while others are faculty members, and still others are students: Should you demonstrate leadership in that type of setting? If your president or chancellor then joins the group, is it still appropriate to demonstrate leadership?

As a way of answering these questions, note that there are both similarities and differences from leading formal and informal groups. Obviously, in an informal setting, there are no agendas, minutes, bylaws, or written policies to govern how to make decisions, disagree with others, and conclude the discussion. Moreover, informal meetings are substantially less task oriented than the work of a committee or task force. But other principles, such as the desirability of making each person feel that he or she is a valued member of the conversation and of protecting the rights of the minority in the discussion, still apply.

To review Peter Northouse's terminology from chapters 1 and 8, leading informal groups depends far more on our emergent leadership authority than our assigned leadership responsibility. The type of leadership we demonstrate in informal groups is a function of what has traditionally been called *moral suasion*: the ability to influence and spur people to action based on the level of respect one receives, not on force or direct commands. Academic leaders might not dominate the discussion in informal groups. They might even speak very rarely. Nevertheless, when they do speak, their comments should have added impact because they are viewed as respected authorities, not because people are afraid to disagree. For this reason, the composition of the group matters very little. No matter whether people report to you, hold positions equivalent to you, hold positions to which you report, or are simply members of the general public, it is the power of your argument that makes you a leader in this situation.

Nevertheless, several steps can increase your level of authority and make your arguments more powerful:

○ Express opinions that you truly believe in, not merely ones that you believe will score you points. There are few other ways of destroying your credibility more quickly than being perceived as someone who adopts positions for convenience or humiliates others by out-debating them.

○ State your thesis calmly, reasonably, and while maintaining good eye contact with others in the discussion. While it is commonly asserted that people admire leaders who show passion for what they believe in, too much passion is often viewed as a triumph of emotion over rationality.

○ Respect the right of other people to disagree. People will have differences of opinion even about matters that seem crystal clear to you. The more you insist that there's only one correct way to interpret the facts, the more you will undermine your own persuasiveness.

○ Use actual evidence, not merely anecdotes or opinions, whenever possible. While a good story can be rhetorically powerful, academic leaders are often held to a higher standard than are politicians and other public figures. Academics are trained to value evidence and discount arguments that appear to be based on feelings or innuendo alone. Always try to support your assertions with facts.

○ Allow others to speak; then genuinely listen to what they have to say. You don't have to dominate the discussion to demonstrate leadership in the discussion. Be respectful of other people's views and freely acknowledge when they make a good point. Don't spend the time while others are talking by simply thinking of the next thing you'll say.

○ Ask questions. This essential principle is particularly true when you're demonstrating leadership in informal groups. Adopt a Socratic method as you might in a graduate seminar where you're helping students discover their own solutions. If you feel you need some practice in the art of asking the right kind of question in each particular environment, Dorothy Leeds's *Smart Questions* (2000) and Michael Marquardt's *Leading with Questions* (2014) are excellent resources.

> Effective leaders aren't always the people who know all the right answers. Often they're the people who ask the right questions.

○ Don't base your self-worth on whether you "win" or "lose" a discussion. Remember that your primary concern is the good of the institution and the programs you supervise. Pride, ego, and self-esteem have to take a back seat.

Conclusion

The vast majority of the leadership that provosts and deans demonstrate occurs in groups. To a large extent, these groups are formally structured with defined offices, responsibilities, and bylaws. Leading in that type of environment requires a thorough familiarity with both parliamentary procedure and the group's own policies. For leaders who are in charge of such groups, designing a well-constructed agenda can go a long way toward making the best use of the group's time and effort. In groups that do not have a formal structure, leadership more often arises from moral suasion than from title or assigned responsibilities. In these cases, academic leaders can enhance their authority by expressing only opinions they genuinely support, basing their arguments on evidence, and adopting the other strategies of effective argumentation described in this chapter.

REFERENCES

Buller, J. L. (2014). Six myths about conducting effective meetings. *Department Chair*, 24(4), 16–17.

Jones, O. G. (1990). *Parliamentary procedure at a glance: Group leadership manual for chairmanship and floor leadership*. Harmondsworth: Penguin.

Leeds, D. (2000). *Smart questions: The essential strategy for successful managers*. New York, NY: Berkley Books.

Marquardt, M. J. (2014). *Leading with questions: How leaders find the right solutions by knowing what to ask*. San Francisco, CA: Jossey-Bass.

Robert III, H. M., Evans, W. J., Honemann, D. H., & Balch, T. J. (2011). *Robert's rules of order newly revised* (11th ed.). New York, NY: Da Capo.

Sturgis, A. (2000). *The standard code of parliamentary procedure* (4th ed.). New York, NY: McGraw-Hill.

RESOURCES

Chan, J. F. (2003). *The Jossey-Bass academic administrator's guide to meetings*. San Francisco, CA: Jossey-Bass.

Doyle, M., & Straus, D. (1986). *How to make meetings work*. New York, NY: Jove/Penguin.

Hunter, D. (2009). *The art of facilitation: The essentials for leading great meetings and creating group synergy*. San Francisco, CA: Jossey-Bass

Kelsey, D., & Plumb, P. (2004). *Great meetings! Great results*. Portland, ME: Great Meetings!

Morgan, N. (2014). *Power cues: The subtle science of leading groups, persuading others, and maximizing your personal impact*. Cambridge, MA: Harvard Business Press.

Neal, C., Neal, P., & Wold, C. (2011). *The art of convening: Authentic engagement in meetings, gatherings and conversations*. San Francisco, CA: Berrett-Koehler.

Parker, G. M., & Hoffman, R. (2006). *Meeting excellence: Thirty-three tools to lead meetings that get results*. San Francisco, CA: Jossey-Bass.

Schwarz, R. (2002). *The skilled facilitator*. San Francisco, CA: Jossey-Bass.

Smelser, N. J. (1993). *Effective committee service*. Thousand Oaks, CA: Sage.

Streibel, B. J. (2002). *The manager's guide to effective meetings*. New York, NY: McGraw-Hill.

11

LEADERSHIP IN PROMOTING TEAMWORK

Few other responsibilities of a provost or dean reflect the distinctive nature of academic leadership as well as promoting teamwork. As we saw in chapter 8, leading a college or university isn't quite the same as leading a rigidly hierarchical organization like a military unit or business. Shared governance, collegiality, and the goal of empowering others, not merely controlling them, are much more integral to how we interact with our stakeholders than it is for leaders of other kinds of organizations. And as we saw in chapter 10, moral suasion rather than outright commands or orders is a key component of how we get things done, particularly with informal groups. So if we want to transform the units we work with from mere collections of individuals to smoothly functioning teams, we can't achieve this goal simply by instructing people to act in a certain way. We have to create the type of environment in which teams flourish and model the sort of behavior we want our stakeholders to imitate.

To understand how this process works in the academy, I begin by considering what a team actually is and how it differs from other types of groups. We might define a group as a collection of three or more people who see themselves as having a common identity or purpose. A random collection of people on the street isn't a group; it's a crowd. Together they don't see themselves as a unit and don't share a common purpose: one person may be going to work, another may be out for a stroll, still another may be headed to lunch, and so on.

An academic department is a group: its members share both identity and purpose. They're likely to include the department's name as part of their signature, and if you ask each of them what they have in common, they may not use exactly the same words, but they'll probably say very similar things. Groups can be closely or loosely knit. A family is a tightly knit group that shares many different aspects of their identity—including, in most cases, even part of their name—and common purposes. Sociologists term that kind of group a *primary group*. But the relationship of people in a subway car is very loose; although they may be said to share an identity ("those of us in this subway car") and purpose ("to reach a destination"), they probably know next to nothing about one another, and although they all want to reach a destination, they don't all have the same destination. To sociologists, they form what is termed a *secondary group*. We see that same range of loosely and tightly knit groups in departments, colleges, and universities. Some just seem to jell effortlessly; members of the group value their time with one another, work cooperatively toward a single purpose, and derive a great deal of satisfaction and meaning from their activities together. Others barely interact with one another, put in the minimal amounts of time and effort needed to do the job, and rarely view membership in the group as an important part of who they are. What accounts for the difference?

Groups and Teams

One way of answering this question is to say that some groups develop an intangible quality that we call *team spirit*, while others don't. A team is a particular type of primary (very tightly knit) group in which members contribute complementary skills, play identifiable roles, and work together cooperatively so as to achieve a significant goal. For example, a baseball team will have a pitcher, catcher, infielders, outfielders, and so on. They all have an individual role and contribute different skills, but they share a clear group identity and work together to achieve a common goal. (We can argue about how significant the goal of winning a game actually is, but the important thing is that this goal is clearly important to the team itself.) In an academic unit too, people play different roles. A small history department may have an American historian, an Asian historian, an African historian, a European historian, and so on. But as I suggested in *Positive Academic Leadership* (2013), we can also think of the faculty and staff of a college in the following way:

- The *contributions* each person makes: the technology guru who can solve any software problem, the precision czar who can catch every typographical error, the visionary who can see what's possible, not merely what currently exists, and so on
- The *roles* each person plays: the class clown who sees the funny side of everything, the devil's advocate who always takes an opposing

point of view, mom or dad whom people turn to when they have a problem, and so on

○ The *networks* each person forms: the clique that always votes together, the lunch bunch that frequently eats together, the rivals who are jealous of (but may secretly admire) one another, and so on

Identifying those different contributions, roles, and networks requires a provost or dean to adopt a systems approach to academic leadership, an understanding of the complex ways in which the individuals who constitute a group affect and are affected by each other. And here's the key:

In order to promote teamwork within a group, provosts and deans need to approach academic leadership from a systems perspective. They need to devote at least as much energy to nurturing the right culture as they do to making the right decisions and developing the right vision.

What this essential principle means in practice is that academic leaders are more likely to see their departments and colleges functioning as teams if they view creating an environment that promotes teamwork as an important part of their jobs. Such an environment comes about by treating people with respect, viewing them as partners and not merely as employees, allowing them enough independence to exert their own creativity, and demonstrating genuine appreciation for their accomplishments.

In many ways, academic leaders tend to fall into three categories:

1. *Purpose-focused leaders* keep their eye on the prize. It's the goal or vision that motivates them, and they see their legacy as reaching that goal or fulfilling that vision. They tend to treat people as means to an end: the workers who are there to help the institution fulfill its purpose.

2. *Process-focused leaders* want the machinery of an organization to run smoothly. It's the set of policies or procedures that occupies their attention, and they see their legacy as leaving behind a more efficient and effective organization. They treat people as cogs in a machine, paying them little attention when everything's operating well but viewing them as problems to be fixed when the process breaks down.

3. *People-focused leaders* practice organic academic leadership (Buller, 2015), believing that if they act like a responsible gardener and take

care of the "plants," the "fruits" will take care of themselves. Thus, rather than becoming preoccupied with goals, results, or processes, they invest their time in people. They're genuinely concerned about the welfare of all their stakeholders (not just donors or tuition-paying students), trusting people to know how to do their jobs, making as many decisions collectively as possible, and demonstrating confidence in the system of shared governance.

If we can imagine the purpose-focused leader as pointing toward a goal on the distant horizon and the process-focused leader as constantly tinkering with an idiosyncratic and often unreliable mechanism, the people-focused leader can be pictured as a caring gardener, hands dirty, willing to tackle the little chores as well as the heavy lifting, and even more concerned about the needs of the flowers in the garden than about his or her own.

In this way, organic academic leadership shares many features with what William Ouchi, Distinguished Professor of Management and Organizations in UCLA's Anderson School of Management, has called leadership in a theory Z organization or how Daniel Wheeler, formerly a professor of leadership studies at the University of Nebraska-Lincoln, has applied the concept of servant leadership to college administration (Ouchi, 1981; Wheeler, 2012). Make no mistake about it: the practice of organic academic leadership doesn't guarantee that people will come together as a team, and teams sometimes do emerge even in environments where administrators are purpose focused or process focused. But making the welfare of the people who work and study in their programs their central concern is an important way in which academic leaders increase the likelihood that people will come together as a team and decrease the likelihood that academic units will become increasingly splintered. When people feel insecure or believe that they're competing with one another, they place protecting themselves ahead of advancing the work of the team. Fragmentation occurs, and members of the faculty and staff become focused only on their own best interests.

Preparing the Soil for Teamwork

Organic academic leadership recognizes that just as gardeners have to prepare the soil before they can expect bumper crops to be produced, so do they have to prepare the environment before teamwork can emerge. Some of the steps they may take include the following.

Establish opportunities for casual socializing

When we really get to know people on a personal basis—knowing what motivates them, who their family and close friends are, which unexpected hobbies and other interests they may have, and who they are as human beings, not merely as employees of the university—we tend to empathize with them more. We become less irritated by their idiosyncrasies because we understand them better. Annoying oddballs begin to become lovable eccentrics. Since, as we've seen, a team consists of people with identifiable roles who are working cooperatively toward a common goal, casual socializing has a dual benefit. It gives every member of the program greater insights into one another's contributions, roles, and networks and promotes the sort of bonding that can transform a group of colleagues into a team.

Make people feel safe and valued

Fragmentation and isolation tend to occur when people feel insecure and unappreciated. By being more transparent in communications, particularly in very difficult times such as budget cuts or new upper administrations, sharing as much information as possible helps people overcome their fear that they're in the dark about decisions that may affect their livelihood. Recognizing contributions frequently, publicly, and specifically also helps produce the environment that makes team-work possible. Saying things like, "Thank you all for everything you've done this year," may improve morale a tiny bit, but saying things like, "I want you all to know how much appreciation we all owe Jordan for setting up the new advising system and working with all the advisors to create a unified set of guidelines for all students," does much more. It lets people know that they're working in an environment where their contributions are recognized and appreciated.

Help people achieve their goal

When members of the faculty and staff believe that all the provost or dean cares about is how they help advance the institution's goals, they can feel used. When members of the faculty and staff truly believe that the provost or dean cares about his or her own goals, they begin to feel part of a team. The mistake too many deans and provosts make is limiting their role as mentors to problem solving or, at best, problem avoidance.

Mentoring people toward achieving their own personal and professional goals improves the quality of the work that's being formed, aids in succession planning, and helps make sure that the right people are placed in the right positions.

> Never feel threatened by someone who seems out to take your job. That person isn't really a competitor, but rather a possible successor who can open the way for you to be promoted.

If you try to shut out someone you regard as a rival, you can create an enemy and destroy the very environment of teamwork you're trying so hard to establish. But if you train and mentor that rival, you'll leave your unit in excellent shape when the next attractive opportunity comes your way.

Yield control

People who feel they have to be in charge of every decision made in their areas rarely create environments conducive to teamwork. People meld as teams when they take ownership of what happens in their programs. By including more group decision making into your standard practices, you aren't abdicating responsibility; you're helping people develop buy-in for whatever decisions they reach by consensus. A team isn't a group of people with one person in command and everyone else simply obeying orders. While you may see your role as that of being a team coach, it's counterproductive to see it as team "owner" or dictator. One simple way to start this process is to include the entire group in decisions about how to renovate a common area like a break room or lounge. Taking their advice and opinions into account will have a much greater effect than covering the walls with the sort of motivational posters seen in too many corporate conference rooms.

Identify an external benchmark

People unite in the face of a common enemy. (That's one of the reasons you want to make sure that the perceived enemy isn't you.) It can be a good team-building strategy to identify an external competitor and set the challenge of beating that competitor in some important benchmark. For example, if there is a department similar to yours at a rival institution, you might considering trying to exceed that program's student retention rate, overall enrollment, productivity in publication, or some other meaningful standard. If the rival is another program within the institution, it's best to keep the rivalry friendly and light. Work out with that dean or vice president a challenge over which program can have bragging rights for the highest participation rate in contributing to the annual fund, attending a campus event, or assisting the students moving into the residence halls. The benchmark you choose should represent a real challenge but still be attainable. If your six-year graduation rate is only 36 percent, it's counterproductive to set a goal of beating a rival program's 85 percent graduation rate within a year. With external competitors, the other program may not even realize that it's involved in your competition. The goal of the exercise is, after all, to promote teamwork within your area, not necessarily to strengthen ties to another institution.

The Role of Retreats

Perhaps the most common way administrators try to promote teamwork is by sponsoring retreats. The idea certainly seems promising: if you get people away from their daily routine for an extended period and get them working together on a project of common interest, it seems likely that they'll discover areas of shared concern, get to know one another better, and begin to form bonds. Moreover, retreats actually can work—as long as we keep three rules in mind: don't overuse them, don't expect them to work miracles, and don't go into them with only the vaguest of intentions.

Some administrators seem overly fond of retreats. They conduct one each summer or before the start of the fall term. Or perhaps they even hold one or two each semester. The general idea seems to be that if one retreat is good, more are even better. "We get so much done during the time we spend together," the academic leader may say, overlooking all the things that *aren't* getting done back on campus while so many key players are off on the retreat.

> Retreats are valuable when they're infrequent and special. Their usefulness decreases in inverse proportion to their frequency.

Once people start thinking of retreats as part of an annual routine, they lose their impact and become just one more long meeting. A retreat can be an important team-building exercise if it's seen as a true break in standard operating procedure. A good time for provosts and deans to hold a team-building retreat is early in their terms and then not again for at least three more years. Reinforce the idea that the time spent together in the retreat is something out of the ordinary if you hope to achieve results that are out of the ordinary.

At the same time, don't set your expectations for the retreat too high. You're not going to transform a highly politicized and fragmented unit into a team overnight. A retreat may provide a useful kick-start to a process of improving a work environment, but it should never be viewed as the entire process. It can provide some ideas of where the group needs to go and which values they share, and those ideas can form the framework of a new working relationship. But a framework alone isn't a complete structure, and it isn't particularly sturdy when the winds of discord or the hurricanes of turmoil begin to blow. Follow up quickly on some of the action items that resulted from the retreat. Form working groups and discuss their progress at your regular meetings. It's simply a waste of people's time to gain some insights in the hothouse atmosphere of a retreat, only to lose them in the crush of day-to-day business once the retreat is over.

Finally, retreats are most successful when they have a clearly identified objective. If the purpose of the retreat is simply to get to know one another better and start building a team, those objectives are going to be hard to achieve. They seem to people to be too amorphous, and cynics are going to dismiss them as a ploy to get them to "play nice with one another." Retreats are valuable if they are held to produce a definite product, like a self-study report for an accreditation visit, an outline for a unit's strategic plan, a more workable course rotation, or something similar. Improving teamwork has to be a desirable by-product of the retreat. As paradoxical as it may sound, if you make it the main focus (or even state that it's one of the objectives) of the retreat, it will probably be a much harder goal to attain.

One useful activity that encourages team building at the beginning of a retreat is asking the group to set its own ground rules. The very act of working to reach consensus about something that matters to people but that they don't invest a lot of ego or emotion in helps set the tone for productive discussions. However, if you simply ask a group to come up with the operating procedures they'll use during the retreat, the discussion is likely to run on very long, and the results may not be particularly useful. It's often better to start with a set of recommended ground rules that other groups have found to be helpful in their retreats and then work with the group to edit, expand, or modify them. As a way to begin this discussion, here are a few policies that are commonly used during academic retreats:

1. Everyone will be treated equally throughout the retreat. For the purposes of this meeting, ideas count, not rank.

2. We will speak for ourselves at all times. We will not duck responsibility by using passive voice ("it has been said that … "), an anonymous or undefined "they" ("they say that … "), a vague reference to "certain people" or its equivalent ("people are saying that … " or "there are those who believe … "), or allusions to "perception" ("the perception out there is that … ").

3. There will be no hidden agendas. If we have something to say, we will admit it and own it.

4. We will respect one another's boundaries. We don't want anyone to feel compelled to reveal personal information or anything else that may cause that person discomfort if he or she does not wish to share it. No one should leave this retreat feeling that attacked or humiliated.

5. To whatever extent possible, we will focus on the things we share, not the things that divide us. Since the goal of this retreat is to achieve consensus, we will not make that goal harder to obtain by overemphasizing the obstacles to compromise and agreement.

6. We will own the problem. We will not act as though the problem is caused by others or that our job is merely to identify the problem for others to fix.

7. We will own the solution. Once consensus has been reached, we will not distance ourselves from it, undermine it, or leave it to others to implement.

After presenting a list of this kind, there may be a temptation for people in the group simply to accept its provisions with a dismissive, "Sure, these are fine." That's actually a red flag for what you're trying to do. It means that people are not yet invested enough in the activity for any true discussion or compromise to occur. Try to encourage a bit more reflection before simply adopting a prefabricated list of ground rules. Perhaps insist that the group add at least three new guidelines to the list while deleting or modifying at least one of the recommended policies. By having to meet these goals, you'll have engaged people in a productive icebreaker and set the tone for the type of discussion you expect to have about the retreat's more substantive issues.

Patrick Lencioni's Five Dysfunctions of a Team

In *The Five Dysfunctions of a Team* (2002) and *Overcoming the Five Dysfunctions of a Team* (2005), management consultant Patrick Lencioni outlines the major ways in which teamwork falls apart:

○ *Absence of trust.* The reason that effective teams blend so perfectly is that each member trusts everyone else to know their job, perform it at a high level, have the right priorities, and be aware of the team's best interests. Once that level of trust vanishes, people start looking out for themselves rather than the group, and the team becomes unglued.

○ *Fear of conflict.* The sign of a well-functioning team isn't absence of conflict; it's the ability to handle conflict constructively and convert it into a creative force. Well-functioning teams value differences of opinion because it keeps them from lapsing into groupthink. Once people become so focused on not rocking the boat that they begin censoring themselves just to avoid conflict, the boat stops moving forward.

○ *Lack of commitment.* If group identity is an important element of what constitutes a team, lack of buy-in characterizes a team that's falling apart. Teams function best when all members contribute their ideas, work out their differences, come to consensus, and then take action. If people begin holding back, it's a sign that the spirit of teamwork is being lost.

○ *Avoidance of accountability.* Each member of the team takes a great deal of responsibility for everything the team does. If people start believing things like, "That's not my job," "Don't ask me; ask the boss," or "It was the majority that made the decision; I don't really support it," this lack of accountability saps the team's cohesiveness, and soon what once made the group strong will be lost.

○ *Inattention to results.* While effective teams don't fixate on results, they don't ignore them either. They take pride in the work they do collectively, and members don't allow their self-interests to distract them from the importance of the work they are doing together. Good teams are neither paralyzed by nor indifferent to setbacks. They understand that what they're doing is important and work to make their results the best they can achieve.

These five descriptors provide administrators with a quick checklist to see how they're doing with their team-building initiatives. (There's a more extensive evaluation checklist in Lencioni, 2005.) They also indicate which steps the dean or provost might take in order to promote a greater sense of team spirit. For example, if there's a high level of trust, willingness to deal with conflict, and strong commitment among group members but little follow-through or sense of responsibility for collective decisions, at least we know where to begin. When decisions are reached, we can begin having each member of the group outline three or four actions that he or she will do personally so as to implement the plan. Each proposed action can be given a time line for completion as to keep the work on track, and regular team meetings can include updates from each person of the progress that's being made.

Lencioni (2005, 2012) also offers specific suggestions on how to make team-building retreats more productive, particularly when there's a need to address one or more of the five dysfunctions. For example, he recommends use of personality inventories like the Myers-Briggs Type Indicator, the DiSC Personal Profile, or the Thomas-Kilmann Conflict Mode Instrument to enable members of the team to learn more about how they each deal with conflict and generate greater understanding of these differences. As a way of promoting group commitment and a focus on results, he recommends a two-part exercise. The first part requires members of the team to answer the question, "What is the single most important goal that we must achieve during this period if we are to consider ourselves successful during that time?" In the second part, they break this overarching objective into specific action items, with each group member assigned to different parts of the strategy. Specific tasks of this sort are likely to be a much more effective use of people's time in a retreat than asking vague questions like, "Where do we need to go from here?" or, "What can we all agree on?" Even if people begin to revert to old patterns once the retreat is over, a foundation will have been laid on which further team-building activities can be built in the future.

Maximum Collegial Flow

The holy grail of teamwork at a college or university is something that I've termed *maximum collegial flow*. Everyone is familiar with the state that the psychologist Mihály Csíkszentmihályi (1990) has termed *flow*: that frame of mind we get into when we're so absorbed in what we're doing that we lose all track of time. Teams can develop flow in much the same way that individuals can. You witness it when a basketball team is "in the zone" or when the members of a string quartet seem to respond to one another with a single will (Buller, 2013). It doesn't happen for every team, and it doesn't always happen consistently even for teams that develop it. But when it does occur, the results can be astounding. Productivity (however we choose to measure it) increases dramatically. Morale is good. Work becomes refreshing rather than exhausting. And people derive great satisfaction and meaning from their work together.

There is no magic formula for guaranteeing maximum collegial flow, but there is one for preventing it from occurring: focus on purpose or process rather than people. When the objective becomes raising retention rates, increasing student credit hour production, or lowering the cost of a degree, there will be some progress (typically fairly minor) in the short term, and certain people will conclude, "See? Our plan is working!" But those initial gains are rarely sustainable for the long term. Members of the faculty, staff, and student body begin to feel used, and that impression that they are merely regarded as a means to an end is fatal to teamwork. If there's to be any chance at all of maximum collegial flow emerging, there has to be enough organic academic leadership for people to feel safe and important. As the psychologist Abraham Maslow (1943) noted in his hierarchy of needs decades ago, you can't focus on self-actualization if your physical needs and desires for safety, companionship, and esteem aren't being met. When we approach programs as though they were living, breathing organisms—the very meaning of organic academic leadership—rather than as machines for the production of whichever metric we have decided to monitor, we take the first step toward making maximum collegial flow possible.

One critical role that provosts and deans can play in promoting teamwork is to act as a buffer and translator between the legislature, governing board, president, and at times even parents on one side and students, faculty, and staff on the other. The first group has a tendency to focus on measurable results, and rightly so: they're either paying the bills or accountable to those who do. But the second group needs to be protected from a sense that the only part of them that matters to anyone is how much they produce and how fast they produce it. Provosts and deans are thus perfectly positioned to speak the language of each group and translate it into the language of the other group as necessary. To those whose primary concern is the ability to document results, they can explain that the best way to reach a destination safely isn't simply to press the accelerator to the floor, oblivious to things like speed limits, fuel efficiency, vehicle maintenance, and the traffic; the best way is to travel at a swift but reasonable rate and make sure that the car is well maintained. To those who work or study in the academic programs that report to these administrators, they can explain that part of looking out for their needs is making sure that they're making appropriate progress and that the resources they depend on are sustainable for the future. It's not that leaders who hope to promote maximum collegial flow see themselves as advocates for one group and opponents of the other. They're actually advocating for the best interests of both groups by understanding their needs and translating them into language that everyone can understand.

Conclusion

In the end, promoting teamwork is more art than science, more long-term goal than short-term objective. The emphasis that higher education has developed on accountability and documentation, often simply measuring the measurable and assessing the assessable, seems to leave little place for more humanistic leadership approaches. There aren't many places to record efforts undertaken to promote leadership on an annual report. Nevertheless, provosts and deans who place the welfare of their teams ahead of the desire to reach specific performance metrics are more likely to achieve both goals than if the focus is on those metrics alone.

REFERENCES

Buller, J. L. (2013). *Positive academic leadership: How to stop putting out fires and start making a difference.* San Francisco, CA: Jossey-Bass.

Buller, J. L. (2015). *Change leadership in higher education: A practical guide to academic transformation.* San Francisco, CA: Jossey-Bass.

Csíkszentmihályi, M. (1990). *Flow: The psychology of optimal experience.* New York, NY: Harper.

Lencioni, P. M. (2002). *The five dysfunctions of a team.* San Francisco, CA: Jossey-Bass.

Lencioni, P. (2005). *Overcoming the five dysfunctions of a team: A field guide for leaders, managers, and facilitators.* San Francisco, CA: Jossey-Bass.

Lencioni, P. (2012). *The five dysfunctions of a team: Facilitator's guide.* San Francisco, CA: Jossey-Bass.

Maslow, A. H. (1943). A theory of human motivation. *Psychological Review, 50*(4), 370–396.

Ouchi, W. G. (1981). *Theory Z: How American business can meet the Japanese challenge.* Reading, MA: Addison-Wesley.

Wheeler, D. W. (2012). *Servant leadership for higher education: Principles and practices.* San Francisco, CA: Jossey-Bass.

RESOURCES

Katz, J. H., & Miller, F. A. (2013). *Opening doors to teamwork and collaboration: Four keys that change everything.* San Francisco, CA: Barrett-Koehler.

Maxwell, J. C. (2009). *Teamwork 101: What every leader needs to know.* Nashville, TN: Thomas Nelson.

Parker, G. M. (2008). *Team players and team work: New strategies for developing successful collaboration.* San Francisco, CA: Jossey-Bass.

Salas, E., Tannenbaum, S., Cohen, D., & Latham, G. (2013). *Developing and enhancing teamwork in organizations: Evidence-based best practices and guidelines.* Hoboken, NJ: Wiley.

12

LEADERSHIP IN MAKING DECISIONS

The responsibilities typically assigned to provosts and deans may be categorized in several ways. For example, we could organize them according to the areas in which these administrators work, such as the curriculum, personnel, research, academic policies, accreditation, and the like. Or we could organize them according to the activities they do, such as conducting meetings, writing reports, managing conflict, interviewing candidates, and making decisions. If we take the second approach, the skills in making decisions assume a special prominence over those associated with other activities. After all, any action we take requires us to make a decision. When we conduct meetings, we have to make decisions about which agenda items to include, how to order them, and when to urge participants to complete their discussions and reach a conclusion. When we interview candidates, we have to make decisions about whom to include as a finalists, what questions to ask, and which applicant should be offered the job. Making decisions, in other words, cuts across nearly everything we do as deans and provosts. For this reason, it's odd that we devote a great deal of time to learning more about the areas in which we work and the different activities that we do, but relatively little time learning how to make good decisions. Ultimately it matters very little how skilled you are in writing reports and managing conflict. If you make the wrong decision about what to include in the report or how to move forward positively from the conflict, you have simply replaced one problem with another.

A decision may be defined as a judgment involving risk that is put into effect. There are three major components of this definition:

1. *A decision involves a judgment.* We can think of each decision point as a fork in the road. When we make a decision, we make a judgment

about which path to follow. The corollary to this component is that each decision leaves one or more paths untaken. Each time we decide to do something, we're simultaneously deciding not to do something else. You can't simultaneously choose to be a bachelor and to get married. In the same way, if we have only a thousand dollars to allocate, we can't simultaneously choose to allocate the entire amount to a faculty member for travel and split the amount between two other programs. Regret occurs when we later realize that we've taken the wrong path. In relatively minor matters, these regrets are fleeting and insignificant. In truly monumental matters, however, that regret can haunt a person throughout the rest of his or her career.

2. *A decision involves risk.* Opting for Chinese food rather than Italian for lunch involves making a choice, but it hardly rises to the level of the type of decision making we're exploring in this chapter. A choice merely requires acting on a personal preference. That preference may be ongoing ("Oh, I always prefer to watch baseball rather than golf, given the option"), momentary ("Let's see. I think I'll order the salmon today. No, wait. The cod."), or something in between. But the consequences are minimal or nonexistent if we had chosen differently. Decisions have significant consequences.

> An essential part of genuine academic leadership is not only recognizing that decisions have consequences, but also living with them and recognizing the role one played in bringing them about.

3. *A decision involves putting an option into effect.* If I decide to travel to India but never go, I've never really made a decision. At best, I've set an intention or perhaps articulated a wish. In order for me truly to have made a decision, I have to purchase my ticket, complete the flight, get off the airplane, and experience India firsthand. While this point seems obvious, it's at this level that many so-called decisions in higher education go awry. Think of the last time you witnessed an institution taking great pride in the "tough decisions" it made in developing a new vision and strategic plan, only to continue doing business as usual and never achieve any of the lofty goals it set itself. Truly making a decision requires acting on that decision. You have to venture down the path you've selected and face the risks that may await you.

The Decision-Making Process

One of the first things to realize as effective decision makers is that we're not going to get it right all the time. There are simply too many unknown factors in the complex types of decisions we make as deans and provosts for us to anticipate all the consequences of what we decide. So how do you reduce the likelihood of making wrong decisions, particularly in important, costly, or irreversible matters? In their book *Winning Decisions* (2002), J. Edward Russo and Paul Schoemaker note, "Your best hope for a good decision *outcome* is a good decision *process*" (3). And that observation leads inevitably to the question: What's the best process for academic leaders to use in making decisions? For a large number of decisions, the most effective process in making a good decision may be nothing more complicated than a quick cost-benefit analysis (a weighted list of pros and cons for each option) or utilitarian scan (Which option produces the most good for the most people?). But some of the most important decisions don't lend themselves to these easy approaches. If we engage in them, we end up either with a list of several options that all have roughly similar costs and benefits or with no option that benefits anyone, merely a menu of unpalatable choices.

The toughest decisions are never those that involve choosing between good and bad options. They're always those that force us to select among several competing good alternatives or where no good alternative exists.

In these instances, we need a more nuanced approach than is possible with a cost-benefit analysis or utilitarian scan. Let's consider three approaches you might take when you're faced with some truly difficult decisions.

The Expected Utility Method

The expected utility method of making decisions is a strategy derived from game theory that attempts to incorporate emotional and rational processes into determining which option a person should choose. If we try to make decisions based on rational processes alone, we often reach conclusions that we either can't bring ourselves to implement or deeply regret later. One famous example of why emotional processes must be included in decision making is often referred to as the trolley problem. The problem is often posed in various forms, but for our purposes, let's look at the following version:

> A villain has tied five innocent people to the tracks. From a bridge overlooking the tracks, you see what is occurring and have the ability to pull a lever that diverts the trolley to a different track from where the people are tied. The problem is that a passerby, unaware of what is taking place, happens to be strolling down this other track. If you divert the trolley, you kill the passerby. Do you pull the lever?

Most people when confronted with this problem decide to pull the lever. It's strictly a rational decision for which a utilitarian scan seems sufficient: the decision is whether to have one person die or five people, and most people conclude that the greatest good for the greatest number of people means that the lever should be pulled. But what if the situation is slightly different?

> A villain has tied five innocent people to the tracks. From a bridge overlooking the tracks, you see what is occurring and notice a button below by which you can divert the trolley to a different track, saving the people. The problem is that the only way to push this button is to shove an innocent person who's standing next to you off the bridge, causing the person to suffer a fatal fall but saving the other five people. Do you throw the person off the bridge?

Given the scenario in this format, most people decide not to murder the person next to them. Being actively involved in throwing someone off a bridge seems different to them from causing a person's death remotely by pulling the lever. But that decision isn't made for rational reasons alone. In each scenario, one person dies and five people are saved. But our emotional response is different because we have a different level of activity in the two scenarios.

That difference is not just hypothetical. It's not uncommon for people to want to take a hard line with a faculty member or a student when it's merely a matter of telling someone else what to do, but to be unable to fire or expel someone when they actually have to look the person in the eye and do it. It's not just in issues of empathy or compassion that emotion can affect the decision-making process. Emotion causes us at times to place utility (the importance of something) ahead of value (the importance of something *as a medium of exchange*). For example, if I visit a number of pawnbrokers and discover that the highest amount any of them will give me for my wedding ring-is one hundred dollars, that is its value. But if I refuse to part with it for any price, it has infinite utility for me. Value is largely a matter of rational calculation. But emotion plays a key role in utility. That difference, too, is one we deal with all the time as academic leaders.

For instance, when we conduct program reviews, we usually focus on three aspects of the program we're examining: quality, viability, and centrality to mission (Buller, 2012). Questions of viability are largely focused on value: Is the program sustainable? Does the amount of money the program brings in through tuition and other sources at least equal the money paid out in salaries and other expenses? What are these trends likely to be in the future? Questions of centrality to mission are largely focused on utility: Would this institution be significantly different without this program? How committed do we feel to maintaining and investing in this program? Questions of quality often combine elements of value (What is the return on our investment in this program?) and utility (Do stakeholders generally believe that this is one of our best programs?), and so both considerations tend to be incorporated in a thorough program review.

Initially many people find the question, "Which of my options has the greatest utility?" a bit subjective. As a way of making such decisions more systematic, the expected utility method attempts to convert our thought process into a formula that begins by identifying three aspects of the decision that must be made:

1. *States*, mutually exclusive boundary conditions that affect the decisions that we're making. When we compare head count enrollment in any given program on this same date five years ago, it will be higher than, lower than, or the same as it is now. It can't simultaneously be both higher and lower than our current headcount enrollment.

2. *Options*, the different possibilities we're considering. For example, during a program review, we may be considering whether to eliminate, maintain, or expand a current program.

3. *Outcomes*, the likely results of each option available within the context of each possible state. That is, the outcome of our decision to eliminate a program with far lower enrollment now than five years ago may well be very different from the outcome of a decision to expand a program with far lower enrollment now than five years ago. We assign this outcome a number that represents how important each outcome is to us or how closely that outcome brings us to achieving a significant goal. The bigger the number, the greater we expect the utility of that outcome to be.

With the example listed, all we need to do according to the expected utility method is to determine which state is true and then select the option within that state that has the highest assigned outcome value. So if what actually occurred is that enrollments plummeted and we assigned the highest utility value to "eliminate the program and redirect funding towards greater priorities," then that option represents our best decision under the circumstances.

But the real advantage of the expected utility method comes when we're not dealing with states that we can verify by examining past or current conditions, but those that deal with what might occur at some point in the future. To turn the example on its head, let's not compare current enrollments to those five years ago but imagine a situation in which we're trying to determine our best option now in light of what enrollments are likely to be five years from now. In this case, we have to make some educated guesses. We have to predict the likelihood of enrollment rising, declining, or remaining the same. Our calculations then are a bit more complex, and we use the following formula:

$$EU = \sum_i p_{i \times o_i}.$$

In this equation, EU stands for expected utility, i stands for the individual option we're considering, p stands for the probability of the state associated with that option, and o stands for the outcome value we've assigned to the result associated with that option.

How this method works in practice may become a bit clearer with an example. Suppose you're in the midst of a program review and having a tough time deciding what to do about the undergraduate program in formulaic decision making. For simplicity, we're going to consider only two states (increasing or decreasing enrollment, with level enrollment eliminated) and three options (maintaining, eliminating, or expanding the program, with consolidating or replacing it with another program, reducing it in size, restructuring it, and other such options eliminated). We'd begin by drawing up a table (table 12.1).

In this case, the dean or provost who drew up the table believed that it was slightly more likely that the undergraduate program in formulaic decision making would decrease rather than increase in enrollment over five years and assigned each outcome a value ranging from 1 to 10. Since none of the outcomes was decidedly more desirable than all the others, none of them was assigned an outcome value of 10. That's not unusual when you're actually applying the expected utility method. If you had an outcome that was so clearly preferable to all the rest, you wouldn't

Table 12.1. Example of the Expected Utility Method

Status	Probability	Options	Likely Outcome	Outcome Value	Expected Utility
Enrollment increases	40%	Maintain	Increased revenue from tuition but much larger classes	4	1.6
Enrollment increases	40%	Eliminate	Loss of revenue from tuition and angry alumni base	1	.4
Enrollment increases	40%	Expand	Level tuition revenue but high quality of program and student satisfaction	8	3.2
Enrollment decreases	60%	Maintain	Loss of revenue from tuition but save faculty jobs	3	1.8
Enrollment decreases	60%	Eliminate	Loss of faculty jobs but opportunity to redirect the budget elsewhere	7	4.2
Enrollment decreases	60%	Expand	Wasted investment but potential increase in quality	1	.6

take the trouble to draw up a table like this one; you'd already know what to do. In a similar way, you'll notice that the scale chosen for the outcome values didn't include zero or negative numbers. That's because any choices to which we'd assign values of that kind would automatically have expected outcome values lower than even those with extremely small positive values. If it's so certain that you'd never consider that option anyway, don't give it a zero or a negative value. Simply eliminate it from consideration.

You can see from the table why the academic leader regarded this decision as difficult. Improving the quality of the program and increasing student satisfaction was more important to the administrator than being able to redirect its budget, since the latter option eliminated faculty positions. That's why he or she assigned those two options different outcome values. But when the probability of the two possible states was considered, eliminating the program and redirecting its funding elsewhere seemed the better decision.

In this way, the expected utility method lends itself particularly well to decisions in which we can quantify the probability of future states and assign values to our preference for various outcomes. It might be used, for example, in the process of prioritizing academic programs (Dickeson, 2010) or hiring candidates with slightly different combinations of strengths and weaknesses. The free software application CHDecide uses the expected utility method to calculate values automatically (it is available for Macintosh computers at freecode.com/projects/chdecide). On the expected utility method generally, see Baron (1988) and Lindley (2006).

The Analytic Hierarchy Process

The analytic hierarchy process is similar to the expected utility method in that it uses a formula to rank various options on the basis of the weights assigned to criteria, but it breaks those criteria down more finely than can be done with a single expected outcome value alone. For example, when we're trying to make a tough tenure decision, it can be extremely difficult to fold all the factors to consider into only one possible outcome per option. In addition, it may be meaningless in this situation to talk about different states since the states would be identical to the options we're considering. The state of having Professor A on our faculty five years from now and the state of not having Professor A on our faculty five years from now are precisely the same as our options of tenuring or not tenuring Professor A. So in this case we have to think of our decision differently.

○ I could tenure Professor A, with the result that Professor A remains a member of my faculty.

○ I could not tenure Professor A and choose to search for a faculty member with a different profile.

○ I could not tenure Professor A and choose to redirect the salary savings elsewhere.

Moreover, I would base my decision on the quality of Professor A's teaching, research, and service. I may even break those categories down further and talk about, for example, the quality of classroom teaching, online teaching, and new course development; the quality of peer-reviewed research, grant acquisition, and support for undergraduate research; the quality of committee work; the quality of service to the profession; and the quality of community service. In order to engage in the analytical hierarchy process, I'd have to assign a weight to each of those factors, a score for Professor A on each of those factors, a score for my hypothetical replacement for Professor A on each of those factors (which is simply an estimate based on how well I think a candidate my institution could reasonably attract would probably do), and the impact on each of those factors by the way in which I would redirect Professor A's salary to such things as hiring adjuncts and funding more research and travel.

The result can be both precise and complicated. First, I'd assign weights to the categories of the evaluation, perhaps using those that my institution selected for teaching, research, and service. This process begins to establish the hierarchy mentioned by the name analytic hierarchy process. Then I'd continue to refine that hierarchy by assigning weights to the different components of each category, such as classroom teaching, online teaching, and new course preparation within the category of teaching. Finally I'd score each of my three options (tenuring Professor A, hiring someone else, and redirecting Professor A's salary to other purposes) on the basis of how well they'd help me achieve my overall goals. Finally, I'd calculate values for each option by multiplying all those weights and scores, then summing the scores for each of my three options. The option with the highest number should then reflect my best decision given the circumstances.

Different resources provide other means of using the analytic priority process, some of them with additional steps and other refinements (see, e.g., Saaty, 2001, 2014; Hubbard, 2010; and Golden, Wasil, Harker, and Alexander, 1989). Yet even the simplified version that I have outlined requires a great deal of calculation and effort. Imagine, for example, trying to use this process to narrow a list of twenty semifinalists for a job interview in a search where the job description cites eleven criteria and eight preferred qualifications. As a result, there are websites, apps, and computer programs that perform the calculation automatically. These resources include mDecide for IOS, AHP Decision for Macintosh computers, and the web-based BPMSG AHP priority calculator (bpmsg.com/academic/ahp_calc.php).

The Seven-Step Method

There are two common objections to decision-making systems like the expected utility method and the analytic hierarchy process. The first is that such approaches seem to fall into the fallacy of false precision, the mistaken belief that information that can be quantified—particularly if it can be measured down to several decimal places—must be more reliable than qualitative information. Although quantitative decision-making systems rely on numerous, at times complicated, calculations, they almost always include a significant amount of data based on feelings or impressions that are extremely difficult to quantify. In our hypothetical case about the undergraduate program in formulaic decision making, we assigned a number from 1 to 10 based on how much we favored each outcome, and in our hypothetical case about Professor A, we had to assign values to a large number of weights and scores. While some of those weights may have been derived from institutional policies, a large number of them were quantities that reflected our judgment and feeling at that moment. On another day, we might have assigned each item a higher or lower number if we happened to be in a different mood or approached the matter from a slightly different perspective. So even if we end up with a final value that seems precise, that value will have been based on data that are largely irreproducible and very imprecise. In fact, if we decided we didn't like the result our system produced, we could go back and adjust a few numbers so as to yield the result we preferred. (As you'll see in a moment, the desire to engage in this sort of data manipulation is itself an important part of decision making.)

The second objection we might make to these formal decision-making systems is perhaps best phrased as a question: Does anyone actually ever do that? Even in the most challenging sort of decisions we have to make as academic leaders, can we really envision ourselves going through all the steps and calculations of these numerical processes? Most people would answer that as intriguing as that kind of decision-making system may be theoretically, it doesn't relate well to the way in which deans and provosts work when confronted with genuine problems. What we therefore need is a systematic approach to decision making that draws on some of the best features of numerical processes but does so in a way that matches how we actually work.

One alternative might be to engage in what I call the seven-step method for making decisions. Like the numerical systems, this method is carefully structured so that we don't omit any crucial considerations when we make a decision, but it also doesn't force us into quantifying phenomena like feelings and impressions that resist reproducible quantification. Moreover, while this method doesn't force us to perform any quantifications, it permits us to do so if we believe that quantifying our results would be appropriate for the decision we're trying to make. The steps in the seven-step method are as follows:

1. *Write it down.* Put the decision you're trying to make in the clearest language you can. In many cases, once you see your problem written out, you'll know exactly what you need to do, and the other steps won't be necessary. Even when the decision doesn't seem obvious at

this point, articulating precisely what the issue is will make the effort you invest in the succeeding steps more fruitful.

2. *Gather it up*. Collect as much information as you possibly can about relevant aspects of the issue. For deans and provosts, that information often includes personnel data (such as is commonly found on a curriculum vitae), practices at other institutions, pertinent data from the office of institutional research, and national data from sources like the National Student Clearinghouse (www.studentclearinghouse.org), the Education Resources Information Center (eric.ed.gov), the National Center for Education Statistics (nces.ed.gov), and College Results Online (www.collegeresults.org).

3. *Think it through*. Identify all the paths that are possible within the boundary conditions governing this decision. It's easy, when trying to figure out what to do, to fall victim to the fallacy of alternative blindness—the tendency to reduce many decisions to a this-or-that decision without considering whether other options are possible. Use whatever process you find effective in identifying additional alternatives: brainstorming, systematic inventive thinking (a formalized process used to look at a problem from different perspectives; see Boyd and Goldenberg, 2013), lateral thinking (approaching issues indirectly rather than simply using deductive or inductive logic), or whatever other method you have found to be effective.

4. *Weigh it out*. Consider the advantages and disadvantages of each alternative. At this stage in the process, you can use a systematic process like the expected utility method and the analytic hierarchy process, you can conduct a traditional cost-benefit analysis, or you can create your own approach. Some people find that the method that Ben Franklin describes in his autobiography and that Daniel Defoe attributes to Robinson Crusoe—simply listing pros and cons for each idea in two columns on a piece of paper—helps them weigh the issue quickly and easily. Microsoft Excel even includes a pros-versus-cons list among its templates; this spreadsheet draws on aspects of formal decision-making systems by permitting users to assign an importance value to each item and then calculating the results.

5. *Check within*. An important part of making a decision that's often omitted from many other processes is reflecting on how a decision "feels" after it's made. I alluded earlier to the tendency people may have, after using a quantitative decision-making system, to adjust the data if they get a result they don't like. Checking to see whether a decision feels wrong is actually an important part of how we make daily

decisions. We can add up all the costs and benefits, run the numbers through the most elaborate quantitative system, and generate a result, but if we can't bring ourselves to execute that decision, we haven't reached a conclusion at all. So pausing to determine whether what the evidence suggests lines up with what your gut tells you is part of making wise choices. If it doesn't feel right, then it probably isn't the best thing to do.

6. *Move it along.* After you've weighed out your options and reflected on how you feel about the path that seems best, it's time to act. Extensive vacillation doesn't benefit anyone. In many instances, any decision at all is better than no decision. You're not going to get it right every time, and you have to be willing to take a calculated risk. If you've been diligent about the first five steps of this process, you're ready to take action. People are waiting for your decision, and they can't move forward until you announce what you'll do. So don't take too long to reach a conclusion.

7. *Check it over.* Once the decision has been made, don't just go on to the next decision. See what happens and what you can learn from those results. Sometimes you'll gain insights into how to make better decisions next time. You may discover, for instance, whom you can trust and whom you cannot trust when gathering data, advice, and perspective. You may discover that you have good instincts and should trust them more or that your instincts are unreliable and you need to trust the data more. In either case, the lesson is valuable. Sometimes, too, you may discover that the decision was absolutely wrong. In many cases, you can correct it. There are actually relatively few situations in academic administration when you can't undo something you've done. Even when it seems absolutely impossible to change a decision—as when you've fired someone and only realized afterward that you made a mistake—there are often corrections you can make. In the case of the poor firing decision, you can admit your error, work actively to find the person a job, and perhaps even hire the person back. The important thing is to admit the error, take responsibility for it, and correct it in any way that you can.

Conclusion

Like many other aspects of serving as a dean or provost, decision making may never be easy, but it can become less onerous and more effective if you adopt a systematic way of approaching difficult decisions. Lacking a good system, we're too likely to make a decision based on the last thing we heard, regardless of whether that information was complete and accurate. A systematic process prevents you from acting too soon or too late and makes sure that you've done all the right things before you reach your conclusion. Remember, too, that we rarely have to make decisions alone in higher education. We always have supervisors to help us sort the way through truly difficult matters, and we frequently have policy manuals, committee recommendations, and precedents as guides. It's rarely the case that we need to make decisions in a vacuum. In fact, there's a good essential principle to rely on before you even conclude that you're the proper person to be making the decision:

Decision making is best done at the lowest possible level of any institution. The people who deal most directly with an issue know most about it and have to live with the consequences of the decision on a daily basis. In addition, making decisions helps groom them to become potential academic leaders in the future.

REFERENCES

Baron, J. (1988). *Thinking and deciding*. Cambridge: Cambridge University Press.

Boyd, D., & Goldenberg, J. (2013). *Inside the box: A proven system of creativity for breakthrough results*. New York, NY: Simon & Schuster.

Buller, J. L. (2012). *The essential department chair: A comprehensive desk reference*. San Francisco, CA: Jossey-Bass.

Dickeson, R. C. (2010). *Prioritizing academic programs and services: Reallocating resources to achieve strategic balance*. San Francisco, CA: Jossey-Bass.

Golden, B. L., Wasil, E. A., Harker, P. T., & Alexander, J. M. (1989). *The analytic hierarchy process: Applications and studies*. New York: Springer-Verlag.

Hubbard, D. W. (2010). *How to measure anything: Finding the value of "intangibles" in business*. Hoboken, NJ: Wiley.

Lindley, D. V. (2006). *Understanding uncertainty*. Hoboken, NJ: Wiley-Interscience.

Russo, J. E., & Schoemaker, P.J.H. (2002). *Winning decisions: Getting it right the first time*. New York, NY: Currency.

Saaty, T. L. (2001). *Decision making for leaders: The analytic hierarchy process for decisions in a complex world* (2nd ed.). Pittsburgh, PA: R W S Publications.

Saaty, T. L. (2014). *Models, methods, concepts and applications of the analytic hierarchy process*. Dordrecht, Netherlands: Springer.

RESOURCES

Abdellaoui, M., Hey, J. D., & International Conference on Foundations of Utility and Risk Theory. (2008). *Advances in decision making under risk and uncertainty*. Berlin: Springer.

Ariely, D. (2010). *Predictably irrational: The hidden forces that shape our decisions*. New York, NY: HarperCollins.

Braun, M. J. (2014). The art and science of good decision making. In L. L. Behling (Ed.), *The resource handbook for academic deans* (pp. 79–82). San Francisco, CA: Jossey-Bass.

Brockman, J. (2013). *Thinking: The new science of decision-making, problem-solving, and prediction*. New York, NY: Harper.

Hammond, J. S., Keeney, R. L., & Raiffa, H. (2007). *Smart choices: A practical guide to making better decisions*. Boston, MA: Harvard Business School Press.

Heath, C., & Heath, D. (2013). *Decisive: How to make better choices in life and work*. New York, NY: Crown Business.

Kahneman, D. (2014). *Thinking, fast and slow*. New York, NY: Farrar, Straus and Giroux.

Mooz, H. (2012). *Make up your mind: A decision making guide to thinking clearly and choosing wisely every time*. Hoboken, NJ: Wiley.

13

LEADERSHIP IN POLITICALLY CHARGED ENVIRONMENTS

In higher education, the politics are particularly vicious because the stakes are so small.

That truism, attributed to everyone from Woodrow Wilson to Laurence J. Peter (of the Peter principle), probably originated as an observation by Wallace Stanley Sayre (1905–1972), a political scientist at Columbia University who codified various forms of this statement as Sayre's law. It began appearing in print in 1970, when the context implied that it was already a familiar remark. (See, for example, Wingfield, 1970, and Far Western Philosophy of Education Society, 1970.) And it's been repeated ever since by faculty members and administrators at American colleges and universities since it so aptly describes the environment in which they work.

Higher education seems to be involved in more than its share of political maneuvering for a number of reasons. First, the lack of trust that often exists between faculty and administration, different administrative divisions (such as academic affairs and student affairs), and different administrative levels cause people to think in terms of power differentials rather than more cooperative approaches like consensus building and negotiating compromises. Second, the tendency of faculty members and administrators to view themselves more as private contractors than as employees undermines the command-and-control relationship commonly found in more rigidly hierarchical organizations. Third, highly educated people have been trained to solve problems and prefer to see themselves as in control of a situation than as subject to the advice and direction of others.

The modern university is thus often like a kitchen in which everyone believes themselves to be the chef de cuisine. It doesn't matter what title people have on their business cards; each of them knows (although only a few will admit it) that what he or she does is the most important thing done at the institution. And so, in the words of Arthur Miller's Linda Loman in *Death of a Salesman*, "Attention must be paid" (Miller, 1998, 40). We can be amused by this situation or complain about it, but we can't escape it. And so all deans and provosts find themselves having to negotiate their way through a politically charged environment, some perhaps more fraught with difficulties than others. As a result, a few of the questions that these academic leaders ask themselves are these:

- If deans and provosts are indeed trying to become #1 in the #2 business, as we saw in chapter 1, what does that mean in terms of what they can and can't do because of the political landscape around them?

- How does the ecosystem of the dean or provost affect the job in terms of how he or she needs to interact with others?

- How do the president's ambitions (or the provost's, if you're a dean) affect what academic leaders are able to accomplish and how they're able to accomplish it?

- How do the ambitions of one's peers and the faculty shape the environment in which an academic leader works?

- Where do other types of leaders, such as influential members of the faculty senate or union, come into the picture?

- What if your supervisor really only wants you to be a manager and not a leader?

- Perhaps most troubling, what if you're viewed as a threat to your supervisor or others even higher on the organizational chart?

The answers to these questions fall into the area of realpolitik (i.e., power politics), an aspect of academic life that's rarely addressed at conferences or in leadership training programs. But since they affect the success of a dean or provost more than any other factor, at least at some institutions, they're worth exploring in some detail.

Determining the Lay of the Land

In terms of simple political realities, the first thing a new provost or dean needs to do is figure out who the real power brokers are at the institution. Power doesn't always flow precisely in accordance with the way in which things are supposed to work on the organizational chart. Presidents are sometimes either powerful or strong-willed enough that nothing gets done at the institution without their blessing. But presidents can also be mere figureheads or so compromised because of prior mistakes and conflicts with the governing board that their support means nothing; in fact, it could be detrimental to be seen as too closely associated with an unpopular or failed president. In a similar way, governing boards vary greatly in how much influence they have at an institution. Some merely rubber-stamp every decision made by the administration; others are so hands-on that they serve nearly as a shadow administration, calling the shots that the president, provost, and deans merely implement. If you've come to your position from inside the institution, you probably already know where power lies. But the challenge of determining the lay of the land is much more difficult if you've been hired into your position from the outside.

Ideally, of course, you should have found out about institutional politics before you accepted the job. It's frustrating at best and career limiting at worst to learn that you're expected to be the mouthpiece for a president or board that's so powerful you can't make any decisions on your own. But if you're already in the position, it's probably a good idea to start having a series of frank and confidential conversations with those at the institution whose work is affected by the political landscape. Begin with your peers: other vice presidents if you're the provost or other deans if you're a dean. This type of conversation is probably best handled casually, off campus, and with food and beverages readily available. Ask where the real power lies, how much influence the board has, and what the president is like when confronted by new ideas or constructive opposition. Candidly inquire where you need to build alliances and whose opinion is usually reliable. Look for patterns in the responses people give you. And take nothing on face value.

> Discussing politics at a college or university is the academic equivalent of the observer effect in science where the use of an instrument necessarily influences the phenomenon being observed. Merely by asking questions, you're not just learning about local politics; you're participating in them.

As confidential as you'd like these conversations to be, the very fact you're having them may get back to the president or governing board. Moreover, at the same time that you're gathering information, the people you're talking to will be drawing conclusions about you. ("Why is he or she asking these questions? What's his or her game anyway? Is this someone I can trust?") Be sure that you can explain your reasons for these conversations to anyone who may ask you about them, and be aware of the impressions you're conveying by the sort of questions you ask and how you ask them.

The Academic Leader's Ecosystem

What we might term the ecosystem of the dean or provost—that network of stakeholders and relationships that affects everything the academic leader does—is so important that I've devoted part 3 of this book to examining it in detail. For now, however, suffice it to say that it's this ecosystem that determines what's possible, what's difficult, and what's worth the political investment that has to be made.

In terms of what's possible, deans and provosts soon realize that the realities of how work gets done at a college or university means that unless their stakeholders go along with their strategies and decisions, very little is possible. Legal counsel and human resources personnel may claim that a supervisor has all the authority necessary to enforce a policy, but the political realities are often far more complex. If students collectively refuse to do what the dean or provost wants, what sanctions are really meaningful? "Don't let them graduate," some might say. "Expel them. Freeze their transcripts." Those solutions are all well and good, and they can be quite effective in certain situations. But if your school's budget is heavily tuition driven, does it really make sense to alienate the people who are paying the bills? If your school depends on high retention and graduation rates in order to qualify for performance-based funding, is it a realistic strategy to impose sanctions that are going to lower those rates substantially? Similarly, in the case of the faculty, enforcement options are often fewer than we may believe. Does a provost or dean really want to endure numerous hearings on the revocation of tenure (along with the negative publicity that would result) simply to enforce a policy? Is the threat to withhold salary increases a serious deterrent in an environment where those increases are often minimal or even nonexistent anyway? Is the goal that is achieved truly worth the consequences of pursuing it?

In terms of what's difficult, academic leaders always have to pay attention to where resistance to their proposals is likely to come from. As we saw in chapter 5, people are naturally resistant to change, even if they claim to support it. They fear the possibility of higher workloads or looking less competent in a new environment. They oppose efforts that appear to be negative judgments on their past efforts. They begin to identify likely problems with the plan that they claim will make its implementation impossible. Moreover, that resistance can occur from anywhere within the open system in which the academic leader operates. (On the concept of the open system, see chapter 9.) It may seem as though the faculty will be the major hurdle to a curricular change, when the real obstacle turns out to be the president, accrediting body, or alumni. Academic leaders who are new to their positions are thus confronted with a dilemma. They often feel they have a window of opportunity or honeymoon period soon after they are appointed when they're expected to launch new initiatives and when it's easiest to see them through; at the same time, that's when they're often least aware of the true nature of the ecosystem in which they're operating. For this reason, it's crucial for new deans and provosts to engage in the sort of organic academic leadership discussed in chapter 11, investing their energy in cultivating relationships with people and not simply acting on enticing visions of the future.

Finally, in terms of the political investments deans and provosts make, it's important to realize that each of us has only a limited amount of political capital. The favor you call in today makes it less likely that the same person will grant you another favor tomorrow and the day after that. It pays at times to think of our relationships in economic terms. As we build good relationships with our stakeholders, we earn a certain amount of political capital with them; they're more willing to give us the benefit of the doubt when we propose an idea because they feel positively about us, and we've proven ourselves in their eyes. But each time we call on them for support, we spend a certain amount of that capital. We always have to ask ourselves whether the expenditure is worth the investment of that capital. If the people in our ecosystem get the impression that we're simply using them to advance our goals, they're less likely to remain cooperative for very long. They can easily move from being our allies and supporters to falling into the first two categories discussed: members of our network who make our goals impossible or at least difficult. It's not cynical to think of our professional relationships in terms of earning or spending political chits. It's merely a practical matter of recognizing the realities of how academic leaders get things done.

The Ambitions of the Upper Administration

Relatively few people reach the highest positions at a college or university without at least some ambition and, in most cases, a fairly healthy ego. While there are occasional stories about someone agreeing to serve as chancellor or president not because they ever coveted that job but simply because there was no one else available to do it, those situations are extremely rare. Searches for university CEOs regularly attract at least a hundred applications, and often far more. The majority of those applicants also apply to other institutions, considering the opportunity to work as a college president to be a worthy career goal. For this reason, one of the factors that most affects the political environment in which provosts and deans work is the precise nature of the ambitions of those above them on the organizational chart. Are those people striving for even more prestigious positions at other institutions? Are they trying to leave a legacy where they are now? Are they seeking to fulfill a mandate from the board? If you don't have at least a general understanding of the answers to these questions, you're operating in the dark. It's unlikely that you'll attain more than a small part of your overall goals if you can't help the upper administration understand how your goals will help advance *their* goals.

> The political reality for most provosts and deans is that they stand a much better chance of accomplishing what they want if they can find a way of helping their chancellors and presidents understand that they want those things too.

In *Positive Academic Leadership* (2013), I explain one of the most effective ways in which administrators communicate their needs and desires to their supervisors: they describe those needs and desires as a means to obtaining the supervisor's own needs and desires. Usually we go about this type of communication all wrong in higher education. We describe our needs and desires as goods that are valuable for their own sakes or as means to obtaining goals that are important to us.

Think of the last time you were in the middle of a severe budget cut, and a faculty member came to you wanting a raise, several new faculty positions, additional staff support, or perhaps all three. There was probably a moment in the conversation where you thought, "Is this person crazy? Doesn't (s)he understand that we're cutting budgets, not increasing them? How can anyone be so blind as to think only of themselves when we've got a real crisis on our hands?" What you were experiencing was the disconnect that can occur between the needs and desires on one level of the institution and those on another level of the institution.

Now consider this issue differently. Remember the last time you presented what you thought was a perfectly valid case for something important to your supervisor, only to have your proposal turned down before you thought you had the chance to make your case complete.

There was probably a moment in the conversation when you thought, "Why is this person so inflexible? All I'm asking for is a small request that could easily be granted. Doesn't (s)he care at all about the long-term good of this institution?" Those thoughts were likely to be going through the head of the faculty member who wanted the funding increase when you refused it. And your reaction to that request was probably going through your supervisor's mind in response to your own proposal. What was happening is that both you and the faculty member were thinking of what you wanted only in terms of its being an absolute good or as a means to obtaining a goal that was important to you. You weren't thinking of your supervisor's ambitions.

Let's approach the situation differently. Suppose now you've taken the time to understand what motivates your supervisor. You understand that what he or she really wants is to impress the board with greatly improved enrollment figures, become the head of a major university system, rebrand your institution as the best in the world at this or that, or whatever it may be. At the same time, what you really want is additional positions that can reduce the massive workload of your faculty and staff, equity salary adjustments that will prevent your best performers from taking jobs elsewhere, having your supervisor's job, or whatever else most motivates you. The challenge then is to cast what you want as a way of your supervisor obtaining what he or she wants. For example, how can you present higher faculty and staff salaries as a means of improving enrollment or new positions as a means of rebranding the institution? If building your own career is a significant goal, consider asking your supervisor to serve as your mentor, delegate a few additional responsibilities to you (thus freeing up more of his or her time while gaining important experience for yourself), and keep you in mind as opportunities arise. These requests then help your supervisor achieve his or her own goals of succession planning and documenting success as a mentor while you also send a signal that you'd be grateful to be nominated for the right opportunity if it came along.

The Ambitions of Others

Just as both you and your supervisor have goals and ambitions, so does every other stakeholder you work with. The political reality of the environment in which we work is that everyone has an agenda. Some of these are open (and for your own success as an academic leader, it's best for your agenda to be as open as possible), but many of them are hidden. That's why it's so important to begin determining the lay of the land when you're new in a position: you don't want to doom an initiative that's important to you by inadvertently doing or saying something that threatens someone's hidden agenda. When you understand what someone else's ambitions are, you can approach them in the same way you did with your supervisor, seeking areas where your goals overlap or finding a way in which your goal serves as a means of achieving the other person's ambitions. (See figure 13.1.)

The difficulty comes when this approach isn't possible. The environment you're working in may be so fragmented that no areas of common interest may be found or the stakeholder may have ambitions that are irreconcilable with your own. For example, the two of you may both have an interest in the same position, or you may want to expand a program while the other person wants to reduce it and redirect its funding elsewhere. In situations like these, you have several options:

o *Pick a side.* There are times when the environment in which we work becomes so toxic that we simply have to take a stand. Doing so can be very difficult when we're new at an institution and don't understand all the issues. As a result, we could end up on the side that limits our effectiveness for a long time to come. So, how do you decide which side to choose? You can be Machiavellian and simply support whichever position you believe will triumph. That's a dangerous strategy, however, since you can never be certain that the situation will turn out as you suppose. The morally superior decision is actually the one that makes the best political sense: let your core beliefs guide you. In that case,

---

**Figure 13.1 Finding Areas
of Commonality**

even if it turns out that you made a poor choice, you can at least defend it on philosophical or ethical grounds. There are few things that will destroy your credibility faster than being exposed as someone who placed expediency ahead of principle and backed a cause only because you believed it would help your career.

○ *Be an honest broker.* Even the most politicized environment requires someone who is trusted by all parties. In many situations, the ethical as well as the politically wise thing to do is to seek to become that honest broker. When someone challenges you to declare whether you side with this or that person, respond by saying that you're not on anyone's side; you're on the institution's side. But rather than just straddling the fence, make it clear that you're willing to work with all the different parties in the matter to reach an effective way of moving forward. Your role could be that of a mediator (someone who facilitates negotiations among people who have found it difficult to do so on their own), arbitrator (someone who objectively considers all position and either imposes a compromise or decides in favor of one position or the other), or intermediary (someone who acts as a go-between for two or more parties who can no longer have productive discussions in one another's presence). There is still a danger that if your efforts aren't successful, your credibility and influence will be damaged. However, the personal and professional rewards of succeeding as an honest broker are so great that this option is particularly attractive for academic leaders.

○ *Negotiate trade-offs.* In cases where your goals are completely incompatible with those of another person, neither taking a side nor becoming an honest broker seem viable options. You can simply try to prevail, adopting an attitude of "let the best person win," or you can use this potential conflict to form a new alliance. For example, would you be willing to yield on this issue if the other person agreed to support you in a matter that you regard as even more important? Or could you persuade the other person to yield in turn for your willingness to make concessions elsewhere? We frequently come to these political bottlenecks not because we're too different in our outlook from those of other people, but because we're too similar to them. That shared interest can be helpful. If we understand what motivates us, we have come a long way toward understanding what motivates them. That creates an opportunity to negotiate a solution not only to the current problem but also to obtain future goals since we can use our similar interests as a foundation for a new partnership.

When seeing administrative issues presented in these terms, some administrators are put off by what appears to be political maneuvering and taking advantage of other people for professional gain. Keep in mind that the topic in this chapter is how to be effective in politically charged environments. Although all colleges and universities are politicized at least to some extent, the spectrum you'll find in higher education is fairly broad. At an institution or in a unit where most things are done with great collegiality, introducing an element of political maneuvering is likely to be seen as destructive and ill considered. But there are institutions so rife with conflict that no dean or provost can survive without approaching each situation from a political perspective. In the oft-cited observation of the Prussian statesman Otto von Bismarck, "Politics is the art of the possible" (Bismarck and Poschinger, 1895, 248). Without this tool in your toolbox, there will be situations in which achieving the goals that are important to you simply won't be possible.

Emergent Leaders

Some of the most important allies to have or enemies to avoid in a highly politicized environment are the emergent leaders discussed in earlier chapters (see, for example, chapters 1, 8, and 10): people whose authority is independent of their actual positions. In many cases, these emergent leaders include influential members of the faculty who may have a base of power in the faculty senate, assembly, or union. They often don't aspire to an administrative position but can make your life either much easier or far harder depending on whether they view you as a partner or an opponent. If their ideas are good, these emergent leaders can be some of the most important people to bring into your professional circle. They can help you with work behind the scenes that's impossible for you to do yourself. They can build coalitions that bring about key votes in committees and can serve to protect you from others at the institution who may see you as a rival or threat.

Unfortunately, not all emergent leaders have good ideas. Indeed, one particularly aggravating type of emergent leader is what I call a Cleon, after the fifth-century demagogue described by Aristophanes and Thucydides. Like their namesakes, Cleons have never held formal positions of authority but that doesn't stop them from believing that they'd be better at everyone's job than the incumbent. Cleons are better at pointing out what's wrong with an idea than at coming up with ideas of their own, and they often seem to oppose whatever initiative the administration supports, even if they themselves had supported that idea in the past. They gain their popularity and political power by being loud, abrasive, and antagonistic to figures of authority. Other faculty members may ridicule Cleons behind their back, but they often delight in their ability to slow down processes they're afraid may increase their workload and make the administration uncomfortable. Cleons are articulate and think quickly on their feet, which is probably why so many college faculties tend to produce them.

In relatively harmonious environments, Cleons are nothing more than a nuisance. In highly politicized environments, they can do real damage because they can transform minor disagreements into true rifts and antagonize an already severe atmosphere of us versus them. Fortunately, the situation is one in which history provides some guidance. After years of hearing the tirades of the historical Cleon, the Athenians finally decided to put his "expertise" into effect. He was sent as a general to fight in the battle of Amphipolis, where he was easily outmaneuvered by the Spartans and killed. The same strategy often works with modern Cleons: make them responsible for the success of what they propose. If, as almost never happens, they are actually able to make their ideas work, you can take credit for empowering them. If, as is more likely, they fail, that very failure undermines their authority. And if, as is most likely, they refuse to take responsibility for their proposals, they can be exposed as the hollow frauds that they are.

Diverging Expectations

Another political challenge deans and provosts may encounter occurs when their supervisors have very different expectations about what their role is than they do. Frequently this situation occurs when an academic leader is working for a particularly strong supervisor who insists on being the source of all initiatives, setting all policies, and having final authority in all decisions. To be accurate, we should say that this situation usually occurs when a supervisor wishes to seem particularly strong, since truly strong and authoritative leaders frequently decide to empower others throughout the institution. Only administrators who are insecure about their own authority or can't abide sharing credit with others go out of their way to make sure everyone in the organization understands who's in charge. When that occurs, the administrator often feels as though his or her supervisor may give lip-service to the importance of academic leadership, but actually wants other people to be managers, not real leaders. Even worse, it may not be possible even to carry out those important management functions discussed in chapter 8. What the supervisor really wants is a staff of minions to carry out his or her instructions.

As we've seen, the first strategy to consider in such a situation is to try to get your supervisor to understand how the initiatives that are important to you actually do advance his or her own goals. That strategy is not always effective, however, particularly when your supervisor mistrusts any idea that he or she didn't originate. Perhaps the most tempting approach to take in that case is to become calculatedly passive-aggressive. That is, you support the supervisor publicly and face-to-face but in private "forget" to follow up on certain agreements and pursue, whenever possible, actions that advance your own goals. Such an approach commits all five of Patrick Lencioni's five dysfunctions of a team explored in chapter 11 and is likely to result in severe repercussions if you get caught in the act. Morally it falls into a gray area at best. Nevertheless, there are times when it's the best of several bad options. For instance, if open revolt is likely to cause significant programs you supervise to be closed down or greatly harmed in some other way, it can be effective as a means of buying some time. Having that additional time is valuable, however, only if you have good reason to believe that your supervisor will soon be replaced or move to another position. Fortunately, most headstrong, rigidly hierarchical administrators cause their own undoing, so it's a gamble that may be worth taking.

More morally defensible is giving serious reflection to how badly your supervisor's expectations will cause you to violate principles you hold dear. For each of us, there are probably dozens of matters about which we can compromise in good conscience but only a few hills we're willing to die on. Only you can decide which of these a given situation falls into. If, after serious consideration, you conclude that you're still able to do your job in the way you need to do it and that following your supervisor's directives doesn't flout your core beliefs, there's nothing wrong with living to fight another day. But if the situation is one in which you couldn't live with yourself after participating in an action that is truly indefensible, then it may be time to take your stand, even at the cost of your position. (See chapter 46.)

The Academic Leader as Threat

Strong, confident academic leaders aren't afraid to surround themselves with the most talented people they can find. If you hire bright, effective people, their success becomes your success. If they're your peers, their achievements provide an incentive for you to become even better at what you do. If you work for them, they can be excellent mentors and role models. And if they happen to exist on your staff when you enter your position, you can count yourself lucky to have a head start toward building the type of program most provosts and deans can only dream about. Unfortunately, not all administrators have this degree of confidence, and you may well find yourself working for someone who sees you as a threat. In a way, that's quite a compliment. Even though you're not at that person's level on the organizational chart, he or she sees you as smart, creative, or promising enough to be a rival. In other ways, however, working in that type of environment can be miserable. You can feel as though every decision you make is mistrusted and every idea you propose is shot down, not because it may not work but because it probably will.

Some administrators are so insecure that anything you try to do to reduce this level of paranoia will only increase it. In that case, just as when you and your supervisor have widely divergent expectations, you need to think very carefully about whether you can still be effective at your job. In other situations, however, you can help change the atmosphere by being proactive. Talk to your supervisor about your own career goals and try to elicit his or her support in achieving them. Be generous in making sure that your good ideas include at least some acknowledgment of your supervisor—even if you may have to be a bit inventive in identifying his or her contributions. If you feel unequivocal support for your supervisor, say so clearly and often. Since your supervisor's view of you as a threat stems from his or her own insecurity, whatever you do to help make your boss feel more secure will ultimately serve to improve the relationship you two share. The steps you take to advance his or her own career will also be steps in advancing your own.

Conclusion

Strategizing about how to succeed in highly politicized environments always makes academic leaders feel as though they're reverting to the tactics found in Machiavelli's *The Prince* or Sun Tzu's *The Art of War* rather than engaging in the broad-based consensus building they claimed to support while they were being interviewed. After all, realpolitik is all about practical means of achieving ends, not humanitarian ideals or lofty principles. But effective academic leadership is rarely all one thing or another. Our ideals and principles do usually drive our goals, even if we need to engage in some hardball politics to achieve those goals from time to time. For this reason, knowing how to be effective in politically charged environments is a tool you need in your administrative toolbox, but it shouldn't be the only tool there. Provosts and deans who approach every issue as a power struggle are soon as ineffective as provosts and deans who are oblivious to the role that power can play in their environments. If it becomes inevitable to think of power politics in militaristic terms, consider the ideas outlined in this chapter to be defensive armaments, not first-strike weapons.

REFERENCES

Bismarck, O., & Poschinger, H. (1895). *Fürst Bismarck: neue Tischgespräche und Interviews*. Vol. 1. Stuttgart, Germany: Deutsche Verlags-Anstalt.

Buller, J. L. (2013). *Positive academic leadership: How to stop putting out fires and start making a difference*. San Francisco, CA: Jossey-Bass.

Far Western Philosophy of Education Society. (1970). Proceedings of the Annual Meeting of the Far Western Philosophy of Education Society.

Miller, A. (1998). *Death of a salesman: Certain private conversations in two acts and a requiem*. New York, NY: Penguin.

Wingfield, C. J. (1970). *The American university: A public administration perspective*. Dallas, TX: Southern Methodist University Press.

RESOURCES

Bess, J. L., & Dee, J. R. (2014). *Bridging the divide between faculty and administration: A guide to understanding conflict in the academy*. New York, NY: Routledge.

Godwin, J. (2013). *The office politics handbook: Winning the game of power and politics at work*. Pompton Plains, NJ: Career Press.

McIntyre, M. G. (2005). *Secrets to winning at office politics: How to achieve your goals and increase your influence at work*. New York: St. Martin's Press.

Reardon, K. K. (2005). *It's all politics: Winning in a world where hard work and talent aren't enough*. New York, NY: Currency/Doubleday.

14

A SCENARIO ANALYSIS ON THE NATURE OF ACADEMIC LEADERSHIP

For a discussion of how scenario analyses are structured and suggestions on how to use this exercise most productively, see the beginning
of chapter 7. A scenario analysis for deans appears in the online content
accompanying this book.

Case Study for Provosts

Your institution has recently hired a new president who, almost immediately on arrival, got rid of more than half the school's vice presidents,
including the former provost. No one was fired in an obvious way—there
were the usual resignations with administrators saying they were eager
to return to the classroom, pursue another opportunity that was just too
good to resist, or spend more time with their families—but everyone at the
institution knew that these were face-saving excuses. The governing board
had long been eager for the institution to adopt a more aggressive strategic plan, phase out programs with low enrollments, improve retention
and graduation rates, and secure more external funding for research. The
previous president was a pragmatist who understood how difficult the
challenges were in pursuing all these goals simultaneously. The new president is cut from an entirely different cloth. Supporters describe the new
president as entrepreneurial, goal oriented, and data driven. Detractors,
of whom there is already a small but vocal number, prefer to character-
ize the president as fixated on the bottom line, a bean counter, and more
interested in building a résumé than strengthening the institution.

While you weren't necessarily a strong supporter of your predecessor as provost, you were concerned that too much transition in the upper administration might not be good for the institution. For that reason—along with the significant salary increase plus a guaranteed two full years of sabbatical at your full provost's salary should you leave the position after five years—you set aside your reservations and accepted the president's invitation to be the school's second in command. At first, you believed that your concerns had been unjustified. In several meetings of the executive staff, the new president stressed the importance of teamwork and said all the right things about wanting decisions to be made collectively about whatever was best for the students, faculty, and community. Lately, however, you've increasingly realized that this rhetoric doesn't match the president's actions very well. After an initial pretense of getting everyone's views out in the open, the president has begun making more and more decisions alone. You've tried to raise respectful objections in several meetings, only to be shut down. Even the notion of teamwork that once gave you hope has begun to take on a distinct edge: if you're not enthusiastically in favor of whatever it is the president decides to do, you're accused of not being a member of the team and urged to "get on board with the rest of us. There's no I in *team*, you know."

As you begin to reach the first anniversary of your term as provost, you find yourself increasingly wondering whether you made the right decision in accepting the job. Even worse, you wonder whether the board made the right decision in hiring this president. If you resign your position after such a short amount of time, you worry about the professional problems such a decision might cause. Certainly you'd alienate the president and not be able to count on support from that quarter if you tried to find another job or wanted to advance any new initiatives at your institution. You'd also be giving up the chance to have that very attractive two-year sabbatical that is guaranteed for you if you can hold out just four more years. In addition, there's always the chance that someone less effective than you would become provost in your place, and you'd no longer have any opportunity to temper what you see as the president's poor choices for the school. You're also not certain that you can be effective if you remain as provost. The president seems to view your position more as one that will implement executive decisions, not make them. And you don't feel you're receiving much support from the other vice presidents, all of whom seem either worried about losing their own jobs or genuinely supportive of the president's style of leadership.

These thoughts are going through your mind one day when you receive a call from the president. "Get in here right away!" you're told. "I'm sick of you going around behind my back and trying to undermine everything I'm trying to do for this school. You need to tell me right now whether you're with me or against me." With that, the president hangs up. What thoughts are going through your mind as you walk to the president's office?

Considerations

1. The case study says that the other vice presidents are "either worried about losing their own jobs or genuinely supportive of the president's style of leadership." Suppose you were to learn that they're as concerned about the president's leadership as you are but simply too afraid to do anything about it. Would that change how you respond?

2. Would you feel differently if the previous president had left behind some genuine problems that the new president is being forced to solve?

3. If you had a close contact on the governing board, would you involve that person in your efforts to find a solution?

4. If becoming a president of a college or university were an important goal for you, how might that affect how you handle this situation?

5. If one of the president's plans were to phase out the department in which your academic discipline is based, how would that possibility factor into your thinking?

6. If the president were the type of person to fly into a rage quickly but then calm down and apologize after an angry outburst, how might that knowledge influence what you say when you enter the president's office?

Suggestions

At first glance, this case study doesn't seem very complex to many people. You've been thinking about whether you can remain effective in your position anyway, and now the president's outburst seems to have decided the matter for you: clearly you should go to the president's office and tender your resignation as provost. But while that response seems tempting, is it the *best* decision to make? As satisfying as turning your back on the president (possibly even slamming the door as you do so) may be at the moment, that action could have long-term consequences for you. It could end your administrative career, harm the institution by opening the provost position to someone who simply agrees with whatever the president says, be detrimental to your income both now and after you retire, cause problems for your academic discipline by alienating the president, and have other effects that you may not see for quite some time. For this reason, even if you do decide that resigning your position as provost is your best option, you should probably not do it in the heat of the moment. Try to listen calmly to what the president has to say. Then add that information to the other issues you've been considering and make your decision when you've had time to give the matter due consideration.

The president, of course, may not give you that option. The phrase, "You need to tell me right now whether you're with me or against me," seems to suggest that you'll be called on to render a decision immediately. Even so, you could say something like, "I want to do what's best for the institution, myself, and frankly you as well. Please give me the weekend to think matters over, and let's talk again on Monday morning." That may not be good enough for the president described in this case study, but it is worth a try.

Remember that even though the president may be acting rudely (and even childishly) toward you, there's no reason for you to respond in kind. If you decide to step down, doing so graciously will be to your credit later. As secure as the president seems with the board right now, that situation can change quickly, particularly if other people start receiving phone calls similar to the one you just had. By burning bridges with an angry response now, you may limit your options to help the institution in the event the president fails. So do whatever you believe to be best for you, but only after due consideration and not in the heat of the moment.

PART THREE

THE ECOSYSTEM
OF THE COLLEGE
OR UNIVERSITY

15

STUDENTS

In chapter 13 we saw how important it was for provosts and deans to understand the workings of their institutional ecosystem: that network of personalities, needs, desires, and relationships that defines their professional environment. In that earlier context, we were concerned with why this knowledge is valuable when academic leaders find themselves thrust into a politically charged situation. But it's also crucial for provosts and deans to understand their institutional ecosystems even when things are going well. These networks consist of the stakeholders whose needs the institution was created to meet, as well as the people who devote their careers to meeting those needs. Not every member of an ecosystem (or any system for that matter) will necessarily have the same function as every other member. Think for a moment about your computer system where the keyboard, hard drive, monitor, central processing unit, printer, and mouse all have their own function and purpose but work together collectively to bring about a certain result. Colleges and universities are systems too. The students, parents, faculty members, department chairs, staff members, upper administration, and others all have different parts to play in the work of the institution. Moreover, like a natural ecosystem (and less like a computer system), they all have an impact on the environment of their network, affecting and being affected by one another.

In terms of sheer numbers, the largest group that composes the higher education ecosystem is the student body. They are also, most administrators would agree, the most important part of that system. Although it's possible for a university to exist without students solely as a think tank or research center, that's not a common model. When most people think of a college or university, they think of it as a source for postsecondary education, and indeed that's how most people have their contact with the institution: they arrive as students, leave as graduates, and unless they remain actively involved with the school as alumni, they view the impact of the university almost solely in terms of how it affected themselves and others like them.

Students are also the most important stakeholders in higher education in an economic sense. At tuition-dependent institutions, they either pay the fees themselves or someone else pays on their behalf. At state-assisted institutions, budgets are often based on enrollment. Even as many states move away from enrollment-based budgeting to performance-based models, most of the metrics tracked by the legislature relate to students: retention and graduation rates, job placement rates, minority access to education, and the like. And although provosts and deans rarely spend as much time in the classroom as does the teaching faculty, students still have a disproportionate effect on the state of their ecosystems.

There are many reasons that students may interact with the dean or provost, either directly or indirectly through a member of the administrative staff. Students may need help in understanding how the college's academic rules and regulations apply to them. They may be unaware of certain procedures they will need to follow. They may be encountering some barrier to their academic success that's appropriately addressed at the level of the dean or provost. They may be seeking letters of recommendation or verifications that they are in good academic standing. They may have exhausted all of their preliminary appeals in addressing a concern with a faculty member or in filing a request for reconsideration of a grade. They may be pursuing an independent major that's supervised at the level of the dean or provost or require assistance in applying for graduate school, an internship, or a study-abroad experience. They may need the administrator's permission for an incomplete, late withdrawal from a course, or a change of grading system (such as letter grade to pass/fail or vice versa). They may be the recipients of a major award, and the academic leader is the person selected to congratulate them. They may be in such severe academic difficulty that an office above the level of the academic discipline needs to intervene, either to help them get back on track or to have them removed from the institution for academic reasons.

Some administrative offices include formal centers of academic advisement, tutoring support, and other forms of assistance that students may require from time to time. At some institutions, too, various forms of records are stored in either the provost's or the dean's office, and students who need information from their files may be required to submit a request through that office. Moreover, even if your position doesn't require extensive interaction with students, this group of stakeholders is so central to everything we do that there are certain issues you need to consider.

Are Students Our "Customers"?

One of the issues about students that's often debated throughout higher education is: Are our students customers of our institutions and, if so, what does that mean in terms of our relationship with them? (See Eagle and Brennan, 2007; Lomas, 2007; and Tight, 2013.) Obviously there are several aspects of a student's interactions with colleges or universities that bear strong similarities to the way in which a customer interacts with a business. For instance, students pay fees to the institution, receive services from it, and are entitled to have certain expectations about how they will be treated by it. Moreover, in specific aspects of their experience on campus, students literally *are* customers. When they purchase items in the bookstore, lease space in a residence hall, or acquire a meal plan, students enter into precisely the same relationship with the institution that any customer enters into with any business.

Nevertheless, in the academic sphere, the relationship of the student to the college or university is significantly different from that which a customer has with the provider of a good or service. Sometimes students or their parents don't understand this difference. Their attitude is, "I'm paying the tuition. Why can't you offer my program at the time I want, give me all and only the courses I want to take, reward me with a grade that reflects my effort and aspirations rather than my performance, and provide me with a degree that certifies I'm ready to advance in my career?" What's misunderstood in this scenario is that in higher education, the relationship that a student has with an institution is much less like that which a customer has with a store or service provider than it is like the relationship a patient has with his or her doctor. That is, academic performance is less of a customer/business relationship than it is a client/professional relationship (Buller, 2013).

An illustration may be helpful in understanding why this distinction is important. In a customer relationship, the purchaser pays a fee and has the right to expect whatever he or she wants and has paid for. It's an even exchange. For example, customers in a restaurant are entitled to purchase as much as they can afford, receive everything they pay for, and be the final arbiters as to whether the food and drink meet their expectations. Any restrictions on those entitlements are limited. A restaurant may refuse to serve a customer who is inebriated, disturbing other customers, or acting in a manner that's otherwise detrimental to the restaurant's business. They may require customers to be dressed in a certain way, such as "No shoes. No shirt. No service," or "Jacket and tie required." But those restrictions aren't particularly onerous. Even if the patron's requests are utterly irrational—for example, if I ask to be served only menu items that begin with the letter *p*—the restaurant, if it cares to remain in business, will most likely be happy to comply and bring me pasta with prawns, potatoes primavera, parsnips, pumpkin pie, and a Pepsi. And if I complain ("These aren't prawns! These are shrimp! I wanted prawns!"), they'll do whatever they can to make me happy.

Something quite different occurs in a professional relationship. In these cases, the client pays a fee and has the right to expect his or her needs—not his or her desires—to be taken seriously, subject to the professional's training and sound judgment. Thus, in a doctor's office, a patient may request a certain treatment or medication, but the physician is not obliged to provide it. If I ask for only medications beginning with the letter *z*—"I'd like prescriptions for Zoloft, Zostrix, Zantac, and Zebutal, please"—I'm not likely to be treated as an interesting eccentric, as I was in the restaurant, but as a candidate for psychological evaluation. What the doctor *is* obliged to do is consider my genuine health needs in light of his or her own ethical and professional code. "Well, rather than simply prescribing those medications for you," my doctor might say, "let me run a few tests, and I'll use those results to plan the best course of treatment for your needs."

In much the same way, students sometimes tell professors, advisors, and other academic professionals what they want, but it's the academic professional's duty to determine what a student actually needs. Prerequisites, general education requirements, graduation requirements, and other aspects of a well-constructed academic program are designed in such a way that they reflect the experience and judgment of educators. Part of what a student "pays for" in college is the exercise of that judgment while having his or her needs addressed, just as would be the case if the student were consulting any type of professional. The professor can't promise a student a passing grade or a degree any more than a doctor can promise to cure a patient; all he or she can do is to make a sincere effort to create the conditions that are most conducive to success. Too many other factors are dependent on the student or patient (whether the student has the natural ability to perform work at a high level and studies sufficiently, whether the patient follows the plan for therapy and takes the medication as directed) as external forces beyond anyone's control (whether the job market has sufficient positions in the student's area of interest, whether the patient's condition is terminal).

There's also evidence to suggest that students who see themselves as customers are actually creating impediments to their own success. In a study of 1,025 students from the University of South Alabama, Treena

Gillespie Finney and R. Zachary Finney (2010) found that students who viewed themselves as being in a customer relationship with institution were more "likely to hold attitudes and to engage in behaviors that are not conducive to success as a student. Students who perceive themselves as customers of the university are more likely to complain and to feel entitled to receive positive outcomes from the university; they are not, however, any more likely to be involved in their education" (286). These students, the Finneys discovered, often viewed complaining and negotiating (rather than working harder, meeting with tutors, or participating in group study sessions) as effective means of attaining what they wanted and adhered to an exchange theory approach to higher education: in exchange for their tuition payments, they expected to receive the grades and degrees they wanted. Though few of them would have phrased it quite so bluntly, in their minds being a customer meant that they were essentially "buying" their degrees. In contractual terms, since tuition was the consideration they were providing, their side of the bargain was complete. It was then up to the college or university to do its part and graduate them.

Deans and provosts are in an excellent position to provide a corrective to this misunderstanding. In fact, many of their other stakeholders, most notably the faculty, are hungry for administrators to provide leadership in this area by relieving them of the students' unrealistic demands because of a false impression of where "customer rights" end and "student obligations" begin.

Setting Boundaries

Of course, not all that we do as provosts and deans involves enforcing policies and serving as a buffer when students and faculty members are in dispute. We genuinely want students' academic experience to be rich and enjoyable. We want to be accessible to students so that when an issue arises in which they need our help or the help of our staff, they'll feel comfortable using the resources that are available to them. Nevertheless, because of the customer mentality, students occasionally mistake accessibility for a sense that the dean or provost should serve as the complaint department no matter what their individual problems might be. They bring to our office issues that are more effectively handled elsewhere on campus (housing, financial aid, the bursar's office, and so on) or addressed at other levels within our units (a faculty member, a department chair, a tutoring program, and the like). Just as customers in a department store sometimes demand to see the manager, students who view themselves as customers may feel it appropriate to demand to see the provost or dean.

They may expect rights that they possess in other settings and assume they are also found at a college or university. What they may not realize is that while their rights in higher education aren't identical to those they may have in a restaurant, theater, or department store, their academic rights will be in many ways much more significant to them in the long run. Let's explore what some of these academic rights may be.

When an academic leader encounters a situation in which students are making inappropriate demands or looking for a solution that can only be provided elsewhere within the institution, he or she has an opportunity to seize the teachable moment and make the experience instructive for everyone concerned. Requests that are better handled by other offices allow us to explain how universities actually work and why they're structured as they are. After all, the organization of universities may seem inherently obvious to us since we work at them every day. But students are often experiencing college for the first time and may well be the only members of their families to have done so. If your only models of institutions have been high schools, department stores, and restaurants, you're likely to assume that colleges and universities work in the same way. As a result, we have an opportunity to teach students where various decisions are made within a system of higher education and where they should go to receive the answers they require.

This approach doesn't mean shunting students off to other departments, however. No one likes to feel that he or she is being given the runaround, and our goal must be to be helpful, even if the request has been made in error or in an offensive manner. We might consider walking the student to the appropriate office, making the necessary introductions, and resolving the whole situation with good feelings all around. These strolls with a student to another office can actually be the most productive part of your day because it gives you a chance to learn about how the institution looks from the student's perspective. You can ask, "What's been your best experience here so far? Who's been your best professor? What's been your favorite class?" Questions like these give you information that you can't easily obtain elsewhere and help the student to focus on the positive aspects of his or her education at your institution. When accompanying the student yourself isn't possible because of your tight schedule, asking a member of the staff to do so or making a phone call on the student's behalf—immediately and in the student's presence—can often resolve the situation quickly and transform what could have been a conflict into a highly positive experience for all involved.

In a similar way, when students end-run a professor or department chair and come directly to you, you have an opportunity to explain the hierarchy of your institution and why it's important (not to mention fairer to all students) for established procedures to be followed. Students will frequently assume that since you are a faculty member's "boss," you're in a position to overturn a decision that they feel is unreasonable or not as convenient as they might like it to be. In these cases, you can explain in detail the difference between the customer/business relationship and the client/professional relationship. For example, if a clerk in a department store does something that fails to meet the expectations of a customer, it's not at all uncommon for the customer to demand to see that person's supervisor and have the decision reconsidered. In professional relationships, a different expectation applies. A patient who disagrees with a doctor's plan of treatment may well seek a second opinion, but won't be successful if he or she tries to go over the physician's head. A second opinion, in other words, involves a reconsideration of a diagnosis or treatment plan by a peer of the physician. But no patient would reasonably expect a hospital administrator to overturn a decision made by a resident physician. That's simply not the way professional administrators work. In a hospital, for instance, the administrator may hire the physician, work to see that the hospital is functioning smoothly, and become involved if there are serious or repeated allegations of malfeasance. But in the day-to-day responsibilities of decision making, the administrator trusts physicians to use their professional judgment in determining what patients need and how those needs should be addressed.

In a similar way, the dean of a college or provost of a university shouldn't be expected to intervene in an academic decision that a faculty member or department chair has made in his or her delegated sphere of responsibility. As supervisors, we hire academic professionals whom we trust to use good professional judgment. Appropriate mechanisms are already in place (such as performance reviews, tenure and promotion reviews, and grievance procedures) to ensure that this trust continues to be warranted. Once again we have a wonderful opportunity to help students understand that except in a few very specific situations, their dissatisfaction with a decision made by a faculty member or a department chair is unlikely to be addressed by your office.

Because of their lack of familiarity with the way in which colleges function (and perhaps also because of their immaturity), students will occasionally attempt to use pressure on you. The claim that "I'm not paying this kind of money to be treated this way" has become particularly common at many institutions. Also frequent is a subtle threat: "I know you'll want people like me, as future alumni, to continue supporting the university. But I'm unlikely to feel particularly generous unless you resolve this issue the way I want you to. And I'm not quite sure how the president and board might feel about your unwillingness to help me, if I need to take the problem that far."

When this type of threat or implied blackmail is suddenly dropped into the conversation, your first reaction might be to have the student ejected from your office or to reply in anger. Far more constructive would be a response that takes advantage of this teachable moment to instruct this student in the sort of civility that colleges expect to offer—and receive—in communications with their stakeholders. While you appreciate the student's frustration and are happy that you have made students comfortable enough to approach you with these concerns, there are certain expectations of procedure, discourse, and protocol that the student is expected to follow. Such a response won't satisfy the angriest or most arrogant of students, but it's successful a surprising number of times. At the very least, it sends the message that your office is neither a dictatorship nor subject to intimidation by misdirected attempts at power politics. In extreme cases, you may even want to open this book and show the student this paragraph to make it clear that what he or she may regard as a clever and unique threat is common at colleges and universities all over the world and highly unlikely to produce the outcome he or she has in mind.

The Student Perspective

Students are well situated in the overall organization of the college or university to provide insight into certain important matters about which academic leaders need to know. For example, students will be aware when a faculty member is regularly late for class, cancels courses or labs frequently, and fails to distribute a syllabus on the first day of class. Students will know whether the instructor speaks distinctly enough to be understood everywhere in the classroom. They will know whether classes always consist of only one activity—lecture, discussion, experiment, and the like—or tend to be more varied. They will be aware whether the professor is accessible outside class. Certainly, any experienced administrator expects a certain degree of exaggeration to the effect that "I looked for professor So-and-So every day for a week, and s/he's never in the office." Students often resort to this excuse when they're up against a deadline, have checked once or twice at someone's office door, and couldn't find the person they were looking for at exactly the time they were looking. Students can also provide more subjective information, such as whether they enjoyed a particular course, are likely to recommend that course to a friend, or would probably enroll for another course from the same instructor.

Unfortunately, many course evaluation systems ignore these issues and ask questions that a student is not in a good position to know. Too many ratings instruments ask questions about whether the professor has:

o Remained current in his or her field (a judgment far better left to the instructor's peers)

o Been sensitive to the student's needs (a question that's too easy to misconstrue and that at best calls for a type of mind reading on the part of students)

o Motivated the students to do their best work (an expectation that in most cases reflects more on the student than the faculty member)

Moreover, course evaluations generally ask too many questions of every kind for students to respond to them thoughtfully. Ten questions or fewer are likely to prompt serious reflection, particularly if the scale isn't the same for each question (e.g., all the desirable responses on the left and all the undesirable responses on the right). When there are more than ten questions, students stop paying attention to the specific focus of the question, and the halo effect (where they give professors they like high marks regardless of the question being asked and assign low marks across the board to professors they don't like) begins to take over.

For this reason, deans and provides may find it useful to supplement the imperfect information that they gain from student ratings of instruction with some deeper insights that students can provide for them. The time spent in walking with a student to another office on campus can provide an opportunity to discuss the positive aspects of the student's experience at the institution. Even in cases when students have gone to the administrator's office to make a complaint, they can be asked questions that help them view the situation in its larger context and provide follow-up details based on actual situations, not passions or exaggerations. By posing such questions as, "Do you have your course syllabus with you? Could I see it for a moment?" you can begin to direct the conversation into a more constructive and useful direction. You can see if the faculty member has a policy outlined on the matter of the complaint (missing classes, turning in late work, being available outside class, and so on). You can discuss whether the syllabus was followed or changed frequently. You can review the faculty member's description of what the primary focus of the course will be in order to determine whether the student's perspective has been unrealistic.

In every case, however, it's probably unwise to base a decision on this single discussion or complaint. It's always better to check the student's allegations with the faculty member and with his or her chair. In extremely serious matters, you may even want to interview a few other students from the course in order to determine whether the allegations that you have heard are corroborated by others.

When You Must Act

If your institution doesn't have a uniform student complaint or grievance procedure, you should work in concert with other administrators and legal counsel to develop one as soon as possible. In some cases, having such a policy in place is a requirement of the regional accrediting body governing your institution. In all cases, however, the existence of this policy will provide you with some valuable guidance about when you must act on a student complaint and when you are free to use your own judgment about responding.

Allegations of sexual harassment—and more generally allegations of infringement on an individual's rights that are protected by your institution's policy of nondiscrimination—require immediate action on your part. Your college's equal opportunity officer, affirmative action officer, ombudsman, or some other human resources representative will almost certainly need to be notified. Legal counsel should be brought into the matter early in the process so that you will avoid making a mistake that could have serious implications later. Such mistakes might include not responding quickly or aggressively enough, not respecting the rights of all parties in the allegation, or divulging information in an improper manner. Serious allegations are never matters that you should attempt to address or investigate on your own. Always follow policies carefully, include all appropriate parties in the reporting process, and maintain accurate but highly confidential notes.

Including Students on Committees

Student representation is often valuable on committees, as long as the group doesn't deal with matters that are either highly confidential or outside a student's area of direct concern. Approvals of curriculum, promotion and tenure decisions, investigations of professional misconduct, and the like are certainly best left to faculty peers and supervisors. Calendar committees, event planning groups, committees that interview candidates for faculty positions, strategic planning bodies, and a wide variety of other groups essential to the institution's operation could well benefit from a constructive student involvement. These groups provide significant learning opportunities for the students themselves and can help the college or university avoid implementing a policy or procedure that results in unanticipated student resistance. In addition to your regular committee structure, therefore, you might consider creating a number of groups that operate as cross-functional teams—combined committees of faculty, staff, students, administrators, and other constituents of the college who meet to address specific issues. Cross-functional teams help institutions avoid horizontal tunnel vision, the narrowing of perspective that can occur when department chairs discuss major issues only with other department chairs, deans with other deans, students with other students, and so on.

Partnerships between Academic and Student Affairs

Keeling (2004) discusses an important concept for how we might look at the structure of a university. Rather than isolating a student's experience into such artificial compartments as academic affairs, student affairs, housing, and other campus offices, colleges and universities might regard a student's time at the institution in the same way that students themselves do: as a single, unified experience. In its most basic terms, "*Learning Reconsidered* defines *learning* as a comprehensive, holistic, transformative activity that integrates academic learning and student development, processes that have often been considered separate, or even independent of each other" (Keeling, 2004, 4). A student's development of knowledge doesn't occur only in the classroom. A student's leadership skills don't develop only through cocurricular activities. A student's self-image doesn't develop only through extracurricular activities. All aspects of a student's collegiate experience can be improved through careful, intentional integration of the goals that we have, as administrators and faculty members, with the goals that student affairs professionals have.

Breaking down the artificial barriers that many institutions create through their nomenclature and internal structures can be of great value in providing students with the rich, life-improving experience that we want college to be for them. If this philosophy has not yet been adopted by your entire institution, it is even more important for you to begin your own efforts in this regard. If instead of the traditional divisions of the college or university, what programs and offices might fall into a division of student success, division of student research, and division of institutional outreach? Even if you can't actually create this new structure at your college or university, thinking of what the institution does rather than where stakeholders are housed can provide insights that improve the way in which you interact with students.

Conclusion

Although students are the most important stakeholders a college or university has, many of the people who work there have relatively little direct contact with students. Offices in human resources, payroll, building maintenance, purchasing, and community relations exist to help improve the student experience but often do so in ways that don't require much interaction with students. As deans and provosts, academic leaders are well positioned to serve as the students' advocates with these offices when there are needs that aren't being met and as the public voice of these offices when student requests (or even demands) become unreasonable. Although we usually don't interact one-on-one with as many students as faculty members or student life personnel do, our role in providing academic programs of the highest caliber means that our impact on everyone affected by a student is very great indeed.

REFERENCES

Buller, J. L. (2013). *Positive academic leadership: How to stop putting out fires and start making a difference*. San Francisco, CA: Jossey-Bass.

Eagle, L., & Brennan, R. (2007). Are students customers? TQM and marketing perspectives. *Quality Assurance in Education, 15*(1), 44–60.

Finney, T. G., & Finney, R. Z. (2010). Are students their universities' customers? An exploratory study. *Education + Training, 52*(4), 276–291.

Keeling, R. P. (Ed.). 2004. *Learning reconsidered: A campus-wide focus on the student experience*. Washington, DC: National Association of Student Personnel Administrators and American College Personnel Association.

Lomas, L. (2007). Are students customers? Perceptions of academic staff. *Quality in Higher Education, 13*(1), 31–44.

Tight, M. (2013). Students: Customers, clients or pawns? *Higher Education Policy, 26*(3), 291–307.

RESOURCES

Bok, D. (2005). *Our underachieving colleges: A candid look at how much students learn and why they should be learning more*. New Haven, CT: Princeton University Press.

Braskamp, L. A., Trauvetter, L. C., & Ward, K. (2006). *Putting students first: How colleges develop students purposefully*. Bolton, MA: Anker.

Cuthbert, R. (2010). Students as customers? *Higher Education Review, 42*(3), 3–25.

Hutton, J. G., Leung, V., Mak, A.K.Y., Varey, R. J., & Watjatrakul, B. (2011). Students, patients, citizens, and believers as "customers": A cross-national exploratory study. *Journal of Nonprofit and Public Sector Marketing, 23*(1), 41–70.

McDaniel, T. R. (2003). Academic standards vs. customer service. In McDaniel, T. R. (Ed.) *Dean's dialogue* (pp. 5–8). Madison, WI: Magna.

Nathan, R. (2005). *My freshman year: What a professor learned by becoming a student.* Ithaca, NY: Cornell University Press.

Nealon, J. L. (2006). *College and university responsiveness to students-as-customers: The reorganization of service delivery in the enrollment service arena.* Ann Arbor, MI: ProQuest /UMI.

16

PARENTS

There was a time not long ago when neither deans nor provosts would have had much contact with the parents of current or prospective students. Perhaps over the course of a new student orientation or family weekend, an administrator might make a short presentation to parents or mingle briefly at a social event. The presentation itself was likely to focus on the prestige and history of the institution, and it may have included some sober warnings about the intellectual rigor of the program that the parents' child was enrolled in. "Look to the family on your right. Now look to the family on your left," I recall a dean saying on one of these occasions back in the 1960s. "The student who comes to us from one of your three families won't be here at this time next year." Many academic leaders may remember hearing similar pronouncements early in their careers. What was then regarded as a realistic assessment of the institution's high academic standards would today probably be challenged by a parent asking, "So why aren't you doing more to increase your retention rate?"

The days of limited administrative contact with parents are gone, probably forever, and that's a good thing. Parents now expect to play a vital role in their children's academic experience even in college. I vividly remember the event that caused me to walk to my president's office one day and announce, "I've just seen the future, and I don't like it." It was the first day I received a call from the parents of a graduate student, complaining about the grade their son got the previous semester in a PhD course. Those occurrences are still thankfully rather rare, but the age of the student and the level of the degree program they are in are no longer barriers to the very active involvement in their children's education.

There are a number of reasons for this change. Many more parents than in previous generations are themselves college graduates, and these parents often have preconceived notions of what their children's experience should be on our campuses. The ease of communication that's possible because of cell phones, e-mail, desktop videoconferencing, instant messaging, and other forms of technology means that many parents are in contact with their children at college several times every day. The rise of what Cline and Fay (1990) dubbed "helicopter parents" (parents who always seem to be hovering over their children in the background) has had an impact on the way in which colleges and universities everywhere do business.

While in certain situations parents can be strong allies for administrators in helping to secure additional resources, potential students, and media exposure for the school's achievements, parents can also occupy a disproportionate amount of an academic leader's time, provide a great deal of aggravation over extremely minor issues, and require deans to develop a special set of communication skills. What, then, are the most common issues that provosts and deans should be aware of in dealing with parents of students? We can begin answering this question by noting a key principle:

> We're used to considering issues by seeing them through a number of lenses: What will the president/donors/trustees/alumni/faculty/students think about this issue? How does it look from that stakeholder's perspective? To this set of lenses we now must add an additional consideration: How will parents view this decision?

If we do so, we'll understand that parents may not know things about higher education that we as professionals take for granted and that part of our job is to communicate the reasons for our decisions in terms that resonate with them.

What Parents Often Don't Know

The specific duties assigned to deans and provosts vary widely from institution to institution. In addition, people who don't work in higher education on a daily basis may even be confused by the very title *dean* or *provost*. Some parents mistake the dean for the president or chancellor, thinking that he or she runs the entire institution. Others are bewildered by the sheer variety of deans that universities sometimes have (dean of this college, dean of that college, dean of students, dean of admissions, dean of multicultural affairs, dean of advising, dean of residential life, associate dean, assistant dean, and so on). It's not surprising, therefore, that parents are often unaware of the appropriate issues to bring before a particular dean. Thus they may call an academic dean when their child is having a quarrel with a roommate. They may contact the dean of students when their child missed a deadline on a tuition payment. They may write to the dean of admissions on any issue, since that dean may have been the first administrator whom they encountered at the institution and the only one they feel they know. The term *provost* is even more baffling to many people. Very few people outside of higher education (and not even everyone within higher education) understand where the responsibilities of the provost begin and how this position relates to that of the president and dean. If they think about the role at all, they may regard the provost as something like a university ombudsman: the person to call whenever they want to issue a complaint or have a problem solved.

Even parents who have a legitimate academic issue to discuss with you may not always understand the role you play as a supervisor of the faculty. Like the students discussed in chapter 15, they may see you only as a faculty member's "boss," the person who will intervene to change a grade that is lower than they would like, waive a departmental requirement that is proving inconvenient to their child, or permit their child to participate in commencement exercises without having completed the minimum requirements. Just as you may need to explain the difference between a customer/business relationship and a client/professional relationship to a student, so too may you need to engage in this discussion with parents. You may be called on to explain why academic requirements are what they are, what rights academic freedom guarantees to professors, and why certain decisions are delegated by you to individual academic disciplines. It may well be that the policies of your institution are different from what they were when that parent was a student. It may be, too, that your college's policies are different from those of other institutions with which the parent is familiar. "Look," you may be told, "I *know* it's possible to do this at Prestigious University, and obviously you don't know what you're doing." As difficult as these exchanges become, the best approach is often to explain—with firmness but also with civility—why you will not grant an exception and whether the parent has any further avenues of appeal.

If you're a parent yourself, it can be useful to try relating to the student's parent on that basis. "I fully understand how you feel," you might say. "I'm a parent myself, and since we always want what's best for our children, it can be aggravating to be faced with a situation where our children are hurting. But as a parent, I can assure you that I would never do anything that wasn't in the best interests of the students entrusted to us. In fact, the reason that this policy exists is ..." That strategy doesn't always work, of course. Despite your best efforts to calm the parent down, there will always be situations in which you're accused of simply being uncaring and not listening, have the parent hang up (or storm out of your office), or threaten to contact the president, governing board, or an attorney. Even though those threats are not often acted on, a situation that ends in this way should immediately be reported to your supervisor and the institution's legal counsel. You don't want them to be blindsided if this situation turns out to be one of those infrequent cases where the parent does not let it ago after talking to you.

Parental Rights to Information

Helicopter parents are used to being having involved in every aspect of their children's educational, social, and extracurricular lives. As a result, they have no reason to believe this degree of involvement won't continue now that their sons and daughters are in college. For this reason, they may claim certain rights, which they may no longer have, simply because they're paying for tuition, and they may expect you to provide them with information that is inappropriate or illegal to provide.

For this reason, every dean and provost can benefit from becoming acquainted with these essential websites:

- www.law.cornell.edu/uscode/text/20/1232g, which contains the full text of US Code 1232g; 34 CFR Part 99, commonly known as the Family Educational Rights and Privacy Act (FERPA) or the Buckley Amendment. The site also includes notes and updates on the law.

- www2.ed.gov/policy/gen/guid/fpco/ferpa/leg-history.html, which outlines the history of FERPA.

- www2.ed.gov/policy/gen/guid/fpco/ferpa/index.html, the government's official FERPA site, which contains any updates made to or changes in the law.

- www.legalarchiver.org/hipaa.htm and www.hipaasurvivalguide .com/hipaa-regulations/hipaa-regulations.php, which presents the full text of the Health Insurance Portability and Accountability Act of 1996, PL 104–191, 110 Stat. 1936 (HIPAA).

- www.uh.edu/legal-affairs/contract-administration/pdf-documents/ HIPAA%20Guidelines%20%207.14.11.pdf, a concise analysis provided by the University of Houston on what the administration, faculty, and students need to know about HIPAA and its impact on institutions of higher education.

FERPA legislation dates back to 1974 when it was signed into law by President Ford and quickly amended by Senators James Buckley of New York and Claiborne Pell of Rhode Island. The intention of the law was to limit access to confidential educational records of their children to parents—and parents only. Significantly, however, FERPA rights revert to the students themselves when they turn eighteen years of age or enter a postsecondary educational institution. While FERPA does allow certain rights to parents who claim a child as a dependent for the purposes of federal income tax, these rights are not automatic and often require parents to file a request for each specific request for access to a child's educational record. Most colleges and universities, too, have developed forms by which students may waive their FERPA rights, but not all students sign such a form and institutions are highly reluctant even to be perceived as requiring or coercing such a signature. Parents may sometimes ask, "If there was a form on which my child could waive FERPA rights and have me notified of what's going on, why didn't you tell me about it?" From the institution's perspective, completion of these forms involves the surrender of a legal right, and few institutions want to be perceived as encouraging individuals to surrender their rights.

The rights that students have under HIPAA are somewhat similar. This federal law was sponsored by Senators Edward Kennedy and Nancy Kassebaum and signed into law by President Clinton. While its major thrust is to protect the insurance coverage of workers when they leave their jobs and set standards for the electronic storage and transfer of health information, it also imposed stringent new restrictions about who has access to an individual's private health records. In most cases, once a student turns eighteen, his or her health information can no longer be shared with parents without the student's consent. Like FERPA, HIPAA has provisions allowing the student to waive that right, and institutions commonly provide forms to do so. Those forms have combined FERPA and HIPAA waivers into a single document, but it's not at all uncommon for schools to provide separate forms, which are then held by separate offices, since the type of information governed by the two laws is so different.

One of the other ways in which HIPAA requirements affect deans and provosts is releasing confidential health information to those inside the institution. For example, if an administrator has knowledge that a student is undergoing treatment for severe depression, is it permissible to notify the student's faculty members? That information may be helpful to professors who could then take steps that would help the student stay on track in his or her courses, and it may be critical information if there's reason to believe the student's depression could lead to suicide or harming others. Because of the complexity of these issues, most universities have created crisis response teams that are authorized to receive certain types of health information and know the intricacies of HIPAA for the purposes of understanding who also can be informed and under what circumstances. For this reason, it's always better for a dean and provost to work through one of these crisis response teams than attempting to act independently.

When contacted by a parent whose request may require the release of FERPA- or HIPAA-protected information (including a question like, "I just need to know … is my kid going to class/flunking out/turning in assignments/likely to graduate this spring?" or "Why is my son [daughter] going to the health center so often?"), you should never provide this information without thoroughly understanding how your institution handles FERPA and HIPPAA requests, whether the student has submitted a waiver allowing the parent to be given the information that is requested, and whether your institution allows you to disclose protected information orally as opposed to disclosure in writing only. Moreover, even in cases where a waiver has been signed and all institutional policies allow you to speak with the parent, it is probably preferable for you to suggest meeting with the student, the parent, and (in the case of academic or disciplinary issues) any faculty members whose courses are relevant to the matter in question. Having all of the individuals who are involved in the situation gather together in a single place is far preferable to a long exchange of telephone calls or e-mails in which any number of statements may be misunderstood or misreported. When the faculty members themselves are present, the student will be less likely to exaggerate his or her own record of attendance in the course or completion of required course assignments. When the student is present, he or she will know precisely what has been disclosed to the parent and will have the right either to reaffirm his or her FERPA and HIPAA rights or waive them in accordance with the parent's wishes. Moreover, with the parent present, you will know directly what has and has not been revealed in case the parent should raise the issue again in the future.

Helping Students Succeed

Parents naturally want the best for their children. They want their son or daughter to succeed in their academic work, be happy, and graduate with sound career prospects in sight. Frequently, however, they don't know the best way to go about achieving these aims. Sometimes the parents haven't been to college themselves and assume that colleges work in the same way as elementary, middle, and high schools. At other times, parents who have gone to college attended a very different type of institution or at a time when colleges were organized in different ways from the structures of universities today. At the very least, most parents have experienced college only as students themselves and thus may not have a good understanding about how colleges and universities work today. They may not understand the differences between such offices as business affairs and financial aid since both deal with money, and they may not know which course-related questions should be directed to your office and which to the registrar since both of you deal with grades.

As a means of clarifying many of these issues, it can be extremely useful to establish a parents' council. The purpose of the parents' council is to help parents get the information they need and channel their natural inclination to help their children into constructive directions. In order to be effective, a parents' council shouldn't be too large; councils of larger than thirty tend to get unwieldy and are almost impossible to bring together at a single time that's convenient to all members. Moreover, a parents' council should consist of parents of students at all levels of the programs you offer.

Many schools provide a parents' council only for those involved in their undergraduate programs. As we saw, however, parents of graduate students are increasingly remaining actively involved in their children's education. Failing to include them can be a detriment when issues arise that affect the student body as a whole. At the same time, if you're the dean of a professional college, it's likely that the parents you work with would largely be drawn from the families of juniors and seniors, with perhaps only a few representatives of those whose sons or daughters anticipate declaring a major in one of your disciplines. If you're the dean of arts and sciences, you may wish to draw your parents' council membership from those with children completing general education courses (who perhaps rotate off the council if their child declares a major in another college) and those with children who intend to graduate with one of your majors.

Parents' councils can be useful to the dean or provost in a number of ways. First, like any other advisory body, they can give you advance notice of issues that might otherwise blindside you. Second, they can be powerful advocates in helping you make the case for additional faculty lines or facility improvements, since it'll be their own children who will benefit when these requests are granted. Third, they can intervene with other parents who may not understand how the college works or who may be encountering a difficulty with one of their children. Having someone who is able to say, "I experienced that very same problem with my child, but here's why it ended up working out for the best," can make a case to another parent that you, even if you are a parent yourself, may not be able to make due to your position. Fourth, a parents' council can be invaluable in helping you recruit additional students, make contact with potential donors, raise funds for various projects vital to the college, or secure goods-in-kind contributions to benefit your programs. Finally, parents' councils can be good training programs for other boards that your college or university may have. You'll have an opportunity to see who has creative ideas and the stamina to see them through, who has excellent management skills, and who may be well intentioned but is ultimately ineffective.

Conclusion

With the increasing involvement of parents in their children's education, few deans and provosts are likely to be in positions where they have no contact whatsoever with parents of current or prospective students. The more that academic leaders try to anticipate what issues the parents of their students are likely to have and the more they start viewing issues through the lens of "How would I see this if my child were a student in this program?" the more effective they will be in assisting this important segment of any college's external constituency.

There's a relative lack of good resources available to help college administrators deal effectively with parents. Fortunately, some works that deal with matters from the parent's own point of view, such as Bane and Bane (2006), Barkin (1999), Savage (2009), and Cohen (2012), or that are intended for administrators at the precollege level, like McEwan-Adkins (2005), contain a great deal of information that is useful for provosts and deans as well. It can also be valuable to survey the books about college life written for students and their parents because they sometimes contain misinformation that make an administrator's job more difficult. An example of the latter is Traci Maynigo's *A Girl's Guide to College: Making the Most of the Best Four Years of Your Life*, which advises students to move out of their residence hall rooms if they feel threatened or if a relationship with a roommate has become dysfunctional: "If you complain enough (and get your parents involved), your college dean will make the arrangements for you" (Maynigo, 2003, 37). Such misinformation only exacerbates the problems that students and parents have of finding the right office to help solve their problems.

REFERENCES

Bane, M.E.W., & Bane, S. (2006). *I'll miss you too: An off-to-college guide for parents and students*. Naperville, IL: Sourcebooks/Sphinx Publishing.

Barkin, C. (1999). *When your kid goes to college: A parent's survival guide*. New York, NY: Harper.

Cline, F., & Fay, J. (1990). *Parenting with love and logic: Teaching children responsibility*. Colorado Springs, CO: Piñon Press.

Cohen, H. (2012). *The naked roommate: For parents only; a parent's guide to the new college experience*. Naperville, IL: Sourcebook EDU.

Maynigo, T. (2003). *A girl's guide to college: Making the most of the best four years of your life*. Boulder, CO: Blue Mountain Arts.

McEwan-Adkins, E. K. (2005). *How to deal with parents who are angry, troubled, afraid, or just plain crazy* (2nd ed.). Thousand Oaks, CA: Corwin Press.

Savage, M. (2009). *You're on your own (but I'm here if you need me): Mentoring your child during the college years* (Rev. ed.). New York: Fireside.

RESOURCES

Carr, M. P., Carr, K., Carr, A., & Carr, E. (2012). *Sending your child to college, 2011: Prepared parent's operational manual*. Washington, DC: Dicmar Trading.

Coburn, K. L., & Treeger, M. L. (2009). *Letting go: A parents' guide to understanding the college years* (5th ed.). New York, NY: Harper Perennial.

Johnson, H. E., & Schelhas-Miller, C. (2011). *Don't tell me what to do, just send money: The essential parenting guide to the college years* (2nd ed.). New York, NY: St. Martin's.

Spohn, M. (2008). *What to expect when your child leaves for college: A complete guide for parents only*. Ocala, FL: Atlantic Publishing Group.

Whitaker, T., & Fiore, D. J. (2013). *Dealing with difficult parents (and with parents in difficult situations)*. New York, NY: Routledge.
    The following websites have been developed by universities on what administrators and parents need to know about the Family Educational Rights and Privacy Act:

University of North Texas, www.unt.edu/ferpa/

University of Illinois, registrar.illinois.edu/staff/ferpa_tutorial/
    The following websites have been developed by universities on what faculty and staff need to know about the Health Insurance Portability and Accountability Act of 1996:

Tulane University, tulane.edu/counsel/upco/hipaa-training.cfm

University of Florida, privacy.health.ufl.edu/training/

17

FACULTY

In some ways it's redundant to devote a separate chapter to the academic leader's relationship with the faculty: almost everything a provost or dean does involves interactions with the faculty either directly or indirectly. As a result, the issues explored in nearly every chapter of this book affect and are affected by the faculty in some way. And yet because faculty members loom so large in the ecosystem of the provost or dean, the way in which we relate to them deserves its own special attention. Although organizational charts depict administrators as occupying an institutional level above the faculty, the truth is that an excellent relationship with faculty members can be a key to success, a troubled or dysfunctional relationship an almost guaranteed path to failure. You can't say the same thing about any other constituency dean and provosts may have.

As academic leaders, we're often directly involved with departments when they develop job descriptions to hire new faculty members. Most deans and at least some provosts interview candidates for a full-time teaching or research position. We either evaluate faculty members ourselves or have general oversight of the process by which they are evaluated. We sign off on tenure and promotion applications, often playing a critical role in that process by either concurring with or overturning recommendations made at the department level. We participate in posttenure reviews. On rare occasions, we may need to terminate or not renew the contract of a faculty member who's not performing as well as anticipated. We almost certainly were once faculty members ourselves and may still see ourselves primarily as members of our institution's corps of instruction and research, perhaps teaching a course or publishing our own scholarship whenever we can.

It's strange that while administrators often speak at length about their leadership philosophy with regard to students, they rarely have given as much thought to their leadership philosophy when it comes to the faculty. Because of an otherwise laudable effort to reshape our institutions as "student-centered learning environments," we sometimes act inadvertently in ways that cause the faculty, our most important resource, to feel unappreciated. So the major questions to consider in this chapter are as follows:

○ How do we act in such a way as to improve morale and reward outstanding effort without being perceived as weak, gullible, or beholden to the whims of prima donnas (who, we may as well admit, appear on the faculties of nearly every institution)?

○ Is there a way to be supportive of the faculty—to be, in essence, a faculty-friendly administrator—while still keeping the institution's overall needs firmly in view?

○ How can we be advocates of the faculty when we're also responsible for evaluating and, when necessary, sanctioning them?

Maintaining the right balance can be difficult, but it's more likely to be achieved by adopting an intentional approach to building the right relationship with the faculty.

Faculty Development and Developing a Faculty

Nearly every college or university has a faculty development program. Unfortunately, many of these programs are not well developed. They fund travel to conferences and perhaps offer a series of workshops, often on the topic of technology in the classroom. In some cases, a center for excellence in teaching and learning may help faculty members explore the most effective methods of instruction in various settings. Research offices may assist faculty members with grant proposals and identifying sources of funding for scholarly projects that are too large to be pursued within the institution's regular budget. Some institutions, too, may sponsor highly developed First-Year Faculty Experience programs (see Buller, 2012) or teaching circles, scholarship networks, and service alliances (see the online premium content for Buller, 2012) that promote colleague-based support for the various duties assigned to most faculty members.

In addition to these efforts, there's a great deal more that provosts and deans can do to provide truly comprehensive faculty development programs, and the rewards are well worth the effort. A well-constructed faculty development program improves morale, illustrates that the institution's central administration has its priorities straight, and most critically adheres to the following essential principle (see Gillespie and Robertson, 2010).

Genuine faculty development provides training, support, and improvement of every aspect of a faculty member's professional responsibilities.

In other words, faculty development efforts that focus simply on teaching, scholarship, service, advising, or any other single aspect of a faculty member's duties are too limited in their focus to be highly effective. They can send the wrong message about what an administrator considers to be important (e.g., a program that focuses almost exclusively on how to obtain grants to fund cutting-edge research at a "teaching first" institution) and can mislead faculty members about the activities that the institution will reward during the tenure and promotion process.

As you review the faculty development efforts for which you're responsible, begin by asking yourself the following questions:

- What are the central activities at which my faculty needs to excel?
- How can I assist my faculty in performing those activities?
- If the faculty evaluation system at my school assigns differing weights to teaching, scholarship, and service for the purposes of promotion and tenure, do our faculty development efforts address those responsibilities in roughly the same proportion?
- Do we provide training in how faculty members can be most effective as members or chairs of a committee?
- Do we provide guidance to advisors not merely in the requirements of our programs, but also in the role that they should play in mentoring students?
- Do we assist faculty members not only in attending conferences and providing subvention for publication expenses where necessary, but also in learning about how to contact publishers effectively, how to prepare an abstract for consideration, and how to organize their résumés for the greatest impact when applying for research fellowships?
- Do we in academic affairs work collaboratively with the office of sponsored programs in exposing faculty members to ways of finding external funding sources and how to go about writing and submitting a successful grant proposal?
- Do we discuss instruction not only in general terms about "how to teach well at the college level," but also in how to take full advantage of the resources, teaching techniques, and approaches to active

learning that have a demonstrated record of success in the disciplines represented by our programs?

○ Do we assist faculty members with the resources available to them when they suspect that students are facing severe health or psychological problems?

○ Are faculty development activities offered in a variety of formats and at different times so that even adjunct faculty members can take full advantage of them?

If you didn't answer yes to all of these questions, then you have abundant opportunities to expand the faculty development program in your area and meet a broader range of faculty needs. Of course, there's no reason that you need to offer all these services yourself. Partnering with appropriate offices on your campus (e.g., a center for excellence in teaching, an office of sponsored programs, or a human resources center), administrators in other colleges if you're a dean or at nearby universities if you're a provost, or the institution's president can relieve some of the extensive work involved in a truly comprehensive faculty development program. If the programs you supervise are large enough, assigning a faculty member, associate dean, or assistant to the provost to serve as a director of faculty development can also be useful for achieving this goal quickly.

Of equal importance to faculty development, however, is the matter of developing a faculty. In other words, faculty development efforts tend to focus on the needs of individual faculty members, but developing a faculty involves finding ways of helping your faculty work better together as a team. (See chapter 11.) If faculty development focuses largely on people and their individual needs, then developing a faculty involves taking stock of your corps of instruction collectively, balancing the various abilities they have and the contributions they're in a position to make. In fact, developing a faculty begins even before someone is hired. Too often when we set up searches, we focus merely on the area of academic specialty that we want in programs, forgetting about the other factors that can make a faculty member successful as a member of the college. There may be nonacademic areas of expertise (such as grant writing, serving as liaison with accreditation bodies, fundraising, mediation, and long-range planning) that your programs need for their ongoing success. If your institution has a mission that emphasizes excellence in instruction, ask yourself whether your job descriptions and search announcements make it clear that teaching is the most important thing you do. Even more important, ask yourself whether the interview process gives you adequate exposure to each candidate's teaching abilities in realistic settings. If the advising load for a position is likely to be heavy, do you ask prospective candidates to address their prior success in this area? If the faculty member will be working with relatively few colleagues in his or her field of specialty or is expected to cooperate with members of other departments in an interdisciplinary program, is this expectation featured prominently in all of the materials related to the search? As a general principle, it's a good idea to approach each search by asking not merely what academic field prospective candidates should represent, but also what qualities they should have, what value-added components would be most important to your program, and what nonacademic contributions each new faculty member will be expected to make.

Strategic Hiring

Faculty members at times find it difficult to understand why a college or university may wish to view vacant faculty lines not simply as "curricular areas that need to be filled," but as opportunities to meet the institution's larger objectives. For this reason, academic leaders may find it useful to begin the hiring process with a series of candid discussions with faculty about why a "whole institution approach" to staffing is preferable and ultimately benefits everyone. For instance, if the school lacks diversity in gender, race, or ethnicity, it's probably not appropriate to declare, "Rather than searching for a faculty member in such-and-such a discipline, this year we're going to seek an excellently qualified faculty member in whatever area can best diversify our ranks." But if you begin your discussion with the faculty by talking about your current lack of diversity, the reasons that improving in this area is pedagogically important for your students, and your openness to consider any number of solutions that will adequately address this issue (provided, of course, that you really are open to more than one possible solution), you may discover that your faculty can be extremely creative in proposing ways of improving the situation you've outlined.

Similarly, if the program's overall needs lie in some other area—such as improved advising, greater grant activity, a more complete international perspective throughout the curriculum, better cooperation with other units at the school, or whatever other goals you may have, it's probably best to be open about your desire to address this need from the beginning of the search. "Look," you might say, "we know we've got a huge challenge coming up with our accreditation review in three years, and none of us has the sort of expertise we're going to need to be successful with that process. Maybe the most important thing as we begin this search isn't the precise academic specialty someone represents but all the other 'value-added' components we're going to need: success in writing accreditation self-studies, excellent teaching in our general education courses, the willingness to advise students from a broad range of disciplines, and so on. I think that if we're creative enough, we can create a job description that reflects what we really need rather than define our positions too narrowly in terms of academic field. After all, we're not going to find someone who has the capabilities we're looking for if we're not clear about what we really want."

One of the most critical areas of developing a faculty arises when it comes time to identify candidates who are likely to be good colleagues. Nevertheless, "success in supporting an atmosphere of collegiality" is rarely seen in search announcements. As a result, committees tend not to emphasize collegiality in their screening of candidates, in the questions they ask references, and in the hypothetical situations they discuss with the candidates themselves. The result, all too often, is a new professor who fills a desirable academic niche but whose uncooperative behavior is ultimately destructive for the program. As the business executive Mac Anderson says in the title of his book about hiring the right people, *You Can't Send a Duck to Eagle School* (2007). You can hope all you want that you can ignore the red flags that arise during a search and make a candidate change his or her behavior once on the faculty, but that hope is almost certainly doomed to failure.

> You're more likely to be able to transform a nice person into a brain surgeon than you are to transform a noncollegial brain surgeon into a nice person.

Given the opportunity, most faculty members are willing to be flexible about a candidate's academic field provided that he or she is likely to contribute to overall morale and make the institution a more productive place for faculty members to work and students to learn. Strategically hiring individuals who have demonstrated their willingness to work cooperatively as members of a team, refrain from harping on pet issues or perceived injustices, and promote both civility and the free exchange of ideas can contribute immeasurably to a college's overall growth and success. As you've probably already discovered, even one noncollegial faculty member in a unit can greatly increase everyone's dissatisfaction with the institution and, in extreme cases, send productivity plummeting.

Another type of strategic hiring, often called *cluster hiring*, occurs when you set out to hire an entire team of faculty members with complementary specialties who together can greatly improve an existing program or position the institution as a leader in a new area. Cluster hiring typically occurs across disciplines and is often used to address needs that can't be met within any single academic field. For example, hiring a bioengineering cluster might involve bringing in a group of faculty members in biology, engineering, chemistry, nursing, and business. Although all of them would have their own specialties, they would each work in areas that contributed in a significant way toward the goal of providing a strong core of teaching and research related to bioengineering. Although it can be valuable to hire a "prepackaged" team of faculty members in a new area where the institution wants to establish an instant reputation, financial realities are such that most provosts and deans will use this type of strategic approach to strengthen an existing area of excellence. In doing so, the questions to ask are, "In which important fields are we already very good? What is missing from the areas that stands between use and true distinction, even greatness?"

Faculty-Friendly Policies

One way of building a sense of teamwork with the faculty is to examine current policies and procedures for signs of anything that may be serving as an obstacle to faculty success. For example, we sometimes lose highly desirable faculty members to other institutions not because we are outbid in terms of salary, but because faculty members have complicated lives that we could make easier if only we thought to do so. Among the policy changes that you might propose for discussion with your president and governing board are the following.

A tenure stop-clock policy

A six- or seven-year probationary period for untenured faculty members was originally created for the protection of the faculty. Such a policy prevented institutions from keeping faculty members untenured for long periods of time and then suddenly dismissing them so that they could be replaced with lower-paid junior faculty members. For this reason, an up-or-out tenure policy has proven to be in the long-term best interests of the faculty as a whole. However, the inflexibility of tenure policies can create unnecessary problems for certain individuals. For example, instructors who have young children or must care for an aged parent may have difficulty meeting the challenges of their day-to-day lives while at the same time meeting all of the institution's expectations in the areas of teaching, scholarship, and service. To address these needs, institutions may consider developing a tenure stop-clock policy. Truman State University in Missouri has such a policy:

> The University recognizes that unique, individual circumstances can play a significant role in the professional development of its faculty and that consideration should be given in instances when those circumstances impose extraordinary disruption to a faculty member's professional life. The birth/adoption of children, illness, military service, and other similar occurrences may delay or disrupt professional accomplishment that should be considered in the tenure decision. Tenure-eligible faculty who find themselves in a position where personal circumstances might impair their capacity to build the record of accomplishment judged appropriate for the tenure review may exercise the option to request "stopping the tenure clock" for a specified period. A request for stopping the tenure clock may be made for a one-semester or one-year period. A second request may be made for a second year, but in no case will a faculty member be permitted to stop the tenure clock for more than two years. Any faculty member who may desire a tenure clock stoppage should consult with his/her dean, who will consult with the Vice President for Academic Affairs. (facultyhandbook.truman.edu/FacHndbkCHPT-4.pdf)

A spousal placement policy

Academics frequently are members of two-career families. There are numerous cases of faculty members who have had to forgo full-time academic appointments because their spouses were offered attractive positions and they accompanied them. "Trailing spouses" (sometimes referred to as the "two-body problem") can have a significant effect on the family's happiness, likelihood of remaining in the region, and quality of life. For this reason, institutions may wish to develop policies for appropriate career placement of faculty members. At some institutions, full-time positions are created for spouses to the extent that budgets allow. At other institutions, spouses have access to placement services that work aggressively to locate appropriate full-time positions for them. The University of Notre Dame provides an example of the second approach:

> Candidates for faculty and staff positions at the University of Notre Dame often have a spouse or partner who is also seeking professional opportunities in the area. The University of Notre Dame Dual Career

Assistance Program offers customized job search assistance to qualified couples who face the dual career challenge. hr.nd.edu/employment -opportunities/dualcareer/

Our services are available to:

○ A spouse or partner of a new permanent faculty or staff member who is being employed by the University through a regional or national recruitment effort, or

○ A spouse or partner of a continuing faculty or staff employee who is seeking job search assistance.

Priority is given to those individuals whose spouse or partner has been employed at the University less than one year.

The Dual Career Assistance Program does not create an entitlement to employment nor does it guarantee a position. Assistance will be extremely hampered if a client does not have authorization to work in the United States. hr.nd.edu/employment-opportunities/dualcareer/ eligibility/

Services Available

○ Pre-offer spousal or partner consultations during the interviewing stage.

○ Job search assistance.

○ Contact information of network partners and networking assistance.

○ Access to job openings at the University.

○ Introductory letter to area employers or hiring officials at the University.

○ Resume/curriculum vitae and cover letter critique.

○ Assistance with interviewing techniques and salary negotiations.

○ Information about local employment demographics.

○ Other information that may be useful in a job search. (hr.nd.edu/ employment-opportunities/dualcareer/services/)

A residential assistance plan

In some areas of the country, there is a wide discrepancy between levels of faculty salaries and the cost of affordable housing. Residence assistance plans consist of any number of approaches to address this problem, including subsidized housing in university-owned homes, low-cost mortgages, down payment assistance, programs where institutions and owners share the equity in a home, reduced rent, incentives to purchase homes in economically depressed areas, and interest-free second mortgages. For instance, the office of the president at the University of California oversees an innovative Office of Loan Programs to assist with faculty retention:

> The Office of Loan Programs designs, delivers and manages housing assistance programs for the recruitment and retention of faculty and senior managers in support of the education, research and public service missions of the University of California. (www.ucop.edu/facil/olp/)

Merit and Equity in Setting Salaries

Throughout most of higher education, faculty members assume that their salaries will reflect seniority, merit, and (in many cases) market factors relative to their discipline (Arreola, 2007). While certain faculty reward systems emphasize one of these factors over the other, the assumption tends to be that the longer a faculty member's service is and the higher the quality of that service has been, the more the faculty member will be paid. All too frequently, however, the systems in which we work lack adequate mechanisms by which to determine whether faculty salaries are truly equitable. Certainly we can compare average salaries for the various ranks at our institutions to the averages found at our own list of peer or aspirational institutions or by consulting the American Association of University Professor's annual salary study, the Oklahoma State University annual salary study (irim.okstate.edu), and the average salary studies conducted by many professional organizations. But these data, while certainly informative, fail to provide everything that we need to know. They almost always provide only salary information without either longevity or quality indicators. They usually include institutions far different from our own. And they're of relatively little help when we want to ask ourselves the question, "Is it appropriate that Professor A is being paid more than Professor B?"

Fortunately, it's fairly easy to perform your own internal salary analysis using readily available software and a bit of creativity. It doesn't take a great deal of technological expertise to set up a database or spreadsheet containing the following fields for each full-time faculty member in the programs you supervise.

- o Name.
- o Rank.
- o Discipline.

○ Base salary for the current academic year. Be sure to convert everyone who's not paid on a nine-month basis to an equivalent nine-month salary. This process will help you make more accurate comparisons, comparing apples to apples, as it were. Use base salary only, ignoring overloads, administrative stipends, externally funded research salaries, summer school, and the like. These factors certainly add to an individual's overall compensation package, but for comparison purposes they simply distort the statistics.

○ Years at the institution.

○ Years in current rank.

○ Years of college-level teaching. Use only full-time years. Ignore years of part-time work as a graduate teaching assistant and the like, which will provide you with a more consistent set of data.

○ Years of teaching, including any years of full-time service that people may have had teaching at the pre-college level.

○ Years of experience—years of teaching plus years of all other full-time adult service in the workforce in any capacity.

Once you've entered this information in a database or spreadsheet, you can easily generate charts or scattergrams that plot salary on the vertical axis against years of experience (determined by years of college-level teaching, years at the institution, years in the workforce, and so on) against the horizontal axis. The name field will allow you to identify individuals whose information appears on your chart, particularly those who are outliers. The rank and discipline fields allow you to separate out different groups of faculty members for more precise comparisons if you need them. For various groups, you may find that different ways of quantifying experience (at the institution, in rank, college-level teaching, all teaching, or workforce experience) may be more useful or descriptive than others. You can also use the database or spreadsheet to generate averages of both your salary figures and your preferred indicator of experience. The result might be an initial graph that looks something like the chart in figure 17.1.

This graph, which is easy to generate, provides a great deal of information. First, the linear regressions or trend lines (which a spreadsheet can generate automatically) provide a sense of how salaries at each rank have been progressing over time. For assistant professors, there is a steep rise. It appears that you've been doing well with those recently hired in terms of having salaries reflect seniority. The trend line flattens substantially for associate professors and begins to rise again for the full professors.

Figure 17.1 Sample Graph of Faculty Salaries

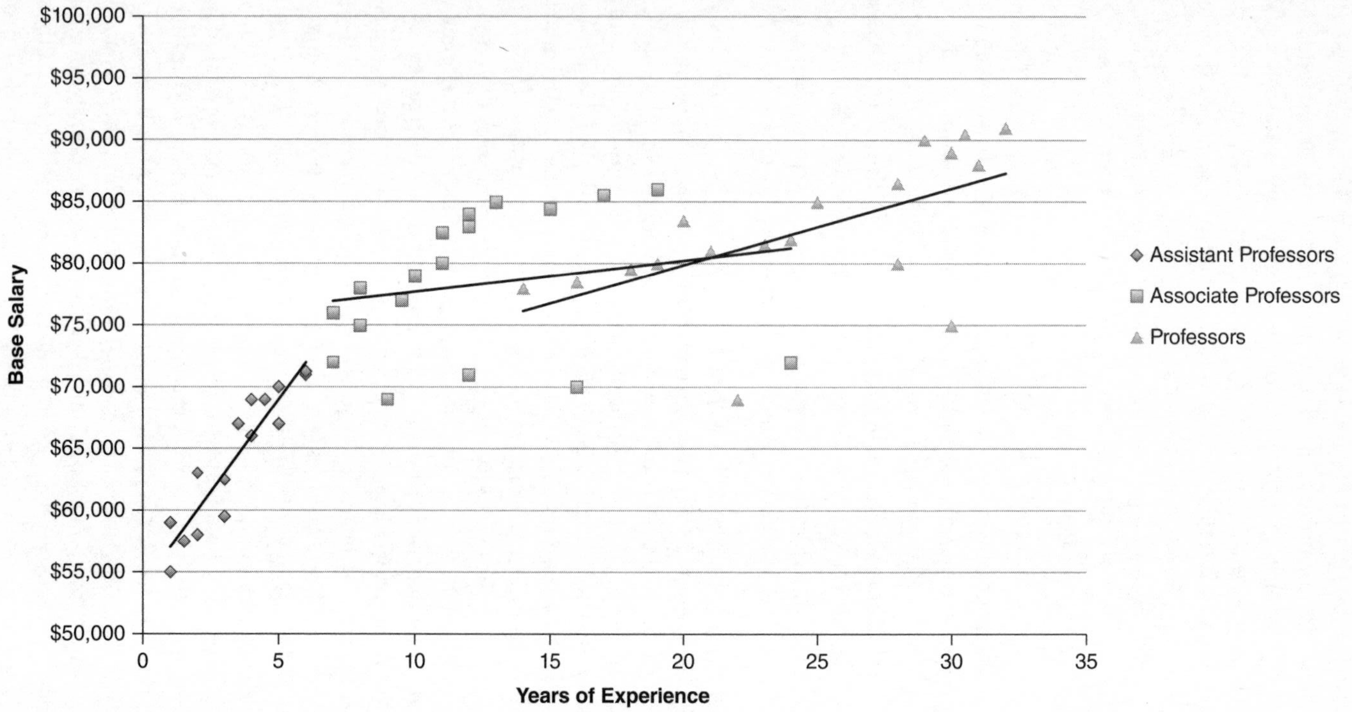

That result is fairly typical. There are almost always a number of people on the faculty who are sometimes referred to as terminal associate professors: their performance was good enough to earn them tenure and their first promotion, but their research was never abundant enough to earn them promotion to the rank of full professor (Buller, 2014). Since these faculty members are often those whose merit increases are low due to limited performance and never receive the adjustment that accompanies becoming a full professor, their salaries are often modest relative to their years of experience, thus flattening the trend line for their rank. The fact that the slope increases again for full professors is a good sign, but there's reason to be concerned about how much flatter that line is than the one for assistant professors: it means that you could have some severe cases of salary compression or inversion on your hands within a few years.

Second, the graph shows that a certain amount of salary inversion has already begun. Notice how the full professor line intersects the associate professor line. There are several faculty members with roughly twelve to twenty-five years of experience whose salaries may require some investigation. For example, an associate professor with thirteen years of experience is making $85,000, while a professor with fourteen years of experience is making $78,000. Similarly, an associate professor with nineteen years of experience is earning $86,000, while a professor with twenty-two years of experience is making only $69,000. There may be reasons for these discrepancies—the associate professors may be rising stars in fields with a great deal of market pressure on salaries, but the professors may be underachievers in fields with little market pressure—but you'll want to know what those reasons are. If you find that the discrepancies cannot be reasonably explained, you may want to be proactive about addressing these cases of salary inequity before they begin to affect morale and staff retention.

Third, there are other individual cases on the graph to explore. At twelve years of experience, three associate professors have different salaries: $71,000, $83,000, and $84,000. Since you can't explain these differences in terms of seniority, what other factors account for such a broad range? If you can defend those differences in terms of performance, market factors, and career path—such as might occur if the faculty members with the two highest salaries worked all twelve years in higher education, but the lowest-paid faculty member worked more than half that period in an unrelated industry—then you've at least done your due diligence. But if the only difference you can find is one of race, gender, or ethnicity, that's a red flag of a problem that needs to be addressed.

To aid in this process of determining whether salary differences are justifiable, it can be valuable as a next step to separate each rank and

Figure 17.2 Sample Salary Trend Analysis

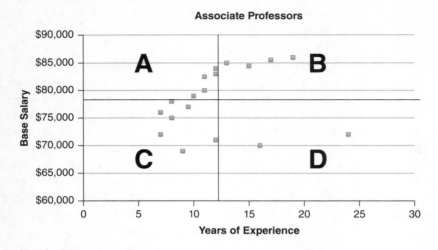

study it individually in greater depth. For instance, if we isolate associate full professors on this chart and then plot the point where their average salary meets their average number of years of experience, we discover that faculty members in this rank have an average of 12.25 years of experience with an average salary of $78,306. (For small faculties where extreme outliers would skew the data, it's better to use medians than averages, but for this example, the differences are negligible.) By breaking the graph into four quadrants around that point of average salary and average years of experience, we get a good illustration of how the associate professors in our program are trending. (See figure 17.2.) Faculty members whose information falls into quadrants B and C are trending normally. Their salaries are rising fairly consistently with their years of experience. The bulk of the faculty should fall within these two quadrants. Quadrant A contains faculty members whose salaries are rising faster than the average in terms of their experience: these should be the best performers or those in fields with the greatest market pressure. Quadrant D contains faculty members whose salaries are rising more slowly than the average in terms of their experience: these should be the weakest performers or those in fields with extremely little market pressure. Graphing the data in this way gives you an opportunity to ask several important questions:

o Do the people in quadrants A and D deserve to be there? If someone challenged me about this information, would I have a reasonable explanation?

○ If I don't have a reasonable explanation, what's my plan for fixing the problem?

Once all of this information is recorded in a spreadsheet, you can easily add other fields and perform further analysis. For instance, if you have some statistical expertise, you could use more advanced linear regressions or mathematical modeling to determine precisely which combination of factors tends to correlate most closely with a faculty member's salary. That insight can become a key element in planning for how you go about making faculty compensation more equitable and faculty rewards more closely tied to the goals of your institution and programs.

Workload Equity

Just as research takes on different forms in different disciplines, so do other types of faculty workload vary by discipline. While there may be an institution-wide standard of the number of credits a faculty member is expected to teach, these standards are usually based on what used to be typical fifty-minute periods of lecture and discussion. The problem is that very few disciplines are really typical anymore. In addition to the relatively common deviations from regular lecture/discussion courses—such as laboratory sections, private studio instruction, thesis supervision, student teacher supervision, and internship supervision—the changing nature of higher education continually offers new challenges. How, for instance, do we count a course in load if the same lecture/discussion section simultaneously involves students at multiple sites through distance learning and podcasts, while other students are also enrolled in the course online? As technology continues to evolve, the number of questions like these will only increase. While disciplinary accrediting bodies frequently provide guidance in establishing equivalences between, say, private music instruction and standard lecture sections, it's all but impossible to develop a table of equivalencies for every new technology that may arise. For most provosts and deans, the result is either inequity resulting from failure to recognize the added workload created by new technologies ("It doesn't matter how many different delivery mechanisms are involved in this course; you're only getting credit for one section") or inequity resulting from instituting numerous "private deals." For this reason, you're far better off being proactive by establishing a committee that provides recommendations on how to resolve questions of load. Workload is simply one of those matters where equity may not be the same as absolute equality. At some level, professional judgment will always have to come into play.

Faculty Senates and Assemblies

Faculty senates (which usually include elected representatives) and faculty assemblies (which may include representatives but also are sometimes open to anyone who cares to participate) are part of the political reality of the ecosystem in which deans and provosts operate. It's not uncommon for these groups to be among the most challenging constituencies for academic leaders to deal with. The faculty members who are attracted to service in a senate or assembly are sometimes those who have a particular issue to advance or complaint to air. They're often senior faculty members who, protected by tenure, are not intimidated by the status of a senior administrator. And since work on a faculty senate or assembly is time-consuming, the people who serve in these capacities are frequently those who care about issues deeply and insist on having their voices heard. Since the political environment of institutions is so different, strategies for working with groups that are quite effective in one environment may not work at all in another. Nevertheless, here are a few principles to consider that are useful as starting points:

1. To the greatest extent possible, treat the members of the faculty senate with civility and respect. Even if they adopt an antagonistic attitude toward you, there's no reason that you need to adopt a similar attitude in return. Remember that although you're an administrator, you're also a faculty member. If the situation were slightly different, you might be making the same arguments to your own dean or provost. As aggressive as some members of the faculty senate or assembly may be at times, you're really all on the same side. You all want what's best for the students, the institution, and the academic disciplines you represent, so there's no profit to be gained from being confrontational when you don't need to be.

2. Although a faculty senate or assembly can sometimes be quite vocal, these bodies actually have quite limited power. Ultimately it's the administration that's charged with developing and enforcing most policies, and even when the faculty may disagree with a decision you've made, they usually can't overturn it. If they're protected by tenure, you're protected by your job description and your supervisor's support for you. As bad as having the faculty pass a vote of no confidence against you can be, even an action that extreme is in reality only a recommendation to the president and the governing board. Academic leadership means refusing to be intimidated by confrontational situations, no matter how unpleasant they may be. The best advice is to be polite but to stick up for your own principles at the same time.

3. Probably the most important principle to keep in mind is to be candid in your dealings with faculty governing committees. Nothing will undermine the authority of an academic leader faster than the perception that he or she isn't acting with integrity and is trying to take action behind closed doors. Just as you don't want the faculty senate to blindside you, so you should take care not to blindside its members. Give them advance warning if a policy change is being considered. Make clear who will be making the decision and what the process will be. Most people would rather be aware of a decision they disagree with than be in the dark about issues they regard as vital to their welfare. Candor doesn't earn trust immediately, but it lays the foundation for trust that can be built on over time.

In fact, with regard to this third principle, it's often useful to keep in mind the following:

> In the end, candor is always preferable to secrecy.

Given the choice, you're better off having the faculty disagree with you than distrust you. As academics, we're all used to disagreement. We respect diversity of opinions and, regardless of our personal perspectives, tend to be convinced that in a free exchange of ideas, the most reasonable argument will win out in the end. Once you sacrifice trust, however, you'll never gain it back. You'll find that even your best intentions are treated with suspicion, and you'll have made your job much more difficult than would have been the case if you'd been open and honest with your faculty from the beginning.

Curricular Committees

Curricular committees are different from other faculty bodies because in the system of shared governance, matters dealing with the curriculum are delegated from the administration to the faculty. What can a dean or provost do, therefore, in a situation where the faculty is clearly making a curricular decision that is not in the best interests of the students or the institution as a whole? For example, what can you do if a faculty curriculum committee decides to eliminate a program that you regard as absolutely vital or refuses to implement reforms that you think are desperately needed? Here again the unique political environment of each institution makes it extremely difficult to articulate hard-and-fast rules about interacting with every kind of curricular committee that may exist. In general, however, there are several good guidelines to keep in mind:

1. Since responsibility for the curriculum almost always resides with the faculty, the power relationship you have with regard to this issue is different from what occurs with most other issues. For this reason, when dealing with a curriculum committee, it's wise to remember everything discussed about moral suasion in chapters 10 and 11. Make the strongest case that you can, being sure to point out the benefits to the students (and, whenever possible, to the faculty members themselves) that would result from what you suggest. Emphasize the logic of your argument. Don't pull rank, but also don't underplay the experience you've gained in higher education. You have perspectives that the members of the committee may not have. Share those perspectives, but in a way that recognizes the authority the curriculum committee has to make decisions in certain areas.

2. If after making the best case that you can, the decision still doesn't go your way, choose your battles. Is this a matter that'll still seem relevant five or ten years from now? Or is it a situation where you can afford to let it go without any great damage being done? If the impact won't be critical, it's better to focus on other issues than to keep this one alive after a decision has already been made. Deans and provosts who can't tolerate "losing" on any issue are putting personal image above the good of their programs. Even many issues that seem very important at the time don't prove to be worth all the aggravation they once caused. So reflect carefully on whether keeping the matter alive will be worth it in the end.

3. If the matter does prove to be important, work to build coalitions but not conspiracies. You may be able to get the matter reconsidered if you can persuade a core group of opinion leaders that your arguments have merit. In doing so, however, it's important not to appear as though you are simply trying to undermine a matter of faculty prerogative. Redirect attention as often as necessary to the issue itself, not to your desire for the position taken by faculty on the curriculum committee to be ignored. Let others in your coalition help make the case. Yours shouldn't be the only dissenting voice ever heard on this issue.

4. In truly critical matters, rely on the authority you do have. In the US Congress, if there's a disagreement with a policy set forth by the president, the House and Senate have the power of the purse, set forth in the appropriations clause of the US Constitution, to withhold funding for that policy. You may have similar powers at your disposal. You could

refuse to allocate the funding, faculty lines, or permission to fill a vacant position as a way of preventing an inappropriate curricular decision from being implemented. By doing so, of course, you are adopting an antagonistic response that could widen the rift you have with the curriculum committee and perhaps even the faculty as a whole. This strategy is something of a nuclear option to be used only in the most serious circumstances.

Conclusion

Virtually everything a provost or dean does affects the faculty in one way or another. If academic leaders approach their responsibilities with an attitude that they're part of the faculty and seeking common goals, it's possible to achieve impressive goals while still maintaining high morale even in the most troubled of times. But once administrators start thinking of faculty members as "them," a group with entirely different priorities from "us," morale and productivity are almost always guaranteed to suffer. Good provosts and deans work in such a way that faculty members trust them. Excellent provosts and deans work in such a way that faculty members trust themselves. And the best provosts and deans understand the importance of investing in people.

> The best provosts and deans don't really build programs.
> They build people.
> And the people build the programs.

REFERENCES

Anderson, M. (2007). *You can't send a duck to eagle school: And other simple truths of leadership*. Naperville, IL: Simple Truths.

Arreola, R. A. (2007). Making merit pay decisions. *Department Chair, 17*(3), 5–6.

Buller, J. L. (2012). *The essential department chair: A comprehensive desk reference*. San Francisco, CA: Jossey-Bass.

Buller, J. L. (2014). Mentoring the terminal associate professor. *Department Chair, 25*(2), 15–17.

Gillespie, K. H., & Robertson, D. L. (Eds.). (2010). *A guide to faculty development*. San Francisco, CA: Jossey-Bass.

RESOURCES

Alstete, J. W. (2000). *Post-tenure faculty development: Building a system for faculty improvement and appreciation.* San Francisco, CA: Jossey-Bass.

Bain, K. (2004). *What the best college teachers do.* Cambridge, MA: Harvard University Press.

Buller, J. L. (2007). Mentoring challenges: Tailoring advice to the individual. *Department Chair, 17*(3), 22–25.

Buller, J. L. (2010). *The essential college professor: A practical guide to an academic career.* San Francisco, CA: Jossey-Bass.

Cambridge, B. L. (Ed.). (2001). *Electronic portfolios: Emerging practices in student, faculty, and institutional learning.* Washington, DC: American Association for Higher Education.

Gerber, L. G. (2014). *The rise and decline of faculty governance: Professionalization and the modern American university.* Baltimore, MD: Johns Hopkins University Press.

Heath, M. (2004). *Electronic portfolios: A guide to professional development and assessment.* Worthington, OH: Linworth.

Kelly, T. (2006). *A case study of a college faculty's use of technology, professional development and perceptions of organizational support.* Ann Arbor, MI: ProQuest /UMI.

Kramer, G. L. (2004). *Faculty advising examined: Enhancing the potential of college faculty as advisors.* Bolton, MA: Anker.

McDaniel, T. R. (2003). Leading the faculty: A dean's definition. In McDaniel, T. R. (Ed.) *Dean's dialogue* (pp. 9–12). Madison, WI: Magna.

Middaugh, M. F. (2000). *Understanding faculty productivity: standards and benchmarks for colleges and universities.* San Francisco, CA: Jossey-Bass.

Murray, J. P. (2000). *Successful faculty development and evaluation: The complete teaching portfolio.* San Francisco, CA: Jossey-Bass.

Poskaner, S. G. (2001). *Higher education law: The faculty.* Baltimore, MD: Johns Hopkins University Press.

Quinn, S. S. (2006). *The organization-based self-esteem, institutional belongingness, and career development opportunities of adjunct faculty at a small northeastern college.* Ann Arbor, MI: ProQuest /UMI.

Saroyan, A., & Amundsen, C. (Eds.). (2004). *Rethinking teaching in higher education: From a course design workshop to a faculty development framework.* Sterling, VA: Stylus.

Shadiow, L. (2013). *What our stories teach us: A guide to critical reflection for college faculty.* San Francisco, CA: Jossey-Bass.

Smith, D. G., Wolf, L. E., & Busenberg, B. E. (1996). *Achieving faculty diversity: Debunking the myths*. Washington, DC: Association of American Colleges and Universities.

Sorcinelli, M. D., Austin, A. E., Eddy, P. L., & Beach, A. L. (2005). *Creating the future of faculty development: Learning from the past, understanding the present*. Bolton, MA: Anker.

Turner, C.S.V. (2002). *Diversifying the faculty: A guidebook for search committees*. Washington, DC: Association of American Colleges and Universities.

18

DEPARTMENT CHAIRS

Like provosts and deans themselves, department chairs play roles that can vary considerably from institution to institution. Particularly at small schools, the department chair may simply be a member of the faculty who serves as a clearinghouse for routine administrative matters such as course schedules, textbook requests, and budget requisitions. Chairs of this kind may have no supervisory authority over other members of the department whatsoever and may not be compensated with either release time or even stipend. At more complex institutions, the department chair may be hired from the outside specifically to work as a chair. In these cases, department chairs function as first-level administrators who may supervise their departments' mission in the areas of teaching or scholarship while doing relatively little teaching or research themselves. Between these two points on the spectrum, there are almost endless varieties of department chair responsibilities in between.

Whatever the job description is for chairs at your institution, it's likely that if you're a dean, you'll have significant interaction with department chairs. If you're a provost, you'll work extensively with deans who are themselves interacting with chairs daily. As a result, building strong relationships with department chairs can make all the difference between having your plans succeed and having to deal with seemingly endless problems. This chapter explores some of the best ways to promote the best possible relationship between your office and your department chairs, including how you can help your chairs succeed (thus encouraging them, in turn, to help you succeed).

Provide Training

Chairs frequently rise to their positions because they've demonstrated some level of administrative acumen, have the confidence of faculty members in their departments (at least at first), and have shown their willingness to balance their scholarly pursuits with the challenges of administration. All too frequently, however, institutions provide little or no specific training for chairs—or for any other kind of administrator, for that matter. While nearly every university has established a center dedicated to the improvement of instruction and the scholarship of teaching and other programs exist to help those wishing to pursue research or service projects, very little training tends to be available for those who are expected to perform administrative tasks. For most chairs, the only training they receive in the area of budgeting occurs by trial and error when they've been put in charge of a budget.

> The worst thing about learning through trial and error is that it requires you to make a lot of errors. Effective training is a shortcut to experience.

In many cases, the sole guidance that's provided to chairs in making decisions and resolving complex personnel issues is provided by a mentor, and only when a serious problem already exists. The experience they gain in how to interview a candidate properly may derive from their own experience with other searches. For all these reasons (as well as many others), colleges and universities need to offer better administrative training, and you, as an academic leader, are in an excellent position to begin making these improvements.

The quickest way to begin providing training for department chairs is to tie into an existing program that already offers administrative training:

o The American Council on Education (ACE, www.acenet.edu/leadership/Pages/default.aspx) and the Committee on Institutional Cooperation (CIC, www.cic.net/faculty/academic-leadership-development) conduct successful leadership training programs that can benefit chairs at any type or size of institution.

o IDEA Education offers a feedback system for department chairs (ideaedu.org/services/department-chairs), as well as access to consultants in a wide variety of administrative areas (ideaedu.org/services/consulting-services).

o Kansas State University sponsors the annual Academic Chairpersons Conference that assembles experts on a variety of topics related to leadership issues in higher education (www.dce.k-state.edu/conf/academicchairpersons).

○ Each summer Harvard University conducts several intense programs in academic leadership development. Among these offerings, the Management Development Program best fits the needs of department chairs and other midlevel administrators (www.gse.harvard.edu/ppe/programs/higher-education/portfolio/management-development.html).

○ Publishers that specialize in topics related to higher education, such as Jossey-Bass (www.departmentchairs.org/online-training.aspx) and Magna Publications (www.magnapubs.com/online/seminars/), regularly sponsor webinars on issues important to chairs and offer short DVD courses.

Private training firms, such as the Center for Creative Leadership (www.ccl.org), ATLAS: Academic Training, Leadership, and Assessment Services (www.atlasleadership.com), the Center for the Study of Academic Leadership, the Academy of Academic Leaders (www.academicleaders.org), and Elite Leadership Training (www.eliteleadershiptraining.com) conduct workshops on site at host universities or at regional conferences (or both). They also offer the services of consultants who can coach individual chairs on possible solutions to their most pressing problems.

To complement these external resources—or if you prefer a more highly focused program for department chairs that addresses your own institutional needs—you might consider offering a series of administrative training workshops that you develop yourself (Gmelch and Buller, 2015). Many outstanding models for such a program exist. Yen, Lange, Denton, and Riskin (2004) discuss an innovative program that began at the University of Washington's ADVANCE Center for Institution Change and offers guidance to department chairs on such issues as these (advance.washington.edu/apps/resources/docs/WEPAN_paper_UW_Leadership_Workshop.pdf):

○ Dual-career hires

○ Making the transition from associate to full professor

○ Faculty development opportunities

○ Dealing with difficult people

○ Offering feedback and delivering bad news

○ Providing family leave and tenure clock extensions

○ Nominating faculty members for awards and recognition

○ Building consensus among the faculty

○ Making job offers

Other topics that department chairs are likely to find useful in a training program include:

o Planning and implementing budgets
o Leading change
o Communicating effectively
o Promoting student leadership
o Conducting faculty evaluations
o Promoting teamwork and collegiality
o Coaching or mentoring a colleague
o Using data to inform decisions
o The chair's role in assessment
o Legal issues
o Work/life balance
o Time management
o Conflict management
o Departmental outreach
o Responding to an emergency or campus crisis
o Strategic and tactical planning
o Developing departmental mission and vision statements

Rather than simply bringing in guest experts who lecture in the workshops, it's usually far more effective to include pedagogically effective techniques such as role playing, case studies, what-if situations, and scenario analyses. Just as students tend to benefit more from active and interactive methods than from passive learning, so will partici-pants in your administrative development series. By offering practical, hands-on experience for your chairs, you'll help them understand the principles you're trying to convey and relate them to their day-to-day professional activities.

One other way of structuring your own series for department chairs is to organize it around one of the many books that address the respon-sibilities of academic administrators. Such works as Barron (2003), Bennett and Figuli (1990), Buller (2012), Buller and Cipriano (2015), Chu (2012), and Hecht, Higgerson, Gmelch, and Tucker (1998) provide topics and discussion points for workshops. Alternatively, you might begin with your institution's own job description for department chairs and build a series that addresses each of the primary responsibilities contained in that document. Of course, if your institution doesn't already have a clear job description for department chairs, you now have a great opportunity to work cooperatively with your fellow academic leaders in creating such a document.

Provide Mentoring and Coaching

All chairs can benefit from working with a mentor or coach from time to time. But new chairs in particular find it valuable to work closely with a mentor (a more experienced chair who provides guidance in various aspects of administrative responsibility) or a coach (an expert in a particular administrative function, such a decision making or public speaking, who works intensively with the chair in an area of demonstrated need). The mentoring relationship might be informal, such as a lunch every month or so in which the new chair has an opportunity to ask questions, or it may be arranged much more systematically with set meetings, formal reports on progress, and a designated date at which the series of sessions will officially end.

It's often easier for chairs to ask questions and request help in individual meetings than in a group setting. Many people are intimidated by the thought of asking a "stupid question" in front of a group or of expressing publicly their need for help. Local mentors are most useful when the chair needs to learn about aspects of the job specific to that institution, such as whom to ask about various issues, how to complete required paperwork, deadlines that are likely to rise with very short notice, and so on. External mentors or coaches may be more valuable when dealing with administrative tasks in general, such as how to deal with difficult personnel problems, how to balance the many competing demands for one's time, the challenges of working with other administrators, and making decisions effectively.

In certain cases, it may be necessary for you to serve as the mentor for a new chair, but this solution is rarely desirable. It blurs the distinction between your roles as a supervisor and as the chair's confidant and advisor. Mentoring a chair may prevent the person you are advising from being as candid with you as he or she needs to be. Moreover, this type of arrangement gives chairs no opportunity to vent or receive advice when the greatest frustration that they're facing has been caused by you as the provost or dean!

Informal Meetings

We often end up playing some sort of role in our official capacities. For example, we present ourselves to stakeholders as defenders of our disciplines, advocates for the underdog, upholders of high academic standards, guardians of tradition, gadflies of the elite, or any of the numerous other identities we may assume in order to advance our personal agendas. At times, these roles are so familiar and natural to us that we're hardly even aware that we're still playing them. After all, assuming a public identity in this way is something that pretty much everyone does when dealing with people who aren't in their family or close circle of friends. It allows us to understand people because we can pigeonhole them. "Ah, she's a liberal," we conclude and thus have an immediate context against which to evaluate her future words and deeds. But playing that kind of role can also be quite limiting. The persona a chair assumes in public can prevent the dean or provost from getting to know that person as an individual. It can similarly prevent chairs from being able to see their provost or dean as a person rather than simply as a voice for the administration. One effective way to surmount this obstacle is to establish opportunities for you to interact with chairs in unofficial and informal ways.

For example, some academic leaders have monthly book discussions with chairs where novels, current nonfiction, and other works that have absolutely nothing to do with either management or college adminis-tration are discussed for an hour or so at a time. Other administrators sponsor informal lunches on the days when they meet with department chairs where the ground rule is that no one may discuss matters that have anything to do with the college, the university, or their jobs. Still others hold discussion groups where each chair in turn is responsible for intro-ducing a topic of personal interest (with preference given to pursuits that are not directly related to the business of the institution) and to initiate a brief discussion. All of these approaches help you to get to know your chairs better outside their official roles and allow them to view you as someone other than just "the boss."

Focused Meetings and Mini-Retreats

While deans (and sometimes provosts) certainly benefit from regular meetings with their department chairs in which decisions are made and policies are discussed, there's also value in conducting mini-retreats—meetings focused on specific topics once or twice a term. These focused meetings allow you to explore a single issue in greater depth than you have the luxury for in the course of a regular meeting. Focused sessions might be devoted to such matters as legal issues and the changes in higher education law that are relevant to department chairs. In another meeting, you might explore assessment with the chairs, allowing them to learn from one another about best practices for assessing whether students are attaining their learning outcomes and giving you an informal progress report on how these assessment efforts are progressing. Another meeting might be devoted to enrollment trends, where you explore likely student demographics for the future, how these enrollment patterns may affect each discipline, and specific courses where there have been histories of over- or underenrollment. Still another session might be devoted to the university budget and include a presentation by the vice president for finance or operations who could provide an overview of how the institution receives and allocates its funding.

Every institution has its own unique needs in the area of mini-retreats and focused meetings, but you'll find that occasional sessions of this sort are far more productive than a series of regular meetings devoted to a miscellany of items that happened to be proposed for that particular agenda.

Effective Retreats

Retreats can be effective uses of time—as long as they aren't overused and have a clear goal (see chapter 11). That's especially true for chair retreats. Many schools host retreats for department chairs every year, even when there's no compelling reason for asking busy people to carve a day or two out of their schedules. The assumption is that the retreat will serve for team building, provide an opportunity to accomplish a good deal of concentrated work, and reward the participants for their past effort by offering them meals and, in most cases, a chance to work in an attractive setting off campus. The problem is that even the most luxurious of retreats rapidly lose their effectiveness when they become commonplace. Without a genuine reason for taking people away from their other responsibilities, annual retreats often cause department chairs to resent the loss of time they could have been spending on other (and, in their minds, more productive) pursuits.

Even worse, some provosts and deans aren't careful about when they schedule chair retreats. They set them at awkward times, such as just before courses begin in the fall or between terms when the workload for chairs can be particularly heavy. Since the provost or dean is the person who has mandated the retreat and since the chairs report to this person, they may not feel comfortable expressing their feeling that the time and money spent on this activity could be better directed elsewhere, but they often feel that way all the same. The practice thus leads to complaints behind the scene, lowering morale and ultimately undermining the authority of the provost or dean.

These problems don't mean that you should never conduct a retreat with chairs, however. Just be sure that a retreat is the best possible way of fulfilling the task you've planned. You'll need a substantive agenda, such as occurs when an institutional reaccreditation is about to begin, there's a new strategic planning effort under way, or a capital campaign is ready to be launched. "Planning for the coming year" is rarely a sufficient reason for scheduling a retreat. It leads to cynicism among the chairs and the suspicion that the provost or dean is simply inventing work for them to do. (See Liteman, Campbell, and Liteman, 2006.) So if you find yourself scheduling retreats every year and have difficulty filling all the time you've set aside, it's probably a good idea to reconsider whether formal retreats are the best possible means of achieving the goals you have for your chairs.

The Internal Advisory Council

It's important for you as an academic to develop a well-rounded view of how your stakeholders view your institution, what its needs are, and what its potential for the future may be. Different groups see issues and priorities in different ways. As we saw with regard to students in chapter 15, including broad representation on cross-functional teams can be valuable in helping you make decisions that won't have unforeseen consequences for those who are currently enrolled in your programs and to attain the greatest amount of support from your student body. Moreover, as we'll see in chapter 24, an external advisory council, if properly organized, can help promote your college in the community, alleviate town-gown conflicts, and move you more easily from "friend raising" to "fundraising." As beneficial as all those groups are, however, it's still a good idea to have an internal advisory council, and a committee of chairs can easily fill this need.

An internal advisory council provides academic leaders with access to a sounding board for new initiatives and can help them avoid policy decisions that are poorly conceived or difficult to implement. Nevertheless, many department chairs aren't used to functioning as advisory bodies. Since you supervise the chairs (either directly or through the dean), they may be reluctant to offer you their candid recommendations, which is the very sort of advice you need the most. At the opposite extreme, some groups of chairs, when canvassed for their opinions, may immediately assume that they are now the decision-making body on all policy matters in the college, objecting angrily when they haven't "approved" or even "been consulted on" matters that you don't regard as within their purview.

In order for your committee of chairs to act as a true advisory council, you'll need to guide them in how such bodies function. One of the essential principles all academic leaders should keep in mind is:

> Never ask an advisory body for its opinion unless you truly wish to be advised.

In other words, an advisory council should never be abused. Don't try to get the group to feed you a recommendation for a plan or policy you've already decided to adopt. At best, the members will sense that they have been duped and become increasingly cynical about the role they're being asked to play. At worst, they may become adamant about a plan or policy quite different from the one you prefer, and your task in advancing your own ideas will now be all the more difficult. If you already know what you're going to do, simply announce your decision, defend it, and try to enlist your council's support. In matters where you truly need advice, however, your chairs can be invaluable. They bring a great deal of experience to the table and understand how certain decisions will play with their students, faculty, and members of the staff. They can help you evaluate decisions from a perspective that you may not have.

Explain to the chairs that in their role as an advisory council, their task is to give you their best professional judgments on matters that you bring to their attention. While the decision as to whether to implement the advice will always remain yours, you are committed to listening to the advice they give you. If you decide to pursue a different path, keep them informed of your decision, explain the reasons that led you to prefer a different path, and value them all the more because they helped you understand an opposing point of view. Explain the difference between the bodies to which you've delegated various decision-making responsibilities (such as a curriculum committee, which may or may not be the same as the committee of chairs) and those to which you turn merely for advice. Discuss the difference between talking a matter through and talking it to death. While you want to allow enough time to consider all the different perspectives on a issue in a thoughtful manner, there will come a time when it's appropriate to move on and to rest the urge to reconsider issues already decided in the past.

Conclusion

Chairs are among the most important constituents you have in performing your job effectively. It's essential for deans and provosts to develop their chairs properly, discuss issues with them candidly, and rely on their expertise respectfully. If you were once a department chair yourself, always keep in mind the special demands of that position. Don't try to continue chairing your own academic discipline—that's no longer your job—but provide the sort of mentoring, guidance, and support that chairs need in order to fulfill this critical administrative role professionally.

REFERENCES

Barron, D. (2003, September 26). Learning to be a department head. *Chronicle of Higher Education*, C5.

Bennett, J. B., & Figuli, D. J. (1990). *Enhancing departmental leadership: The roles of the chairperson*, New York, NY: American Council on Education/Macmillan.

Buller, J. L. (2012). *The essential department chair: A comprehensive desk reference*. San Francisco, CA: Jossey-Bass.

Buller, J. L., & Cipriano, R. E. (2015). *A toolkit for department chairs*. Lanham, MD: Rowman & Littlefield.

Chu, D. (2012). *The department chair primer* (2nd ed.). San Francisco, CA: Jossey-Bass.

Gmelch, W. H., & Buller, J. L. (2015). *Building academic leadership capacity: A guide to best practices*. San Francisco, CA: Jossey-Bass.

Hecht, I., Higgerson, M. L., Gmelch, W. H., & Tucker, A. (1998). *The department chair as academic leader*. Phoenix, AZ: American Council on Education/Oryx Press.

Liteman, M., Campbell, S., & Liteman, J. (2006). *Retreats that work*. San Francisco, CA: Jossey-Bass.

Yen, J. W., Lange, S. E., Riskin, E. A., & Denton, D. D. (2004). Leadership development workshops for department chairs. *WEPAN [Women in Engineering Programs and Advocates Network] 2004 Conference Proceedings*. WEPAN: Albuquerque, NM.

RESOURCES

Coombs, V. (2014). Production relationships with department chairs and program directors. In L. L. Behling (Ed.), *The resource handbook for academic deans* (pp. 241–248). San Francisco, CA: Jossey-Bass.

"Dean X." (2006). Working with an academic affairs council. *Department Chair*, 17(2), 9–13.

Gmelch, W. H., & Buller, J. L. (2015b). *Building academic leadership capacity*. San Francisco, CA: Jossey-Bass.

Gmelch, W. H., & Miskin, V. D. (2011). *Department chair leadership skills.* Madison, WI: Atwood.

Higgerson, M. L. (1996). *Communication skills for department chairs.* Bolton, MA: Anker, 1996.

Lucas, A. F. (2000). *Leading academic change: Essential roles for department chairs.* San Francisco, CA: Jossey-Bass.

McDaniel, T. R. (2003). Dean-department chair relationships. In McDaniel, T. R. (Ed.) *Dean's dialogue* (pp. 25–26). Madison, WI: Magna.

Seagren, A. T., Cresswell, J. W., & Wheeler, D. W. (1993). *The department chair: New roles, responsibilities and challenges.* Washington, DC: ASHE-ERIC Higher Education Report No. 1, George Washington University.

Walvoord, B.E.F. (2000). *Academic departments: How they work, how they change.* San Francisco, CA: Jossey-Bass.

Yen, J. W. (2007). Proactive leadership development for department chairs and emerging faculty leaders. *Department Chair, 17*(3), 12–16.

19

STAFF

The staff in the office of a provost or dean can vary from the large and complex to the nonexistent. "Nonexistent" isn't an exaggeration. In a very small college, the dean or chief academic officer may be assigned, at best, only a single administrative assistant to help with the routine details of day-to-day business. This situation contrasts sharply to what can occur in a large university, where the staff of the provost or a college dean may include several assistant and associate provosts or deans, a communication officer, a budget officer, a number of directors (dealing with a broad range of administrative functions, including advising, faculty development, research, and alumni relations), a webmaster, an event planner, and possibly other administrators as well. Despite these differences, there are similar challenges that academic leaders face in managing their staff regardless of its size. For instance, the most important factor in making sure that a support staff functions effectively is determining not only that all the essential duties of the office are adequately covered, but also that the skills of the staff complement those of the administrator. A provost who tends to focus more on the big picture needs access to staff members who can handle the details. A dean who's not comfortable speaking before large groups needs an associate dean who is skilled in making presentations. An administrative office, when it's functioning smoothly, should operate as an efficient system. Each member of the system should maintain his or her own unique individuality and area of responsibility, but together the office should function as a supportive team, compensating for one another's deficiencies and building on one another's strengths. (For more on how to promote teamwork, see chapter 11.)

As a way of determining how well your own office has progressed toward achieving this ideal, it can be helpful to conduct an internal audit of your staff. If you already have a team in place, this exercise will help you determine where additional training, reassignments of responsibil-ities, or (in the most extreme of situations) replacement of individual members of that team may be necessary. If you have one or more staff openings, the audit will help you develop a clearer picture of the type of person you'll need to seek when you bring in someone new.

A Staff Audit

To conduct an internal audit of your staff, take a blank sheet of paper. Down the left side, identify all the functions, duties, and responsibilities associated with your office. Be as comprehensive as you can, even if the final version of your audit requires several more sheets of paper. As you conduct this exercise, ask yourself questions like these:

- Is our office responsible for overseeing student advising?
- Does it propose and allocate budgets?
- Does it interact with parents?
- Does someone in our office sign off on curricular proposals?
- Are hiring decisions made at this level? (If so, don't forget about all stages of the search process that someone in your office may supervise: requesting positions, approving job descriptions, placing advertisements, collecting dossiers, screening candidates, schedul-ing interviews, selecting a finalist, making an offer, notifying unsuc-cessful applicants, processing paperwork for the new employee, and the like.)
- Does our office run a faculty development program?
- Does our office run a leadership development program for adminis-trators, faculty, or student leaders?
- Do we approve requests for travel?
- Do we evaluate faculty members or other employees, such as department chairs?
- What roles does our office play in the promotion and tenure process?
- If faculty members have complaints or concerns, are they likely to bring them to our office? Who would be the first person to review them?
- Are salary increases recommended or approved here?
- Is our office involved in termination decisions or contract nonre-newals?

○ Does anyone in our office ever interact with the media, plan events, or finalize publications?

○ What is our role during a campus emergency, such as a weather event or campus intruder?

○ What is our role in assessment, accreditations, and program reviews?

○ Do we approve faculty credentials and, if so, is that documentation stored here?

As you create this list of responsibilities, don't overlook seemingly minor functions your staff may have. Does your office ever have visitors who need to be greeted? Does it receive phone calls? Does it file documents? Does it shred confidential materials? Does it prepare items for the mail or for routing to other campus offices? What are the other critical functions that someone in your office must be responsible for?

Once you've filled the left side of the audit with a comprehensive list of the functions, duties, and responsibilities that involve your office, on the right side of the paper list by name and title all the members of your staff. Then draw a line from each item on the left side of the page to one or more of the names on the right side of the paper. Don't draw a line to yourself if you merely have ultimate responsibility for a particular duty but don't actively perform it regularly. Do, however, draw multiple lines if several members of your staff are actively involved in one of the responsibilities you have indicated. Continue through the list until you have connected each duty with at least one staff member. If you find that you have an area of responsibility that isn't clearly assigned to one or more members of your staff, that's the first red flag raised by this audit. Either you have an unmet staffing need (which means that you require additional employees to meet the basic responsibilities of your office) or you haven't designated anyone to be in charge of that responsibility. Both situations are cause for concern.

A responsibility that no one owns is likely to be a responsibility that no one performs.

After you've matched all of your office's areas of responsibility to different members of your staff (noting any area of responsibility that doesn't appear to belong to anyone), the next step in the audit is to examine your results from another perspective. Are there any responsibilities that are connected to too many members of the staff? In other words, are there duties that are so broadly distributed among all the people in your office that it's unclear who's really in charge of them? Certainly it's valuable to cross-train members of the staff in different duties. For example, if only one person knows how to advise students, there can be a real problem if someone suddenly needs a time-sensitive approval in order to override an enrollment limit. If the only advisor in your office is out sick or on vacation, the student either won't be helped at all or will be helped in a way that could cause additional problems down the road. So it's perfectly fine for two or three people to know how to do some task, particularly if it's critical to your mission. But you'll have a real problem if no one in your office can identify the logical first point of contact for students to meet with when they have advising problems. In fact, for certain areas of responsibility, having too many people in charge is worse than having no one in charge. It means that no one will feel authorized to make a final decision or that people may get different answers to their questions depending on whom they ask. So review your duty assignments with an eye toward determining whether there's clearly one person who is known by everyone else in your office as the individual who heads up that task.

Finally, look at your audit to make sure the assignment of responsibilities to particular staff members makes sense. Particularly if the staff is in place for a long time, certain duties tend to fall to certain people because they have the best skills or are the most willing to do them. But from a strictly logical point of view, that allocation of responsibilities may make an office less efficient than it can or should be. For example, having the associate provost make routine updates to the web page because he or she was the first person who learned how to do it may not be the best use of that person's time any longer. Therefore review the audit asking questions like the following:

- Are these duties better reassigned so that one person handles most student matters, another person handles most faculty matters, and a third person handles most staff matters?

- Are responsibilities currently assigned in an inefficient manner so that one person initiates the process but then has to interrupt someone else for a routine signature or approval?

- Are duties assigned in such a way that people who come to your office feel that they're getting the runaround, going to one person for this, another person for that, and a third person (who will end up being at lunch or in a meeting) for yet another aspect of their request?

As you complete this part of the audit, ask yourself how duties might be reallocated in such a way as to get a better or more efficient result while keeping the workload equitable. See, too, if you can explain each person's primary assignment in a few words. If you find that you can't introduce a member of your staff with a short, easily understood phrase, such as "our associate dean primarily deals with faculty matters, ranging from setting up searches through overseeing the promotion process and ultimately to handling requests for emeritus status," then you probably don't yet have a sufficiently clear set of duties assigned to each individual.

Assess Skills

In addition to the areas of responsibility that your office supervises, it's also valuable to identify the various types of training that members of the staff need in order to perform those duties. You can conduct this kind of inventory in the same way you did the last one: outline on the left side of a piece of paper the different skills your office relies on and then record the members of your staff by name and position down the right side. Here are a few of the skills that are needed in the offices of most provosts and deans:

○ *Technology.* What level of technological skill is necessary for at least one member of your staff to have? At some schools, it'll be important for a member of the staff to have advanced knowledge about how to analyze and repair networking problems, set up new hardware and get it running, and interact on a highly technical level with members of the information technology staff. At other schools, such complex technical skills need only be found in a single office that serves the entire institution; someone in a individual administrator's office needs to know about only a few common software applications and whom to call when more difficult problems arise. Remember, too, that mastering your technological needs isn't limited to computer skills. Your office may need someone who can solve problems in smart classrooms, assist faculty members with distance learning and audiovisual problems, perform basic maintenance on research equipment, and the like. It's a good idea to think about all the ways in which your office depends on technology and then consider whether you need at least one person on your immediate staff who can address those issues.

○ *Fact checking.* Administrative offices tend to be inundated with details. Contracts must be issued accurately. Deadlines must be kept.

Information that's shared with the public must be free of grammatical and typographical errors in order to convey a high degree of professionalism. Documents must be easily understood. Names must be remembered. As you think of all the tasks for which your office is responsible, try to determine where accuracy seems the most crucial. Don't just dismiss this part of the inventory by saying, "Everywhere." While it'd be wonderful if every single e-mail, document, and spreadsheet produced was completely without error, there are always going to be aspects of work in which mistakes have a far greater impact. Consider where the biggest problems or greatest embarrassment would result if an error occurred. Then who on the staff has the best skill set to prevent that type of error from occurring?

○ *Budgeting.* All administrative offices tend to be involved with budgeting at least on some level. At smaller or less complex institutions, the skills needed for effective budgeting may require little more than basic bookkeeping or the ability to create a spreadsheet. In more complex environments, a far more highly developed knowledge of accounting practice may be required. Try to determine the level of budgeting skills that are required for your office to do its work. What are the skills you rely on others having when you make a budget proposal for future years, defend that proposal, implement financial decisions made by the president or board, deal with cutbacks, and develop plans for new programs, positions, or facilities?

○ *Event planning.* Next, consider the activities and projects your office oversees. What are the skills needed to ensure that those initiatives proceed in a timely fashion? Do you need someone with formal training in event planning, or is familiarity your institution's calendaring system sufficient for your purposes? What systems do you have in place—or, even better, what systems should you have in place—to make sure that critical deadlines are met and that adequate preparation goes into reports and proposals before they're due? Keep in mind not only lecture series and other major events that are sponsored by your office, but also annual processes at your institution such as promotion and tenure considerations, issuance of contracts, preparation of budget proposals, performance reviews, and other responsibilities for which steps must be completed in a certain order and by a certain deadline. What are the skills that you need in order to make sure none of those deadlines are missed?

○ *Vision.* Is there anyone on your staff who assists you in clarifying your vision for the future? You may be working in a dynamic environment in which your office is responsible for developing and implementing a shared vision for a major new initiative. (See chapter 4.) Or you may be working in a fairly stable environment where the only goal your office has is to do its job this year a little better than it did the previous year. In any case, do you have anyone on your staff who can give you a candid critique of any ideas you may have about improving the curriculum, identifying new sources of funding, or updating your mission as student needs change? Are you in need of someone who can help you think about how to structure programs in radically new ways, an entrepreneur who can address unmet needs in your region, a problem solver who can find practical new solutions to vexing problems your programs are facing, or someone with a great deal of creativity who can introduce new ideas and help you see familiar matters from a fresh perspective?

○ *Interacting with other units.* What sort of relationship does your office have with other units on campus? What sort of requests must be submitted for review elsewhere? What sort of information needs to be retrieved from outside your area? Do you have cooperative programs with other divisions at the institution or your counterpart at another school? Do you supply or receive seats in classes that function as service courses for programs outside those you supervise? Do you share faculty members with other units or offer release time to faculty members to teach outside your unit (perhaps in an honors program, graduate school, or institution-wide core curriculum)? Once you've outlined all the ways in which you might interact with offices outside your own, consider the skill sets you'll need in order to accomplish those goals. Is it a simple matter of completing a form, or does it require the ability to negotiate and the authority to make a decision? Is some degree of institutional memory necessary because of past problems or procedures that aren't written down? Does your institution operate on the basis of "it's not what you know; it's whom you know," with the result that being well connected is an important skill for someone on your staff to have?

Just as you did with the earlier inventory, pay close attention to any skills listed on the left side of the page that you can't associate with any name on the right side. But this time, it doesn't matter if you have lots of people on the staff who have the same skill set. For example, if three or more members of your staff are all excellent proofreaders, prepare highly complex spreadsheets, and are very effective in serving as a liaison to other units, you don't have a problem. It's good to have a high level of cross-training in these skills. But if you can't think of anyone who can perform the necessary task you've listed on your inventory, you've got a problem. Either you don't have the right people in the right jobs, haven't adequately met your staff's needs for training, or are severely understaffed. In these cases, review the missing skills and ask yourself: Which people on my staff should have these skills? It may be that you realize there's a need for a position you don't yet have (e.g., you may need a dedicated budget analyst or event planner), or it may simply suggest to you the type of training you need to provide. In either case, you come away from this exercise with specific information about how to make your staff more effective.

Appointing and Developing Staff Members

Deans and provosts can learn a great deal about how to hire or appoint members of their staff from strategies pioneered at Southwest Airlines, the idiosyncratic company begun in 1971 by Rollin King and Herb Kelleher. Freiberg and Freiberg (1996) summarize the counterintuitive approach to employee development that simultaneously made Southwest Airlines both a highly desirable place to work, with extremely low staff turnover, and a financial success story in an industry where many of its competitors failed. Several of the Freibergs' conclusions about what made Southwest Airlines prosper aren't transferable to an academic setting; they require the profit-centered, hierarchical nature of the corporate world in order to succeed. But other strategies will work in any organizational environment. While provosts and deans are more concerned with producing educated and innovative students than ending the year with a profit, four principles represent important lessons that an academic leader can learn from Southwest Airlines.

Principle 1: Appoint staff members on the basis of qualities you can't teach someone; then teach the other things they need to know

One of the most common mistakes made in appointing staff members is hiring people for all the wrong reasons. For instance, since we use a particular database or student information system at our college or university, we may immediately start screening out any candidate who's not completely familiar with that specific application. Or we need an administrative assistant to help with the clerical functions in our offices, and we reject any candidate who hasn't already worked in higher education. The problem is that we've then made these decisions on the basis of a single litmus test—what we might call the applicant's *surface credentials*, that is, the details that can be easily quantified or reported on a résumé. What then occurs all too frequently is that the person hired proves able to perform that particular function but fails to become an effective member of the team for reasons we never thought to consider while we were evaluating applicants.

Employees succeed on an administrative staff not only because they have the skills needed to perform the tasks that are assigned to them but also because they have certain attributes and characteristics that make them a good fit for the environment in which they're working. As we've all experienced at least once in our careers, a person who's quite effective in one type of institution or program can be utterly disastrous in a different type of professional situation. In our haste to find someone with the perfect surface credentials, we sometimes overlook the intangible factors that affect whether the person will become a valuable asset to our unit.

Southwest Airlines inverted the traditional hiring process by searching for people demonstrating certain attributes and characteristics—in their case, a sense of humor, a willingness to take calculated risks, and an independent spirit—rather than experience in the job they'd be assigned. As Southwest's board chairman and cofounder, Herb Kelleher, once said to prospective employees, "We'll train you on whatever it is you have to do, but the one thing Southwest cannot change in people is inherent attitudes" (Freiberg and Freiberg, 1996, 68). The company's statement of philosophy also summarizes this important principle: "It's difficult to change someone's attitude, so hire for attitude and train for skill" (68). As an academic leader, you might consider appointing staff members in much the same way. Perhaps your next public relations officer doesn't need to have extensive experience in higher education, just excellent people skills, a willingness to learn, a good service ethic, and the ability to be a self-starter. Perhaps everything else can be learned.

As you look at your own staff, it's useful to think of it not just as a collection of discreet job responsibilities, but also as a web of personal attributes. What are those intangible qualities that members of your staff need in order for your entire office to be effective? What qualities are necessary for everyone on the staff to have? What qualities are necessary for at least one person on the staff to have? By thinking about how your office works as a system, not as mere boxes on an organizational chart, it becomes easier to develop a strong and successful administrative team.

Principle 2: Students come second

The next step in building a strong administrative staff is to inculcate a philosophy that in a surprisingly large number of areas, your institution's students are your office's *second* highest priority. Admittedly, this approach runs contrary to the philosophy we hear at nearly every conference and from nearly every professional group. "We exist solely for the students," we're told over and over. "We are a student-centered institution. We always place their interests first." To be sure, that's a perfectly good philosophy for your institution as a whole to have, and it's admirable to see members of the faculty and staff going out of their way to do everything they can in the best interest of their students. (See, for example, Braskamp, Trautvetter, and Ward, 2006.)

The problem is that when everyone is focusing exclusively on the needs (and often also the desires) of the students, no one is looking out for what's in the best interest of your faculty and staff. That's *your* job. If you and your administrative staff also give everyone at the institution the impression that the students are the only people who matter, you're likely to see significant problems in faculty and staff morale, high turnover rates, and an actual decline in service to the students. As counterintuitive as it may seem, your office can serve your college's students better by putting their interests second and the interests of your employees first. By increasing professional satisfaction among those who work at your institution, you'll end up educating your students better.

Keep in mind that a philosophy that "students come second" doesn't mean your office should convey the attitude that "students don't matter." In fact, by putting faculty and staff first, you're creating the best possible environment for students to be served. Members of the faculty and staff will feel that they are truly valued for their contributions, not merely seen as unappreciated laborers whose interests are always insignificant when compared to those of students. By looking out for your college's most valuable assets—literally the most valuable, since personnel costs probably account for between 90 and 95 percent of your total budget—you set your faculty and staff free to look out for the needs of the students. In such a situation, everyone feels valued, and everyone wins. That result does not often occur at institutions driven by a mentality of "it's all about the students." By putting the faculty and staff first, your office is modeling the best possible practice of how a college or university should work. In other words, your focus on the faculty and staff demonstrates the way in which the faculty and staff should focus on the students, who in turn should focus on their studies.

Moreover, the "students come first" philosophy can backfire. As everyone in higher education knows, there will be some students who have an exaggerated sense of entitlement—students who believe that paying tuition (or even having their parents pay the tuition) gives them the right to be rude to faculty and staff, demand to have "inconvenient" policies waived for them whenever they wish, and appeal each negative decision to the next level. By underscoring the sense that "only the students are important," administrations may be exacerbating this culture of negativity, creating a poor learning environment not only for the students who are guilty of this rude behavior but for the rest of the student body as well. By demonstrating to your faculty and staff that you expect them to be courteous to students and focused on their needs but that you will back them up when students have clearly overstepped their boundaries, you end up serving both your school and its students far better.

As the Southwest Airlines statement of philosophy puts it, "Employees are number one. The way you treat your employees is the way they will treat your customers" (Freiberg and Freiberg, 1996, 15). In an academic setting, we might say that the way an administrator treats the faculty and staff helps determine the way that the faculty and staff will treat the students. Moreover, Southwest Airlines has demonstrated a willingness to pursue this philosophy even at the risk of offending a few customers. "While [Southwest Airlines's board chairman] Kelleher gives his customers a great deal and a great time, he's clear that the people of Southwest come first—even if it means dismissing customers! Are customers always right? 'No they are *not*,' Kelleher snaps. 'And I think that's one of the biggest betrayals of your people you can possibly commit. The customer is frequently wrong. We don't carry those sorts of customers. We write them and say, 'Fly somebody else. Don't abuse our people'" (Peters, 1994, 165). Students too are frequently wrong, and in extreme situations it may be up to the dean or the provost to suggest that they find another college.

Putting students second must be carefully distinguished from arguing inflexibly that your faculty and staff are always right. There will be times when, having heard the entire story, you'll have to agree that a student was poorly treated or denied full consideration of his or her rights. Nevertheless, by giving members of the faculty and staff the benefit of the doubt as much as possible, demonstrating that you're interested in their welfare and not just the satisfaction of the students, and supporting your employees in the professional decisions you've delegated to them, you will end up serving all your constituents' best interests.

Principle 3: Stand for something

Every good college or university has a mission statement. Your unit—and probably every program or department within your unit—also has its own mission statement. But now ask yourself, "If I had to write a mission statement for myself and my administrative team, what would it be? Do we actually stand for something as a team or do we just work together for the sake of working together?" In *Joy at Work* (2005), Dennis Bakke writes, "Purpose matters.... People want to be part of something greater than themselves. They want to do something that makes a positive difference in the world" (149). Having a sense of purpose, a sense that being a member of your office matters, a conviction that all of you on the administrative team are on a mission to do something important, can be a vital factor in developing positive staff morale.

How do you go about having a clear administrative philosophy? You begin by thinking about your core values and how these values set you apart from other offices at your institution and other units that may be similar to yours at other institutions. Create a mission statement for yourself if you don't already have one or review it critically if such a document already exists. Be brutal in editing the document to ensure that it doesn't consist merely of attractive but empty verbiage. Too often mission statements are overly general. Poorly written institutional mission statements tend to give lip-service to vague and unassailable principles, focusing more on how the authors want their organization to be perceived than any real set of values to which it aspires. If you deleted the name of the institution or unit from the document, would anyone reading the mission statement be able to identify where it came from? (For an exercise related to this challenge, see Buller, 2015.) If your administrative team is truly going to stand for something, you'll need to give careful consideration to the factors that truly set your office apart from all others, identifying what makes your administrative team distinctive.

What is it that you believe your office does—or could do—better than anyone else? Perhaps your goal is accessibility, a dedication to serving anyone with the help they need, without an appointment, whenever they need it. Perhaps you see your role as facilitating communication, both listening to the concerns of everyone in your unit and making certain that "as soon as I learn something, you'll know about it too." It could be that you see your strengths as supporting scholarship, a willingness to be flexible with workload and aggressive in seeking external funding for projects that are truly innovative. You may have a mission based in student-faculty collaboration, working to reduce enrollment caps in key classes and encouraging faculty support of undergraduate research. Perhaps the unique quality of your office is a more intangible value—something like creativity, leadership, teamwork, entrepreneurship, or vision—that you're trying to instill in every single course, program, and degree your university offers. Only you and members of your administrative team can decide the most appropriate elements of your administrative creed. The important thing to keep in mind is that you must have a sense of purpose that you sincerely believe in and that your unit's overall theme needs to be distinctive enough to give your office a clear and recognizable identity.

Principle 4: Never underestimate the power of celebration

As academic administrators, we believe that higher education is important and serious business. Moreover, a great deal of our work requires us to do important and serious things, such as solving difficult problems, handling crises, making major decisions, initiating policies, developing visions for the future, and coping with the sheer quantity of issues that are brought to our attention every day. As a result, it can be easy in an environment that is preoccupied with what is important and serious to give short shrift to the many wonderful successes that are occurring all around us. Students are being accepted into graduate school, law school, or medical school. Articles and books are being published. Awards are being won. New insights are being formed. Diseases are being cured. The mission of the institution is being fulfilled. Lives are being changed. *Our fundamental role as educators is paying off.* So why is it that we so rarely celebrate these successes?

Nearly every institution has an awards ceremony once a term or once a year in which major academic achievements are touted. Nearly every institution has some sort of internal newsletter or website in which people are praised for publications, awards, and other achievements. But this type of recognition isn't enough. A college should engage in frequent, abundant, and spontaneous celebrations of all the terrific things that are happening in it. Colleges should celebrate when enrollment is up and a history of enrollment decline appears to have tapered off. They should celebrate whenever a grant is received, but they should also celebrate the effort required for a grant application to make it out the door. They should celebrate all of the routine milestones of employees (birthdays, years of service, promotions, and the like), and they should celebrate the sheer good fortune you have in working together. They should celebrate the adoption of a new platform for administrative computing and bid farewell to the cumbersome technology that's been holding the institution back for so many years. Celebrations should be frequent, and they should be joyous. When you can't think of any other reason to celebrate, invent your own occasion and then celebrate the start of a new tradition.

Celebrations build esprit de corps by reminding us why we entered higher education in the first place. They remind those we work with that we value them enough to set aside time just to show them our appreciation. By providing a temporary diversion from work, they help us to be more efficient at our work when we return to it. They dispel the notion that an academic leader's office is just the complaint department for the rest of the institution by providing people with access to you when they don't have a problem or criticism. Most important, celebrations among members of your staff help reinforce a positive working environment. To cite one final example from this history of Southwest Airlines, "Southwest's formal and informal celebrations are opportunities for relationship building. Terry 'Moose' Millard, a pilot and alumnus of Southwest's Culture Committee, explains: 'If you want your company operating at maximum efficiency, you have to have trust. In order to have trust, you must have some kind of relationship. So all the things we celebrate give us opportunities to establish and strengthen our relationships'" (Freiberg and Freiberg, 1996, 178).

Conclusion

As you reflect on your work with your staff, it can be beneficial to keep the following points in mind.

- ○ Staff members of an administrator's office frequently have maximum responsibility with minimum authority. They are asked to get things done and to get people involved with important tasks, but they rarely have the sort of supervisory authority they need in order to get the job done. As a result, staff members can cajole, charm, barter, and wheedle others, but they can rarely order them to do anything. You can help members of your staff by providing them with the gravitas that's derived from your own position, intervening on their behalf if required, and understanding that their approach may at times need to be less direct than your own.

- ○ Few members of an academic leader's staff have academic degrees directly related to their job responsibilities. If your institution

STAFF 267

doesn't provide adequate in-house training for administrators, work with members of your staff to find conferences, seminars, and workshops that can expose them to best practices in academic administration and to keep them informed about issues directly related to their roles in your office.

○ Few young people look themselves in the mirror and say, "When I grow up, I want to be an administrative assistant." Certain members of your staff may view their positions as a stepping-stone to something else. Don't resent them for thinking this way. Rather, understand that a certain amount of flux in your staff is desirable: every resignation is an opportunity for you to balance your team according to your shifting need for different areas of responsibility, additional skill sets, and the appropriate mix of personality types. You'll be more helpful to your staff and receive better support from them as a result if you actively assist them in meeting their career objectives than if you appear to begrudge them their dreams.

In short, building a strong staff is a combination of searching internally or externally for the right kind of people (not just the right kind of qualifications), making their success your highest priority, uniting them in a common purpose, and rewarding them for all the good they do. In most institutions, it can be difficult to effect this type of change overnight, particularly when other habits are already ingrained and you were not the one who hired members of the current staff. Nevertheless, even incremental changes of attitude can produce profound benefits in the long run. The important thing is not to be overwhelmed by the enormity of changing everything, but be energized by the possibility of changing something.

REFERENCES

Bakke, D. W. (2005). *Joy at work: A revolutionary approach to fun on the job.* Seattle, WA: PVG.

Braskamp, L. A., Trautvetter, L. C., & Ward, K. (2006). *Putting students first.* Bolton, MA: Anker.

Buller, J. L. (2015). *Change leadership in higher education: A practical guide to academic transformation.* San Francisco, CA: Jossey-Bass.

Freiberg, K., & Freiberg, J. (1996). *NUTS! Southwest Airlines' crazy recipe for business and personal success.* New York, NY: Broadway Books.

Peters, T. (1994). *The pursuit of WOW!* New York, NY: Vintage.

RESOURCES

Bright, D. F., & Richards, M. P. (2001). *The academic deanship: Individual careers and institutional roles*. San Francisco, CA: Jossey-Bass.

Christy, S. (2010). *Working effectively with faculty: Guidebook for higher education staff and managers*. Berkeley, CA: University Resources Press.

Krahenbuhl, G. S. (2004). *Building the academic deanship: Strategies for success*. Portsmouth, NH: Praeger.

Lester, J. (2013). *Workplace bullying in higher education*. New York, NY: Routledge.

20

ASSISTANT AND ASSOCIATE DEANS

While all the members of an academic leader's staff play a crucial role in the success of the office, there are few other people who are as integral to the work of the team as assistant and associate deans. (For ease of reference, I'll continue to use the expression *assistant and associate deans* throughout this chapter even though everything I explore applies to assistant and associate provosts as well.) Often dismissively referred to as *deanlets*, assistant and associate deans represent the ultimate level of maximum responsibility with minimum authority that affects all members of the dean's senior staff. Without any supervisory power, they are expected to meet deadlines, prepare reports, convey news (sometimes good, although often bad), and get results on the dean's behalf. Whatever they do well will probably get credited to the dean. Whatever mistakes they make will probably be blamed on them. It can be thankless work, and it certainly isn't for everyone. For the right person, however, work as an assistant or associate dean can be an interesting complement to an academic career, a launching pad toward an administrative career, or a welcome but temporary interruption of ordinary responsibilities.

The difference between an assistant and an associate dean depends on the institution. Often there's little or no difference at all. An associate dean may simply have more seniority in the position or a more proven set of skills, similar to the difference between an assistant and an associate professor. At other times, the difference can be great. Assistant deans may be staff members who lack terminal degrees, tenure rights, and classification as faculty members according to the institution's policies or union contract. (See chapter 43.) Associate deans, by contrast, would then be faculty members with an administrative assignment, qualify for tenure, and may be part of the bargaining unit for contract purposes.

The simplest way to view this distinction is to say that the difference between an assistant and associate dean is whatever your institution says it is. There's no general rule, and the precise descriptions of these positions can vary widely. Regardless of these differences, however, it's almost universally the case that the relationship between a dean and his or her associates becomes very personal. If you've inherited a staff from a previous dean, they may suit your needs very well or they may not. It's not uncommon for a new dean to replace one or more members of the staff during his or her first year in the office. That doesn't suggest that the previous dean appointed the wrong people. It simply means that the new dean needs people with different skills, attributes, and background.

Appointing the Right People

A common mistake deans make is to choose assistant and associate deans who are just like them. It's a natural temptation: they want people who bring the same attitudes and work ethic to the job that they have themselves. If they're workaholics, they want staff members who will stay late into the night with them. If they take a more easygoing attitude when running the office, they want staff members who are as laid back as they are. The problem with this approach is that it tends to generate a type of groupthink that can permeate the office. If deans surround themselves with people who think about most issues exactly as they do, they don't get the benefit of learning different perspectives and hearing a voice of caution when their ideas may be ill considered. Offices that are too homogeneous frequently develop an us-versus-them mentality toward the rest of the institution. They assume that their ideas are better and more widely embraced than they are because they so rarely hear opposition (at least during staff meetings). They distance themselves from members of the faculty and staff who look at the world differently or don't fully support their style of interacting with others. They end up becoming an enclave instead of an office where people feel welcomed and respected.

When appointing assistant and associate deans, therefore, it's valuable to take a candid look at where your strengths and weaknesses lie. No one's perfect at everything, and you need to know what you tend not to do well. That's not the same thing as identifying what you don't *like* to do. Naturally deans frequently assign to a staff member those functions that they find unpleasant. The phrase "and other duties as assigned" in the job descriptions of most assistant and associate deans is very handy when it comes to delegating boring or burdensome tasks. But if those are the only responsibilities you're assigning your staff, you're missing out on a significant part of their value to you.

Assistant and associate deans can provide a degree of balance to the office. If you're a big picture sort of person, they can help keep track of the details. If you're an introvert, they may be able to deal with certain groups more effectively than you can. If you're a better speaker than writer, they can assist you with polishing reports and other documents. But even beyond these basic functions, it's useful to think of other ways in which your staff can help balance your office. For example, if you tend to be overly optimistic about how much can be achieved within tight deadlines and limited budgets, you might want to have an assistant or associate dean who's realistic, maybe even a bit pessimistic, in such situations. If you tend to push yourself and others too hard, someone who can help remind you about the need to set reasonable limits can be an asset to your work. Harmony isn't the same thing as complete uniformity, and a dean's office is often richer for the different talents and personalities of the staff.

While the precise profile you'll want for your assistant and associate deans will thus depend on your own personality and needs, there's one trait that's all but essential in these staff members: a good balance of academic insight and administrative talent. That mix isn't always easy to find. Some faculty members are excellent in their disciplines and may even be superstars when it comes to teaching and research, but they don't work well with bureaucracy. They may spend more time fighting the system than they do working within the system or be indifferent to details of policy and regulations. Some potential candidates don't have the right people skills that will enable them to interact with others collegially but with sufficient authority to get the job done. There are plenty of people who can handle all the bureaucratic functions of the position but don't have the right academic credentials, of course. As much as we pride ourselves on our democratic spirit in higher education, colleges and universities are still places where advanced degrees and impressive résumés matter. An assistant dean who lacks authority because he or she "has just a master's degree" can be a liability in certain situations. You have to spend time justifying that person's role on your staff or finding an alternative way of achieving the goal you want. While it's not necessary for your assistant or associate dean to be your most productive scholar—in fact, it can be counterproductive to divert such a person from his or her research—it's very helpful for staff members to have a good personal understanding of what the work of a college professor is like. For this reason, most deans find that they need to screen candidates carefully to find the right blend of academic depth, experience with the world of higher education, and administrative acumen.

You may also need to make a judgment call on the proper time in someone's career to enter one of these administrative staff positions. An untenured faculty member is likely to find the demands of being an assistant or associate dean so heavy that it proves difficult to earn tenure, and an associate professor may well be delayed in his or her attempts to become a full professor. That risk, along with the other sacrifices required for work on a dean's staff, is perfectly acceptable to some faculty members and utterly abhorrent to others. So before anyone agrees to take the position, it's a good idea to try to explain to the candidate exactly what he or she will be getting into. If at all possible, a trial period of an academic term or a year may be desirable, with the option available for either party to end the relationship without stigma and with no questions asked. If your system allows a tenure-eligible faculty member to stop the tenure clock while on your staff or to shift temporarily to a non-tenure-track line, you may wish to offer these options to the person you select.

Another good conversation to have would be about the person's reasons for being interested in serving as an assistant or associate dean. Some faculty members view these positions simply as temporary departures from their regular faculty work and intend to return to full-time teaching and research within a few years. Others regard the position as a springboard into higher administrative positions. And still others may be attracted by the possibility of moving up the hierarchy on the staff side, such as becoming an associate provost or president's chief of staff someday. Understanding how your assistant and associate deans view their career trajectory can help you best make use of their talents (and career ambitions) while giving you valuable insight into the type of training they're most likely to need.

Providing the Right Training

Developing that insight is important because even if you select an assistant or associate dean with all the right attributes for success, he or she will almost certainly need to learn a great deal in order to become a valuable member of your team. For instance, faculty members tend to understand their own curriculum and its requirements quite well, but they often don't have that level of knowledge for all the disciplines you supervise. They may know a bit about the paperwork that departments submit to your office, particularly if they've served as chairs, but they're unlikely to know all the policies that govern what happens to that paperwork at your level. Moreover, if your assistant or associate deans are hoping to advance to higher administrative positions, the training they need provides you with opportunities to mentor them and pass along lessons you've learned in your own work as an academic leader. Providing that type of training is good for your staff, and it's also good for you. It helps you reflect on why you lead your programs in the way that you do. It causes you to consider your own leadership style and how you've discovered that certain approaches are more effective than others. And it can cause you to become more intentional and less reactive in your work as a dean.

One useful resource to turn to in providing training to your assistant and associate deans is Tammy Stone and Mary Coussons-Read's *Leading from the Middle: A Case-Study Approach to Academic Leadership for Associate Deans* (2011). This book addresses such issues as developing an appropriate leadership style even when you're not technically in charge of an area, communicating effectively, interacting with department chairs, managing conflict, working with students, and adapting to change. Part of the training you provide could consist, therefore, of simply having your assistant and associate deans read the seventeen chapters of *Leading from the Middle* and meeting with you after every chapter or two to discuss the principles and case studies they've encountered. After each case study they present, Stone and Coussons-Read provide a discussion and offer some guidance in how the situation might be addressed. These discussions are an opportunity to review the case with the members of your staff, examine their thought processes as they work their way through the problem, and describe how you'd prefer them to handle similar situations. The book is written in a breezy, conversational style that lends itself particularly well to casual mentoring sessions one-on-one or in small groups.

In addition to these training opportunities you can provide independently, your assistant and associate deans are likely to find a number of national programs valuable. While programs explicitly designed for members of the support staff are rare, many of the workshops and conferences for academic leaders noted in chapters 2 and 18 cover topics that are identical to those that members of your team need to master. A good team-building activity can be for you to attend one of these programs with your entire support staff, set aside some time each day to meet as a group, compare notes from different sessions, and respond to any of the exercises or case studies that have been presented. Social time at these events enables a group to jell more completely and produces benefits that will continue long after the workshop is over. It can even be a leadership initiative of your office to use the lessons learned from these programs to begin offering training to other members of the support staff on your campus in such topics as time management, conflict resolution, work/life balance, promoting collegiality, and the like.

Staff Meetings

Meeting with the staff, either as a group or individually, with a frequency that suits everyone is more difficult than it may appear. People have widely different expectations for how often they believe members of a work group should meet. For each person who feels as though they've been put at a disadvantage and are out of the loop if they don't hear immediately about even the most minor new development or initiative, there will be someone else who feels that even occasional meetings are a waste of time and "I could get all my work done if only we didn't have so many meetings." Hitting the right balance depends on knowing the needs and personalities of your assistant and associate deans, discovering a format that works best for you, and adapting your approach as members of the support staff change. Just because you inherited a particular schedule of staff meetings from your predecessor or were familiar with one at your previous institution, you don't have to follow that schedule if it doesn't work for the team you have now. Staff meetings are rarely addressed in bylaws or policy manuals. They exist for the benefit of those who participate in them and can change as people's need and expectations change.

At the beginning of each academic year, therefore, you might consider conducting a survey of your assistant and associate deans that looks something like exhibit 20.1.

Exhibit 20.1 Staff Meeting Preference Survey

Directions: In order to increase the likelihood that we meet with a frequency that suits most people's needs but doesn't detract from their work, please complete the following survey of your preferences. In the first column, check all the possibilities that you find attractive or desirable. In the second column, check the *one* possibility that you like best.

Check ALL Preferred Options	Check the ONE Most Preferred Option	Meeting Options
☐	☐	No regular meetings. Update one another by e-mail, impromptu conversations, and (when necessary) specially scheduled meetings
☐	☐	Daily brief (5–10 minute) updates at the beginning or end of the day to keep one another informed about current projects and activities
☐	☐	Weekly staff meetings and weekly one-on-one meetings
☐	☐	Weekly staff meetings with less frequent (biweekly, monthly) one-on-one meetings
☐	☐	Less frequent staff meetings (biweekly, monthly) with weekly one-on-one meetings
☐	☐	Biweekly staff meetings and biweekly one-on-one meetings
☐	☐	Monthly staff meetings and monthly one-on-one meetings
☐	☐	An annual retreat followed by shorter, regular staff meetings
☐	☐	A retreat at the start of each term, followed by shorter, regular staff meetings
☐	☐	Weekly staff meetings with one-on-one meetings only as needed
☐	☐	Biweekly staff meetings with one-on-one meetings only as needed
☐	☐	Monthly staff meetings with one-on-one meetings only as needed
☐	☐	Weekly one-on-one meetings with staff meetings only as needed
☐	☐	Biweekly one-on-one meetings with staff meetings only as needed
☐	☐	Monthly one-on-one meetings with staff meetings only as needed
☐	☐	Other schedule (please specify): _____ _____ _____.

By collating the responses you receive, you can determine how wide the range of responses is among the members of your staff and whether there are any clear areas of consensus. In general, people who are introverts (e.g., those whose four-letter profile on the Myers-Briggs Personality Inventory begins with the letter I) tend to prefer meeting less often, while those who are extroverts (those with a Myers-Briggs profile beginning with E) prefer to meet more frequently. Moreover, teams where several members are new or are working for a dean who is new to the institution usually benefit from meeting more often than well-established work groups. When only one assistant or associate dean is new, that person may prefer to have individual meetings with you as the supervisor, where questions can be asked and responsibilities clarified, rather than having to admit in a larger setting that he or she doesn't understand a certain policy or procedure.

The focus of staff meetings will also vary according to the needs of your group. For example, the usual rule of thumb for meetings in higher education is that they should be primarily task oriented rather than opportunities simply to share information. (See chapter 10.) But that principle becomes inverted for most staff meetings. Deans get together with their assistants and associates less often to make decisions collectively than to find out what everyone is doing, coordinate work assignments, and make certain that all members of the group are on the same page. When collective decision making does occur, it is more often a matter of the dean asking for advice from other members of the staff than a formal process of voting or seeking to reach a consensus. For this reason, it pays to put a certain amount of planning into staff meetings rather than to go into them unprepared and ask, "So what's everyone up to this week?" Reflect on other meetings that you've attended and the information shared there that can help your assistant and associates do their jobs most effectively. Don't just burden them with reports and other documents for the sake of getting them off your desk; rather give serious consideration of what may blindside them if you don't alert them that a certain policy is being considered or a particular action is pending. Unless your supervisor declares that all discussions held at meetings you attend with the provost and other deans must be kept confidential, you might also consider sharing minutes or your own updates of those meetings with your staff. At certain institutions, it can even be valuable to share that information with all the faculty members in your programs as a way of keeping everyone informed as to ongoing issues and developments.

Office Politics

In the best of all possible worlds, you'll get along both personally and professionally with the members of your support staff, they'll respect your authority even when they don't agree with you, and you'll all have confidence that everyone on the team makes the interests of the students and institution his or her highest priority. Unfortunately, that optimal scenario doesn't always occur. You may find yourself working with an assistant or associate dean who disrespects you, believes that he or she is more qualified than you are, places personal desires ahead of his or her professional work, or is otherwise not a loyal and productive member of your work group.

If you're new to your position, it's often useful to state from the beginning your expectations from your assistant and associate deans and receive their individual commitments to live up to those expectations. Among the principles you might include in this discussion are the following (Buller, 2010):

o "We'll speak about one another only with respect and support when talking with people outside of our team."

o "We'll share our views openly and candidly with one another, but once a decision has been made, we'll do everything in our power to support that decision rather than undermine it."

o "If a decision that we opposed, later proves to have been wrong or unwise, we'll work collectively to fix the problem rather than gloat in our superior judgment."

Discussing your expectations in this way places people on notice that failure to act cohesively as a unit is destructive to the goals you intend to pursue as dean and gives you an opportunity to remind others of these principles when they fail to live up to the goals you've established for the office.

Differences of opinion are bound to occur. In fact, differences of opinion are highly desirable because they keep your team from lapsing into groupthink and help you consider likely objections that other stakeholders will make. But there's a world of difference between constructive and destructive differences of opinion. Since the whole purpose of having assistant and associate deans on your staff is to make your job easier and your work more effective, if they fail to achieve this goal because of their words or actions, their value to you becomes nonexistent. Except in the cases of the most egregious betrayal of your principles, it's probably best to treat the first (and possibly even the second) failure to meet your expectations as an opportunity to mentor the person. Treat the lapse as a learning experience, point out the reasons that the person's actions were harmful to the effectiveness of the office, and set a clearer goal for the future.

Repeated lack of support from an assistant or associate dean is a far more serious matter. It suggests a pattern of behavior that advice and possibly even sanctions have failed to correct. In these cases, your best option is probably to replace that person at your earliest opportunity. Although a commonly cited dictum tells us to "keep our friends close and our enemies even closer," the small size of the staff in most deans' offices means that you probably can't afford the luxury of having even one negative influence on your team. In these cases, the damage that someone can do from the outside is likely to be far less than the damage that person can cause by remaining on your staff.

Good Cop/Bad Cop

One practice that some dean's offices follow—at times intentionally and at other times inadvertently—is dividing responsibilities for positive and negative roles among different members of the staff. In one version of this approach, the dean assumes the role of "good cop." In order to maintain as constructive a relationship with the faculty as possible, the dean becomes the person who meets with successful candidates for promotion, grants exceptions to established policies, allocates additional funding for research and travel, and generally becomes the person others meet with when the answer is yes. An associate dean then is either assigned or simply lapses into the role of "bad cop." He or she is the person faculty members meet with when they're being terminated or turned down for promotion, informed that a policy must be enforced to their disadvantage, refused additional money for a request they've made, or given the answer no to whatever it is they may happen to want.

The reverse situation also sometimes occurs. The assistant or associate dean either claims or sincerely means that he or she would like to help if only it were possible, but the dean (the faculty member is told) is such a stickler for established procedures that a waiver is simply out of the question. Deans or associate deans may be attracted to this "good cop" role because it's unpleasant to give people news they don't want to hear or because they're guilty of the practice known as managing through, that is, passing the hard decisions to someone else who's more removed from the situation and often does not have to look the faculty member in the eye when refusing the request. There may also be a desire for at least one person in the dean's office to be viewed publicly as a good cop so that the faculty and staff will at least have the illusion that they have an advocate at the college level.

All of these reasons, while understandable in many situations, are ultimately insignificant in comparison to the damage that adopting a good cop/bad cop approach can cause. First, it's manipulative, and as soon as people figure out that that's how the dean's office is operating (and they always will), the damage to your credibility will be immense. Second, if you assign the bad cop role to a member of the staff, you're being derelict in your own duties and creating a working environment that's unpleasant and soon demoralizing for the assistant or associate dean you've made responsible for conveying all the negative decisions. No one relishes being "the dean's hatchet man" for very long; people begin to fear and avoid those who adopt or are assigned this role because they know that encounters with them are likely to be dissatisfying, unpleasant, and frustrating. Third, if you take on the bad cop role for yourself, you're potentially erecting a major barrier between yourself and members of the faculty and staff. People will stop trusting you and feeling free to share information with you because they know in advance that you're unlikely to help, support, or advocate for them if they need you. As a result, you'll stop learning things that you need to know in order to do your job effectively and miss opportunities that could make a positive difference for the programs you're supervising.

Conclusion

In general, the relationship that deans have with their assistant and associate deans should be close, candid, and mutually supportive. Having members of the staff who are too similar to you in thought and personality can be just as destructive as having people on your team who are actively trying to undermine the work that you're doing. When you appoint new assistant or associate deans, it's useful to consider the skills you need, the attributes the different candidates have, the career paths they are on, and the way in which different people are likely to fit into the system you've created with administrative assistants and other members of the support staff. A good assistant or associate dean should be comfortable enough to challenge you in private whenever necessary and loyal enough to respect the decisions you make even if he or she would have chosen a different option.

REFERENCES

Buller, J. L. (2010). Serving under Commander Queeg. *Academic Leader*, 26(2), 4–5.

Stone, T., & Coussons-Read, M. E. (2011). *Leading from the middle: A case-study approach to academic leadership for associate deans*. Lanham, MD: Rowman & Littlefield.

RESOURCES

Buller, J. L. (2008). The "Spider-Man Principle" and the "categorical imperative": How to address the problem of "managing through." *Academic Leader*, 24(4), 2–3.

Hendrickson, R. M., Lane, J. E., Harris, J. T., & Dorman, R. H. (2013). *Academic leadership and governance of higher education: A guide for trustees, leaders, and aspiring leaders of two- and four-year institutions*. Sterling, VA: Stylus.

Sloat, J. M. (2014). Developing productive relationships with assistant and associate deans: What they might want you to know. In L. L. Behling (Ed.), *The resource handbook for academic deans* (pp. 249–254). San Francisco, CA: Jossey-Bass.

21

PEERS

Unless you're the sole academic officer at a very small institution, one of the most complex, challenging, and potentially rewarding constituencies you will have can be found among your peers or colleagues: fellow deans if you're a dean or the other vice presidents if you're a provost. Those relationships can run the gamut from constructive and supportive to absolutely toxic. At some institution, peers view one another largely as competitors; the budget, they feel, is a zero-sum game, and so any gain in one area must mean that someone else has lost. As a result, there's perennial conflict over how important one division of the institution is relative to another, and the deans continually jockey with one another—as the provost may with the other vice presidents—for position in the eyes of the president and governing board. At other institutions, interactions are far more collegial, with the deans and vice presidents all viewing one another as members of the same administrative team, working on behalf of the school as a whole. Of course, the variations along this spectrum of possibilities are almost infinite. Your college or university probably falls somewhere between the two extremes, and it may even be that one group of peers interacts with one another in one way, while another group has an entirely different way of interaction. So how should you try to interact with your own peers? And if the relationship you have with them is already strained, how might it be improved?

It's natural for deans and vice presidents to view themselves as competitors with one another, at least for certain resources. New facilities are relatively rare commodities; if one college or division is granted priority in a major building project, it may be years before the new facility you want can ever be approved. Similarly, continuing lines for members of the faculty or staff are limited resources, and every new position granted to one area means one less position that's possible in another area. Seats in courses cannot expand infinitely, and a dean who is stingy about providing other deans with space in a desperately needed service course can be a real detriment to the success of your program. A vice president for financial or student affairs who's not receptive to the needs of the provost can make every meeting seem like a battle.

Nevertheless, your peers also face many of the same problems that you encounter year after year. Policies and initiatives developed by accrediting bodies or the governing board can either ease or complicate the work of your peers in precisely the same way they help or hinder you. In other words, there are other people at your university who can understand the complexity of the issues you're called on to address and feel your pain when budgets are tight, enrollment is down, or members of the faculty and staff seem to be in a particularly annoyed (or annoying) mood. There's good reason to form a common cause with your peers, and this chapter sets out a few best practices to consider for doing so.

Meet Together Informally

It's not uncommon for institutions to have a deans' council, executive staff, or some similar body where peers meet together as a group. Usually these bodies are chaired by the group's supervisor or include people in related but not precisely parallel positions. The result is that those in attendance sometimes feel pressure, even if they're not aware of it, to affirm their status, show off for the person in charge, or establish their authority over others.

One way to develop a good working relationship with your peers is to propose periodic meetings in which you meet only with one another to discuss items of current concern, keep informed about issues that cut across all your areas, and get to know each other better in a more relaxed, less formal setting. Meetings such as these can give you an opportunity to discuss the different approaches you take in your individual areas in a constructive, nonthreatening manner. For instance, if one of the other deans or vice presidents has intimated that the enrollment caps in your courses have prevented his or students from getting the courses they need or that your frequent requests for additional positions have unfairly increased the workload in his or her area, you can explore this issue together without worrying about what either your supervisor or the people who report to you might conclude. In the case of the enrollment caps, for instance, you might explain that there are only a certain number of lab stations available or that the amount of writing required in the course limits the number of students each instructor can teach. In the case of your position requests, you might learn that people in your area would be better off if you go without a few faculty positions this year in order to allow staffing in the registrar's office, financial aid, or admissions to increase. Since you're just having an informal conversation, you can explore together such options as reserving a certain number of seats in your courses for those in other programs, joining forces with a colleague in making a joint budget request for additional positions, modifying degree requirements to ease the bottle-necks that are now occurring, reassigning certain staff members to other duties, and the like. In short, by having this conversation "offline" rather than in a formal meeting, you'll be freed to be more creative in the way you solve problems.

Other issues that can result from miscommunication during formal meetings can also be addressed in these casual meetings. For example, you could explore why the workload for staff members in your area seems so different from that in other units, why more or less stringent entrance requirements may be desirable for the institution, and why certain areas may require a different ratio of students to staff members that's either higher or lower than your own. Most important, by meeting with your peers as colleagues rather than competitors, you establish a new working relationship with them that can carry over into your other meetings. You'll have an opportunity to ask questions that'll minimize the likelihood of being blindsided by someone who used to take delight in discussing, in a very public setting, the one disastrous problem in your area that affected his or her own. In fact, in many cases, your colleague may be more reluctant to embarrass you publicly with information that makes you look bad because the two of you have formed a new kind of relationship during your informal meetings.

Seek Common Ground

Either in these informal meetings or in individual conversations with your colleagues, you may find it useful to explore areas of common interest or shared opportunities. Seeking common ground in this way helps improve the relationships you have, sends a positive message to the president about the harmony present in the administration, makes better use of scarce resources, and sometimes leads to innovative programs that better serve the needs of students. Some issues you may have in common with your peers include the following:

o *Faculty and staff development.* Providing all the workshops and leadership development you might like to offer can be expensive and time-consuming. Particularly for deans or provosts at small institutions, it can be difficult to justify an entire series of sessions for new department chairs if they have only a handful of new chairs each year. Partnering with another dean or vice president in offering leadership development programs in both your areas can create good ties between your areas and help ensure that the programs you offer draw the critical mass of participants they need.

o *Create interdisciplinary programs.* Many of the challenges facing the world can't be solved within the confines of individual disciplines. Creating a problem-based or issue-based approach as an alternative to a discipline-based institutional structure can offer numerous opportunities for creative interactions among vice presidents or deans that prove highly beneficial to the instructional and research missions of your programs. In one qualitative study, John Benedicto Krejsler of Aarhus University in Denmark provided evidence of how important this type of cross-fertilization can be for universities. He traces the development of two academic departments—one that embraced opportunities for collaboration with other units and another that sought to preserve disciplinary integrity by remaining entirely separate and self-sufficient—and noted the problems and vulnerability that resulted from the latter approach (Krejsler, 2013). In times of budget cuts and rapid institutional change, the connections that deans and vice presidents develop with their peers can be the difference between success and failure. They can even be the factors that allow certain programs to survive while others are cut back or eliminated.

o *Externally funded grants.* Foundations and government agencies like to see partnerships among administrative units when they consider grant applications. Such collaboration demonstrates that the need for the grant transcends the individual interest of a single department, college, or division. They also realize that any funding they provide will have a greater impact and be more likely to result in activities that continue once the grant period is over. Working cooperatively with peers thus demonstrates to both the funding agency and your internal constituents that you're open to seeing connections among disciplines, free from the silo mentality that causes people at many institutions to view things only from their perspective, and a good team player when it comes to sharing responsibility and credit.

o *Internally funded grants.* If you have access to funds that your college or university provides for research, scholarship, or creative activities, you may want to explore with a peer the possibility of pooling resources as a way of offering grants to members of the faculty or staff who collaborate on projects between your two areas. With funds drawn from two sources in this way, you may be able to support proposals that produce much more impressive results than those you were able to support using only your own resources. For instance, a college of arts and sciences could develop a grant jointly with a college of education for faculty members interested in developing innovative ways of incorporating access to primary sources of information into elementary or secondary school education. A division of academic affairs could partner with a division of student affairs to fund new approaches to promote student success, retention, and timely graduation. The individual focus of your grants will depend on your institution's needs as well as your own interests, but those grants, planned carefully, can help bring about new partnerships among those who work in different areas of the school. And that collaboration can begin with something as simple as a telephone call to a peer.

o *Personal invitations*. Every institution has a number of lectures, exhibits, recitals, concerts, or other events that are open to the public. All too often, the people who attend these events are simply the usual suspects—the same few members of the community who have an interest in that particular topic. We'd all like our events to be more widely attended, particularly by those who are outside our own areas. One way to achieve this goal is to issue personal invitations to your peers, making it clear that they're being personally invited to attend the event. A handwritten note, a phone call, or an office visit is far more effective than a general flier or a mass e-mail. In person, you can explain why you think that particular person would enjoy or be enriched by that event. Be sure, of course, to reciprocate. Go out of your way to attend events sponsored by other colleges or divisions too. This simple exchange of visits can help immeasurably with improving the relationship among the different areas of the institution (Irwin, 2014).

Express Disagreements in Private

If after all your efforts to reach out and build constructive relationships with your peers prove to be ineffective, it might be time for a candid heart-to-heart talk with the individual involved in the impasse. Offer to meet for lunch or at an off-campus location. A conversation of this type should not be held in either person's office, where there can be a sense you're speaking on one person's turf and the other person is the outsider.

Begin the discussion candidly by saying something like, "I keep noticing that there's a sense of antagonism or competition between us that I think is hindering our ability to work together. Have you noticed that too? Or am I wrong? Do you think there's a reason I'm getting this impression?"

After raising this issue, be sure to listen to and consider the answer. Don't be defensive. Don't try to explain away or justify your actions immediately. What you want to do in this conversation is to get your colleague's perspective. Perhaps there's some policy in your area that's been detrimental to the success of the other person's programs. Perhaps you've been inadvertently acting as though you have little respect for the other administrator, his or her students, or the programs that person supervises. Perhaps there's a matter of history that began even before your arrival at the institution. Give the other person plenty of time to discuss the issues that he or she believes to be at the root of the problem.

Once you know what the basic issue is, explore ways of solving the problem. Ask the other person, "What would you like to see happen?" You don't necessarily have to agree to that particular course of action—it may not even be within your power to do so—but at least you will better appreciate your colleague's position. In certain cases, you may be surprised to find that the solution the other person requested is so minor it seems incredible that there's been friction over so small a matter. In other cases, you'll find that there are genuine philosophical differences between the two colleges that can't be bridged and that the best you can do is agree to disagree. Most frequent, however, you'll need to develop some compromise that'll address the problem without undue detriment to your own programs. Whatever you learn in this conversation, be sure to follow the three principles of diplomacy outlined in McDaniel (2003):

1. Identify real interests and needs as opposed to the surface issues and conflicts that are sometimes advanced for rhetorical purposes rather than because people actually believe what they are saying. Be sure to perform this check on yourself as well as on your colleague.

2. Work on developing patience. "Patient deans do not force unwise, ephemeral solutions but do nurture the processes of dialogue, debate, and decision-making" (McDaniel, 2003, 34).

3. Be flexible. Remain true to your actual needs and core values, but remember that there may be more than one way to achieve your goals.

By following these simple principles of diplomacy, you may well find yourself asking the other person at the end of the conversation, "Why did we wait so long to discuss this?"

Constructive versus Destructive Conflict

Just as with your own staff, don't assume that all conflict and differences of opinion are a bad thing. When you find yourself disagreeing repeatedly with a peer, a good question to consider is, "What harm is being done by this conflict?" If the only answer you can think of is, "It makes me feel uncomfortable," or, "I don't like it when other people oppose my ideas," it may be that the situation isn't really one that needs to be changed.

Our work in higher education gives us a wonderful opportunity to have a profound impact on people's lives and improve the world through the discovery of important new knowledge; we didn't become deans and provosts just to be comfortable. There'll always be people who don't like or appreciate us. It just goes with the territory of being a dean. You can't allow the fact that you've been unable to win all the hearts and minds of your colleagues to distract you from your primary goals. Just as a faculty member can't be expected to be the idol of every student in every course, so will there be people at your institution who see the world differently from the way you view it. But that's a good thing: it helps us gain new perspectives. We've all had the experience of knowing (or even better, being) a professor who, years after a course is over, hears from a former student who hated a class when enrolled but now regards it as a turning point in his or her life. It could be that your experience with your colleague will be somewhat similar but on the administrative level. Whenever it gets uncomfortable, remind yourself that no real harm is being done and use the opportunity to expand your comfort zone. Although the two of you may disagree about fundamental ideas, your work is still being done at a high level, and so is that of the other administrator. You're a big enough person to endure a few unpleasant moments every now and then.

It may even be the case that you and your colleague are involved in a constructive conflict. Perhaps you get frustrated when the other person seems to nitpick at every detail but find that you're double-checking documents so that they're perfect. Even if you're only being particularly careful so that your colleague doesn't annoy or humiliate you, a positive result has emerged from the conflict. Or perhaps another dean or vice president is in the habit of belittling one of the disciplines you supervise. Although that behavior may be childish, if you find his or her comments causing you to think of better ways of defending that field to people who may not understand it, your colleague has actually done you a favor. Or you may find yourself exasperated by one of your peer's self-congratulatory attitude when that person repeatedly wastes valuable meeting time trumpeting his or her latest achievement. If you can channel your frustration into ways of getting larger grants, identifying more generous donors, and encouraging your faculty members to apply for a larger number of national awards, the conflict has become constructive for you. Just as the pressure exerted by a coach or personal trainer can make you reach new levels of success (even though you may hate them at the time), so can this type of constructive conflict cause you to become an even better academic leader.

The real problem occurs when you can't find any positive outcome arising from a disagreement with a colleague and realize that the two of you are in a state of destructive conflict. You'll know that a conflict is destructive if you find that you're missing out on collaborative opportunities because you can't work with another person, meetings are becoming unproductive due to repeated arguments that are never resolved, or damage is occurring to the reputation of your programs because the ongoing disagreement is public, bitter, or petty. In that case, action is necessary, and even if you regard the other person as more culpable, it's up to you to make the first move.

Differences and conflicts always flow in two directions. When you are in the middle of a conflict, it's frequently difficult to see how that may be the case, even though it may be abundantly clear to everyone else. "But they started it," we often say, unaware of how juvenile such a reaction sounds. "Yes, but it's up to you to resolve it," someone needs to remind us. Fighting hostility with hostility, coldness with coldness, or contempt with contempt only escalates differences among peers. In order to overcome a difficulty with another administrator, you frequently have to take the initiative to defuse a situation that wasn't your creation. You may find it unpalatable to have to do so repeatedly, particularly when the other person appears to be acting with impunity, but your focus has to be on whatever is best for the institution, and often that means enduring the unpalatable.

We often find ourselves saying things like, "He infuriates me so!" or, "She makes me feel as though I don't even exist!" But the truth is that no one can make us feel angry, hurt, or ashamed. We always have more choice about how to respond and even whether to respond than we realize. Have you ever noticed someone in a situation where another person was angry, rude, or insulting but the first person simply shrugged it off or even smiled in mild amusement, although you wouldn't have been quite so forgiving? For whatever reason—and it may only have been that the person who was mistreated happened to be in a particularly good mood that day—he or she was able to look at what was happening objectively and decided that it wasn't worth it to carry the problem to the next level. "That person's anger doesn't have to become my anger," he or she may have thought. "This unacceptable behavior isn't about me; it's about the other person. Maybe he or she has been upset about something or has difficulty dealing with anger or was reminded of a bad experience from the past by something I did inadvertently. Whatever may be going on here, just because I've been treated poorly, there's no reason that I should treat others poorly in return." It's surprising the number of conflicts that we can resolve with colleagues by acting in this way. It's possible at times to end even a long-term clash simply by refusing to add to someone else's negativity.

In certain situations, when you can't figure out any other way to end differences with a peer, you can try making progress by killing them with kindness. Sometimes academic leaders are reluctant to adopt this approach because they feel that it'll make them appear to be weak or lacking in authority. This fear is certainly misdirected. As a strategy, repaying rudeness or hostility with kindness can often be effective because it's difficult for another person to keep a disagreement going if you refuse to play along. More important, you'll discover that this approach will both decrease your stress as an administrator and help you model a more effective interpersonal style to others. You'll have chosen not to be "made" angry or offended, electing instead to be guided by an essential principle that is said to have originated with Abraham Lincoln:

People are just about as happy as they make up their minds to be.

In other words, you've made up your mind to be happy by acting as a supportive colleague despite what the other person may do. In a surprising number of instances, that decision will eventually cause the other person to make the same choice as well.

Peers and Other Stakeholders

When your relationship with one of your peers isn't going well, the proper place to begin is working directly with that person and keeping the conflict as invisible as possible to other stakeholders. Academic leaders sometimes feel that they're being hypocritical when they act supportive toward a difficult colleague if the governing board, president, faculty, donors, parents, or students are around but speak their minds with the person in private. "I just can't be two-faced like that," someone might say. "As academics, we're supposed to respect honesty and stand up for what we believe in. I'm not going to act as though I can tolerate so-and-so, because that would be insincere, and I just have to call things as I see them." This attitude may seem to be based in a commitment to integrity, but ultimately it is self-serving and counterproductive. It's a matter of complete indifference to students we like or don't like, what our personal disagreements may be with our colleagues, or who's making our jobs more difficult by being rude and unreasonable. What students are interested in is getting a good education, and that means learning in an environment where people treat one another with professionalism. Parents, donors, and board members won't respect you or your programs more if you impose your professional disagreements on them. In fact, they're likely to lose respect not for the person you're complaining about but for you if you're airing dirty laundry in public. Every college and university has interpersonal tensions lurking just below the surface. Sometimes these tensions are petty; at other times they're extremely serious. At no time, however, should these conflicts be visible to the stakeholders we're serving. This is a case where brutal honesty only makes matters worse. After all, it's always possible that we'll resolve our differences with our colleagues. If that occurs, it can be difficult to undo any damage we may have caused by making public a conflict that should have remained private.

We can easily imagine someone asking, "Shouldn't I at least tell my supervisor what's going on?" That can be a beneficial approach, particularly if your supervisor is the sort of person who likes to know about everything that's going on in your area, but it's probably best not to do so too often. It can look as though you're tattling or unable to solve your own problems if you make a habit of sharing lots of petty disagreements with your boss. When you do mention these issues, it's probably best to ask for advice rather than direct intervention. Third-party intervention can be effective in conflict resolution, but only if the mediator is viewed as an honest broker—someone who's not biased toward either one of the parties. Since you're the one who mentioned the problem to your supervisor first, he or she is unlikely to be trusted by the other person as completely impartial. Moreover, as soon as a supervisor begins to intervene in interpersonal relations, the dynamics of a problem can change radically. What before was just a dispute between the two of you has now escalated to a higher level of the institution. Your supervisor can give you general advice about conflict resolution, discuss formal mediation options you may have, and sometimes give you some helpful insight into the other person's reasons for acting as he or she does. But you should never expect the person to solve the problem for you or leave the impression that you want the supervisor to take your side in the dispute.

Conclusion

Too frequently provosts and deans operate independently, losing sight of the common cause they share with the other units at their institution. Provosts are commonly regarded as first among equals in the vice-presidential rank and supervise a budget that's often many times that of other vice presidential areas. Deans too often view their academic programs as the most important part of the institution; after all, that's why they pursued an advanced degree in one of those fields. But there's much to be gained from collaboration with peers if these possibilities are explored with creativity, a willingness to compromise, and an entrepreneurial spirit. If the process of frequent constructive communication among your colleagues hasn't already begun at your institution, you may be the person in the best position to begin bringing about some positive change.

REFERENCES

Irwin, B. D. (2014). Working with other deans. In L. L. Behling (Ed.), *The resource handbook for academic deans* (pp. 233–236). San Francisco, CA: Jossey-Bass.

McDaniel, T. R. (2003). The art of diplomacy. In McDaniel, T. R. (Ed.), *Dean's dialogue* (pp. 33–35). Madison, WI: Magna.

Krejsler, J. B. (2013). Plug into "the modernizing machine"! Danish university reform and its transformable academic subjectivities. *International Journal of Qualitative Studies in Education*, 26, 1153–1168.

RESOURCES

Bolton, R. (1986). *People skills: How to assert yourself, listen to others, and resolve conflicts*. New York, NY: Touchstone/Simon and Schuster.

Cloke, K., Goldsmith, J., & Bennis, W. (2005). *Resolving conflicts at work: Eight strategies for everyone on the job*. San Francisco, CA: Jossey-Bass.

Cupach, W. R., & Canary, D. J. (2000). *Competence in interpersonal conflict*. Prospect Heights, IL: Waveland.

Edelmann, R. J. (1993). *Interpersonal conflicts at work*. Leicester, UK: British Psychological Society.

Irwin, B. D. (2014). Working with other deans. In L. L. Behling (Ed.), *The resource handbook for academic deans* (pp. 233–236). San Francisco, CA: Jossey-Bass.

Kaye, K. (1994). *Work place wars and how to end them: Turning personal conflicts into productive teamwork*. New York, NY: AMACOM.

Pickering, P. (2006). *How to manage conflict: Turn all conflicts into win-win outcomes* (3rd ed.). Franklin Lakes, NJ: Career Press.

Wilmot, W. W., & Hocker, J. L. (2014). *Interpersonal conflict* (9th ed.). New York, NY: McGraw-Hill.

22

THE PROVOST

Since so many responsibilities of deans and provosts are similar, most chapters in this book are directed to both audiences simultaneously. But as part of your professional ecosystem, it's important to talk about your interactions with your supervisor. And who that supervisor is obviously differs for deans and provosts. This chapter is directed primarily at deans, although provosts might find it useful to learn a bit about how they're perceived by the people who report to them. For this reason, the primary questions here are:

- How do deans work most effectively with the provost for the benefit of their programs, students, and faculty?
- How do deans repair a relationship with the provost once it has become strained or damaged?
- What should deans do when their relationship with the provost has become toxic and unsustainable?

To begin on as positive a note as possible, let's start by assuming your relationship with the provost is already good and you're looking for ways to make it even better.

Sharing Information

No one likes to be blindsided, just as no one likes to feel as though they're drowning in a sea of useless information. We all have some point of comfort along this spectrum that divides what we feel we must know from what we're perfectly content letting others worry about. A healthy relationship with the provost depends on knowing what that point is for your boss. If you share too much information, important details will get lost and you'll run the risk of being perceived as not able to distinguish between the vital and the trivial. If you don't share enough information, the provost may feel that you're keeping secrets or trying to undermine his or her authority. So how do you know how much to share? You can begin by asking. Particularly if either you or the provost is relatively new to the position, it can be useful to inquire, "Am I providing the level of detail you'd like to see in my reports? Am I giving you all the information that you need? Or would you prefer merely to know what's going on in broad outlines?" It's not a sign of failure to be told that you're under- or overreporting information. In fact, you'll probably receive credit just for asking the question. If your provost is not forthcoming with an answer and you have to guess, it's probably better to err on the side of providing too much information rather than too little. You can always scale back the amount of detail your provost feels is necessary in future meetings. But if you happen not to tell the provost something he or she regards as really important, the damage can be significant. So until you're sure, offer too much rather than too little.

When sharing this information, it's a good idea to do so through formal means: in scheduled meetings, by e-mail, or in printed memoranda. You're not the only dean who's passing on important items to the provost, and he or she must also keep track of items shared by the president, members of his or her staff, and many other stakeholders throughout the institution. It's easy to forget something that someone tells you in passing in the hallway or at a public event. While it's inappropriate to record certain types of information, such as personnel matters or unproven allegations, in writing, it's also unrealistic to expect that the provost will give you an immediate response to complex issues that will require time to investigate and reflect on. Any experienced administrator knows that it's difficult to understand the intricacy of a problem after hearing only one side of an issue, even if the person who's presenting the matter is a highly trusted dean. One of the reasons you're sharing the information with your supervisor is that the issue is significant and perhaps difficult to address. The provost will want to think more about the matter and probably collect additional information. He or she will know that until it's clear whether there are multiple dimensions to the problem, it can be dangerous to commit to pursuing a specific course of action—or even being perceived as unwilling to hear whether there are other sides to the story. So don't be surprised if the answer you receive is little more than, "Let me think about it."

The Three Cs

In chapter 2, I discussed the importance of collegial candor to academic leadership. Now in building strong relationships with the provost, I expand on this notion:

> In order to develop a strong and mutually supportive relationship with the provost, deans need to base their interactions on what we might call the three Cs: candor, collegiality, and confidentiality.

Candor

Just as much as you rely on the provost for support, advice, and timely information, so does he or she rely on you for your perspective and sound advice. If you believe that the provost is about to embark on a new course of action that you believe is ill advised, it's your obligation to point out the problems the decision might cause. A dean who simply agrees with everything the provost says may find these conversations quite pleasant in the short term, but ultimately does a disservice to the institution and the programs in his or her college.

It's a dean's professional obligation to give candid advice to the provost, regardless of whether giving that advice entails supporting a good decision that's likely to be unpopular in the college, offering an alternative perspective that the provost may have overlooked, pointing out the dangers likely to occur from a proposed plan, or something else. The dean's role is to be neither the perpetual gadfly nor the administration's toady but rather a reliable counselor who provides the provost with the information and insight he or she needs in order to be effective as a chief academic officer.

Collegiality

While you should feel free to disagree with your supervisor, that disagreement rarely, if ever, needs to be made in an unpleasant manner. Collegial disagreement means being specific about why your views on a matter are different from those of the provost—perhaps they involve a policy that will be seen one way by the president and the governing board but quite differently by the students, faculty, and alumni of your college—and engaging in a constructive conversation about other possibilities. Just as you would expect a faculty member or department chair who disagrees with you to focus on the issue itself and not attack you as a person, so should you adopt this same approach when dealing with your boss. You want to make it clear that it's the initiative, proposed change, or decision with which you disagree, not the provost personally, who may well have given this issue great thought and care. In short, collegiality entails dealing in a professional manner with all issues, no matter whether you and the provost happen to agree about the best way to proceed.

Confidentiality

As candid and collegial as your disagreements with the provost may be, those discussions are best conducted behind closed doors. Having this type of private discussion with the provost is quite different from concealing important information from your faculty, acting deceptively, or operating in an underhanded manner. Confidential conversations mean that you and the provost have developed a relationship in which you can air your differences constructively in private while working together for the institution's benefit in public. There will inevitably be issues on which, although you have done your best to dissuade the provost from pursuing a particular course of action, your recommendations will be overruled. If that ever happens in a matter of such dire consequence that you feel your entire working relationship with your supervisor has been damaged irreparably, then you'll need to do some serious thinking about whether you can continue in your position. (See chapter 46.) But a situation that severe shouldn't happen more than once or twice in your entire career. If you find yourself faced with a dilemma of this kind more often than that, you might want to examine your own role in creating these situations. It's simply not worth going to the wall over most policy decisions. In a surprising number of cases, matters that look as though they're likely to have a negative effect on our programs actually turn out to make very little difference. Sometimes we even find ourselves better off than we were before.

In the vast majority of cases, therefore, your most productive approach will be to state your position candidly in private and then leave these differences of opinion behind when you speak about the issue in public. Support what you can in whatever way you feel you can. You don't have to lie. You don't have to call an initiative "wonderful" if you feel it is seriously flawed. Nevertheless, you can say such things as, "The provost has outlined several important benefits that may arise from this initiative," or, "I think we need to evaluate the merits of this proposal in terms of how it'll help the institution as a whole." The important thing is to avoid undermining your supervisor's idea simply because you disagreed with it. There are times when being a member of a team means working supportively on behalf of an idea that you yourself had privately not endorsed.

Assuming the Provost's Perspective

Many conflicts arise between deans and their provosts because each side assumes that the other shares its priorities. While this assumption is undoubtedly true to a certain extent (no one, for instance, would object to a goal that deals with improving the institution's academic reputation), you shouldn't assume you know all the provost's primary concerns unless the two of you have discussed them openly. If your institution has a solid strategic plan, particularly one that was authored or revised by the upper administration currently in place, that document can be an excellent guide to many of these priorities. You'll still want to check, however, to make certain your interpretation of how the institution's strategic goals relate to your college accurately reflects your provost's own view of these matters. Never assume that simply because you're using similar language, you both are talking about the same things. To you, "strengthening academic programs across the institution" may mean expanding the number of majors and reducing your overall student-to-faculty ratio. To your provost, that same phrase may mean reducing the number of majors the school offers so as to create a more focused curriculum and free up funds that can be redirected to the largest and most popular majors. Until you have a clear conversation about how you intend to implement the plan's strategic goals, you'll never know if your priorities really reflect those of your provost.

Of course, understanding your provost's priorities doesn't necessarily mean the same thing as agreeing with them. You'll still have an opportunity, using the candid, collegial, and confidential approach, to clarify where you think these priorities need to be reconsidered. Nevertheless, you'll never get to this point unless you make a concerted effort to find out precisely what your supervisor's most important goals really are and which of those goals may be nonnegotiable. At the very least, you'll emerge from these conversations with a much clearer understanding of where you and your college stand in relation to the upper administration's vision for the future.

Aligning Objectives

Once you understand what your provost's priorities are, you have an opportunity to reevaluate your college's own mission and objectives within the framework of those overarching goals. For instance, suppose you're the dean of a liberal arts college and your provost has told you that "economic development for the region" and "placing graduates in high-paying jobs" will be the single highest priorities of his or her administration. This knowledge will provide you with several opportunities:

- You can shift your rhetoric in discussions with the provost to focus on the ways in which liberal arts disciplines develop effective written and oral communication, critical thinking skills, and leadership abilities—all qualities that employers say they're looking for when they hire people—and thus are well aligned with the goals the provost outlined.

- You can start a new conversation with the provost in which you clarify the ways in which economic development has to go hand-in-hand with cultural development and intellectual development, as suggested by authors like David Brooks in *Bobos in Paradise* (2000) and Richard Florida in *The Rise of the Creative Class* (2002).

- You can gather data that highlight the success of your graduates in contributing to the economic development of your region either directly after their graduation or by placement in highly desirable graduate programs.

- You can supplement that information with data about the rate at which graduates from your college have remained in or returned to your region after their positive experience in your programs.

In a similar way, if you are dean of the graduate school and your provost has indicated that undergraduate education will be the highest priority of his or her administration, you can begin demonstrating how the presence of graduate students as teaching assistants enhances the institution's undergraduate program, how the availability of graduate assistants for research has helped retain the very faculty members who are most critical to the success of your undergraduate program, and how the prestige of your graduate programs has played a significant role in recruiting students to all levels of the institution. Nearly every administrative priority can be related in some manner to the mission of a dean's college. Your challenge as an academic is to help interpret those vice-presidential goals into objectives that your college can help to achieve.

Respecting Boundaries

One of the mistakes some deans make is to adopt a course of action that falls within the province of the president or provost. For example, directly contacting a member of the governing board, soliciting donors for gifts without first checking with the development office, or speaking with the media on behalf of the institution without the appropriate clearance can all be regarded by upper administrators as infringements on their areas of authority. Deans should never initiate contacts of this kind without prior discussion of your intent with the provost and receipt of his or her express approval. Most deans understand this principle and would never initiate such a contact.

But what do you do if it's the donor, reporter, or member of the governing board who's contacting *you*? Even in these cases it's a wise practice to keep the upper administration fully informed as soon as possible. Deans who neglect to do so often find themselves in trouble—at times, they even lose their positions—for the mere appearance of overstepping their bounds. For this reason, any interaction with external constituencies that could be regarded as falling within the prerogative of the upper administration should be cleared with the appropriate offices before proceeding. If you're the one who is receiving the call, ask if you can call back at a more convenient time. Then immediately notify your supervisor and anyone else who needs to be in the loop on the matter. If it's best for you to return the call yourself, you'll have a better understanding of what the institution's message should be. If there's some reason that you shouldn't be the person who returns the call, the reply can then be handled at what the upper administration decides is the appropriate level (perhaps the president or provost directly), with you simply informed of the outcome in case the external constituent asks you about it later.

Repairing a Relationship

So far this discussion has been about ways in which deans can build and maintain a good relationship with their provosts. But the second question was, "How do deans repair a relationship with the provost once it has become strained or damaged?" In other words, suppose you haven't been following the principles I've been discussing until now, and you have a tense or dysfunctional relationship with your boss—or suppose you have been following these principles but they just haven't worked for you. How do you turn things around? First, do a quick review of your interactions with the provost and make sure that you're consistently applying the three Cs:

○ *Candor*: Discuss the matter openly with your supervisor. Indicate that you sense the relationship isn't as positive as you'd like it to be. Ask the provost for his or her ideas about why that may be so. Listen carefully and not defensively to the responses. Initiate a candid conversation about how matters could be improved.

○ *Collegiality*: Reflect on whether you've been acting professionally at all times. Are there instances you can recall where you might have taken matters personally when a more objective approach was called for? Have you ever acted in a way that undermined the provost's authority? Have you been supportive of the provost's policies once decisions were made, even if you didn't initially agree with them? Do you repay coldness or hostility with kindness in an effort to set a positive tone?

○ *Confidentiality*: Consider whether there have been occasions when you shared information with others that the provost intended to be for you alone. Are there ways in which you may have made the provost's job more challenging by releasing privileged information without permission?

Then, after laying the groundwork through these reflections, continue to build on your positive relationship with the provost by asking yourself the following questions:

○ In the grand scheme of things, how important are the issues that appear to be causing tension between the provost and me? Is it in the long-term best interests of my programs, students, and faculty members for me to be more flexible or even to concede the point entirely?

○ Can I identify a particular date or event after which my relationship with the provost began to break down? For example, do the problems seem to have arisen largely after the new president arrived? Did the provost begin treating me differently after I openly disagreed with the upper administration on some issue?

○ Is it possible that what I'm sensing isn't a matter that I should take personally? Could it be, for instance, that the provost treats everyone, or at least all the deans, this way? Could I be misinterpreting an issue that's causing the provost concern in his or her own life as one that involves me when in fact it has nothing to do with me?

○ To what extent is this problem making it more difficult for me to do my job as effectively as I would like?

If, after considering these questions, you find that your problem with the provost is truly serious, ongoing, and resistant to your efforts to resolve it, it's time for the two of you to have another frank conversation. Ask the provost what outcome he or she would like to see regarding your continuing impasse. Even if the answer is, "I'd like you to step down," at least you'll know where you stand and can begin to respond on the basis of knowledge, not mere imagination. Or if the outcome the provost suggests is both nonnegotiable and completely unacceptable to you, you'll have clear confirmation that your relationship has broken down irretrievably.

In most cases, however, what you learn will provide a path that you and the provost can use to begin moving toward a more satisfactory working relationship. The two of you may never become close or develop the level of mutual respect you'd prefer, but you'll have a chance to work together professionally in a way that best serves the needs of the institution as a whole and your college in particular.

Being Undermined

I noted how important it will be for you as a dean to avoid undermining (or even being perceived as undermining) the provost's authority once a decision has been made. But what do you do if the provost is the one doing the undermining? How do you respond if, as one of my colleagues puts it, you're working for a boss who appears to be after your scalp?

Situations like these—and they occur more frequently than some deans expect—require you to weigh three, sometimes competing, sets of needs simultaneously: your own, your programs', and your institution's. In terms of your own needs, you have to consider the toll that working in such an environment is likely to have on your health, piece of mind, and career. Some people can cope with an environment in which their boss is unsupportive or hostile far better than others. They can leave their concerns at the office and distinguish between the tensions they have with the provost and their own sense of self-worth. For other deans, however, the level of stress and anxiety that's produced by a boss who seems bent on undermining them creates an intolerable working environment. They lose sleep, the ability to focus on important details, and their general enjoyment of life. Also a factor in the personal needs of many deans is their career path. If they're only a few years from retirement, they may either decide that they'll just tough things out for the short term or that they don't need the unpleasantness their supervisors are causing and will return to the classroom or retire early rather than tolerating the situation. If they're just starting out in their administrative careers, they may feel that failure now could compromise all their plans for future work as an academic leader. And if they're somewhere in the middle of those two situations, they may feel trapped in an environment where there's no escape: they've interrupted their research agenda sufficiently that it would be difficult to return to life as a professor but find it impossible to be effective in their current role. These midcareer deans may face the most difficult choice of all. The dilemma they confront can lead to a full-blown midlife crisis as they struggle to consider if what they've done and still hope to do will be meaningless if they change paths now.

These serious thoughts about one's personal needs, well-being, and legacy become coupled with concerns about the best interests of the institution and its academic programs. Would the college or university be better served by having the dean step aside so that the provost could work together more effectively with a replacement? Or are the students and faculty better served by a dean who pushes back against the provost's efforts to undermine his or her efforts and becomes a strong advocate for an alternative academic vision? There can't be one answer to these questions that suits everyone's situation, but the following are some of the issues you will probably want to consider if you find yourself working with a provost who appears to have it in for you.

○ *Where is your base of support?* As you'll see in chapter 46, academic leaders can survive (at least for a while) if they have the strong support of their supervisor or their faculty. If the provost has turned against you for whatever reason but you've got strong faculty support, it may be worthwhile sticking it out if you feel you can still make a valuable contribution to your college. But if faculty support is weak or nonexistent, your position may be untenable; start looking for an exit strategy.

○ *How would you describe the president's relationship with the provost?* There's one possible exception to the rule that you can survive without either the provost's strong support or your faculty's, but not without both: when the president likes you but has a stormier relationship with the provost. In this situation, unless the president's own position is in jeopardy, you've got a strong ally to defend you against the provost's efforts to undermine your authority. In fact, depending on how Machiavellian you are, you might be able to parlay the situation into your chance to become the provost's successor, either temporarily or permanently.

○ *How secure is the provost's position?* In light of the possibility of the provost's departure, you probably wouldn't want to give up your position and then find the provost stepping down or forced out only a short time later. It may well be that if you're not having a good relationship with the provost, no one else is either. If you have reason to believe that your current unpleasant situation won't last forever, then it becomes a matter of deciding whether the stress and anxiety that you're experiencing now might be compensated by contributions you'll still be able to make in the future. Take your time before making a final decision in this case. You've got a lot of pros and cons to consider, and the result could mean significant damage to your career if you make the wrong choice. You may also want to consider adopting some of the decision-making strategies explored in chapter 12.

Conclusion

Despite all the attention I've paid to repairing a bad relationship with the provost and exploring your options when the environment is truly toxic, it's appropriate to close this conversation with a reminder that most provosts prove to be good partners with the deans, generally interested in their colleges, and eager to help them succeed. On those rare occasions when that's not the case, the flexibility and understanding adopted by the dean will go a long way toward a way to resolve or cope with the situation. The most important principle to remember as academic leaders is that we ourselves need to model the cooperative, collegial, and confidential approach to our responsibilities that we're expecting from others.

Good administration can be contagious. If we do our jobs in the way that we believe all academic leaders should, our supervisors may be guided by our own example.

In cases where reflection on a matter suggests that we've played a role in causing a relationship to sour, we should never underestimate the power of looking someone straight in the eyes, admitting what we've done, and uttering a direct, clear, and sincere apology. When that occurs, we should always remember to apologize for what we have done, not just for making the other person feel bad. Otherwise we're not really taking full responsibility for our actions, but rather assigning partial fault to the other person for giving in to a negative emotion. Being accountable for our actions is an important ingredient of academic leadership and an essential prerequisite for success as a dean.

REFERENCES

Brooks, D. (2000). *Bobos in paradise: The new upper class and how they got there*. New York: Simon & Schuster.

Florida, R. L. (2002). *The rise of the creative class: And how it's transforming work, leisure, community and everyday life*. New York, NY: Basic Books.

RESOURCES

Dufour, G. (2011). *Managing your manager: How to get ahead with any type of boss*. New York, NY: McGraw-Hill.

Futterman, S. (2004). *When you work for a bully: Assessing your options and taking action*. Montvale, NJ: Croce.

Nielsen, L. A. (2013). *Provost: Experiences, reflections, and advice from a former "number two" on campus*. Sterling, VA: Stylus.

Scott, G. G. (2006). *A survival guide for working with bad bosses: Dealing with bullies, idiots, back-stabbers, and other managers from hell*. New York, NY: AMACOM.

23

THE PRESIDENT

Perhaps no other administrative position has changed as dramatically in the last century as that of the university president. Whereas once presidents were almost always faculty members who had risen through the ranks and served as department chairs, deans, and provosts before being selected as chief executive officer, now that pathway is the exception, not the rule.

Presidents and chancellors come to their positions by any number of routes, but the traditional academic track is increasingly uncommon. Presidents may have worked in higher education as vice presidents for development, community relations, or business affairs. They may come to the academic world after success in business. Many are political appointees, often former governors or legislators who failed in a reelection bid, reached the end of their term limit, or decided on their own to pursue a different career. Those different pathways to the presidency reflect the changing nature of the job itself. Many presidents spend very little of their time dealing with curricular issues, evaluating research proposals, or interviewing candidates for faculty positions. They're far more likely to be devoting their energy to fundraising, lobbying the government, or representing their institutions to the public at large. That's why the skill set of the successful corporate leader, politician, or development officer is often more important for presidents than the skill set of the successful teacher, researcher, and academic citizen.

What all of this means is that the relationship a dean or provost has with the president is likely to be significantly different from the relationship he or she has with any of the other internal stakeholders of the institution. At times, interacting with a president can be more like interacting with an external constituent—a board member, potential donor, legislator, community supporter, or parent—than with any other member of the faculty, staff, or administration.

It's possible that the last time the president was on a college campus was when he or she was a student and thus may bring to the job certain assumptions about universities that are no longer relevant. The president may assume that the organizational culture of the university is similar to that of a corporation, senate committee, or brigade and thus can be managed or directed in much the same way. None of this is to say, of course, that presidents don't ever understand the academic ecosystem or that you never encounter a chancellor who rose through the academic ranks, merely that the challenges facing presidents and chancellors have changed, and so the background of the people who are hired as presidents and chancellors has often changed as well.

Building a Relationship with the President

It's a truism in higher education that what you see depends on where you sit. As a provost or dean, you understand the extent to which issues can seem very different from your perspective than they do from that of faculty members and department chairs at your institution. It isn't merely that you deal with more academic disciplines than they do, but also that the issues themselves take on added complexity. That complexity intensifies geometrically at the presidential level. For now, it's not just academic issues that are involved, but also the full range of activities that occur at a modern university: athletics, housing, student conduct matters, contracts, dealing with the governing board and/or legislature, construction, maintenance, legal challenges, employee benefits, contract negotiations, fundraising, emergency planning, interacting with the media, and much else besides. Those elements don't just change the way presidents see things; they change what presidents see. So the first important ingredient in building a good relationship with the president is to look at the world through his or her lenses and adjust your rhetoric accordingly.

For example, when deans and provosts are interested in adding faculty lines or seeking major renovations to facilities, they tend to focus on issues like meeting student demand, attracting and retaining the best faculty members, increasing the international reputation of their programs, promoting student engagement, and the like. Presidents are interested in those issues too, but they may have to set these concerns alongside such matters as keeping occupancy rates of residence halls high enough to pay for the outstanding bonds on their construction, providing adequate staffing in areas like admissions and development to sustain the institution's future growth, balancing the expectations of the governing board and legislature that a sufficient number of students are prepared for jobs in particular fields, making sure that athletic teams meet all the Title IX requirements, and so on. In addition, presidents have certain priorities either because those are their own particular interests or because certain expectations were made when they were hired. They may be expected to increase enrollment, raise the endowment, clean house after a previous administration, embark on a capital campaign, or engage in any of a full range of responsibilities that provosts and deans rarely think about. If they're still trying to staunch the flow of donors who are withdrawing their pledges to the university because of an ill-considered remark by their predecessor, then your white paper about restructuring the general education program to meet the needs of today's students, as important as that goal may be, is likely to be met with indifference. It could even cause a rift between you and the president because you appear to be harping on an issue that's clearly not his or her priority.

Managing Up

What you need to do instead is engage in what Roseanne Badowski and Roger Gittines (2003) call "managing up": going beyond your assigned duties to accomplish tasks that make your boss's job easier. In other words, if deans and provosts see their roles as not merely advocating for and supervising the programs assigned to them but also engaging in activities that make the president more successful, they become important assets for the president, not simply paid administrators.

Suppose you are working for a president who was hired by the governing board with a clear mandate to get the budget under control, improve student retention, and end the athletic sanctions that the institution is currently under. "Managing up" means that these concerns should also now become your concerns. The first step in this process is to ask yourself what possibilities you have within your sphere of responsibilities to help the president achieve these goals. Among the possibilities that might exist are these:

- Devoting a larger portion of your student employment budget to hiring current students as tutors, which could improve student retention by helping struggling students succeed and engaging the tutors themselves more fully in the life of the institution while also providing them with a source of income. This strategy might even remove the athletic sanction if it happened to be related to the academic performance of student athletes.

- Reducing expenditures by conducting a study to improve efficiency in course scheduling, use of classrooms, and faculty loads.

○ Cutting the budget further by aggressively seeking external funding for program support wherever possible and thus shifting costs from institutional accounts to development sources.

○ Examining the programs under your supervision to determine where student attrition is the highest and then redirecting current funding to eliminate obstacles, disincentives, and bottlenecks that are causing problems for students.

○ Identifying best practices in the institution's programs that are currently most successful with student retention and timely graduation and then adopting those practices in other areas.

By helping the president succeed, you're actually helping your own area, even though that result may not be immediately obvious. You're building a relationship with the president, and in the future when it comes to your own needs and priorities, he or she will regard you as an important member of the team and thus be more willing to help.

The next step in managing up is to look for ways in which meeting your own needs also helps the president reach his or her goals. As we saw in chapter 13, a particularly effective way of getting your supervisor to buy into something that you want is to find a way to describe your desire as a means of achieving a goal important to your boss. But an even more effective strategy is to discover areas of actual overlap where your goals and the president's clearly align. For example, you may have decided that it's best to merge two departments since enrollments in both have been low, and there's an excellent chair in one but no acceptable candidates in the other to replace a chair who's retiring at the end of the year. What you regard as a logical move because of administrative efficiency can also be incorporated into the president's goal of reducing costs. Or perhaps you're interested in providing incentives to faculty members who present their research at conferences and then convert that presentation into a peer-reviewed publication within two years. Although your motivation may be to increase the faculty members' chances of earning tenure and promotion, you can incorporate this goal into your president's initiative to improve the university's reputation for research.

Possible Warning Signs

Managing up is thus a highly effective way of establishing or improving a relationship with your president. There are, however, two warning signs you should be alert for that might suggest a need for a more cautious approach.

The first is when the president actively encourages you to manage up. While it may seem paradoxical to argue that it's ineffective to adopt this strategy when the president expresses a desire for it but desirable to do so when he or she demonstrates little interest or awareness of it, doing so actually makes sense. Supervisors who feel a need to state that they want those who report to them to be particularly mindful of how they can make their bosses look good are demonstrating a high degree of insecurity, lack of trust in their employees, and self-interest that surpasses their desire to help the institution. While it's a good idea for provosts and deans to manage up sometimes, they also have to manage down a lot too. They have to think of the needs and desires of the students, faculty members, and other stakeholders in their programs. If the president expects that the provost and deans will devote all (or at least a significant part) of their energy to looking out for his or her own interests, those other constituents will soon be overlooked. Even more important, Managing up works when it can be done as a welcome and often unexpected addition to one's ordinary responsibilities, not a required substitute for them. It's also important to remember that insecure, mistrustful, and overly self-interested presidents often don't last very long. It's a poor strategy to ignore the needs of your programs in an attempt to benefit a supervisor who may not be around in a few years.

The second warning sign is if you and a number of your peers feel a sincere reluctance to benefit the president by managing up. Protecting your supervisor and advancing his or her agenda is something that provosts and deans should regard as an important part of their responsibilities and eagerly want to do. But if they feel a serious reservation or concern about doing so, that's a bad sign. It means that their relationship has broken down to the point that helping their supervisor succeed is no longer viewed as a priority. There's a reason that votes by the faculty against administrators are called "votes of no confidence": it means that the faculty no longer has confidence in the administrator's ability to lead the area or institution in an effective, honest, or successful manner. If you feel that you'd be managing up only grudgingly or half-heartedly, that feeling is in itself a personal vote of no confidence in the president. On at least some level, you must sense that the institution's success and your programs' success are no longer tied to the president's success. You and your peers have already begun to pull away from the president, and if a crisis were to occur, you might be content to let the president suffer the consequences while you protect your own students, faculty, and staff. It is likely that within a fairly short time, either you or the president will be exploring other professional opportunities.

The question then arises what you should do if either of these two warning signs occur. The wisest strategy, of course, is to try to maintain as cordial a relationship as possible with the president while strengthening your programs in a way that helps secure their future. People often feel hypocritical acting this way because they appear to be supporting the president while in actuality they're planning for his or her replacement. But the reality of administrative positions is that people rarely keep the same job for very long anyway. We all know presidents who have been in their positions for fifteen or twenty years, but they're rapidly becoming a rarity. A president who serves the same institution for ten years is now regarded as having held the position for a very long time, and presidencies of only five or six years are no longer uncommon. For this reason, maintaining good relations with the president while keeping an eye on your own future and that of the programs you supervise isn't being insincere; it's being realistic. Particularly when you sense that others are beginning to pull away from the president as well, you don't want your area to suffer because the president's position has weakened. You want to survive whatever happens to the president and be well situated to make certain that your area isn't harmed in the transition. (For other possible signs that the president's position may be in jeopardy, see Trachtenberg, 2013.)

The President as Mentor

In the majority of cases, however, where the president is effective and the relationship the two of you have is good, there are other possibilities for how you can strengthen your rapport with the president in a way that is of mutual benefit.

The first is to ask the president to serve as your formal mentor. Particularly in situations where you might envision yourself as the president of a college or university someday, this mentorship can be extremely valuable. Simply by virtue of having reached the highest level of the university, the president knows something about how to identify the appropriate executive position, write an effective letter of application, interview in a manner that leads to a job offer, and negotiate an acceptable hiring package. These are skills that all academic leaders need. In addition, the president, whether in his or her first executive role or merely new to this institution, will be undergoing a process of figuring things out, making decisions, and building a team for the future. By mentoring you, the president will have access to you as a sounding board for new ideas. You can begin crafting your own executive vision at the same time that you help the president refine his or her own. Moreover, if the president likes the way you think about various issues, you might secure yourself a leadership role on the team the president is assembling at your current institution—and possibly beyond.

Depending on your own needs and the amount of time the president has available, your mentoring relationship might be formal or informal. Formal mentoring relationships occur when you agree to meet on a set schedule in order to discuss specific tasks that are undertaken with definite expectations. Informal mentorships are far more casual. You get together when your schedule allows, perhaps over a drink or a meal, and simply talk about how things are going. While formal mentorships might include assigned projects with expectations for follow-up and reflection on the lessons learned, informal mentorships are far more likely to consist solely of conversations about the issues you're facing and whatever guidance the president can offer based on his or her own experience. While formal mentoring usually has a defined beginning and end date ("Let's get together the first Wednesday of the month for the rest of the academic year"), informal mentoring may simply fade away when either participant finds it no longer useful, or it may develop into an ongoing, even lifelong relationship. Table 29.1 summarizes some of these major differences between these two types of mentoring.

Although you'll be the one receiving most of the benefits from this mentoring relationship, it's the president's needs and personalities that should shape its development. For example, if the president would be lost

Table 23.1. Formal versus Informal Mentoring

	Formal Mentoring	Informal Mentoring
Goals	Goals are clearly established.	Goals are often unspecified.
Outcomes	Outcomes are measured.	Outcomes are unknown.
Duration	Mentoring span is often limited (i.e., one semester, one year).	The mentoring span is often indefinite (i.e., "as long as we find our meetings useful").
Action plan	Sometimes it is tied to an action plan (i.e., mentoring veers off into coaching).	Rarely is it tied to an action plan (i.e., conversations tend to be general).
Frequency	Often there is a set timetable (e.g., every other Tuesday at noon).	Mentor and protégé meet as needed.
Content	Usually it has a set agenda (e.g., developing a strategic vision or securing external funds).	Meetings are often free-form and flow easily from one topic to the next.

without a tight daily schedule, relishes academic ceremonies (the more elaborate, the better), and speaks frequently about following the chain of command, then he or she would probably prefer a more formal mentoring relationship, regardless of what you may wish. However, if the president is on a first-name basis with absolutely everyone, strolls around campus frequently, loves to have impromptu conversations, and enjoys dressing down for casual Fridays, then an informal type of mentoring is likely to be best even if you feel more comfortable with something that's scheduled a bit more tightly. Remember that you're likely to gain the most from an arrangement in which the president feels free to act however he or she wishes than if you try to make your style set the tone. Most important, be sure to keep in mind the following essential principle:

> Respect your boss's time.

Nothing can turn a positive mentoring relationship into a dreaded chore faster than a belief that a protégé is going to outstay his or her welcome, prove to be a distraction from other responsibilities, and abuse your generosity by mistaking an offer to help as a ticket to special access not accorded to others.

Special Projects

The second way to help strengthen your rapport with the president is to display a willingness to assume a leadership role in special projects that help advance the president's vision. Even the most hands-on president understands that he or she can't do everything alone. While you'll be expected to play a significant role in carrying out the president's initiatives in your capacity as provost and dean, you'll increase your value to your supervisor by going above and beyond these expectations. When volunteering for a special project, don't limit your offer to activities that are enjoyable or glamorous. Everyone wants to participate in the pleasant opportunities. Instead be the first person to step up for some of the less visible but important activities that can help the president succeed. Volunteer to edit the reaccreditation study. Collect the data that are not stored centrally. Serve on the community board that seems to meet too often and for far too long. Take on activities that can save the president's time and energy for things that can be done only at the executive level. No matter how tedious the responsibility may be, you'll learn something from it, earn the president's gratitude, and have a new achievement to record on your résumé.

In choosing which special projects are most likely to help you build a strong relationship with the president, ask yourself the following questions:

○ What are the three or four highest goals of the president? What are the steps along the way that will have to be accomplished in order to achieve each of those goals? Which of those steps will others least be willing to do, thus leaving an important need that I can fill?

○ What are the skills I have that best complement those of the president? In other words, what am I good at that he or she finds challenging, unpleasant, or time-consuming?

○ What are the tasks at which I am most likely to exceed the president's expectations? Where might it be possible for me to under-promise and overproduce?

Volunteering for special projects provides you with a lot of opportunity, but it also carries some risk. Once you offer to help, you have to follow through. More than that, you have to succeed. If you don't, it's likely to be the case that an activity you thought might bolster your relationship with the president could actually end up harming it.

Maintaining Perspective

The last way to develop good rapport with the president is to approach your relationship with the right perspective. Try not to interrupt any single action or comment. If you fixate on everything the president does or says, scrutinizing it for signs of whether he or she respects and values you, you'll probably take steps that are counterproductive. For instance, you might hesitate to state an important objection to one of the president's plans because you feel that he or she has been cold to you lately; that objection may have been the very thing that would have stopped the president from making a serious mistake.

For the most part, presidents like the people around them to be confident, secure people. If you begin acting as though every compliment given to someone else is an insult to you, you'll come across as full of self-doubt and overly reliant on the opinions of others. Presidents have bad days too. Whatever is upsetting them or causing them to be more abrupt with you than usual probably isn't about you; it's about something else that's going on in his or her life. Don't take it personally. Continue to demonstrate loyalty suffused with candor, a willingness to help wherever needed, and a commitment to go beyond the responsibilities outlined in your job description, and the relationship you have with the president is likely to get stronger over time.

Conclusion

Remember that presidents value loyalty but often feel contempt for groveling. Be authentic: vigorously support what you can, speak your mind about genuine concerns, and seek the right place on the spectrum between being a sycophant and an opponent. As confident as presidents may appear and as much as they admire confidence in others, they too have moments of self-doubt. There's truth in that old saying about it being lonely at the top, and if you adopt the right tone and attitude, you can build a strong relationship with the president by making him or her feel a little less lonely.

REFERENCES

Badowski, R., & Gittines, R. (2003). *Managing up: How to forge an effective relationship with those above you.* New York, NY: Currency.

Trachtenberg, S. J. (2013). *Presidencies derailed: Why university leaders fail and how to prevent it.* Baltimore, MA: Johns Hopkins University Press.

RESOURCES

Bowen, W. G. (2011). *Lessons learned: Reflections of a university president.* Princeton, NJ: Princeton University Press.

Brown, D. G. (2006). *University presidents as moral leaders.* Westport, CT: Praeger.

Buller, J. L. (2012). Leading upward. *Academic Leader, 28*(3), 1–2.

McDaniel, T. R. (2003). President-faculty relations: A dean's dilemma? In McDaniel, T. R. (Ed.) *Dean's dialogue* (pp. 1–3). Madison, WI: Magna.

Padilla, A. (2005). *Portraits in leadership: Six extraordinary university presidents.* Westport, CT: Praeger.

Pierce, S. R. (2012). *On being presidential: A guide for college and university leaders.* San Francisco, CA: Jossey-Bass.

Trachtenberg, S. J., & Blumer, T. H. (2008). *Big man on campus: A university president speaks out on higher education.* New York: Simon & Schuster.

Tulgan, B. (2010). *It's okay to manage your boss: The step-by-step program for making the best of your most important relationship at work.* San Francisco, CA: Jossey-Bass.

24

FRIENDS OF THE COLLEGE

The term *friends of the college* encompasses many different groups of external stakeholders, all of whom have a vital interest in supporting your programs and seeing them flourish. This general group of supporters may include alumni, parents of alumni, community members who have an interest in the disciplines you supervise, donors, potential donors, community leaders, and other individuals who have a high likelihood of contributing to and benefiting from the work of students and faculty members at your institution. Skillfully handled, your relationship with these external supporters can help you achieve objectives that are impossible to attain otherwise. Poorly conducted, relationships with external stakeholders can lose you friends of the college, destroy your reputation in the community, and create problems that could easily have been avoided. With that sobering truth in mind, how should provosts and deans go about creating the best possible relationship with their external stakeholders?

Using and Abusing Advisory Councils

It has become commonplace for institutions as well as the various colleges and departments within them to have formal groups of external constituents who meet periodically in an advisory role. Pioneered by colleges of business administration, where groups of successful representatives of different professions often served as mentors to students and provided insight into new curricular possibilities needed by the commercial world, these advisory councils quickly became common in all types of academic units. Many such groups were highly successful endeavors and proved invaluable to the colleges and departments that established them. Many more such entities languished, however; they had difficulty in taking root and ultimately were disbanded. What accounted for the difference? One factor appears to be that too many colleges set up their external advisory groups without a clear understanding of what they were going to do.

> Advisory councils succeed only when they have a clear purpose, a sense of direction, and, most important, a genuine opportunity to provide meaningful advice.

In other words, many advisory councils were formed with little thought and planning other than, "Lots of other groups have successful advisory councils; we need to have one too." The problem with this approach is that the people you'll want to serve on your council will be those whose time is extremely valuable. They're most likely to become disillusioned with your initiative if they feel that their time is being wasted. As a result, before forming any sort of external advisory council, ask yourself several questions:

- Will I have enough substantive business for this group to perform every time it meets?
- Is it likely that there will be a significant amount of substantive business for the foreseeable future?
- Is it truly advice that I'm seeking?
- Do I actually want some other type of involvement from my external constituents besides their advice?

Unless your answer to each of these questions is an emphatic yes, you probably should look for other ways in which friends of the college can contribute their expertise. For example, if you have an issue for which you need advice and support now but are unlikely to have substantive business for this group to perform every time it meets, you're probably better off creating a short-lived planning group with a well-defined mission that will solve the problem it's given and then dissolve. If you have a number of issues about which you want advice but don't foresee the ongoing utility of such a group, you might want to consider establishing an ad hoc advisory body that will consult with you for a semester or an academic year and then graciously disband when it's no longer needed. Furthermore, if you're not actually seeking advice but want other types of participation from the community—financial contributions, volunteered labor, guest speakers, and the like—you might consider forming a group with a different focus and mission, such as a development committee, a leadership board, a speakers' bureau, or simply "friends of the college."

Remember the essential principle from chapter 18: *Never ask an advisory body for its opinion unless you truly wish to be advised.* If you call a group an advisory board, it's going to advise you, and it's probably going to advise you about matters that you regard as beyond its purview. So even if you repeat at every meeting that the group is there simply to advise your programs on possibilities for internship placements, don't be surprised when it starts offering its advice on curricular changes, recruitment strategies, and hiring decisions. Don't be surprised either when its members become dissatisfied because "you never take our advice." What you probably should have done from the very beginning was to call the group an "internship placement board" and thus having avoided giving the members the wrong idea of their role.

In short, institutions and the programs within them use the term *advisory council* far too loosely, applying it to groups that are really in no position whatsoever to provide useful advice or offer well-informed opinions. They also form too many competing advisory boards, such as one for community supporters, another for alumni, a third for parents of current students, and so on. Distinguishing among these groups by calling them the community relations board, alumni assembly, and parents' council—each with its own charter and clearly delimited spheres of influence—helps prevent you from receiving advice that's useless or inconsistent from one group to the next. As you set up the bylaws of these groups, be aware of several important guidelines about working with external stakeholders:

○ Be honest with people about the group's purpose. Most friends of the college would prefer to know that they're being appointed to a group that's expected to raise and contribute funds than to assume their professional expertise is most important to you.

○ Be respectful that busy people have competing interests. Don't schedule meetings once a week or once a month if there's not enough serious work for the group to do. If service on the board becomes an imposition, people will resent the institution, college, or department and will not be favorably disposed to helping it.

○ Be generous in expressing your gratitude for any type of contribution—including nonfinancial contributions, such as time devoted to planning a project or professional services that you would otherwise have had to pay for—made by any member of the group. Recognize these contributions individually, specifically, and (unless the board member would not want you to do so) publicly. A once-a-year, "Thanks, everyone, for all you do," isn't sufficient.

Conducting Travel Programs with External Stakeholders

Most faculty members already know that if you really want to get to know your students well, you can do one of two things: work with them on an extended project like a play or concert or take a long trip with them. Seeing a group of students daily for several weeks, having meals with them, engaging in prolonged conversations, dealing with unexpected challenges together, and all the other experiences that result from a period of enforced togetherness creates a bonding experience that can't be duplicated in the classroom alone. And what's true for students is at least as true for getting to know the supporters of your program.

These opportunities, collectively known as *affinity travel programs* (because everyone in the group shares a common interest or affinity to some cause), benefit academic leaders in a number of ways. First, a ten- to fourteen-day trip to a highly attractive destination can provide an immediate source of external funds. It's not uncommon for schools to add a premium of a thousand dollars or more to the cost of travel packages as a required contribution to the annual fund. With an average group size of about thirty people, that contribution to your unrestricted funding may not be massive, but it's still a significant amount that can be used to augment faculty research, student travel to conferences, special events, and other activities for which funding is often scarce.

Second, affinity travel programs also provide a high degree of access to potential donors. During the trip, your external stakeholders will get to know you on a personal level, and you'll have an opportunity to learn about issues that are important to them. Photographs you take while on the trip will provide an opportunity to follow up with your travel companions after you return. For example, you could send a letter with a few photos and a handwritten card that reads, "I was just going through the photos from our trip, and I found this great picture of you. Here's a copy for you to keep as a memento of the wonderful time we had together. I'd also like to give you a call sometime to talk about [some upcoming event or fundraising initiative]." Depending on your clientele, you might even consider having the trip conclude with a final dinner at which travelers are asked for multiyear commitments or to increase their level of giving for the coming year. Even in cases where that approach might be viewed as too aggressive or where not all the participants are likely to become donors, the trip itself will serve to establish a closeness with these stakeholders that you couldn't get just by asking them to join you for lunch or an athletic event.

Technology also makes it easy for you to customize gifts for your travelers, giving you a reason to stay in touch with them after you return:

○ Many photographic programs and websites allow you to generate photo books, calendars, greeting cards, and slideshows from the photographs that you and other travelers have taken during the trip.

○ Film editing software like iMovie, Adobe Suite, Final Cut Pro, and Corel VideoStudio Pro make it easy to develop creative films from your trip, complete with previews of upcoming trips and professional-looking titles, that go far beyond the routine home movies of the past. You could even host a "premiere" of the film as an opportunity to bring the travelers to campus for a formal event.

○ Images from the trip can be transferred to cakes, mugs, passport cases, luggage tags, and other giveaways that remind the participants of what a good time they had traveling with you during your program.

There's a certain appeal that traveling with the provost or dean has for community leaders and other external supporters that's difficult to describe. They feel that they're getting special access to you and a behind-the-scenes glimpse of your programs. Another lure for friends of the college might be a travel opportunity in which they can mingle with current students, faculty members, and alumni who "come back to school" for a short period in order to relive the intellectual and cultural experiences of their youth. These mixed groups tend to be very popular. Current students frequently find mentors among the alumni and members of the community. Older travelers gain insight into what today's college students are thinking, and faculty members frequently add to the academic richness of the program by discussing topics related to their discipline. In some cases, the group bonds so closely that the same people return to take trips with one another year after year.

While travel experiences outside the country are usually the most popular with donors and other friends of the college, they aren't the only kind of affinity travel program that works well at a college or university. Domestic trips, possibly led by a popular faculty member who has expertise in a certain region of the country or historical events related to the sites you visit, can also provide an excellent "friend-raising" opportunity. (For more on friend raising, see chapter 25.) Among the destinations you might consider are:

○ Theatrical or operatic performances in New York City, combined with pre- and postperformance discussions with members of the faculty

○ Tours of the space centers in Florida or Texas, featuring special lectures by physicists, electrical engineers, or historians

- ○ Visits to film and television studios in California, enriched by presentations from film historians and faculty members with backgrounds in film, video, and multimedia studies
- ○ Exploration of national parks, including conversations with ecologists, geologists, and botanists
- ○ Trips to Wall Street, with explanations and investment advice from faculty members in finance, economics, and political science

The goal is to ask, "What expertise do I have among the faculty that could be combined with an appealing trip to a highly desirable location?" Because what you're offering can't be provided by an ordinary travel company, external stakeholders are willing to pay a premium for this special content.

Finally, short-term events such as day trips to away games, cultural events, performances, or festivals also offer possibilities for affinity travel. While they don't provide you with the extended time for getting to know the participants that you have on longer trips, they do give you a chance to test the waters without taking you away from campus for an extended period. If a short trip works well, you can always follow up with a longer private meeting with a friend of the college who seems a good fit for your vision and institutional mission.

Offering Special Premiums

One final way of strengthening the ties that external stakeholders have for your programs is to provide them with special premiums or perquisites that demonstrate how much you value their support. All colleges and universities are likely to have some sort of gift or promotional item that both advertises the school and is highly desirable to receive. Logos can be placed on such items as leather bookmarks, wine glasses, lapel pins, portfolios, note pads, and other products of this sort. Even more creative are packages of services that can be offered to friends of the college to thank them for their service, recognize certain levels of contribution, or build a closer relationship—for example:

- ○ *The golden ticket.* Guaranteed seating at certain performances, lectures, and other cultural events, perhaps combined with reserved parking, dinner, or other perquisites
- ○ *"Friends-only" lecture series.* Opportunities to meet in smaller and more personal settings with outstanding members of your own faculty or distinguished lecturers when they come to campus
- ○ *Dessert with the dean.* Periodic evening events in which friends of the college can meet with you in a casual setting and you can update

them on upcoming initiatives, allowing them to be in the know
before the rest of the general public

○ *Pregame with the provost.* A special tailgate event for select external
   stakeholders that could lead to reserved seating at the game itself

○ *Academic privileges.* Access to special collections in the library,
   opportunities to sit in on certain classes (on a space-available basis),
   the use of the institution's electronic databases, and a reserved
   parking permit

○ *Electronic perks.* Nearly every school has a section of its website
   devoted to its friends and alumni. You can take this approach one
   step further by providing password-protected access for a select
   group of external supporters that allows them to view special materials, transcripts or videos of lectures, advance news items, and
   other information that may be of interest to them

Conclusion

There is no single way to serve all the friends of your programs. The best
approach is to offer a broad menu of possibilities so that supporters can
choose opportunities that fit best with their own interests. If you do decide
to have an advisory council, it can advise you on the needs and desires of
external stakeholders. If seen as a key component in your open system (see
chapter 9), friends of the college can become powerful allies in advancing
the mission of your programs. Even better, they can become some of your
institution's most loyal donors, a major part of your ecosystem that we
consider in chapter 25.

RESOURCES

Buller, J. L. (2008). Creating an affinity travel program. *Academic Leader*,
   24(10), 4–5.
Carter, T. (2003). *Customer advisory boards: A strategic tool for customer rela-
   tionship building.* New York, NY: Best Business Books.
Carver, J. (1997). *Boards that make a difference: A new design for leadership in
   nonprofit and public organizations.* San Francisco, CA: Jossey-Bass.
Pekkanen, R., Smith, S. R., & Tsujinaka, Y. (2014). *Nonprofits and advocacy:
   Engaging community and government in an era of retrenchment.* Baltimore,
   MD: Johns Hopkins University Press.
Worth, M. J. (2008). *Sounding boards: Advisory councils in higher education.*
   Washington, DC: Association of Governing Boards of Universities and
   Colleges.

25

DONORS AND POTENTIAL DONORS

Although chapter 14 explored several aspects of how to build strong relationships with donors and prospective donors, fundraising is so important to what academic leaders do today that we need to consider this topic in greater depth. It wasn't that long ago that provosts and deans weren't expected to interact with donors very much. That situation has changed dramatically. With the increasing dependence on external funding to support academic programs, almost all academic leaders engage in at least some type of fundraising. But if provosts and deans reach their positions with relatively little formal training in many aspects of their responsibilities, they often know even less about fundraising and initially feel rather uncomfortable doing it. This chapter looks at what it is that provosts and deans need to know about working with donors and potential donors, where academic leaders go to find out how to be more effective in securing external funds, and how to avoid the pitfalls that can appear when you're engaging in an activity that seems so different from the rest of your formal responsibilities.

Using a Team Approach

Academic leaders who are new to fundraising sometimes assume that they'll receive more credit and possibly have more success if they make direct contact with people they already know, develop their own proposals, and return to campus with a check or pledge in hand. In fact, that approach could be a recipe for disaster. By acting independently, deans and provosts deprive themselves of the expertise that a development office can bring to their efforts. They risk complicating relations with a donor who may already be under solicitation for another (possibly much larger) gift by the institution. And they may make serious mistakes when it comes to finalize a complex gift agreement. For all of these reasons, the rule of thumb for academic leaders is to never go it alone in fundraising. Academic leaders are well advised to involve members of their institution's development staff from the very beginning in planning and conducting visits with donors or potential donors.

Development officers have a vast amount of information at their disposal that can be invaluable to academic leaders and help tailor a proposal that best suits the overall needs of the institution. For example, from public records, they can ascertain a potential donor's financial capacity. They may also be able to determine a prospect's giving history, thus indicating what that person's philanthropic interests are and the likelihood that a specific request might be successful. They will certainly have a record of someone's history of giving to your own institution, and that information can help you in developing future proposals. For instance, one general rule of thumb is that people who have contributed small to medium amounts (e.g., $250 or more) to a school's annual fund each year for at least twelve years are often likely to respond favorably to a request at the next significant tier (such as $10,000 or more), as long as the request is tied to an area of their interest. Because of their experience in dealing with many donors or potential donors, development officers have a good sense of how different people need to be approached. Often they can even determine which potential donors are most likely to respond favorably to a blunt request for a specific amount, which of them should be handled more circumspectly, and which of them fall somewhere in the middle. Their experience guides them in knowing whether now is the right time for what advancement professionals call the *ask*, the formal request for a specific gift.

Moreover, unless you work closely with your development office, you probably won't have a clear idea of which donors may be in the process of being recruited by your institution for possibly far larger gifts. As a result, it could end up that although you feel proud that you landed a $250,000 gift to your college's scholarship fund, what you've actually done is interfered with other plans that your college or university had for that person. Perhaps the president's desire to secure $10 million from this donor to name a building is now in jeopardy because he or she will regard the gift you received as sufficiently generous. In this way, proceeding blindly into the world of advancement brings with it a significant chance that you could alienate your president and governing board, as well as your fellow deans or vice presidents if you're ever perceived as "pinching" someone else's prospect. Only the development office tends to know all the solicitations that are in the works or anticipated, and they can guide you, when necessary, toward appropriate prospective donors for the project you have in mind.

Finally, you should be aware that the work involved in handling a gift is far from concluded once the ask is made and the gift is offered. There are legal implications in receiving, recording, and allocating contributions. Unless you have been trained as an attorney, those aren't details you'll want to be responsible for. Development officers will be experienced in the language necessary for executing valid gift agreements, the timing of when a gift may be booked, and the restrictions on when the funds will be available to your program. (On the term *book a gift*, see the glossary at the end of this chapter.) At the very least, that office will prevent you from making promises you won't be able to fulfill. Even more important, development officers can warn you against actions that would place both you and the institution at legal risk in the future.

Identifying Your Best Prospects

Once you've established a good relationship with the development office, sit down with members of that staff and begin creating a list of people with connections to your institution who do not already play a significant role in your school's fundraising efforts. Your list might include untapped or underused donors who have significant private resources, regular contributors to the annual fund who appear to be ready for a major gift request, foundations that are in your area or have a history of supporting institutions like yours, and funding agencies or government programs that have a focus related to the work you do.

Once you've created your list, go through it name by name or foundation by foundation, exploring where there may be possible overlap between the philanthropic interests of the donor or grantor and the focus or needs of the programs you supervise. For example, someone on your list may be an alumnus and thus best contacted by a favorite professor. Or the person may have attended another institution but majored in a field represented in your college; the best way to cultivate someone like this may be through the appropriate chair or dean. Someone with a successful career in a profession that relates in some way to a particular discipline may relate well to a student who's majoring in that discipline. You could reach out to a potential donor who has been active in a field like construction, architecture, or contracting about an idea for a new building, with their services donated as an extremely generous gift-in-kind. By the time you've completed this review, you'll probably notice that perhaps two to six of the names on your list have both the personal resources and the most logical connection to your greatest needs. These are the people with whom you'll want to begin your development efforts.

Raising More Than Money Alone

Development professionals frequently distinguish *friend raising* from *fundraising*. Friend raising involves creating close relationships with people, making them feel positive about what the faculty and students do in your programs, and instilling in them a strong desire to help you succeed. People rarely contribute to causes they care nothing about. Your first task, therefore, shouldn't ever be to ask for donations, but to get people excited about what it is you're trying to do and to increase the esteem they feel for the achievements of your programs. Much of the work you'll do as a provost or dean is initial cultivation of prospects who may contribute only later when a specific request is made by the president or member of the development team. Your goal is to prepare the groundwork that will make an eventual proposal successful, regardless of whether you or someone else makes the ask.

In many ways, every contact you have with a stakeholder, from today's first-year student through highly wealthy captains of industry, is friend raising that could eventually become fundraising. You never know when someone who looks favorably on something you say or do will help your institution later by encouraging an excellent student to enroll there, introducing you to someone else who will become one of your largest donors, or helping you to publicize an important event. Fundraisers often say that people contribute to causes in three basic ways: by donating their time, talent, or treasure. Through your friend-raising activities, you'll encounter many people whose resources or other commitments don't allow them to donate treasure themselves, but whose generous gifts of time and talent are even more meaningful to you in the long run.

Cultivating relationships with prospective donors takes time. It may take several visits for prospects to feel comfortable enough with you to discuss issues that they care deeply about. Even more visits may be necessary before they fully understand what your funding priorities are and how their goals might align with yours, either directly or indirectly. Despite what academic leaders sometimes believe, it's rarely the case that you meet once with a prospective donor, outline a proposal for an idea, and walk away with a check supporting the plan you have in mind. Donor relations often require protracted discussions before you ever reach the point of discussing specific plans. People who have substantial resources usually feel that they have more to contribute to projects than money alone. Paying respectful attention to their ideas may result in some highly beneficial improvements to your original concept. In addition, people have a stronger commitment to ideas they've helped create.

> If you ask for money, you'll probably just get advice. But if you ask for advice, you may also get money.

Donors, like everyone else, want to feel that they're in charge of situations where they're making a substantial contribution. No one likes to feel that they have been taken advantage of and then ignored. As a result, it's often the case that when you ask for a gift, the prospective donor will take charge of the situation and give you advice on how to raise the money elsewhere or focus your proposal more effectively. Conversely, when you ask for ways in which your proposal might be strengthened or improved, people may be impressed by your willingness to learn their ideas. If they're interested enough in seeing those ideas come to fruition, they may even provide you with some of the resources that can turn those dreams into reality.

Dreaming Creatively

Gifts that are large enough to transform an institution are rarely given for ordinary things. Your greatest need might be in the area of day-to-day concerns, such as a few more computers, extra travel money, or a bit of additional adjunct support, but these aren't the projects that'll fire the interest of large donors. Truly transformative gifts must be impressive enough to make a statement. They have to symbolize something fundamental about your college and the donor or foundation that supports it.

> If you want to produce extraordinary results, you need to start with an extraordinary idea.

If you don't typically come up with ideas like that on your own, you'll need some help. Consider putting together a dream team, an advisory group that develops innovative ideas that help the institution, have great appeal to potential donors, and are capable of moving your programs (and possibly your career) forward. You and a development officer will need to be part of this group. An experienced grant writer is also a useful addition. Beyond that, who has the proper mixture of vision and practicality to succeed in this capacity? Working with this group will be a good preparation for future leadership roles, so you probably don't want to restrict the committee to your senior faculty or the usual suspects, the people tapped for every significant role at the school. In order to develop a group that is as creative as possible in the ideas it generates, you'll need to be as creative as possible in staffing it.

The charge you give your dream team will depend on your precise needs, but you might consider the following:

○ Ask the group to get you a prioritized list of fundable projects that are simultaneously exciting to the imagination, relevant to the disciplines you supervise, and practical enough to be accomplished.

○ Have them reflect on the questions, "What would put us on the map?" and "What can we do better than anyone else?"

○ Challenge them to think in terms of ideas that are appealing enough that they would want to contribute to them.

If your development office has already determined that a certain level of gift is the largest your prospective donors are likely to be capable of, you might also say something like, "We know that we're much more likely to be successful if our request is no larger than $[amount], so that's the amount that we're going to be pursuing. What I need from you, then, is advice about the sort of project that can do something incredible but still fall within that range."

Fairly generic ideas that the group may come up with include:

○ A new facility or extensive renovation of an existing structure

○ An endowed professorship

○ An endowed scholarship fund

○ A large annual award that recognizes the recipient for contributions made to some particular area

○ A high-profile annual conference

If you're given suggestions like these, encourage the team to probe more deeply. Say, for instance, "A new building is great, but what would be really remarkable about this building? What's going to make a student want to come here, a professor want to work here, and a donor want to contribute here? What's going to get us favorable coverage in the *Chronicle of Higher Education*?" Challenge your committee to use its creativity to the utmost so that their proposal isn't for "just another" building or endowed chair, but something that they'll be proud to have as part of their legacy.

Developing this proposal in concert with an ad hoc committee like the dream team is far preferable to relying on your own ideas for everything. You may be a remarkably imaginative person, but even the most visionary person can't think of everything. While a group process may take longer, in the end you'll get better ideas, a team of committed stakeholders who will be your allies in promoting the idea through any required review process, and a ready body of advocates when you go out to present the idea to your potential donor or foundation. Moreover, if you don't think creatively on your feet, a dream team can help compensate for your own challenges. It's a sign of good leadership that you're wise enough to understand when you need help.

Doing Your Homework

Those you solicit for donations are busy people for whom both time and money are important. They're not likely to have accumulated their wealth by wasting time in idle chatter. As a result, you never want to go into a meeting with a potential donor unprepared. We've already seen that your school's development office can be a great source of information about a prospect's capacity for giving, record of contributions, and social or philanthropic interests. In addition, you'll also want to know as much as possible about the prospective donor's characteristics:

o *Style of interaction*: Will he or she expect you to get down to business immediately, or will there be an expectation that you'll talk about other issues, get to know one another, and discuss philanthropy only late in the process?

o *Hot buttons*: Are there any topics that are off-limits with this person? Is he or she so strongly committed to a certain political or religious perspective that reference to certain matters will cause the conversation to become sidetracked or prove an impediment to a possible donation?

o *Connections*: Does the person have family members or friends who might shape the donor's philanthropic interest? For instance, you might be seeking a contribution to a medical program because the prospect was successful as a physician; but the person might have a child whose goal is to become a concert pianist, and thus this donor prefers to talk about music rather than medicine.

As you go into the meeting, have a clear but flexible strategy in mind for what you're hoping to accomplish in that particular conversation. You'll be expected, of course, to do some talking as well as some listening, but it's useful to know how much of each is likely to suit each donor. If you're perceived as not talking enough, certain prospects may assume that you aren't as interested as you should be either in them or in the proposal you're discussing. But if you're perceived as talking too much, certain donors may assume that you're too full of yourself and don't care what they think. If the development staff can't give you insight into the personality and expectations of the person you're meeting, pay attention to any indications the person gives you that you need to hold back more or do a better job filling the awkward pauses. People tend not to give donations to those who make them feel uncomfortable, so part of your preparation for the meeting should be to consider ways of making the other person feel as comfortable as possible.

In the same way that you want to do your homework about the donor, you also want to know your proposal inside and out. Many donors, particularly those with careers in business or public service, have a great deal of experience evaluating pitches for investment, business models, and strategic plans. They're likely to spot weak areas quickly. You'll need to think through the proposal to such an extent that you can answer even the most detailed questions imaginable about how the plan might be implemented. At the same time, don't become so committed to every detail of the plan that you're unwilling to modify it. Donors almost always want to improve the projects that are brought to them. If you insist on the purity of your original concept, you could end up with a pure and (to your mind) perfect idea that no one wants to fund. If it fits your style to do so, let your own excitement for the idea emerge in the way you discuss it. Donors and investors are often motivated by what's sometimes called the *FOMO factor*: the fear of missing out. If the prospect leaves your conversations with the feeling that you've shared an irresistible opportunity rather than made a plea for money, you're much more likely to be successful in your solicitation.

One important step in doing your homework occurs with the development of a case statement for the request you're making. A case statement is a concise summary of what you're trying to accomplish with the proposal, whom it benefits, why it's important, how it relates to your college's mission, whom it serves, and its specific need in terms of the project that you are proposing. A good case statement should make it clear why your proposal is the best (or perhaps the only) way of meeting the need you've identified. Case statements shouldn't be lengthy; a reader should be able to understand them quickly and easily. But although they're short, case statements should represent clear ideas that will seem important to the people reading them, inspire them to become part of the projects you've outlined, and make it clear that the projects you're proposing are both realistic and significant. Cases statements are sometimes divided into three parts so that they can be skimmed in only a few minutes:

1. *Concept*: Two or three sentences outlining the proposal. The description of the concept should be brief and written in a way that immediately engages the reader.

2. *Need*: Information about why it's important to achieve the goal you've suggested. The statement of need should make the problem you're trying to solve clearly visible to the reader and inspire the reader to solve it.

3. *Opportunity*: A description of how the reader can make a positive difference in the world by satisfying the need you've outlined.

A good case statement should be specific enough that the reader can visualize the project but general enough that he or see could still modify it so that it aligns more fully with his or her own philanthropic interests.

Thinking Sideways

Ordinarily when we're trying to achieve a goal, we think in terms of the most direct and efficient path that leads us to the objective. But there are times in dealing with donors when it's useful to "think sideways," that is, to consider not just how to get from A to B, but how moving from A to B can be a way of getting to C and then D. A donor's area of philanthropic interest may not bring you closer to one of your most important goals in any obvious way, but there may be aspects of that interest that you can leverage in a manner that will accomplish that goal. For example, suppose that you're losing valuable faculty members because your institution's salaries aren't competitive and you need to find a way to increase the rates you're able to pay. You could ask a donor outright for a gift to help achieve this goal, but donors rarely contribute funds just to increase faculty salaries. By thinking sideways, however, you may be able to achieve your goal as a secondary result of what you propose to a donor.

Suppose you have a faculty member who's about to retire with a base salary of $128,000 and that your institution has an average rate of benefits that runs approximately 24 percent of the base. You could hire an entry-level faculty member on this line at $65,000 which, when benefits are included, amounts to an investment of $80,600. Of the $158,720 in salary and benefits that is being paid to the retiring faculty member, you will still have a pool of $78,120 that you can use to boost the salaries of current faculty members. That would be an example of effective academic leadership, and it's the sort of strategic thinking that provosts and deans engage in all the time.

Now suppose that instead of following the plan we just considered, you could interest a donor in endowing a position for an eminent scholar as a replacement for the retiring faculty member. In this case, you could fulfill an objective of the donor (who may want to have his or her name on an endowed chair), a second goal of enhancing your institution's reputation through the hiring of a distinguished professor with an international reputation, and also have a full $158,720 available to increase faculty salaries. By thinking sideways instead of proceeding on a strictly linear path, you're able to accomplish a lot more than simply one goal funded by one gift. That's not just strategic thinking; that's visionary leadership.

Demonstrating Support

There's a careful balance that a case statement should achieve. It should make it clear that the problem will go unsolved if the donor doesn't become an active supporter, but it also shouldn't leave the impression that no one else cares enough about the problem to want to participate in the solution. In order to achieve this balance, there are two ways in which you can demonstrate the support you already have.

Levels of contribution within the institution

Donors are more likely to support a project if they know that the people most closely connected to it care about it as deeply as they do. You can demonstrate the support the project has within the institution in several different ways.

If only a few people have contributed so far, but at least one of those gifts was rather large, you can demonstrate support through the total amount raised: "We launched this project only a month ago, and already members of the faculty have contributed more than twenty-five thousand dollars to bring it about." If the total amount raised is rather small, but many members of the faculty have contributed five or ten dollars each, you can cite the depth of participation: "We launched this project only a month ago, and already more than half the faculty have made contributions to help bring it about." If neither of those approaches makes a very strong case, you may be able to discuss the rate of participation:

"We launched this project only a month ago, and each week the number of faculty members who contribute to it has doubled."

If contribution levels of the faculty and staff aren't sufficiently impressive, consider which other stakeholders might help you make a stronger case. Numbers or percentages of current students who have contributed to the project may seem large even though each participant in the campaign may have contributed only a few dollars. Being able to say "100 percent of the members of the parents' council have contributed" sounds a lot better than "2 percent of the parents have contributed" or "Eight parents have contributed," even though all three figures might reflect the same situation. In a similar way, contribution levels by the president, advisory council, or governing board can help you make your case: "This project has received such strong support from the president that she's pledged to match dollar-for-dollar every contribution we raise in the first month. More than three-quarters of the people on our advisory council and governing board have already contributed. I think that demonstrates just how seriously the institution takes this issue. And with the president's match, it's also an important way to make your own contribution go further."

The human element

As impressive as those statistics may be, nothing makes a need seem as compelling as meeting the people who are affected by it. For instance, if the project that you are proposing concerns increased support for scholarship, visit the prospect with one or two of your most articulate students who either have already been helped by similar programs or could stand to benefit from the project you're proposing. Immediately the pitch you're making will cease being an abstract idea and become a matter of helping real people who have real needs.

Other projects might be better served by having faculty members, previous donors, or friends of the college accompany you on your visit to the prospective donor. Faculty members can discuss the impact of projects in their disciplines with a passion and vision that is quite compelling to many donors. Previous contributors can help form a bond with the prospective donor. They interact as equals. Since they won't be benefiting directly from the gift, their motives are not suspect, and they can invite the prospective donor to "join me in helping to make this vision a reality." In a similar way, friends of the college can provide a broader community perspective, demonstrate ways in which the college helps people other than its own students, and illustrate the breadth of support that the project has in the school's service area.

Following Through

Once a gift has been received, your work with the donor has really just begun. Too many academic leaders assume that the development process ends as soon as the gift has been booked. That mind-set can produce strained donor relations and ruin a once promising relationship. Donors expect follow-through in return for their financial support. Not only should they be kept in the loop about absolutely everything connected to the project itself, but they should also be made to feel like members of the college or university community. Be certain that they're invited to college events; send these invitations, whenever possible, in the form of handwritten notes or personal telephone calls, particularly to donors whose gifts have been substantial. Let them be the first to hear about publications and grants for which the faculty has been responsible, honors bestowed on students, and other projects that are ongoing at the institution.

Donors can sometimes feel that they were actively sought out, courted, and consulted during the solicitation phase of a gift, only to be ignored entirely once the gift has been made. Proper stewardship of a gift involves both the appropriate use of the gift in a straightforward and accountable manner and the display of sufficient respect, gratitude, and interest in the donor who made the gift in the first place.

Follow-through on a gift also involves assessing its impact. Donors want to know that their gift mattered. Fortunately, as academic professionals, we're used to assessment and evaluation in many other aspects of what we do. It's a good practice therefore to evaluate the impact of the gift carefully and report these results to the donor:

o How many people benefited from the project? Who were these individuals? How was their situation improved by the project?

o What were the goals of the project? What were the benchmarks or key performance indicators you used to indicate whether the project was as effective as you had hoped? If a benchmark wasn't reached, how did you respond?

o If the project is still continuing, what did you learn from the assessment process that will help you make the next phase of the project even more successful?

Report what you've learned about how to make the project even better next time to the donor, and be sure to thank the donor yet again. It's possible that by following up on the gift so thoroughly and attentively, the donor may even increase the size of the gift or be willing to fund other projects you may have in the future.

Conclusion

Building relationships with donors and prospective donors takes time. Fundraising isn't simply about making a pitch and receiving a check. It's about creative thinking, developing long-term relationships, and following through on your commitments. Effective provosts and deans make sure that their donors know the faculty and staff and that the faculty and staff know the donors. Moreover, they see their internal stakeholders as key partners in building strong relationships with donors. Periodically when meeting with groups of the faculty, staff, or students, it can be useful to engage them in a joint fundraising exercise with you. Ask them:

- ○ What would you do with a gift of $20 million if a donor gave it to our institution right now? Why would that particular use be interesting and meaningful to the donor?
- ○ What would you describe as our school's single biggest need? Why does that particular need matter more than all the other challenges we have?
- ○ If you could look ten years in the future and conclude, "The entire school was positively transformed by a single gift," what changes do you believe you would have seen? How large would the gift have had to be to make that vision a reality?

The discussions that arise from these questions are important on a number of levels. They can help your college or university develop a shared vision along the lines discussed in chapter 4. They can give you a source of excellent ideas that you can use in your own fundraising efforts. And the energy generated by your stakeholders when they begin to think about future possibilities might turn out to be contagious, making them want to join with you in making these dreams come true.

Glossary of Terms

In order to be successful in your relationships with donors, there are a number of technical terms from the field of fundraising that deans and provosts need to know. The following list provides an overview of several concepts that academic leaders are likely to encounter when they seek external funding for their programs.

Bequest. A legacy or gift of personal property that comes to the institution through the terms of a donor's will.

Book a gift. The official recording of a gift's receipt and incorporation into the institution's resources. Institutions have specific accounting rules regarding when a gift may officially be booked (such as, "gifts must never be booked before a formal agreement has been signed by both the donor and institution") and how the value of the gift must be calculated. In the United States, determination of a gift's value is subject to restrictions set forth by the US Internal Revenue Code and by either the Governmental Accounting Standards Board for public institutions or the Financial Accounting Standards Board for private institutions.

Corpus. The principal of a sum of money as opposed to the interest it generates.

Endowment. The permanent transfer of money or property to an institution for a particular purpose. In most cases, the endowment of a college or university is a corpus of funds, the interest of which (or some portion of, usually 3 to 5 percent) may be used for operation of the institution while the principle must remain intact.

Gift agreement. A document that sets forth the terms under which a gift is offered by the donor and accepted by the institution. Gift agreements usually specify the donor's charitable intent, what would happen to the gift if the original purpose is no longer appropriate at some point in the future (or, in the worst-case scenario, if either the program itself or the institution as a whole ceases to exist), who will be responsible for making certain decisions about how the gift will be used, and which operating procedures will be in effect as the project proceeds.

Gift-in-kind. A gift made in a form other than cash. Tangible gifts-in-kind may consist of property or services. Intangible gifts-in-kind may consist of rights (such as patents or copyrights) that have the potential of providing value in the future.

Lead trust. Also *charitable lead trust.* A trust in which the income or some specified portion of the income created by a corpus is donated for charitable purposes during a set period. When the period expires (e.g., on a certain date or at the death of the donor), the corpus reverts to the donor or the donor's beneficiaries. Lead trusts are frequently attractive to individuals who want to reduce their tax liability for a specific period. Currently they have an added advantage in the United States because the federal government taxes only what the Internal Revenue Service (IRS) projects the likely value of the principal will be at the end of the trust period. If, as is often the case, the value of the principal increases beyond what the IRS has calculated, that additional increase passes to the donor's heirs free of transfer taxes. *See also* trust.

Remainder trust. Also *charitable remainder trust.* In many ways the opposite of a lead trust. A remainder trust occurs when the income of a trust is distributed to beneficiaries until some particular time in the future, after which the trust is donated to the specified charity. Remainder trusts are frequently attractive to donors who wish to reduce the amount of tax that will need to be paid from their estates at their deaths or wish to provide a guaranteed income to a beneficiary while also achieving a second charitable goal at a later date. *See also* trust.

Trust. A right of property that a person or institution holds on behalf of (and for the benefit of) another.

RESOURCES

Alexander, G. D., & Carlson, K. (2005). *Essential principles for fundraising success: An answer manual for the everyday challenges of raising money.* San Francisco, CA: Jossey-Bass.

Axelrod, T. (2006). *The joy of fundraising: How to stop suffering and start enjoying asking for money for your favorite cause.* Seattle, WA: Benevon.

Buller, J. L. (2008). Stewardship in fundraising. *Department Chair, 18*(4), 1–3.

Buller, J. L. (2009). Conducting an annual fund campaign. *Department Chair, 19*(4), 8–9.

Buller, J. L. (2011). Fundraising 201: What to do after you've learned the basics. *Department Chair, 21*(3), 6–9.

Ciconte, B. L., & Jacob, J. G. (2009). *Fundraising basics: A complete guide* (3rd ed.). Sudbury, MA: Jones and Bartlett.

Greenfield, J. M. (2002). *Fundraising fundamentals: A guide to annual giving for professionals and volunteers* (2nd ed.). Hoboken, NJ: Wiley.

Hall, M. S., & Howlett, S. (2010). *Getting funded: The complete guide to writing grant proposals* (4th ed.). Seattle, WA: Word & Raby.

Hunt, P. C. (2012). *Development for academic leaders: A practical guide for fundraising success.* San Francisco, CA: Jossey-Bass.

Miller, P. W. (2002). *Grant writing: Strategies for developing winning proposals* (2nd ed.). Munster, IN: Miller.

Schaff, T., & Schaff, D. (1999). *The fundraising planner: A working model for raising the dollars you need.* Hoboken, NJ: Wiley.

Schiller, R. J. (2013). *The chief development officer: Beyond fundraising.* Lanham, MD: Rowman & Littlefield.

Timmerman, D. (2014). Productively working with advancement and development. In L. L. Behling (Ed.), *The resource handbook for academic deans* (pp. 211—214). San Francisco, CA: Jossey-Bass.

Worth, M. J. (Ed.). (2002). *New strategies for educational fund raising.* Westport, CT: Praeger.

26

BOARDS, TRUSTEES, AND LEGISLATORS

Various kinds of boards that are of interest to provosts and deans. Some, like the advisory councils discussed in chapter 24, play only an informal role in the life of the institution. Others, like the governing board or state legislature (which sometimes acts as a type of board, designing policies, approving recommendations, and sometimes even setting tuition rates for colleges and universities), can play a formal and direct role indeed. It's this latter type of board—sometimes known as a board of trustees, regents, governors, or visitors—that is the focus of this chapter.

Governing boards require a special level of care when a provost or dean deals with them. Many presidents view interactions with members of these boards as their own personal prerogative and don't want other administrators to complicate that process. Even so, there are certain things about governing boards and legislatures that every academic leader needs to know. In addition, there may well be an occasion when the provost or dean is asked to fill in for the president at a board meeting or make a presentation related to the programs that he or she supervises.

For example, there may be an issue about which the provost or the dean is better situated than the president to provide the type of information that the board needs. The institution may be about to invest in a major new program or scholarship opportunity for students in a particular discipline, an academic conference with a controversial focus, or a highly specialized new facility. In less pleasant situations, there may be a serious issue involving certain members of the faculty or student body that the dean or provost needs to comment on. Moreover, depending on the management style of your president, other academic leaders may be encouraged to become closely involved with the board because the upper administration regards teamwork as an important part of its identity and approach to governance.

If you find that your work as a dean or provost places you in a position where you'll be in contact with your governing board, a trustee, a regent, or a legislator, what's the best way to handle this situation? Is dealing with a board similar to dealing with other external stakeholders, like parents or members of the community? Or since they set the institution's policies and have final approval over many decisions, is a governing board just a different kind of internal constituent?

Seeing Issues from the Board's Perspective

Board members and legislators are internal and external constituents simultaneously, and that unique type of "dual citizenship" makes interacting with them different from an academic leader's dealings with any other group. On the one hand, much of the information that boards receive about a college or university is fairly detailed. They often see budget figures that are known to few of the faculty and understand the details of contract negotiations, construction plans, and the institution's investment portfolio with great precision. On the other hand, not many board members or legislators have ever been professionals in higher education. For that reason, even fairly basic aspects of how institutions of higher education are structured and operate may not be familiar to them. They may have only the most rudimentary idea of what a dean or provost actually does, and they may not have a clear understanding of how disciplines are organized into administrative units. They may assume that a chair is a faculty member's boss in the same way that a department head is the boss of an employee in a company. They may have completely erroneous views about the role of academic freedom, tenure, and other principles that are highly prized in higher education.

That different perspective doesn't make them ineffective in their positions or demonstrate that "they just don't care" about issues of vital concern to people who work in academia. If the roles were reversed and any of us were asked to serve on an advisory board to the state legislature or a business operated by a particular trustee, we'd find ourselves in the same situation. We'd want to do a good job, and we'd take our responsibilities seriously. But we'd also find our knowledge rather limited in terms of how the day-to-day business of the legislature or corporation is actually done. For this reason, we have to keep in mind when we're working with a legislature or board that even though most (if not all) of their members care deeply about higher education, they may have a limited or distorted understanding of how higher education actually functions.

As a result, we have an opportunity in our interactions with board members and legislators to inform or remind them gently of things that we and our colleagues may take for granted. We can say things like, "Well, you know that as the provost, I have ultimate responsibility for all academic programs at our school. Other aspects of collegiate life—such as housing, financial aid, student organizations, and so on—report to other vice presidents. My main concern is with hiring and developing an excellent faculty, keeping our curriculum focused and up to date, and ensuring that we can meet our educational objectives within our budget. In fact, that's why I'm here today. I'd like to suggest that together we ... " Or, if you're a dean, you could say something like, "Now, as dean of the university's college of liberal arts, I'm responsible for a significant portion of the institution's general education program (the required courses that every student has to take), service courses (the supplemental courses we offer to majors outside our college), and undergraduate majors in eleven disciplines: American studies, art, classics (ancient Greek and Latin language, civilization, and literature), communication, English, foreign languages, history, international studies, Latin American studies, philosophy, and women's studies." By phrasing your remarks in this way, you've been respectful of your audience at the same time that you reminded them of information they needed to know. You set the context for your conversation and helped the board avoid making false assumptions. You've neither insulted them by assuming they don't know what you're telling them nor risked miscommunicating with them by assuming that they understand everything. You've sought to preserve a collegial and informative balance.

Seizing the Teachable Moment

Board members who work in fields other than higher education on a daily basis are likely to assume that colleges and universities function exactly like other kinds of institutions with which they're familiar. Many trustees or legislatures know how to get things done in a corporation, faith-based community, public service organization, military unit, or political body and approach your school as though it works in the same way. As a result, board members may misinterpret your relationship to your "employees" (i.e., the faculty) and your "customers" (i.e., the students), unaware that even the use of such terms rankles many within the academy. That can be a challenge when dealing with a member of the governing board because the two of you are often not speaking the same language or basing your views on the same assumptions. Faced with these challenges, academic leaders can simply give up, conclude that the gap between them is too wide to bridge, and reduce their interactions with the board to the bare minimum, or they can seize the teachable moment and try to find some common ground from which to improve their mutual understanding. The latter approach has the greatest number of advantages, but it isn't easy.

To begin, provosts and deans have to resist every natural urge they have to lapse back into professor mode and regard the board member as a struggling student who doesn't comprehend even the fundamental principles of how higher education works. If any of us were asked to give advice to a type of institution vastly different from our own, we'd probably draw conclusions about how that organization works that would be just as erroneous as are many of the views that legislators have about colleges and universities. We may be shocked at how dictatorial some corporate executives act when making decisions that affect the lives of thousands of employees; they may be shocked by how long it takes to get a simple decision made at a university, with multiple levels of committees, consultations, and formal votes. Seizing the teachable moment in this case doesn't involve merely "setting someone straight" about what higher education is really like. It means systematically broadening the perspective of the board members we work with at the same time that we allow them to broaden ours.

For example, if you have a conversation with a legislator or board member who can never seem to get past "all the problems that tenure keeps causing us," you might try explaining the benefits of the tenure system in terms that resonate with the other person's values. As deans and provosts, we're so used to arguing about the need to protect academic freedom that we sometimes forget that legislators and board members typically work in a world where this concept sounds more like a luxury than a necessity. It might be far better to say something like, "I think it's useful sometimes to look at how the advantages of the tenure system outweigh its disadvantages. We both can agree, I'm sure, on how important it is for the university to promote student success and produce the type of research that helps us all. In order to do that, we have to be able to attract the best possible faculty members who share those goals. The tenure system is just one of the things that helps us attract those highly competitive professors. You can think of it as part of our benefits plan. If an outstanding faculty member has an opportunity to work either for me or at another university, I'm at a competitive disadvantage if I can't offer that faculty member the level of security that the other school can. The faculty member will choose the other offer, and why not? For many people, the freedom from worry that tenure provides is worth tens of thousands of dollars that otherwise our budget would have to absorb. If I can't attract the type of faculty member we need to build our future, the quality of education our students are going to receive will inevitably suffer, and I don't think either of us wants that. In fact, I think there are several ways in which we can improve the educational opportunities available to our students, and that's really what I'd like to talk with you about today."

By handling the conversation in this way, you're relating a concept that the board member finds foreign and irrational ("Isn't tenure just a guaranteed job regardless of how badly you perform? You can't get anything like that where *I* work") to concepts that he or she both recognizes and values: employment benefits, cost savings, socially useful research, and improved graduation rates. That same approach can work with other types of misunderstandings a board member may have about higher education. For example, suppose you have a tense encounter with a trustee who wants to know why you don't simply fire several faculty members who used an exercise in class that he or she found offensive or at least forbid them from using that exercise in the future. Once again, relying on the importance of academic freedom may not be very persuasive if the trustee works outside higher education. You could try a different approach, saying, "It's true that those faculty members report to me, and I'm their boss. But the relationship that faculty members have with their supervisors is more like what you're familiar with on one of your own legislative committees [or nonprofit boards] than the relationship an employee has with a supervisor in a corporate setting. Just as the chair of the legislative committee [or nonprofit board] functions more as a first among equals than as a traditional corporate manager, that's how we work with the faculty at the college. I assign them their workload, set their salaries, and evaluate them. In rare but extreme cases, I may even have to terminate someone. But much of what I do, just like much of what you do, is accomplished more through persuasion and mutual respect than through direct orders. I hire the best possible faculty members I can find, and then I give them the freedom they need in order to do their job effectively. So rather than what you're suggesting, I think the most appropriate way for us to address this issue is for me to … " Once again, you've related how your relationship with faculty members relates to the trustee's own frame of reference, respectfully helping that person understand both the similarities and the differences of your two professional worlds.

Promoting Diversity

Just as members of governing boards and legislatures may not understand the organizational culture of higher education, they also may not understand the importance of diversity, including a broad diversity of options, to the success of students and our communities. Part of this problem is simply rhetorical. It's common for people to speak of students "going to college" as though they were all sharing a single experience. In fact, higher education is highly diverse and becoming even more so in terms of the educational experiences students are offered, the formats in which their programs are provided, and the backgrounds of the other people who will be sharing their courses.

Diversity is not simply a goal in higher education; it's an accomplished fact. What students encounter in the undergraduate program of a large public research university will be distinctly different from what students encounter at a small, private liberal arts college, seminary, conservatory, online university, community college, preprofessional school, for-profit institution, or any of the many other opportunities students have to choose from today. Even more important, the substance of that experience—what the students will learn and how their lives will be changed by the curricular, cocurricular, and extracurricular elements of their college years—will be different as well. The skills developed in a three-hundred-seat lecture hall where all the examinations are delivered electronically in a multiple-choice format simply can't be identical to the skills developed in a twelve-member seminar where a reaction paper is due every week, a research paper is completed before the end of the semester, and each meeting requires everyone in the class to defend his or her conclusions when challenged by the professor and other students. In a similar way, what students learn when they have access to state-of-the-art scientific equipment and professors who are leading researchers in their field can't be the same as that gained from reading a textbook or watching a video about that discovery.

This vast diversity found in the types of higher education currently available benefits everyone. Not all students learn best when they're continually put on the spot and challenged by highly articulate peers, just as not every student is prepared for the challenges and responsibilities of independent scientific research. But this breadth of options is important to more than just those who enroll in our programs. The complex tapestry of educational choices helps prepare a citizenry with the broad range of insights and skills that will be necessary to respond to future challenges. Many members of a governing board and legislature understand this; others do not. They focus on how much more cost-effective fully online courses would be, unaware that your programs specialize in art and design where studio space, peer critique, and access to physical galleries are all central components of your curriculum. Similarly, they may question the high cost per credit hour that your program requires, even though the curriculum of your college relies on technology that must be upgraded extensively every year or two in order to remain relevant.

In these situations too, provosts and deans have an opportunity to explain the mission of their programs in terms that will resonate with the board or legislature. As academic leaders, we realize that the goal of higher education is never as simplistic as "getting students to graduate on time," "developing a knowledge-based society," or any of the other slogans commonly heard in state senates and during board meetings. We understand that we're also trying to develop skills in critical and creative thinking, oral and written communication, creativity, innovation or entrepreneurship, leadership, teamwork, civic engagement, responsibility, conducting independent research, and self-understanding. We're attempting to build our community's intellectual, economic, social, and cultural capital. We're preparing students both to make a living and to lead a life worth living. All of these issues are matters about which governing boards and legislatures care deeply. But it's up to us as academics to draw the connection between how the diversity of our programs and the benefit to society are connected—how academic freedom, tenure, and the other issues we care about are inseparable from generating student credit hours, helping students graduate on time, and the other things they care about. Sometimes we have to try to speak their language in order to get them to understand ours. Doing so is just another part of the same effort to promote diversity that imbues everything we do.

Listening Effectively

It may seem in this chapter as though I regard board members and legislators as necessary evils who never understand anything about the colleges and universities they affect by their decisions. That's far from the case. To be sure, there are times when certain aspects of our institutions, programs, and needs do have to be clarified for them, as they do for any of our external stakeholders. But they are also important things that we can learn from those who serve on governing boards or the legislature. Just as meeting with a potential donor involves perhaps 80 percent of your time listening to that person's goals and aspirations and only about 20 percent of your time talking about yourself and the programs you're trying to help, so should a meeting with any other external constituent give you an opportunity to learn even more than you explain.

By listening carefully to the member of the board or legislature, you can better understand what that person's priorities are. You'll then be in a better position to understand how the programs you offer can address those priorities. Even if, by listening attentively, you learn that the person who's talking to you has a highly distorted understanding of your institution or higher education as a whole, that's still a valuable conversation. You can't dispel those misconceptions unless you first know what they are. You may even find that you learn important information about other topics that help you do your job better, either because they give you a deeper understanding of how the governing board or legislature works or because they give you insight into how your programs are perceived by their external constituencies. For all these reasons, it pays to listen carefully whenever a member of your board or state legislature starts talking about higher education.

Keeping the President Informed

Even if your president has given you carte blanche in meeting with your institution's external constituents, it's still a good idea to keep him or her in the loop about the nature of any private conversation you have with a member of the board or legislature. At the very least, the person with whom you were speaking may meet with your president at a later date and assume he or she is fully informed about the conversation you've had; you don't want your president to feel blindsided by a situation you could have alleviated through a short memo or e-mail. In other situations, your president may even need to follow up on or even head off some of the actions the board member or legislator decided to pursue as a result of your conversation. A quick document titled "Summary of My Conversation with [name] on [date]" can be valuable in keeping everyone in the administration informed about your contact with the board, creating a paper trail that may prompt further action and avoiding misunderstandings that could occur due to faulty memories after the meeting has occurred.

Conclusion

The most important thing for every dean or provost to understand before meeting with a regent, trustee, or legislator is how that individual's own governing council functions and makes its decisions. No dean should go into any conversation with an external stakeholder unprepared. Fortunately, there's a significant amount of material available on governing boards and state legislatures for those who may have little, if any, prior knowledge about their structure or operation.

If you're dealing with a legislator, the best place to begin is your institution's own historical account of its origins and developments. Nearly every state institution has a written history that details the legislature's initial role in establishing the university and subsequent issues that have guided its development. These sources can then be supplemented by review of your state legislature's website (so that you can familiarize yourself with the names of key players and important committees) and such work as Cohen and Kisker (2010), Alexander and Alexander (2011), Budig (2002), McMillen (2010), Kuh and Whitt (1998), and Altbach, Berdahl, and Gumport (2011). If your interactions are more likely to be with a board of regents or trustees, be sure to consult the website of the Association of Governing Boards of Colleges and Universities (www.agb.org), as well as Hendrickson, Lane, Harris, and Dorman (2013), Ewell (2006), Houle (1997), and Bastedo (2012).

REFERENCES

Alexander, K. W., & Alexander, K. (2011). *Higher education law: Policy and perspectives* (3rd ed.) New York, NY: Routledge.

Altbach, P. G., Berdahl, R. O., & Gumport, P. J. (2011). *American higher education in the twenty-first century: Social, political, and economic challenges.* Baltimore, MD: Johns Hopkins University Press.

Bastedo, M. N. (2012). *The organization of higher education: Managing colleges for a new era.* Baltimore, MD: John Hopkins University Press.

Budig, G. A. (2002). *A game of uncommon skill: Leading the modern college and university.* Phoenix, AZ: American Council on Education/Oryx Press.

Cohen, A. M., & Kisker, C. B. (2010). *The shaping of American higher education: Emergence and growth of the contemporary system* (2nd ed.). San Francisco, CA: Jossey-Bass.

Ewell, P. (2006). *Making the grade: How boards can ensure academic quality.* Washington, DC: Association of Governing Boards.

Hendrickson, R. M., Lane, J. E., Harris, J. T., & Dorman, R. H. (Eds.). (2013). *Academic leadership and governance of higher education: A guide for trustees, leaders, and aspiring leaders of two- and four-year institutions.* Sterling, VA: Stylus.

Houle, C. O. (1997) *Governing boards: Their nature and nurture.* San Francisco, CA: Jossey-Bass.

Kuh, G. D., & Whitt, E. J. (1998). *The invisible tapestry: Culture in American colleges and universities.* San Francisco, CA: Jossey-Bass.

McMillen, W. (2010). *From campus to capitol: The role of government relations in higher education.* Baltimore, MD: Johns Hopkins University Press.

RESOURCES

Amaral, A., Jones, G. A., & Karseth, B. (2011). *Governing higher education: National perspectives on institutional governance*. Dordrecht, Netherlands: Springer.

Duryea, E. (2000). *The academic corporation: A history of college and university governing boards*. New York, NY: RoutledgeFalmer.

Guston, D. H., & Keniston, K. (Eds.). (1994). *The fragile contract: University science and the federal government*. Cambridge, MA: MIT Press.

Kezar, A. J. (2006). Rethinking public higher education governing boards performance: Results of a national study of governing boards in the United States. *Journal of Higher Education*, 77, 968–1008.

Morill, R. L. (2002). *Strategic leadership in academic affairs: Clarifying the board's responsibilities*. Washington, DC: Association of Governing Boards.

Schloss, P. J., & Cragg, K. M. (2013). *Organization and administration in higher education*. London: Routledge.

Weerts, D. (2002). *State governments and research universities: A framework for a renewal partnership*. New York, NY: RoutledgeFalmer.

27

A SCENARIO ANALYSIS ON THE ECOSYSTEM OF THE COLLEGE OR UNIVERSITY

For a discussion of how scenario analyses are structured and suggestions on how to use this exercise most productively, see the beginning of chapter 7. A scenario analysis for provosts appears in the online content accompanying this book.

Case Study for Deans

Each year your college sponsors a major series in which one member of your faculty presents several public lectures before an audience that mixes current students, alumni, supporters of the college, parents of current students, representatives of the media, and even a few members of your school's governing body. This year's series will commemorate an important anniversary in the institution's history, so the attendance is expected to be even larger than usual.

Due to your development efforts, these lectures are now a specially budgeted item, and because this year's series will be so important to the institution, you have made arrangements with a number of additional external donors who have agreed to provide supplemental funding. For this reason, a commemorative volume of the faculty member's lectures will be published for the first time, and a gala banquet will follow the first night of lectures. You have handwritten invitations to many of the college's most generous donors, and you are hoping that several of them may be sufficiently impressed by the event that they'll increase their contributions, possibly even endowing a second such series.

The evening of the first lecture arrives. So many people are in attendance that at the last minute, you have needed to move the lecture to your institution's largest auditorium. Even with that late change, however, the audience is in a particularly festive mood as the ceremony gets under way. The faculty member who will be speaking was selected by a collegewide committee, and since you aren't personally acquainted with much of the speaker's work, you've had your introductory remarks prepared by a member of your staff. Nevertheless, you've practiced your introduction carefully and feel quite comfortable reciting the speaker's many accomplishments. You note that the faculty member who will be speaking is relatively new to your campus community but has already developed a reputation as a distinguished scholar, a highly popular teacher, and a dedicated member of your community. Your introduction is glowing, and the speaker comes to the stage with thunderous applause.

The first few minutes of the presentation go quite smoothly. Suddenly, however, you are rather startled to hear the faculty member utter a rather coarse obscenity. It's clear from the context that the speaker had planned all along to use this language, and so far as you can tell, it was included in the speaker's written notes from which the publication will be made. The remark makes you uncomfortable because the audience includes children, members of the press, your institution's president, parents of students, and several important members of your community, not to mention your college's largest donors, several of whom you know to be quite socially conservative. You assume, however, that the faculty member's language was simply a single statement intended for shock effect, and it's certainly clear that if that was the intention, it worked: the room is completely silent, and all attention is directed toward the speaker. Several minutes go by, and the speaker utters the same obscenity again. Then again. Before the presentation is over, you estimate that the speaker has used what you believe most members of the audience would regard as a highly offensive term more than twenty times. It's with great trepidation that you exit the auditorium with the rest of the crowd and proceed to the gala banquet.

The reaction of the audience is immediate. As you had feared, many people feel that the speaker's choice of words was completely inappropriate to the occasion, offensive, and not justifiable under any circumstances. Other members of the audience come to the speaker's defense; they call the ideas that were presented "innovative and challenging," arguing that the speaker was perfectly justified in using whatever language seemed most effective in stirring the audience from its complacency and causing people to grapple effectively with such difficult material.

You're being asked what you think of the presentation and why, if you knew the speaker was likely to use such obscene and offensive language, you'd been so lavish in the praise you used during your introduction. You've barely had time to think about what you might do or how you might react to the evening's turn of events when you reach your table for the banquet. There you discover your president on one side of you, your college's largest donor on the other side, both of whom "want to have a word with you" about "*your*" speaker's choice of language this evening.

Considerations

1. Does the type of constituent who responds negatively to the faculty member's presentation affect how you respond to this situation?

   a. Suppose that both your president and your big donor are strongly in support of the speaker, while a small but vocal group of students and their parents are offended by the speaker's remarks. Does this strong support from these constituents change how you respond?

   b. Suppose that students and their parents were excited by the speaker's "use of contemporary language to draw attention to an ongoing social problem," while your president and donor are shocked and angered by what the speaker has said. Do you react differently?

2. Imagine that the important donor who stops you after the presentation is extremely angry because of the speaker's conduct. You're told that unless you either terminate or severely reprimand the speaker, your college will never again receive a gift from this particular donor. How do you respond?

   a. Is your response any different if the donor is the very person who endowed the lecture series?

   b. Is your response any different if your college has been named in honor of this donor?

3. Does the type of obscenity affect your response in any way? For instance, do you respond any differently if the repeated vulgarity were a

   a. sexual term?

   b. scatological term?

   c. term offensive to a particular racial or ethnic group?

   d. term offensive to members of a particular sexual orientation?

4. Suppose that the obscenity the speaker used was a term widely considered offensive to a particular racial or ethnic group or to members of a particular sexual orientation. Would your response be any different if the speaker

   a. were a member of the very racial/ethnic group or sexual orientation that would be most likely to be offended by the term?

   b. had made it clear that he or she was not endorsing the term but used it as an example of "the very sort of stereotyping we are all fighting"?

   c. suggested that "if we keep repeating these words ourselves, then they cease to be effective as weapons against us. By constant repetition, even the most disgusting words lose their power"?

   d. proposed that the term be adopted in an academic context for a new cutting-edge field of scholarly studies that would henceforth be called [offensive term] Studies?

5. Would your response be any different if you and most of your colleagues were not offended by the term that the speaker used but you were aware that it caused strong reaction on the part of a certain, very vocal religious minority?

   a. Suppose that this religious minority had staged violent protests in the past when similar occurrences had occurred at other institutions. Does this change your response?

   b. Suppose instead that the religious minority in question was widely regarded as a cult by most people you knew. Do you react any differently?

   c. Does your institution's nature as a public or private college or university affect how you might respond?

6. How do you react since members of the media were present at the lecture?

   a. Do you try to be proactive and contact them immediately, even before you know what their reaction will be?

   b. Do you wait until stories about the event appear in the media and respond to them on a case-by-case manner?

7. Since there are additional lectures remaining in the series, do you take any action in advance of those lectures?

   a. Do you ask the faculty member to make any changes in future lectures?

   b. If so, do you

      i. give a direct order that changes be made? (What would the consequences for the faculty member be if your order is not followed?)

     ii. try to persuade the faculty member that changes should be made?

  c. If not, do you at least talk to the faculty member about the incident before the next lecture in the series? What is the purpose of the conversation?

8. How concerned are you by the presence of students in the audience? If you're concerned, is it because you're worried that the students

  a. may transfer out of your college because they were offended by the speaker's remarks?

  b. did not receive a good educational experience because of the speaker's remarks?

  c. may be more reluctant to attend such presentations in the future?

9. Suppose that several days after the presentation, you received a letter from a parent who was very angry about the language the speaker used. The parent is demanding that you "take immediate and serious action" against the faculty member who spoke at the lecture series.

  a. How do you respond to the parent?

  b. What form of communication do you use in responding to the parent: A phone call? A letter? An e-mail? A personal visit (if the parent happens to live in the immediate vicinity)?

10. Would your reaction be different if, after the night of the first speech, you heard from only a single concerned individual than if you had received numerous angry letters and calls about the incident?

11. Since the offensive term appears to have been part of the speaker's written notes, do you seek to excise it before the commemorative volume is published?

12. Is your response any different if the faculty member were untenured rather than tenured? If so, is your response directed more toward assisting the faculty member, protecting the institution, or with some other goal?

Suggestions

Give yourself time to sort through your own reaction to the presentation. If the speaker's language did upset you, did you have this reaction because you were embarrassed that you might be considered responsible for the speaker's remarks or because you found the remarks truly offensive and inappropriate? Had you known in advance what the speaker was going to say, what would you have done? Maintaining good relationships with your many constituents is difficult enough without the unexpected disasters that occur along the way. Those disasters are certain to occur, however, and one of the best tests for you as a dean will be in handling them capably, decisively, and with good grace.

Specifically, situations involving proprieties in public speech are among the most complex any dean may face. Certainly the right of free speech is protected by the US Constitution. Certainly too the legal system has ruled continuously that one's right to free speech is limited by certain "time, place, and manner" restrictions. That is, the context in which remarks are made always has a bearing on whether the remarks themselves are deemed to be appropriate or justified. In the situation in this case study, the very context of where you work will have some influence on your response. If you're a dean of a small, conservative, church-related institution, for instance, your response may well be different from what it would be if you were dean of a large, diverse, state-supported institution. Similarly, the type of obscenity the speaker uttered may well guide you in your response. If the speaker simply engaged in a use of vulgarities that seemed out of place in very formal and public setting of the lecture series, you have an issue resulting from a lapse of professional judgment. But if the speech involved outright insult to any group of individuals protected by your institution's equal opportunity or diversity statement, then both you and the speaker may have a much more serious legal problem on your hands. Failure to act in such a situation could leave you liable to charges of fostering a hostile environment for the protected class. Your college, as the official sponsor of the lecture series, may need to disassociate itself more clearly from the speaker's remarks than would have been the case with a simple lapse of judgment.

As you consider your response to the situation, one factor to consider is the degree to which the speaker's remarks seemed gratuitous and unnecessary as opposed to having genuine pedagogical or scholarly merit. In other words, was the term that was used in some way essential to the point the speaker was trying to make, or was it adopted merely for its shock value or as a result of the speaker's carelessness? If there was some important relevance of that particular term to the speaker's thesis in the speech, then its use, while unfortunate in light of the difficulty that it creates for you with your external constituents, may well be justified and needs to be defended. One of the goals of higher education must always be to inform people and help them see the world in new ways; higher education is not about making people comfortable. As we all tell our students from time to time, there are situations in which being offended is the best thing you can do for your education; it reminds us that we have left our comfort zone and are being forced to reflect on our most cherished convictions. If you find, however, that the speaker's use of the term was gratuitous, unnecessary, and irrelevant to the point being made, then your reaction is likely to be different. It's difficult to justify an individual's use of language in a public setting that alienates a significant portion of the audience for no pedagogical or scholarly reason. The question then becomes, How do you best deal with the situation?

In one sense, according to the scenario outlined in the case study, much of the damage has already been done by the time you have become aware of the issue. Moreover, it is not clear what steps you could have taken to avoid the situation before it occurred. You can, of course, demand to see a copy of each lecturer's remarks in advance of every public presentation and schedule rehearsals for any time a member of the faculty or staff in going to address your external constituencies. If you do so, you will both put a chill on the free exchange of ideas in your unit and increase your workload by an unsustainable amount. Yet even if you take those steps, you will not be guaranteed against every form of public embarrassment. Moreover, you are likely to lose more than you gain, being dismissed as a "micromanager" or "control freak." This case study, in other words, is more an exercise in damage control than it is in planning for risk avoidance.

Since there are other lectures remaining in the series, the best course of action is probably to schedule a meeting with the faculty member as soon as possible and discuss the situation candidly. How that conversation develops will depend largely on the seriousness of what the faculty member said. If the incident involved a violation of the institution's equal protection code, it may be necessary to have one of the campus attorneys explain to the faculty member why the term used in the speech is unacceptable and could leave the speaker open to a grievance or even a legal challenge. With other speeches remaining in the series, the speaker could be encouraged to open the next presentation with an apology or retraction as a way of trying to alleviate the damage. If the speaker proves recalcitrant and refuses to take any action, the institution may need to decide how it will respond on its own. Options might include canceling the remaining lectures in the series, issuing a statement to the press, or offering a disclaimer before the speaker begins the next presentation. The disclaimer or statement to the press might make it clear that while the institution supports a free exchange of ideas, the speaker's views and terminology do not necessarily reflect those of every member of the community and certainly should not be regarded as an official statement made on behalf of the institution.

In situations involving a lack of judgment rather than a serious breach of policy, your conversation with the faculty member might take a number of different directions. You might explore why the faculty member chose the language that he or she did. You could outline why it created difficulties for the college in light of the wide range of your constituents who were present. If the individual resorts to invoking the right of free speech, you might respond by saying, "That's all well and good. But what I'm talking about is not restricting your right of free speech. What I'm talking about is whether you were effective as a speaker. There are situations in which the way that we say something causes our message to be lost, and I'm afraid that's what happened last night. For instance, you wouldn't expect a nonprofessional audience to understand the technical terms of your discipline; you'd have to explain them or use more conventional words in order to be understood. Well, in a similar way, when you've got an audience similar to the one we had last night, you can't expect people to listen to what you have to say if you use language that makes them stop wanting to hear your message. So let's talk a bit about how you might be more effective in your future lectures with tailoring what you have to say to whom you are saying it."

RESOURCES

Bowen, W. M. (2014). *End of academic freedom: The coming obliteration of the core purpose of the university*. Charlotte, NC: Information Age.

Casper, G. (2014). *The winds of freedom: Addressing challenges to the university*. New Haven, CT: Yale University Press.

Downs, D. A. (2004). *Restoring free speech and liberty on campus*. Cambridge: Cambridge University Press.

Fink, K. (2012). *Sex, race, and politics: Free speech on campus*. San Diego, CA: Cognella.

Golding, M. P. (2000). *Free speech on campus*. Totowa, NJ: Rowman and Littlefield.

Nelson, C. (2010). *No university is an island: Saving academic freedom*. New York, NY: New York University Press.

Wolfson, N. (1999). *Hate speech, sex speech, free speech*. Westport, CT: Praeger.

PART FOUR

THE ACADEMIC LEADER AS SUPERVISOR

28

EVALUATIONS OF FACULTY

At most colleges and universities, faculty evaluations are performed by department chairs or special personnel committees. But at very small institutions, the dean (who is usually also the chief academic officer) may be directly responsible for performing these evaluations, which could require a significant portion of each academic year. In addition, even where other administrators or groups conduct the evaluations, the faculty member's dean and provost often sign off on it, verifying that procedures were followed, standards were applied consistently, and appropriate conclusions were drawn. For this reason, we can divide the possible roles deans and provosts might play in evaluations of faculty members in the following way:

- o Developing evaluation standards and procedures
- o Clarifying expectations to both the evaluator and the person being evaluated
- o Empowering department chairs and others to conduct meaningful evaluations

Since not every academic leader will be involved in all these aspects of faculty evaluation, it's best to address each of these functions individually.

Developing Appropriate Standards

At some colleges and universities, the faculty themselves set the standards by which they'll be evaluated. The thinking is that only those who are themselves professionals in that discipline can determine meaningful expectations for teaching, research, and service. At other schools, administrators set the evaluation standards. In this case, the thinking is that evaluation is an administrative responsibility, and thus administrators should be the ones to determine the procedures and criteria. Besides, it is sometimes said (and even more commonly thought than said) that if you allow people to set their own evaluation standards, won't they set them unacceptably low? For this reason, provosts and deans may be called on occasionally to develop or revise evaluation procedures and, in order to do so effectively, they may want to keep several principles in mind.

Match evaluation criteria to the assignment of the person being evaluated

In chapter 1, I cited Bob Cipriano's dictum that "what gets rewarded gets repeated." That's a concept too often ignored when evaluation criteria are set. It's not uncommon for administrators to complain that faculty members simply aren't pursuing major strategic goals of the institution to the extent they should. But if you ask those same administrators how each faculty member's progress on those goals is evaluated, you'll frequently get the answer, "But that's not what evaluation is for. It's for appraising performance in teaching, research, and service." Therein lies the problem. If you want faculty members to become more active in institutional priorities like student advising and mentoring, promoting undergraduate research, advancing student success, engaging in community outreach, or whatever else the institution regards as a priority, you have to evaluate and reward it. When faculty members seem to ignore goals that deans and provosts regard as important but fail to include in the evaluation process, they're making a simple but logical economic decision: they're focusing their efforts on what counts. And no matter how much you may claim that a particular strategic goal counts, if it's not included in standard evaluation criteria, it actually counts for nothing at all.

Even when specific strategic goals aren't a major concern for academic leaders, it's important that there be close alignment between what is expected of faculty members and how they're evaluated. At most institutions, faculty responsibilities are set forth in a handbook, set of bylaws, or policy manual that divides each person's assignment into the standard academic triad (sometimes called the three legs of the academic stool) of teaching, research, and service. Frequently, too, either the institution as a whole or specific units within that division assign specific weights to these three responsibilities, such as teaching (50 percent of performance), scholarship (45 percent), and service (5 percent). Weights like these suggest to both the evaluator and the person being evaluated the relative importance of each responsibility. But in so doing, it's important that the weights truly reflect the extent to which the institution or unit values that activity. In the weighting example just outlined, for example, it's unreasonable for an administrator to expect that a faculty member is going to regard service as much of a priority. By assigning it a weighting of only 5 percent, the institution is sending a message that service is of low economic value. "Spend your time teaching and doing research," the system is saying. "Service doesn't matter here." If the institution's strategic plan claims that community engagement is a priority but lumps it in the category of service for the purposes of evaluation, it's undermining its words by its actions. Faculty members will invest their time in the areas where that investment will pay the largest dividends.

Include, but also distinguish between, formative and summative reviews when creating evaluation standards and procedures

Many faculty evaluation processes attempt to achieve two goals simultaneously: draw a conclusion about the quality of past work and improve the quality of future work. Those are laudable goals, but they require evaluators to assume very different roles. In formative evaluations, the reviewer is acting as a mentor, guide, or coach who's seeking to offer constructive advice on how the faculty member can do better in the future. In summative evaluations, the reviewer is acting as a judge who's concerned with whether a certain standard of performance was reached in the past. Since we combine these formative and summative roles all the time when we grade student work, we're sometimes unaware of the different forces they place on a reviewer during the faculty evaluation process.

Suppose that you work at an institution where department chairs conduct annual evaluations of their faculty members and then you, as dean or provost, use those evaluations to allocate merit salary increases for the coming year. The system in place at your institution confronts department chairs with a dilemma. They'll want to be candid in their evaluation of the faculty so they can address any areas of concern and improve teaching, research, and service over time. But they'll also want to be as positive about their faculty members as possible, since they know that the more glowing an evaluation is, the more likely that person is to receive a merit increase. Even if a chair thinks that a certain faculty member performed poorly, there'll be a temptation to inflate his or her scores on the evaluation. If more money is placed on that faculty member's line, more can be reallocated after the faculty member leaves or retires. In fact, the department's entire salary pool increases, and any funding decision based on the size of the entire pool is an incentive for the chair to assign higher evaluations. That's why so many sets of faculty evaluations appear to suffer from the Lake Wobegon effect, a term drawn from Garrison Keillor's traditional ending of each story about the fictional Minnesota town of Lake Wobegon on his radio program *A Prairie Home Companion:* "where the women are strong, the men are good looking, and all of the children are above average." It isn't that chairs can't bring themselves to make qualitative distinctions among the performance of different faculty members; it's that they have an economic disincentive for doing so.

The solution to this problem is to encourage the development of evaluation standards and procedures that impose a firewall between formative and summative components. One way of achieving this goal is to establish peer committees with the sole purpose of providing formative advice at certain checkpoints during a faculty member's career:

- *Formal probationary reviews:* Often called *second-year reviews* or *third-year reviews*, these evaluations note the rate of progress that tenure-track faculty members are making in key areas when there is still time for improvements to be made before their final tenure review, which usually occurs in the sixth year of full-time service
- *Promotion progress reviews:* Informal evaluations conducted about three years after faculty members are tenured to determine whether they are on track toward promotion to the rank of full professor within a reasonable period of time
- *Posttenure reviews:* Evaluations that are more comprehensive than an annual review and occur regularly, beginning about five years after the receipt of tenure or the faculty member's most recent promotion

Two mistakes that a lot of institutions make in developing their evaluation standards and procedures are not conducting promotion progress reviews at all and making formal probation reviews and posttenure reviews largely summative in nature. But these checkpoints are valuable precisely because they're suitable occasions for addressing and fixing problems, not punishing faculty members for them. To the extent that you can do so as a provost or dean, therefore, it's desirable to advocate that the checkpoints remain wholly or largely formative in nature, while other evaluations (merit salary increase reviews, promotion and tenure reviews, contract renewal reviews for nontenured faculty members) remain summative in focus. Moreover, while the outcome of a summative review can sometimes help guide a formative process ("I'm sorry that the personnel committee didn't recommend you for promotion to full professor last year, but in our formal evaluation this year, let's explore some goals that can get you there eventually"), the findings of a formative review should never be used in any subsequent summative evaluation. To do so is to betray the open spirit of collegiality and mentoring that's essential to the success of a formative evaluation.

Encourage your institution to use both qualitative and quantitative dimensions in its faculty evaluation standards

Too frequently institutions create evaluation standards that encourage reviewers simply to count things: average scores on student course evaluations, numbers of pages in peer-reviewed journals, number of committees on which a faculty member has served, and so on. The problem is that this numerical approach doesn't always provide useful information. The most popular professor may not be the best instructor. The most prolific author may not be the best scholar. The most frequently elected committee member may not be performing the type of service that really matters. To help provide a clearer picture of someone's performance, qualitative methods can supplement what review committees learn from their quantitative approaches to evaluation.

As their name implies, qualitative methods of evaluation are techniques that enable reviewers to make more effective judgments about the quality of a faculty member's work as opposed to its mere quantity. One of the most common qualitative forms of evaluation used in faculty reviews is the portfolio, which allows the reader to gain a sense of how a faculty member has developed in various areas over time and gives the faculty member an opportunity to provide a full context for his or her achievements. For example, in a portfolio, a faculty member could contrast a current course syllabus to one that he or she used five years ago, explaining the reasons that the most important changes occurred. Rather than burdening committees with binder after binder of printed material, portfolios give faculty members an opportunity to include and discuss their "five most significant contributions to scholarship since the last promotion," "three most successful pedagogical techniques," "best exam or essay prompt within the last four years," and so on. Instead of including copies of publications, which reviewers almost never read anyway, the portfolio might include one or two examples that the faculty member considers representative, along with an explanation of why that work was important. Similarly, instead of mere lists of committees, faculty member can include a statement describing his or her philosophy of service, followed by an annotated outline of service activities that illustrate how that philosophy has guided his or her activities.

The recognized authority on the portfolio approach to evaluation is Peter Seldin, whose publications with J. Elizabeth Miller and others address nearly every aspect of compiling and reviewing faculty portfolios. Seldin describes this approach to qualitative evaluation as

> a reflective, evidence-based collection of materials that documents teaching, research, and service performance. It brings together, in one place, information about a professor's most significant professional accomplishments. It includes documents and materials that collectively suggest the scope, quality, and significance of a professor's achievements. As such, it allows faculty members to display their accomplishments for examination by others. And in the process, it contributes to sounder personnel decisions as well as the professional development of individual faculty members. (Seldin and Miller, 2009, 2; see also Seldin, 2006, and Seldin, Miller, and Seldin, 2010)

In addition, just as many colleges and universities require their students to develop electronic portfolios as a way of assisting them in being more intentional in setting learning goals and evaluating their progress toward achieving those goals, so can e-portfolios be used in the faculty evaluation process. When this information is placed on a secured website, it enables reviewers to examine materials no matter where in the world they may be. They can even make the reports of external reviewers more meaningful by providing scholars in the discipline with a much more fully developed picture of a faculty member's work than can be gained from a résumé alone.

Clarifying Expectations

If you already have clear, meaningful evaluation standards in place for the programs that report to you (or if you decide to take a leadership role in developing them, once these standards and procedures have been approved), the next step is to communicate those standards to everyone involved: those who are going to be expected to live up to those standards, as well as those who will consult those standards as criteria when making personnel decisions about others. Clarifying evaluation standards is a continuous process. Each year new faculty members arrive at the institution, and they'll need to be brought into the loop. Even faculty members who have been at the school for a long time need to be reminded of these expectations. Their role may change; perhaps they're now going to be evaluating someone whereas before they were the ones being evaluated; or perhaps they're due to be evaluated in a way they've not previously experienced, such as in a posttenure review or application for promotion to the rank of full professor. For all these reasons, clarifying expectations can never be viewed as a task that's been fully completed. It's more of a perennial duty of deans and provosts than it is merely a short-term goal.

Provide formal training sessions annually for evaluators and those who are being evaluated

Faculty members have long understood that students are far more likely to perform at the level expected of them if they know in advance what those expectations are and how grades will be assigned. That's why they so often use rubrics not only to grade student work but also to share with the students what they're looking for from them.

The same principle applies when it comes to faculty performance: you're much more likely to receive the type of performance you hope for if you provide formal training sessions in faculty evaluation than if you rely on people picking up what they need to know along the way. These training sessions need to occur every year. Standards of performance do change over time. An institution may be attempting to increase its research portfolio. Another school may find that in order to promote the highest level of student success, it has to raise the bar for pedagogy. But even if the criteria by which faculty members are evaluated and the process used to evaluate them doesn't change, routine reminders are important. With all the other activities that institutions require of the faculty, it can be easy to overlook certain details of the evaluation process until they become a matter of immediate performance for the person. When that occurs, the response of a faculty member is likely to be, "Why didn't you ever tell me this?" if you haven't provided a regular series of training workshops. Simply outlining these expectations in a faculty handbook or online isn't enough. Institutions need to conduct workshops on these topics each year, and those workshops should be as interactive as possible. Give people a chance to see how their own performance stacks up against the written criteria or offer them an opportunity to practice their evaluation skills through hypothetical case studies. If those attending the workshop simply listen to a laundry list of expectations or procedures, they're unlikely to retain more than a small portion of that information.

For those who will be conducting the evaluations, it's helpful to clarify what their role is and is not. In most cases, faculty evaluators aren't making the final decision about a colleague's performance; they're simply making a recommendation that a member of the administration will consider but is free to accept, reject, or modify. At certain institutions, even department chairs may only be making a recommendation to the dean or provost, and so they need to hear from you what you expect from them, in what format, and by what deadline. If there will be an oral component to the evaluation process, such as a promotion interview or an informal summary of findings before the recommendation is passed to the next level, chairs and faculty evaluators need to be trained in what to say and how to say it. For example, criticism that is intended to be offered in a wholly constructive way may cause the faculty member to become defensive and resist any offers of help and guidance if that criticism isn't presented properly. In a worst-case scenario, the faculty member may even have grounds to appeal and possibly nullify the entire procedure because a single participant in the evaluation process didn't live up to the institution's expectations and thus violated its procedures. Training for evaluators could also include exposure to some of the major systems for faculty evaluations, such as Raoul Arreola's (2007) quantitative approach or Peter Seldin's qualitative approach already discussed. Finally, training might include some guidance on how to handle the very difficult conversations that can occur after a chair or faculty evaluator has recommended that someone's contract not be renewed. (For advice on how to handle these conversations, as well as recommendations on other aspects of the faculty evaluation process, see Buller, 2012.)

For faculty members who will be undergoing evaluation in some form (which at most institutions means every single faculty member), an annual workshop or even a series of workshops is probably a useful idea. Those who will be going up for promotion or tenure soon probably have not been through that process before. In fact, if they have been through that process before, they're repeating it because they weren't successful the first time and need to do better now. For this reason, even though it's valuable to outline due dates, required matters of formatting, and the general expectations of the institution in terms of procedures, it's even more important to outline the program's criteria and effective strategies in making the case that someone has met those criteria. Because so many elements of a successful promotion or tenure application have to be amassed over time, this type of training workshop shouldn't just occur once in the very year that the faculty member will be applying. If it is held annually, people can be encouraged to attend this program every year or two as a way of determining whether they're on track and what they still need to do in order to make the strongest case possible when they apply. Moreover, since nearly everyone undergoes an annual evaluation, a separate session on the criteria used in these reviews and the resources that are available to help them meet those criteria is a valuable service for any dean or provost to provide.

Develop faculty flight plans to set specific and appropriate goals

One of the best tools academic leaders can develop to help faculty members perform more successfully on their evaluations is the faculty flight plan. When we want students to be successful, we frequently create a plan of study with them that outlines what courses they need to take during which terms in order to graduate in a timely manner. Student plans of study also regularly include other advice, such as when to visit the career center to begin investigating employment possibilities in different fields, when to try to build an internship or study-abroad experience into their program, when to have a formal degree audit conducted, and so on. A faculty flight plan is a similar document. It outlines the criteria that the program has for various milestones, such as promotion to the rank of associate professor or posttenure review, and the recommended time line for achieving those milestones.

Consider a hypothetical example. Suppose Riley Neophyte is a brand-new faculty member in the Department of Victimology at Aspirational State University. Shortly after the academic year begins, a mentor meets with Riley and discusses the criteria that apply to promotion and tenure decisions in the program and the qualifications of several recent successful candidates. The mentor explains that at Aspirational State University, tenure-track faculty members undergo a preliminary, formative evaluation of their progress in their third year of full-time service and a summative tenure evaluation in their sixth year. Tenure, if granted, becomes effective at the start of the seventh year; otherwise the faculty member is on a terminal contract for that year. Although Riley isn't given any promise that achieving this level of performance will guarantee promotion and tenure, the mentor explains that certain standards will have to be achieved in order for an application to have a reasonable chance of success. The mentor notes that over the past five years, successful applicants for tenure in the Department of Victimology have met the following standards:

o Their scores on peer evaluations of teaching and student course evaluations averaged at least 3.8 on a 5-point scale where 1 is unsatisfactory and 5 is excellent.

- Each had at least four refereed articles as first or sole author in print or in press.
- Each had a book of research in print or in press at a major university published.
- Each had served on one department-level and one college-level committee.

Using these standards as a basis, the mentor and Riley then jointly develop the flight plan presented in table 28.1.

In their meetings, the mentor is careful to explain to Riley that the flight plan is intended to be a guide, not an inflexible contract. Unforeseen developments, whether negative like a severe illness or positive like the receipt of a Fulbright Fellowship, might cause them to revise the plan along the way. In addition, there will be specific points, such as each spring of the third through fifth years, when together they'll take a formal and thorough look at the progress that's being made toward tenure and conclude whether Riley seems to be on track. Even with these formal reviews, however, the mentor reiterates yet again that successful completion of the flight plan is not a guarantee of tenure, but rather an indication that Riley has performed at an appropriate level to be given serious consideration by the tenure committees at various levels of the university.

Explain the criteria by which decisions will be made in a manner that reduces subjectivity as much as possible

In clarifying expectations of both the evaluators and those being evaluated, it's important to stress the need for all review criteria to be applied as objectively as possible. Any form of performance appraisal will have at least some degree of subjectivity in it. Even if you try to create the most elaborate type of checklist of performance criteria imaginable, it can't account for every eventuality. Moreover, if you do try to create such an elaborate checklist—for example, specifying minimum word counts for articles that must be published in certain first-tier journals and achieve at least a certain impact factor—the standards will end up becoming so narrow that you'll stifle people's innovation for making contributions in ways you can't yet imagine.

It's far better to have a series of discussions with evaluators about what terms like *excellent*, *good*, and *unsatisfactory* mean in your system so that everyone's applying roughly the same standards. Necessarily at this point you'll be discussing conceptual definitions of these terms with the evaluators. Conceptual definitions provide the theoretical framework of a

Table 28.1. Sample Faculty Flight Plan

Year 1

Fall
Prepare and teach 2 courses
Prepare and submit abstract for conference presentation

Spring
Prepare and teach 1 new course; repeat 1 course from fall
Present paper at conference
Review course evaluations with mentor; discuss action plan

Summer
Teach 1 course (repeated from spring)
Begin revising conference paper for article
Begin draft of book proposal

Year 2

Fall
Prepare and teach 1 new course; repeat 1 course

Complete and submit article for publication

Serve on departmental committee

Spring
Repeat 2 courses
Begin drafting second article
Continue book proposal
Review course evaluations with mentor (work with center for excellence in teaching, if needed)

Summer
Repeat 1 course
Revise first article as necessary
Continue drafting second article
Prepare items for third year review

Year 3

Fall
Prepare and teach 1 new course; repeat 1 course
Complete and submit book proposal
Submit items for third year review

Spring
Prepare and teach 1 new course; repeat 1 course
Complete and submit third article for publication
Discuss third-year review with mentor; adjust flight plan

Summer
Work on book
Begin drafting third article
No teaching

Year 4

Fall
Repeat 2 courses
Continue work on book
Revise second article as necessary
Complete and submit third article

Spring
Repeat 2 courses
Complete and submit book manuscript
Discuss progress on flight plan with mentor

Summer
Repeat 1 course
Revise third article as necessary

(*continued*)

Table 28.2. (Continued)

Year 5

Fall	Teach 1 new course; repeat 1 course
	Serve on college committee
	Begin writing fourth article
Spring	Teach 1 new course; repeat 1 course
	Continue writing fourth article
	Discuss course evaluations and progress with mentor; remediate any weaknesses indicated
Summer	Prepare promotion and tenure materials
	No teaching

Year 6

Fall	Teach 1 new course; repeat 1 course
	Conduct research for ongoing publications
	Submit promotion and tenure materials
Spring	Teach 2 new courses
	Complete work with mentor: develop plan going forward
	Prepare research for publication (fifth article? second book?)
Summer	Repeat 2 courses
	Continue research and writing

---

standard that can be applied to any academic discipline. Once they understand the concept, people will be able to develop more specific operational definitions that apply that framework within their own fields. They'll be able to say things like, "Well, if we're going to say that the rating of stellar should be reserved only for performance that's truly extraordinary and goes well beyond what we've defined as excellent, then I guess in our case, we'd use that rating only for people who have brought in a grant that year of $10 million or more or who have won some major international prize."

One other way of minimizing the impact of subjectivity in faculty evaluations is to make use of rationally normed rating instruments or those that have been field-tested for interrater reliability at a number of institutions. For student ratings of instruction, examples of these standardized instruments include the widely used IDEA Form distributed through IDEA Education (ideaedu.org/). For reducing the impact of subjectivity in a controversial area such as collegiality, many institutions use the Collegiality Assessment Matrix and the Self-Assessment Matrix available through ATLAS Leadership Training (www.atlasleadership.com/ATLAS_Leadership_Services/CAM_and_S-AM.html).

Empowering Evaluators

Even in situations where you may not have an opportunity to improve the evaluation standards and criteria used at your institution, you can still play an important role in improving the effectiveness of faculty evaluations by empowering those who are involved in various levels of the process. Empowering people doesn't mean giving them carte blanche to do whatever they like, regardless of the criteria and procedures that are in place. It doesn't entail a promise never to overturn a recommendation made to you by a person or committee that reports to you. Rather it's a commitment that you'll take seriously any recommendation that's made to you, respect the professionalism of those who made it, and support the right of evaluators to hold those being reviewed to high and consistent standards of achievement. In order to provide this type of academic leadership, deans and provosts may wish to consider adopting several principles.

Encourage anyone participating in a review process to adopt truly evaluative language

When chairs, personnel committees, and others participating in the faculty evaluation process don't feel empowered to render candid, straightforward appraisals, they often resort to cataloguing accomplishments without actually evaluating them. They end up saying things like, "Since your last promotion, you submitted two first-author research papers for editorial review and had one additional paper for which you were second author appear in print." The difficulty with such statements is that they don't indicate whether the achievement they mention exceeded the expectations the institution has for a faculty member at that rank, meets those expectations, or falls short of what the person should have been doing. When items are listed and not really evaluated, the faculty member may draw a completely different conclusion from what the reviewer had intended. Moreover, evaluators who make this kind of remark aren't doing their jobs. The task of a reviewer isn't simply to count items from a faculty member's résumé but to report whether, in his or her professional judgment, that level of achievement was appropriate. Without truly evaluative language, a statement may be regarded by a faulty member as acceptance or praise when the person who wrote it actually considered that level of achievement mediocre at best.

One of the great advantages of supplementing quantitative measures of achievement (numbers of articles published or committees served) with qualitative measures (such as the portfolio approach mentioned above) is that reviewers can better distinguish between how much work was done and how much work was done well. If they simply list accomplishments instead of appraising them, they ignore the great value in this method of faculty evaluation.

If your institution or unit doesn't already have clearly evaluative categories by which to rate a faculty member's performance in each area under review, empower them to develop their own. Even if next year's chair or review committee adopts a different system, the categories used by this year's evaluators will function as something similar to a rubric used to grade a student's paper. It will encourage greater consistency of results and reduce the likelihood of subjective factors distorting the results. Some approaches that you might consider recommending are the following:

○ A *Likert scale* or a similar form of numerical rating scale. A Likert scale (commonly mispronounced as "LIKE-ert," but correctly pronounced "LICK-ert") is a numerical ranking, usually consisting of five sequential categories. For instance, on faculty evaluations, a Likert scale of rating might look like this: "On a scale of 1 (low) to 5 (high), I would rate your achievement in the category of scholarly activity for the past year as . . . "

○ A *verbal Likert scale*. This type of evaluative ranking is essentially identical to the numerical Likert scale but substitutes descriptive adjectives for numbers. Common categories used on faculty evaluations as part of a verbal Likert scale are excellent, very good, good, satisfactory, and unsatisfactory.

○ A *graded Likert scale*. Since academics are comfortable with letter grading, some evaluators prefer to use an A to F scale in appraising faculty performance. The advantage of such a system is that it allows more specific gradations (B+, C-, and so on). The disadvantage is that the type of grade inflation expected by many students routinely carries over to this evaluation system; faculty members thus sometimes find even a rating of B, which should imply "above average," to be insufficiently favorable.

○ A *statement of meeting expectations*. In many ways, this approach is similar to the verbal Likert scale, merely substituting a statement about the unit's expectations for a simple adjective. These statements may include, "Significantly exceeded/exceeded/met/failed to meet the institution's expectations for a faculty member at your rank and in your discipline." If you encourage evaluators to use this type of phrasing, it's important that there be some document (frequently part of a faculty handbook or policy manual) that sets forth what the expectations are in each category of evaluation so that there can be little confusion over what it means to meet them.

Some of the drawbacks to using Likert scales and their equivalents is that they suggest to some reviewers that each category should include roughly the same number of people, the categories are all equidistant from one another (that is, that the distance from satisfactory to good is identical to the distance from very good to excellent), and that no one ever falls into the space between the categories (in other words, a person's performance has to be either satisfactory or good; it can't be somewhere in between). A model that seeks to avoid these drawbacks is presented in table 28.3. In this model:

- Both numerical ratings and descriptors are used so that people who feel more comfortable with one system or the other don't need to choose between them.

- Evaluators are given some leeway in assigning numerical scores within the middle three categories. For example, a faculty member whose performance is rated as good can be assigned a score as high as 7 or as low as 4, indicating that this category encompasses a fairly broad range of achievement. The highest and lowest ratings, Outstanding and Unsatisfactory, are each associated with only a single score (10 and 1, respectively), indicating that these categories are intended to be reserved for performance that is truly exceptional.

- The middle range of the scale is termed good rather than satisfactory since a college faculty should not represent a normal distribution of achievement. The rigor of the process of hiring, annually appraising, and promoting faculty members means that even typical performance should be at a fairly high level.

- The system compels reviewers to be truly evaluative. The recommended guidelines discourage evaluators from simply concluding that everyone under review is outstanding or very good and guides them toward making candid assessments of each faculty member's performance.

- Conceptual definitions are given, allowing the individual discipline or specialty to apply these principles more specifically through operational definitions.

Table 28.3. Sample Faculty Evaluation Standards

Rating	Descriptor	Definition
10	*Outstanding*	To achieve this rating, the faculty member must demonstrate truly extraordinary performance in the category under consideration during the review period. This rating should be reserved for recognition of achievements that *far* exceed expectations based on the faculty member's assigned duties and are demonstrably superior to those that would merit a rating of Exceptional. *Recommended guidelines*: In ordinary circumstances, it is expected that not more than 10 percent of the faculty will receive a rating of Outstanding in the category under consideration during the review period.
9–8	*Exceptional*	To achieve this rating, the faculty member must demonstrate performance that exceeds expectations in the category under consideration during the review period. This rating should be reserved for recognition of substantive achievements that go above and beyond the faculty member's assigned duties and are demonstrably superior to those that would merit a rating of Good. *Recommended guidelines*: In ordinary circumstances, it is expected that no more than a third of the faculty will receive a rating of Outstanding or Exceptional in the category under consideration during the review period.
7–4	*Good*	To achieve this rating, the faculty member must demonstrate meritorious performance in the category under consideration during the review period by fully attaining the high standards of performance expected of the faculty at this institution. This rating serves as a recognition that the faculty member's accomplishments have been commendable and that challenging objectives have been met. *Recommended guidelines*: In ordinary circumstances, it is expected that a significant majority of the faculty will receive a rating of Good in the category under consideration during the review period.

(*continued*)

Table 28.3. (*Continued*)

Rating	Descriptor	Definition
3–2	*Needs Improvement*	To achieve this rating, the faculty member must demonstrate performance that does not meet expectations in one or more aspects of the category under consideration during the review period. The designation of Needs Improvement serves as an indication to the faculty member that future progress in this category is expected and that a performance improvement plan will be developed to clarify standards and set a timetable for remediation. *Recommended guidelines*: In ordinary circumstances, it is expected that relatively few of the faculty will receive a rating of Needs Improvement in the category under consideration during the review period.
1	*Unsatisfactory*	To achieve this rating, the faculty member must demonstrate performance that either egregiously fails to meet expectations in at least one aspect of the category under consideration or generally fails to meet expectations in several aspects of the category under consideration during the review period. The designation of Unsatisfactory serves as a warning to the faculty member that significant improvement is urgently required, a performance plan will be developed to clarify standards and a timetable set for remediation, and sanctions may be imposed if these standards and/or timetable are not met. *Recommended guidelines*: In ordinary circumstances, it is expected that very few of the faculty will receive a rating of Unsatisfactory in the category under consideration during the review period.

Recommend that when evaluators identify problems, they also propose solutions

One of the best ways to empower chairs and others involved in evaluating faculty members is to give them the freedom to suggest ways in which the person being evaluated can remediate any difficulties recognized. Two important benefits derive from this approach. First, since the evaluators are expected to come up with a reasonable action plan for any problem they identify, they're less likely to become preoccupied with relatively minor issues that don't have a great impact on the faculty member's performance. Sometimes evaluators are tempted to regard something as wrong simply because the person being evaluated doesn't do it exactly as they would. By encouraging them to specify workable solutions to any challenge they see, you're urging them to devote their time to thinking about performance issues that truly affect teaching, research, and service, not those that are merely the result of the faculty member's individual style. Second, you're making the best use of the knowledge and creativity of a broad range of highly qualified people. Instead of limiting yourself to only ideas you can come up with yourself, you now have one or more "consultants" who may generate solutions you'd never have imagined. The evaluators will also be more likely to buy into the solution and work actively to make it effective, since the suggestion was theirs in the first place.

Empowering evaluators to develop solutions means helping them understand that general advice—such as "You need to work on your people skills" or "You have to stop wasting so much time"—is rarely productive. A good solution to a problem is one that presents a clear action plan with specific expectations and a time line for when those expectations are to be met—for example:

- "From this point forward you should be sure to arrive at class sufficiently early for the session to begin on time, remain present for the full duration of the period, and conduct at least five office hours for students every week. If for any reason you are not able to attend class, you should notify your chair in advance so that students may be notified that class is canceled for that day."

- "No later than June 15, [year], you are to prepare at least three proposals for external funding. One or more of these proposals must be submitted to the National Science Foundation, the National Endowment for the Humanities, or the National Endowment for the Arts."

- "By the end of the workday on Friday, [date], you are to have removed from your office computer all items not permitted by our college's Policy on Appropriate Use of Electronic Resources, a copy of which is enclosed with this letter. "

- "By October 1, [year], you must have attended and completed one of the monthly sessions offered by the Department of Human Resources on Interpersonal Relations in the Workplace and submitted to your department chair a letter, signed by the director of human resources, indicating that you have completed this requirement."

- ○ "During the spring semester of [year] you must participate in at least four workshops sponsored by the Center for Effectiveness in Teaching and document how you will improve the quality of your instruction based on those sessions. "
- ○ "Effective immediately, you will not engage in any written or verbal communication whatsoever with [name]. "

If you feel it's appropriate to do so, you could also encourage the evaluators to recommend to you what they believe an appropriate sanction to be if the required activity does not occur by the deadline. Among the options you might give them are the following.

- ○ "Failure to do so will result in an official reprimand being placed in your personnel file."
- ○ "Failure to do so will result in your forfeiture of any cost-of-living or merit increase for the coming fiscal year."
- ○ "Failure to do so will result in your loss of any departmental travel funding for up to three years."
- ○ "Failure to do so will be regarded as potential cause for termination of your contract, in accordance with the institution's policy on tenure and contract renewal."

Academic leaders are sometimes surprised to find that department chairs and faculty members of personnel committees can be even more demanding of their peers than they themselves would be. Having the evaluators recommend a performance improvement plan to you in this way shouldn't lock you into any particular option. However, empowering the evaluators to propose solutions gives you valuable insight into alternative approaches to those you may be considering on your own.

Remind those who are conducting faculty evaluations that they don't have to be experts in the same areas as the person they're evaluating in order to provide a meaningful and accurate appraisal

You will sometimes hear from chairs and faculty evaluators that they don't feel qualified to comment on the quality of someone's performance because they don't share that person's field. That belief sometimes exists even within the same department where physical chemists will tell you that they couldn't possibly evaluate the work of organic chemists or that historians of modern Asia feel unprepared to render an opinion on the work of early medieval historians. As a dean or provost, you have an excellent opportunity to empower evaluators by describing why this reluctance is unwarranted and what you envision their role to be.

You might start by explaining that there are indeed times when intimate familiarity with a faculty member's specialty is desirable. For example, many institutions include an external review component as part of the review for promotion and tenure, requiring the applicant to send his or her curriculum vitae to specialists in the discipline who can comment about the significance of the person's research, the type of grant support he or she has been receiving, the quality of the journals in which the applicant's publications have appeared, and so on. If a chair or faculty personnel committee has sufficient knowledge to render an informed judgment on these issues, that's wonderful. But that's rarely the expectation institutions have for their internal evaluators. They don't have to be specialists in the field to determine whether a colleague's syllabi are well constructed and adequately informative to students. They don't have to know a field in order to distinguish between a course in which students are actively engaged and one where they're passive, unchallenged, and simply the recipients of one dry lecture after another. They don't have to publish in the same journals as the person they're reviewing to know whether his or her work on committees and other contributions to the institution constitute solid academic citizenship.

In most departments it's not feasible to have every evaluator be in the same field and specialty as the person being evaluated. And if chairs and faculty members on personnel committees reject the idea of evaluating their colleagues, the alternative is something they wouldn't want either: major personnel decisions made solely by upper administrators and governing boards who may well have even less insight into the faculty role than they do. By reminding them of the important role they play in the evaluation process, you're empowering them to assume their rightful role in a system of shared governance. There are times when having a less than fully informed opinion is far preferable to leaving important decisions to those who may have different agendas and priorities from those of the faculty.

Conclusion

While the role of provosts and deans in faculty evaluations at some institutions may involve conducting those evaluations themselves, it's far more common for provost and deans to take a more supervisory role, signing off on the work of others, hearing appeals, and ensuring that consistent standards are applied. In so doing, it's helpful to remember that no faculty evaluator, regardless of the position he or she holds at the institution, is qualified to deal with every issue that might occur during the evaluation process. For example, Deryl Leaming (1998) noted the level of caution that must be exerted when a matter of performance appears to be related to a problem like alcoholism or substance abuse. The vast majority of institutions have formal processes for referring a faculty member for counseling and professional assistance when there are psychological issues, challenges that may be covered under the Americans with Disabilities Act, and serious personal problems. Make sure that everyone involved in the faculty evaluation process in your area understands what aspects of performance they should address themselves and which are better left to others. Finally, there's one piece of advice that's valuable for anyone who serves as a faculty evaluator or is in charge of the evaluation process:

Every reviewer should be able to summarize his or her overall conclusion about each person being evaluated in fewer than twenty words. If someone cannot state a conclusion that clearly and succinctly, the faculty member who is being reviewed is unlikely to understand the nature of the recommendation that's being made. In fact, if a review panel as a whole can reduce its conclusion to fewer than twenty words, it's an excellent practice to include that statement in boldface type at the beginning or the end of each evaluation it conducts.

REFERENCES

Arreola, R. A. (2007). *Developing a comprehensive faculty evaluation system: A guide to designing, building, and operating large-scale faculty evaluation systems* (3rd ed.). Bolton, MA: Anker.

Buller, J. L. (2012). *Best practices in faculty evaluation: A practical guide for academic leaders.* San Francisco: Jossey-Bass.

Leaming, D. (1998). *Academic leadership: A practical guide to chairing the department.* Bolton, MA: Anker.

Seldin, P. (2006). *Evaluating faculty performance: A practical guide to assessing teaching, research, and service.* Bolton, MA: Anker.

Seldin, P., & Miller, J. E. (2009). *The academic portfolio: A practical guide to documenting teaching, research, and service.* San Francisco, CA: Jossey-Bass.

Seldin, P., Miller, J. E., & Seldin, C. A. (2010). *The teaching portfolio: A practical guide to improved performance and promotion/tenure decisions* (4th ed.). San Francisco, CA: Jossey-Bass.

RESOURCES

Berk, R. A. (2013). *Top 10 flashpoints in student ratings and the evaluation of teaching: What faculty and administrators must know to protect themselves in employment decisions.* Sterling, VA: Stylus.

Blumberg, P. (2014). *Assessing and improving your teaching: Strategies and rubrics for faculty growth and student learning.* San Francisco, CA: Jossey-Bass.

Cheldelin, S. I., & Lucas, A. F. (2003). *The Jossey-Bass academic administrator's guide to conflict resolution.* San Francisco, CA: Jossey-Bass

Coffman, J. R. (2005). *Work and peace in academe: Leveraging time, money, and intellectual energy through managing conflict.* Bolton, MA: Anker.

Falcone, P. (2005). *2600 phrases for effective performance reviews: Ready-to-use words and phrases that really get results.* New York, NY: AMACOM.

Falcone, P. (2010). *101 sample write-ups for documenting employee performance problems: A guide to progressive discipline & termination* (2nd ed.). New York, NY: American Management Association/Society for Human Resource Management.

Grote, R. C. (2011). *How to be good at performance appraisals: Simple, effective, done right.* Boston, MA: Harvard Business Review.

Higgerson, M. L., & Joyce, T. A. (2007). Managing interpersonal conflict. In Higgerson, M. L., & Joyce, T. A. *Effective leadership communication: A guide for department chairs and deans for managing difficult situations and people* (pp. 83–98). Bolton, MA: Anker.

Max, D., & Bacal, R. (2011). *Perfect phrases for performance reviews: Hundreds of ready-to-use phrases for describing employee performance* (2nd ed.). New York, NY: McGraw-Hill.

29

EVALUATIONS OF CHAIRS
AND DEANS

This chapter shifts focus from the role that provosts and deans can play in evaluating faculty members to the role they can play in evaluating other administrators. This discussion begins by considering what you may wish to keep in mind when you're evaluating academic administrators who report directly to you: deans if you're a provost and department chairs if you're a dean. The first thing to notice is that certain aspects of faculty evaluations explored in chapter 29 apply when you're conducting administrative evaluations:

- ○ It's important to tie each evaluation to the person's actual assigned responsibilities.
- ○ Using clearly evaluative language, not mere lists of achievements, offers better guidance on how to build on strengths and improve weaknesses.
- ○ If you can't summarize the overall conclusion of your evaluation in fewer than twenty words, the person you're evaluating will probably be unable to understand the message you're trying to send.
- ○ In all reviews, it's essential to distinguish formative advice from summative assessment.
- ○ Using both qualitative and quantitative methods of evaluation provides a more complete picture of someone's performance than using either of these methods alone.
- ○ Performance plans, or "flight plans," can be effective ways of setting and achieving goals.
- ○ Seeking ways of reducing the subjective element in evaluations is highly desirable.

○ When identifying problems, you aren't being helpful if you don't also propose solutions.

Administrative evaluations also have important differences from faculty evaluations. For example, although administrators may engage in teaching and research, they typically do so as part of their faculty responsibilities, not their administrative responsibilities. So regardless of how well or poorly a dean teaches a course, that factor probably won't enter into your evaluation of that person at all as a dean. (In his or her evaluation as a faculty member, however, teaching effectiveness would be highly relevant.) Moreover, even though faculty evaluators don't have to be experts in the specific discipline of the person they're reviewing, it'll be much easier for you to conduct an administrative review if you have a great deal of familiarity (and perhaps some firsthand experience) with the responsibilities performed by the person you're evaluating. Although the work of provosts, deans, and chairs has many similarities, chairs deal with issues on a far more personal level than most deans, and deans serve as advocates for a specific group of disciplines far more than do provosts, who are expected to represent all disciplines. Deans and chairs can't devote all their energies to managing up (see chapter 23), so to evaluate them effectively, you often have to see things from their perspective and how circumstances frequently require them to manage down.

In this vein, Gary Krahenbuhl (2004, 226–227) has outlined five principles for conducting administrative evaluations, basing his recommendations on those developed for the evaluation of deans by the Council of Colleges of Arts and Sciences:

> There should be clarity and consistency on all aspects of the administrative evaluation.... An institution's policies on the review of academic administrators should be congruent with the following principles:
>
> 1. The scope and mechanics of all evaluations of administrative performance should be known, codified, and exist as an aspect of institutional policy.
>
> 2. Those individuals asked to provide input should be well informed about the requirements of the position and the job-related accomplishments (or lack thereof).
>
> 3. Reviews should occur on a known, regular cycle....
>
> 4. The collection, statistical treatment, and conclusions drawn from evaluative data should be handled with the same rigor and objectivity that would be viewed as sound practice in research.

5. Successful administrative evaluations feature an appropriate balance between (a) the right of the [department's] members to have input that is appropriately confidential and access to summary results that are disseminated in a timely way, and (b) the right of the [chair] being evaluated to receive appropriate summary data and to enjoy the same level of privacy normally associated with other related personnel actions in the institution.

The first principle parallels the observation in chapter 29 that evaluation ought to be tied to specific standards of performance (something like a grading rubric) and that those standards should be shared in advance with the person being evaluated. The second principle is related to our discussion about the need for regular training for evaluators so that they understand their role and the criteria that they'll be using.

The other three principles are extremely important additions. We can't simply review the administrators who report to us sporadically or only when a problem arises; performance review helps people to grow in their positions, reflect on what they've learned, and set new goals for the future. With regard to Krahenbuhl's fourth principle, we should remember that data about administrators are too frequently collected and analyzed in a manner that we'd never find acceptable in our own academic research. For example, we sometimes generalize from a very small sample size. It may sound informative to tell a dean or a chair, "100 percent of those who responded to the survey we distributed think that we need new leadership in your area." But if that conclusion is based on only two people who completed the survey out of a pool larger than a hundred, the statement (although still technically accurate) is utterly meaningless. In addition, if we simply use averages with a relatively small sample size, the results may similarly be distorted. Saying something like, "Your score at serving as an effective advocate for your area averages 4.2 on a 5-point scale" means something quite different if four people gave the person a perfect score of 5, with one disgruntled person giving a score of 1 (on this and every other question) than if that average results from a sample size of 239 respondents, all of whom considered each question carefully. As we saw in chapter 17, for small data sets it's better to calculate medians, which are less sensitive to outliers than arithmetic means. Moreover, means are not really the best way to calculate an aggregated score when the survey or evaluation form requires responding with discrete data, such as occurs with a Likert scale or any format in which only integers are used, as opposed to situations where a respondent is free to provide continuous data, that is, any rational number, such as 2.487.

Looking to the Future

Evaluation of all kinds is most effective when it combines appraisal of past work, well-considered advice on specific ways in which to improve, and practical goals for the future. Too frequently evaluators focus only on the past when reviewing someone's performance. The very word *review* suggests a backward look on achievements that have already occurred, so it's a natural inclination to devote an entire evaluation, oral or written, to appraising only what the person did during the review period.

But an evaluation process that leaves a person being reviewed with a sense that he or she hasn't lived up to expectations (or, conversely, that provides blanket praise without any indication of how to build on those successes) doesn't take full advantage of the type of administrative development that these processes can provide. If you've never used evaluation sessions to set goals for the future as well as to discuss achievements of the past, it might be a good idea to begin including in your discussions with the dean or chair some strategies for the future that seem most desirable because of the person's past challenges and accomplishments. For instance, if the person has been responsible for something particularly successful, language like the following can use that achievement as a springboard for even more notable accomplishments in the future:

> Your outreach efforts during the past year have been nothing short of excellent. In addition to the new (and highly successful) Distinguished Lecture Series, you have used presentations by visiting scholars and other public events to bring a great deal of positive attention to your program and to the institution as a whole.
>
> For this reason, I would like you, during the coming year, to increase public awareness of the Distinguished Lecture Series even further by working cooperatively with the University Development Office on a plan for maximum media exposure and targeted invitations to prospective donors.
>
> As part of our series of administrative training workshops, I would also like you to make a presentation to all the deans and chairs on ways of increasing community engagement in their areas. Your expertise in this regard would make you very effective in helping the institution expand its outreach efforts even more broadly.

In a similar way, constructive criticism can also be used as a springboard for developing future goals, such as in the following example.

The paperwork that leaves your office is too frequently late or poorly completed. Typographical errors are common and tend to create a poor public image for your program. To improve your performance in this area, I am setting the following goals for you during the coming year.

○ Have all memoranda and nonroutine e-mail messages proofread for spelling and grammar before sending them out. Nonroutine e-mail messages include any communication sent off-campus, to the president or governing board, or as part of an official exchange that may become public or part of a permanent record.

○ Put all deadlines on your calendar. Set aside sufficient time in advance to complete routine reports and recommendations. List appropriate start dates and milestones along the way, as well as final due dates.

○ Delegate to others those tasks that seem to be scattering your efforts. Give faculty members a chance to accomplish some of the tasks you would normally handle. For instance, you might consider sending a faculty member to an occasional meeting in your place or putting that person in charge of an ongoing project. As you do so, be sure to monitor the person's progress closely and provide appropriate guidance.

Once this type of systematic goal setting has become a regular part of how you perform evaluations, you'll probably find that your review meetings with chairs or deans become far more productive. You'll be able to monitor progress in achieving the goals of the previous evaluation at the same time that you establish new goals for the future, a process that's known as *formative-summative evaluation*. (See Buller, 2012.) In this way, you'll have an opportunity to measure the quality of the administrator's work against both the institution's established list of job responsibilities for the position and any more focused list of goals you may have developed for the specific challenges facing that particular person.

Interviewing Faculty Members

Whenever possible in an administrative review, conduct oral interviews with the faculty members who report to that person even if you receive written or electronic evaluation forms from those same people. One-on-one conversations provide you with a far more comprehensive view of how the dean or chair is doing than what you will learn from even the best written evaluations. Those paper or electronic evaluations give you a great deal of information that you can usually summarize very quickly. Often those summaries even occur automatically. On items that require the evaluator to supply a numerical score, the medians that you calculate often provide a useful comparison between colleges or departments; they allow you to see how one chair or dean is doing relative to others, at least in terms of how the faculty members perceive them. Since these evaluations are usually submitted anonymously, this part of the evaluation process can elicit greater candor from faculty members who may fear (rightly or wrongly) that they will suffer retribution for their criticisms. But as useful as these standardized evaluation forms may be, they frequently don't tell you as complete a story as you would learn if you conducted brief private interviews with each member of the department. Just as certain faculty members will be reluctant to be straightforward with you unless they have the anonymity of a written response, others won't be as open as you might like if they have to put their comments in writing. For this, private interviews give an evaluator a more complete picture of a unit's operation, morale, and plans for the future than you would ever have gleaned from a stack of printed evaluations or a list of aggregated data.

In the course of these individual conversations, you'll be able to ask follow-up questions about items that cause you special concern or that you don't fully understand. Particularly if you don't know the individual members of that program very well, you'll gain insights into their personalities that can offer a broader context to the insights gained from the written evaluations. For example, you might learn that people in the program tend to be overly negative about even small disappointments or are positive about their chair or dean because they aren't being challenged as much as they should be. Moreover, if you've seen a pattern in the written comments that appeared on evaluation forms, you can explore the reasons for those remarks and ascertain just how widespread the sentiment may be. You can say, for example, "On the written evaluations, several people seemed to indicate that Dr. Jones was a bit too [fill in the blank]. What's your opinion on this issue?" or "Do you know why people may feel this way?"

One particularly useful suggestion you may want to keep in mind as you conduct these interviews is to meet the faculty members in their offices, not yours. You'll learn more about the program that way, and it's a more efficient use of your time since it reduces the likelihood that someone will forget the appointment or arrive late. Most important, it allows you to end an unproductive or excessively long conversation gracefully. After all, it's far easier to leave someone's office than to get that person to leave yours. Just be aware of how far loud voices (including your own) may carry where walls are thin.

Giving Clear and Specific Advice

Most provosts and deans are able to be quite specific when making criticisms. They know the problems caused by poor performance, and they probably have at least a few ideas on how to fix them. But sometimes academic leaders aren't able to be quite that specific when it comes to praising others for a good performance. They make comments like, "You're doing well," "You conduct efficient meetings," or "Your reports are always submitted on time." Statements like that don't have enough emotional punch to make someone want to repeat and then surpass their past accomplishments. For this reason, it's beneficial to take enough time to be specific when praising another administrator. Allow the person to bask in the glow of a job well done. Here are a few ideas about good, specific, compliments during an administrative evaluation:

○ "You're an excellent role model for everyone who works in your area. The type of leadership you provide is just what we need in order to accomplish our goals and serve the needs of our faculty, students, and community. What I'm particularly impressed with is the degree to which you have a clear vision of precisely where you want your programs to go. In addition to that, you inspire people so that they're able to carry out that vision. I've never known you to micromanage the faculty on any issue. People sense—and I believe they sense correctly—that you regard them as full and equal partners in your leadership. Some of the faculty members I spoke to told me how much they value the amount of freedom you give them to make their own decisions about matters that affect them directly. What I conclude from those remarks is that you respect the strengths of individuals by allowing them to be individuals."

○ "Your faculty members admire you greatly for your historical insight into how to get things accomplished at this institution. You're credited with knowing whom to contact to get projects moving and with having the kind of authority that makes the impossible suddenly become possible. Every single person I spoke to on the faculty said that you're well respected throughout the entire school. I concur with their impression, and I've come to respect your expertise and advice as well."

○ "One of the most impressive things I learned from your faculty
members is the extent to which they regard you as open and receptive to new ideas. People feel free to voice their needs, state their
concerns, and disagree with you when necessary. They know that
your office is always open to them. Probably the most common
phrase I heard in my conversations with the faculty is that you are
'easy to talk to.' They find that you support them personally in their
professional goals and treat them with a great deal of collegiality
and respect. Since I also respect your perspective on the numerous
challenges and opportunities we face, I'm delighted that we'll continue to be working together in the months ahead."

○ "The faculty members in your program have great confidence in
you as their advocate. Regardless of whether they share your vision,
everyone I spoke to knows that you'll always act in what you regard
as their best interests, as well as the best interests of the students and
institution as a whole. People know that you'll be candid in presenting their needs to me, even at times when that may be difficult for
you because of all the competing priorities our institution has. But
I want you to know that I appreciate your openness just as much
as I appreciate your support when issues don't always go your way.
We happen to have a great administrative team right now, and I'm
delighted that you're on it."

Deans and chairs will remember statements like these on days when
everything seems to be going wrong and the people around them are
blaming them for their frustrations. They have an impact that a mere
rating of Outstanding or advice to "keep up the good work" can't have.
In a similar way, when you have to provide criticism, don't just say, "You
do such-and-such poorly," or, "Your performance in this area needs to
improve." Take time to explain what the problem is, why you see it as a
problem, and how the situation might be addressed more productively in
the future. Here are a few examples of how you might take this approach:

○ "Members of your program tell me that they often feel they don't
have a clear sense of where their area is going or what your vision
is for the future. This lack of clarity is a particular concern to me
because of our upcoming reaccreditation visit. Without a shared
sense of purpose and mission, I'm concerned we may face tougher
questions about our goals and plans in your area than for other
parts of the university. For this reason, I'd like you to take some time
at your next faculty meeting to outline to everyone in the program
your vision for the future and your strategy for getting there."

○ "Junior faculty members in your program report that they're not receiving the degree of mentoring from you that they feel they need. They're uncertain what your expectations are of them and don't understand the criteria you'll use for their annual evaluations. In addition, many of your recent hires would like you to do a better job explaining to them both the overall design of the curriculum and their own job responsibilities as they proceed toward promotion and tenure. As a result, I'd like you to consider developing a series of sessions specifically aimed at junior faculty members in your discipline. In these workshops, make your expectations clear. Go over institutional policies, as well as those that are specific to your discipline. Follow up afterward so that you can be sure all the members of your program understand their responsibilities, the way the curriculum works, and the standards used to make personnel decisions at various levels of the institution. If you sense even the slightest confusion over these matters, try to put the person at ease (since some have said you can come across as a bit intimidating in individual conversations) and encourage them to ask you specific questions."

Making Possible Sanctions Clear

We've already seen how important it is to follow criticism with advice on how to improve. It's even more important, when offering serious criticism (that which can lead to a formal reprimand, reassignment, or even dismissal from the institution), for provosts and deans to be as specific as possible about what behavior was unsatisfactory in the past, what corrective measures are needed, and what sanctions may result if improvement doesn't occur in the future. Following is an example of how you might write a section of an evaluation that contains this type of criticism, advice, and warning:

> As you and I have already discussed several times, you're prone to demonstrate fits of anger when things don't go your way. On your 360-degree evaluation this year, the single most common adjective people used to describe you was *mercurial*. In my professional judgment, anger and general moodiness are interfering with your managerial effectiveness. I myself have had to redirect time and energy from important academic business to deal with several grievances in your area. As you know, at least one junior faculty member has left the institution, citing the tension that exists in your program as a reason.

In order to improve your performance in this area, I am encouraging you to take the following steps immediately:

○ When you find yourself tempted to reply to someone in anger, delay responding for as long as possible. Say something like, "Please ask my secretary to set up an appointment so that we can discuss this in greater detail later this week. I want to get some information together." Then give yourself a chance to cool down.

○ Don't immediately send an e-mail if there's any chance at all that you wrote it in anger. Delay a day or two and see if your attitude toward the matter changes or softens. On highly sensitive issues, consider hand-writing a memo that your staff has to word-process for you rather than resorting to e-mail.

○ Remember that your opinions and attitude profoundly affect others in the program, especially untenured junior faculty members. Try to make the most out of challenging or difficult situations by focusing on the positive aspects rather than finding fault with others over relatively minor issues.

Because I regard this issue as serious, I'll be conducting a follow-up evaluation one year [or, in very problematic situations, three to six months] from today. If I continue to receive what I regard as substantive complaints from your faculty about unwarranted displays of anger and the level of your interpersonal skills, I will require you to step down as dean [chair] before the conclusion of your current term. Moreover, if I learn of a particularly egregious example of anger displayed to any of the college's constituents even before that date, I will require you to step down immediately.

Conclusion

Evaluation of deans or department chairs should be an integral part of your comprehensive development plan for administrators in your area. In most cases, it's probably best to conduct informal reviews annually with a particularly thorough review (performed with 360-degree input from you as the supervisor, the person's colleagues in his or her same rank, and the people who report to that person) every three to five years. Don't forget to include members of the staff since administrative assistants, budget directors, and communication officers can provide you with insight you won't get elsewhere. For a nationally normed perspective, IDEA Education offers an evaluation instrument for reviewing department chairs that provides constructive criticism, analysis of successful areas of achievement, and a customized plan for professional development based on priorities determined by the chair (ideaedu.org/services/department -chairs). The same instrument can also be used for evaluation of deans if you provide a little extra instruction to those who will be completing the form.

Properly conducted, evaluations of chairs and deans can forge a stronger administrative team, improve leadership skills, and reward individuals for exceeding your expectations. Poorly conducted, evaluations waste your time as well as that of the person you're evaluating, lead to endless appeals, and increase distrust of the administration among the faculty. Evaluate the administrators who report to you as a model to how you would wish to be evaluated by your upper administration and how other academic leaders should evaluate their faculty and staff. The time spent in doing an evaluation properly will more than repay you in effective leadership throughout the programs you supervise.

REFERENCES

Buller, J. L. (2012). *Best practices in faculty evaluation: A practical guide for academic leaders*. San Francisco, CA: Jossey-Bass.

Krahenbuhl, G. S. (2004). *Building the academic deanship: Strategies for success*. Westport, CT: Praeger.

RESOURCES

AAUP Report on Faculty Evaluation of Administrators, www.aaup.org/report/ faculty-evaluation-administrators

Administrator Evaluation, www.connecticutseed.org/?page_id=445

Administrator Evaluation Questionnaire, provost.uncc.edu/policies/evaluation -academic-administrators

Faculty Evaluation of Administrators, www.gru.edu/universitysenate/feoa.php.

Faculty Evaluation of Administrators: University of Idaho. www.webpages .uidaho.edu/fsh/wordforms/2010-Oct_3320Form2.doc

Principles and Procedures for Evaluation of Academic Administrators, policy.unt.edu/policy/15–1–25

UNC Charlotte Academic Policy and Procedure: Evaluation of Academic Administrators, provost.uncc.edu/policies/evaluation-academic-administrators

30

POSITION REQUESTS AND DESCRIPTIONS

Colleges and universities use the expressions *position requests* or *position descriptions* to refer to several different types of documents. At your institution, someone might use one of these terms when speaking of any of the following:

- A section of a budget proposal that justifies the creation of a new faculty or staff position (see chapter 34)
- An application made to the dean or provost for retaining a position that has recently been vacated or adding a new position through reallocation of existing funds
- A document, usually required by the office of human resources, that outlines the primary job responsibilities associated with a position and the percentage of workload that the person is expected to devote to each of those responsibilities
- A detailed description of the duties associated with a particular job that is prepared for candidates who might be interested in applying for that position
- A somewhat more abbreviated discussion of a position that is used for advertising purposes when conducting a search

Since these uses of a position request or description have such different purposes and audiences, it's rarely the case that a single document can fit every need. For example, if a department chair is trying to justify to you why an extra faculty member is needed, he or she may well include information about workload, the retirement plans of current staff members, and the history of the program that would be too long for an advertisement and out of place in a document shared with potential candidates.

When you create any type of document, always ask two questions: Who is my audience? and What does this audience need to know in order to reach the result I desire?

Being Holistic

As we saw in chapter 19, academic leaders sometimes think about current and prospective employees in excessively narrow terms. They focus on someone's surface credentials rather than the aspects of that person's work they really need, such as the attributes and experiences that can help the person truly succeed at the institution. In the same way we might make this mistake when choosing a member of the staff, we might also focus on the wrong things when hiring a faculty member. For example, we might create a position description that tells the reader everything he or she could possibly want to know about the specific academic specialty we're looking for but nothing at all about our expectations for collegiality, positive energy, a sense of humor, an ability to be flexible, and other factors that are just as important to us. We can also become so preoccupied with what a potential faculty member knows that we lose sight of whether the person is successful in conveying that information to others, instilling in them a passion for the discipline, and elevating the students' skills in such areas as critical thinking, independent learning, and creative thought. We give a great deal of thought to which courses the person will teach and how much research productivity we'll require from the successful applicant but pay little or no attention to any of the ways in which we could tell whether someone is a good fit for our institution.

In a similar way, an academic department might hope to increase its gender or ethnic diversity as the result of a new position, but fail to take the steps that will diversify the applicant pool. We saw in chapter 6 that one successful strategy can be to replace such statements as "PhD required at time of application" to something more inclusive, like "doctorate required by time of appointment," since the latter phrase doesn't exclude people who haven't yet completed their graduate programs or those who may be pursuing the EdD, PsyD, or other types of doctorates. But what do you do if it's a strategic initiative of your institution to increase the percentage of faculty members who hold research doctorates and every search is expected to contribute to this goal? In such a case, you're going to need to determine how these different priorities rank in importance with one another, and the time to do that is while you're developing the position description, not once the search is already in progress.

In a similar way, if such matters as collegiality, excellence in teaching, and willingness to advise undergraduate nonmajors are important to your institution, be sure to consider whether these expectations should be featured prominently in job announcements and advertisements. Including these items can send a strong message about the values you'll be screening for during the search, but at very prestigious institutions, there may be a feeling that such remarks at best merely state the obvious and at worst sound trivial at a university that built its reputation on cutting-edge research. You'll know best how these statements of expectations will be viewed by your own school, but if you do include them in ads, be sure to incorporate them in your process of selecting candidates.

How can you screen for intangible qualities like collegiality and the ability to work as a member of a team? One way might be to ask applicants to define and address *collegiality* in their letters of application. (Requests of this sort also give you a good indication of who has read your ad carefully as opposed to sending the same letter to every institution with an advertised position in that field.) You can then follow up on this request by:

- Including expressions like *team player*, *strong institution-wide citizenship*, and *cooperative attitude* elsewhere in the job description
- In the longer job descriptions that are sent only to applicants (or sometimes only to those who are likely to be interviewed), discussing why collegiality is essential to the mission of teaching, scholarship, and service of your programs
- Asking questions about collegiality when you call the candidate's references

Similarly, if enhancing excellence in teaching is a major goal of your college or university, you might consider, as part of the application process, having all candidates submit a statement outlining their philosophy of teaching and its application in the classroom. In this case, you might construct the position description so that it's clear that all finalists will be expected to demonstrate their teaching techniques in different pedagogical settings, such as lecture/discussion, seminar, master class, or tutorial. You might suggest too that development of a successful teaching portfolio will be expected during the successful candidate's probationary period.

This same approach can be applied to any area in which your institution or program has a strong strategic interest. In cases where community service or attending student events is important, it's a good idea to note this expectation in the position announcement that's published online or in professional journals. While such statements may dissuade a few candidates from applying for your position, in the long run they're unlikely to be those who succeed at this position anyway.

> You may not always get the type of person you advertise for when you develop a position description. You are certain not to get that type of person if you don't mention your most important expectations in the advertisements seen by possible applicants.

Setting Priorities in Screening

Just as you may need to determine whether a desire to broaden an applicant pool is more important than a desire to hire only candidates with terminal degrees, so is it important to set priorities among all the qualities you hope to find in the successful candidate. If you brainstorm the qualifications, skills, and attributes you're looking for—particularly if you move beyond surface credentials to such matters as collegiality and institutional fit—you're likely to end up with a very long list indeed. A common joke made at meetings of search committees on seeing this kind of impossibly detailed catalogue of desired traits is, "Maybe we should add ' ... and can walk on water' at the end." But even if getting everything you hope for is unrealistic, thinking through what you'd like to find in the best person for the job is an important stage of developing a good position description.

Once you've done so, it's time to start going through this laundry list of what you hope to find and begin identifying the qualities you need to find. If you were serious about identifying important personal attributes and qualities as well as matters of experience and credentials, it may surprise you to find that the items that rise to the top of your list differ from the sort of information you've usually included in job descriptions. It may well be that collegiality, diversity, and the ability to teach effectively on different platforms now matters a lot more than having done extensive research in some specific field. It may even be that you find you can be quite flexible about the discipline the person works in as long as he or she is the right fit for the students and faculty already in your program. In any case, you should now begin to focus on the top five or six items on your priority list. These items should suggest to you the points to emphasize in the position request, description, or advertisement you write.

Writing Ads with Applicants in Mind

When you're writing advertisements for jobs, your audience consists of potential applicants for the position, and what they need to know covers a fairly broad range of issues. If you look at the announcements posted in journals like the *Chronicle of Higher Education*, you find that they vary greatly in terms of their usefulness to candidates. Some consist of nothing more than a reference to a website. That's very inexpensive for the institution posting the advertisement, but it provides little inducement for the reader to take the extra step to go online, find the URL, and read the full announcement there. Someone might object, "But that's okay. If someone doesn't even have enough interest to go to a website, I don't want that person applying for this job. I want someone with more motivation than that." Think of the various assumptions that lie behind this objection:

- It assumes that the only people who will apply for the position are those who are actively engaged in a job search. The best possible candidate, however, might be a person who already has a position and isn't actively looking for a new opportunity but could become interested in applying if he or she knew the right things about this position. What would those things be?

- It assumes that the people who will apply for this job already know enough about your institution to want to work there or care enough about finding a position to learn more about you. That may be true if you're working at Harvard, Princeton, or Yale, but you can't assume that readers of the ad are all familiar with Middle Backwoods State University or Obscure Private College. What makes your institution distinctive enough to make the right person want to find out more?

- It assumes that potential applicants will be looking only for positions within their fields of specialty: that marine biologists will be looking only for positions in marine biology, pre-Columbian art historians will be looking only for positions in pre-Columbian art history, and so on. But much of higher education doesn't work that way. At some small colleges, faculty members are expected to teach broadly across their disciplines and to be active in freshman seminars, honors programs, and many other activities that reach outside their specific fields. Moreover, a great deal of current research addresses questions that span disciplines and can't be answered within the confines of any single field. Without more information about what the job entails, the best person for the position may pass the advertisement by without taking the time to investigate further by visiting the website indicated.

It's important, therefore, to think carefully about what applicants need to know about the institution, unit, position, and responsibilities in order to understand if they'd be interested in applying. If an ad provides only the address of a website or speaks only about the qualifications required for the position, it doesn't communicate as effectively as it could in order to attract the right candidates for the position.

Persuading a candidate you want to hire that he or she should come to your institution doesn't begin only when you make the offer. The treatment someone receives throughout the application and interview process plays a vital role in the candidate's decision whether to accept an offer, even if you're able to meet every one of that person's expectations in terms of salary, start-up costs, teaching load, moving expenses, ongoing research support, and anything else the candidate might want. You're recruiting from the very moment you draft a position request or description. Perhaps you're fortunate enough to work at an institution that everyone's heard of and immediately receives respect and admiration because of its prestigious name. Most deans and provosts aren't that lucky. They're trying to recruit highly talented people who have excellent teaching skills, a strong commitment to collegiality, and a host of other desirable attributes even though the salaries they can offer are modest, the challenges are great, and the opportunities for advancement are relatively few. In these situations, it's often the intangible benefits of a position—a beautiful campus or location, the opportunity to work closely with interesting students, the chance to make a real difference in someone's life—that attract and retain members of the faculty and staff. As you're creating a position description, reflect on the intangibles you have available for candidates. What is it that tends to keep employees at your institution even when they could earn higher salaries elsewhere? What would excite an energetic newcomer to the discipline? By including information of this sort in your position description or advertisement, you're more likely to attract applicants who will succeed in your environment and be happy as a member of your community.

Moreover, most applicants for positions have rather vague notions of what it would be like to hold the position that you're posting:

○ Is the job you're advertising primarily a teaching position, primarily a research position, or some mix of the two?

○ If it's primarily a teaching position, what's the course load?

○ How many courses will the faculty member you hire probably teach at the introductory level?

○ How many are likely to be at an advanced or graduate level?

○ Will there be any opportunities for the person to develop new courses?

○ Will there be chances for or expectations of interdisciplinary work?

○ If the position is primarily in the area of research, what are the expectations you have that will determine whether the faculty member is successful?

○ Will start-up funds be available?

○ Will there be an expectation that the successful candidate secure external funding (and, if so, will there be the support of an office of research and sponsored programs to help him or her do so)?

○ If the position requires a mixture of instruction and scholarship, in what proportions are those two activities likely to occur?

○ Will there be an expectation that the person hired involves students in his or her research, or are duties in the areas of teaching and scholarship usually unrelated?

○ What will the opportunities and requirements be for service?

○ Is the committee load usually high or low in this discipline?

You can undermine the effectiveness of a position description by being too vague about what your institution is looking for. If the advertisement states that you're seeking an assistant professor, would you also accept applications from people holding higher ranks? If you state, "Minimum of one year experience preferred," how will this preference be used in selecting candidates? What sort of experience will you consider? Does it have to be experience in a faculty position at a college or university? And what precisely does it mean that you *prefer* this type of experience? Does it mean that any experienced candidate will automatically be given an edge over any inexperienced candidate or that you're reserving the right to give precedence to experienced candidates, all other factors being equal? If you don't make these matters clear, candidates may well make incorrect assumptions.

As you draft your position request or description, it's a good idea to give careful consideration to the types of qualifications and experience that you regard as absolutely essential to the position. For instance, a requirement such as, "Minimum of three years teaching experience at a regionally accredited four-year college or university," is clear, but it also means that you won't be able to consider any candidate who does not meet that criterion, no matter how desirable the candidate may be in other ways. Above all, you're well advised to avoid meaningless phrases like, "Some teaching experience preferred." This kind of requirement is so general that even a candidate who has taught only one Sunday school class for ten minutes has technically met the criterion. It's far better to have hard-and-fast requirements for the qualifications that you really need and to forgo taking up advertisement space with statements that only appear to express preferences.

Asking for the Application Materials You Truly Need

For search advertisements, request that applicants send you only materials you really need in order to make an informed decision during the first screening. Avoid requiring any item you won't need until later in the search process or can obtain in another manner. Here's an example of what you regularly see in job postings from even very well-established colleges and universities: "In addition to a letter of application and current curriculum vitae, submit three letters of reference, official transcripts of all college work, and samples of publications." The problem with statements of this kind is that they require submission of materials that are of relatively little help to search committees in their initial screening of candidates and, at the same time, may discourage the most desirable candidates from applying in the first place.

Letters of reference

These references will probably tell you a good deal less than you're likely to learn by asking for a list of three to five references and their mailing addresses, telephone numbers, and e-mail addresses. To begin with, anyone can locate three people who are willing to write positive, upbeat letters on their behalf. What you really want is the opportunity to ask follow-up questions, describe your precise position and inquire whether the candidate is a good fit for it, and ask the one question that you really need to know (and will almost never learn from reference letters): "Are you aware of anything about this candidate that if I were to learn it, might make me hesitant to offer this person a job?" (There's only one correct answer to this question: an immediate and unmitigated no.) In addition, many of the most qualified candidates will choose not to apply for your position because you've asked for letters of reference up front. No one likes bothering references for letters regarding positions they may not even receive a telephone interview for. And the more desirable a candidate is, the more likely he or she is to have distinguished references whom they won't want to trouble for a letter early in the search. Finally, many candidates don't want their current employers and colleagues to know that they're considering new positions; these highly experienced candidates are likely to rule out applying for any position that requests letters of recommendation too early in the process.

Official transcripts

There are almost no searches for which a college or university needs to request official transcripts up front as part of an initial application. Make no mistake about it: most accrediting agencies do require institutions to obtain official transcripts—that is, transcripts marked with an official seal and sent directly from the registrar of the issuing institution to the institution requesting them, without ever being in the possession of the candidate—*once a faculty member is hired*. For this reason, providing official transcripts is often required in a faculty member's contract for employment.

But it's an unnecessary burden and expense for candidates to have to submit official transcripts simply to apply for a job. Setting this requirement restricts the applicant pool. Many desirable applicants who are just starting out won't apply because they can't afford the fees their schools charge them to send these transcripts. And even more experienced candidates may decide not to apply because they don't want to be inconvenienced by what they'll regard as a gratuitous complication. So if you feel that it is absolutely necessary to review an applicant's course work and grades in order for you to prepare your short list of semifinalists, be sure to request unofficial transcripts or photocopies of transcripts.

Scholarship

Evaluating the scholarship of applicants is certainly an important part of every academic search process. But ask yourself whether it's truly necessary to review every single publication of the people who apply for your position or whether it would be more effective to request these materials only from a select group of applicants after you've completed your initial screening. Mailing books and offprints is another expensive proposition for candidates. Returning these items at the end of a search, should a candidate request them (and the vast majority of the candidates will), will be an expensive and time-consuming process for your institution. Besides, depending on the position, you're likely to receive between sixty and two hundred applications in most searches. Is it going to be worth the time it takes your committee to examine all the scholarly products submitted (in fact, are they really going to examine them or just glance at them?) and is it going to be worth the space to store these items, even temporarily? In most cases, the answer to these questions will be no. For that reason, screen applicants on the basis of the information that they provide in their cover letters and résumés. Then request actual samples of publications only later in the search or ask that they be brought to the interview.

Documentation that is useful

By eliminating items from the search process that you don't really need, members of the search committee can better focus on the documentation that really does help them select the best group of finalists:

- A statement of the candidate's philosophy of teaching, administration, scholarship, or service
- A sample syllabus or final examination so that you can learn something about that person's approach to teaching
- A brief description of the best student project ever submitted to that candidate
- Suggestions about the one book every student (or faculty member) should read, as a way of learning more about the applicant's perspectives and priorities
- A short faculty development plan for teaching, scholarship, and creative activity over the next five years so that you'll better understand where the applicant is heading in his or her work

Should Position Advertisements Mention Salary?

Certain decisions about position descriptions can be made only in the context of particular institutions and particular positions. For instance, do you ever refer to salary in a job advertisement and, if so, do you provide a range or merely say something general like "salary commensurate with experience"? In this case, while your institution may have guidelines, there can be no hard-and-fast rule that will suit every situation. If you provide a salary range, you may lose certain candidates who believe that the range offered is inadequate for their current needs. Such a situation may be preferable to incurring the expense of bringing a candidate to campus only to discover that this person was out of your price range anyway.

Nevertheless, your school may offer certain intangible benefits—a beautiful location, extensive cultural opportunities, a safe and congenial community, and so on—that candidates will need to experience in order to appreciate. In any case, you should never state that a salary range is commensurate with experience if the remuneration for this position is already largely fixed. That would be tantamount to lying; at the very least, you may end up with an awkward encounter with an applicant whose idea of what is commensurate with his or her experience is highly different from your own. In a similar way, many institutions make the mistake of terming their salaries as highly competitive and their benefits packages as excellent when neither of these is actually the case. Be very careful about using phrases that sound appealing but end up advertising what you can't actually provide.

One situation in which it's preferable to avoid mentioning a specific salary in a position description occurs when institutions in the United States are posting jobs that may be filled by noncitizens. If a candidate is hired on an H visa, which permits foreign nationals to work in the United States on a temporary basis and later seeks to obtain permanent resident status, posting a specific salary range can cause problems. Those problems might occur, for example, if the wage indicated doesn't correspond with the government's prevailing wage determination for that type of position, which could mean that the position would need to be readvertised. Then if a US citizen with comparable credentials applies for the position during the new search, it may not be possible to retain the foreign national as an employee, regardless of how badly the college or university wishes to keep that person on the faculty. In general, therefore, it's wise never to list a specific salary or even a salary range if there's the slightest chance you may be hiring someone from outside the United States.

Checklist for a Position Request

There are other items, however, that should always appear in a position request or announcement. A good checklist to use when developing job announcements or proposals for faculty positions would include the following.

- Is the position tenure track, nontenure track but open-ended, or temporary with a set term?
- Is it clear by what date candidates must have attained qualifications required for the position (such as at the time of application or by the starting date)?
- What is the starting date for the position?

❑ Which documents must be submitted in order for an application to be considered complete?

❑ Have you provided the full name and contact information of the search chair?

❑ Have you indicated whether applications are acceptable in hard copy, electronically, or both? If both are acceptable but the search committee or institution has a preference, have you stated that preference?

❑ Have you clarified whether deadline dates are postmark deadlines or deadlines for receipt of material?

❑ If candidates are permitted to mail application materials, have you checked to make sure the deadline doesn't fall on a Saturday, Sunday, or postal holiday?

❑ When will the committee begin reviewing applications?

❑ Have you listed a website where applicants can find additional information about the position and/or school?

Position Descriptions for Internal Use

Most of this discussion so far has been about position descriptions that will be viewed by external constituents, such as possible applicants for a job. But what about the documents you create for internal use, such as a request to your supervisor that you be granted a new position or a job description that human resources will use to classify a position? Although these may initially appear to be very different from the types of position descriptions you'd use in creating an advertisement, many of the same factors go into creating them. You still consider who your audience is and reflect on what that audience needs to know in order to lead to the result you desire. For example, if you're a dean who's requesting a new position from a provost or a provost requesting a new position from the president, how does adding this new line help your supervisor get closer to his or her own goals? In most cases, your supervisor will be interested in making progress toward meeting objectives laid out in the institution's strategic plan and possibly making improvements in certain performance metrics that have been established by the legislature or governing board. How can you make a legitimate case that this position helps achieve one or more major strategic planning goals or is likely to cause significant improvement to key performance metrics? If retention and graduate rates have been a challenge, how can this position request be written as a partial solution to that problem? If increasing research productivity has been an important goal, how can this position be cast as a major part of your strategy in achieving that goal?

When creating these internal documents, remember that the people who will be reviewing them have different needs from the candidates who might apply for the job. They're likely to care about the following:

- The average number of students majoring in the faculty member's discipline over the last three to five years
- The average number of students enrolling in introductory, advanced, and graduate courses in the faculty member's discipline over the last three to five years
- The anticipated teaching and research load you project for the new faculty member
- How much you are contributing to the position for salary, benefits, and start-up costs
- Current utilization rates for classrooms, studios, and laboratories assigned to the discipline
- National enrollment trends and demographic information that might affect the ongoing need for this position
- Other responsibilities, such as advising and thesis direction, that affect workload in the discipline

Similarly, if your request is for a staff position, you'll need to identify the unmet needs that the person you hope to hire will address, how those unmet needs relate to issues critical to the concerns of your supervisor, and why current staffing is insufficient to address those needs. Official documents used by the office of human resources to classify positions are usually brief descriptions of the essential duties performed by someone in that position, regardless of who that person may happen to be, and the minimum level of competency required for a person to perform each of those duties successfully. For this reason, preferred qualifications usually don't appear in documents of this kind, nor do any accommodations that may have been made to the position simply to fit the needs of a specific person who used to hold that job.

Conclusion

Although many different types of documents are all referred to as position descriptions or announcements, the audiences for these documents can vary widely. What a potential applicant needs to know in order to decide whether to apply for a job will be very different from what a president or governing board might need to know in order to decide whether to allocate funding for new positions. As a result, position descriptions shouldn't be written with a one-size-fits-all mentality. Provosts and deans can benefit from reflecting on who will be reading the specific version of the position description they're creating, what the particular needs and concerns of that audience might be, and how the position description can be specifically tailored to address those individual needs and concerns.

RESOURCES

Mader-Clark, M. (2013). *The job description handbook* (3rd ed.). Berkeley, CA: Nolo.

Martin, C. (2010). *Perfect phrases for writing job descriptions: Hundreds of ready-to-use phrases for writing effective, informative, and useful job descriptions*. New York, NY: McGraw-Hill.

31

POLICIES AND PROCEDURES

Every institution has its own time-honored ways of making decisions, reaching consensus, or implementing strategies for the future. Unfortunately, in too many cases, these policies and procedures exist solely in the form of oral tradition, with no written record maintained in a printed manual or on a website. But as colleges and universities become more complex and as society itself becomes more litigious, having a reliable set of written policies and procedures assumes increased significance.

At least once in your administrative career (and probably far more often), you'll be asked to develop some type of new policy or procedure unit. There may also be times when you decide that you want to create a new policy or procedure, not because there is any external reason compelling you to do so but simply because you believe it would be more equitable or efficient to have a clearer system in place. In fact, there are three major reasons for developing a new policy or procedure.

○ A law or the regulations of an accrediting body requires it.

○ It is desirable for such reasons as efficiency, consistency, and quality assurance.

○ A problem has occurred due to the lack of such a policy.

Of these three reasons, the last is the one that should cause deans and provosts to proceed with caution. Many administrators are familiar with Oliver Wendell Holmes's dictum: "Great cases, like hard cases, make bad law." But few of them probably recall Holmes's following line in which he explained his reasoning: "For great cases are called great, not by reason of their real importance in shaping the law of the future, but because of some accident of immediate overwhelming interest which appeals to the feelings and distorts the judgment (*Northern Securities Co. v. United States,* 1903, 400–401). In other words, it's a poor practice to develop a policy in response to a single unfortunate situation that's unlikely ever to occur again.

We've all seen the syllabi of faculty members who impose a lengthy set of strict rules, each of which is a response to a single incident in which a student gamed the system in a way that the professor regarded as unfair. As academic leaders, we need to avoid making similar mistakes when developing policies and procedures for the programs we supervise. While it's important to learn from painful experiences and develop any policies that might prevent similar problems from occurring in the future, we don't really need a policy that precludes relatively minor difficulties that are highly improbable. Rules of that kind merely waste the time of the people who develop, read, and enforce institutional policies.

> The goal of a good policy or procedure is to make people's work easier, safer, or better, not harder.

Always Ask, "What Problem Are We Trying to Solve?"

Policies and procedures are never created in a vacuum. They're always intended to fix or avoid some problem. While poor policies tend to result from an attempt to respond to single, relatively minor, uncommon situations, a single egregious situation—for example, an act that caused a scandal, financial disaster, termination, or the departure of large number of students—is an entirely different matter and may well be the reason for creating or changing policies and procedures. In fact, sometimes policies may be created out of political necessity. If an institution has suffered a great deal of negative publicity because of the misdeeds of one of its members or the poor treatment that someone received, developing a policy that prevents the recurrence of that problem can be a sign to the community that the institution is taking the situation seriously. But for the most part, if a situation is not of the utmost importance and is unlikely to become a problem again in the future, simply learn a lesson about the frailties of human nature, regard it as a bad experience, and move on.

Good policies and procedures aren't attempts to create elaborate filters that can screen out every conceivable way of abusing the system. Faculty members and students in higher education are clever people. Given a chance, some of them will find a way to turn nearly any set of policies and procedures to their advantage. So whenever you're about to develop a new policy, ask yourself exactly what you're trying to achieve and what you're trying to avoid. Steer clear of the tendency to brainstorm every possible eventuality and build ways of dealing with every one of them into your plan. That will only extend your process indefinitely and create a document so cumbersome that it'll be all but unusable. Worse, the spirit of the law will become lost in all those pages of unimportant accretions.

Most of all, remember that the primary purpose of a policy and procedure is never simply to make more rules for their own sake. With well-written policies and procedures, everyone knows what is expected, when it is expected, and how decisions will be made when there are competing priorities. If, in the midst of developing a policy, you find yourself getting too far away from this primary purpose, it's time to stop, step back, and reconsider what you are doing and why.

Don't Reinvent the Wheel

Another common mistake provosts and deans make in developing policies and procedures is starting from scratch. Almost any conceivable policy matter—from intellectual property disputes to issues of faculty load and overriding enrollment caps—has been explored dozens, even hundreds of times at other colleges or universities not unlike your own. It's valuable for each institution to see itself as distinctive, even unique, when presenting its advantages to prospective students, donors, and candidates for faculty positions. It can be extremely detrimental, however, for any institution to assume it's so unique that it must create every single policy or procedure out of whole cloth.

An Internet search using key words related to the policy you're trying to create will probably result in more examples of well-designed policies and procedures than you or your committee can possibly read. But don't simply cut and paste sections from these documents; even less desirable is merely adopting another institution's policy or procedure wholesale. Rather, examine what approaches comparable schools have taken to similar situations, consider how these ideas can be adapted to your own environment, and explore the ways in which useful approaches from several different institutions can be combined to create the best possible policy for your institution.

Focus on Clarity

We all have numerous opportunities to be creative in our lives, use evocative language to create a memorable, lasting impression, and amuse readers with our wit, charm, and cleverness. *Writing policies and procedures is not one of these opportunities.* The hallmark of a well-written policy statement is clarity. If you develop a statement that contains ambiguity or can have multiple interpretations, you've not solved the problem that you set out to fix. After completing a draft of your new policy or procedure, reread it sentence by sentence, asking the following questions as you do so:

- ○ Is each statement free from ambiguity, capable of being interpreted in only a single way, and specific enough that it applies precisely to the situation I'm trying to address?

- ○ If I omit one word at a time in each sentence, does each word I leave out significantly change the overall meaning? (If it doesn't, the word is probably unnecessary.)

- ○ Are there adverbs or qualifying phrases—such as *normally* and *in most cases*—that provide undesirable vagueness? Remember that an ambiguity that may work in your institution's favor may also be used against the institution by someone who's seeking a loophole.

Seek Appropriate Guidance

In the case of truly major policies and procedures, always have the document reviewed by the human resources staff and your institutional counsel or office of legal affairs. Those who work in these capacities have a great deal of experience in the unintended consequences that can result from the way in which a policy is phrased. They can help you see what the results will be in different situations. In addition to screening your document for unnecessary ambiguity and multiple interpretations, they can also serve as a good counterbalance against any desire you may have to develop too simple a policy. As we saw earlier, one of your guiding principles should be to create the clearest policy you can. But those who work in human resources or legal affairs sometimes encourage you to make a new policy as comprehensive as possible, covering every imaginable contingency.

Out of these two competing motivations, you're likely to find a good compromise—a policy that's specific enough to address your institution's unique environment but also general enough to cover different circumstances as they arise. For instance, you may be the chief academic officer at a liberal arts college and want your school's policy on intellectual property to be as generous as possible, rewarding your faculty for their creativity and scholarship by allowing them to retain ownership of all the books, software, and course enrichment materials they develop. The staff members in your human resources and legal affairs offices, however, may propose a number of contingencies—such as the creation of marketable products, patentable inventions, and developments in biotechnology with applications in the health care industry—that you regard as inconceivable in your liberal arts setting.

By causing you to think through various contingencies and scenarios, the advice you receive may well cause you to develop a far better policy or procedure. You may not include every single contingency people recommend to you, but you may decide that surrendering rights carte blanche to faculty members for everything they create on the college's time while using the college's resources isn't the best strategy either. In this way, the tension that arises between your desire for simplicity and your reviewers' desire for comprehensiveness can become a healthy and advantageous part of your policy development process.

Plan for Appeals

Almost every policy and procedure should have a formal appeal process. The objection might be made that the very reason you're developing a new policy or procedure is to avoid appeals. But some people will appeal a decision that's not in their favor regardless of how carefully constructed the policy may be, so you may as well design a method for dealing with those requests effectively.

> A properly designed policy can help reduce unwanted appeals, but it can never prevent them.

When developing an appeal process, the first decisions you'll have to make are:

1. To whom the appeal will be made
2. In what forms (orally, in writing, electronically) the appeal can be made
3. On what grounds a decision is appealable
4. At what level a decision becomes final

The last question is particularly important. In many areas where a decision must be made, you may wish to include in your policy a statement that the individual or group making the decision, such as a department chair, review committee, or you as dean or provost, has final jurisdiction in this matter; you probably don't want routine academic matters being appealed all the way to the president and governing board.

At the same time, you'll want to give careful consideration to the third question, which deals with the grounds for an appeal. You can reduce the number of decisions that have to be reconsidered (and possibly over-turned) if you specify that appeals can be made only on the basis that whoever made the original decision didn't follow the institution's estab-lished procedure or criteria. No policy can eliminate every element of subjectivity. And certain questions of quality and priority require people to make a professional judgment. As long as they're acting within their assigned professional responsibilities and following the procedures and criteria that have been duly established, they should be protected from having their conclusions questioned once they've been made. Moreover, limiting the acceptable grounds for an appeal means that the person or group performing the review doesn't have to reexamine the entire issue from top to bottom for every appeal. If they find that the original decision was made properly, they can simply let it stand. That type of policy also sends a strong message to the faculty and members of your administrative team that you support them and trust their judgment.

Communicate the Policy to Those Affected by It

After your new policy has been approved by all appropriate bodies, it's important that its content and purpose be explained to the stakeholders who'll be affected by it. It's not sufficient simply to post a new policy or procedure on a website or include it in a new version of the per-sonnel manual. No one can be expected to reread all existing policies each year, noting any differences that were made from what was pre-viously in effect. Training can occur any way your institution finds most appropriate—in a public forum, by e-mail, by paper flier, or by some other appropriate means—as long as it reaches all of the appropriate parties. At times, you may be tempted to downplay the significance of a policy change because you anticipate resistance and opposition. But anything less than perfect candor in such matters is highly undesirable. It's far bet-ter to face criticism head-on than to be accused both of deception and poor policymaking. By taking a formal opportunity to teach members of the community about the new policy or procedure, you have the opportu-nity to explain its rationale, summarize its benefits, and counter resistance early on. Moreover, if you have adopted an open and collegial process in generating your proposal, people are unlikely to feel blindsided by a change that they were unaware was imminent. You may even be pleas-antly surprised that the amount of opposition you receive is less than you expected.

Training members of your college in policies and procedures should not be a single occurrence. Certainly all new members of the faculty and staff should receive training in existing policies and procedures, but the entire faculty and staff should receive a refresher course periodically. It isn't necessary to review every policy at every training session. But taking a few moments at a faculty meeting or staff retreat to review current policies and procedures is time well spent. It's really just another part of your development plan for members of the faculty and staff since it enables them to do their jobs more effectively.

Pay Attention to the Politics of It All

Many aspects of what deans and provosts do, from how they themselves are chosen for the position to the pressures that may eventually force them to look for other employment opportunities, are affected by politics. Some deans and provosts revel in this aspect of the job; others (and I'd include myself in this number) believe it's simply an unfortunate part of the job and is often given far more attention than it deserves. Certainly, one might think, such a routine matter as the development of policies and procedures should be free from such political concerns. That isn't the case.

Policy matters become political from the start:

○ Who is authorized to develop the new policy? Answering that question assigns power and responsibility to that person or group.

○ Who decides when a new policy is needed? Answering that question bestows a certain amount of decision-making authority on someone.

○ Who decides whether a policy is even necessary? Answering that question conveys the right of executive leadership to someone or some committee.

For this reason, policy development can be more controversial and fraught with problems than we may initially expect.

Generally policies and procedures in higher education are made in an environment that we might call a Tenth Amendment default. The Tenth Amendment to the US Constitution states, "The powers not delegated to the United States by the Constitution, nor prohibited by it to the States, are reserved to the States respectively, or to the people." For colleges and universities, we might rephrase this principle as follows: the right to make any decision not delegated to a specific person or group by an established policy is reserved to the person or unit most immediately affected by that policy. In other words, if an institution doesn't have an overarching policy on academic dishonesty, a case of plagiarism or research impropriety that occurs, for example, in the department of chemistry can and should be handled by the department of chemistry. But if an institution's policy on academic integrity says that all such issues must be brought before a central council that oversees the school's honor code, then that policy imbues that body with a great deal of power. It can even be sending a political message: if the council consists mostly of students, the message is that the institution regards questions of integrity as part of a student's compact with his or her peers; it's not a question of rules imposed from higher up the organizational chart.

This type of Tenth Amendment default also explains why the responsibilities of a dean or provost at one institution can differ in so many ways from what a dean or provost does somewhere else. Either through conscious decision or habit over time, decision-making authority accrues to certain offices because the community feels that those offices are the ones most immediately affected by the decision. Is an excused absence a matter for an individual faculty member to decide, for a larger unit within academic affairs to decide, or a student affairs issue? If that excused absence involves a student athlete who has to compete in an intercollegiate athletic event, how might that change the dynamic of who is in charge of making the decision? If the professor claims that the student must be physically present in class for an activity that's integral to the nature of the course, at what level is this decided? And to whom could an appeal be addressed if there are still disagreements after a decision has been made? All of these questions are not merely procedural issues; they are also political matters of who has final authority over what areas, under what circumstances, and for what reasons. Deans and provosts need to be aware that creating or amending policies and procedures is sometimes not a simple matter but an issue that takes them directly into areas of personal power, authority, and privilege.

Conclusion

Writing policies and procedures entails a different sort of writing from that which we use when we write articles, reviews, letters, and grant proposals. If your institution has one or more faculty members with training in technical and professional writing, or if your institution maintains a designated writing center, running a draft of your proposed policy or procedure past individuals trained in this type of communication can assist you greatly with structure, clarity, and precision. For political reasons, it's also desirable to make certain that your supervisor is on board with the policy you're seeking to implement. Otherwise you could face some difficult and potentially embarrassing disagreements over the policy when its development is already well under way.

REFERENCE

Northern Securities Co. v. United States. (1903). 193 U.S. 197.

RESOURCES

Campbell, N. (1998). *Writing effective policies and procedures: A step-by-step resource for clear communication.* New York, NY: AMACOM.

Page, S. B. (2007). *Best practices in policies and procedures.* Westerville, OH: Process Improvement Publishing.

Page, S. B. (2007). *Establishing a system of policies and procedures* (Rev. ed.). Westerville, OH: Process Improvement Publishing.

Page, S. B. (2012). *Seven steps to better written policies and procedures.* Westerville, OH: Process Improvement Publishing.

Peabody, L. (2013). *How to write policies, procedures and task outlines: Sending clear signals in written directions* (3rd ed.). Lacey, WA: Writing Services.

Wieringa, D., Moore, C., & Barnes, V. (1998). *Procedure writing: Principles and practices* (2nd ed.). Columbus, OH: Battelle.

32

A SCENARIO ANALYSIS ON THE ACADEMIC LEADER'S RESPONSIBILITIES AS SUPERVISOR

For a discussion of how scenario analyses are structured and suggestions on how to use this exercise most productively, see the beginning of chapter 7. A scenario analysis for deans appears in the online content accompanying this book.

Case Study for Provosts

Imagine that you're about to develop a new policy on what should be included in the various types of position requests and descriptions that your university requires. For the purposes of this case study, assume that your institution uses variations of a position request and description in the following ways:

1. As a request for a new faculty line that you would submit to the president

2. As a request for a new faculty line or to fill a currently vacant line that a dean would submit to you

3. As an official record of the duties and responsibilities associated with a position, as kept on file by the office of human resources

4. As an abbreviated advertisement that would be placed in print publications

5. As a more complete advertisement that would be used online, in e-mail announcements, and to provide additional information to candidates who request it

6. As a summary of qualifications required and responsibilities assigned
that accreditation bodies can use to determine whether faculty members
are appropriately credentialed for the courses they teach

In exhibit 32.1, check which items are appropriate for these six purposes and would thus be required in the policy you're developing. Note that you may want to require that certain items be used for several different types of position requests and descriptions. You may also leave certain rows blank if you don't believe they should be required for any of the different position requests and descriptions.

Exhibit 32.1 Items for Position Requests and Descriptions

	Request from You to the President	Request from a Dean to You	Official Record for Human Resources	Short Print Ad	Longer Electronic or Mailed Ad	Record for Credentialing and Accreditation
Human resources job classification for the position						
Line number and cost center of the position						
Academic department in which the position will be located.						
Discipline and specialty of the position						
Initial rank of the position						
Permanent or temporary nature of the position						
Tenure eligibility						
Starting date of the position						
Ending date of the position, if temporary						
Required degree						
Date by which required degree must be completed						
Years of experience required						
Type of experience required (e.g., college teaching, corporate or professional experience, working in a multicultural environment)						
Anticipated starting salary for the position						

	Request from You to the President	Request from a Dean to You	Official Record for Human Resources	Short Print Ad	Longer Electronic or Mailed Ad	Record for Credentialing and Accreditation
Approved salary range for the position						
How much each level of the institution (provost, dean, and chair) is expected to contribute to the salary, benefits, and start-up costs of the position						
Teaching load for the position						
Anticipated courses to be taught by the successful candidate during his or her first year						
Research expectation of the position						
Other responsibilities, such as advising and thesis direction						
Background information on the institution (e.g., size, mission, location)						
Average number of students majoring in this discipline for the previous three to five years						
Average number of students enrolling in introductory, advanced, and graduate courses in this discipline for the previous three to five years						
National enrollment trends and demographic information that might affect the ongoing need for this position						
Preferences for the position (e.g., a preference for a higher degree than that required, preferred additional years of experience)						
Materials that are required in order for the application to be considered complete						
Application deadline for the position						

	Request from You to the President	Request from a Dean to You	Official Record for Human Resources	Short Print Ad	Longer Electronic or Mailed Ad	Record for Credentialing and Accreditation
Indication as to whether the deadline is a postmark deadline, a final date on which materials will be accepted, or the date on which screening will start						
Equal opportunity or affirmative action indication, if appropriate						
Information for candidates requiring accommodations, if appropriate						
How materials are to be submitted (electronically, surface mail, or other)						
Name of the search chair						
Contact information for the search chair						
Website where additional information may be found						

Considerations

1. Would your answers be different if any of the following were true?
   a. The president has demonstrated a reluctance to approve more faculty positions because he or she believes that the division of academic affairs is already overstaffed.
   b. Your institution is prestigious; its name is instantly recognizable.
   c. Your institution is practically unknown outside your immediate area.
   d. Salaries at your institution are not at all competitive relative to those of your peer institutions.
   e. Your institution is about to enter a period of rapid expansion of faculty positions because of the school's innovative strategic plan.
   f. The director of human resources is a stickler when it comes to policies, wanting every "i" dotted and every "t" crossed.
   g. The institution recently lost a large lawsuit because a search was conducted improperly due to a poorly written advertisement.

2. Review the items that you believe should be included in the abbreviated advertisement that's placed in print publications. In what order would you recommend that these items be placed to make the ad as effective as possible?

3. Are there any additional items that you'd want to see in any of the six kinds of job description categories listed above?

Suggestions

This case study is a good exercise in reflecting what information different stakeholders need most in order to make effective decisions. While the unique nature of your institution and your relationship with others, such as the president and director of human resources, will cause some of your answers to be different from those of other provosts, you should expect a certain degree of agreement about which items should be included in which particular type of position description. For instance, technical items of solely internal interest (such as the line number of the position, its cost center, and specific classification) are perhaps needed only for the documentation kept by the office of human resources. You may want to include them in the documentation you forward to the president (or have a dean include them in the documentation submitted to you) if they're useful for you or the president to understand precisely what type of position is being requested; otherwise they're just extraneous material that clutters the job description.

Matters like the department and academic specialty of the position should probably be included in every type of job description. You and the president need this information in order to understand what the successful applicant will teach and what type of research he or she will perform. Candidates for the position need the information in order to determine whether the position is appropriate for them. The office of human resources and accrediting bodies need this information in order to determine whether there's an appropriate match between the duties of the position and the credentials and level of experience it requires. For this reason, exhibit 32.2 is completed in the way that would probably be appropriate for most provosts at most institutions. In completing this table, I've adopted the following symbols:

○ An X indicates an item that possibly should be included in that type of job description, depending on your individual circumstances.

○ A check mark indicates an item that probably should be included in that type of job description under almost all circumstances.

Exhibit 32.2 Recommended Items for Position Requests and Descriptions

	Request from You to the President	Request from a Dean to You	Official Record for Human Resources	Short Print Ad	Longer Electronic or Mailed Ad	Record for Credential-ing and Accredita-tion
Human resources job classification for the position	✗		✓			
Line number and cost center of the position	✗	✗	✓			
Academic department in which the position will be located	✓	✓	✓	✓	✓	✓
Discipline and specialty of the position	✓	✓	✓	✓	✓	✓
Initial rank of the position	✓	✓	✗	✓	✓	✗
Permanent or temporary nature of the position	✓	✓	✓	✓	✓	✓
Tenure eligibility	✓	✓	✓	✓	✓	✓
Starting date of the position	✓	✓	✗	✓	✓	✗
Ending date of the position, if temporary	✓	✓	✓	✓	✓	✓
Required degree	✓	✓	✓	✓	✓	✓
Date by which required degree must be completed		✗		✓	✓	✓
Years of experience required			✓	✓	✓	
Type of experience required (e.g., college teaching, corporate or professional experience, working in a multicultural environment)			✓	✓	✓	
Anticipated starting salary for the position	✗	✗				
Approved salary range for the position			✓	✗	✗	
How much each level of the institution (provost, dean, and chair) is expected to contribute to the salary, benefits, and start-up costs of the position	✓	✓				
Teaching load for the position	✓	✓	✓	✓	✓	✓

	Request from You to the President	Request from a Dean to You	Official Record for Human Resources	Short Print Ad	Longer Electronic or Mailed Ad	Record for Credentialing and Accreditation
Anticipated courses to be taught by the successful candidate during his or her first year				×	✓	
Research expectation of the position	✓	✓	✓	✓	✓	
Other responsibilities, such as advising and thesis direction	✓	✓	✓	✓	✓	
Background information on the institution (e.g., size, mission, location)				×	✓	
Average number of students majoring in this discipline for the previous three to five years	✓	✓				
Average number of students enrolling in introductory, advanced, and graduate courses in this discipline for the previous three to five years	✓	✓				
National enrollment trends and demographic information that might affect the ongoing need for this position	✓	✓				
Preferences for the position (e.g., a preference for a higher degree than that which is required, preferred additional years of experience)				×	✓	
Materials required in order for the application to be considered complete				✓	✓	
Application deadline for the position				✓	✓	
Indication as to whether the deadline is a postmark deadline, a final date on which materials will be accepted, or the date on which screening will start				✓	✓	
Equal opportunity or affirmative action indication, if appropriate				✓	✓	

	Request from You to the President	Request from a Dean to You	Official Record for Human Resources	Short Print Ad	Longer Electronic or Mailed Ad	Record for Credential-ing and Accredita-tion
Information for candidates requiring accommodations, if appropriate				✓	✓	
How materials are to be submitted (electronically, surface mail, or other)				✓	✓	
Name of the search chair				✓	✓	
Contact information for the search chair				✓	✓	
Website where additional information may be found				✓	✓	

PART FIVE

THE BUDGET
OF THE COLLEGE
OR UNIVERSITY

33

SETTING BUDGETARY PRIORITIES

When provosts and deans become involved in budgeting, their role falls largely into three main categories:

1. Budgetary planning: Developing requests for additional funding, real-location of current resources, and tying the spending they control to the overall strategic goals of the institution
2. Budgetary supervision: Tracking how funds are spent over time to ensure that the programs for which they're responsible remain within their budgetary limits throughout the entire fiscal period
3. Budgetary modification: Reconsideration of budgeted amounts during the fiscal year as a result of changing situations

In the next three chapters, we'll examine some of the ways in which provosts and deans can be most effective in each of these three areas, beginning with budgetary planning.

Budgetary Planning

Budgetary planning concerns the development of an estimate of anticipated income and expenditures that are likely to occur within a specific, predetermined period, usually a fiscal year. A fiscal year consists of any contiguous twelve-month period over which an institution plans and tracks its use of funds. For some institutions, fiscal years are identical to calendar years, but most institutions have found that some other twelve-month period, most frequently July 1 through the following June 30, better suits their academic calendars, state legislative cycles, and student enrollment habits. It's traditional to denote a fiscal year by using the abbreviation FY, followed by two or four digits that specify the calendar year in which the fiscal year ends. For example, most institutions use the designation FY25 or FY2025 to indicate a fiscal year that begins sometime in the calendar year 2024 and concludes on a predetermined date in the year 2025.

Nearly every state institution and many private institutions require that budgets be closed out at the end of each fiscal year. In other words, funds and deficits usually can't be carried over from one fiscal year to the next. In these systems, all unexpended monies must be spent and all unreconciled deficits must be covered by the last day of the fiscal year. This practice leads to the allocation of what are frequently called year-end funds—amounts that can become an important factor in the budgetary planning of any academic leader.

Systems that allow for the transfer of unexpended funds from one fiscal year to the next (a category of funding generally known as carry forward) are likely to have stringent rules about what types of funding may be transferred in this way, what accounts may be involved, and what the maximum amount of a unit's carry forward may be. For example, it may be possible to bank unexpended equipment funding in order to make a very large purchase the following year but impossible to carry forward personnel funding. Or it may be possible at a state institution to carry forward income derived from an investment or foundation account, while all the funding that comes from the state has to be either spent or returned to the government. You will know from your upper administration or budget office whether the use of carry forward is allowed in your system. In situations where transfer of positive balances from one fiscal year to the next is permitted, planning the use of carry-forward funding can become a significant element of the dean or provost's strategic plan. In addition to a large equipment purchase, carry-forward balances could be used for such items as:

○ Costly vehicle purchases like a bus or specially outfitted van that can't be accommodated within the budget of any single fiscal year

○ Furniture, casework, and equipment needed to furnish new facilities, particularly when (as frequently occurs) construction costs rise after the initial estimates have been received and the project can be completed only by transferring the funding set aside for furnishing the building to completing the construction

○ Unanticipated one-time expenses, such as matches for grants, repairs after natural disasters, start-up costs for a faculty member, and opportunities that, while unplanned, meet a critical need

Carry-forward accounts are useful, but they also pose some risk for the academic leaders overseeing them. In years of fiscal exigency, they are almost always the first type of account scooped to meet a sudden institutional shortfall. It's not uncommon, therefore, for deans and provosts to bank carry-forward amounts for a large future expense, only to have the account raided during a particularly bad budgetary year. For this reason, if your institution or system permits carry-forward balances, you need to be fully aware of both the benefits and risks associated with this type of account.

As you begin to develop the budgetary plan for the programs you supervise, a good practice is to draft it within the framework of a single, comprehensive philosophy of budgeting. That philosophy may be one of your own creation, or it may be determined by your institution, university system, or state law. While there are many ways of describing these different approaches to the budget, all of them fall largely into three main categories: zero-base budgeting, historical budgeting, and performance-based funding.

Zero-base budgeting occurs when an institution resets all budgetary sources and allocations each time a new budget is created. The income and expenditures of previous years don't matter; the entire budget is designed from scratch or, as the name of this approach implies, from a zero base. The advantages of zero-base budgeting are that it's extremely flexible, helps free institutions from budgeting patterns that no longer make sense, and causes every single revenue and spending goal to be developed with a clear and defensible rationale. The disadvantages are that it's highly time intensive, can exacerbate divisiveness within an institution (since it forces each unit to compete every year against all other units for a share of the limited resources that are available), and frequently doesn't result in budgets that are significantly different from what would have occurred if the previous year's allocation had simply been used as a template for the current year.

Historical budgeting, the most common type of budgeting at colleges and universities today, relies on the institution's past record of income and expenditures to help plan for the future. The advantages of historical budgeting are that it's quicker to implement than the two other approaches, gives institutions an initial plan they can adjust according to their needs, and has the merit of having been tested by the experience of previous years. The disadvantages of this system are that a poorly designed initial budget continues to guide decisions for years into the future even though the needs of the institution can change significantly over time. With historical budgeting, it can be quite difficult for institutions to change poor practices that have become well entrenched; it can also be relatively easy to overlook poor financial planning since every category of income and expenditure need not be justified each time the budget is set.

Performance-based funding allocates amounts in such a way that rewards institutions or units that meet certain predetermined targets by redirecting funds from those that fail to meet those targets. The advantages are that it closely ties budgeting decisions to the strategic plan and goals of the institution and encourages units to be serious about how funds are allocated. The disadvantages are that it sometimes rewards the wealthy and penalizes the poor since wealthy institutions and units have more resources to direct toward achieving the goals specified in the formula and that the priorities of the administrative unit setting the goal may not always align with those of the unit implementing them. For example, imagine a system in which one of the funding metrics is based on the salaries earned by a program's graduates within six months of their graduation. That type of goal may work very well for programs in accounting and engineering, but they will almost certainly penalize programs in philosophy and art history, even though those programs may be more reflective of the institution's mission than its professional programs. (For more on performance-based funding, see Herbst, 2009.)

Regardless of the system of budgeting that an institution uses, almost all budget planning processes are hierarchical in nature. Departments submit budget proposals to colleges, colleges to the university, and the university to the university system. Even at small institutions, private colleges, and autonomous state institutions, the budgetary planning process follows at least some sort of hierarchical structure: plans and proposals generally move from smaller units to larger units, from the bottom to the top; budgetary decisions then are passed on from larger units to smaller units, from the top to the bottom. Most institutions also have specified formats for budget requests. In other words, there's a standardized design that you will use in requesting new funding or reallocation of existing funding, justifying your request, and tying that request to the institution's strategic plan. At other institutions, particularly at small colleges, budget proposals may be developed in a more informal manner. The chief academic officer might contact chairs and program directors, saying, "Get me a list of your most critical needs for the coming year by [date]." He or she will then collect these statements of need, arrange them in a priority order, and decide which of them to include in his or her own budgetary proposal to the president or governing board.

At some institutions, a formal budget hearing will be an important part of the planning process once proposals have been received from all units.

In a budget hearing, each unit is given an opportunity to elaborate on and justify its requests for the coming fiscal year. The requests made by all units are discussed, and the relative merits of the competing proposals are debated before the budget is set.

A budget hearing process can be useful because it allows upper administration to see the big picture of the institution's anticipated needs as it works to set its priorities. It also allows deans and the provost to discuss whether increases in various academic units are really in the best interest of the institution as a whole. For instance, a dean of business administration who has known that students who majored in one of his or her disciplines were unduly delayed in their program because of insufficient seats in English composition or calculus may prefer that additional faculty lines be added to the college of arts and sciences rather than his or her own. Similarly, several deans may support a request for an additional member of the staff in the advising or counseling center because needs in those areas are having an impact on their own academic programs. At institutions where formal budget hearings are not conducted, the president's cabinet, a special budget committee, or even, at times, the chief financial officer alone will collate the individual requests of the various units and establish an overall budget for the coming year. This type of approach can result in a budget that's set more quickly than one developed through a long period of budget hearings, but greater efficiency often comes at the expense of the consensus building that those meetings can provide.

A Guide to Decision Making

As you establish you budgetary plan and proposal each year, there are several questions you may find it useful to ask yourself as a guide to your decision-making process.

1. On what basis am I setting my budgetary priorities?

The temptation for most deans and provosts is to base their budgetary plans on their reactions to specific problems. For example, during the current academic year, there may have been problems resulting from higher-than-expected enrollments in particular courses. Students and their parents may have been angry because certain courses closed early and the demand for particular sections far exceeded the supply of seats.

The temptation for an academic leader might then be to try remedying this situation with a new faculty line as a way of demonstrating that the problem is being taken seriously and avoiding similar complaints in the future. But it could well be that this year's enrollment pattern isn't indicative of the institution's continuing needs. Demographic patterns may suggest that a current overall increase in institutional enrollment is likely to be followed by several years of steep decline. In other words, the current high enrollment may be the result of a temporary fad rather than a more lasting trend. Economic situations in other countries, international crises, and even shifting fashions in popular culture and entertainment may result in enrollment spikes for certain courses that are not sustainable in the long run. For example, immediately following the Watergate scandal and the publication of Woodward and Bernstein's *All the President's Men* (1974), many universities experienced a sudden, but temporary, increase in enrollments for introductory journalism courses. A similar fad arose for archaeology courses in the wake of the Steven Spielberg film *Raiders of the Lost Ark* (1981) and its sequels, for Japanese language and culture courses during the surge in the Japanese economy between 1985 and 1991 (which vanished at many schools in the wake of the prolonged stagnation of the Japanese economy), for Arabic language courses following the attacks of 9/11, and for courses in STEM (science, technology, engineering, and math) disciplines after the popularity of a number of television series about crime scene investigation and lovable, though quirky physicists (e.g., *CSI* and *The Big Bang Theory*).

Enrollments in business courses increase during a tough economy; enrollments in humanities courses increase during times of social crisis. While it can be extremely difficult for a dean to distinguish between a temporary fad and a trend, it's always important to consider what may be the root causes of a change in enrollment patterns. Shifts that occur because of changes in demographics that are likely to continue or because of new professions that arise may cause you to seek permanent staffing for courses that you will probably need for an extended period. But shifts that are the result of events in the news, vogues in popular culture, or the specific initiatives of individual political administrations are unlikely to be sustained over time. You're far better off meeting these needs not by seeking or reallocating tenure-track lines but through the creation of temporary or grant-funded positions, visiting scholars, or short-term changes in your course rotation. These approaches make it far easier to adjust your schedule once the fad is over and don't leave you with a staff of tenured faculty members who suddenly have little demand for their courses.

Another ineffective way of setting budgetary priorities is by greasing squeaky wheels. Every college or university will have certain constituents who voice the loudest and most frequent complaints about some perceived need. Deans and provosts can be tempted to address the issues raised by these squeaky wheels simply in order to placate their troubling demands. Moreover, because these faculty members mention their specific needs so often and so forcefully, academic leaders may begin seeing these needs as having a higher priority than they merit.

It's important when setting budgetary priorities to see each request not in terms of how stridently it was made but in terms of its overall benefit to the college or the department making the request. Ask yourself, "If this complaint were not one that I heard so frequently from this one particular person, how would I evaluate it on its own merits? In terms of absolute, lasting benefits to the college or department, does this request outrank the other items in my budget proposal?" To the greatest extent possible, try to separate the value of a request from the person who's making it. Consider the likely possible benefits that would result if the demand were met and the likely possible problems that would result if the problem went unaddressed. Which seems more compelling?

Perhaps the best way to evaluate your priorities objectively as you develop your budgetary plan is to tie all of your requests to either your institutional or your individual unit's strategic plan. Keep in mind the following essential principle:

> At institutions with well-designed strategic plans, the budget is guided by the plan; at institutions without well-designed strategic plans, the budget *is* the plan.

Or to put it another way:

> It's better to budget to a plan than adjust a plan to a budget.

In other words, budgets are always manifestations of institutional priorities. If your school has taken the strategic planning process seriously, you already have a clear framework in place for ranking your area's budgetary needs. A request for an expenditure that's not supported by planning and data is unlikely to be taken seriously by the individuals making decisions at your college or university. Moreover, why would you advocate on behalf of a need that doesn't help your institution pursue its stated objectives and fulfill its mission? There will always be unexpected situations that arise—unanticipated opportunities to take advantage of, unforeseen emergencies to address—but these situations should be rare and sufficiently compelling that everyone will understand why an exception is required. If you find that you're regularly giving high priority to items not easily tied to your institution's strategic plan or mission statement, you probably need to reevaluate the way in which you've been planning your budget.

Have you given due attention to revenue as well as expenditure in planning your budget?

Budget planning must take account not only of where resources will be spent but also of how those resources will be acquired. Frequently you will discover that an increase in institutional funding is not the only way in which your college can achieve a goal that it regards as important:

○ Is a particular budgetary item a suitable goal for a development project?

○ Can a fee be established that will fund the item that you need?

○ By charging admission for a particularly popular college event, can you accumulate a pool of funds that can be directed toward some other pressing needs?

○ Are there foundations that can be approached for seed money for a project? (A good source of information about funding opportunities, including tools for matching the interests of your faculty with existing funding programs, is pivot.cos.com.)

Even more immediately, look at your existing funds to determine whether resources could be redirected from a low-priority item to this new higher priority.

It can be an informative exercise for deans and provosts to examine their budgets each year and see what might occur if they were to redirect 5 percent of their operating budgets from items that are of relatively low priority to the institution or its strategic plan to clearly established new priorities. (This exercise is particularly useful for focused meetings or mini-retreats of the people who report to you.) While most administrators initially approach this exercise merely as a hypothetical experiment, they frequently discover that there are indeed ways of achieving important goals without increases in funding simply by reallocating current resources.

Budget plans that take account of both resources and expenditures tend to be more compelling when you're making a case to your president or governing board. They demonstrate that you've grappled with the difficult challenge of finding ways to pay for new initiatives and that you're aware of the importance of tying spending levels to your highest priorities. Academic leaders who view the budgeting process merely as an opportunity to present new wish lists to the upper administration are ultimately less likely to have even their most pressing needs taken seriously. They will have made the mistake of paying attention only to what they want, not to what they already have and how they may use it more efficiently.

3 Have you clearly examined the difference in budgetary implications of your one-year expenditures and your continuous expenditures?

As every administrator knows, not all spending is alike. Buying an extra piece of equipment affects a single year's budget. But a new faculty line, a permanent increase in scholarship aid, or the start of a distinguished lecture series requires ongoing support year after year. In budgetary planning, deans and provosts have to treat each of these categories differently. One-year expenditures may be addressed through year-end funding, outright gifts, annual fund contributions, temporary salary savings (e.g., the savings that result from hiring a temporary replacement who earns less than a faculty member who's on an unpaid leave), or budgetary transfers that are effective for only the current academic year. Continuous expenditures may be addressed through permanent increases to your budget, endowments, long-term salary savings (e.g., hiring a new faculty member who earns less than a retiring faculty member), and budgetary transfers that endure beyond the current fiscal year. It's a good practice to be as creative as you can in moving funds from one type of continuous expenditure to another. For example, if a highly paid senior faculty member is leaving the institution and you have consistently found your unit short of faculty travel funding, try to address the problem through innovative use of the resulting salary savings. A faculty member who currently earns $112,000 plus 23 percent in fringe benefits requires a continuous expenditure of $137,760. If an entry-level replacement is hired for $65,000 plus 23 percent in fringe benefits, there will remain a continuous pool of $57,810 that could be redirected into faculty travel. While some systems will have rules against transferring funds from personnel lines into nonpersonnel services accounts, it's at least worth investigating whether some of your college's priorities can be addressed not by increasing your entire budget but by reallocating current resources from one type of expenditure to another.

Conclusion

Deans and provosts need to keep in mind these fundamental principles in budgetary planning:

- Budgetary priorities should always reflect the overall priorities of the institution and the programs that the academic leader supervises.
- If a need can be met in ways other than an increase in overall funding, it's usually easier and often better to pursue those other options.
- Whenever possible, it can be beneficial to partner with other units in seeking ways to meet mutual needs. This kind of collaborative endeavor almost always benefits the institution as a whole.

Finally, if you've never formally reflected on your budgeting philosophy, such as how you set priorities and what happens when one of your programs has funding it no longer needs, doing so at this point is probably a very good idea before proceeding to the topic of the next chapter: drafting a formal budget proposal.

REFERENCES

Bernstein, C., & Woodward, B. (1974). *All the president's men.* New York, NY: Touchstone.
Herbst, M. (2009). *Financing public universities: The case of performance funding.* Dordrecht, Netherlands: Springer.

RESOURCES

Barr, M. J., & McClellan, G. S. (2011). *Budgets and financial management in higher education.* San Francisco: Jossey-Bass.
Goldstein, L. (2012). *A guide to college and university budgeting: Foundations for institutional effectiveness* (4th ed.). Washington, DC: NACUBO.
Goldstein, L., & Meisinger, R. J. (2005). *College and university budgeting: An introduction for faculty and academic administrators.* Washington, DC: NACUBO.

34

BUDGET PROPOSALS

HISTORICAL ✓

Once you have your philosophy of budgeting clearly in mind and have set your priorities, how do you go about making the best possible case for the items you feel you need? How do you create budget proposals that are compelling and will be most likely to result in the funding that your unit needs in order to flourish?

By this point in your administrative career, you're probably well aware of the following essential budgetary principle, although it's frequently unknown to faculty members and even to a surprising number of department chairs:

> A statement of need alone never makes a case that this need must be addressed, particularly when there are insufficient resources to meet all of an institution's competing needs.

Stephen Crane once phrased this principle in more philosophical terms: "A man said to the universe: 'Sir, I exist!' 'However,' replied the universe. 'The fact has not created in me a sense of obligation.'" What both these principles mean when it comes to academic budgets is that a good proposal doesn't merely argue that a need exists, even though it may make such an argument quite persuasively; it must also take the needs and interests of its audience into account. As we saw in chapter 30, whenever you create any type of document, it's important to ask two questions: Who is my audience? and What does this audience need to know in order to reach the result I desire? We'll begin this discussion of budget proposals by posing these two questions and then proceed to several other important questions that are specific to requests for funding.

• Who is my audience
• What do they need to know
for me to reach my desired
result

437

Who Is My Audience for This Proposal?

Every budget proposal has a target audience of people who'll be reading, evaluating, and deciding on the recommendations you propose. In many cases, there will even be multiple audiences for a budget proposal as it winds its way through a committee structure, is modified at the vice-presidential level, and possibly then modified again at the presidential level. It's important to keep these different audiences in mind as you create your budget proposal because not all the people reading it may share the same knowledge, values, and outlook as they make their decisions. In fact, each of these three areas—knowledge, values, and outlook—may cause you to phrase your budget proposal differently depending on your audience. Let's consider why.

Knowledge   Don't Assume others know

Do you take particular terms, acronyms, or concepts for granted that may be unclear to those who are outside your field? In terms of equipment requests, be sure to specify in nontechnical terms the reasons that the item is essential to or highly desirable for your academic programs and their pedagogical or research missions. Don't just talk about why you need the item but also point out the benefit to the institution that will result from its acquisition. Why is an outright purchase preferable to rental of the equipment or entering into a consortium agreement with another institution that would allow occasional use of similar equipment? With regard to position requests, how is the discipline represented by the prospective hire vital to your institution's overall mission and plan?

Values

It's a bad idea to develop a budget proposal on the basis of values that are completely different from those of the audience for your request. For instance, you may be trying to decrease your student-to-faculty ratio by requesting additional faculty positions because you believe that small classes are better pedagogically, but you may be making this request to people for whom productivity and maximizing student credit hour production are the most important principles. In such a case, consider providing statistics indicating that increasing section size beyond a certain point produces diminishing or even negative returns because it leads to increased rates of failure or attrition. In the long run, you could argue, decreasing the student-to-faculty ratio actually produces a higher sustainable student credit hour production in your area. You won't realize that you need to make this argument, however, if you don't consider how your intended audience's values are likely to color their interpretation of your request.

Outlook

We all see things differently because of our individual vantage points within the institution. Making a case for increasing faculty lines so as to reduce course load and increase scholarly productivity may not be the most useful approach if your audience consists primarily of representatives from student life, the business office, and the registrar's office. Take time in structuring a budget proposal to consider what outlooks may be shared by the people reviewing your proposal. If many members of your audience tend to see the world from a student service perspective, then a proposal that's based in a more faculty-oriented approach may be doomed to fail. View how the institution works from their perspective and then consider what would motivate them to think that increased funding in your area would be to their benefit.

What Are the Primary Concerns of That Audience?

Once you have established the knowledge base, values, and outlook of your proposal's primary audiences, you're ready to ask: What are my readers' primary concerns? What do they need most, care deeply about, or wish to see happen? What would cause them to react negatively to a new idea or request? For instance, you will always want, whenever possible, to tie your budget proposal to your institution's strategic plan. But if your institution is at the beginning of implementing its latest strategic plan—particularly if that plan has been the pet project of a new president—then it's all but essential for each item you request to be closely connected to the major objectives of that plan. The audience for your proposal will be concerned with making clear and demonstrable progress on the school's main objectives; whatever you can do to demonstrate that funding your request will be a key to that progress will best serve the interest of the programs you supervise.

Following is a list of common concerns held by many decision-making constituencies in higher education. If you go through this list and identify the concerns that are most likely to be the driving forces affecting the people who'll be evaluating budget proposals for the institution, you'll have found a basis from which to make your requests. Then you simply have to communicate a compelling reason why what you need will serve to meet that need or address that concern.

DRIVING FORCES THAT AFFECT BUDGETARY DECISIONS

- Increasing head count of full-time equivalent enrollment
- Retaining a higher percentage of students from term to term
- Improving graduation rates (overall or within a specific period such as four-year or six-year graduation rates)
- Improving graduation rates in certain fields, such as STEM, health professions, or education
- Improving job placement rates for graduates (either overall or within a certain period, such as six months or a year after graduation)
- Improving placement rates of graduates in graduate and professional schools
- Increasing starting salaries for graduates
- Increasing research productivity (among students, faculty, or both)
- Increasing external funding for research
- Developing spin-off companies for research
- Improving the institution's profile and academic reputation (regionally, nationally, or internationally)
- Internationalizing the curriculum
- Promoting active learning
- Promoting service-learning
- Raising minimum standards for admission
- Attaining a higher ranking in annual surveys of colleges and universities, either nationally or internationally
- Increasing external giving (either overall or by a specific stakeholder group such as alumni or parents)

Once you identify the primary concerns of the audience who will be reading and evaluating your proposal, you'll be in a good position to reread your draft through their eyes. Have you tied your requests to the priorities that these readers will have? If not, your budget proposal is unlikely to be effective. You'll be arguing on the basis of one set of fundamental assumptions, while those who make the budgetary decisions will have a completely different set of assumptions. When that happens, it's time to rework your draft.

Now that you've identified your audience and its likely concerns, you're ready to move on to three other questions you'll need to answer in order to strengthen your proposal.

What Do You Do in the Case of a Genuine Need That Can't Be Tied to the Strategic Plan?

Effective budget requests are those that present the expenditure being proposed as a solution to a problem recognized by the audience reviewing the requests. Does that mean that you can never request anything that isn't obviously related to the institution's strategic plan or another major goal of the president and governing board? Not necessarily. In the case of a truly idiosyncratic or irrelevant request, it's probably diplomatic to wait for a more opportune moment. In the midst of massive retrenchment, you aren't likely to be successful asking for a dozen new positions, an increase in travel funding, and cosmetic upgrades to an existing facility. But if the things you've requested are really important to the programs you supervise, you don't necessarily have to give up on them. You just have to think of them from the perspective of those who have the authority to fund your request.

Writing an effective budget proposal is a lot like writing a successful grant proposal. Every granting agency has specific concerns or a defined philanthropic focus to which you tailor the rhetoric of a grant proposal. Only rarely will you ever have a faculty member who wants to secure external funding for a project that fits exactly the goals of a foundation or other external source. Grant applications always involve a process of refining a project idea so that it better addresses the interests of the funding agency. That's exactly the process that academic leaders need to follow with regard to budget proposals. The only difference is that now the granting agency is your own institution.

As you review your school's strategic plan and any tactical goals that the president or governing board have set for the coming year, look for possible linkages that could occur between what your programs need and what the institution is trying to accomplish, even if you will have to explain to others what those linkages are. At the very least, most strategic plans have a section devoted to enhancing the quality of academic programs; it's a good idea to tie the vast majority of your budget requests to that goal. Even beyond that general objective, however, find ways to speak the language of the budget review committee, demonstrating that granting a request that helps you actually helps them too and serves the best interests of the institution as a whole.

You may well find that the arguments you need to justify a budgetary priority to those who report to you ("We really need this new position to reduce our workload, which has become unmanageable lately") are quite different from those that you use to justify the request to others ("Having this new staff member will help us improve our student retention and increase the likelihood that our professional programs will continue to be accredited"). Changing arguments in this way is not a matter of being disingenuous. Budgetary priorities usually reflect many different needs. Your task is to identify the needs that will be most compelling to a particular audience and then to highlight those needs in your request.

④ Which Other Factors Strengthen the Case for a Budget Proposal?

Submitting a budget proposal is a lot like applying for a grant in terms of how you relate your needs to someone else's goals. But budget proposals are like grant applications in another way as well. Just as many funding agencies look more favorably on proposals that provide at least some matching funds for the project, so is your budget proposal likely to be strengthened if you can find ways to demonstrate your own commitment to its priorities:

- Are there sources of funds that you can transfer from lower-priority areas to the higher-priority areas of the budget proposal? If so, you can make an argument like the following: "Now that I've outlined all the reasons that it's better to advertise this new position at the senior level than at the entry level so that we can achieve our strategic goals, I'd like to demonstrate how important this position is to us. Within my unit, I've identified sixty-five thousand dollars that I intend to shift from our adjunct budget—which, by the way, also gets us closer to another strategic goal of reducing our institutional reliance on part-time faculty members—to this new position. In other words, if you'll simply allocate to us funding for an entry-level position, I'll be able to make up the difference and elevate the position to senior rank."

- Are there other types of contributions that your area can make that would result in a stronger proposal? For instance, if the readers of your proposal are concerned about productivity, can you tie a slight increase in the enrollment caps for certain courses to the funding of your budget request? If the concerns are about promoting undergraduate research, can you reassign another faculty member to take charge of this endeavor once the position you are requesting is funded?

- Are there ways in which you can leverage this request so as to obtain other items of great concern to the readers of this proposal?

For instance, can you argue legitimately that if your request is granted, you'll be in a better position to secure external funding for other priorities of the institution? Are there ways in which the position or item will pay for itself over time? Could this particular budgetary priority account in any way for increased revenue to your department through providing services for a fee to other entities, increasing enrollment in your area, or justifying a fee for use?

⑤ How Might Alliances Help Your Budget Proposal?

Those who allocate funding at an institution want to get the largest impact they can from their expenditure. If you can build an alliance with one or more of your peers at the institution that will allow you to share a costly item or position, you'll stand a much better chance of getting it funded. Here are a few examples of ways in which provosts and deans can partner with peers in developing persuasive budget requests:

- A provost could work with a vice president for student affairs to receive funding for a new position that would be used to hire a director of campus leadership programs. The new director would be responsible for leadership development opportunities that could meet the needs of faculty, students, and administrators simultaneously. If certain programs were also opened to members of the staff, the director of human resources might be brought into the alliance so as to make it even stronger.

- A provost could cooperate with a vice president for enrollment management to propose a new building in which student success initiatives would be housed. As an additional classroom facility, the building would also serve the needs of the division of academic affairs. As a center where tutorial services, supplemental instruction, advising, and career counseling would occur, the building would be equally valuable to the division of enrollment services.

- A dean of business administration, a dean of education, and a dean of science might partner to request a number of new faculty lines in statistics that would be of equal value to programs in mathematics, psychology, educational research, management, and entrepreneurship.

- A dean of visual arts joins forces with a dean of health sciences to propose retrofitting an existing facility to configure it as a center for art therapy that could serve a critical community need at the same time that it prepares students for a career in an expanding field.

Can we develop alliances

Through collaborations like these, academic leaders gain one or more partners who can join with them in making a stronger case for the request than they could make on their own, demonstrate good stewardship of resources by identifying opportunities than benefit several areas of the institution simultaneously, and exhibit creative solutions that may not be possible within the confines of a single department or college.

Conclusion

Ineffective budget proposals frequently result from the assumption academic leaders make that simply because an item appears compelling to them, it must be compelling to everyone. A budget request is, in the end, a rhetorical document: its author is trying to persuade someone to do something. For this reason, the basic rules of argumentation that are taught in Rhetoric 101 apply to drafting all budget proposals.

1. Know your audience.
2. Know what motivates your audience.
3. Find a way to connect what you want to occur with your audience's motivation or chief concerns.

RESOURCES

Goldstein, L., & Meisinger, R. J. (2005). *College and university budgeting: An introduction for faculty and academic administrators.* Washington, DC: NACUBO.

Kosten, L. A. (2009). *Decentralized budgeting and the academic dean: Perspectives on the effectiveness of responsibility center management.* Saarbrücken, Germany: VDM Verlag.

Miner, J. T., & Miner, L. E. (2013). *Proposal planning and writing* (5th ed.). Santa Barbara, CA: ABC-CLIO.

35

SUPERVISING A BUDGET

Once you've developed your budget proposal, presented it, and received
your allocation for the fiscal year, one important fiscal duty still remains:
monitoring expenditures to make sure that the programs reporting to you
keep within their budgetary limits for the year. At small institutions, you
may perform that duty yourself; at larger institutions, you may have a
budget officer on the staff who takes care of this responsibility for you.
Basic budgetary supervision can also be an appropriate responsibility to
delegate to an associate provost or assistant dean. But since you'll ultimately be held responsible if someone exceeds his or her budget, you'll
want to be kept in the loop on a regular basis. In short, although it can
be useful to assign the technical and time-consuming aspects of budget
supervision to someone else, be sure to retain ownership of the major
decisions that lead to those expenditures and of the budgetary philosophy
that guides those decisions.

Regardless of whether you delegate the technical details or look after
them yourself, it's important to remember that budgeting requires proactive monitoring and supervision, not simply keeping an eye on the transactions. Anyone who has ever told a child, "Watch your little brother,"
only to be told later "But I *did* watch him. I watched the whole time
he climbed up on the counter and the whole time he fell off," understands that there's a big difference between active and passive monitoring.
Supervising a budget requires a special type of vigilance—the kind of
involvement where you check on every detail that seems unusual and
intervene before, rather than after, a shortfall occurs. At most institutions, budgetary information is provided to deans and provosts electronically and updated continually. At some institutions, printed statements
are still distributed every week or every month, listing income, transfers,
and expenditures according to the specific category in which the change
has occurred.

Supervising budgets involves tracking transactions according to the department, program, object code, or category in which they have occurred. Institutional systems of tracking transactions can be highly complex, depending on the mission and size of the college or university, its organizational structure, the type of accounting software it uses, and the set of accounting standards it follows. As we saw in the glossary at the end of chapter 25, the boards that set these standards are the Governmental Accounting Standards Board (GASB) for public institutions and the Financial Accounting Standards Board (FASB) for private institutions.

> One major difference . . . involves the number of allowable cash-flow reporting categories. The FASB requires the cash flow statement to report cash flows from operational, investment and financing activities. The GASB requires the cash flow statement to report cash flows from operational, investment, capital and related financing and non-capital financing activities. The effect is increased transparency and a more accurate representation of financing activities from private sector agencies. (Jackie Lohrey at smallbusiness.chron.com/difference-between-fasb-gasb-effects-statement-cash-flows-76401.html)

Unless you've become so used to working with one system that the other method puzzles you when you move to another type of institution, these differences probably won't matter much. For most of the issues that are dealt with by the provost and dean themselves, GASB and FASB standards are identical.

In most cases, the object codes that institutions use are nine or more digits, with each digit or group of digits providing such information as the specific campus on which the transaction took place (in multicampus systems), the source of funding (education and general, foundation, sponsored programs, and the like), the unit responsible for the transaction (college, division, department, program, and so on), and the precise nature of the income, transfer, or expenditure (which can include a vast array of types, such as full-time salaries, part-time salaries, casual labor, benefits, postage, telephone: local, telephone: toll, subscriptions, memberships, equipment over a certain amount, equipment under a certain amount, travel, food, lodging, and office supplies).

Since institutions almost always allow at least some types of transfer among different funds, it's probably best—unless institutional policies say otherwise—to tie each transaction as closely as possible to its actual object code, not simply to any account that happens to have sufficient funding remaining in it. For instance, in a year when a particular department's small equipment account has already been depleted, you may be tempted to allow the program to purchase an additional piece of equipment with money that remains in its postage or supplies account. But it's much better (and in certain systems required) for that purchase to be funded from the small equipment account, even though it's depleted, and then to conduct a one-time transfer of funds from another account to cover that expense. Not only does this procedure make it much easier for accounts to be reconciled and audited, but it also provides the unit with a far more realistic picture of its needs when each budget year is compared to others. If you notice that funds are being transferred from operating supplies and expenses to small equipment in the same department several years in a row, you may decide that it's preferable to realign those accounts permanently. Moreover, if you're chronically short of funds in one account and must repeatedly cover those expenditures by piecing together remaining bits from several other accounts, you can use this pattern as support for an argument that the underfunded account ought to be increased by your institution.

It may at times be impossible to transfer funds between certain accounts at your institution. As we saw in chapter 33, there may be restrictions on transfers between personal services accounts (those used to pay for salaries and benefits) and expense accounts, thus limiting your ability to use salary savings to fund expenses like travel, photocopying, and equipment. Other institutions may have restrictions on whether funds in the regular operating budget—the type of accounts usually known as education and general accounts (E&G accounts)—may be used for such purchases as student travel, entertainment, the purchase of food or alcoholic beverages, and the like. Your school's business office or chief financial officer can give you an overview of the restrictions that apply to your program. But it's always a good practice to explain what you're trying to do rather than how you intend to do it. For example, if you say, "I'd like to move the funding on the line that remains from Dr. Smith's sabbatical to cover the cost of a new photocopier," you may be told, "We can't do that. We can't transfer funds between personal services and equipment accounts." But if you say instead, "I'd like to purchase a new photocopier, and I have enough money on the line that remains from Dr. Smith's sabbatical to cover it. How can I make the purchase?," you're likely to get an entirely different answer. You may be able to swap the cost in some way. For instance, perhaps there was another expense that you were going to pay for out of E&G funds that you are allowed to fund from Dr. Smith's salary savings. That may leave you with enough E&G funding that you can then pay for the photocopier out of an account that permits equipment purchases. Foundation accounts also tend to have fewer restrictions than do institutional accounts. It's sometimes possible, therefore, to swap expenses between E&G funding and donations in a way that achieves your ultimate goal while still adhering to your system's accounting guidelines.

It can take quite a while to discover all the intricacies of an institution's budget procedures, so don't assume that there's only one way of accomplishing a goal. If you're informed that a certain type of purchase or transfer isn't possible, rephrase your request. Say something like, "Well, here's what I need to do. Explore with me some of the ways in which we can get that done while still adhering to our policies."

Tracking Expenditures

No matter how much budgetary information your institution provides, many deans and provosts find it useful to maintain their own shadow budget in the form of a simple spreadsheet. Items are occasionally coded incorrectly at other levels of an institution, and shadow budgets allow you to detect discrepancies when you're either charged for something that should've been charged to a different unit or not credited with funding that should properly be yours. It's often the case, too, that official institutional reports lag behind actual activity by weeks or even months; keeping a shadow budget prevents you from accidentally spending the same money more than once, resulting in a deficit at the end of the year. Think of your shadow budget as something like the check register in a checkbook: reconciling this record with your bank statement helps you spot errors and avoid overdrawing your account. It also assists you in identifying funds that you've already encumbered or promised to use for a particular purpose, although you haven't technically spent them yet.

On both your shadow budget and official budget, one important figure to track is the percentage of each account expended versus the percentage of the fiscal year that's gone by. Most budget offices calculate this ratio for you, but if yours doesn't, it's easy to set up a spreadsheet formula that provides you with the same information. Here's how you'd make the two calculations:

(Amount expended ÷ original amount) × 100
= percentage of that account expended to date

(Day within fiscal year ÷ 365) × 100
= percentage of the fiscal year that has passed to date

After you've tracked this information for several years, you'll learn the budgetary patterns and rhythms of the programs you supervise and can recognize the red flags you need to watch for in your budget. As an example, an account that's 98 percent expended with only 35 percent of the academic year gone may or may not be a cause for concern. This apparent discrepancy could result from an equipment account that supports only one or two purchases each year, or it may be that the account is used to pay for certain supplies or services that are regularly needed at the start of the academic year but rarely again afterward. But a photocopying account that is depleted too rapidly may leave an academic program vulnerable when final exams must be copied at the end of the term. Your own familiarity with the needs of the disciplines in your area, coupled with a healthy dose of common sense, will guide you in determining which percentages are problematic and which are not. You may need to explain these spending patterns to budget managers outside of academic affairs who may not know the rhythms that occur in the spending of individual disciplines.

Another budgetary item you may wish to track is each program's cost in relation to similar programs at peer institution. How much does it cost to produce, for instance, one student credit hour of introductory French at your school compared to others that resemble your institution in size and mission? Frequently the business office of a college or university has a system in place to calculate these figures. But if your institution doesn't provide you with this, you can calculate a crude approximation of cost by adding all of a particular department's expenditures in salaries, benefits, and all categories of operating expenses (being sure to include travel funding and other accounts that may not be managed within the department itself) and then dividing that figure by the number of student credit hours the discipline produced during the same fiscal period. The reason that the resulting figure is crude is that it doesn't account for overhead and other institutional expenses (such as the department's share of the salaries paid to your president, other administrators, librarians, members of the support staff outside that department, the registrar, and the like). Provided that you calculate rates for other programs the same way, you'll get a good general sense of how expensive each program is to maintain. If you discover that it costs significantly less to produce one student credit hour in one department than it does in that of a peer program, you can use this information to demonstrate that program's efficiency and sustainability. If you find that a particular program's costs are much higher, you can be proactive in developing a strategy that will reduce those costs. In either case, this type of very basic cost accounting is beneficial to academic leaders.

You might even begin using this approach to determine the cost-benefit ratio of making certain types of equipment purchases. For example, if two

How much does it cost
for us to run a program

programs both request a new videoconferencing system, cost accounting allows you to calculate the efficiency of funding a single system that the two programs can share versus making two purchases or none at all. How does the new system affect the cost per credit hour in the two programs? Will it allow more students to enroll in certain courses (thus potentially lowering the cost), or will it be used by faculty members only occasionally to participate in meetings occurring elsewhere on campus (thus increasing the cost)? Will use of a single system by two programs require the purchase of a more durable system that's less cost effective than buying two simpler systems? Are there other factors that are more important than cost alone in making this decision? Cost accounting may not answer all these questions for you, but it will provide an important set of data that can help you make a more informed decision.

Budgetary Intervention

Simply because a department or program is expending its budget more rapidly than the fiscal year is passing doesn't mean that that unit is doing anything wrong. Certain spending patterns just don't correlate well with the passage of the fiscal year even when they make perfect sense to the program. At times, too, a particular department or program will have an unusual budgetary year because of an emergency, a sudden increase in enrollment, the needs of a new or visiting faculty member, or some other unusual occurrence. It's also possible that what appears to be an excessive expenditure at the moment will be covered later by student fees paid into an agency account or custodial account. These accounts are so named because the institution is merely acting as the agent or custodian for funds that are paid into the account through such revenue sources as student fees or ticket sales and then expended as needed. For instance, an account into which students pay laboratory fees that are used to purchase chemicals and glassware for lab sessions is an agency or custodial account. As long as the person responsible for this department or program is fully aware of this situation and has incorporated it into his or her own budgetary planning, the situation is probably being addressed appropriately and requires no intervention on your part.

Nevertheless, if you're unable to find a compelling explanation for the spending pattern of a unit you supervise, it's probably a good idea to meet with the person in charge of that area to review income and expenditure patterns from the start of the fiscal year. He or she may be well aware of circumstances that explain the financial situation that you have observed. But if that person isn't able to offer any persuasive reason for the pattern you've observed, it may be time for the two of you to explore strategies that will help the department or program end the year without a deficit. In certain cases, it may be possible to transfer funds to this unit from resources that you know will not be expended elsewhere. One-year salary savings for a sabbatical or leave replacement and carry-forward accounts can provide a few options. In other cases, expenditures may need to be reduced for the rest of the year in order to avoid the deficit. Nonessential purchases could be deferred or made only in the event that year-end funding is available. (On year-end funding and carry-forward accounts, see chapter 33.) Photocopying expenses might be reduced by providing course materials to students electronically rather than through hard copies. Mail and telephone charges could be trimmed by encouraging Internet communication rather than surface mail or toll calls. In certain cases, merely making a department chair or program director aware of the severity of a budgetary issue will prompt that person to come up with creative solutions to what would otherwise be a severe problem.

Greater Challenges

Frequent budgetary overruns by a department or program could be an indication that the unit is insufficiently funded, isn't a good steward of its resources, or has been affected by some other factor that's complicating its budget. In order to determine which of these possible causes is the true culprit, you'll probably need more information than you can glean from the budget and ledger listings alone. Here are some of the areas you may wish to address.

Synchronic analysis

How do the revenue and expenditure patterns of this unit compare to those of similar units during the same period? Compare the unit with similar departments or programs at your institution, if any exist. Try to think not necessarily in terms of the number of faculty members in each department or the number of majors served, but in terms of the unit's overall mission, reliance on equipment or travel to fulfill that mission, and other factors that most directly affect the budget. In addition to these intrainstitutional comparisons, see if you can locate several departments or programs in comparable academic areas at peer institutions. Then examine each major area of the units' budgets (supplies, copying, postage, adjunct and overload hiring, and so on) divided by such factors as the number of student credit hours produced by each unit per fiscal year, the number of majors graduating from the unit as a rolling five-year average, the number of full-time or full-time-equivalent faculty members in the unit, and the like. Examined in this way, are there areas of the budget in which the unit you're examining is atypical? Where does the difference appear to be: in insufficient funding or excessive spending?

Diachronic analysis

[handwritten: TRACK Expenditures over time]

Next examine the unit's expenditures over time. If at all possible, trace these patterns over at least the past five years. Has the overrun been consistent in size relative to the unit's entire budget over time, or did it increase? (If you discover that the size of the overrun is actually decreasing, you may have encountered evidence that the problem is already being addressed in an appropriate manner; all that the unit may need is your help and support.) Is there a specific turning point when the unit suddenly passed from balanced budgets into deficits? If so, what factors changed in the department or program at that time? Was the chair or director new? Did the department receive a new faculty line while its nonpersonnel services budgets were not increased? Did enrollment start to rise? By pinpointing the time frame in which the unit's fiscal situation changed, you can begin to isolate the factors that may have accounted for the difference.

Proactive Intervention

Just as you monitor the expenditures of the programs that report to you in order to ensure that your unit remains in budget, so will the president or provost monitor your own enrollment and spending patterns to ensure that the institution as a whole remains fiscally stable. While you'll want to be proactive in assisting your individual units to keep their spending in line with their allocations, there will inevitably be years in which your area may be unable to adhere to its spending limits. Reasons for a budgetary shortfall at the dean or provost's level include enrollment declines, budget cuts imposed by the legislature or governing board, emergencies, rising costs that affect academic affairs disproportionately, one-time situations (such as the need to furnish a new facility), and similar factors. Whenever a situation of this sort is likely to occur, be sure that your supervisor is informed as quickly as possible so that plans can be made and to prevent your boss from being blindsided. In sharing information of this sort, you'll need to do your homework so that you can address each of the following areas:

[handwritten: Projection]

- The likely *size* of the anticipated shortfall. Estimate to the best of your ability the probable scope of the deficit. Be as specific as you can. After all, if you say, "It looks like we're going to be short in our equipment fund this year," you don't want your president to assume you are speaking of a few thousand dollars of deficit when the actual shortfall is many times that amount.

o The likely *cause* of the anticipated shortfall. Try to determine, before meeting with your supervisor, what seems to be producing a deficit this year. If it's a factor that can be controlled or compensated for at your level, you'll be asked for your plan to deal with the problem. Even if it's a factor beyond your control, you'll still be expected to have some ideas about how to address the impact of the problem.

o Some possible *plans* for dealing with the anticipated shortfall. No administrator likes to be handed problems by people who seem to have given no thought at all to seeking a solution. Come to your meeting ready to propose possible solutions to the deficit. In doing so, be sure to give attention to what you intend to do internally within your unit, not simply to what other units or your supervisor can do for you. In fact, to the extent possible, you should come to this meeting ready to cover the preponderance of the shortfall through reallocation of resources within your area.

For suggestions on how to trim budgets in order to meet this reallocation, see chapter 36.

Conclusion

*TRack Rev + exP
determine if funds used wisely*

Supervising a budget means more than just tracking income and expenditures. It also means determining whether the funding that's allocated to different programs is being spent wisely and for its intended purposes. Deans and provosts don't need advanced knowledge of accounting in order to supervise a budget, but they do need to know how to read a journal, a ledger, and any other type of budget report their institutions may generate. In many cases, the dean or provost may delegate day-to-day budgetary supervision to a budget manager, associate provost, or assistant dean, but budgets are one area in which delegating responsibility doesn't mean delegating accountability. A mistake that someone makes in your name is still your mistake. It's a good idea to become sufficiently knowledgeable about general accounting practices and the expenditure patterns of individual programs in your area so that you'll be able to make the most informed decisions possible.

delegating responsibility does not mean delegating accountability

RESOURCES

Horner, D. (2014). *Accounting for non-accountants* (10th ed.). London, UK: Kogan Page Limited.

Label, W. A. (2013). *Accounting for non-accountants: The fast and easy way to learn the basics* (3rd ed.). Naperville, IL: Sourcebooks.

Stenzel, C., & Stenzel, J. (2003). *Essentials of cost management*. Hoboken, NJ: Wiley.

36

IMPLEMENTING BUDGET CUTS

If you serve as dean or provost long enough, you'll almost certainly experience a period during which your institution undergoes a severe financial challenge. At private institutions, budget crises tend to occur when enrollment fails to meet projections or the return on the institution's endowment is so low that it cannot cover shortfalls occurring elsewhere in the budget. At public institutions, budget cuts similarly tend to occur when enrollment projections are not met (in cases where appropriations are tied to enrollment), but also when the state is experiencing a financial downturn and all state allocations must be reconsidered or reduced. With the expansion of performance-based funding (see chapter 33), public institutions may also have to cut their budgets if they don't meet the targets set by their state legislatures.

In the best situation involving a budget cut, you'll have plenty of warning so that you can make plans and deal with your reductions in a deliberate, careful, and well-considered manner. All too often, however, budget cuts occur unexpectedly. For instance, a state appropriation may be cut midyear. Enrollments that looked solid in May can prove to be surprisingly soft as classes begin in August. A sudden stock market plunge could make it impossible for an institution to take its anticipated annual draw from the endowment. How you handle these situations will prove to be one of the clearest tests of your academic leadership. Good administrators help their institutions fulfill their missions during times of economic strength. Excellent administrators help their institutions fulfill their missions even during times of severe budget cuts. This chapter looks at the most important principles to keep in mind when implementing budget cuts.

Develop Contingency Plans

The time to think about how to make budget cuts isn't in the heat of the crisis; it's before the economic challenge has occurred. Good times never last forever. Even if your institution is prospering at the moment, eventually there'll be a budget cut that affects your programs. As a result, good budgetary planning includes preparing for those cuts before they're ever required. Chapter 33 discussed some of the ways to go about creating a budgetary plan for your area. In chapter 34, we explored ways of formulating those plans into proposals that help explain your needs and their rationale to others.

Part of every good budget planning process, whether strategic (tied to long-range goals that extend more than one year in the future) or tactical (tied to more immediate goals, particularly those of the current or next fiscal year), should be the development of contingency plans that outline what you'd do in the event of a budget reduction:

- Suppose that you're severely understaffed, but a budget cut imposes a hiring freeze before any of your available positions are filled.
- Suppose that travel budgets are eliminated, but you have several junior faculty members who need to present their research in order to submit a successful tenure application.
- Suppose that you receive a mandate to reduce the number of sections you offer (and thereby reduce what you spend in personal services) by 5 percent.

How would you address each of these situations? More important, how would you address these situations and still fulfill the mission of your institution?

As part of your regular budget planning process, it's a good idea to develop contingency plans exploring how you'd respond to several scenarios if they arose with very little warning:

- *Across-the-board cuts.* How would you implement a 5 percent budget cut if you were given the liberty to reduce your existing budget in any way you wished as long as you met the 5 percent target? How would you handle the same situation if a 10 percent budget cut were mandated? Most academic units find that approximately 95 percent of their budgets are dedicated to salaries and benefits and approximately 5 percent to everything else in the budget. Nevertheless, it is the rare program that can sustain even a 5 percent budget cut without affecting salaries or reducing the number of sections taught by temporary faculty members, such as part-time or adjunct employees. After all, course materials still have to be photocopied. Telephones still have to be connected. Mail still needs to be sent. For this reason, study carefully both the operating budgets and staffing patterns of the units that report to you as you consider how you would implement budget cuts. Develop a plan that you could actually put into effect, not merely one that meets the reduction goal on paper.

o *Specified cuts.* How would you reorganize to fulfill your area's objectives if specific areas of your budget were reduced or eliminated? For instance, how would you respond to restrictions in travel? Supplies? Equipment? Maintenance? Part-time faculty? Overloads? If one of these areas were greatly reduced or eliminated, could you alleviate the situation by transferring funds from other areas of your budget to help cover the shortfall? Can you make cuts in other areas so that a reduction that is mandated in a particular part of the budget is less severe? Anticipating how you would address cuts in certain areas is important because that is the way deans and provosts often receive budget reductions. State legislators or governing boards target an area of the budget, perhaps without regard to how that one area affects the entire mission of our units. By forming contingency plans, you may be able to transform a specified cut into a more general (and for your planning purposes, more flexible) across-the-board cut by shifting funds from different areas to cover the reduction.

One way of making contingency plans is to engage in the practice known as STEEPLED analysis. (See Cadle, Paul, and Turner, 2010, and Buller, 2015.) The idea behind this approach is to consider the eight main drivers of change in higher education that spell out the acronym STEEPLED: drivers that are Social, Technological, Economic, Ecological, Political, Legislative, Ethical, and Demographic. For each driver, you speculate on the best case, worst case, and most likely case scenario for what could occur. For example, in terms of the best-case scenario for the demographic driver of change, you might come up with contingency plans for each of the following.

- o Best-case scenario: Steady increase of qualified high school graduates of 7 percent per year for a decade
- o Worst-case scenario: Sustained annual decreases over 15 percent or increases over 30 percent of qualified high school graduates for a decade
- o Most-likely case scenario: Fluctuations year to year but a net 11 percent decrease of qualified high school graduates in a decade

Even better, you can mix and match the scenarios from different drivers to plan for more complex contingencies. What would you do,

Figure 36.1 Considering Different Combinations of Contingencies

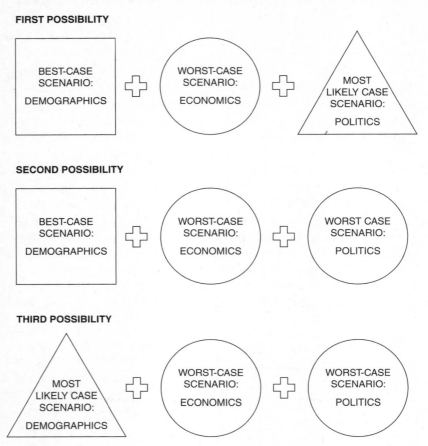

FIRST POSSIBILITY

BEST-CASE SCENARIO: DEMOGRAPHICS + WORST-CASE SCENARIO: ECONOMICS + MOST LIKELY CASE SCENARIO: POLITICS

SECOND POSSIBILITY

BEST-CASE SCENARIO: DEMOGRAPHICS + WORST-CASE SCENARIO: ECONOMICS + WORST CASE SCENARIO: POLITICS

THIRD POSSIBILITY

MOST LIKELY CASE SCENARIO: DEMOGRAPHICS + WORST-CASE SCENARIO: ECONOMICS + WORST-CASE SCENARIO: POLITICS

for instance, if your best-case scenario were to develop in demographics but your worst-case scenario in economics and your most likely case scenario in politics? Would that response change if instead of the most likely case scenario in politics, the worst-case scenario occurred? Some of the ways in which you can visualize these different combinations appears in figure 36.1.

Don't Abandon the Strategic Plan

If you originally set your budgetary priorities properly by aligning them with the strategic plan of your institution and unit (see chapter 33), now is not the time to abandon strategic thinking. Moreover, if you didn't originally establish your budgetary priorities as part of an overall strategic

STRATEGIC
plan is prime

process, it's imperative that you now think strategically as you plan your cuts. After all, a strategic plan outlines for you where your institution or area intends to go and how it intends to get there. If you don't incorporate this plan into your approach to identifying possible cuts, you run the risk of stalling in your momentum toward achieving goals that are far more important than the transitory situation of the current fiscal year. Make no mistake: for most institutions, dire financial times, like prosperous financial times, come and go. The challenges that appear so pressing at the moment will be a distant memory within just a few years. Don't abandon your most important initiatives simply because you've hit a bump in the road.

As you consider cuts, examine each of them in the following light: To what extent does this cut threaten the realization of the vision that I've outlined in our strategic plan? For instance, if your school's vision statement is that "within ten years, this institution will be one of the top five research universities in this region of the country," that very goal provides you with a key tool for planning your budget cuts. So if you have to make a choice between increasing course enrollments and cutting equipment funding for scholarships, you won't hesitate to expand the size of courses. If instead your strategic plan says, "Within ten years, this institution will be recognized throughout its region as a premier 'teaching first' university with high retention rates and improved measures of student engagement," your decision will be quite different. If your strategic plan doesn't provide adequate guidance—if it's so generic, for instance, that it promises to do all things for all people—the fault lies not with the principle of tying budgetary decisions to the strategic plan but with the quality of the strategic plan itself.

Think Like a Chess Player

Provosts and deans need to approach budget cuts in the same way that they'd approach a game of chess: studying the implication of each decision several moves hence. While it's obvious that every budgetary cut will have consequences, you don't want a cut to have unanticipated consequences if there's any way to avoid them.

Suppose that you're a dean of a college with eighty full-time faculty members. Travel budgets are allocated to the college, not the individual department, and your annual budget for faculty travel is $100,000. By January of the current academic year, just over $80,000 remains on this budget line. Because of a midyear budgetary crisis, you're asked to return $75,000 of your budget to the central administration. "This seems to be a slow year for travel," you conclude, "so I'll take the cut from that account.

After all, we have to copy exams and provide supplies for our classrooms and labs. No one has to travel." You transfer the funds back to your president and inform your chairs of what you've done. There's an immediate outcry. The reason so much money has remained in your travel budget until January, you're told, is that most conferences for the disciplines in your college are held in the spring. Faculty members have already submitted abstracts for numerous programs, made commitments to attend, and assumed financial obligations that will now not be reimbursed. Even worse, several faculty members *must* attend these conferences because this last bit of professional development will be just enough to ensure a positive decision for them on tenure and promotion. Also, several of your chairs are outraged that your unilateral decision has privileged those few faculty members whose conferences happened to be in the fall. What had once seemed such an obvious decision is now beginning to look like a very poor choice.

This difficulty arose because as dean, you failed to anticipate all the implications of your budget cut. Midyear cuts are particularly challenging because they don't allow sufficient time for planning and adjusting goals in light of a new financial situation. Nevertheless, this crisis could have been avoided through better understanding of your unit's spending rhythms throughout the year for each category in its budget. If you'd been aware that travel commitments are usually made in the fall while the travel itself occurred in the spring, you might have investigated other options, such as requiring funding to be encumbered before travel commitments are made. Perhaps a less wholesale reduction in the travel budget, complemented by the reduction of a few sections taught by adjunct faculty members and modest cuts in supplies and equipment budgets, would have allowed you to meet your target less destructively. Moreover, remember that your chairs can serve you well as an advisory body. (See chapter 18.) A focused meeting in which you establish a $75,000 reduction as the goal and explore with your chairs strategies for attaining that target would almost certainly produce a more carefully considered plan than one you developed on your own.

Transparency Is Essential

All the considerations we've reflected on so far lead us to the most important principle in implementing budget cuts: be as candid as possible as soon as possible with as many people as possible. Budget reductions are difficult for everyone. Students complain about sections of courses becoming larger or more difficult to get into. Faculty members are disturbed by loss of funding for research, travel, or instructional materials.

Parents can't understand why they're "paying all this money when our children can't even get the classes they need." Donors and potential donors become skittish because they're afraid their contributions will be wasted. As difficult as all these situations are, however, there is one essential principle that should serve as your guide:

> When you aren't candid in giving bad news in a bad situation, people will always imagine that the truth is even worse than what you would've told them.

By not sharing disturbing news about the need for a budget cut early in the process, rumor and innuendo will fill the void that should have been filled by your effective leadership. Given the facts, the vast majority of our constituents are reasonable people who both can handle bad news and think constructively about possible solutions. Attempting to fix the problem by yourself or with a small group of trusted advisors only exacerbates the situation. It creates distrust of your leadership methods and resistance to any solution you may propose. It's far better to inform people about the extent of the problem as early as you can, demonstrate that you're taking the situation seriously, and enlist them in finding a way of resolving the matter. *yes* (handwritten)

Conclusion

At its core, budget reduction doesn't involve strategies that are any different from those you'd use in planning or expanding a budget. The goal is to be guided by your strategic plan, vision for your unit, and good common sense. Avoid draining any particular line item simply because it's a convenient target. You're not a lion and budget items aren't herds of wildebeests that you should attack, looking for the slowest-moving victim as your earliest prey. Your approach to budget cuts should be one that allows your unit to advance toward its strategic goals at the same time that it tightens its belt in less-than-critical areas. Above all, be forthright in presenting what needs to be done and encouraging sound, constructive ideas from others for achieving that objective.

REFERENCES

Buller, J. L. (2015). *Change leadership in higher education: A practical guide to academic transformation.* San Francisco, CA: Jossey-Bass.
Cadle, J., Paul, D., & Turner, P. (2010). *Business analysis techniques: Seventy-two essential tools for success.* London: British Computer Society.

RESOURCES

Dickeson, R. C. (2010). *Prioritizing academic programs and services: Real-locating resources to achieve strategic balance* (Rev. and updated ed.). San Francisco, CA: Jossey-Bass.

Eckel, P. D. (2009). *Changing course: Making the hard decisions to eliminate academic programs*. Lanham, MD: Rowman & Littlefield.

MacTaggart, T. J. (2010). *Academic turnarounds: Restoring vitality to challenged American colleges and universities*. Lanham, MD: Rowman & Littlefield.

Schuster, J. H., Smith, D. G., Sund, K. C., & Yamada M. M. (1994). *Strategic governance: How to make big decisions better*. Phoenix, AZ: American Council on Education/Oryx Press.

Shin, J. C., & Teichler, U. (2014). *The future of the post-massified university at the crossroads: Restructuring systems and functions*. Heidelberg, Germany: Springer.

Wolverton, M., Gmelch, W. H., Montez, J., & Nies, C. T. (2001). *The changing nature of the academic deanship*. ASHE-ERIC Higher Education Research Report, vol. *28*, no. 1. San Francisco, CA: Jossey-Bass.

37

A SCENARIO ANALYSIS ON THE BUDGET OF THE COLLEGE OR UNIVERSITY

For a discussion of how scenario analyses are structured and suggestions on how to use this exercise most productively, see the beginning of chapter 7. A scenario analysis for provosts appears in the online content accompanying this book.

Case Study for Deans

Imagine that it's time for you to start preparing your budget proposal for the coming fiscal year. Your institution follows a practice of historical budgeting rather than zero-base or performance-based budgeting, so unless you propose a change or an overall cut is mandated by your upper administration, next year's budget for your unit will essentially be identical to your current year's budget. (On these different approaches to budgeting, see chapter 33.) Nothing that you have heard to date leads you to expect that upper administration will impose a budget cut over the coming year. In fact, because enrollment has been increasing, it's likely that you'll be able to request the first significant increase to your budget in many years.

As you sit down to organize your thoughts for the budget proposal, you find that you have unmet needs that could form part of your request. The order in which these needs are listed next doesn't represent a priority order, merely the random order in which you've encountered them in your notes or in the requests that you've received from your department chairs:

A. The department that offers your institution's largest major is desperately in need of a new full-time faculty line in order to meet the demand for students. You've already increased section size in as many courses as you possibly can and adjusted the course rotation to its maximum efficiency. Without a new full-time faculty line, this large program will see reductions in quality that could soon hurt enrollment as well as the department's national reputation.

B. Salaries in your college lag behind those of other colleges at your university, as well as those of similar colleges at other universities. In part, this problem has been caused by rapid growth in the disciplines that you supervise, causing you to devote a portion of your raise pool each year to new faculty and staff positions rather than salary increases. You've been waiting for a good budget year to remedy that situation, which has become critical. Last year, several of your best faculty members left the institution for better-paying jobs elsewhere.

C. The disciplines in your college are highly dependent on technology. The institution's technology funding has been insufficient to upgrade this equipment as often as your college requires in its effort to remain competitive. You're in desperate need of a large, permanent increase in your college's technology fund to address this issue.

D. Travel funding in your college has remained flat for many years. It is now woefully insufficient. You are currently able to fund only about $350 per faculty member per year in travel for scholarship. Because of rising costs for airfare, hotels, and conference registration, the actual need per faculty member in your area is at least five times your currently budgeted amount. Several tenure decisions have recently gone against faculty members in your college whom you believe made an important contribution and deserved to be tenured; the reason cited for these decisions was "insufficient presentation of scholarship at national meetings." You're convinced that your meager travel budget is at least partly responsible for your faculty members' inability to attend national meetings.

E. There has long been discussion of adding a new emphasis to one of the departments in your college. In order to achieve this goal, however, you'll need to begin phasing in several new faculty positions and one additional staff position over three or four years. If you don't begin pursuing this initiative soon, your college is likely to fall behind its peer and aspiration institutions, which have already established strong programs related to this area of emphasis.

F. Students in one of the disciplines contained in your college are failing at an alarming rate in introductory-level courses required for their major. You've conducted a study exploring the reasons that this has occurred and you've discovered that successful programs in this discipline maintain a well-staffed tutorial center. Since the discipline is declining in majors, you've concluded that its long-term success can be achieved only if it creates one of these intensive, well-staffed, discipline-specific tutorial centers.

G. A department in your college has requested three additional full-time faculty members. Without this expansion, the department chair states, it's highly unlikely that the discipline will be successful in its bid for reaccreditation from its professional accrediting body.

H. Your institution has recently allowed colleges to have their own development officers—as long as the college can fund the position from within its own budget. To achieve this goal, your college would require an increase in its continuing budget. Nevertheless, you believe that having your own development officer might return to your college many times what it pays out each year in salary and benefits to retain such a person.

I. The dean from another college has told you repeatedly that students majoring in that college's disciplines are being delayed in their programs because the service courses that your college offers keep closing out too soon. You've raised enrollment caps as far as you believe to be appropriate, and you can provide the relief the other college requires only by hiring four additional full-time faculty members.

J. A recent needs assessment indicated that students in your college would be much more successful in finding employment or being accepted into graduate school if they had experience presenting and defending their original research at an undergraduate research conference. No appropriate conference of this type takes place anywhere near your school. In order to achieve this goal for your college, you'd have to fund the conference yourself each year or create a large enough fund to pay the students' expenses to travel to conferences that are at least five hundred miles away.

K. Aside from your meager travel budget, your college has never had its own faculty development program. You have no resources to conduct workshops and other forms of training on effective classroom techniques, promoting active learning, increasing student engagement and academic success, grant writing, submitting research proposals, and the like. Since the institution itself has no plans on the horizon to provide such training, you believe that the faculty of your college will be best served if you can start your own faculty development program. You can't do that without increased funding.

L. Because you are short-staffed in a number of key academic areas, you know that the most cost-effective way of providing additional sections of courses would be a permanent increase to your adjunct budget. Because adjunct faculty members are hired at your institution on only a per-term basis, this solution provides you with the most flexibility in meeting the course demands of your students. Also, because adjunct faculty members do not receive benefits, you have calculated that for approximately the same cost of a full-time, tenure-track faculty member, you could add more than twenty sections taught by adjuncts.

M. Your own office has been insufficiently staffed for many years. Because you have no one assigned to monitor the budget, deal with student requests for course overrides and policy exceptions, and provide administrative support to faculty searches, you have had to handle most of these responsibilities yourself. This situation has limited the time you're able to spend on grant development, donor visits, and meetings with program officers at major foundations, all of which could significantly improve your college's financial situation. You believe that requesting another assistant dean, who would then be assigned many of the duties you can't tackle yourself, would quickly pay for itself and produce additional revenue that could help fund your college's other pressing needs.

How do you go about determining which of these needs are among your unit's highest priorities? If you were to rank all of the items in a single list by their importance, what would your ranking look like?

Considerations

1. How might your budgetary priorities change if your institution's strategic plan contained each of the following statements? (As you conduct this exercise, assume that only one of the statements may be found in the strategic plan at any one time. Then reconsider your priorities in light of the new information.) "Within ten years, this institution will be nationally recognized as . . . "

    a. " . . . having given the first priority to the full range of student needs in every decision that it makes."

    b. " . . . one of the top five research-oriented institutions of its region."

    c. " . . . providing the highest quality of instruction and dedicated to the academic success of its students."

d. " . . . a model for efficiency in all of the services that it provides, fully respectful of the sacrifices students make to pay tuition, donors make to contribute support, and the taxpayers of the state make to defray costs."

e. " . . . having attained discipline-specific accreditation in every program for which such accreditation is possible."

f. " . . . a national leader in both its retention and graduation rates."

g. " . . . on the cutting edge technologically in all the disciplines it teaches."

h. " . . . placing a priority on the needs of all its constituents: students, their parents, community supporters, faculty members, staff members, and alumni."

2. Suppose that your institution's strategic plan included a goal that you believed was philosophically wrong or ill considered. For instance, what if your institution's strategic plan gave high priority to . . .

a. . . . granting students access to classes by increasing the number of adjuncts hired, thus increasing the total number of sections offered? Nevertheless, you believe that the quality of education provided to the students suffers through an already excessive reliance on adjuncts, and you fear that accrediting bodies will look adversely on this trend. How do you handle budget item 1L in this case, since the strategic plan and your personal outlook are in conflict?

b. . . . expanding existing academic programs into innovative, even experimental new areas? You believe, however, that the institution's actual funding has barely been sufficient to maintain current programs, much less expand into risky new areas. How do you handle budget item 1E, since the strategic plan and your personal outlook are in conflict?

3. Two possible items for your budget, 1H and 1M, concern positions that you believe will more than pay for themselves, probably even generating enough additional income to fund other priorities on your list.

a. How do you make the case (to both upper administration and members of your own college) that it may be preferable to secure funding for an item that isn't itself a high priority but that could increase funding for several items that are high priorities?

b. Suppose you're preparing your budget request in a highly politicized environment. The dean who preceded you frequently requested additions to the dean's office staff and operating budget while departmental needs went unaddressed. This practice has made your faculty highly cynical of any request from the dean's office that doesn't immediately serve the needs of academic programs. You're new to your deanship and do not yet have a track record of strong faculty support that has enabled you to earn their trust. Nevertheless, you believe that adding a college development officer and associate dean will truly serve the faculty's needs better in the long term. At the same time, you're aware that most members of the faculty will be skeptical, perhaps even hostile, to such a proposal. Do you make this proposal anyway?

4. Suppose that item 1A was, according to both your strategic plan and your personal conviction, your highest priority. Nevertheless, funding this position would be so expensive that you believe this request may be ignored by the budget review committee if you give it precedence in your proposal. Items 1D, 1J, and 1K are, respectively, your second, third, and fourth priorities. You believe that all three of them could be funded for less than the position outlined in item 1A. Nevertheless, your upper administration is unlikely to fund these requests unless you argue that they are your top priorities. Is it ever legitimate to resort to realpolitik and structure your priorities according to what's more likely to be funded than according to your actual convictions? Assume that all these items are needed, but that the position discussed in item 1A is simply needed far more than the other items.

Suggestions

The way in which you evaluate these funding priorities will reveal a great deal about your own decision-making processes in developing a budget proposal. You'll probably have a very obvious preference in situations where you have an established mandate from your institution's strategic plan that corresponds well with your own beliefs and convictions. But what about those messy situations where the plan tells you one thing but your gut tells you another? Certainly you don't want to ignore the guidance of your strategic plan casually or frequently. If you find yourself setting budgetary priorities year after year that deviate from your institution's strategic plan, then something is decidedly wrong. Either the plan itself is poorly designed (and you need to have a serious discussion with the upper administration about why it should be changed), your personal priorities are distorting your ability to see what is in the best interest of your institution as a whole, or you just aren't the right person for your position. It would be a good idea to conduct a candid, objective analysis of why your priorities seem so frequently to be different from those that your institution as a whole has deemed to be important. Once you're able to discern precisely where this disconnect resides, you'll have a better understanding of how you should act in response.

If you truly believe that it is better for your unit to pursue a priority different from that suggested by your institution's established strategic goals—and you've come to this conclusion only once or twice in the time you've held your current position—then go ahead and make the strongest case you can for your priorities. Remember the following important principle:

> One of the most important items in any dean's job description is chief exception maker. If it weren't occasionally necessary to make exceptions to existing policies, plans, or procedures, colleges would simply have rule books; they wouldn't need deans.

In other words, effective deans realize that strategic plans are important road maps for an institution's future, but they are only road maps. They can't cover every contingency that may arise after they're created. Just as only foolish pilgrims completely ignore their road map and thus are unlikely to reach their appointed destination, so do only foolish deans completely ignore their institution's strategic plans. But pilgrims are also foolish if they thoughtlessly adhere to their map despite changing circumstances, such as a washed-out route, a potentially productive side trip, or the construction of a new bridge that can shorten their journey. You should be willing to advocate for the rare departure from your institution's strategic plan as long as you can legitimately defend its importance to others.

PART SIX

THE OPPORTUNITIES AND CHALLENGES OF BEING AN ACADEMIC LEADER

38

DEALING WITH EMPLOYEE CHALLENGES

In the best of all possible worlds, everyone who works at a college or university would be productive, dedicated, efficient, and a good colleague. Unfortunately, most academics have to contend with at least one person (and often many more) who either cannot or will not work cooperatively and effectively as a member of a larger institutional team. For this reason, deans and provosts need to consider how to deal with the problems caused by employees whose work is not meeting standards in terms of their productivity, quality, or attitude. Addressing these issues requires explore questions like these:

- Under what circumstances should you attempt to change an employee's behavior?
- At what point should you conclude that changing a person's behavior is no longer possible and that the employee should be terminated?
- Are there other strategies to use when termination isn't an option or isn't desirable, and yet someone's behavior isn't improving despite your best efforts?

In most cases, academic leaders will find that their efforts at dealing with employee challenges are much more effective if they adopt an eight-step plan.

Step 1: Clarify the Problem

In many cases, our initial awareness of a serious issue with an employee's behavior can be rather vague or based on a feeling rather than clear and indisputable facts. For example, we might think something like, "That person's ruining morale around here because (s)he's so negative all the time," or, "Those two people just need to get along better; the constant tension they produce is hurting our whole program." But such general impressions don't help you solve the problem. If you're going to fix the problem, you need to determine precisely what behavior is causing your challenges, where those challenges tend to occur, and why that particular behavior is problematic enough that it needs to be addressed. In other words, there are three questions to ask.

1. What harm do I see being done?
2. What specific behaviors are causing that harm?
3. What changes in behavior would be sufficient to bring about more desirable results?

It's important to distinguish relatively minor but annoying behaviors—pet peeves that may get on your nerves but don't really have a negative effect on anyone's work—from truly disruptive behavior.

> People are entitled to their own personalities, even if we may not happen to like their attitudes or mannerism. What employees are not entitled to is behavior that makes it harder for you or others to get your work done.

For instance, if people are reluctant to speak their minds in meetings because someone on the faculty or staff resorts to bullying tactics and ridicules or insults other people for their ideas, it's important to focus on the actions, not the person's attitude. Saying something like, "Stop thinking you're better than everyone else," isn't appropriate; the employee has a perfect right to think that he or she's better than everyone else. What you're really concerned about is the chilling effect that this person's behavior has on others at the meeting. Similarly, if excessive gossiping is ruining morale or causing deadlines to be missed, you would address what the employee is doing that's causing the problem, not his or her nosiness or interest in issues that you don't think are very important. If an employee's style of dress is interfering with work because it's distracting, that's an issue you can deal with. But if it's merely out of style or not something that you'd wear yourself, it's probably not the sort of concern that requires intervention. (As the employee's mentor, you may at some point want to have a diplomatic coaching session with the person on how his or her dress may be limiting any possibilities for career advancement, but if the employee chooses not to take this advice, it's usually not worth pursuing.)

Each of us has idiosyncrasies and other personal traits that through constant exposure can be annoying to others. But each of us is also entitled to a certain degree of personal freedom, and even in the workplace, that freedom should be respected.

Step 2: Create an Action Plan

Since employee problems vary in severity, different issues require different levels of response. You don't want to fire someone because of a problem you could address through a less extreme measure. Replacing employees is almost always an expensive, time-consuming process. Besides, there may be positive ways in which the employee is contributing to the work of your area that will be lost if you resort to termination at the first sign of a problem. When someone's fired, it's a trauma for the person, and it can also be hard on the people left behind. Their workload is going to increase, at least until a replacement can be found, and they may wonder whether they'll be the next person to be let go for a relatively minor breach in protocol. For these reasons, it's usually best to help the employee improve rather than proceed to termination if there's a reasonable chance that the problem can be fixed.

In medical emergences, the term *triage* (from the French *trier*, meaning "to sort out") is often used to describe the process of distinguishing the severely wounded from those suffering less life-threatening injuries and focusing attention on those most likely to benefit from medical care from those whose injuries are so extensive that they're beyond hope. In a similar way, we can perform triage on employee challenges as a way of determining the best action plan to address the problem. This type of triage would place the employee challenge into one of the following four categories:

1. The problem is likely to be solved through intervention
2. The problem is unlikely to be solved, but its negative effects can be managed
3. The problem is unlikely to be solved or managed, but its negative effects can be isolated
4. The problem is unlikely to be solved, managed, or isolated

Each category has a different course of action. A problem that's likely to be solved through intervention is one that we might address by coaching the employee, reassigning certain responsibilities, changing the location of the person's office or desk, providing more specific guidance on how to perform certain tasks, calling the person's attention to the issue in a performance evaluation, and the like. This category usually includes problems the person is either unaware of or for which he or she currently lacks the skills needed to improve. The assumption in such a situation is that with proper instruction or minor changes to the employee's environment (such as moving a talkative person away from the copy room so that there will be less of an opportunity to engage passersby in prolonged conversations), the problem can be solved and better results obtained.

While everyone would agree that it's desirable to solve problems whenever you can, the realities of interpersonal relationships suggest that certain types of problems can't be completely solved. Nevertheless, a number of these more intractable problems can be managed or isolated. What's the difference between managing and isolating a problem? A problem is managed if steps are taken to reduce its severity, even though the difficulty doesn't go away completely. A problem is isolated if its severity can't be reduced, but steps can be taken to contain or limit its effects.

Suppose two people in your area can't get along, and their animosity toward one another is preventing key committees from doing their work and driving valued members of the faculty to apply for jobs elsewhere. Despite repeated discussions and attempts at mediation, you've been unable to solve the problem and have concluded that both parties are at fault to a roughly equal extent. Managing the problem might include meeting with each person separately and then gathering the two of them together to establish ground rules for their conduct in the future. You might also reorganize committee assignments or other responsibilities so as to reduce the amount of contact between the two faculty members. You might even consider establishing some incentives for the two parties to work together more collegially, such as assigning them each an extra teaching assistant if they can get through an entire year without causing problems at faculty meetings. In taking these approaches, you haven't solved their problem, but you've managed to keep it in check for the benefit of the program.

Isolating a problem is a more extreme solution than merely managing it. It's the approach you might take if, for instance, you have a tenured faculty member whose noncollegial treatment of the junior faculty is bad but not bad enough to warrant revocation of tenure. If you've tried solving the problem and failed, then tried managing the problem and failed, your last resort might be to separate the problem from the people who are affected by it—in other words, separate the person who's causing the problem from others in the program. For example, the problematic faculty member might be "excused" from certain committee work, not as a reward for his or her poor behavior but as a purely practical response to an ongoing concern in your area. It's not the most desirable solution by any means, but it is a solution, and it's sometimes the most expedient way a dean or provost can fix a problem. No one likes to hear about cases where troublesome faculty members were given extended periods of leave with pay or other incentives as an encouragement to retire early. But if it comes down to a choice between ongoing problems and a less-than-satisfactory solution to them, many deans and provosts opt for an imperfect solution over an enduring problem.

Another situation in which you may decide it's appropriate to isolate a problem can occur when someone's being rude or offensive at a public meeting. Passions often run high when faculty meet, and the occasional outburst can be safely ignored as an indication of how committed people are to their positions (or how much they enjoy grandstanding in order to provoke a reaction). But sometimes a remark will be so inappropriate that your intervention will be necessary in order to prevent more serious problems. Shutting down faculty members who are truly being abusive is actually in their own best interests, since it may prevent them from saying things that could have serious repercussions. While you never want to interfere with genuine debate or silence the voices of anyone who has the right to express an opinion, you may occasionally find it necessary to isolate someone who's being offensive by saying something like, "That comment has absolutely nothing to do with what we're discussing here. At the right time and in the right place, you can express your opinion about the issue, but at no time do you have the right to abuse a colleague. I think Dr. Patrick was making an important point before your interruption. Don't interrupt again. You're out of order, and I'm not recognizing you as having the floor. This meeting is going to focus on the topics we came here to discuss. If you interrupt again, I'll have to insist that you leave. In fact, you may feel free to leave now if you like." This type of response should be reserved as the nuclear option since it's likely to cause a lasting, and perhaps even permanent, breach between you and the faculty member. It's an approach to consider only when the person's interruptions have been so frequent or so detrimental to the work at hand that no other choice is available to you.

In the most extreme cases, you may need to terminate an employee when the problem cannot be solved, managed, or isolated, an issue that I address in chapter 39. In all such cases, be certain to follow your institution's written policies for dismissal. Keep both the president and the office of human resources fully informed of what is occurring. If your institution has a staff attorney or legal counsel under contract, you should be in touch with that person before you engage in any irrevocable action. When giving notice of the dismissal, present it in the form required by your institution's procedures and, if at all possible, have a witness present. A witness will be able to clarify any misstatements about what was said or left unsaid if the faculty member who was dismissed challenges the procedure. Give a clear, documented reason for the dismissal if you're required to do so. Certain situations, such as nonrenewal of untenured faculty members or dismissal of hourly employees, may not require giving a justification at your institution; your legal counsel can provide guidance about which situations fall into this category. Always be sure not to offer more detail than is absolutely necessary. The more of an explanation you provide, the more opportunity you are creating for a later challenge.

Step 3: Look for Underlying Causes

If you've concluded that the personnel problem you're addressing can be solved or managed, your next step will be to explore the root causes of the problem. Sometimes people cause trouble in meetings merely because they're unaware of how others perceive their negativity and brusque tone. They believe they're "just telling it like it is" and have no idea that their colleagues see them, and not the issues that they bring up, as the real problem. Other employees are so focused on their narrow specialties that they don't understand how every aspect of what's done at the institution must fit into a larger picture. Some people become fixated with rules or traditions, believing that if you don't adhere to every letter of every policy or do things exactly the same way they were done decades ago, chaos will result. Still others have a need for attention or a desire to feel in control of their lives. And other employees simply find it difficult to let go of past grievances or perceived injustices, continually dredging up matters that their colleagues have long since ceased to care about or find relevant to their current situations.

By identifying the underlying causes of someone's difficulty with others, you'll develop a much more constructive course of action than if you simply conclude that the person has poor interpersonal skills or is habitually rude. As part of a development program for the faculty and staff, periodic workshops in constructive ways of working in groups, developing plans, and making suggestions can help people acquire the skills they need to do their jobs better. People who have been particularly in need of this advice might even be required, perhaps as part of their performance appraisals, to attend the workshops and work with a mentor to explore possible ways of implementing what they've learned. You will then have an opportunity to refer to the content of these workshops whenever you need to provide guidance about an inappropriate behavior. "Well, as we've been discussing in our sessions on positive group dynamics," you might say, "how we should really be addressing that concern is . . . " Resources such as books by Patrick Lencioni (2002, 2005) can be particularly effective as starting points for any sessions you might wish to conduct on how your area can work together more effectively as a team.

For people whose behavioral problems appear to stem from sources other than a lack of knowledge about how to contribute constructively, a different tack will be necessary. You may need to enlist the help of others at your institution to ensure that the negative behavior isn't inadvertently being reinforced. For example, if certain members of your area always seem to confront a particular faculty member after a public outburst (thus increasing the duration of the outburst), you might discuss with those faculty members more effective ways of handling these situations: they can change the focus of the discussion to a different topic, respond in a manner less likely to push the buttons of whomever is causing the outburst, or simply ignore the situation rather than feeding its intensity. You can even use other members of the program in a more passive way to redirect negative behavior by saying, for example, "From the looks that I'm getting, many of you aren't interested in addressing this issue yet again. Is that correct? Shall we move on to something else instead?"

Step 4: Provide Specific Expectations

We saw in chapter 28 that attempting to improve problematic behavior through general advice (such as, "Try to be more collegial," or, "You need to care more about your job") is rarely productive. Just as in faculty evaluations, the best way to deal with all types of employee challenges is to be clear about precisely what change in behavior you expect to see and set a deadline by which that improvement must be made. Since we've already considered several ways of phrasing statements of this sort for faculty members, the following examples reflect the types of issues that may arise with administrators who report to you or with members of the staff:

o "Effective immediately you are to be on time and ready for work each day when the office opens at 8:00 a.m. and to leave no earlier than when the office closes at 5:00 p.m."

○ "No later than March 15, [year], you are to have completed the office of human resources' training program in customer service."

○ "In order to bring your computer skills up to the level required by your job description, you must complete at least an advanced level of spreadsheet training and an intermediate level of database training by the end of this academic year. You may acquire this training either in-house through the staff development center or off-campus through an external agency such as CareerTrack or Microsoft. When your training is complete, your skill level is to be reassessed by the office of human resources, with the results approved by me as your supervisor."

○ "Following our discussion today, there are to be no further outbursts of anger or hostility toward me, any of your coworkers, students, or visitors to our campus. As I explained to you in our meeting, I alone will serve as arbiter of what constitutes an inappropriate level of anger or hostility."

○ "Beginning immediately, you will limit your personal calls during business hours to no more than ten minutes per day and will restrict the volume of your conversation to a level that doesn't interfere with the work of your colleagues."

Also as with such statements in faculty evaluations, these expectations should be followed by an indication of what sanction will follow if the goal is not met:

○ "Failure to do so will result in your ineligibility for any salary increase funding for up to three years."

○ "Failure to do so will result in your reclassification and reassignment."

○ "Failure to do so will result in your immediate termination."

Step 5: Focus on the Positive

It's certainly true that many challenging employees can't be "fixed" no matter what we do, and their negative behaviors are too deeply ingrained in habit to be altered even by our best efforts. But in other cases, the threat of sanctions, combined with clear advice on how to improve, can produce a significant change in a person's work and the start of an entirely new working relationship for that employee. When that occurs, it's often helpful to find some appropriate way for the person to begin making a more positive contribution to the institution.

The idea behind this strategy is to start replacing the person's old identity as "the troublemaker" or "that rude administrative assistant in the dean's office" with a new identity as a constructive and valued member of the community. Even more important, it gives the people who are offered these opportunities a way to see themselves in a different light and distance themselves from the problems of the past. Examples of what you might suggest include heading up the office's effort for a charitable campaign, serving on a significant committee designed to bring in external speakers, or editing an important document as part of a reaccreditation effort. By offering this opportunity, you demonstrate that you haven't lost confidence in the person. Now that the problem is behind you, you're putting that negative energy aside and beginning to work together on a new basis.

Step 6: Use Mentoring to Build on Progress

At times, your very status as the provost or dean hinders your ability to mentor an employee effectively. Regardless of how you may view your role, the people who report to you may see you as the "boss" and fear that any discussion they have with you about their problems or frustrations may be giving their supervisor information about their own failings. In these cases, assigning a trusted colleague of the employee as a peer mentor may be an effective way to build on the person's progress in improving his or her behavior. A peer is able to say things that you simply can't say ("I want you to consider for a moment how your behavior is affecting me and everyone else who works with you") and to provide advice in a non-threatening manner. If you offer to respect the confidential nature of the discussions between the mentor and the employee, then you must do so absolutely. The peer mentor may learn personal details of the employee's life or hear about problems that that person would feel uncomfortable sharing with you directly. In all respects, the peer mentor's role should be formative and constructive, complementing the summative and evaluative role that you will need to take at some time as the employee's ultimate supervisor. (On the difference between formative and summative evaluation, see chapter 28.)

Step 7: Reward Ongoing Progress

Anyone who has served as a supervisor eventually learns that positive reinforcement (carrots) has more value in the long term than do punishments (sticks). Threats of sanction may initially be necessary in order to get an employee's attention and to underscore the severity of a situation. They may also produce an initial dramatic change of behavior. But ultimately it's much more effective to provide support for good behavior than to focus solely on threats. Sincere praise for a job well done, restoration of certain privileges that were removed as the result of a sanction, and other means rewarding the employee's constructive efforts can help make a temporary change become permanent.

Step 8: Keep a Paper Trail

As much as you want to emphasize the positive in helping the employee change his or her behavior, it's also important for you to keep detailed documentation of all you've done to help the person, indicating what your expectations were and what he or she has done differently as a result. Maintain a written record of all conversations with the employee, and record the advice that you've given in each of them. Remember that not every problem is fixable and even when improvements do occur, some backsliding is possible.

In the event of a negative personnel decision, you need clear documentation outlining precisely when you first recognized the problem, how you brought it to the faculty member's attention, what steps you took to improve the situation, and why you remain dissatisfied with that employee's behavior. Your written record will also be an important training device for you as you consider which approaches worked and which approaches were ineffective the next time a similar problem arises.

Conclusion

Not every type of employee challenge is something you should handle on your own. For example, in dealing with complex matters like substance abuse, your office of human resources probably has guidelines on what type of intervention should occur and who should do it. Many colleges and universities have formal processes for people to obtain counseling for problems that may be covered under the Americans with Disabilities Act. Take special care to follow your institutional guidelines scrupulously in all such situations.

REFERENCES

Lencioni, P. M. (2002). *The five dysfunctions of a team: A leadership fable.* San Francisco, CA: Jossey-Bass.
Lencioni, P. M. (2005). *Overcoming the five dysfunctions of a team: A field guide for leaders, managers, and facilitators.* San Francisco, CA: Jossey-Bass.

RESOURCES

Bruce, A. (2005). *Perfect phrases for documenting employee: Performance problems*. New York, NY: McGraw-Hill.

Cheldelin, S. I., & Lucas, A. F. (2004). *The Jossey-Bass academic administrator's guide to conflict resolution*. San Francisco, CA: Jossey-Bass.

Coffman, J. R. (2005). *Work and peace in academe: Leveraging time, money, and intellectual energy through managing conflict*. Bolton, MA: Anker.

DelPo, A., & Guerin, L. (2013). *Dealing with problem employees: A legal guide* (7th ed.). Berkeley, CA: Nolo.

Falcone, P. (2009). *101 tough conversations to have with employees: A manager's guide to addressing performance, conduct, and discipline challenges*. New York, NY: AMACOM.

Falcone, P. (2010). *101 sample write-ups for documenting employee performance problems: A guide to progressive discipline and termination* (2nd ed.). New York, NY: AMACOM.

Higgerson, M. L., & Joyce, T. A. (2007). *Effective leadership communication: A guide for department chairs and deans for managing difficult situations and people*. Bolton, MA: Anker.

Leaming, D. (1998). *Academic leadership: A practical guide to chairing the department*. Bolton, MA: Anker.

Lieberman, D. J. (2005). *How to change anybody: Proven techniques to reshape anyone's attitude, behavior, feelings, or beliefs*. New York, NY: St. Martin's Press.

Lloyd, K. (2006). *Jerks at work: How to deal with people problems and problem people* (rev. ed.). Franklin Lakes, NJ: Career Press.

Masters, M. F., & Albright, R. R. (2002). *The complete guide to conflict resolution in the workplace*. New York, NY: American Management Association.

Scott, G. G. (2004). *A survival guide for working with humans: Dealing with whiners, back-stabbers, know-it-alls, and other difficult people*. New York, NY: AMACOM.

Topchik, G. S. (2001). *Managing workplace negativity*. New York, NY: American Management Association.

39

TERMINATING A FACULTY MEMBER

By far the most difficult situations any administrator will face are those that involve negative decisions about major personnel matters. Turning someone down for promotion, hiring another candidate into a position, and refusing a request for a salary increase all present significant challenges and can result in unpleasant, even highly confrontational discussions. Of all these difficult cases, however, there's none that's more challenging for deans and provosts than terminating a member of the faculty. Even staff terminations, while difficult, aren't usually as complex and don't often have as many stages of appeal. Unlike those on the faculty, staff members usually have annual contracts and carefully delineated job descriptions; they're subject to policies supervised by an office of human resources, a unit that can give academic leaders a great deal of guidance and flexibility when dealing with these difficult situations.

Faculty members typically have a type of job assignment that makes it more difficult to quantify or demonstrate conclusively why it's necessary to let a specific person go. For instance, what indicators can administrators point to as clearly establishing a lack of collegiality? How easy is it to document unsatisfactory teaching? What can one do to illustrate "insufficient progress in research" when the way in which one discipline manifests scholarship is often completely different from that of another discipline?

In most situations that deans and provosts will face, the decision to terminate a faculty member falls into one of six categories:

1. The faculty member receives annual contracts, and his or her services are no longer needed.

2. The faculty member receives annual contracts and is being nonre-newed for reasons other than because his or her services are no longer needed.
3. The faculty member receives annual contracts but is being terminated "for good cause" before the expiration of a contract.
4. The faculty member is tenured and is being terminated "for good cause."
5. The institution is facing severe financial exigency and is eliminating an entire program or class of employee in an effort to preserve its long-term survival.
6. The faculty member's program is being phased out for reasons other than financial exigency.

Each of these situations involves different considerations and may well require different actions from the dean or provost.

A Term Employee Is No Longer Needed

At most institutions, faculty members on annual or noncontinuing con-tracts include all part-time or adjunct faculty members, instructors with temporary appointments, and probationary faculty members who are on tenure track but have not yet been granted tenure. Some institutions and systems also permit the hiring of nontenure-earning instructors who may have heavier teaching responsibilities than their tenure-earning colleagues but consequently also have lower service and research expectations than do tenure-track faculty members.

In the vast majority of cases when the services of individuals on annual contracts are no longer required, the institution has significant lead time during which the individual can be notified. For example, if there's a plan to collapse several part-time positions into a single tenure-track line on which a national search will be conducted, the supervisor will have ample opportunity to notify those affected by the institution's intentions so that they can either apply for the full-time position or make arrangements for employment elsewhere. Similarly, faculty members who are hired as sabbatical replacements or to fill other short-term needs have reason to assume (and can easily be informed if they don't initially understand) that the nature of their employment is necessarily confined to a specific period after which they will need to seek other opportunities. There may at times be uncomfortable situations when a term employee's hopes for continued employment triumph over their more realistic expectations, and these situations become more common the longer a temporary employee is employed.

Nevertheless, there are clear reasons that the institution can't be expected to offer annual contracts beyond its need for the service of someone on a replacement contract. Of all the situations that we'll consider, these tend to be the easiest to handle and to involve relatively few challenges or confrontations.

A Term Employee Is Dismissed for Other Reasons

Aside from no longer needing someone's service, the most common reason for terminating a person who holds an annual contract is that the employee's work hasn't been suitable in one way or another. Perhaps you can point to a demonstrated cause such as insubordination, misuse of funds, or the failure to follow established procedures. Perhaps there isn't any demonstrated cause for the termination other than that the person is "a bad fit" for the position or "we think we can do better."

The most important thing that deans and provosts need to know about this type of termination is that no reason is actually required when you're not renewing the contract of an annual employee. Indeed, some institutions and university systems will not even permit you to provide the employee with the reason for a nonrenewal at the end of an annual contract. Furthermore, even if you are permitted to do so, you shouldn't ever state the reason or put it into writing. Why? Stating a reason for a nonrenewal does little more than open the door to a legal challenge that could easily have been avoided. Think of it this way: an annual contract is a self-contained, self-limiting agreement, much like the contract that you might give someone to build your house or paint your kitchen. The builder or painter works for the duration of the contract and, when that task is complete, has no right to expect any future employment from you unless you explicitly offer a new contract. If you aren't satisfied with the work performed by the painter or builder, you don't owe that person a reason for hiring a different painter or builder the next time; you simply hire someone else. Moreover, you're perfectly entitled to hire someone else in the future for any reason or for no reason at all. The terms of the contract with the original worker were fulfilled, and you're free to do whatever you like in the future. Those same rules apply to annual contract employees at a college or university. When you don't renew someone's annual contract, providing a reason isn't required. Doing so only creates the possibility of problems that could easily have been avoided.

As an effective academic leader, you'll want to balance your legal rights and responsibilities to your institution with your professionalism as a supervisor. For this reason, you should always keep in mind that when employees hear that they aren't being continued at your institution, it can be rather similar to hearing a death sentence. Their initial reaction is often one of shock, and for the rest of your conversation, they may not effectively process everything you tell them. Consequently, after they digest the news you've given them and discussed it with their family and friends, they'll frequently have additional questions, concerns, and possibly even anger. You should expect that the employee will try to engage you in further conversations about the nonrenewal. Your challenge will be that while you carefully prepared for the initial conversation and planned what you would and would not say, you can easily be caught off-guard by subsequent conversations. In the best of such circumstances, the employee may make a follow-up appointment. Nevertheless, later discussions can just as easily occur without warning in the hallway, washroom, or a location off campus.

Because of the complexity of these situations, it's a good idea always to expect follow-up conversations when giving someone a notice of nonrenewal. Think through in advance precisely what you'll say and where you'll draw the line in revealing anything more. In truly difficult situations, you may need to say, "I've told you everything I have to say about this matter. From this point on, you'll need to direct those questions to the office of human resources [or to the institution's legal counsel]."

Most important, if you didn't provide reasons for the nonrenewal during your original conversation, don't allow the impromptu nature of subsequent encounters to cause you to deviate from this plan. Out of sheer goodwill, you may be tempted, in a casual chat with the employee, to provide additional information about what he or she could have done better because you'd like to help that person in the future. This type of mentoring too frequently backfires. Even the informal guidance you offer an employee can be construed as a reason for the dismissal. Be as humane and supportive as you can, but don't provide any information in a later conversation with the employee that you intentionally omitted from your initial meeting.

A Term Employee Is Dismissed for Good Cause

Situations where it's necessary to break a contract before it expires tend to be far more complicated than simple nonrenewals that occur after the expiration of a contract. In these cases, you'll need to provide a reason for the dismissal and, in many instances, allow the individual some recourse for due process or appeal.

It should be obvious that breaking a contract must never be done lightly. In anything but the most extreme of situations, it's usually better simply to endure inferior performance until the contract reaches its stated term or to reassign the individual to tasks where he or she can make a more positive contribution. Nevertheless, there are situations where termination for good cause is fully warranted. According to *West's Encyclopedia of American Law*, "good cause" may be defined as

> legally adequate or substantial grounds or reason to take a certain action. The term good cause is a relative one and is dependent upon the circumstances of each individual case.... An employee is said to be dismissed for good cause if the reasons for the termination are work related. However, if the employer simply did not like the employee's personality, this would not ordinarily constitute good cause, unless the employee held a position, such as a salesperson, for which a likable personality was required. (www.encyclopedia.com/doc/1G2–3437702006.html)

The faculty handbooks or human resources manuals of many colleges and universities state that individuals may be dismissed before the expiration of a contract for cause. This use of the phrase *for cause*, while common, is inadvisable for a number of reasons. To begin with, court-established definitions of the phrase deal almost exclusively with the removal of individuals from public office. (See, for example, Nolan and Nolan-Haley, 1990.) That's why the more correct terminology for what colleges and universities are trying to describe is the expression we've been using: *for good cause*. (On the legal precedents for this expression, see Nolan and Nolan-Haley, 1990, and Gifis, 2010.) Most institutions of higher education recognize incompetence, gross immorality, felony, insubordination, violation of contract terms, and failure to follow stated policies as among the reasons for which a faculty member may be terminated before his or her contract expires. At other institutions, the precise definition of the phrase *for good cause* is left undefined but generally involves extremely serious violations of a faculty member's responsibilities as a teacher, scholar, and colleague: plagiarism, violation of the rights of protected classes, contributing to an atmosphere in which an individual's rights of free inquiry and expression are diminished, and abuse of one's position for inappropriate personal gain, for example.

Dismissals for good cause are almost always contentious matters and must be preceded by careful planning, analysis, and consultation. In each instance, you should be sure that at the very least, you have taken the following five steps:

1. *Follow all of your institution's internal procedures.* More challenges to dismissals are upheld because of an institution's failure to follow its own written procedures than for any other reason. Take extra care that each step in your institution's policy on dismissal has been followed to the letter. Adhere carefully to all timetables for notification. If your institution requires a series of oral and written warnings before you can break a contract, be certain that these warnings have occurred. Notify everyone that your institution requires you to bring into the loop. Prepare a checklist of all the steps your institution requires you to take, and then check and recheck that all these steps have been taken.

2. *Maintain proper documentation.* It's in your college's best interests for you to have a clear paper trail that leads up to the faculty member's dismissal. In the best possible scenario, you'll have a series of performance appraisals indicating that the employee was informed of improvements that needed to occur, a timetable by which these actions were required, and indications that the needed improvements didn't occur. With many employees who are on annual contracts, however, performance appraisals don't occur, at least not on a regular basis. The faculty member may have been under contract for too short a time to have been evaluated, or the renewal of the contract itself may have been regarded as the performance appraisal. Even in these situations, however, it's extremely useful to document conversations in which someone spoke to the employee about concerns with his or her performance, e-mail messages illustrating the problems for which the employee is being dismissed, time cards, minutes from meetings, or attendance records suggesting that the employee failed to perform the full functions of the position, or other clear, written evidence that will suggest, to a reasonable observer, that you were justified in terminating the employee before the contract expired.

3. *Work in conjunction with the appropriate offices.* No dismissal for good cause should ever occur without extensive prior discussion with your institution's human resources staff and your legal affairs office or campus attorney. Those offices will help you crosscheck that all your institutional policies have been followed and the proper notifications have been given at the proper times. They will evaluate whether the reason for dismissal is adequate and advise you on such matters as whether you even ought to be taking an action as severe as dismissal in the first place.

Moreover, your consultation with capable, discreet individuals who have probably dealt with many more terminations than you have will provide you with an external scan to make sure that you've asked the right questions, followed the right steps in the right order, and prepared yourself to be asked some potentially difficult questions.

4. *Give all notices of termination with at least one witness present.* It's always advisable to have a third party present when you're dismissing someone. The third party's testimony can be extremely useful if there's ever a question at a later date about what specifically was said, promised, and done. Particularly in cases where you and the employee are of different genders or sexual orientations or where there has been a history of tension and animosity, a witness can verify that the proper policies were followed and that nothing inappropriate occurred behind closed doors. When selecting a witness, it's best to recruit someone from your institution's human resources or legal affairs office who's dealt with other terminations and can offer you guidance about precisely what to do. Meet privately with the witness before joining the employee you will dismiss in order to plan your strategy, go over precisely who will say what, whether a written notice of dismissal will be given to the employee on the spot or at a later date, and remind one another of the importance of discretion and common courtesy in matters of this sort.

5. *Confirm that the dismissal does not violate a protected employee's right to be discharged.* Many laws and statutes protect certain classes of workers from being discharged. These laws and statutes change from time to time. For this reason, begin by consulting the summary of laws relating to protected classes that appears in Anglim (1997) and then consult with legal counsel to determine whether any modifications to Anglim's list have occurred.

A Tenured Faculty Member Is Terminated for Good Cause

Despite common misperceptions to the contrary, tenure does not provide faculty members with lifetime job security. At least, faculty members don't have a right to expect a guarantee of employment without any continued obligations on their part. Tenured faculty members must fulfill all the terms of their contract, demonstrate that they remain competent in their disciplines, and refrain from violating any of the standards that would make them liable to dismissal for good cause. Before the abolition of mandatory retirement ages at American colleges and universities, it would occasionally occur that an institution would endure a tenured faculty member's lack of productivity or declining performance temporarily, knowing that at age sixty-five or seventy, the professor would be compelled to retire in accordance with university policy. But now that mandatory retirement ages are forbidden in the United States, institutions are often compelled to initiate agonizing and often confrontational processes to revoke the tenure of senior faculty members who are no longer performing their responsibilities at an acceptable level.

Posttenure review procedures at many institutions have helped make the evaluation of tenured faculty members somewhat more rigorous and equitable; with posttenure review, every tenured faculty, not just those who are suspected of incompetence or dereliction of duty, must undergo a periodic review of his or her performance. Some tenured faculty members see the handwriting on the wall when they receive an unsatisfactory posttenure review and volunteer to retire. Nevertheless, there are occasional cases in which a tenured faculty member must be forced out of the institution. Even with a well-designed review process in place, the revocation of any faculty member's tenure for good cause is likely to involve a high degree of acrimony and multiple levels of appeal, making it one of the most challenging situations that any dean or provost can face.

While tenure isn't the lifetime sinecure it's frequently depicted as in the popular media, it does provide a faculty member with two things that a nontenured faculty member has no right to expect: being informed of the reason for a dismissal and receiving access to some form of due process. When you give a tenured faculty member a reason for dismissal, you'll probably adhere to the standards of dismissal for good cause that were discussed earlier in this chapter. But the due process that you make available to the faculty member can vary widely from institution to institution. The type of due process that someone is entitled to depends to a great extent on the right or interest that has been affected by a negative decision. As a right or interest becomes greater, so does the amount of due process a person is entitled to. For example, students applying to an institution aren't entitled to any due process at all if they're not accepted for admission. Since they haven't yet enrolled, they have no right or interest that's being taken away. But current students who are being expelled for disciplinary reasons have a greater right of due process because they have a current right of enrollment that's being withdrawn. The same principle holds true for faculty members. In cases where a major interest such as one's livelihood is at stake, they are entitled to a higher level of due process than if they were merely given a strong verbal censure by a provost or dean.

Whatever form the due process takes must be established in advance of the particular case (there can be no development of procedures simply to make it easier to get rid of a specific employee), and in most situations, it should offer the faculty member at least some opportunity to dispute the grounds for his or her dismissal. One important fact to observe is that due process doesn't always have to involve a formal hearing. From a legal perspective, there are two different kinds of due process:

- Substantive due process, which essentially consists of making sure that the faculty member is treated fairly and that his or her basic rights have not been violated
- Procedural due process, which means that a person has been given due notice of the reason for his or her dismissal and the right to present his or her side of the story

In neither of these senses of the term does the concept of due process guarantee the right of a formal hearing. The opportunity for the faculty member to present his or her perspective as to why the dismissal is unwarranted can consist simply of a forum at which the person is permitted to speak. But because terminations so often lead to grievances or lawsuits, it's not uncommon for the type of due process accorded a faculty member facing dismissal to take the form of an in-house hearing. If your institution follows this practice, you may want to find out whether there are procedures in place that address the following issues:

- Who will be involved in the hearing as active participants or observers? Does the faculty member get to choose any representatives to serve on the board that will render the final decision? Is the faculty member entitled to legal counsel or some alternative form of advocacy or representation? (If lawyers are present representing one side, it is best for both parties to have legal representation in the interest of basic fairness.) Is the session open to other observers, or is it closed? Who is allowed to speak at the hearing? Is it possible for both sides to call witnesses and cross-examine the testimony of those who speak at the session?
- When must the request for due process be received? Is there an automatic review of all decisions to revoke tenure, or must a hearing be requested by the faculty member? Are there restrictions on how soon the hearing must take place? How long are records kept after the hearing?
- Where can an appeal be directed if the result of the hearing is that the decision to revoke tenure is upheld? Where are the official records or transcripts of the hearing stored?

Revocation of tenure is an extremely serious decision for any institution. If you become involved in an issue of this sort, you might experience it only once or at most twice during your tenure as dean or only a handful of times during your service as provost. If you discover that you're facing dismissal of tenured faculty members more frequently than that, there may well be something wrong with your institution's tenure policy, posttenure review procedure, or treatment of its senior faculty.

Finally, it's important to understand the distinction between the denial of tenure and the revocation of tenure. Denial of tenure is a decision not to grant a benefit to a person who doesn't already have it. In effect, a denial-of-tenure case is identical to nonrenewing a faculty member who holds an annual contract. Your system may require, allow, or forbid you to disclose the reasons for this decision, depending on its philosophy with regard to tenure rights. Unless you're specifically required to provide a reason for withholding tenure, you should probably refrain from doing so. An individual who has been denied tenure may have recourse for appeal through the institution's grievance process. Revocation of tenure, however, is a decision to withdraw a benefit from a faculty member who has already earned it. You will always be required to state and defend your reasons for such a weighty decision. A faculty member from whom tenure has been revoked may have recourse for appeal through the institution's disciplinary process.

A Faculty Member Is Terminated Because of Financial Exigency

Although it rarely happens, there can occur a situation in which an institution's financial situation is so precarious that it becomes necessary to reduce staffing in order to prevent economic disaster. The time to plan what steps will be taken in a financial exigency is not, of course, in the midst of the crisis itself, but well in advance of such an emergency, so that planning can be done in a well-considered and dispassionate manner. The strategies that institutions commonly use to reduce staffing during periods of extreme financial exigency often include these:

○ *Last-in, first-out.* In this system, seniority provides a certain degree of job protection. The most recently hired faculty members are those who are released first in difficult financial times, with the order of reductions determined by the longevity of one's employment.

○ *Reduction by contract type.* In this system, types of employment status are placed in a hierarchical order, with reductions determined by that order. Usually this means that part-time faculty members are reduced first, full-time temporary faculty members second, tenure-track assistant professors next, tenured associate professors after that, and tenured full professors last.

○ *Reduction by program demand.* With this approach, academic programs are ranked according to some measurable standard, such as number of student credit hours generated per academic year or average number of majors who graduate during an academic year. Programs that have less demand according to this standard are phased out first.

Regardless of the system used, it's important that the financial exigency policy be established and discussed with the faculty long before there is a need to implement it. If this approach isn't taken, there's likely to be a perception, whether justified or not, that the system was fabricated simply in order to eliminate certain troublemakers on the faculty. Reductions because of financial exigency cause a great deal of tension and distrust even in the most collegial of institutions. These problems will be exacerbated if the institution is perceived as inventing policies out of retribution or as a way of targeting the most highly paid of the faculty.

A Faculty Member Is Terminated Due to Elimination of a Program

Programs are also eliminated for reasons other than financial exigency. At the conclusion of a program review, for instance, it may be determined that a given program is no longer viable because of enrollment trends or projected demands for its majors, incompatibility with institutional mission, or an irremediable lack of quality. In addition, institutions may shift their programmatic emphasis as part of a strategic planning process, mandate from a state legislature, or revised institutional mission as determined by the governing board. In most cases, when eliminating programs for reasons other than financial exigency, institutions attempt to reassign tenured faculty members and other long-term employees to whatever extent possible. A good example of a policy on staff reductions due to the elimination of a program may be found at Utah State University.

> Program discontinuance for academic reasons . . . means the cessation of a program, center, institute, school, department, or college based upon educational and academic considerations. For the purposes of [this policy], educational and academic considerations do not include cyclical or temporary variations in enrollment and/or budgets, but

must reflect long-range judgments that the basic teaching, research, and extension mission of the University will be strengthened by the discontinuance of the program, center, institute, school, department, or college. Program discontinuance does not preclude the reallocation of resources to other academic programs with higher priority based on academic and educational reasons. (www.usu.edu/hr/files/uploads/policies/406.pdf)

This policy makes it clear that positions are not going to be eliminated simply because of a temporary dip in enrollment, but only as part of an ongoing, reflective, well-considered strategy. It also suggests that the resources of these discontinued programs—human resources as well as financial resources—could, at the institution's discretion, be reassigned to programs that are deemed to have a higher priority as a result of this long-term strategy.

A particularly comprehensive policy about how program discontinuations are to be handled is found at California State University, Stanislaus. The process begins with a request for a special program review that may be made by several institutional bodies, including the faculty of the program, the academic senate, the university educational policies committee, and others. A review committee is then appointed that reviews this information:

1. The program's current data profile
2. The perspectives of all available full-time faculty members who have taught courses in the program within the last two academic years
3. Projected future enrollments
4. Anticipated impact of the program discontinuation on students (including community college students within the university's service area) as revealed by a survey
5. Any existing plans or alternatives to allow enrolled students to complete the degree program or a related one should the program be suspended
6. Any recovery plan that administrators of the program have developed, including alternatives that might increase student enrollment in the future
7. The results of public meetings with various university stakeholders, including faculty, staff, students, administrators, and community members, about the program's possible suspension or discontinuation

8. Any plans for providing financial support that would permit continuance of the program

If, on consideration of these materials, the special review committee recommends that the program be suspended, no additional students are accepted into it. The program is given a five-year period (which may be extended by one-year increments, if warranted) during which current students are permitted to complete the program and restructuring or improvement plans may be developed to reactivate the program. If, at the end of the suspension period, continuation of the program still seems undesirable, it is terminated by the campus president in consultation with the university's chancellor. This extensive review and suspension process helps avoid the trauma that could result from sudden dismissals of tenured faculty members by giving them sufficient time to improve the program or to seek other employment possibilities.

Conclusion

No matter how easy your relationship with a particular employee has been, it's important to realize that termination will be stressful for both you and for the faculty member. Indeed, termination can be devastating to a person's career and self-esteem. You will want to extend all the courtesy, respect, and professionalism you can possibly bring to the situation.

As you review in your mind how you'll approach the situation, ask yourself how you yourself would wish to be treated—or how you would wish your child to be treated—if you were in a similar position for whatever reason. Remember too that our tendency to want to improve a painful situation can lead us to say things we don't really mean. Because of a terminated employee's tears or discomfort, we may start to praise aspects of the person's performance that in other situations we might not regard as having been of particularly high quality. That can be a serious mistake. It's important not to send mixed messages about someone's performance that can end up complicating your task later. Be clear and direct in stating what you had planned to say, but do not be unnecessarily heartless in your phrasing or demeanor. Finally, it should be noted that collective bargaining agreements can play a major role in the steps that academic leaders must pursue in terminating a faculty member, the timing of the notice that must be given, and the levels of appeal to which the faculty member is entitled. (For more on the impact of unionized environments on academic leadership, see chapter 43.)

REFERENCES

Anglim, C. T. (1997). *Labor, employment, and the law*. Santa Barbara, CA: ABC-CLIO.

Gifis, S. H. (2010). *Barron's law dictionary* (6th ed.). Hauppauge, NY: Barron's Educational Series.

Nolan, J. R., & Nolan-Haley, J. M. (1990). *Black's law dictionary* (6th ed.). St. Paul, MN: West.

RESOURCES

Berk, R. A. (2013). *Top 10 flashpoints in student ratings and the evaluation of teaching: What faculty and administrators must know to protect themselves in employment decisions*. Sterling, VA: Stylus.

Covey, A. (2000). *The workplace law advisor: From harassment and discrimination policies to hiring and firing guidelines: What every manager and employee needs to know*. New York, NY: Perseus.

Falcone, P. (2006). *The hiring and firing: Question and answer book*. New York, NY: AMACOM.

Fleischer, C. H. (2005). *The complete hiring and firing handbook: Every manager's guide to working with employees—legally*. Naperville, IL: Sphinx.

Horowitz, A. S. (1999). *The unofficial guide to hiring and firing people*. New York, NY: Macmillan.

Kaplin, W. A., & Lee, B. A. (Eds.). (2013). *The law of higher education: A comprehensive guide to legal implications of administrative decision making* (5th ed.). San Francisco: Jossey-Bass.

Levin, R., & Rosse, J. (2001). *Talent flow: A strategic approach to keeping good employees, helping them grow, and letting them go*. San Francisco, CA: Jossey-Bass.

National Business Institute. (2014). *Human resource law from A to Z*. Eau Claire, WI: National Business Institute.

Repa, B. K. (2000). *Firing without fear: A legal guide for conscientious employers*. Berkeley, CA: Nolo.

Weiss, D. H. (2004). *Fair, square, and legal: Safe hiring, managing & firing practices to keep you and your company out of court* (4th ed.). New York, NY: AMACOM.

40

REPLACING A CHAIR

Colleges and universities use the expression *department chair* to refer to everyone from a full-time faculty member who receives little or no release time in return for performing a few administrative tasks on behalf of the discipline to a full-time administrator who evaluates the faculty in the program, serves on a twelve-month contract, and has few if any expectations in the areas of teaching and research. Department chairs may be hired into an institution from the outside as part of a national search, appointed from within the discipline through an internal search, elected by the members of the discipline, appointed by the dean, or given their position as part of a regular rotation that eventually includes every full-time member of the department. At some schools, department chairs can't succeed themselves after a single term; at others, they can retain their positions indefinitely until they either step down or are forced to resign.

The different combinations that you can mix and match from all these scenarios are almost limitless. But despite the vast flexibility of the position, all department chairs share one thing in common: they can create a real challenge to the dean or provost when they're not working out. This chapter thus addresses several questions:

- What factors might lead you to suspect that a department chair should be replaced?
- Under what circumstances should you act on those suspicions?
- What steps should always be taken when replacing a chair?
- How do you keep the department functioning effectively during what could be a difficult and anxiety-producing transition?

These questions are so important that it's best to deal with each of them individually.

Factors to Observe

It's only natural that when several people report to you, some of them will be better at their jobs than others. As you look across the range of department chairs you know at your institution, you're unlikely to find that they all have equally impressive people skills, equally stellar records of meeting the needs of their stakeholders, and equally admirable strategies for helping their disciplines improve. Aside from all of these practical considerations, there are probably going to be some chairs you like and others you don't particularly care for. Does that mean that you should replace the chairs you don't like or who don't perform their jobs quite as well as the best chairs you know? Not necessarily. Not liking someone doesn't mean that he or she isn't effective in the position, and even the worst chair in your area could easily be the most competent person available.

The real issue arises when you see a chair whose style, decisions, or actions are causing demonstrable harm to the discipline or the institution. If you can't point to specific opportunities that have been missed, work that hasn't been performed, or problems that haven't been solved, then the question facing you is: Do I really have an ineffective department chair or merely a personality conflict with the person who happens to serve as chair? We all encounter people at work we don't like or who do things differently from how we would've done them. But if you can't reasonably demonstrate that there's been damage caused by a chair's personality, management style, actions, or decisions, then maybe the situation isn't as bad as you think. It may even be possible that *you're* the one who's causing the personality conflict and that some candid self-reflection may be in order.

> The problem isn't always them. Sometimes it's us.

But if your objective assessment is that the department chair is causing real problems for the discipline, a good next step is to ask yourself the following questions:

o Is the problem fixable? Can the chair be given guidance or support that will eliminate the problem or at least reduce it to a manageable level? Is it reasonable to expect the chair to change his or her behavior and act in the way that you hope?

o Is the problem unfixable but endurable? If the situation, for whatever reason, can't be improved, is it something that has to be addressed right away? Is a better strategy simply tolerating a less than perfect situation until the chair's term is over? Which would cause the greater harm to the most people: gritting your teeth and waiting it out or dealing with the disruption that may be caused by replacing the chair now?

o What's the best you can expect to achieve through replacing the chair? Does that advantage outweigh the disadvantages that may arise from changing departmental leadership? Is your action likely to unite the faculty in the program behind the chair you're replacing? Do you have a reasonable candidate to replace the chair, and is that person likely to have support within the program?

The degree of disruption that replacing a chair can create depends on the history of the program, the way in which the chair was initially selected, and the personality of the people involved. For example, replacing a department chair who was elected by the faculty is almost always more contentious than replacing one you chose yourself. In any case, the important considerations are what outcome you'd like to occur, whether it's likely that your desired outcome will actually come about, and where the department will be heading if the chair doesn't significantly change his or her behavior.

Circumstances Requiring Action

Even in situations where you conclude that the chair is causing serious difficulties for the department and that his or her behavior isn't likely to be improved significantly by mentoring or your explicit instructions, it's not always the case that you'll want to go so far as replacing the chair immediately. The key question must be: Is the improvement that will result sufficient to justify any disruption in or loss of progress that the discipline may experience?

Tensions in the program may run high since replacing a chair is likely to be perceived, at least initially, as a demotion for the person who's forced out. Although in many cases the chair ultimately will be relieved to be assigned duties that he or she can perform more successfully and to be freed of the frustrations that may have led to your decision, there's almost always an initial resistance to the loss of authority (and, in many cases, salary as well) that accompanies this reassignment. To make the situation more palatable, many supervisors have simply let the former chair retain his or her administrative stipend, rolling it over into annual salary. This approach may ease the immediate situation, but it can cause serious problems in the long term. If successful chairs who return to the faculty after several well-respected tours of administrative duty aren't rewarded in the same way, you can end up giving the impression that you only recompense chairs for poor service. The ultimate impact on morale is usually not worth the short-term benefit that this approach can offer since it affects the best and most productive people in the program.

Replacing a chair can also cause other kinds of disruptions. After all, nearly every chair, no matter how ineffective, has at least some supporters. It's an extremely rare case where every member of the department agrees that they'd like to have the chair removed. In fact, all too often one of the problems caused by an ineffective chair is intense departmental factionalism, with cliques either siding with the chair or becoming members of a departmental insurgency. In these situations, replacing the chair may convey the impression that you've taken sides in the departmental dispute, declaring one faction the winner and the other side the loser.

Unless you clearly believe that one bloc is fully in the right—and are prepared to defend this perspective to both the department itself and the rest of the faculty and administration—it's a good idea to reflect long and hard on the possible implications of this decision. Only if you're absolutely convinced that extensive or irreparable damage to the department will occur if the chair remains in position should you bypass less drastic alternatives, such as meeting with the department yourself regularly to serve as an broker for disputes and to ensure that arguments within the program don't degenerate into unprofessional and personal attacks.

Offering the department access to outside mediation, providing faculty development training in conflict resolution and constructive group dynamics, and assigning a skilled mentor to the department chair may be much better alternatives to a staff change. At the very least, you may want to try these approaches before resorting to a replacement of the chair and all the disadvantages such an action could bring.

Admittedly there are situations in which replacing a chair is the most appropriate course of action a provost or dean can take—for example:

o *Budgetary mismanagement.* As we saw in chapter 35, it's not always an academic leader's fault when his or her unit consistently exceeds its allocated budget. But there are situations in which the person who supervises the budget doesn't exert an appropriate level of care when monitoring expenditures. You may have this situation in an academic department if the program was able to remain within its budget under previous chairs and began having difficulties only under the current leadership. Careful budgeting is something that administrators often have to learn on the job, so it's probably wise to address a few small problems early in a chair's tenure with training and mentoring. But if a lapse in judgment is egregious enough or the budgetary shortfalls continue despite the guidance and warnings you've given the chair, you may best be served by appointing a replacement.

○ *Serious failure to follow institutional policies.* Lack of adherence to established procedures that results in major harm to the institution—such as a lawsuit, the need to cancel a search very late in the process, the resignation of a highly valued employee, or an increase in students transferring from the institution—is sufficiently serious to call for intervention from the dean or provost. If you believe that the chair's mismanagement of the situation, negligence, or incompetence caused the problem (particularly if the chair doesn't appear to have gained appropriate insight from the situation), the time may be right to look for a replacement.

○ *Other types of problems that can cause severe or ongoing harm to the discipline.* There are also problems caused by chairs that don't neatly fall into any particular category. You can't really regard them as a failure to follow a procedure because they are situations for which no policy was ever established. They don't qualify as insubordination, fiscal mismanagement, or violating the terms of a contract because you couldn't possibly have predicted them, and the institution doesn't have any guidelines explicitly forbidding them. But they pose a significant challenge to the program or institution anyway. Perhaps the chair has demonstrated such a lack of professionalism that his or her continued effectiveness in the department has been compromised. Or perhaps the chair has taken actions behind your back that have irreparably destroyed your confidence in his or her ability to work with you effectively. Situations like these can be among your most trying challenges as an academic leader and require a great deal of professional insight and decision-making acumen. As always, the major question to ask yourself is: Has the chair's actions in the past so fully compromised our ability to work together effectively in the future that the cost of replacing the chair is less than the cost of retaining the chair? In making this consideration, the term *cost* involves not merely money but also effort, likely problems, hindrances to further progress, the investment of your time, and the overall impact on stakeholders.

Steps to Take

Your institution undoubtedly has formal policies that you need to follow if you decide to replace a chair. In most cases, those policies will tell you everything you need to know in terms of which offices need to be informed or consulted, what type of notification has to be provided to the chair and faculty in the discipline, and which procedures you'll have to adopt when electing, appointing, or hiring the new chair. What your institution's written policy is unlikely to give you, however, is the following important advice.

Be direct

It benefits neither you, the department, nor the chair you're replacing for you to beat around the bush or try to work behind the scenes once you've made your decision to replace this person. Make an appointment with the chair specifically for the purpose of discussing his or her performance. If you're asked the reason for the meeting and don't want to give too much away in advance, say that the session is about planning for the future or matters related to staffing for next year. Once the appointment begins, state clearly and directly your reasons for deciding to replace the chair. Be specific in saying that the decision has already been made and that this meeting isn't an opportunity for further discussion or debate. You're there to announce a decision, not critique it. Then proceed to outline your plans for the next steps in the department's future.

Be charitable

In the case of a chair who's being forced to step down as the result of a disciplinary matter or a serious failure, you have few options for taking the sting out of your decision. (In fact, you may well not wish to do so. The chair has failed in his or her responsibilities, and it can send a mixed message if you begin acting as though this failure was a minor matter.) But other situations sometimes call for a gentler touch. The chair who's simply in over his or her head, has been assigned the wrong responsibilities, or is basically a very good person unfortunately placed in the wrong job is best treated with all the compassion and generosity you can muster. In certain cases, allowing the chair to step down voluntarily can be an appropriate face-saving measure. In other situations, offering a new assignment that better suits the individual's talents will ease this transition. In each case, praise what you can honestly regard as the person's successes, being careful neither to exaggerate nor to make the chair feel bad if the reasons for this action were beyond his or her control.

Be transparent

Rumors spread quickly throughout an academic community. Meet with the entire department as soon as possible after informing the chair of your decision. If too much time elapses, a distorted version of your decision will quickly become accepted as the truth. Morale will suffer, and the entire situation will soon get out of control. Moreover, don't convey this news first by memo or e-mail: meet face-to-face with members of the department. They'll have questions, some of which you'll be able to answer immediately, others of which you'll need to defer. In any case, state the result of your meeting with the chair without too much elaboration. If you've allowed the chair to resign as though the decision were his or her own idea, say nothing that will undermine this face-saving measure. If you've forced the chair out, say so in clear terms, but avoid revealing any information that could be regarded as personal or confidential. Keep the focus of your meeting with the faculty on what will take place in the future, not on reliving the past.

Be quick

The transitional period between chairs is often difficult. A dynamic department may lose some of its momentum during this interim period. A highly polarized department may find that its wounds can't heal until new leadership is in place. A truly dysfunctional department may even be reduced to anarchy or open hostility before the entire matter is resolved. For this reason, it's a good strategy to proceed with appointing, hiring, or electing a new permanent chair at the earliest possible opportunity. While you'll naturally want to move forward with due thought and careful planning, a certain amount of dispatch is also in order. A long delay will make an unsatisfactory situation even worse.

Actions to Maintain Progress

Since the purpose of replacing a chair is always to improve a department, you don't want the transitional period following the removal of a chair to cause the program to lose momentum or fragment even more. How you approach this situation is likely to be different depending on whether a new chair is appointed immediately or only after a process that necessitates a slight delay, such as an election or search.

If the new chair is appointed immediately, it's helpful to give this person an opportunity to establish himself or herself in the department and develop his or her own identity as the program's new leader. Don't visit the department too frequently at first. In particular, don't visit the department too often in a formal capacity since frequent visits may be regarded as your way of undermining the chair's authority, "checking up on things" that you don't believe will be done properly. Rather, give the new chair the freedom to act independently, meeting occasionally with you in your office so that you can get updates, lend support, and, *if requested*, provide a bit of advice. When the transition from an old chair to a new chair occurs immediately, in other words, one of the best things you can do is to provide that person with a little bit of space to get the feel of the position and establish a new identity.

The situation is a little bit different in cases where there's a clear transitional period between chairs. For instance, the department may be under the direction of an acting chair for a few months during a national search. There may be need for a departmental election to vote for a new chair, with the outgoing chair remaining in office until this election can be completed.

In these situations, the opposite strategy from the one outlined above is usually in order: you should meet with the department on a fairly regular basis, perhaps every week or so. These visits can help demonstrate that the department is not being forgotten during its transitional period, that there's still a high-ranking administrator in place who can help the program achieve its goals, and that there's not going to be a gap in leadership. You may even want to use this transitional period to reorganize the department more extensively. This may be a good time to revise the departmental mission statement, establish a departmental code of conduct, or update the department's strategic plan. Your goal, in other words, is to keep the department's energies focused on the future throughout the transitional period. Ask questions like these:

o Where can we go from here?

o How can we assist the next chair in understanding who we are by reaffirming our core values?

o What do we hope this department can become in the next five to ten years?

These questions will result in a far more productive use of time than continually revisiting the past and asking, "What went wrong?"

Conclusion

Perhaps the most difficult challenge you may face when replacing a chair can occur when you and the department are in clear disagreement over the next step. For instance, you may require a chair to step down after years of budgetary mismanagement that has been disastrous for the institution but fairly invisible to the department itself. If you then hold an election for the next chair and, to your great disappointment, the former chair is reelected by a sizable majority, what do you do? Nearly every institution has some type of policy in place that allows the dean or provost to override a departmental vote in the election of a chair. You may well need to apply this policy in the situation just described, but it'll also require some further effort on your part. For example, you might explain to the department as candidly as possible (without revealing information that is regarded as privileged under your institution's personnel guidelines) why you couldn't accept the situation as it was unfolding and why the faculty must either reconsider its vote or accept your appointee. It would also be a good idea to lend the new chair extra support since he or she may well meet additional resistance from the faculty and be regarded as your pawn. And you'll need to negotiate the situation in a way that doesn't come across as mere stubbornness or authoritarianism, but as a strategy that's genuinely in the best interests of the department. If you decide to accept the department's vote, you probably should establish some clear parameters for the chair's performance and explain in no uncertain terms, to both the department and the chair, what results will occur if these expectations aren't met.

A good department chair has an effect on a discipline's morale, efficiency, and productivity that's almost incalculable. Nearly every academic leader is surprised to find that a department that seemed completely dysfunctional under one chair can improve dramatically under new leadership. Conversely, it's not uncommon for even the best department to become fractious and unmanageable simply because a new chair proves to be ineffective in his or her role. The most important thing you can do as an academic leader is to gauge your chairs not on the extent to which you like them or they seem to reflect your own administrative style, but on the degree to which they add to a department's quality in fulfilling its central mission of teaching, scholarship, and service.

RESOURCES

Pollan, S. M., & Levine, M. (2011). *Workscripts: Perfect phrases for high-stakes conversations.* Hoboken, NJ: Wiley.

Ryan, K. (2012). *You have to say the words: An integrity-based approach for tackling tough conversations and maximizing performance.* Orlando, FL: Achievement Press.

Schyns, B., & Hansbrough, T. (2010). *When leadership goes wrong: Destructive leadership, mistakes, and ethical failures.* Charlotte, NC: Information Age.

41

RESPONDING TO EMERGENCIES

People sometimes speak of leadership styles as though they were innate aspects of someone's personality. "I have a consultative leadership style," we can imagine a dean or provost saying. "I never do anything without getting all the facts, letting people voice their opinions, and achieving consensus." But being locked into a single leadership style or approach in every situation is not only excessively limiting; it's also counterproductive. That same consultative style that works so well when revising the curriculum or planning a new initiative isn't going to be very useful when the building's on fire: "Okay, everyone, let's consider our options. We can call 911. We can flee the building. We can try to put out the fire ourselves. But before we act on any of these very useful suggestions you've made, I'd like to consider whether we have any other alternatives we need to discuss. Then I'd like a subcommittee to get me a recommendation and a timetable for action. Once I have that report, we'll all reconvene and . . . " By the time you reach that point, you'll have lost most of your coworkers to smoke inhalation.

Emergencies require a different leadership style from most other situations we encounter as deans and provosts. Authoritarian, top-down management is usually out of place in the community of scholars that constitute a college or university. But it's exactly what's needed—and what your stakeholders will expect of you—when a genuine crisis occurs.

Note, however, a key word in that last sentence: a take-charge attitude is a useful approach in a *genuine* crisis. And genuine crises do occur. Hurricanes, floods, earthquakes, fires, or tornadoes unexpectedly destroy facilities. Members of the faculty or staff are charged with serious crimes. Armed intruders invade campuses. Students are hospitalized after a drug overdose, car accident, or injury from athletic events. People are assaulted in our facilities. Bomb threats are issued that involve buildings for which we're responsible. Suspicious packages are discovered. Dangerous materials are discovered to be missing from our laboratories. Students threaten or commit suicide. Terrorist attacks in our communities cause us to go on lockdown. Any of these situations mean that we as academic leaders have to act in ways that are different from our normal way of working with our stakeholders.

Crises require a specific type of response because of the danger they pose and the rapidity with which they unfold. While these challenges are severe, they're also relatively rare. Most deans and provosts face a genuine emergency only a few times in their administrative careers; some are fortunate enough that they never have to deal with such events at all. For this reason, it's important for academic leaders to distinguish between actual threats to life, safety, or well-being and incidents that, although troubling or unpleasant, don't rise to the level of an emergency. If we operate in crisis mode too often, we're likely to be far less effective when actual disasters occur. We undermine our credibility by giving the impression that we regard a faculty e-mail war and the death of a student as somehow equivalent. By crying, "Wolf!" once too often, we may find people's response lagging when we really do need fast and decisive action.

Disaster Preparedness Plans

The most important action you can take before emergencies occur is to develop an effective disaster preparedness plan that can help guide your decision making when there won't be time to think clearly and calmly about what to do next. Obviously it's impossible to create a plan so comprehensive that it covers every possible contingency. One of the reasons emergencies so frequently turn into disasters is that many of them can't be foreseen and the institution isn't ready to respond to them. But even if you can't plan for everything, a good disaster preparedness plan puts you in a much better position for emergencies that are most likely to occur and gives you a general working procedure for what to do even in the most unexpected of situations. The plan includes such considerations as these:

- Who should be notified, in what order, and how each person may best be reached

- The location of medical supplies, along with a calendar for when different supplies should be replaced to make sure they remain effective

- Instructions for what to do during a lockdown, how to shelter in place, and where to meet once a facility has been evacuated

○ The names and contact information for the people who are responsible for various facilities

○ How stakeholders and the public should be notified once the crisis has past

In many cases, an emergency preparedness plan will consist of several complementary and at times overlapping documents: an emergency response plan details the actions to be taken during the crisis itself; a continuation of operations plan details how the institution or program will return to ordinary function after the crisis is over; and one or more individualized plans that detail how to deal with hazardous materials, expensive equipment, or other items that may be specific to that individual program. The continuation of operations plan is particularly useful because it gives thought in advance of the emergency to how a program might continue its educational and research missions if its facilities are damaged or otherwise unusable for an extended period of time.

Most institutions have all of these plans already in place. Your task as dean or provost therefore will likely be to become as familiar as possible with your institution's existing procedures (since, in an emergency, others will be turning to you for advice and the ability to make decisions rapidly), make sure that as many people in your unit as possible are aware of these procedures, and take steps to ensure that copies of the plans are available online and in hard copy (in the event that the plan must be consulted during a power failure) at numerous convenient locations throughout your facilities. Also, it's possible that the programs you supervise may involve facilities, equipment, or supplies that could result in an emergency that's impossible or at least highly unlikely in other areas. For example, you may be responsible for laboratories that store corrosive, inflammable, radioactive, or explosive materials. Or there may be fitness equipment in one of your programs that could potentially cause injuries. In such cases, you should work cooperatively with your faculty (who know the nature of your facilities, equipment, and supplies the best), your security office, and your environmental health and safety officer or department to develop the specialized emergency response plans needed for these contingencies.

You may also find yourself in that somewhat rare situation where your institution doesn't have an existing plan for emergencies or the current plan is inadequate, confusing, or out of date. Even more common may be the situation where multiple emergency response plans exist at the institutional, collegiate, and departmental levels with little consistency or coordination among these competing and incompatible plans. If this is the case for your area, you now have an excellent opportunity to exercise forward-looking academic leadership and fix a problem before it becomes a true emergency.

In developing your plan, you don't have to start from scratch. Henderson (2004, 2007) provides useful examples of plans that can be adapted to your institutional needs, and many other colleges and universities already have posted their own manuals for public access online. No matter how you begin this process, however, these are several best practices to keep in mind so that your document is as useful as possible:

○ *Make the first step clear, short, and easily understood.* When an emergency occurs, people don't have the time or mental focus to review an extensive or complex policy. Each disaster preparedness policy should thus begin with a brief initial course of action that tells the reader what to do first. That course of action should be impossible to misunderstand, consist of a single brief sentence, and refer to the most important procedure that needs to get under way—for example, "Call 911 and report the nature and location of the emergency," or, "Get everyone out of the building immediately." Place this information in large, bold print on the emergency procedures web page or at the front of an emergency preparedness manual. If you have additional information to provide, such as, "Then call campus security and remain on the telephone until help arrives," or, "Assemble the building occupants at the predesignated gathering area and wait for help to arrive," put this information in a smaller type size after the major instructions, but make sure that it doesn't make the first step appear too complicated or overly long to read. The very first step should always be something that people can read, understand, and act on in a matter of seconds.

○ *Provide hyperlinks or clear page references about what someone should do during different types of emergency.* Since different sorts of crisis situations require different responses, after providing a general first step that applies to all emergencies, your plan should next have a clearly delineated set of subsequent actions that are appropriate for particular crises. Even in these more focused instructions, however, it's important to keep all directives short, simple, and as easily understood as possible. On a website, the best way of providing this information is through a sidebar or secondary menu with hyperlinks for categories like fire, earthquake, armed intruder, chemical spill, serious injury, and the like. In a printed manual, a simplified table of contents or section tabs can serve the same purpose. The University of Minnesota, Duluth's emergency preparedness website is an excellent example of this type of crisis management plan: a clear instruction tells readers that they should "Always dial 911" is followed by several secondary instructions.

1. Always dial 911 from a safe location.
2. Provide operator with the following information:
   - Your name and phone number;
   - Your location: building name, floor and room numbers;
   - Nature of emergency (fire, medical, chemical spill, etc);
   - Number of injured people if any, and nature of injuries if known;
   - Nearest building entrance where emergency personnel should go.
3. Ask someone to or meet the emergency personnel outside of the building, and direct them to the emergency location.
4. If it is safe to do so, stay on line until you are excused by emergency operator.

A sidebar then gives hyperlinks for more detailed instructions about dealing with such emergencies as mail threats, bomb threats, biohazards, radiation leaks, severe weather, and other potential dangers. (www.d.umn.edu/ehso/emergencies/general.htm). Other good websites to use as examples are for Arizona State University (cfo.asu.edu/emergency?destination=node%2F2481); the University of Washington (www.washington.edu/emergency/), where the emergency management office has the delightful motto, "Everything we do is a disaster!"; the University of Miami (www.miami.edu/ref/index.php/ep); and the University of Denver (www.du.edu/emergency/whattodowhen/). A good example of a written emergency preparedness plan can be found in the *Stop. Think. Act.* guide (spu.edu/info/emergency/stopthinkactbook.pdf).

You'll notice how in all these examples, the actions the reader is urged to take are outlined in a simple step-by-step manner, free from unnecessary verbiage and the need to look for information like names and telephone numbers on other web pages or in other parts of the manual. They recognize that the person who will be reading them is likely to be nervous or distraught. Everything that's unnecessary has been removed; the reader can focus immediately on exactly what he or she needs and take the appropriate actions.

Provide a contact tree of people to be informed of the emergencies and train them in any subsequent calls they'll be expected to make. After calling 911 or campus security, there will be other people who will need to be notified about the emergency. It can be a time-consuming task for the person who makes the initial call (and who may need to tend to others who require help) to make all of those subsequent calls on his or her own. A well-designed contact tree allows the initial caller to contact one person who then calls several others, each of whom then calls several others as well. In order for this system to work effectively, people need to know in advance what their responsibilities will be, have ready access to an accurate and updated contact list, and be reachable even when they're not in their offices. Unless careful thought is given in advance to how this type of contact tree will work and under what conditions it will be used, mistakes are likely to be made in the heat of the moment. At the very least, one of your supervisors or colleagues can end up being offended because he or she wasn't notified and "had to learn about all of this from the evening news." Even more serious is the possibility that the problem may become worse because the right people didn't receive the information they needed in a timely manner.

Safety Always Comes First

When you're faced with an emergency, it's likely that a thousand different thoughts will occur to you. But as all-consuming as each of those thoughts may be, none of them will be as important as this one: *What do you have to do immediately to make sure that everyone's safe?* Your first priority must always be securing people's safety, providing the emergency treatment that they need, and reducing the likelihood of further injury or trauma. Facilities if damaged can be restored. Feelings, if hurt, can be repaired through apologies and explanations. But actual physical harm to someone is the one thing academic leaders must be on the greatest alert to avoid or alleviate. For this reason, even if it means that someone else will end up looking more heroic or decisive than you will, your first thought in every emergency should be, "How can people best be protected?" If you let thoughts of how the incident will look in the newspapers, whether you yourself might be regarded as blameworthy, the impact such an incident may have on enrollment or donor support, or anything else get in the way of safety, you're neglecting your most important responsibility.

There will be many opportunities during your service as an academic administrator to burnish the image of your programs, build your own résumé, and receive praise for your creativity and initiative. This isn't one of them. Don't even begin to consider other factors until you know that everyone's safety has been secured.

A Second Set of Three Cs

Everyone responds differently in a crisis. It's possible that as the emergency unfolds, you'll be tense and nervous, uncertain what to do next, and feeling that your self-assurance is badly shaken. But despite this very natural feeling, it's important to remember that during crises, people turn to their leaders for decisiveness and comfort. If you act as though you're flustered or convey an attitude of despair, it can complicate the emergency even further.

Panic tends to be contagious, and it will be important for you to remain as calm as possible, even if everything around you appears to be falling apart. In chapter 22, we saw that positive interactions between deans and provosts required what I called the three Cs: candor, collegiality, and confidentiality. Emergencies require three Cs too, but these qualities are different from those you want to exhibit in normal circumstances.

> In the midst of crises, effective academic leaders remember to guide their actions by a new set of three Cs: confidence, composure, and certainty. Academic leaders' sense of being in charge will prevent others from panicking and allow the problem to be addressed with as much calm determination as possible.

Conveying an attitude of confidence, composure, and certainty does not imply that you should come across as coldly indifferent or dispassionate to the suffering of others. Your goal should be to reach that valuable middle ground between composed decisiveness and deep, caring compassion. Particularly in cases where a student is killed or seriously injured, your expression of compassion to the parents, siblings, and friends of the student will be of the utmost importance. Those conversations or telephone calls are the hardest that you'll ever have to make, but they're essential to the healing process of those to whom you demonstrate concern. At times, parents may even unleash their anger at you as a representative of the institution that "allowed this to happen." If that occurs, you should allow the person to vent his or her anger, and then express your compassionate understanding of the person's suffering without admitting liability on the part of the institution. As we saw in chapter 9, demonstrating concern isn't the same as committing to any particular course of action. There'll be plenty of time later for blame to be assigned and punitive action taken if it is warranted. But don't allow the eventual need for a thorough and systematic review of what caused the problem prevent you from treating those affected by this disaster humanely.

Treat the Media with Care

Crises are news. Reporters sometimes appear on your campus even as an emergency situation is unfolding and want to know how you feel about it or what you intend to do about it. That's their job. They have a duty in a free society to report the news, and emergencies taking place on university campuses attract a great deal of public interest. You'll want to assist the media in carrying out these duties responsibly, while not being distracted from your own immediate response to the crisis or answering their questions while still in a state of high emotion. For this reason, it's a good practice to defer questions from reporters to your school's office of public relations, and even in situations when it's difficult to worry about policies and procedures, keep in mind the guidelines for dealing with the media explored in the next chapter.

Conclusion

Every emergency that a dean or provost faces will be different. In the end, one of the best possible preparations you can make is to brainstorm or role-play possible responses to a crisis situation during a mini-retreat or a focused meeting with your staff. Not only will doing so help you think through what you might do in these crisis situations, but you'll also be training those who work with you in how to respond better to these very difficult challenges. By making this practice a group activity, you'll all learn from one another techniques for solving problems that will be invaluable should a crisis ever arise during your tenure as dean or provost.

REFERENCES

Henderson, D. (2004). *Crisis management protocols for colleges and universities: A crisis management template.* Brookfield, CT: Rothstein Associates. CD-ROM.

Henderson, D. (2007). *Comprehensive crisis and continuity program for colleges and universities on CD-ROM: Risk and impact analysis, continuity of operations plan (COOP), departmental/division plans and crisis/risk management plan development templates.* CD-ROM. Brookfield, CT: Rothstein Associates.

RESOURCES

Augustine, N. R., Sharma, A., Kesner, I. F., Smith, N. C., Thomas, R. J., Quelch, J. A., . . . Hill, L. (2000). *Harvard Business Review on crisis management.* Boston, MA: Harvard Business School Press.

Barton, L. (2008). *Crisis leadership now: A real-world guide to preparing for threats, disaster, sabotage, and scandal.* New York, NY: McGraw-Hill.

Crandall, W. R., Parnell, J. A., & Spillan, J. E. (2014). *Crisis management: Leading in the new strategy landscape* (2nd ed.). Thousand Oaks, CA: Sage.

Dezenhall, E., & Weber, J. (2011). *Damage control: The essential lessons of crisis management.* Westport, CT: Prospecta.

Dreshman, J. L., Crabb, C. L., & Tarasevich, S. (2001). *Caring in times of crisis: A crisis management/postvention manual for administrators, student assistance teams and other school personnel.* Chapin, SC: Youthlight.

Fagel, M. J. (2014). *Crisis management and emergency planning: Preparing for today's challenges.* Boca Raton, FL: CRC Press.

Warner, D., & Palfreyman, D. (Eds.). (2003). *Managing crisis.* Philadelphia, PA: Open University Press.

42

DEALING WITH THE MEDIA

Once they reach the dean or provost level, nearly every academic leader will need to interact with the media in some way. As chief administrators of our units, we need positive media relations in order to publicize events, convey our message effectively, and reach potential students and donors. However, when problems arise at our institution—particularly when there are problems that are serious enough or appear scandalous enough to have high "news value"—we may have to deal with the media in situations we'd much prefer to avoid.

Any dean or provost who's been interviewed more than once has probably experienced the discomfort of being misquoted, misunderstood, or having his or her remarks taken out of context. These problems can cause a great deal of tension between the dean or provost and the president or governing board. Even worse, misleading or inaccurate news stories can do serious damage to enrollments, donations, and the opportunity to recruit and retain the most desirable faculty members. For this reason, every academic needs at least a little preparation for situations that may involve the media. The information in this chapter is intended to serve as something of a primer on the most important guidelines to keep in mind when interacting with reporters.

I begin the discussion of media relations with one essential principle that you should remember in every situation involving the press, radio, or television:

Never interact with the media without having first contacted your institution's office of public relations.

In the vast majority of cases, media inquiries are best directed solely to the public relations office. You can save yourself a considerable amount of frustration and regret simply by answering every request for a statement or interview with the words, "I'm sorry, but I always refer all media requests to our institutional office of public relations. Let me give you their number, and then I'll forward your call directly to them. Hold a moment, please." The professionals in that office are trained in how to deal with reporters, know precisely what the institutional message is on nearly every issue, and are skilled in diplomatic ways of delaying a request for information if the institution is not yet ready to go public on an issue. Even if it turns out that an interview with you is absolutely essential, the staff of your public relations office can help you prepare for it, make the appropriate arrangements, and even participate in it with you, amplifying or clarifying any information where you might need a little help. In situations where you find yourself ambushed by a reporter or are otherwise caught unaware, contact the public relations office as soon after as possible. Someone from that office may be able to contact the reporter or redirect the focus of the story, provide more complete background information, or otherwise assist you in telling your college's story.

In addition to this one basic rule, the other guidelines that you should follow in dealing with the media fall into several categories.

In All Situations

o *Limit yourself to factual information.* Reporters will frequently want you to speculate on the reasons a problem occurred. While you'll often have strong opinions on this matter, it's unwise to share them with the media. Your speculation may well be proven incorrect later or it may contradict an equally valid alternative explanation favored by your president. You're far safer sticking to the facts, and you'll have less to retract later if you do so.

o *Never answer a question off the cuff.* If you're asked a question to which you haven't given careful consideration in advance, defer the question whenever possible. As difficult as it may be to say, "I simply don't know," that admission may be your wisest answer. Don't be goaded by repeated iterations of the same question into providing an answer about which you're less than completely confident. If you absolutely must answer a question that surprises you, either say, "Let me think about that for a moment," or, "Give me some time to consider that question, investigate the matter a bit, and them I'll get back to you later." A glib or improvised response increases the likelihood that you'll be embarrassed by how your remarks are interpreted.

○ *Stay on message.* As academic leaders, we like to listen carefully to the questions we're asked and provide clear, complete answers that address every aspect of the questions we're posed. Many of us, in fact, were offered our positions because, unlike other candidates, we actually *answered* the questions we were asked at our interviews. Nevertheless, a press interview isn't at all like an employment interview. And it isn't like a final examination: No one is going to grade you lower for not answering the question you're asked.

For this reason, you should take any opportunity when a reporter or interviewer asks you a question to get out your message even if your answer is utterly irrelevant to the question you've been asked. Remember that your ultimate audience isn't the reporter or interviewer but the community at large. What message do you want the public to hear? Prefacing sentences with the phrases, "Well, the most important thing we need to keep in mind is . . . ," and, "As I said earlier, the really critical idea here is . . . ," reinforce the central message that you are trying to convey. Particularly when you're interviewed by a reporter, remember that although your answers may be quoted, the questions themselves never appear in print. So talk about what's important to you, even if it doesn't seem relevant to the question you've been asked.

○ *Avoid filling silences.* Silent pauses are awkward, and we're often tempted to keep speaking so as to fill them. It's in these situations when you're more likely to reveal something you don't want to or make a comment that will be misunderstood. The reporter isn't there to evaluate your social skills. When you've said all that you intended to say, be silent and allow the silence to continue for as long as necessary.

○ *Use clear and accurate statistics.* If there's an issue that you are most eager to have others learn about, talk about it with a few carefully chosen and accurate statistics. Reporters like to quote quantitative information in their stories—which makes the story seem more "researched"—and, by offering the reporter something that he or she can best use, you'll increase the likelihood that the information you would like to see in the final story is ultimately reported.

○ *Demonstrate compassion.* Since you're using statistics whenever possible, avoiding questions that you don't know the answer to, and redirecting the conversation toward the message you want to convey, you may run the risk of appearing cold and indifferent to anyone who may be suffering because of the situation that's unfolding. For example, a reporter may blindside you with a question about an accusation of sexual misconduct in a program that you supervise. If you don't have any information about the issue yet, your temptation may be to say that you have nothing yet to share on the topic and that you'll get back to the reporter as soon as you can. That response can seem excessively indifferent to the suffering of the person who's the victim in this situation. At the same time, you don't want to rush to judgment, assume that every allegation is true, and defame anyone who may later be found to be innocent. In this case, it's useful to demonstrate compassion without assigning fault. Say something like, "I think the very first thing we need to be concerned about are the people who are the victims in situations like these. I want to make sure first that everyone's all right and that all their needs are being taken care of. That concern has to be paramount. Second, we need to be sure that we know precisely what occurred so that we can take appropriate action and make sure nothing like it ever happens again. And third, we want to be careful that we don't rush to judgment and assume that we already have the full story. There's a lot that's still unknown and that we're trying to find out as soon as we can."

Resorting to legalisms makes academic leaders sound cold even when they're in the right. Showing compassion for others can help win listeners over even when your case isn't as strong as you'd like it to be.

If you have additional information to provide to the reporter, follow up with that information as soon as possible, but do so only once. Particularly in situations where you've had to answer a reporter's question with, "I'm afraid I don't know," you may wish to follow up later with a bit more information. Do this as soon as you can so that these additional insights reach the reporter before his or her deadline. But don't allow yourself to be drawn into an additional interview about matters that you're not prepared to discuss; provide only the information that you promised (e-mail and voice mail is extremely useful for this purpose). Also, don't keep contacting the reporter with multiple additional clarifications or amplification. You will find that repeated calls only cloud the issue even more and make it appear as though you are defensive or trying to conceal something.

o *Don't use disciplinary jargon.* Even if you use the technical terms of your discipline on a daily basis, remember to define them or rephrase them in ordinary language for the reporter. Outside of academia, people don't always understand the difference between an assistant professor and an associate professor, computer science and computer information systems, the department of biology and the college of medicine.

You should never use terms that you're not absolutely certain are clear to both the reporter and the general public. If you sense in any way that you need to define a term, do so in the course of the conversation. "Well, the most important thing for us to remember is that we didn't actually fire this person. The matter was really a nonrenewal of a contract, and here's the critical difference between those two concepts . . . "

When You Have Time to Prepare for an Interview

○ *Learn the purpose or focus of the story in advance.* Since you have time to prepare, use that time to your best advantage. Gather as much specific information as possible so that you can make your case effectively. Anticipate the sorts of questions you're likely to be asked. Decide what you'll say and, even more important, what you *won't* say no matter how hard the reporter may push your buttons. If the interview is being conducted by a student newspaper or television station, you may even be able to insist on receiving a list of all the questions you're going to be asked. You can say something like, "My policy, whenever I'm interviewed by a student newspaper, is always to make the process as educational for the student body as possible. For this reason, I'll need to be shown all of the questions I'm going to be asked at least twenty-four hours in advance so that I can be certain that they adhere to proper journalistic standards."

You'll rarely be accorded this privilege with a professional newspaper, radio station, or television program. Nevertheless, this ploy does work from time to time even in those situations, and it never hurts to ask if you can be sent the questions before the interview "so that I can have all of the information at my fingertips when you get here." At the very least, you'll want to know the general subject of the story so that you can prepare for the interview adequately.

○ *Identify three to five talking points.* By knowing what message you intend to convey in the interview, you'll be more likely to direct its focus to issues that are positive for your institution. If you find it necessary, a single index card or printed sheet with these bullet points can lie on the table in front of you, and you can glance at it from time to time. Preparing your ideas will also help you at those times when you intend to answer the question you wished you were asked rather than the question actually posed by the reporter.

○ *If you haven't done a lot of interviews before, conduct a practice session.* It can be very useful to ask a colleague to help you prepare for your interview by asking you potential questions, even grilling you aggressively on issues that are likely to make you uncomfortable. This rehearsal will help you feel more comfortable during the interview itself, and your colleague may be able to suggest ways in which, by providing additional information or slightly altering your choice of words, you can be more successful in your efforts to remain on message.

○ *Prepare several sound bites.* Short, pithy, catchy phrases are likely to be included by the reporter in the printed article or broadcast because they're quickly understood and make the story more interesting. Few of us are creative enough to think of something immensely quotable on the spur of the moment. Since you have time to prepare for your interview, devote some of your creativity to developing a few memorable phrases that will help you convey your message most effectively.

○ *Include anecdotes.* Talking in general about what students need or the purpose of higher education is less compelling than stories people can relate to. So rather than speaking vaguely about the student body, provide an anecdote about a particular student (always having received permission from the student to do so, of course) that brings the story to life. Talk about your own educational experience so that people see you as a human being, not simply as a college administrator.

> The data you provide will demonstrate that your information is correct. The stories you tell will demonstrate that it's important.

When the Interview Is Impromptu

○ *Defer the discussion whenever you can.* The best possible strategy when ambushed or blindsided by the media is to direct the reporter to your institution's public relations office. But there will be times when that's just not possible. In such cases, it's still a good idea to try delaying the discussion until you can compose yourself, think through the message you wish to convey, and develop an overall strategy for your conversation. You can say something like, "I'm terribly busy right now, and I have a meeting that I simply have to prepare for. Is there a time later when I can call you or when we can meet?" This strategy will give you at least an hour or two to prepare for the interview. In that time, you can contact your public relations office and strategize with them how you will proceed at the interview itself.

○ *Be on guard.* A great deal of what's considered news involves matters that are controversial, scandalous, or embarrassing. We could all wish that reporters would communicate only our successes, but in the real world, this is not going to happen. The vast majority of news conveyed by the media is bad news, and reporters are inevitably interested in anything negative or disreputable that occurs on your campus. Those issues may run the gamut from a possible enrollment decline to the preventable death of a student, from consistently poor attendance at an event "paid for by the public," to the most personal details involving a staff member's dismissal.

When an institution refuses to speak at all to the media on these topics, it doesn't make the stories disappear; in fact, it can end up looking even worse for the school if a reporter has to say something like, "Despite repeated contacts, no one from the university returned this reporter's calls." For this reason, it's important for you and the public relations staff to get ahead of all stories, particularly those that can be damaging to the institution's reputation. Your message may be nothing more than that an internal investigation is continuing so that situations like the one being reported may be prevented in the future. Or you may wish to say that the institution is committed to ensuring that all personnel decisions are made in an equitable and appropriate manner and it's your understanding that this high standard was followed in the current situation. Whatever response you or your public relations office provide in difficult situations, you'll be better off if you seek a good balance between compassion and professionalism than if you try to stonewall the reporter.

○ *The reply, "No comment," is often worse than any comment you could have made.* In certain situations, it would be inappropriate, illegal, or unwise for you to provide the media with information about an issue. Frequently these situations arise when confidential personnel matters are involved or where student records are protected by the Family Educational Rights and Privacy Act. (See chapter 16.) Stating a simple, "No comment," to a reporter may be your constitutional right, but it is usually an ineffective strategy that makes it look as though you have a great deal to conceal. It can even lead to speculation that is far worse than the actual situation.

For this reason, it's far preferable to give a reason that you're unable to comment than to simply refuse to speak at all. You might try saying, "Well, unfortunately, our institutional policy is not to discuss publicly the reasons that confidential personnel decisions are made. We find that this policy helps protect the individual's privacy better and serves that person's best interest in the long run. What I *will* tell you, however, is that we do have in place a detailed policy on how these types of decisions are made and that, in this case, we followed that policy to the letter. In fact, I can get you a copy of the procedure that we used. It's in the public domain and is even posted on our website at . . . "

When You Want Publicity

Sometimes it's not a reporter who's pursuing you, but you who are pursuing the media because you have an event that you want to publicize or a success that you'd like recognized. In these cases, there are also several important guidelines to keep in mind:

o   *Keep press releases short and compelling.* It's often easy to tell the difference between press releases done by academic leaders and those prepared by media specialists. While deans and provosts write stories that are several pages long, professionals in the field typically keep press releases to a single crisp paragraph. If you try to draft your own press release, make it no longer than a single side of a page. Put the most interesting or eye-catching information first; if the press release doesn't interest the recipient after a brief glance, he or she will probably ignore it. Include several brief quotes that could be inserted into the article or paraphrased during a broadcast. Attach a good, clear photograph that could be used as part of the print article or as a background during a television report. For everything else, supply contact information so that the reporter can follow up with you for more details.

o   *Make events easy for members of the media to attend.* Good publicity can come not just when you're promoting an event but also when you're celebrating its success. If it's a ticketed event, provide free admission to members of the media. Send them these tickets well before the event itself, along with maps that indicate where to go, passes for special parking arrangements, and a schedule of when it might be possible to have a private conversation with the speaker, performer, or special guest. Identify in advance a few good locations for photographs or a video to be made. Offer to be available if you're needed for background information or other assistance.

Conclusion

Academic leaders frequently find dealing with the media frustrating. Only a fraction of what they say ever appears in the final report. Often the fraction that does appear is, in the minds of the deans and provosts themselves, the least important part of the story. Despite their best attempts to provide the media with facts, errors all too often appear in the final story. And yet despite all these frustrations, good media relations are an important component of every college or university's success. Try to maintain good relations with the journalists in your area. Don't set your expectations too high. And most important of all, never say anything—even off the record or in a private conversation—that you don't want made public.

RESOURCES

Bonk, K. (2008). *Strategic communications for nonprofits: A step-by-step guide to working with the media.* San Francisco, CA: Jossey-Bass.

Bonk, K., Griggs, H., & Tynes, E. (1999). *The Jossey-Bass guide to strategic communications for nonprofits: A step-by-step guide to working with the media to generate publicity, enhance fundraising.* San Francisco, CA: Jossey-Bass.

Frazier, L. J. (2014). Representing your institution well: Engaging with the media. In L. L. Behling (Ed.), *The resource handbook for academic deans* (pp. 195–198). San Francisco, CA: Jossey-Bass.

Hoffman, J. C. (2011). *Keeping cool on the hot seat: Dealing effectively with the media in times of crisis* (5th ed.). Highland Mills, NY: 4 C's.

Leroux, M. K. (2010). *The nonprofit marketing guide: High-impact, low-cost ways to build support for your good cause.* San Francisco, CA: Jossey-Bass.

Stewart, S. (2004). *Media training 101: A guide to meeting the press.* Hoboken, NJ: Wiley.

Wade, J. (1992). *Dealing effectively with the media: What you need to know about print, radio and television interviews.* Mississauga, ON: Crisp Learning.

Walker, T. J. (2011). *Media training A-Z: A complete guide to controlling your image, message and sound bites* (6th ed.). New York, NY: Media Training Worldwide.

43

THE UNIONIZED ENVIRONMENT

There are two essential principles that academic leaders are well advised to keep in mind about organized labor and its relationship to higher education. The first is:

> Working with a unionized faculty and staff can simplify matters greatly.

And the second is:

> Working with a unionized faculty and staff can complicate matters almost unimaginably.

The challenge is that these two principles are equally true. In other words, there are numerous aspects of an administrator's relationship with the faculty and staff that become much clearer in a unionized environment. Workload considerations, the distribution of salary increases, evaluation standards, and many other complex decisions that other deans and provosts have to struggle with are addressed through a much more systematic and organized process when a collective bargaining agreement is in place. A negotiated contract will usually spell out many important details of the job responsibilities that can and can't be assigned to different classes of employees, specify the standards that must be used in performance evaluations, outline the process that must be followed for arbitrating differences, and provide a great deal of additional information that otherwise would have to be decided on a case-by-case basis by individual administrators. That's the strength of a union contract: it seeks to treat everyone fairly and establishes clear parameters within which certain processes must occur.

Simultaneously, however, there's also a great deal about an administrator's working relationships with the faculty and staff that becomes far more challenging in a unionized setting. For example, the ability that a dean or provost has to launch new initiatives may be severely restricted because of limitations on adding to a faculty member's workload. Academic leaders may not have the freedom they would like to modify job descriptions in order to free up certain members of the faculty or staff for tasks that you regard as important to the future of their programs. They may be limited in the way in which they can reward employees for a job particularly well done, just as they may not be free to choose the ways in which they can impose sanctions on those who consistently underperform. In addition to the challenges provosts and deans always face when terminating a tenured faculty member (see chapter 39), there are usually extra levels of appeal and documentation that can complicate the situation even more when the employee is covered by a union contract.

Above all, many academic leaders find that unionized environments introduce an unwanted adversarial relationship into their association. Although provosts and deans understand that they have a supervisory relationship with faculty members, they also usually see faculty members as their colleagues, not their subordinates. After all, most academic leaders were themselves once full-time faculty members and still think of themselves largely as playing a faculty role. The corporate division between labor and management creates an us-versus-them dichotomy that strikes many academic leaders as incompatible with the collegial, consensus-based approach of shared governance that they hope to develop. They'd prefer to create a better balance between their supervisory responsibilities of ensuring high quality in their programs, providing an appropriate level of accountability to their stakeholders, and maintaining the level of productivity they need in order for their units to remain viable with their collegial responsibilities of forging a strong sense of community, building a close academic team, and preserving a high level of morale. (See figure 43.1.) While understanding the inherent complexities of working in a unionized environment can help prevent academic leaders from making serious mistakes, there's little that can be done to make this type of employment relationship any less complicated.

Figure 43.1 Balancing the Administrative Role

Take Full Advantage of Legal Counsel

According to one of the most widely used guides to legal issues in higher education,

> The mix of factors involved, the importance of the policy questions, and the complexity of the law make collective bargaining a potentially troublesome area for administrators. Heavy involvement of legal counsel is clearly called for. Use of professional negotiators, or of administrators experienced in the art of negotiation, is also usually appropriate, particularly when the faculty have such professional expertise on their side of the bargaining table. (Kaplin and Lee, 2013, 318)

In simple terms, provosts and deans should never presume to engage in negotiations directly with a union unless they have the full support of their institution's legal counsel, prior experience in negotiations (at least to the point of having observed previous negotiations on numerous occasions), and a clear mandate from their institutions to do so.

Even beyond this general principle, academics must be aware that there are many gray areas that others may claim fall within the domain of negotiation with the union or contract modification. For example, changes to workload that free a faculty member from teaching duties to prepare annual evaluations of his or her colleagues may, under certain conditions, be construed as improperly delegating management responsibilities to a nonmanagement employee. Particularly in situations where department chairs are regarded as first-level managers or classified as *out of unit* for contract purposes, the unilateral creation of new assistant chairs, directors, program supervisors, or project coordinators can have unforeseen contract implications if these new positions are assigned responsibilities clearly falling to the chair according to the collective bargaining agreement. If you work in a unionized environment, receiving the advice of college counsel or the office of legal affairs should be a part of your standard operating procedure whenever you contemplate a change that would affect someone's workload.

Naturally any action that has a negative impact on an employee (ranging from mild sanctions such as an oral reprimand or the placement of a letter in one's file to severe sanctions such as salary reductions or terminations) should also be discussed in advance with both an attorney and the office of human resources before it is implemented. There may well be initial steps that must be followed before you can proceed with the sanction or a timetable that will guide what you can do when. Proper guidance will prevent you from pursuing a course of action that you'd regret later. At best, violating the terms of a contract could be an embarrassment to you if your decision has to be reversed. At worse, such an action could threaten your position if others conclude that you violated policy, acted irresponsibly, sought retribution, or violated the rights of a member of a protected class.

Issues of Academic Freedom

Ronald B. Standler, in an excellent survey of the issues involved in academic freedom, notes that this concept consists of two not wholly synonymous principles in American higher education:

> There are two distinctly different kinds of academic freedom, which should have distinct names:
>
> 1. *Individual academic freedom* protects an individual professor.
>
> 2. *Institutional academic freedom* protects universities from interference by government, a right that applies to the community of scholars, *not* to individual faculty. (www.rbs2.com/afree.htm; see also Kaplan and Lee, 2013.)

As Louis Menand (1998) noted, those very ambiguities have greatly complicated the discussion of academic freedom at colleges and universities. When using the expression *academic freedom*, administrators and legislatures frequently are adopting it in the sense of what Standler (http://www.rbs2.com/afree.htm) calls "institutional academic freedom." However, unions and many professional organizations like the American Association of University Professors usually assume that the term is identical to what Standler calls *individual academic freedom*. Therein lies the problem.

Much of the case law involving academic freedom, especially *Regents of the University of Michigan v. Ewing* (1985), *Edwards v. California University of Pennsylvania* (1998), and *Urofsky v. Gilmore* (2000), has concluded that the First Amendment rights involved in academic freedom apply only to institutions, not to individuals employed by those institutions (Rabban, 2001). In general, US courts have recognized four major areas of institutional academic freedom.

- The right to decide who will teach its programs
- The right to decide what will be taught in those programs
- The right to decide how that material will be taught
- The right to decide who will be admitted into its programs (provided that public institutions do not violate antidiscrimination laws in doing so)

But those freedoms are very different from the attitude of "I can do whatever I want in my own classroom" that many professors believe is the meaning of academic freedom. As a result, faculty unions often represent themselves as defenders of a type of academic freedom that may even conflict with court-sanctioned, institutional academic freedom. As Steven Poskanzer (2003), the president of Carleton College, notes,

> In upholding a faculty union's statutory right to consult with administrators on matters of college governance (and conversely denying parallel rights to individual faculty outside the union), the Supreme Court noted that it had "never recognized a constitutional right of faculty to participate in policymaking in academic institutions." Indeed, both line academic administrators (chairs, deans, provosts, and presidents) and nonacademic officials (vice presidents for human resources, student affairs professionals) will rightly assert that they are the ones charged with responsibility for managing the affairs of the institution and that—both by knowledge and by breadth of perspective—they are much better suited to do so than faculty (who, perhaps out of self-interest, often resist change and efforts at increased accountability). In light of such tension, the answer to the question of who benefits from academic freedom in intra-university affairs depends almost

> entirely on whose claim of autonomy prevails. Faculty gain stature and influence over college and university operations if their bid for independent speech and action is upheld; administrators will be the direct beneficiaries if claims of *institutional* autonomy are honored. (105–106)

As a result, working in a unionized environment means that provosts and deans may need to clarify which type of academic freedom, individual or institutional, they have in mind when they're making official pronouncements about this issue. In addition, the president and the governing board, not the provost or deans, should really be serving as the voice of academic freedom in both senses of that expression. Since the upper administration constitutes the level of the organization that sets fundamental institutional policies and direction, it's the decisions of the president and board that are ultimately protected by institutional academic freedom. But even in the matter of individual academic freedom, the principle that's involved is defined and protected almost exclusively by the history, mission, and values of the individual institution, not, as many provosts and deans believe, by clearly established case law. For this reason, individual academic freedom means something very different at a seminary than it does at a state college, and no matter how strong a union may be, it won't be successful in disputing that point. If you're at all unclear about how the concept of individual academic freedom is being applied at your institution, it's a good idea to discuss this issue with your supervisor, representatives of your office of legal affairs, and perhaps the director of human resources to make sure that everyone is on that same page and that mixed messages aren't being sent to the faculty.

The Importance of Clear, Regular Communication

Conflicts between the union and administration tend to be at their most severe when the two sides communicate only during periods of contract negotiation or when there's a problem to be solved. It can feel natural for each side to see the other as an adversary when the bulk of the issues that they're dealing with have to do with conflicting views about salary and benefits, workload, the role of faculty evaluations, and appeals resulting from attempted terminations. Deans and provosts can develop a far more constructive relationship with the union if they meet with it regularly when there isn't an obvious conflict. In your own conversations with the union, consider allowing its representatives to state their hopes and concerns to you in regular, informal conversations. Build in an opportunity for you to discuss your own ideas with them. While you should avoid giving any impression that these discussions are either unofficial negotiation sessions or that you're improperly relinquishing your right to make administrative decisions, you can use these talks to build a more constructive, trusting relationship over time. Even if you're in disagreement with the union's stand on certain issues, you're likely to come away from these discussions with a better understanding of why its members have adopted their points of view. These informal conversations can serve as an outgrowth of what Poskanzer (2003) called "a faculty union's statutory right to consult with administrators on matters of college governance" (105).

By providing some regular venue for informal consultation, you'll have an opportunity to demonstrate that your visions for your programs have significant value and that they're not merely a stance that the administration takes during times of negotiation so as to reduce faculty salaries or increase faculty workload. Conversely, you'll learn, in a clearer manner than is possible during what may be tense contract negotiations, where there really are problems that affect the quality of life of the faculty and staff and how teaching, research, and service are viewed by those who are daily involved in these activities.

Union Contract Limitations for Staff

One other issue that deans and provosts need to consider in an environment governed by collective bargaining is who is affected by a union contract and who is not. Depending on tradition and the agreements arising from past negotiations, chairs, assistant and associate deans, program directors, and others with limited administrative responsibilities may be considered to be in unit for the purposes of the contract, or they may qualify as management or part of some other entity that stands outside the contract. In some cases, everyone who is part of the corps of instruction—which, depending on the institution, may be defined as something like "all full-time employees at least half of whose assignment is devoted to teaching and/or research"—falls under the terms of the union contract. In these instances, provosts and deans have to be careful when adjusting the salary or workload of these employees. It can seem unfair that academic leaders may not be able to give bonuses to an assistant dean or associate provost whose work has been exceptional. Nevertheless, such policies are sometimes created specifically to prevent administrators from rewarding cronies to an extent that is not possible for the faculty in general. In order to avoid making promises that you won't be able to keep, therefore, be sure you know who's governed by the union contract before offering to discuss possible compensation with members of the faculty or administrative staff.

Conclusion

Although the organizational culture of higher education does not fit easily into the labor-management division of a unionized environment, many colleges and universities have had a long history of collective bargaining and union contracts. With the rising cost of higher education, competition between for-profit and nonprofit institutions, growing enrollments in many courses, and an increasing dependence on adjuncts, it can be expected that unionized environments will become even more common in the future. For this reason, even deans and provosts who do not currently work at an institution that practices collective bargaining can benefit from understanding the issues that arise in a unionized environment and how those issues might affect their work in the future.

REFERENCES

Edwards v. California University of Pennsylvania. (1998). 156 F.3d 488 (3rd Cir.).

Kaplin, W. A., & Lee, B. A. (2013). *The law of higher education: A comprehensive guide to legal implications of administrative decision making* (5th ed.) San Francisco, CA: Jossey-Bass.

Menand, L. (Ed.). (1998). *The future of academic freedom.* Chicago: University of Chicago Press.

Poskanzer, S. G. (2003). *Higher education law: The faculty.* Baltimore, MD: Johns Hopkins University Press.

Rabban, D. M. (2001). Academic freedom, individual or institutional? *Academe,* 87(6), 16–20.

Regents of the University of Michigan v. Ewing. (1985). 474 US 214.

Urofsky v. Gilmore. (2000). 216 F.3d 401 (4th Cir.).

RESOURCES

Alexander, K. W., & Alexander, K. (2011). *Higher education law: Policy and perspectives.* New York, NY: Routledge.

Arnold, G. B. (2000). *The politics of faculty unionization: The experience of three New England universities.* Westport, CT: Bergin and Garvey.

Benjamin, E., & Mauer, M. (2006). *Academic collective bargaining*. Washington, DC: American Association of University Professors.

Cross, J. G., & Goldenberg, E. N. (2009). *Off-track profs: Nontenured teachers in higher education*. Cambridge, MA: MIT Press.

Duryea, E. D., & Fish, R. S. (1973). *Faculty unions and collective bargaining*. San Francisco, CA: Jossey-Bass.

Hoeller, K. (2014). *Equality for contingent faculty: Overcoming the two-tier system*. Nashville, TN: Vanderbilt University Press.

Hutcheson, P. A. (2000). *A professional professoriate: Unionization, bureaucratization, and the AAUP*. Nashville, TN: Vanderbilt University Press.

Johnstone, R. L. (1981). *The scope of faculty collective bargaining: An analysis of faculty union agreements at four-year institutions of higher education*. Westport, CT: Greenwood Press.

Mortimer, K. P., & Sathre, C.O.B. (2010). *The art and politics of academic governance: Relations among boards, presidents, and faculty*. Lanham, MD: Rowman & Littlefield.

Pierce, S. R. (2014). *Governance reconsidered: How boards, presidents, administrators, and faculty can help their colleges thrive*. San Francisco, CA: Jossey-Bass.

Wheelan, S. A. (2004). *Faculty groups: From frustration to collaboration*. Thousand Oaks, CA: Corwin Press.

44

THE DEAN AS CHIEF ACADEMIC OFFICER

While much of the discussion in this book is based on the assumption that the dean and the provost are two separate people who share many of the same concerns, there are also many institutions where the dean *is* the provost. Often these schools are small, private institutions where the chief academic officer is called the dean of the faculty, dean of the college, or academic dean. Sometimes in these organizational structures, there are department chairs or division directors who perform various administrative tasks on the dean's behalf; these administrators may have direct supervisory authority over the faculty members in their areas, or they may serve in a more collegial role simply as "first among equals." There are even schools where every member of the faculty reports directly to the dean. Whatever the exact structure that exists at any particular institution, whenever a dean functions as a chief academic officer, he or she will encounter challenges and opportunities that differ significantly from those of colleagues in institutions with more complex hierarchies.

A Conflation of Roles

At institutions where there's a clear chain of command that runs from the faculty through the department chair, dean, chief academic officer, president, and governing board, the organization develops a certain degree of predictability because each of these positions comes with its own role and expectations.

- o The department chair is expected to serve as an advocate for the discipline.

- ○ The dean is expected to serve as an advocate for an established group of disciplines that share a common methodology, history, or approach to pedagogy.
- ○ The chief academic officer is expected to serve as an arbiter among all of these competing needs and also serve as an advocate for the academic mission of the institution as a whole.
- ○ The president (or chancellor) is expected to serve as an arbiter among all of the institution's competing needs and also as an advocate for the institution as a whole.
- ○ The governing board is expected to approve institutional policies, ratify the strategic plan, supervise the overall management of the institution, provide fiscal oversight, review essential operations, and make the final decision in the case of certain appeals. Most governing boards also appoint and evaluate the president.

Whenever one or more of these levels is conflated, it can become much more difficult for an administrator to meet all of the expectations that arise from his or her combined position. For example, when deans also serve as their institution's chief academic officers, they may be torn between their desire to serve as advocates for the academic programs under their supervision and their obligation to protect the budgetary integrity of the entire academic program. The combination of these roles can also send mixed messages to the faculty. "Why are you refusing to fund this project?" the dean may be asked. "I thought you were our advocate." This situation is exacerbated when the institution doesn't grant true supervisory or line authority to department chairs or division directors. In such a case, the dean may feel as though he or she must switch roles constantly—serving at one moment as the chair of a discipline, the next moment as the dean, and the moment after that as the vice president for academic affairs—and end up pleasing no one at all in the process.

Deans who also serve as chief academic officers may need to make an extra effort to explain to others (both those to whom they report and those who report to them) the complexity that results from their role. They may need to say to faculty members on a regular basis, "Of course, I'm your advocate, and I want your program to flourish. But I also know that achieving this goal would be impossible if we end up having to make a lot of budget cuts next year because we exceeded our current allocation. We could fill only two full-time positions this year, and yes, as the college's chief academic officer, I had to make the hard decision to assign those positions to other areas. Sometimes the need to take the whole academic picture into account means that I don't have all the resources I'd like to devote to your area. But I do have a plan for how I think we can move closer toward achieving our goals for your discipline. Here's what I think we need to do . . . " Conversations of this sort help to remind others of the difficult dual role that a combined dean-and-provost must play. They help faculty members distinguish between what the academic leader needs to do in evaluating competing needs and what he or she plans to do as an advocate for the discipline in question.

A Conflation of Decision and Appeal

One of the other challenges that deans can face when their institutions lack multiple levels of hierarchy is the pressure that tends to result when faculty members or students have fewer avenues for appeal. In more complex institutions, a wide variety of decisions are made by faculty members themselves or by department chairs. If a student or faculty member believes that a chair's decision was unfair or violated the institution's procedures, an appeal can usually be submitted to the dean. The dean's decision can be appealed in turn to the provost or vice president for academic affairs. These multiple layers of appeal have an important value in terms of both principle and practicality. From the standpoint of principle, they protect the individual who is affected by the decision from the arbitrary judgment of any one individual. From the standpoint of practicality, multiple levels of appeal often result in a more harmonious or smoothly functioning institution. That's because when individuals have had their cases reviewed at several previous levels, they often feel that their perspectives are being adequately considered. If the appeal is denied by a faculty member, chair, dean, provost, president, and board, it becomes much harder for them to believe that their request has been dismissed due to the bias of any individual administrator. (There are, of course, exceptions to this principle, and that is precisely why appeals sometimes advance all the way to the governing board.)

Nevertheless, when one or more of these levels is removed, the intensity of the appeal process can increase exponentially. The individual who's making the request may view the levels at which the decision is being made and to which an appeal should be directed as identical. Where else is there to go to seek redress? Moreover, since several administrators haven't independently reached the same conclusion, the appellant may feel that it's merely the dean's stubbornness or lack of truly understanding the seriousness of the issue that has prevented the "correct" decision from being made. The result, which will be all too familiar to deans who also serve as chief academic officers, is that the faculty member or student simply refuses to accept the dean's decision, appeals the decision on the spot, becomes increasingly insistent, and refuses to leave the office until being granted what he or she demands.

Because of this situation, deans who are also chief academic officers need to develop not merely excellent but stellar skills in communication, persuasion, and counseling. Whereas at other types of institutions, a decision can often be justified by referring to precedents, this practice is rarely possible at schools with a flat administrative structure. The dean will immediately be challenged to justify the precedent, exhorted to decide on the basis of justice rather than history, and tested to the utmost of his or her rhetorical skills. Emotions tend to ratchet up very quickly in these situations, since the person with the complaint knows that there are no other opportunities for appeal; moreover, if there does exist another avenue for appeal (such as the president and governing board), the person may feel that these levels are impossibly remote and likely to reaffirm the dean's decision. For this reason, deans who serve as chief academic officers must exercise a great deal of patience, remain calm even when the other person's assertiveness begins to morph into abuse, explain the basis for the precedent, and clarify whenever possible how that decision is ultimately in the best interests of everyone involved.

As we have seen repeatedly, superior people skills are almost a prerequisite for deans and provosts. But deans at smaller institutions need to have those skills perfected from the first day on the job because of the frequency with which they'll be required to make and communicate their decisions.

Balancing Workload

The workload of all academic administrators tends to be excessive. Simply balancing all the committees on which they serve, the stakeholders they need to address, the letters and other forms of communication that must be answered, the meetings they must attend, and the reports they have to write can be an all-consuming job. And when there are fewer administrative levels at an institution, this workload increases proportionally. Rather than having a provost who serves on the president's cabinet, the dean must also fill this role. Rather than having department chairs or other directors who oversee the day-to-day operations of individual programs, there may at times be no one else who can take on these duties. While logic might dictate that the larger and more complex an institution is, the heavier and more difficult the dean's workload would be, the reverse is frequently the case. Deans at small institutions regularly feel as though they're pulled in several directions at once, emerging from a meeting unable to accomplish the tasks the committee has just agreed to undertake because there's yet another meeting to attend immediately and no one else can be delegated the task that the dean has been assigned.

In addition to these competing demands for one's time at work, there's also a need for deans to balance these professional duties with their personal lives, work as a scholar, and the frequent expectation that they should be active in service organizations, religious groups, and volunteer activities. While there can be no perfect solution that fits each dean's personality and individual situation, the following recommendations provide some relief when the pressure of responsibilities seem overwhelming.

Plan carefully

Too often the activities that end up consuming our time aren't those that are most productive or even the most important to our institutions. A carefully constructed calendar or day planner should never become your master, but it can be your best asset in the effective use of your time. In your planning, consider marking out time on your calendar for your own scholarship, walking around and talking to people, getting off-campus occasionally, and having some quiet time to think. If you don't block out periods for these activities before other demands arise, less important responsibilities will consume your day before you find the time you were expecting would somehow just emerge.

Don't be embarrassed to ask for help when you need it

Deans sometimes feel that requesting additional staff members or the right to delegate some of their responsibilities to others is tantamount to an admission that they're not up to the job. These fears are almost always unfounded. Presidents expect deans to be candid about their workload and would prefer some reassignment of duties to allowing important work to slip through the cracks or to having to replace a dean who leaves the institution because of job dissatisfaction.

Learn to say no politely

Many deans regard it as a matter of pride to chair every committee they're asked to serve on, agree to every speaking engagement they're invited to attend, and travel to every conference for which they're eligible. But taking on too many obligations increases the likelihood that few of these obligations will receive the dean's full attention. It's perfectly acceptable to decline a few responsibilities so as to place greater focus on others. Remind yourself that no one except yourself ever really expects you to accept every responsibility you're offered.

Take real vacations

Deans who serve on twelve-month contracts almost always earn annual leave time they can use for vacations. Use it! It's true, as every dean says, that there's no good time for a dean to be away from campus. And that's particularly true when you're also serving as chief academic officer. Even when classes are not in session, there's a great deal of planning that needs to be done. Despite your heavy workload (or actually because of it), it's in your institution's best interest for you to be fresh and focused when you perform your duties.

So although it may be difficult, make a practice of taking a week or two off at a time. With enough warning, the institution can make plans to do what needs to be done while you are away. And when you are away, make sure that you're enjoying a real vacation. Attending a conference or checking in by phone and e-mail several times a day doesn't give you the leisure that you need to unwind and recover your full level of energy. Delegate your responsibilities to others while you are away, check in (if you must do so at all) no more frequently than once a week, and leave your laptop, tablet, and—if you can bring yourself to do so—cell phone locked in your desk back at the office.

Getting Perspective

At institutions with relatively flat administrative structures, deans may be accused of simply being stubborn or not "really understanding" the issue when they fail to grant a request that's made to them. The other side of this coin is that situations can sometimes occur when the dean truly *is* being stubborn or not delving far enough into a situation to understand the issue.

All of us have our blind spots and, without multiple levels in the reporting relationship both above and below us, we don't have individuals in place who help us see different perspectives, serve as the devil's advocate when we're working our way through complex issues, or simply challenge us to get out of our comfort zones. Deans who also serve as their institution's provost may need to make an extra effort to understand when waiving a policy or granting an exemption is perfectly warranted. Unless their institution is one that doesn't have department chairs, working with representatives of each discipline as a sort of dean's cabinet or internal advisory council can be an extremely effective way to broaden perspective on a significant number of issues. Gradually changing the focus of meetings that once were used solely for the sharing of information to true decision making or at least advisory bodies will both help manage your workload and give you access to a group of advisors that can prove invaluable. Consider disseminating information electronically, eliminating roundtable updates on routine items, distributing a written agenda in advance of each meeting, and devoting a sizable portion of the group's time to expressing points of views, making plans, and discussing how policies could be improved. At the very least, you may gain the respect of others at the meeting since you took the time to ask their opinions. Even better, you may find that issues you believed to be one-sided or clear-cut are actually far more complex than you realized.

Interacting with the President

We saw in chapter 22 that all deans should interact with their provosts by using the three Cs: candor, collegiality, and confidentiality. When the dean is the provost, this principle then applies to his or her interactions with the president. If you're the chief academic officer, your association with the president is the most critical professional relationship you have. A good rapport with your institution's CEO can make all the difference between success and failure or between loving your job and becoming increasingly dissatisfied with it.

For this reason, you may need to go out of your way to strengthen this relationship, particularly in situations where the president is off campus frequently because of fundraising activities or doesn't have a warm and engaging personality. If you can do so, set aside time for one-on-one meetings where no work is on the agenda but where the two of you can just get to know each other. Get off campus together at least once a month for breakfast or lunch. Offer to drive when attending meetings at some distance from the office to give yourselves time to catch up and perform an "attitude check" on one another. Above all, don't use these private meetings as opportunities to advance your personal agenda or make additional requests. That will change the entire purpose of the conversation and may even make the president reluctant to undergo a sequel. The chief academic officer and the president must be members of a close and harmonious team; if the president isn't laying the groundwork for this relationship to flourish, it's up to you to do so.

Conclusion

Serving simultaneously as dean and as chief academic officer is the best possible illustration of an important essential principle:

> Nearly every institution of higher education has the same committees and needs the same jobs done. The only difference is that at smaller schools, fewer people are available to serve on those committees and perform these jobs. The result is that everyone ends up wearing multiple hats, and work becomes more, not less, complex than at a large university.

What this essential principle means is that many of the tasks that at larger institutions are assigned to department chairs, deans, and provosts all accrue to the chief academic officer at a smaller school. As compensation for the higher workload and level of stress, the dean who also serves as chief academic officer has a greater potential for making a real difference at his or her school and gaining experience in a wider range of important administrative functions. Particularly if you are hoping someday to serve as the president of a college or university, serving simultaneously as dean and provost can be an excellent foundation for the type of complexity you would face in a leadership role at the head of an entire institution.

RESOURCES

Diamond, R. M. (Ed.). (2002). *Field guide to academic leadership*. San Francisco, CA: Jossey-Bass.

Erwin, J. S. (2000). The dean as chief academic officer. *New Directions for Community Colleges, 109,* 9–18.

Krahenbuhl, G. S. (2004). *Building the academic deanship: Strategies for success.* Westport, CT: Praeger.

Martin, J., & Samels, J. E. (2015). *First among equals: The role of the chief academic officer* (2nd ed.). Baltimore, MD: Johns Hopkins University Press.

Nielsen, L. A. (2013). *Provost: Experiences, reflections, and advice from a former "number two" on campus.* Sterling, VA: Stylus.

Wolverton, M., Gmelch, W. H., Montez, J., & Nies, C. T. (2001). *The changing nature of the academic deanship.* ASHE-ERIC Higher Education Research Report, vol. 28, no. 1. San Francisco, CA: Jossey-Bass.

45

A SCENARIO ANALYSIS ON THE CHALLENGES OF BEING AN ACADEMIC LEADER

For a discussion of how scenario analyses are structured and suggestions on how to use this exercise most productively, see the beginning of chapter 7. A scenario analysis for deans appears in the online content accompanying this book.

Case Study for Provosts

The semester is just ending, and everything seems to be going wrong at once. A series of sexual harassment issues involving members of your faculty have led to several lawsuits, not merely against the alleged perpetrators but also against the university for not being sufficiently proactive in making sure that employees and students alike are able to work in a safe and nonhostile environment. An animal rights group has protested experiments conducted on campus that they regard as inhumane, with the result that representatives of this group are now occupying several of your institution's science facilities. Your office has been besieged by angry calls and letters from a religious group because one of your faculty members gave a public speech in which she described the founding figure of the religion as "more mythical than historical" in nature and argued that its sacred texts were not divinely inspired and produced, as the religion contends, within a short period of time but represent several centuries of editing and revision. A higher-than-usual number of athletic injuries have provoked your institution's parents' council to demand a full investigation into the safety of your sports program. Last night a local television reporter ran a story about how he was able to gain access to several residence halls on your campus that are supposed to be closed to everyone but students and even found several student rooms unlocked and unoccupied. An accident in one of the chemistry labs resulted in serious injuries when the facility's safety shower malfunctioned.

You're in a meeting with the rest of the executive staff on how to handle these multiple crises when the president's administrative assistant comes to the door. "Reporters from Channel 8 and Channel 15 are outside," the assistant tells the president. "Apparently there's been a new development, and they need to talk to you right away. This one sounds pretty bad."

The president turns to you: "Look, I'm up to my neck dealing with these other issues. I need you to take the lead on this one. Go talk to the reporters and see what they want."

You're annoyed that the president seems to be sending you to face the media when you regard it as her job to represent the university in situations like this. But she's given you a direct order to handle the situation, so you get up to meet the reporters. When you reach the president's outer office, you discover that it's not just the reporters from the two television stations present but also several print journalists, including the editor of the student newspaper. Cameras and recorders are on, and flashbulbs pop when you enter the room. What do you do?

Considerations

1. How would you respond if the new development were one of the following?

   a. A pipe has burst, rendering your university's largest classroom facility unusable, and a large number of final exams were scheduled there today.

   b. An armed intruder has taken hostages in the student union.

   c. A distressed student is on the roof of one of the residence halls and is threatening to jump.

   d. The press has photographs of the president in a compromising position with someone who's not her spouse.

   e. Evidence has emerged that the vice president for business affairs has been taking kickbacks on various contracts.

2. How would you respond if the new development were something that made one of the existing problems worse, such as the following?

   a. A judge has just ruled that the university was indeed liable for not providing a safe environment for employees and students, had knowingly permitted a hostile workplace to exist, and is subject to damages sufficiently large that they would make the university's continued operation unsustainable.

b. The occupation of facilities by the animal rights group has spread to other buildings. The group has taken hostages and is threatening to "destroy all facilities and equipment involved in animal torture" unless their demands are met.

c. The religious group attacked the professor who has offended them as she was arriving on campus this morning. She is in critical condition in the hospital, and the press wants to know why the university didn't do more to protect her.

d. Your school's athletic conference is threatening to shut down your entire sports program unless the safety issues are addressed to its satisfaction.

e. More than three hundred students have withdrawn from the university because last night's television report made them feel that they were no longer safe in the residence halls. A group of these students is holding a press conference in which they claim that the failure of security noted by the reporter "is just the tip of the iceberg."

f. One of the students injured in the chemistry lab accident has died.

3. Do you think the president was right in continuing to work on addressing the crises and sending you to meet with the press?

a. If you think the president was right, how do you respond to a reporter who says, "We asked to meet with the president herself, not some second-in-command. Does she have something to hide?"

b. If you think the president wasn't right, how do you later discuss this issue with her in a constructive manner?

Suggestions

Although it may be unrealistic to imagine that you'd ever have to deal with this many problems simultaneously, crises do occur, and the provost—like everyone else on the academic leadership team—has to be prepared to deal with them. In fact, it's not uncommon for crises to occur in groups—perhaps not six or seven at once as in this case study but at least two or three at once. That's because when everyone's attention is directed toward one area, problems tend to arise elsewhere, either because people have let their guard down or because critical resources have been shifted in order to deal with the crisis. In addition, the news media react to problems and scandals in higher education rather like sharks in a feeding frenzy. By looking carefully at one problem, they tend to spot others, and thus a single challenge can multiply into a multifold disaster. In fact, certain stories may not really be major problems for a university until the press decides they're newsworthy.

Thinking about how to respond to numerous crises simultaneously is good preparation for an academic leader. It helps you decide how you'd triage the situation and where you'd begin to direct your greatest attention. You may not need to use these skills often in your administrative career, but when a complex emergency arises, you'll be glad you have them.

In this case study, there are several steps you can take in order to handle what is obviously a very bad situation:

○ Immediately after you enter the room with all the reporters present, turn to one of the staff members and ask, "Is a representative from the office of community relations on the way?" The question thus alters the staff member to your expectation that there be a public relations person present for the press conference, and if someone has not already been summoned, you'd like that office to send someone immediately.

○ You might then follow that question with a request: "Also, please ask the president to join us just as soon as she's available." This statement alerts the staff member to let the president know that the situation is one where her presence really is required. At the same time, it indicates to the press that the president is very busy dealing with the various emergencies on campus but will join you a bit later.

○ A good way of starting the exchange is to take control of the process (rather than letting the reporters set the agenda) and to try to demonstrate that you're all on the same side: "First, I'd like to thank you for taking the time to join us here on campus today. Obviously we're facing a number of serious issues right now, and I appreciate your willingness to share in our efforts to get information out to people to help ensure their safety and resolve any concerns they may have."

○ Next, demonstrate concern for those who have been affected by the crises and underscore the institution's commitment to make things right. But don't commit yourself to any specific course of action unless it's already been decided that that's what the institution will do. Say something like, "Of course, our biggest concern right now is for people's safety and well-being. I can assure you that that's my top priority, and also the top priority of the president, our board, and everyone else here at the institution. We take these reports very seriously and are always troubled to find that any member of our community has a problem we need to address. That's the single most important message I want you all to hear today."

○ Take further control of the narrative by focusing it in the way you feel is best for the institution. Don't minimize or apologize for mistakes that were made, but try to put them into a more complete context. You might say, "Like any other complex organization, when problems occur, they tend to occur all at once. So rather than talk about everything all at once, I'd like to be as systematic as I can in terms of what we know about each situation and how we're dealing with it." Then you might proceed by talking about whichever issue you know most about or feel most comfortable discussing.

○ If a reporter blindsides you with new information, don't be lured into saying more than you know. The reporter is likely to present only one side of what may be a highly complex issue, and you don't want to admit fault where there may be none or declare someone guilty of wrongdoing when facts may exonerate that person later. Defer the question by saying, "I'm sorry, but what you've just told me is new information. None of us wants to make a problem worse by acting before we've had time to investigate further and plan the best course of action. I can assure you that we'll explore this matter in great detail, act in the best interests of everyone involved, and get back to you with updates just as soon as we have them."

PART SEVEN

THE NEXT STEP FOR THE PROVOST OR DEAN

46

KNOWING WHEN IT'S TIME TO GO

Deans and provosts serve on average for about five to six years in their positions. Of course, like most other averages, that figure conceals as much information as it reveals. We've all known academic leaders who have served fifteen, perhaps even twenty, years at a single institution, and we've all known administrators who, for whatever reason, left their positions after only a year or two. Besides, knowing the tenure of the average academic leader really tells very little about individual situations. After all, who wants merely to be average?

The length of time you'll serve in your position is a function of your own personality and goals, the needs of your institution, the desires and personality of your supervisor, and your own satisfaction in working with the faculty and staff in your programs. As variable as these factors may be, however, there are several clear warning signs that should suggest to you it may be time to think about investigating other career opportunities. Let's explore several of these warning signs and discuss why each may indicate to you that it's time to go, or at least to reflect seriously on why you may wish to stay.

A Sense of Staleness

We saw in chapter 2 that there are many bad reasons for wishing to become a dean or provost, including a desire to increase your salary, reach a position where you can advance your own discipline at the expense of others, and enjoy the many benefits that can accompany administrative positions. But we also saw a number of excellent reasons to serve as an academic leader that have attracted some fine scholars into administrative roles. These deans and provosts had a passion for making a difference in the quality of their academic programs, a commitment to creating an environment in which both students and faculty members could grow with intellectual freedom, a capacity to understand the needs of higher education on a large scale while still serving as a fervent advocate for the people in their area, and a delight in communicating with a broad range of constituents about the successes, challenges, and opportunities of all the disciplines they supervised. Reflect for a moment on the reasons that you first became a dean or provost, and then ask the following questions:

- Am I still motivated by the same opportunities and challenges? Do I still feel that I have important contributions to make in these areas?

- If I'm no longer motivated by the issues that led me to academic administration, have I found other major opportunities and challenges that I can pursue in my current position? Have I sought out new ways in which I can make a positive difference at my institution? Are these new ways exciting to me?

- Do I find my work challenging enough to engage me but not so challenging as to be a continual source of frustration?

- Do I look forward to returning to my position after I've been away from work for a weekend or longer?

- When I envision the future, do I still see myself happily working in this same position five years from now? Two years from now?

- As I think of my programs' goals for the next five to ten years, do I find them interesting?

- Do I still discover that on a regular basis, I have new ideas to share with my unit, or am I mostly implementing and building on the ideas I had in the past?

- Do I come to work happy to be there on more days than not?

- Do I still find meaning and a desirable level of engagement in my current position?

As Lev Vygotsky demonstrated long ago through his concept of the zone of proximal development, most people learn best and achieve the greatest satisfaction when they are sufficiently challenged to stretch their abilities, but not so overwhelmingly challenged that they feel frustrated and discouraged (Vygotsky and Kozulin, 1986; Vygotsky, 1978). If you feel there are still important contributions to make in your job and find the opportunity to make these contributions both interesting and rewarding, there's probably no compelling reason right now for you to explore a different role in higher education. As we'll see in the next chapter, a new position that looks enticing from the outside may be fraught with disappointments once you accept it. If you're still enjoying the work you're doing and have ideas you want to explore in the future, consider yourself lucky. A large number of people in the world would love to have what you have right now.

But if you believe that you're getting stale in your position—answering the same questions over and over and attending what seem like the same meetings year after year—then it may be time to think about moving on. Lack of challenge isn't good for you, since it can lead to boredom and ultimately to resentment of an institution and career you once loved. Even more important, it isn't good for the people you work with, since someone with fresher ideas or a higher degree of energy may help your area achieve a new level of success. If you suspect that your programs could benefit from new leadership, the best contribution you can make to your institution now is to seek a new type of assignment.

A Lack of Fit

At other times deans and provosts may find that it's not the continuing challenge or interest of their positions that concerns them but rather the specific environment in which they find themselves. A sense that your current position may be a bad fit for you, that you may not be the right person for this job, or that the job may not be the right opportunity for you right now could result from several different factors.

Level of the position

Some people become dissatisfied as deans or provosts because they feel that they're misplaced at this level of the institution. Full-time administrative work may allow them too little time for teaching or research. They may miss the close interactions with students that they had as faculty members. They may feel that they were more effective representing one particular discipline as a department chair. Or a position of academic leadership may not offer them a broad enough canvas for the initiatives they'd like to pursue, opportunities that may be possible only at the level of president, chancellor, or head of a university system.

Focus of the position

Other people may find that they enjoy the work they encounter as a dean or provost but that their current position doesn't suit their talents and temperaments. Perhaps they assumed a role as dean of an honors college or graduate school when their real passion was in the arts and sciences, business administration, or education. Perhaps they took a position as provost at a large university when what they were better suited for was work at a smaller liberal arts college. For whatever reason, it is not being an academic leader that feels wrong, but rather being this type of academic leader.

The specific institution

Other people discover that they feel somehow incompatible with the goals and mission of the institution where they are dean. While this experience is most common for individuals who are hired in from other institutions, it can also occur that individuals rising through the ranks of an institution may begin to see things from a new vantage point and feel uncomfortable with what they observe. They may notice that they can't agree with the institution's plan to balance its budget through expanded enrollments rather than through maintaining a higher level of standards even at the risk of cutting faculty positions. They may be philosophically committed to community service and civic engagement while their institution's new strategic plan compels them to defend an approach to education that emphasizes the importance of securing large research grants. They may find that their religious beliefs can't find adequate expression at a secular institution or that their humanistic outlook seems out of step with a private institution that's growing increasingly fundamentalist in outlook. In other words, these deans and provosts still enjoy their jobs; they simply don't enjoy the environment in which they must perform those jobs.

The people

No job is entirely free of irritating individuals. Even the best position will occasionally force you to interact with difficult students, faculty members, other deans, or bosses who will annoy, frustrate, or offend you. A large potion of part 3 of this book deals precisely with what to do when you find yourself in these stressful and challenging situations. But some academic leaders find themselves in situations where the vast majority of the people with and for whom they work seem to annoy them. At times, this reaction is a sign of burnout. One of the signs that we've been at a task too long is that we lose sympathy for the people on whose behalf we're working. At other times, deans and provosts may be projecting their own dissatisfaction with their jobs onto the people around them. It's always possible, of course, that due to the principle that "like tends to hire like," many people at the institution have outlooks and personalities at odds with those of the academic leader. All of these factors may be cause for you to consider if you're wondering whether your current position is still right for you. If you find yourself out of harmony with most of the people you encounter, it's time for a reality check.

When everyone else seems annoying, stubborn, and irritating, pull back and evaluate the situation as objectively as you can. In most cases, you'll discover that the real problem isn't them; it's you.

When you do discover that you're the one responsible for the irritation, frustration, or problem you're experiencing, you still have a number of options. You can try to correct your attitude. You can explore the root cause of your dissatisfaction. Or if the relationship between you and your constituents seems to be broken irreparably, it may be time to consider whether you should remain in your current position.

A Clear Lack of Support

Leadership, even leadership from someone who's #1 in the #2 business, implies the existence of followers. (It's interesting how willing we are in higher education to discuss the idea of academic leadership but how reluctant we are to identify anyone as a follower.) But discovering an exciting destination for a program to reach means nothing at all if no one wants to go there. And no matter how much of a visionary leader any particular dean or provost may be, that person's vision will remain little more than a dream unless it's shared and actively pursued by faculty, students, and other stakeholders.

For this reason, one of the factors that may cause academic leaders to feel that it's time to look elsewhere is their sense that they don't have the support they need from chairs and other members of the faculty. Obviously a formal vote of no confidence is the clearest possible expression of this lack of support. But there are plenty of informal, less obvious signals people give that deans or provosts don't have the level of support necessary to serve the programs they represent. For example, the increased frequency with which one's proposals are voted down, one's suggestions ignored, or one's opinions firmly rejected in meetings are all indications that support for the academic leader is absent or waning. Make no mistake about it: there will always be opposition to any dean or provost, and the mere fact that there is a certain amount of disagreement on key points isn't an indication of a problem. It's the frequency, severity, and tone of the disagreement that matters. People can disagree with you but still respect you. If that respect is lost, however, there may well be cause for concern.

Early in their positions, most deans and provosts experience a honeymoon period during which they seem to receive widespread backing for nearly every idea they have. But after a semester or, at most, a year or two have passed, the vast majority of academic leaders will begin to encounter greater resistance to their initiatives, an increased willingness of people to be confrontational about the merits of a new proposal, and the rise of grumbling about the way in which they're doing their jobs. That's normal. It doesn't indicate that there's been any substantive decline in faculty support. On the contrary, it often means that members of the faculty and staff are beginning to feel more comfortable with the academic leader. They're treating the person less like a guest and more like a member of the family. Moreover, opposition is not in itself something to be avoided. Differences of opinion can prevent institutions from making mistakes through groupthink, and a certain amount of conflict is all but essential for genuine progress.

A true decline in support feels quite different from the constructive sort of give-and-take that every college should have. Engaging seriously with a person's ideas implies that one is giving those ideas all the respect and scrutiny that they deserve. But when members of the faculty and staff routinely dismiss an academic leader's ideas out of hand, ridicule them without even giving them the courtesy of a true consideration, or ignore them entirely as though the administrator hadn't even spoken, these actions are signs that the leader's authority has been severely compromised. If you sense that you may already be in this situation, try redoubling your efforts to argue persuasively on an issue that you care deeply about. If you still encounter little or no difference in the way people respond to the idea, it may be time to question how effective you still are in your position. You can tough it out, discuss the matter with your supervisor, and conclude that as long as the person who's issuing your contract is satisfied with your work, you can endure these setbacks. You can also try to learn from some of the opinion leaders among the faculty what may have accounted for the reaction you're sensing and work to address those issues. At times, approaches like these will solve the problem, and you can keep making progress. At other times, they will make little difference. When you get to the point that you can't easily answer the question, "Why am I continuing to do this?," you've probably reached the point when you should consider seeking another position.

Serious Incompatibility with Your Supervisor

As we saw in chapters 22 and 23, your relationship to your supervisor is key to your success, happiness, and job satisfaction. Deans need to know that the provost supports them, and provosts need to know that the president supports them. It may be possible for you to survive periods when you don't have strong support from your faculty and chairs. Frequently these rough patches can occur during times of change when there's resistance to new ideas, even though people eventually come around. But without the clear support of the person you report to, your long-term success is all but impossible. In the case of deans, it may well be that their relationship with both the president and provost determines how effective they'll be in their jobs. If the provost is generally an ally but the president's strategic initiatives seem to be taking the institution in a direction that conflicts with the dean's priorities and core principles, it may be impossible for the dean to accomplish everything he or she believes to be essential for the college's success.

While it's important for deans and provosts to have their supervisor's support, it's not the case that they have to see things in exactly the same way or have a rapport that extends far beyond their professional relationship. In cases where you don't feel that you have much chemistry with your boss, your task may be harder at times, but it won't be impossible. At times, the differences between the two of you can be beneficial for your programs. For example, if one of you is more faculty oriented while the other seems more student centered, that difference doesn't have to be a cause for disagreement; it can actually bring the institution a more balanced perspective when issues have an impact on both of these constituencies, as so many of them do. Similarly, if one of you is more outgoing and believes that a key aspect of college administration is public relations, while the other person is highly introverted and prefers to work behind the scenes, what you're doing is complementing each other's skill set, not facing a situation that necessarily poses a problem. So if you and your supervisor are simply different in personality and outlook, you'll have to decide whether those differences serve your program well and whether the occasional challenges you may encounter will, in the end, be worth it.

> A good relationship between academic leaders and their supervisors isn't based on similarities in Myers-Briggs profiles or complete uniformity in thought. It's based on whether both parties can benefit from their similarities as well as their differences and work together on behalf of the institution and its stakeholders.

Conclusion

When academic leaders discover, for any of the reasons outlined, that it's time for them to leave their position, several different options are open to them. They can:

- ○ Retire
- ○ Seek a comparable position at another institution
- ○ Return from administration to a teaching or research position at their own institution
- ○ Move to a higher administrative role

It's also possible to pursue some combination of these goals, such as returning to the faculty but moving to another institution or making a lateral move (e.g., from dean of a college to dean of the graduate school) within their own institution. While making a decision to retire is easy for some and difficult for others, the last three possibilities all involve their own set of choices to be made and preparations to be considered. For that reason, the next three chapters are devoted to an extended analysis of each of these three options separately.

REFERENCES

Vygotsky, L. S. (1978). Interaction between learning and development (trans. M. Lopez-Morillas). In M. Cole, V. John-Steiner, S. Scribner, & E. Souberman (Eds.), *Mind in society: The development of higher psychological processes* (pp. 79–91). Cambridge, MA: Harvard University Press.

Vygotsky, L. S., & Kozulin, A. (Ed.). (1986). *Thought and language* (Rev. ed.). Cambridge, MA: MIT Press.

RESOURCES

Basalla, S., & Debelius, M. (2001). *So what are you going to do with that? A guide for M.A.'s and Ph.D's seeking careers outside the academy*. New York, NY: Farrar, Straus.

Battistella, E. L. (2009). Making soup from rain: My year as provost. *Academic Leader, 25*(5), 1, 6.

Buller, J. L. (2013). The bell-shaped career curve. *Academic Leader, 29*(10), 1, 8.

Dean, X. (2009). Character does matter . . . and working for an unscrupulous boss is no fun. *Academic Leader, 25*(3), 4–5.

Edwards, P., & Edwards, S. *Changing directions without losing your way: Managing the six stages of change at work and in life*. New York, NY: Tarcher/Putnam.

Gerdes, E. P. (2014). When to move on, ready or not. In L. L. Behling (Ed.), *The resource handbook for academic deans* (pp. 135–140). San Francisco, CA: Jossey-Bass.

Gmelch, W. H., Hopkins, D., & Damico, S. B. (2011). *Seasons of a dean's life: Understanding the role and building leadership capacity*. Sterling, VA: Stylus.

Holloway, D., & Bishop, N. (2003). *Before you say I quit!* Gretna, LA: Wellness Institute.

Jansen, J. (2003). *I don't know what I want, but I know it's not this: A step-by-step guide to finding gratifying work*. New York, NY: Penguin.

Martin, R. H. (1997). A graceful (but risky) goodbye. *Trusteeship*, 5(3), 20–23.

McDaniel, T. R. (2003). A dean's demise. In McDaniel, T. R. *Dean's dialogue* (pp. 47–48). Madison, WI: Magna.

McDaniel, T. R. (2013). Checking out? You need an exit strategy. *Academic Leader*, 29(5), 4–5.

Rubin, G. H. (2003). *Quit your job and grow some hair: Know when to go, when to stay*. Manassas Park, VA: Impact.

47

CHANGING INSTITUTIONS

Administrators may decide to change institutions for many different reasons. They may be seeking a higher leadership role than what's currently available to them at their own institutions. They may have decided to return to teaching or research, but prefer to engage in these activities somewhere other than where they were deans or provosts. They may wish to continue at the same administrative level they're in now but want to serve in this role at a different institution, perhaps because they lack the support of their faculty and chair or perhaps because they don't have a satisfying relationship with their president or because they're seeking a new challenge.

This chapter explores the challenges and opportunities that arise when academic leaders are hoping to continue working in very similar roles to what they have at their jobs right now but want to relocate to another college or university. We'll then leave the challenges that face those who wish to return to the faculty or seek a higher administrative role at their own or another institution for the next two chapters.

The Decision to Change

Changing schools can help revitalize deans and provosts who basically enjoy their work but find that the challenges they're facing aren't enough. They may feel that they're getting stale or are becoming disengaged from their jobs. These academic leaders may (and, in fact, probably will) face many of the same challenges in their new positions that they had encountered at their previous institutions, but the people they work with will be new and they'll have an opportunity for a fresh start if they've made mistakes in their earlier jobs. Besides, they may find that at least some of their ideas haven't been tried before at their new school, so people may still find them fresh and exciting.

Keep in mind, however, when changing institutions that there's an old adage about the grass always seeming greener on the other side of the fence. It isn't at all uncommon for academics to look with envy at other institutions where the faculty seems more harmonious, the funding more generous, and the governing board more enlightened, only to discover that the same old problems exist in an altered form at the new institution. If you've spent most or all of your professional life in the private college setting and are tempted to expand your experience by seeking an administrative position at a public university (or vice versa), it's a good idea not to make any binding decisions until you've fully grasped the following essential principle about moving from one institutional type to another:

> People who work at private institutions often assume that budgets are better at public institutions because of funding received from the state. People who work at public institutions often assume that budgets are better at private institutions because of higher rates of tuition. Both are wrong.

This principle surprises many people who haven't had a lot of experience at both public and private universities. The assumption among many faculty members and administrators at private schools is that if they only had access to all that funding that comes from state support, they'd be far better off in terms of resources. At the same time, the assumption among many faculty members and administrators at public colleges and universities is that if they only had access to those higher tuition rates and large endowments they associate with private institutions, they'd be far better off in terms of resources.

What actually occurs is that operating budgets at both public and private institutions are largely comparable for institutions of similar size, while salaries at both public and private institutions tend to be roughly equivalent for institutions of similar prestige. For this reason, if you want a higher salary and access to a larger operating budget, your goal should be to find a position at a larger, more prestigious institution, regardless of whether it's public or private. Before you make this choice, however, it's important to understand that if you succeed, you'll be even busier than you are now, under a great deal more stress, and confronted with significantly more pressure from students, faculty, and the president. In addition, many of the same problems you encounter now will also be found at your new institution. So it'll be a trade-off: more salary with more work and pressure versus a more relaxed pace with a lower level of compensation.

The reason that the size and prestige of an institution matter far more in terms of salary than a school's status as a public or private institution is easy to understand. While public institutions do receive funding from the state, that funding is shrinking. A report by the Center on Budget and Policy Priorities reveals that, between 2008 and 2014, funding for higher education decreased in every state except Alaska and North Dakota (both of which benefited from petroleum production). Those declines ranged from a modest 0.7 percent cut in Wyoming to a massive 48.3 percent reduction in Arizona, with the average being 23 percent. Moreover, political pressure has meant that in many states, tuition rates either didn't increase or even decreased during that period. Moreover, most public universities charge far lower tuition rates for in-state students, who are the bulk of their student bodies. Compared to private institutions, state schools generally qualify for fewer grants from foundations, have lower rates of contribution to their endowments and annual funds, and manage endowments that are usually much smaller than those of similarly sized private institutions. At many public institutions, the cost of each student's education can be divided into three unequal parts: that which is paid for by tuition and externally funded scholarships, that which is paid for by the state, and that which is paid for by all other sources, including contributions, proceeds from the institution's own foundation, and internally funded scholarships. From 1988 to 2013, the size of the part paid for by tuition increased from about a quarter of the total cost of a student's education to nearly half (www.cbpp.org/files/5–1–14sfp.pdf).

We can compare this situation to that of private institutions where the published price of tuition is almost always higher than at state institutions and which generally have larger endowments, but receive little or no money from the state. At these schools, the sticker price of tuition can be misleading since it's often heavily discounted so that students can afford the cost of attendance. A catalogue of a private college may state that the school's tuition plus room and board is $60,000 or so for a year, but few if any students are likely to be paying full freight. A tuition discount rate of 30 to 60 percent is not uncommon, and many scholarships offered by private colleges aren't actual transfers of money but rather simple reductions to what the student must pay (tuition discounting). Moreover, many private institutions maintain a lower student-to-faculty ratio as part of their justification for charging a higher rate of tuition than public schools, with the result that each faculty member's salary must be supported by a correspondingly smaller group of students. As a result, at many private institutions, the cost of each student's education may be divided into two parts: roughly 40 percent revenue from tuition and roughly 60 percent resulting from externally funded scholarships, contributions, and proceeds from the endowment. The important factor to observe is that the total return to the private institution from those two sources will be approximately equal to what a public institution of comparable size and prestige receives from its three sources.

As a result, the real difference in available resources occurs when an institution is larger or more distinguished, with the greatest difference occurring when the institution is both. Larger institutions often have higher student-to-faculty ratios. Since the total revenue to the institution is the same regardless of whether the school is public or private, if the number of students enrolled in each course increases, the size of the operating budget used to support that course can increase as well. Similarly, if the number of students per faculty member at an institution increases, the overall budget that is available for salaries can also be increased. Likewise, if students are attracted to an institution because of its prestige and reputation, it's possible to charge a higher rate of tuition, discount it less, and offer fewer internally funded scholarships. In any of these cases, there is more money available for operating budgets and salaries.

With these observations in mind, it's a good idea to research a new institution carefully before accepting any offer. Among the questions you might consider raising before changing institutions are those that deal with the following issues:

- *The nature of the position.* The responsibilities that fall under the job description of a dean or provost at one institution may be quite different from those at another institution. If you're used to a great deal of independence in your current job, you may be frustrated working at an institution where you'd be expected to function more as a manager, implementing policies developed by the president and governing board rather than actively participating in the development of those policies. It may also occur that the very area in which you have the greatest strength, such as program review or faculty development, is handled at an entirely different level of the new institution. In other words, the attributes that helped you succeed in one job may not relate well to your new position.

- *The flexibility of the budget.* Deans and provosts are frequently in charge of fairly large budgets, but they themselves may control extremely small budgets. The reason for this paradox is that between 90 and 95 percent of most academic budgets are devoted to personnel costs. At institutions where a large portion of the faculty is tenured—and an even greater portion of all employees are in relatively stable positions because they are on tenure track or have been in staff positions for many years—a dean or provost may have little flexibility in how this budget can be used. So if you're considering a position, it's important to find out the size of the operating and discretionary budgets in the areas you'll be supervising. Compare what you learn not only to the size of your current budgets but also to those at institutions of a similar size and mission. Your key question should be: If an opportunity or problem arises, how much budgetary flexibility will I have to address it?

o *Interaction with other administrators.* Your relationship with your new colleagues will play a major role in your job satisfaction. As we saw in chapter 46, your ability to develop a good working relationship with your supervisor will be critical for the success of your college and your ultimate success in your new position. But the way in which you'll be able to interact with your peers and those who report to you will be an important factor in how effective you'll be in your new position. See if you can determine why the position you're seeking is available. If it has been vacated for any other reason than retirement or the previous person's acceptance of a highly desirable new position, ask a few questions about the dynamics that existed between that person and others at the institution. You may be inheriting a situation that is more complicated than it initially appears.

The Learning Curve

Although you've already served as an academic leader and know a great deal about college administration, you should never assume that you have all the answers to administrative questions. Because of a different institutional history and the personalities of the employees, your new school will be an environment where approaches that worked admirably for you earlier may now be less effective than you'd like. For this reason, you should arrive at your new job with a readiness to appreciate fully what makes this opportunity both similar to and different from your former position. Keep the following essential principle firmly in mind:

As much as possible, never begin sentences with the expression "Back at [your former institution]." By the time you've been at the job for six months, you should have eliminated this expression completely from your vocabulary.

In your new environment, there'll be a great temptation to relate many experiences back to the situation that you knew previously. You'll look back on some of these achievements with pride. After all, they're what got you this new job. You'll be particularly tempted to talk about previous schools if your new position is at only the second or third institution where you worked. All of us become familiar with a certain way of addressing issues, implementing policies, and making decisions, and we use that experience to guide us in new situations. Effective academic leaders learn, however, that there are numerous "right" ways to do things, any one of which may be more effective or more appropriate at one institution than another. Just as we expect our students to develop skills at coping effectively with an unfamiliar environment, expand their horizons by encountering different ways of thinking, and question their own assumptions, so must we learn to do so as administrators.

Always feel free to ask, "Why do we do X the way we do?," but always be willing to learn from the answer you receive. Nostalgic "Back at Wistful Memories State University" recollections are pleasant for you, but they tend to grate on your new colleagues and employees. For the first six months in your new position, people will probably accept a few backward glances as long as they remain rather rare. But as you begin to approach a full year in your new position, these statements will increasingly backfire on you. At best, people will assume you have no fresh ideas. At worst, they will conclude that you're making an implied comparison between your former institution's wonderful expertise and their own regrettable incompetence.

Provosts and deans can never afford to give the impression that everyone at their new institution was inept until they came along or that they have arrived to "save" it. For this reason, a good strategy for new administrators is to speak frequently of building on the "already strong foundation" that they discovered when they arrived. Even if you were brought to the institution in order to solve some serious problems, remember that the institution wouldn't have lasted as long as it has if the people there were doing everything wrong. Lavish praise widely. Be particularly generous in extending praise to your predecessor and long-term members of the faculty. Discover procedures to admire. Replace the phrase "Back at [name of previous institution] . . . " with, "One more reason why I'm glad I'm here is . . . " Most of all, be willing to learn as much as you can from your new role. That is, after all, one of the most important reasons why you took the job.

Finally, keep in mind the lesson from chapter 5: few people, if any, are ready for as much change as they say they want. During your interviews for the position, you may be told repeatedly, "We need some new ideas.

We need to change the way things work around here. We want you to be bold, to take some risks." Since you've already held administrative positions elsewhere, you may even have been preferred over other candidates precisely because you have the type of experience that can take the institution in a new direction. Nevertheless, be very careful about regarding any of these statements as a clear mandate for radical change.

Before you go about implementing substantive changes, learn how the institution and the programs that report to you work. Colleges and universities are like ecosystems. Introducing invasive species into an ecosystem can harm the delicate balance that allowed the members of that system to survive. You can't fill one pond without draining another. Just as in the wild, the law of unintended consequences, which you encountered in chapter 5, applies when you introduce something new to your institution's environment. Certainly you'll want to consider some necessary improvements and to make a positive difference in your new position. But you should embark on this course only when you truly understand how the local organizational culture works. For this reason, of two possible errors—proceeding too cautiously or forging ahead too recklessly—caution is always less destructive unless the college is so dysfunctional or in danger of financial ruin that immediate, radical change is imperative (see Buller, 2010, 2015.)

Conclusion

Moving from one institution to another is always a matter of finding that things are both stranger and more familiar than you had anticipated. Problems you thought were unique to your former institution have a tendency to arise at the new institution as well. Procedures you had assumed were universal throughout academia turn out to be quite different at your new school. Use the transferable parts of your skill in being an academic leader—your ability to identify the causes of problems, your communication skills, your critical judgment—as you move to your new job while leaving behind "the way we did things back at" your former institution. After all, you left there for a reason.

REFERENCES

Buller, J. L. (2010). Rearranging the academic furniture. *Academic Leader*, 26(8), 3, 8.
Buller, J. L. (2015). *Change leadership in higher education: A practical guide to academic transformation*. San Francisco, CA: Jossey-Bass.

48

RETURNING TO THE FACULTY

Many academic leaders, after spending some time in an administrative role, either choose or are asked to return to the faculty. If the leaders themselves make the choice, it may be because they miss the direct contribution they once made to their school's teaching and research mission or because administrative work at the level of a provost or dean no longer holds their interest. Moreover, an increasingly common option for academic leaders is to return to the classroom for a year or two before their retirement, rounding out their academic careers by rediscovering what brought them into the field in the first place.

If you're considering a return to the faculty, be sure to explore your institution's policies on your right to choose to do so. Most schools are quite flexible in allowing either the administrators themselves or their supervisor to determine when and in what way an academic leader can return to a faculty role. The assumption in these cases is that no institution is well served by an administrator who's either no longer happy with his or her responsibilities or not demonstrating the level of success that everyone desires. Making it as easy as possible for someone to return to teaching, research, and service thus serves the institution's own best interests in the long run. Nevertheless, some colleges and universities do have restrictions that limit when and how an administrator can change roles. For example, they may offer a certain amount of release time for people to resume their research and revise their courses if they've served as a dean or provost for at least three years. Or they may expect administrators to step down only at the end of their contracts, making it difficult for a person who, for whatever reason, decides that a change is necessary in the middle of an academic year.

Other policies in place may also affect your decision or at least alter its timing. For example, unions may create firm boundaries between management and labor, making it difficult for someone to go back and forth between these categories. Some schools may allow deans and provosts to return to the faculty only when positions become available. The latter situation is the case at Amarillo College:

> A full-time administrator who does not have tenure at the College but desires a faculty appointment shall be given preference for any vacant position for which he or she is qualified and is recommended by his or her administrative supervisor. www.actx.edu/president/index .php?module=article&id=90
>
> Tenured faculty who accept an administrative position shall retain their tenured status in the area (discipline or program) in which they were tenured. However, their return to the tenure area will be subject to need (determined by the administration) and availability of funds. In no case shall another tenured faculty in the same area be released to accommodate this move, even though such person was tenured last. However, a probationary or temporary appointed faculty may be released if necessary to accommodate the transfer. If all faculty in the area are tenured and there is no need for an additional person, then the administrator has no recourse except to be retained in the administrative position or be released from employment at the discretion of his/her administrative supervisor. Any faculty member who accepts an administrative position prior to the receipt of tenure forfeits any progress made toward tenure. www.actx.edu/president/article/id/92/page/5

Moreover, while returning to the faculty can be an attractive option for many administrators for a variety of reasons, this transition can be difficult to accomplish without at least some preparation. Let's consider some of the factors deans and provosts may want to consider before they make their decision to step out of an administrative role.

Loss of Authority and Prestige

Everyone reacts differently to the reality of no longer being the boss. To some, the transition is quite easy; they can yield authority to others without any qualms, immediately settle back into a role that frees them from the burdens of leadership, and devote their full attention to the duties of being a faculty member.

To many, however, this transition is far more difficult, perhaps even more difficult than they had anticipated. They're used to being asked for their opinion on a variety of issues and to having that opinion matter to many people. Once they're no longer in charge, they miss being treated as important, such as having the opportunity to meet dignitaries who are visiting campus. As deans and provosts, these administrators felt connected to significant issues. They learned about important matters before everyone else did, had the freedom to make many decisions on their own, and were granted the authority to solve certain kinds of problems. For these former leaders, giving up many of the job responsibilities they long took for granted, moving to a smaller office, losing all the benefits that came with their position, and finding themselves no longer consulted about major issues turns out to be a greater sacrifice than they had envisioned.

In addition to trying to anticipate your own feelings on this matter, you may want to think about how other members of the faculty will feel about you when you return to their ranks. Will you be treated as one of them once again or be regarded as somehow tainted because you "went over to the dark side" during your terms as an administrator? As you consider these issues, it's a good idea to try answering the following questions:

○ *What sort of relationship do you currently have with the faculty members in the discipline where you'll be working?* Discovering that you have no relationship with them should be just as much of a warning sign as finding that you have a very strained relationship with your future colleagues. If you feel you haven't developed a good rapport with members of your future department, you may end up being resented as a person who hasn't "paid your dues" or who "assumes you can just walk in here and take whatever you want." If you have any reason to suspect that your relationship with your future colleagues isn't particularly good, you may well want to engage in some bridge building now so that you can smoothly rejoin the faculty later.

○ *Have you regularly attended departmental meetings so as to become apprised of issues that are of recent concern to the department?* As the dean or provost, it may have been awkward or impossible for you to attend departmental meetings in your academic discipline. But you'll probably want to start doing so once the announcement is made that you are returning to the faculty. Make it clear that your reason for attending these meetings isn't in any official capacity as an administrator, but rather to learn as much as you can about topics of current concern to your discipline and to ease your transition back to a faculty role.

○ *When you return to the department, are you likely to be perceived as having received advantages that you didn't earn?* In order to smooth their transition back to teaching and research, administrators are sometimes given benefits that the rest of the faculty don't have. If your teaching schedule is lighter than that of other faculty members or filled with only the most desirable courses, if your research space is larger than that of your colleagues, or if your on-campus duties are arranged for your own convenience, you may encounter more resentment than you expect from the members of your department. Particularly in cases where people's teaching loads have been heavier or modified so that your load is easier, you may be treated as an unwelcome addition to the faculty ranks. As you make this transition, think about what it means to accept the whole faculty experience, including inconvenient class times, large numbers of introductory courses, time-consuming committee assignments, numerous advisees, and cramped quarters. If you don't "do your part," you'll be more likely to have an uncomfortable experience as you rejoin your discipline. You also won't have a genuine faculty experience, increasing the likelihood that it'll be a long time before you are treated as an actual colleague.

The Need to Retool

Unless you have served in your administrative position for only a year or two, you'll probably discover that you'll need a good deal of preparation before returning to a faculty role. Most deans and provosts either don't teach at all or teach one or two courses a year at most. As a result, there are going to be new scholarly developments that'll have to be reflected in the courses you'll teach. There may also be new elements of pedagogical technology or improved practices of instruction that you perhaps haven't used yet and require some time to master. It's also quite likely that during your tenure as dean or provost, you haven't been as active in pursuing your scholarly agenda as full-time faculty members have been. That doesn't mean you haven't published or spoken at conferences. It just means that maybe you haven't had all the time to devote to your academic research as you'd have liked or that some of your scholarship may have been on administrative issues rather than concerned with your academic field. That's only to be expected. The time commitments of an academic leader's position make it extremely difficult to continue a full schedule of professional research. As a result, reestablishing a scholarly agenda may require some time and careful preparation.

If you're stepping down from an administrative role, you may want to think about requesting sufficient time to retool for your teaching and research responsibilities. A semester- or year-long sabbatical or educational leave can be vital for making this transition effectively, particularly if you've been out of full-time teaching and research for more than five years. While retraining periods are valuable for former administrators themselves, they can also be useful for the institution. They allow time for students and faculty members to adjust to seeing their former dean or provost as a faculty member. They also provide an opportunity for the new person in that administrative role to establish his or her own identity without the daily presence of the former occupant of the office to complicate the picture of who's really in charge. This period of retooling can be the best gift you can give your successor too, since, when the former administrator is less visible for an extended period, everyone (including the new dean or provost) will be less tempted to ask you how this or that policy has been implemented in the past. Your temporary absence gives your successor both the opportunity and the necessity to begin making his or her own decisions and helping the institution to move in new directions.

As a result, following are a few guidelines you may wish to consider if you believe you may be returning to a faculty role at the end of your administrative tenure:

○ If you're a faculty member who's thinking about an administrative position, try to negotiate your right to a period of educational leave or retraining at the end your contract. Because of all the advantages we've seen from giving former administrators time to get their teaching, scholarship, and service back up to speed, many institutions offer this opportunity when they're considering you for a position as dean or provost. But others won't, so you may need to ask. At times too, there may even be formal policies about who is and is not entitled to an educational leave. For instance, the University of North Texas's Policy on Tenured Administrators Returning to Full-Time Academic Status addresses this possibility directly:

> This policy applies to members of the tenured faculty who serve on at least 50 percent administrative appointments in positions noted above for a period of at least one year. When such person concludes an administrative assignment to return to full-time academic status, his or her faculty salary base (excluding any longevity pay consideration) will be prorated generally at nine times his or her then monthly salary earned while an administrator.... Any development leaves granted by the University to an administrator immediately prior to his or her return to full-time faculty status shall be at the determination of the President and at the salary level as determined [by institutional policy] and in accordance with Section 51.105 of the Texas Education Code. (policy.unt.edu/policy/15–1–10)

Even at institutions without formal policies, it is frequently possible to negotiate either an educational leave or a sabbatical, particularly if you have served your college well for an extended period as dean.

o If you're already serving as a dean or provost but not thinking of returning to the faculty immediately, it's still a good idea to begin laying the groundwork now for your eventual return through incremental measures. Your eventual transition from administration back to the faculty will be easier if you begin your return to teaching and research gradually. Certainly the workload of most academic administrators makes this added effort difficult, but the sacrifices involved will cause the additional challenge to be worthwhile in the end. If you haven't taught for several years, consider having a discussion with the chair of your discipline to see if there's a teaching assignment that could serve the department's needs while benefiting you after your transition. For instance, an evening course or a section that meets very early in the morning may be an unpopular time for most faculty members, but it could fit your schedule far more easily than a course that meets midday. Similarly, a survey course may not be the first choice of many faculty members who often prefer to teach upper-division or graduate courses; nevertheless, teaching at the introductory level may require the least amount of new preparation from you. In the area of scholarship, you might begin to ease back into a more challenging research agenda by attending a conference in your discipline without making a presentation yourself or by offering to chair a session or serve as a discussant. Volunteering to review books for a journal can reacquaint you with recent developments in your discipline, while at the same time giving you a short, easily managed opportunity for publication. Finally, making a presentation or publishing an article on pedagogical or administrative issues in your field of study can help you take advantage of your expertise as both a dean and an academic professional who has a specific disciplinary focus.

o If a developmental leave isn't possible at your institution, think about other ways in which you can effect a more gradual reentry into your faculty role. At some institutions, educational leave before returning to the faculty isn't possible. That limitation may be due to budgetary restrictions or policy restrictions that prevent those in administrative roles from qualifying for sabbaticals. In these cases, your best recourse may be to request more modest adjustments to your teaching and research expectations as you ease back into your faculty role. A reduced teaching assignment, a larger number of lower-level courses (which will reduce your preparation time), multiple sections of the same course (which will reduce the number of weekly preparations you have to make), release from committee work or other service obligations, a lower publication or grant target, and the like can provide you with some extra time to reestablish your scholarly agenda, update your course materials, and accomplish many of the other tasks you'll need to perform in order to be successful once again as a full-time faculty member. Just remember that these adjustments are likely to be viewed as special favors by your faculty colleagues who have to maintain full teaching loads with multiple preparations while still meeting high expectations for research and service. There may well be some pushback due to these adjustments, and you may need to demonstrate an even greater degree of tact and diplomacy as a result.

The Boss as the Boss

Once you step back into your faculty role, it's important to remember that no matter who your successor may be, the new dean or provost is now your boss too. When you see someone doing things differently from how you would've done them, it can be difficult to accept. Most people become deans and provosts because they care deeply about the academic programs they lead. It can be frustrating to learn about decisions you believe are ill advised, crucial tasks that remain undone, or a future being charted for an area you love that you believe is likely to fail. It's important for former academic leaders to remember—as challenging as this can be—that they must give their successors the freedom that they'll need in this position, the same freedom that they themselves were once hoping to have. Avoid the temptation to second-guess the new administrator. Everyone has a unique style of leadership, and what your successor is attempting may not have worked for you but may well work under new leadership.

People who knew you as their dean or provost may occasionally ask your opinion about decisions that have been made, public remarks that have been shared by the new academic leader, or how you would describe your successor's general level of success. It benefits no one for you to be anything less than supportive. Criticism of the new administrator can undermine his or her chances for success at the same time that it makes you seem petty or bitter. Your status as a former administrator doesn't entitle you to any special privileges with regard to the position you once held. Your role is now the same as any other faculty member, except that you have a moral obligation to be generous toward someone who's attempting to do a job you know (better than anyone) is tough. Even if all the other members of the faculty are highly disparaging of the new dean or provost, it's advisable for you to temper your own remarks. A statement that may seem innocuous coming from another faculty member could easily come across as mean-spirited and uncalled for if you make it.

You should also be highly reluctant to serve on any advisory board related to your old position for several years after you leave the deanship. Placing yourself in an advisory role to your successor creates a highly awkward position for that person and encourages others to continue seeing you as the person in charge, with the new dean or provost merely filling in for you temporarily. A clean break from your former administrative role is a far better course to take, and it'll give you the time you need to refocus your energies on your faculty responsibilities.

Some administrators find it preferable to change institutions when resuming their faculty roles. (See chapter 47.) At an entirely different school, they're less likely to still see themselves or to be seen by others as the boss. They discover an opportunity to create a new identity for the next phase of their career and work with colleagues who have never had a different sort of working relationship with them. In fact, leaving an administrative position for a position as a distinguished professor or eminent scholar in one's academic field can be an excellent step in a career. It provides access to a new role, gives one prestige and important responsibilities, and presents an often attractive range of opportunities and challenges.

Conclusion

Administrators frequently believe that a transition back to a faculty role will be easy for them because of their earlier success as scholars and researchers and because they've spent a number of years assisting others in their own development. Nevertheless, in the years one spends away from full-time teaching and research, students change, classroom technology changes, and entire disciplines change. Preparation for return to the faculty is just as essential as was preparation for the administrative role you're leaving, and it has to be approached with at least as much care and prior thought. Becoming a full-time professor again is a desirable option for many deans and provosts, but they need to be ready both for their new tasks and for how they'll feel after returning to a role they once left behind.

RESOURCES

Buller, J. L. (2013). The bell-shaped career curve. *Academic Leader*, 29(10), 1, 8.
Gmelch, W. H., Hopkins, D., & Damico, S. B. (2011). *Seasons of a dean's life: Understanding the role and building leadership capacity*. Sterling, VA: Stylus.
Spitzer, M. L. (2001). Taking over. *University of Toledo Law Review*, 33, 213–216.
Zappe, C. J., & Gerdes, E. J. (2012). Temporary insanity: Deciding to be a dean. *Academic Leader*, 24(12), 1, 6.

49

PLANNING FOR A HIGHER ADMINISTRATIVE ROLE

After serving successfully as a dean or provost, it's not uncommon for many deans and provosts to wonder whether they may be suited for a higher administrative role. Particularly administrators who may have moved up through the ranks, first serving as a department chair or president of the faculty senate, next as an assistant or associate dean, then as the dean of a college or special program, and finally perhaps serving as a chief academic officer, it can seem logical, possibly even inevitable, to continue this progression to a term as a president or chancellor. Nevertheless, the very skills that made you most effective in your past roles—fierce advocacy for certain disciplines, a distinguished reputation as a scholar, and a tendency to view a university's academic mission as its primary function—may be impediments as you try to advance to a new role. Even the very level of your success may work against you. You may have established such a reputation as "the dean" or "the provost" that others have a hard time imagining you in any other way. So if you're considering whether the challenges of an executive position might be an appropriate next step, what are the issues you'll need to consider and the preparations you'll need to make?

Not All Administrative Roles Are Alike

Being a provost or vice president for academic affairs isn't the same as being a dean writ large. Being a president or chancellor isn't the same thing as being a provost writ large. Making one of these transitions will be a much bigger leap than what you encountered when you went from being a department chair to serving as a dean. In fact, if you're a dean whose ultimate goal is to serve as the head of a university or university system, your best choice might not be seeking another position within academic affairs; in certain circumstances, taking such a position can actually hurt your chances of being offered a presidency, as we shall see. For this reason, if you're considering higher administrative roles, there are several good questions to ask yourself:

o What do I see as my long-range administrative career path?

o Why do I believe that that particular path is right for me?

o What would I do in this position that I can't do now?

o When I meet people who currently hold this position, do I like them? Do I see myself as fitting in among them?

o How do I see my skills as relevant to the type of work I'd be doing in these positions?

o What additional skills and experiences do I need to acquire now in order to be prepared for where I eventually want to be?

Answering those questions will help you understand whether a higher administrative role is really your best option or whether you're seeking it simply because it seems to be the next step on the ladder. They'll also help you decide whether you're on track toward reaching your goal in a timely manner.

The job of the provost

At increasing numbers of institutions, the provost or vice president for academic affairs fills a position that looks inward toward the institution. The vice president for academic affairs is responsible for making sure that the institution's academic programs function at a high level, its curriculum is being provided in a way that meets the needs of the students, and its faculty members are being hired and developed in fulfillment of the institution's key instructional, scholarly, and service goals.

Frequently, the term *provost* is used as though it were a synonym for vice president for academic affairs. But in a system where this term adheres more closely to its original meaning, the provost is the administrator to whom all the institution's vice presidents report so as to promote the smooth internal operation of the college or university. The provost is the chief executive officer who's in charge of the day-to-day management of the campus. The president or chancellor acts as the chief executive officer for external affairs. In certain situations, the provost and vice president for academic affairs may be different individuals; the provost thus serves as "first among equals" of the vice presidents, while the vice president for academic affairs is responsible for the instructional and scholarly missions of the institution.

The job of the president

The president of an institution more frequently has an external role, looking outward from the institution toward the community. The president serves as the institution's chief fundraiser, its primary liaison with the governing board or state legislature, and its most active representative to service organizations, the chamber of commerce, and other community bodies. That's why deans who want to be presidents sometimes become sidetracked when they seek positions as provosts as an interim step. As deans, they had both internal and external responsibilities. By becoming provost, they may be moving away from community engagement, fundraising, and public relations responsibilities that are actually their best preparation for a presidency.

If you review the list of people assuming executive positions in works like the *Chronicle of Higher Education*, you'll find it's no longer the case that the vast majority of new presidents come from positions as provost or vice president of academic affairs. Particularly at private colleges and universities, only about a fifth of the presidents who are hired each year enter that position directly from service as a provost or chief academic officer. The majority of private college presidents have immediate prior experience in development, advancement, or public life outside academics. Even at state institutions where it's still somewhat more common for presidents to have recently headed an academic division, a growing number of people reach the presidency after work in fundraising, alumni affairs, business, or politics.

For this reason, if you're a dean, you may want to think carefully about where you ultimately want to go in higher education before your next move. If service as a president interests you, one of the following positions may be a better pathway than seeking to become a provost.

o *A larger and more challenging deanship.* Because deans often have stronger records raising external funds and winning grants than do provosts, your next move might be to serve as dean of a very large college, perhaps as large as the entire institution where you eventually want to be president. In this role, you can point to your advancement successes, document that you've supervised a large staff, and develop a strategic plan for your college that will prepare you for many of your future executive responsibilities.

○ *President of a small college.* Any executive role, even one at an institution far smaller than you may wish to lead someday, can give you much better preparation for a presidency than you'll receive from another stint in middle management. In fact, you may find the transition from dean to president easier than a move from provost to president. Leading a small college will give you opportunities to develop important skills in such areas as athletics, student life, housing, and auxiliary services that you're unlikely to develop if you remain in an academic track.

○ *A nonacademic vice presidency.* You can develop some breadth in your administrative portfolio if you seek a different sort of vice presidency, such as a position as vice president for development, advancement, or alumni relations. After all, you've already proven your academic leadership during your tenure as dean. By gaining experience more broadly across the institution, you can improve your understanding of how other units of the university function at the same time that you accumulate a portfolio of successes that will serve you well in your applications for executive positions.

I am not saying that there aren't many good reasons for people to want jobs as a provost or vice president for academic affairs. You may have found that you receive your greatest satisfaction from dealing with matters of curriculum, program development and review, faculty employment and evaluation, and everything else that goes into building a solid academic program. You may have a personality that best suits you for leading meetings and championing causes within an institutional setting rather than interacting with the full range of a school's stakeholders. Or you may have more personal reasons for wanting to seek a provost's position, such as the fact that provosts can often avoid the requirement to be on duty 24/7 in the way that presidents almost always cannot. The most important thing to realize is that if you're a dean, you don't need to seek a position as chief academic officer if your ultimate goal is a presidency because there are other positions that can help you achieve that goal a lot more quickly and directly.

Building Your Portfolio

If you've decided to seek a presidency, the most important type of experience for you to have comes under the area of development. You may want to start looking now for opportunities that will help you secure multimillion-dollar gifts from private individuals and grants from foundations. Almost certainly, if you're being seriously considered for a presidency, you'll receive questions during your interviews about your biggest ask, whether you were successful in obtaining that gift, and the extent of your cultivation role leading up to it. If you can't document several substantial gifts that resulted either in new facilities or major increases to the endowment or foundation, you'll have a far more difficult time making a positive impression on the search committee.

Take advantage of every opportunity you can to secure fundraising experience. Participate in training workshops offered by your school's development office. Explore the possibility of attending national or regional workshops on fundraising for administrators. The Council for Advancement and Support of Education conducts a number of these programs every year (www.case.org), and the professional organization that represents your academic discipline may also provide fundraising training. Consider asking your development office if they'll assign you your own portfolio of prospects you can cultivate for various kinds of gifts to your programs. These efforts will have the immediate effect of helping to serve your institution better by increasing your sources of revenue for the many needs that your academic programs have. They'll also produce a long-term benefit to you personally by improving your résumé and making it seem more presidential.

In addition to fundraising, there are several other types of institution-wide experiences you'll want to gain if you aspire to a presidency:

o *Athletics*. As a president, you'll be expected to know something about the business of athletics. For this reason, offer to serve as a representative to the athletics committee, institutional representative to the National Collegiate Athletic Association (or the appropriate athletic association for your institution), or on a search committee for your school's next athletic director or major coach.

o *Alumni relations*. As a president, you'll have to represent the institution at numerous alumni gatherings and before other groups. Start now by offering to speak at regional or national meetings of your institution's alumni association, initiating or revitalizing an affinity group for your college within your institution's alumni association, and serving as an institutional representative on committees involved in homecoming and other alumni activities.

o *Physical plant and business operations*. As a president, you'll need to know about ways of preserving an institution's fiscal health and the challenges posed in maintaining a complex physical plant. If you haven't had much experience with the ground-up planning for a new facility, offer to serve as a member of a planning committee for a building in another area of the university. Be sure you can document sound fiscal management for your own unit, and be prepared to describe the course of action you took when departments under you faced serious financial challenges or mismanagement.

o *Cocurricular activities.* As a president, you'll be responsible for student life, housing, judicial affairs, study-abroad opportunities, student leadership programs, and internships. Explore ways of acquiring experience in each of these areas. If you don't have a strong student affairs background, for instance, offer to serve on an appeals committee for a judicial offense, an exemption to the residency requirement, or a violation of the honor code. Participate with search committees in these areas as a way of learning the issues that professionals elsewhere in the university have to face and the types of training that most helps them to succeed.

In a similar way, if you're a dean who's decided to seek a position as a provost, you'll want to begin accumulating the types of experience that you'll need in order to succeed at that level of the institution:

o *Broad academic experience.* During interviews to become a chief academic officer, you'll be asked how you've demonstrated support and advocacy for academic areas beyond your field of specialty. Service you have performed on an institution-wide curricular committee, establishing grant opportunities that transcend the disciplines of your own academic area, chairing search committees for deans of other colleges, and adjusting your course offerings to provide more adequate coverage of the service courses required by other units will all help you make this case in a more compelling manner.

o *Tenure and promotion issues.* As a provost or vice president for academic affairs, you'll need to understand some of the challenges faced by individuals who are seeking tenure and promotion in disciplines outside your area. Volunteering for a university-wide tenure and promotion committee or agreeing to serve on an appeals committee at the institutional level can provide an excellent background into the complexity of these larger institutional issues.

o *Posttenure review.* As a dean, you've probably reviewed a number of tenured faculty members in your area, providing them with guidance where it was needed and praise where it was warranted. For the next level of academic administration, you'll need experience in how these decisions are made in disciplines far different from your own. Service on an institution-wide posttenure review committee (or even a committee that examines the adequacy of existing posttenure review procedures) can provide a wealth of information that'll broaden the perspective you'll need in your role as chief academic officer.

National Training Opportunities

The American Council on Education (ACE) sponsors a number of important training activities that can help you decide on the appropriate next step in your administrative career. These programs change periodically, and the best way of obtaining up-to-date information is by visiting the ACE website on leadership programs (www.acenet.edu/leadership/Pages/default.aspx). Among the programs sponsored by ACE that should most interest you are the following:

○ *The ACE Fellows Program.* Begun in 1965, this program allows administrators to spend an extended period of time on another campus, working directly with a president and other important mentors. In addition to the practical information gained through workshops and discussions, the experience creates a national network of individuals to whom you can turn for advice, career support, and information.

○ *ACE Advancing to the Presidency.* A more condensed experience than the Fellows Program, this multiday workshop exposes those who are considering an academic presidency to the issues that arise at the executive level of university administration, techniques of searching for a presidency, and constructive critique of one's application materials and interviewing style.

○ *ACE Institute for New Presidents.* A nine-month program for presidents within their first three years of service, this series combines meetings, webinars, and personal reflection to expose participants to key issues in higher education and help them make an effective transition to an executive role.

○ *ACE Institute for New Chief Academic Officers.* In this workshop, a group of approximately thirty-five chief academic officers (all in the first three years of their positions) meet three times over the course of an academic year to learn about leadership issues facing vice presidents for academic affairs, the role of their units in strategic planning, and budgetary challenges that confront chief academic officers.

○ *Chief Academic Officer and Chief Business Officer Workshop.* This two-day workshop explores the relationship between the academic and financial components of an institution of higher education.

○ *ACE Presidential Roundtable.* Periodic discussions of small groups of institutional presidents explore how upper administrations can respond to emerging challenges and opportunities in higher education.

Furthermore, chapter 2 noted how useful it can be for deans and provosts to volunteer to serve as a member of an accreditation review committee. If you've not worked in this capacity for some time, serving as a member of an on-site or off-site accreditation review board is an excellent way to gain insight into the ways in which different institutions have chosen to solve various academic problems. At the same time that you perform a valuable act of service, you'll be expanding your own knowledge of how budgets are prepared, curricular proposals are reviewed, student problems are addressed, and strategic initiatives are selected.

Conclusion

No single administrative path is right for everyone. You should never feel pressured by others—or even by yourself—to seek a higher administrative role simply because it's the "logical next step." Many highly effective deans have made very poor provosts, and many highly effective provosts have made very poor presidents largely because different types of personalities and skills are required in these different positions.

Perhaps the most important advice to consider is that which appeared at the beginning of this discussion: seek out opportunities where you can get to know a large number of presidents and chief academic officers. See if they're the type of person you'd like to be. Do they live lives that offer the sorts of challenge and hold the sorts of opportunity that would make you feel excited to come to work in the morning? Just as only the worst sort of deans were attracted to their positions because of the salary and privileges they'd receive, so is this the case with presidents and provosts. Prepare for a higher administrative role if that type of position seems to be your calling. If it's not, there's an essential principle you may wish to keep in mind:

It's far better to be an effective dean than a frustrated provost. It's far better to be an effective provost than a frustrated president.

There are many unsuccessful administrators who failed to heed that advice and reflect on both what they want and are best temperamentally suited to do.

RESOURCES

Bornstein, R. (2003). *Legitimacy in the academic presidency.* Westport, CT: Greenwood Press.

Ferren, A. S., & Stanton, W. W. (2004). *Leadership through collaboration: The role of the chief academic officer.* Westport, CT: ACE/Praeger.

Gunsalus, C. K. (2006). *The college administrator's survival guide.* Cambridge, MA: Harvard University Press.

Hendrickson, R. M., Lane, J. E., Harris, J. T., & Dorman, R. H. (2013). *Academic leadership and governance of higher education: A guide for trustees, leaders, and aspiring leaders of two- and four-year institutions.* Sterling, VA: Stylus.

Kouzes, J. M., & Posner, B. Z. (2003). *The Jossey-Bass academic administrator's guide to exemplary leadership.* San Francisco, CA: Jossey-Bass.

Martin, J., & Samels, J. E. (1997). *First among equals: The role of the chief academic officer.* Baltimore, MD: Johns Hopkins University Press.

Martin, J., & Samels, J. E. (2004). *Presidential transition in higher education: Managing leadership change.* Baltimore, MD: Johns Hopkins University Press.

Martin, J., & Samels, J. E. (2015). *The provost's handbook: The role of the chief academic officer.* Baltimore, MD: Johns Hopkins University Press.

Nielsen, L. A. (2013). *Provost: Experiences, reflections, and advice from a former "number two" on campus.* Sterling, VA: Stylus.

Pierce, S. R. (2014). *Governance reconsidered: How boards, presidents, administrators, and faculty can help their colleges thrive.* San Francisco, CA: Jossey-Bass.

Renewing the academic presidency: Stronger leadership for tougher times. (1996). Washington, DC: Association of Governing Boards of Universities and Colleges.

Schloss, P. J., & Cragg, K. M. (2013). *Organization and administration in higher education.* New York, NY: Routledge.

Trachtenberg, S. J. (2013). *Presidencies derailed: Why university leaders fail and how to prevent it.* Baltimore, MD: John Hopkins University Press.

50

A SCENARIO ANALYSIS ON THE DEAN'S NEXT STEP

For a discussion of how scenario analyses are structured and suggestions on how to use this exercise most productively, see the beginning of chapter 7. A scenario analysis for the provost's next step appears in the online content accompanying this book.

Case Study for Deans

You're serving in your ninth year as dean of one among seven colleges at a large university. For about the first five or six years in your position, things seemed to be going extremely well. You liked your work. You felt that you were accomplishing many of the goals you'd set out for your college. You enjoyed your faculty colleagues and had a mutually supportive relationship with your fellow deans. But since the start of the seventh year in your position, you've been feeling decidedly less satisfied. It's been harder for you to come up with fresh ideas. A new president has arrived at the institution, and the two of you don't seem to have the affinity you had with the president who hired you. Worst of all, you're faced with a faculty situation that seems to drain you of all your time and energy. The details of this most pressing problem are as follows.

Late in your sixth year as dean, your college experienced a challenging tenure case that led to appeals at each level of your institution and resulted in a lawsuit. The institution's decision not to tenure the professor was upheld, and the lawsuit was dismissed by the courts. The faculty member has been gone from the institution for more than a year, but you still feel that this incident caused a significant change in mood at your institution. Four of your tenured senior faculty members have become increasingly hostile to you. Several of your proposals were voted down when considered by the full faculty, with these four "ringleaders" heading the opposition. You've tried meeting individually with these faculty members, but to no avail. They appear to have concluded that you're "the enemy," and they're stirring up as much trouble for you in the college as they can.

What has you most concerned now is that several key items will be up for discussion by your college in the near future. Your institution is about to enter a two-year preparation period for its next regional accreditation. It's time for the strategic plan to be updated. In the next few years, several more difficult tenure cases are on the horizon. The deteriorating relationship that you have with those four faculty members makes you concerned about all of these pending issues. Moreover, after years of strong evaluations from your faculty, the problems that you've been facing seem to be taking their toll. Your faculty evaluation scores slipped this year from among the best of the deans to near the bottom. In written comments, several faculty members described you as "increasingly out of touch with faculty concerns" and "losing a sense of direction." There's been a change of mood in your college, and you can feel it.

Based on what you know so far, does it appear to be time to reconsider staying on as dean? If so, what sort of timetable would you set up for your next step? If not, what efforts would you make to improve this situation?

Considerations

1. If you don't feel that you know enough yet to make an informed decision, what additional information would you want to have?

2. Suppose that your supervisor is the provost. Does your response change at all if the provost says one of the following to you?

   a. "Oh, this is just the sort of bump in the road that happens to all of us occasionally. 'Seventh-year itch,' I call it. I wouldn't take those four faculty members too seriously. You know you have my full support. And the president was just saying to me yesterday that you certainly don't deserve the kind of grief these people are giving you. So don't lose any sleep over it. This too shall pass."

   b. "Are you sure that you're still able to be effective in a situation like this? I mean, I know you've done great things for the college. But how do you feel about the future, particularly with our reaccreditation coming up? Do you have a plan for getting through all of this?"

   c. "I don't want to add to your headache, but the president's really concerned about what's going on in your college. Personally I think you're doing great, and I think we all know that these people are upset for reasons that really don't have anything to do with you. But it sounds to me as though you've got some fences to mend with the president."

3. Do you respond any differently if you are one of the following?

   a. Dean of a very small college and the four problematic faculty members represent a third of your entire faculty.

   b. Dean of a very large college and the four faculty members represent barely 1 percent of your faculty.

   c. Intending to retire within five years.

   d. Likely to have a vote of no confidence taken by your faculty at a meeting scheduled within the next month.

     i. Is the mere fact that a vote of no confidence will occur the most important factor in your decision?

     ii. Does your decision change only if the vote of no confidence goes against you?

4. Does it matter to you if the four faculty members who are leading the opposition against you are widely regarded as

   a. opinion leaders among the faculty?

   b. "cranks, whiners, and crackpots," as another member of your college regularly calls them?

   c. so closely associated with the faculty member who failed to receive tenure that their opinions are highly suspect?

   d. so disaffected by the current situation that they're likely to leave the institution within a year or two?

5. Suppose that during your years of service as a dean, you've developed an excellent reputation among the students of your college and are strongly supported by them.

   a. Does this factor alter your decision about whether to stay in your position or move on?

   b. If you've decided to leave your current position, does this factor help you decide what your next step should be?

6. Of all the pieces of information that you've encountered in this case study, which do you regard as the biggest red flag (i.e., which detail concerns or disturbs you the most)?

7. The case study mentioned that your faculty evaluation scores had declined precipitously this year.

   a. If your actual institution (not the one in the case study but where you work now) conducts a formal faculty evaluation of you, how do you tend to interpret the results? Do you

      i. compare them, whenever possible, to the scores received by other administrators in order to see how well you are performing in relation to the rest of the administration?

      ii. find yourself becoming fixated on negative scores and comments even when the overall evaluation is positive?

      iii. forgo interpreting any of the results too extensively until you can review them with your supervisor?

      iv. regard the evaluations primarily as constructive and formative, scanning them for advice on ways in which you can do your job even better?

      v. dismiss negative results on the basis that the faculty can't really understand what your job is like?

   b. What would you regard as a clear message from your actual faculty (i.e., not those in the case study, but the those at the institution where you work now) that they believe you haven't been successful in your position?

      i. Is there a particular percentage of negative responses or comments that you would regard as a red flag?

      ii. Is there a ranking among your fellow administrators, such as bottom half or lowest fifth, that you would regard as cause for great concern?

      iii. Are there particular types of comments that would cause you to rethink your position if more than one or two faculty members made them?

      iv. Are there particular types of comments that would cause you great concern if even one faculty member made them?

      v. If your institution uses some type of Likert scale on its evaluations, is there a particular score level or ranking that you would regard as cause for alarm?

Suggestions

The decision to leave one's current position is an extremely personal one. Some deans regard moving on from any challenging job as an admission of failure and will redouble their efforts when problems occur until they can make things better. Other deans will ask themselves, "And just why am I putting up with this?" as soon as frustrations begin to build, deciding to "get out while the getting is good." Most deans fall somewhere in between. In general, deans need to ask themselves three questions in situations such as the one outlined in this case study:

- ○ Can I still be effective in my position?
- ○ Can I still receive the satisfaction that I need from my position?
- ○ Is remaining in my current position the best thing that I can do for my college and institution?

Let's consider each of these questions individually.

○ *Can I still be effective in my position?* Sometimes the dynamics of a college reach a point where the dean is no longer able to perform key functions effectively. There may be too many distractions in the dean's personal life (a complicated divorce, care for a chronically sick relative, the lingering shadow of questionable ethical decisions) for critical activities to receive the attention they deserve. It can also happen that the dean's level of support from the faculty and staff, the upper administration, or both is so diminished that the college lacks meaningful leadership. In the situation described by this case study, you would need to decide whether you believe that this point has been reached. Certainly there are several developments that should concern you. The shift of your faculty evaluation scores from among the best to near the bottom of the administrators could be an indication that your effectiveness as a faculty leader has been irretrievably lost. With a reaccreditation visit and several difficult tenure cases coming up, you should reflect on whether you're still as effective as you need to be to represent your college during the challenges that will be occurring soon.

○ *Can I still receive the satisfaction that I need from my position?* Even in situations where deans can still provide effective leadership for their colleges, they may discover that their position no longer suits them on a personal level. It may be that the work that deans do simply doesn't relate well to their strengths and interests. It may be that the school where they are right now is a bad fit. Or it may be that after a period of reasonable satisfaction and success, they're feeling burned out from their professional responsibilities or frequently asking themselves, "Is this all there is?" In the case study, one of the phrases that may have attracted your attention was that "you've been feeling decidedly less satisfied." It appears that even beyond the challenges you've faced in the disputed tenure case, you're sensing that you've already contributed your best ideas to the college and could benefit from some new challenges. Nine years can be a long tenure in a deanship, and if the prospects ahead no longer seem as rewarding as they once did, this may well be time to reevaluate your professional position.

○ *Is remaining in my current position the best thing that I can do for my college and institution?* There are also situations in which a dean's effectiveness may have declined significantly and his or her job satisfaction may be low, but it's still in the best interests of the college for the dean to remain in the position—at least temporarily. For instance, if both the president and provost were planning to leave the institution at the end of the academic year, a dean may decide that regardless of all the reasons for making a new career path attractive, it's better to stay on in his or her position for a year or two in order to provide the unit with some stability.

In the case study, the institution's pending reaccreditation and the difficult tenure cases coming forward from the college may complicate your decision. If you're thinking of leaving the position anyway and the self-study portion of the reaccreditation effort has not yet begun, it may be in the institution's interests for you to hand over your position to someone who can see that process through from start to finish. On the other hand, if the self-study or compliance report required for reaccreditation is already well under way, you may decide to endure your current situation (even if it's less than desirable) until that entire process is complete. Similarly, you'll have to assess whether remaining in your position will make a positive or a negative contribution to the tenure reviews that lie ahead. If you feel that your involvement in the previous case has either affected your own objectivity or reduced the value of your judgment throughout your college, it may be prudent to step down before those cases come before you. Nevertheless, if you believe that your departure may be detrimental to two valuable faculty members for whom you're the best person to make a strong case, it would be in the best interests of your college to remain in place a bit longer.

Certainly nothing outlined in this case study would suggest that you're indisputably in a position that would call for your resignation. What you decide to do will have to depend on all the factors and considerations summarized above, as well as your own personality, career goals, and ability to snatch victory from the jaws of defeat. But one thing is certain: all deans have periods of unpopularity or reduced support. You simply can't find an administrative position in which you're required to make difficult and unpopular decisions from time to time without meeting some resistance from your faculty, upper administration, or both.

> Effective academic leaders make decisions not by taking the easiest path but by doing what is right for the institution as a whole.

One encouraging factor in this case study is the fact that while your faculty evaluations have suffered this year, they were very positive for all preceding years. It may well be that what you're experiencing is simply one of the inevitable rough spots that afflict every dean on occasion. With good communication, mending some fences, an openness to acknowledge anything you did to contribute to current problems, and some simple perseverance, you may be able to put the problem behind you. In addition, although you don't have the same rapport with the current president that you had with his or her predecessor, nothing in the case study would suggest that the relationship between the two of you is irretrievably broken. This situation may require you to discover ways to improve your ability to work together more effectively. At the very least, if you decide to remain in your current position, working to deepen your relationship with the president is a strategy to consider.

The real question is thus, "Do you *want* this deanship to be saved?" If you feel that after nine years, you've contributed all you can to the college, are no longer satisfied in the position, and have little likelihood of being effective for several more years, it may be time to explore your options. While it may be difficult to move to another deanship or a higher administrative role from a position where you are not being as successful as you may like, such a move is far from impossible. Certainly you have at least five or six years of accomplishments to report, and it shouldn't be difficult to find references who can address the positive differences that you have made at the institution. Alternatively, if you have maintained a solid record of teaching and scholarship, particularly if you believe that you have preserved an excellent reputation with students, returning to a faculty role may well be a good option.

The important thing to remember is what we saw in chapter 49: there's no single career path in academic life that fits every administrator. While there are many individuals who move from faculty member to department chair to assistant or associate dean to dean to provost to president, that pathway isn't inflexible. Sometimes in our travels, the best experiences occur on our side trips, unexpected detours, or when we double back to retrieve something we forgot at a previous location. A dean's administrative career can be much the same. Only you can decide what the next best step is for you and, in most cases, when you're ready to take it. Don't make the mistake of assuming that your academic and administrative life must follow the preset itinerary of a packaged tour. Essential academic deans always know that in their own careers as well as in the service that they provide to others, the path they travel will not be the same as the journey taken by anyone else.

EPILOGUE

Throughout this book, you've had repeated opportunities to observe that being an effective dean or provost doesn't require any particular type of personality or administrative style. Good academic leaders come in all kinds and varieties. But there are a few traits in deans and provosts that make a difference at their institutions.

o *The essential academic leader is accessible.* Good deans and provosts know their stakeholders. In the phrase made popular by Tom Peters and Robert H. Waterman (2009), they "manage by walking around" (15). Essential academic leaders have impromptu conversations with students and faculty members wherever they meet them, eat regularly in the dining halls, attend campus events, and create a culture of openness that keeps them informed about the key issues in their programs. The best administrators are those who can make each person they meet feel as though they have all the time in the world just to interact with that one individual.

o *The essential academic keeps things in perspective.* Not every challenge is a crisis. Not every battle is worth fighting. Sometimes when the vote goes against the academic leader, the best policy is to accept the decision and move on. Good administrators tend to focus their energy on what truly matters, not on winning every argument or proving that they were right all along. Letting disappointments go is not a sign of being weak; it's a sign of knowing what your real priorities are.

o *The essential academic leader invests in people.* Administrators who speak dismissively of students or faculty members, think of them as obstacles to rather than the focus of their work, or don't take time to listen to their concerns have forgotten what colleges and universities are all about. Good academic leaders value students and faculty members. They also value parents, trustees or legislators, donors, members of the community, and all their other stakeholders. They approach their institutions as open, not closed, systems (see Chu, 2012) and understand the importance of servant leadership (Wheeler, 2012). Essential academic leaders don't cater to students because they view them as the "customers" of the institution or yield to every faculty whim because it makes their jobs easier. But they do recognize that students and faculty members have valid needs, desires, and dreams. Academic leaders invest in people by respecting those they serve even when they cannot agree with them.

o *The essential academic leader delegates effectively.* Appropriate delegation doesn't consist of foisting off on others the responsibilities that deans and provosts don't like. At the other extreme, effective administration also doesn't mean doing everything yourself, micromanaging, or stifling the creativity and initiative of others. Good academic leaders understand that they can't do everything by themselves. They know that the contributions and perspectives of others are valuable, and they regard shared governance as a fundamental strength of American higher education.

o *The essential academic leader demonstrates quiet confidence.* People are more likely to be persuaded by leaders and managers who, while they're not smug or condescending, have a sense of assurance that most administrative challenges are all in a day's work and that even serious problems will eventually be overcome. Approaching your job with cheer, conveying an attitude that "we can do this if we all work together," and taking subtle pride in a job well done will make people want to work with you and help you achieve the goals of your institution.

o *The essential academic leader neither ignores nor becomes preoccupied with details.* An administrator who pays no attention to the fine points of budgets, policies, and procedures can end up doing a great deal of harm to both the college and the institution. But academic leaders who lose all sight of the big picture because they worry about every minor arrangement and decision aren't working in their programs' best interest. There should always be a balance between healthy respect for the details and a capacity to look beyond them to more global issues. Spending too much time "down in the weeds" is just as destructive as spending too much time "with your head in the clouds." The best academic leaders respect details but don't become obsessed by them.

o *The essential academic leader preserves a healthy work/life balance.* Good administrators are good people, first and foremost. They can't serve their stakeholders effectively if they don't keep their whole lives in balance. Family, private interests, research, and efficient administration must all be part of the essential academic leader's life. The best administrators take vacations, read books unrelated to their jobs, have healthy relationships beyond the confines of the campus, and develop a full range of interests that make them interesting as people even outside work.

o *The essential academic leader has a sense of humor.* Good academic leaders laugh, occasionally even at themselves. They recognize their own idiosyncrasies and understand that not everything they do is fraught with significance. Administrators feel free to share lighthearted moments with faculty members, particularly in public meetings where lightening the mood can be more effective than approaching every issue with solemn earnestness. Essential academic leaders don't confuse being dignified with being dour. At the same time, they don't make light of every situation either. They understand the need for a balance between levity and seriousness. They are never superficial or heartless because they know that many of their decisions affect people's lives.

REFERENCES

Chu, D. (2012). *The department chair primer: Leading and managing academic departments* (2nd ed.). San Francisco, CA: Jossey-Bass.

Peters, T. J., & Waterman, R. H. (2009). *In search of excellence: Lessons from America's best-run companies*. New York, NY: Collins Business Essentials.

Wheeler, D. W. (2012). *Servant leadership for higher education: Principles and practices*. San Francisco, CA: Jossey-Bass.

INDEX

STRATEGIC PLAN   3-5 yr ⟩
Biz/Marketing Plan   1 yr ⟩ Hand   support
BUDGet Proposal   1 yr ⟩ in   SP
                          Hand

GRANTS ⟨ need these
Sponsorships⟩

General accounting practices

Meet weekly w/ Tenille ⟩ Mondays
Budget   ½ hr   / Check when
Misc   ½ hr.   adaptive updated